MAGILL'S LITERARY ANNUAL
1991

MAGILL'S
LITERARY ANNUAL
1991

*Essay-Reviews of 200 Outstanding Books
Published in the United States during 1990*

With an Annotated Categories List

Volume Two

Int-Z

Edited by
FRANK N. MAGILL

SALEM PRESS

Pasadena, California   Englewood Cliffs, New Jersey

LIBRARY OF CONGRESS CATALOG CARD NO. 77-99209

ISBN 0-89356-291-2

FIRST PRINTING

PRINTED IN THE UNITED STATES OF AMERICA

MAGILL'S
LITERARY ANNUAL
1991

INTIFADA
The Palestinian Uprising—Israel's Third Front

Authors: Ze'ev Schiff (1932-   ) and Ehud Ya'ari (1945-   )
First published: Intifada, 1989, in Israel
Translated from the Hebrew by Ina Friedman
Edited by Ina Friedman
Publisher: Simon & Schuster (New York). 352 pp. $22.95
Type of work: Political history
Time: 1987-1989
Locale: Israel and the occupied territories

Two Israeli journalists explore the various causes of the intifada *(Islamic fundamentalism, Arab nationalism, the Palestine Liberation Organization, social and economic pressures) and, after concluding that the* intifada *cannot successfully be repressed, offer their solution to the situation*

> *Principal personages:*
> YASSER ARAFAT, the leader of the Palestine Liberation Organization (PLO)
> KING HUSSEIN of Jordan, former ruler of the West Bank
> YITZHAK SHAMIR, the Prime Minister of Israel

Israeli journalists Schiff and Ya'ari, who also wrote *Israel's Lebanon War* (1984), turn their attention to Israel's "third front," the *intifada*, which they regard as a war wholly new to Israel because it is a popular war fought by civilians using not standard weapons, but rocks, pamphlets, and strikes. Since the war is still in progress, the authors face a substantial interpretive challenge. They must diagnose a patient without the benefit of an autopsy. As the authors point out, the evolving positions of the involved political entities (the PLO, Jordan, the United States, and Israel) since the inception of the *intifada* on December 8, 1987, have also made an assessment of the *intifada* more difficult.

In the foreword to their book Schiff and Ya'ari state that the point of the book is not "to establish guilt, impute blame, or grade the parties on their conduct or performance." If grades were to be awarded, both the Labor and Likud political parties would be issued failing grades because they failed both to anticipate the results of their socioeconomic policies and to control the *intifada* once it began. Though the *intifada* was a "surprise" to Israeli officials, there were many warning signals (a rapid increase in civil disturbances such as demonstrating, blocking roads, throwing stones, and burning tires) that were simply ignored by the Israeli government, which preferred to "touch up reality in pastel colors." In fact, the authors do blame, individually (Ariel Sharon building an apartment in the Muslim quarter of Jerusalem) and collectively (the vigilante actions of the Jewish settlers), the Israelis for making an already bad situation worse.

The authors maintain that their only reason for writing the book is to "contribute to a better understanding of the tempest that has been raging in our country for two years so that the necessary conclusions can be drawn." To that end, they present not a chronological account of what transpired during the two years, but a series of chapters devoted to the separate threads in that pattern. After chapters on the early development of the *intifada*, there are separate chapters, organized chronologically, on the roles played by the proletariat, the Israeli Palestinians, the Unified National Command, the Islamic Resistance Movement, and the United States. Conspicuous by their relative absence, ostensibly because of the minor role they played in the *intifada*, are the Communists, the PLO, and King Hussein of Jordan.

While few Middle East experts believe that the Communists did play an important part in the uprising, the roles of the PLO and King Hussein are debatable. Certainly Yasser Arafat has attempted to associate the PLO with the *intifada* as part of his strategy to gain credibility for himself and for his Palestinian country without a homeland. He may, moreover, have actually been as surprised by the *intifada* as the authors claim, but the authors' assessment of Arafat is hardly objective. According to Schiff and Ya'ari, the PLO simply assumed, through a power play, control of an essentially apolitical popular movement. Understandably unwilling to give their formidable adversary any legitimacy, the authors describe the "astounding degree of estrangement between the self-styled popular leader and the people he presumed to have led." The words "self-styled" and "presumed" reveal the biased attitude toward Arafat, who is elsewhere described as "ideologically supple." Jordan's King Hussein is also denigrated, first snidely as "the once and future regent of the West Bank" and then for brooding "in one of his periodic depressions." Their evaluation of King Hussein hardly squares with his international reputation as a statesman and mediator, and it definitely does not acknowledge how Jordan's tenuous existence— Israel's plan for Jordan becoming *the* Palestinian state is itself a threat—affects policy.

From the authors' perspective, the *intifada* is primarily the product of Israeli socioeconomic policy rather than Palestinian nationalistic pride or Islamic religious fervor. This interpretation has several implications: It fails to address the legitimacy of Palestinian demands for statehood; it suggests that Israeli authorities could have avoided, by using enlightened policies, the *intifada* problem; and it implies that if Israeli authorities had benefitted from their mistakes they could have suppressed the *intifada*, which was, the authors believe, an Israeli creation, not a Palestinian one. Despite their disclaimer about not wanting to establish guilt or impute blame, Schiff and Ya'ari catalogue many Israeli policy mistakes and create the impression that the post-1967 situation could and should have been sustained.

Their insistence that the *intifada* was not politically motivated is the subject of "The Enraged Proletariat," in which the authors assert that "Israel's economic system was the real driving force behind the radicalization of the Palestinian public." The authors state that the initial leaders of the *intifada* were ignorant of politics and that the Palestinians revolted because of economic pressures and social injustices. These policies created a "human time bomb" because the Palestinians were "treated like animals" and made to feel inferior. Such treatment, according to the authors, was the result "less of malice than of sheer thoughtlessness," though they concede that the economic clamp Israel placed on the territories created "a 'slave market' of

sorts" in the territories. Through admitting to Israeli abuses in the territories, however, Schiff and Ya'ari can also claim that since these abuses caused the problem, the
problem could have been prevented through a "more generous and humane policy."

While the authors minimize the role of the PLO and the Communists, they do
devote an entire chapter to the Islamic Resistance Movement or "Hamas." Again
they stress Israeli failure to assess accurately the enemy, the fundamentalist Muslims
whose religious fervor they anticipated would counterbalance the political activity of
the PLO. The authors point out, however, that "the distinction between church and
state does not exist in the mind or creed of the pious Muslim." It is doubtful, though,
that any Israeli tactics could have done more than temporarily impede the growing
influence of the Muslim Brotherhood and Islamic Jihad. After all, fundamentalist
Muslims have become powerful in many other countries which did not encourage
their development.

When Schiff and Ya'ari turn their attention from the Palestinians in the territories
to the Israeli Arabs, they vary their approach. Rather than explaining how and why
nationalism and religious fundamentalism developed, they discuss why the *intifada*
has not been extended to Israel, even though they acknowledge that the voting patterns of the Israeli Arabs are changing, that they are undergoing "Palestinization,"
and that their position is increasingly ambiguous and tenuous. The authors' prediction that "the stronger the feeling of inequality and deprivation grows, the more
Israel's Arabs will stress the Palestinian aspect of their identity" has, in fact, been
proven accurate, for Israel's Arabs have become united with "territorial Palestinians" in their support of Iraq's Saddam Hussein. That support, which should hardly
be surprising, has left the Israelis feeling embittered and betrayed. The projected
"potential for equal rights disappearing in Israel" is closer to reality because Israel
has not reversed the trend toward inequality and deprivation.

Events subsequent to 1989 have reinforced the authors' contention that "if Israel's
Arabs are drawn into the *intifada*, the country will face a genuine disaster." Although the pro-Iraqi demonstrations have not also been pro-*intifada*, those demonstrations have paralleled the Palestinian/PLO demonstrations. Schiff and Ya'ari offer
convincing demographic data that indicate that the rapidly deteriorating situation
can only worsen. By the year 2000 the Arabs will constitute 20 percent of Israel's
population, and already there are Arab concentrations (50 percent or more) in Galilee and in the Triangle and in Wadi Ara. Although the authors suggest that the Israeli
Arabs' best interests depend on their continued support of Israel's democracy, not
on their importing the *intifada*, their suggestion seems a bit naïve because it does
not even consider the legitimacy of the Palestinian homeland or the Arab/Muslim
determination to regain what they regard as rightfully theirs.

When the authors turn their attention to Jordan, however, they are on surer ground.
They point out what Jordanian officials are reluctant to acknowledge, that in Jordan
Palestinians outnumber their Jordanian hosts. Although publicly committed to "national unity," Jordanian officials are concerned about mass deportations of Palestinians to Jordan. The authors claim that Jordanians fear the spread of the *intifada* to

Jordan because a politically and religiously committed Palestinian majority clearly has the potential, despite the Jordanian secret police, to destabilize the Hashemite kingdom. King Hussein's severing his ties to the West Bank thus becomes, for the authors, a defensive measure. The Palestinian demonstrations in Jordan, which began in May of 1990, were initially appeals for a religious war against Israel—these were suppressed by the army, but not before Palestinian realization of their political power, which was also being tested in the elected lower house of the Jordanian Parliament. Since the Iraqi invasion of Kuwait in August of 1990, widespread demonstrations in support of Saddam Hussein, whom the Jordan Palestinians view as the potential savior of "Palestine," attest Palestinian influence in Jordan and account for King Hussein's reluctance to alienate his people by yielding to Western demands for blockading shipments to Iraq.

Equally impressive is the handling of those international factors which make Israeli concessions essential. Schiff and Ya'ari predict Soviet unwillingness to interfere, assess Washington's incapacity for action, anticipate deteriorating American-Israeli relations, criticize the hawkish behavior of the Israeli settlers, and discuss the implications of a stalemate between the Likud and Labor parties in Israel. They seem to believe, however, that the problem is the image of Israeli "intransigence." Israeli peace initiatives, unfortunately, have not worked, primarily because they have been cosmetic efforts in support of a status quo which encourages extremists on the right and left, produces a callous, frustrated military, and threatens Israeli democracy.

In their epilogue, the authors offer a possible solution to what they have presented as a virtually insoluble problem. A first step, they assert, is Palestinian and Israeli acceptance of their situation as one "that precludes an absolute victory for either cause." Israel must consider "how it will be possible to redeem the whole of the Land of Israel"; Palestinians must ask if "the determination to destroy the State of Israel will not in fact prolong the occupation and the suppression of Palestinian national aspirations." Both sides must settle for less. Schiff and Ya'ari advocate Israeli administrative withdrawal from the territories and the transfer, on a trial basis with careful monitoring, of the Gaza Strip to the PLO. The next step would involve a tripartite arrangement: a confederation of Israel, a demilitarized "Palestinian entity" consisting of the West Bank and Gaza Strip, and Jordan, which would have its current national rights severely curtailed. Furthermore, the Palestinians would have to renounce their "right of return" and their plan to dismantle Israel in stages.

Not surprisingly, the concessions for the Israelis are not significant, but those for the Palestinians are so substantial and so basic (the loss of the Jerusalem promised them in the Koran, as well as seriously compromised "national" rights) that they stand little chance of acceptance even by Arab moderates. In addition, King Hussein's acceptance of such a seriously compromised Jordan could well cost him his throne. While the authors freely acknowledge Israeli abuses, their insistence that Israel created the *intifada* also serves to deny the legitimacy and inevitability of Palestinian revolt; and their solution, the "only one meaningful alternative," effectively denies the religious/political motivations of a dispossessed people and curtails Jordan's sovereign rights. Given their backgrounds, Schiff and Ya'ari have written a relatively objective account of the *intifada*, but that reportorial objectivity is counterbalanced by ideological biases, and their compromise is not a concession but the reaffirmation of an earlier (pre-1967) status quo.

Thomas L. Erskine

Sources for Further Study

Chicago Tribune. March 14, 1990, XIV, p. 1.
Commentary. LXXXIX, April, 1990, p. 60.
Foreign Affairs. LXIX, Spring, 1990, p. 184.
Los Angeles Times Book Review. April 29, 1990, p. 12.
National Review. XLII, May 28, 1990, p. 44.
The New Leader. LXXIII, May 14, 1990, p. 19.
The New York Times Book Review. XCV, March 18, 1990, p. 3.
Publishers Weekly. CCXXXVII, January 12, 1990, p. 56.
The Times Literary Supplement. June 29, 1990, p. 687.
The Washington Monthly. XXI, January, 1990, p. 56.
The Washington Post Book World. XX, March 18, 1990, p. 6.

JACKSON POLLOCK
An American Saga

Authors: Steven Naifeh (1950-   ) and Gregory White Smith (1949-   )
Publisher: Clarkson N. Potter (New York). Illustrated. 934 pp. $29.95
Type of work: Biography
Time: 1912-1956
Locale: Wyoming, California, Arizona, New York, Pennsylvania, and Massachusetts

This long, detailed account of the life of Jackson Pollock, one of the leading Abstract Expressionist painters, will be the standard biography for many years, as well as an engrossing history of American painting during the 1930's and 1940's

> *Principal personages:*
> JACKSON POLLOCK, Abstract Expressionist painter and father of "drip" painting
> ROY POLLOCK, Jackson's father
> STELLA POLLOCK, Jackson's mother
> CHARLES POLLOCK,
> JAY POLLOCK,
> FRANK POLLOCK, and
> SANDE POLLOCK, Jackson's older brothers
> THOMAS HART BENTON, painter and Jackson's onetime mentor
> LEE KRASNER, painter and Jackson's wife

Paul Jackson Pollock was born in Cody, Wyoming, on January 28, 1912. His mother was born Stella Mae McClure to "hardshelled" Presbyterian parents in the small town of Tingley, Iowa. His father's original name was LeRoy McCoy. His ancestors had settled in Pennsylvania, which LeRoy's parents left to move west in the 1850's. Hardship and disaster overtook the McCoys, and after LeRoy's mother and sister died of tuberculosis, the three-year-old LeRoy ended up living with James and Lizzie Pollock and took their name. LeRoy and Stella's first child, Charles Cecil, was born without their parents' knowledge before they were married, and the young couple headed west with their baby, stopping to get married in Alliance, Nebraska. They soon settled into the rigors of rural life in Cody.

There LeRoy worked as a stonemason and cement worker to support a family that soon included four more sons: Marvin Jay, Frank Leslie, Sanford Leroy, and Paul Jackson. Ten months after Jackson's birth, the Pollocks packed up and moved to San Diego, California, the first of many moves the restless Stella would impose upon LeRoy and the boys. Less than a year later, in August, 1913, they moved again, this time to Phoenix, Arizona, where LeRoy bought a truck farm.

The Phoenix move was the prelude to a series of transplantations instigated by Stella: to Chico, California, in 1917, and then on to the small California towns of Janesville and Orland before returning to another farm in Phoenix in 1923. A year later, they were back in Chico, finally settling that same year in Riverside, near Los Angeles. By that time LeRoy had left the family to work in road construction jobs until his death in 1933.

Jackson's interest in art was stimulated in 1922 when his brother Charles sent home copies of *The Dial* and *The American Mercury* from Los Angeles, where he was working for the *Los Angeles Times* and studying at the Otis Art Institute. Four years later, Charles was in New York City taking classes at the Art Students League and studying with Thomas Hart Benton. After spending the summer of 1927 working, with his brother Sanford (or Sande) as a surveyor in the Grand Canyon, Jackson entered Riverside High School, only to be expelled the following March. When Stella moved the family to Los Angeles that summer, Jackson enrolled at Manual Arts High School. Jackson's studies there were crucial, for it is there that he met two talented art students, Philip Guston and Manuel Tolegian, and, most important, the eccentric art teacher, Frederick John de St. Vrain, who involved him in Theosophical study. He was expelled from school in his first year, however, spent the summer of 1929 working on a road crew with his father, returned to Manual Arts that fall to study life drawing and clay modeling, and was expelled once more.

Jackson was allowed to return to Manual in the spring of 1930, but only as a part-time student. He became an admirer of the Mexican muralists at about this time, especially after seeing José Clemente Orozco's fresco *Prometheus* at Pomona College. In the fall Jackson made a big decision. He went to New York with his brothers Charles and Frank, dropped the name Paul to go by Jackson, and enrolled in Thomas Hart Benton's class at the Art Students League.

Jackson's life in New York would prove to be a hectic struggle with alcohol and insecurity even as he secured a reputation as an artist. His association with Thomas Hart Benton was an important part of his new life in the East. Not only was he Benton's student, but he also became a more or less regular fixture in the Bentons' home. Rita Benton looked out for Pollock, flirted with him, fed him spaghetti suppers, and finally had to reject his overtures of love. Pollock was a willing baby-sitter for the Benton's young son, telling him stories about the imaginary character Jack Sass. Benton organized an informal musical group, the Harmonica Rascals, to which Pollock belonged despite his meager musical talents. The Bentons took him to Provincetown with them during their rather Bohemian summers of nude bathing and alcoholic socializing. One summer Pollock arrived unexpectedly, rented a bicycle, got drunk, harassed a girl on the road, and had to be rescued by the Bentons from the local jail.

The Provincetown episode was typical of Pollock's behavior whenever he felt abandoned and insecure, and it was held in check mostly by the care of his loyal brothers, especially Sande, and concerned surrogate mothers like Helen Marot and Dr. Violet Staub de Laszlo. Pollock first met Helen Marot in 1934 when he and Sande worked as janitors at the City and Country School in New York. Marot provided valuable emotional support for Pollock until her sudden death in 1940, which precipitated a protracted bout of self-destructive drinking by Pollock. At the time of Marot's death, Pollock had been consulting the Jungian psychologist Dr. Joseph L. Henderson, who found Jungian archetypes in Pollock's paintings and thereby stimulated Pollock, eager to please a father figure, to paint more works with obvious Jungian motifs.

When Henderson moved to California shortly after Helen Marot's death, he turned Pollock over to Dr. Staub de Laszlo, who worked helpfully with the overwrought artist for more than a year.

During the Depression years of the 1930's, Pollock made summer trips to California, working as a lumberjack in 1931 and sketching and studying David Alfaro Siqueiros' murals in 1932. He worked in 1930 and 1933 with stone carver Ahron Ben-Schmuel; later he received government help, first in 1935 working as a stonecutter for the Emergency Relief Bureau and then from 1936 until 1943 in the employ of the Works Progress Administration. He lived in a succession of rooms and apartments in these years—with Charles and his wife, Elizabeth, and with Sande for a while.

His career stumbled along. Benton's mode of painting was not suitable to Pollock's sensibility, and Benton's anti-intellectualism was probably harmful in that Pollock was not a good draftsman (Pollock once pointed to one of his "drip" paintings and asked rhetorically if anyone thought he would do that kind of "crap" if he could draw). Pollock needed a mentor with a more radical view of art and life to help nurse along his personal vision. In 1935, nevertheless, Pollock appeared in his first group show, the Eighth Exhibition of Watercolors, Pastels, and Drawings by American and French Artists at the Brooklyn Museum.

A major turning point in Pollock's career came on November 8, 1943, when his first solo exhibition opened at Peggy Guggenheim's gallery, Art of This Century. The reviews were mixed. The Surrealists acclaimed Pollock as a worthy new member of their group, but the reviewers were less sure of what they had witnessed. All the "right" journals discussed Pollock's startling creations, however, and the publicity helped his career. Best of all, a museum in San Francisco purchased one painting, and a collector in Philadelphia bought another. Peggy Guggenheim gave him a contract and also commissioned a huge mural for her home, and her association with Pollock, though sometimes strained, was the prime mover in his career.

Pollock established another fruitful relationship in 1944. At the urging of Lee Krasner, a painter with whom he had been living and whom he would marry in 1945, he consulted Dr. Elizabeth Wright Hubbard, an M.D. who had given up a conventional medical practice to study homeopathy and to treat the "whole" patient. She was a large woman, imposing in every way, and a solid mother figure on whom Pollock relied for the rest of his life. Dr. Hubbard came into Pollock's life at the right time. Despite his successes in 1944—*Guardians of the Secret* went on a five-city tour, *The Moon-Woman Cuts the Circle* and *She-Wolf* went on an eleven-city tour with the Museum of Modern Art's exhibition Twelve Contemporary Painters— Pollock spent a very difficult summer. His association with Peggy Guggenheim put him in the company of the licentious homosexual brotherhood that surrounded her and set off a new round of self-destructive behavior. Precisely what Pollock's sexual proclivities and problems were cannot be known, but it is one of the themes of Naifeh and Smith's biography that homosexual tensions created one of Jackson's painful inner conflicts. Fortunately for Pollock, Lee Krasner was able to rescue him from his Bohemian rioting around the bars of the Cape Cod gay scene. She summoned Sande, the brother who could always calm Pollock, and Stella, and they chaperoned the wayward artist the rest of the summer.

In 1945, after their marriage, Pollock and Krasner bought a farmhouse in Springs, Long Island. This was also the year of Pollock's first exhibitions outside New York, with shows being mounted in Cincinnati, Chicago, and San Francisco. The combination of marriage, homeownership, and critical recognition proved beneficial, for in 1946 Pollock painted the first of his famous drip paintings. With his drinking largely under control, Pollock had four excellent years—from 1946 through 1950—that enriched his reputation and his self-esteem.

In 1947, Peggy Guggenheim closed her gallery and left for Venice, freeing Jackson to sign a contract with the Betty Parsons Gallery. His career was boosted that year by Clement Greenberg's praise in *Horizon* magazine, eliciting Philistine sneers from *Time* that surely made for good publicity. The article that gained Pollock real notoriety, however, was published in *Life* in August, 1949, a blockbuster photo-essay that told the world about Abstract Expressionism and Jackson Pollock. When *Life* identified Pollock as "the shining new phenomenon of American art," he suddenly became exactly that. Pollock had a hundred copies of the issue delivered to Springs.

Three months later, in November, 1949, Pollock's show at the Betty Parsons Gallery was a tremendous success. Critics and collectors were enthusiastic; only *Time* continued to sneer. The critical success was followed in the summer of 1950 by four of his greatest paintings: *Number 1, 1950*, or *Lavender Mist*; *Number 32, 1950*; *Number 31, 1950*, or *One*; and *Number 30, 1950*, or *Autumn Rhythm.* This was the peak of Pollock's career. He had been off alcohol for two years, but in the fall of 1950 he again mysteriously succumbed.

Hans Namuth came to Springs and made a motion picture of Pollock at work. When he finished, Pollock started drinking heavily. He went to Chicago in February, 1951, to judge a show and was drunk all the time. His work suffered, and he switched to Sidney Janis' gallery, but with no success. By 1954, after three years of dissipation, his career was finished. Pollock and Krasner's marriage broke down completely, and they both underwent therapy. Pollock spent as much time as possible at Manhattan's Cedar Bar during those years and behaved deplorably.

The final blow for Lee Krasner came when Pollock started seeing a worshipful young art student, Ruth Kligman, who occupied all of his time. When Krasner, in desperation, left for Europe, Kligman moved in with Pollock. On August 11, 1956, Ruth brought her friend Edith Metzger with her to Springs, and in a drunken rage Pollock drove the three of them down Fireplace Road, lost control of the car, and killed himself and Edith Metzger in the crash. Ruth Kligman survived.

Naifeh and Smith's biography is long and detailed but gracefully written and copiously illustrated. Much of the material is sensational, even scandalous, in its frankness. The supporting characters are sketched more fully than in most biographies (for example, Thomas Hart Benton's family background seems to have been detailed so completely merely to suggest the contradictions in his sexual life), but the broad canvas is usually engrossing. The result will not satisfy everyone (see the review in *The Times Literary Supplement*, for example), but this is a major work of research that presents a full picture not only of an extraordinarily complicated man but also of a period and a movement.

Frank Day

Sources for Further Study

ARTnews. LXXXIX, April, 1990, p. 109.
Booklist. LXXXVI, December 1, 1989, p. 717.
The Christian Science Monitor. February 14, 1990, p. 10.
Kirkus Reviews. LVII, November 1, 1989, p. 1579.
Library Journal. CXIV, September 1, 1989, p. 200.
Los Angeles Times Book Review. February 25, 1990, p. 4.
National Review. XLII, March 19, 1990, p. 53.
The New York Times Book Review. XCV, January 28, 1990, p. 3.
Newsweek. CXV, January 8, 1990, p. 67.
Publishers Weekly. CCXXXVI, November 17, 1989, p. 39.
The Times Literary Supplement. March 16, 1990, p. 287.
Utne Reader. XL, July, 1990, p. 108.
The Washington Post Book World. XX, January 21, 1990, p. 1.

JEAN STAFFORD
The Savage Heart

Author: Charlotte Margolis Goodman (1944-   )
Publisher: University of Texas Press (Austin). Illustrated. 394 pp. $24.95
Type of work: Literary biography
Time: c. 1915-1979
Locale: California, Colorado, New York, Louisiana, Massachusetts, and Maine

Delineating the connections between Jean Stafford's life and her fiction, this literary biography presents a portrait of Stafford as an extremely talented but troubled individual

> *Principal personages:*
> JEAN STAFFORD, an American fiction writer whose collected short stories won a Pulitzer Prize in 1970
> JOHN STAFFORD, her irascible father, who as a young man published Western fiction under the noms de plume Jack Wonder and Ben Delight
> ETHEL (née McKILLOP) STAFFORD, her loquacious and sentimental mother, who taught school briefly before her marriage to John
> ROBERT (CAL) LOWELL, a Pulitzer Prize-winning poet whom Jean married when she was twenty and to whom she remained married for eight years

According to Charlotte Margolis Goodman, Jean Stafford grew up feeling like an unwanted child. The last of the four Stafford children, she was born July 1, 1915, in Covina, California, to John and Ethel (née McKillop) Stafford. Portrayed throughout this biography as misanthropic, misogynistic, and habitually self-pitying, John Stafford is implicated by Goodman as the primary and most profound cause for his daughter's feeling unwanted, for her eventual estrangement from the family, as well as for the self-destructive choices she made in her personal life, especially where men and marriage were concerned. She was married three times, the first marriage lasting eight years, the second lasting less than two, and the third lasting approximately four—this latter the only one not torn asunder by ongoing verbal and physical fighting. Her parents' relationship, apparently always a tumultuous one, worsened after John lost the family's fortune (approximately $200,000) in the stock market in 1922.

Before that financial devastation, the family of six had lived comfortably, having moved from Covina to San Diego in 1920, but after the great loss John Stafford decided to move his family to Colorado in 1922—first to Colorado Springs and then to Boulder, where they settled even though he had no steady job and his wife was forced to make loaves of bread and baked beans to sell to her neighbors. Eventually Ethel would open a section of the family's home to boarders, while her husband spent his days writing stories and an economic treatise (none of which he published) or exploring the outdoors. According to Goodman, Jean Stafford's writing of stories when still a child was a defense against the pain she suffered in her home, the stories themselves—throughout her life—means of escaping unpleasant domestic situations in which she found herself. Goodman also maintains that, beginning with

Stafford's earliest story, virtually all of her fiction was thinly disguised autobiography, the main characters versions of herself and her immediate or extended family.

Stafford was graduated from the State Preparatory School in Boulder, Colorado, in 1932, and four years later (1936) was graduated cum laude from the University of Colorado, Boulder, being the only student in her graduating class to receive both the B.A. and M.A. degrees at the same time. After spending a year at the University of Heidelberg studying on a fellowship, and the next year teaching composition at Stephens College in Columbia, Missouri, Stafford entered a Ph.D. program at the University of Iowa, but she remained there only through the fall term, 1938, leaving in November. She had met Robert Lowell in 1937 at the Boulder Writers' Conference, and he apparently became obsessively intent upon convincing her to marry him; she resisted his pursuit for three years, but in 1940 they were married. From the time of Stafford's marriage to Lowell, according to this biography, her life consisted of frequent moves from one place to another, chronic alcoholism and heavy smoking, increasingly complicated mental and physical illnesses (such as insomnia, angina pectoris, and chronic lung disease), ceaseless and intense fighting between her and those with whom she became close, and a writing career that never garnered for her the recognition Goodman believes she deserved. Nevertheless, Stafford eventually became a frequent short-story contributor to *The New Yorker*, the recipient of two Guggenheim Fellowships, and the winner of several O. Henry Awards for her short stories. At the time of her death from cardiac arrest (March 26, 1979), Stafford had published three novels and forty-three short stories, having been awarded a Pulitzer Prize in 1970 for *The Collected Stories of Jean Stafford* (1969).

One of Goodman's expressed intentions in this biography is to champion Stafford's short stories and novels as deserving a larger audience and greater critical attention than they have had; unfortunately, the discussions herein of Stafford's fiction seldom extend beyond perfunctory paraphrases of story lines or plots, and what analyses Goodman offers are always reductive, intent as she is upon illustrating the extent to which the stories are all autobiographical. According to Goodman's readings, the central male characters in virtually all Stafford's stories are fictional renditions of her father, her brother, or one of her husbands, and the central female characters represent Stafford herself. It is impressive when one reads that forty thousand hardcover copies of Stafford's first novel, *Boston Adventure* (1944), were sold within a few months of publication, and that three hundred thousand were distributed through book clubs and as overseas editions, but Goodman sidesteps a discussion of the novel's literary merit or Stafford's artistic achievement in writing it and instead reduces it to an essentially autobiographical exposé of the writer's marriage to poet Robert Lowell, a Boston Brahmin, and the female protagonist's (read Stafford's) awkward entry into upper-crust Bostonian stuffiness. In like manner, while Goodman calls Stafford's third novel, *The Catherine Wheel* (1952), her most complex story, Goodman fails to show how it is more complex than the writer's earlier work. While a sense of place was not as important to Stafford in her life or art as it was, say, to Willa Cather or Edith Wharton, it was nevertheless an essential ingredient in almost all of her stories, nowhere more apparent than in her first novel and *The Mountain Lion* (1947), her second. Yet only when discussing this latter story does Goodman give her reader a glimpse of the importance of place or region in Stafford's life and work. While Goodman notes that Stafford and Lowell moved seven times in five years, there is seldom any effort expended by this biographer to pull the reader into a given locale or ethos, as there is, for example, in Roxana Robinson's *Georgia O'Keeffe: A Life* (1989) or David Sweetman's *Van Gogh: His Life and His Art* (1990).

What this biography does present is a portrait of an extremely self-destructive and increasingly isolated individual, who at thirty-one was hospitalized for the first of many times because she suffered acute alcoholism and its deleterious psychological and physiological effects. She thought of herself as a hapless victim of circumstance, and Goodman repeatedly tells the reader that Stafford also believed that her childhood had had a hugely negative effect upon her adult psyche. Goodman presents no information or interpretations of events with which to contradict this latter belief; indeed, Stafford's view of her adult psyche and the events from which it supposedly derived seems to underpin this biography throughout as an unannounced thesis, the overall discussion about her life being therefore inductive. For example, Stafford eventually viewed Robert Lowell, her first husband, as being like her father, as both men were violent—though Lowell was evidently much more so, breaking Stafford's nose twice, once by deliberately driving a car into a wall and the second time by driving his fist into his wife's face. Indeed, Goodman has absolutely nothing good to say about either Stafford's father or Lowell. The latter is scathingly portrayed as a spoiled, egocentric, and psychopathic villain throughout; whatever there may have been that was positive between him and Stafford is nowhere mentioned in this biography.

While Goodman is quite convincing in discussing the extent to which Stafford's early-developed sense of alienation was caused by her family's financial difficulties, the person on whose head the blame rests for those difficulties is, again, John Stafford. Perhaps if he had not lost the family fortune and had not been so aimless, Goodman's supposition seems to go, his wife Ethel's bourgeois inclinations, her craving for material comforts and social acceptance, and her constant striving for a better life might not have created such tension in the Stafford home and thus the youngest daughter's psyche. After all, Goodman maintains, it was because Stafford had had imprinted upon her psyche her mother's inclinations and cravings that she married a Boston Brahmin and entered a social class she gradually learned to detest, satirizing it brilliantly in *Boston Adventure*.

Stafford's marriage to Lowell ended in a permanent separation in the autumn of 1946; yet despite the fact that *The Mountain Lion* was published that same year and she would shortly thereafter begin what would prove to be a long affiliation with *The New Yorker*, during the period between her separation from Lowell and their divorce in 1948 Stafford claimed to friends that, without Lowell and her marriage, writing was not enough to sustain her life. In January, 1950, Stafford impulsively married

Oliver Jensen, a member of the *Life* magazine editorial staff and a man with whom she fought continuously. This marriage was a mistake, according to Goodman, and it lasted less than two years. Her third and final marriage (April, 1959) was to journalist A. J. (Joe) Liebling, who had courted Stafford for almost three years and was eleven years her senior. Although it would end when Liebling died in 1963, the marriage was apparently an exceptionally good one for Stafford. Unlike Lowell, Liebling greatly valued and praised Stafford's artistic talents and creations, seemingly never expecting her to subordinate her career to his, as Lowell had. Whatever destructive factors there were in the marriage were apparently the results of Stafford's own self-destructive impulses—manifested most noticeably in her heavy drinking and smoking. After Liebling's death, Stafford suffered an acute writer's block, complicated by numerous physical maladies, and she wrote very few new stories during the remaining sixteen years of her life.

While Goodman's strictly chronological ordering of her narrative might seem to some readers too rigid and formulaic to convey the felt presence of one such as Stafford, who was often recklessly impulsive and for the most part emotionally confused, the biography is well written. And while it is true that a biography about such a tormented life as Stafford's will inevitably be bleak and even depressing, whatever triumph there was of Stafford's spirit over potentially crippling obstacles between her and her artistic achievements should be highlighted more than they have been by Goodman here. Such a highlighting seems especially necessary in a study whose author repeatedly claims that the artistic accomplishment in question deserves a larger audience and greater recognition. Certainly this well-researched biography thoroughly informs its reader about a woman's profoundly twisted and emotionally chaotic life; but if the reader wants to gauge the extent to which Jean Stafford the writer transcended the tribulations she suffered in her personal life, as well as the extent to which she contributed anything remarkable or memorable to American literature, that reader must delve into Stafford's fiction.

David A. Carpenter

Sources for Further Study

Atlanta Journal Constitution. June 3, 1990, p. N10.
Booklist. LXXXVI, July, 1990, p. 236.
Choice. XXVIII, November, 1990, p. 483.
The Houston Post. July 29, 1990, p. D6.
Library Journal. CXV, June 1, 1990, p. 128.
The New York Times Book Review. XCV, August 12, 1990, p. 17.
Publishers Weekly. CCXXXVII, May 11, 1990, p. 236.
San Francisco Chronicle. October 14, 1990, p. REV5.
The Washington Post Book World. XX, May 13, 1990, p. 13.

KATE CHOPIN

Author: Emily Toth (1944-   )
Publisher: William Morrow (New York). Illustrated. 528 pp. $27.95
Type of work: Literary biography
Time: 1851-1904
Locale: St. Louis, Missouri, and Louisiana

The product of twenty years of research, this detailed yet accessible biography reveals that Kate Chopin's unconventional fiction reflects a life that was equally nontraditional

> *Principal personages:*
> KATE O'FLAHERTY CHOPIN, the author of *The Awakening* (1899)
> THOMAS O'FLAHERTY, her father
> ELIZA FARIS O'FLAHERTY, her mother
> AURELIAN ROSELIUS OSCAR CHOPIN, her husband
> MADAME VICTOIRE VERDON CHARLEVILLE, her great-grandmother
> ALBERT SAMPITE, her Cloutierville lover
> LOCA SAMPITE, Albert's wife
> DR. FREDERICK KOLBENHEYER, St. Louis obstetrician and her close friend
> JOHN ALVAREZ DILLON, the editor-in-chief of the *St. Louis Post-Dispatch* and *New York World* and possibly another of her lovers

The dust jacket of this biography advertises it as "A Life of the Author of *The Awakening*," thus identifying Kate Chopin's primary claim to recognition in the late twentieth century. Canonized by inclusion in the major anthologies of American literature, *The Awakening* has enjoyed critical acclaim and popular success. This biography, the first of Kate Chopin in twenty years, explains how this novel came to be written. Exactly as Gustave Flaubert observed, "Madame Bovary, c'est moi," so Chopin might have said that *The Awakening* is the story of her life. The work unquestionably depends on a literary tradition that includes Flaubert's *Madame Bovary* (1856), Bjørnstjerne Bjørnson's *Fiskerjenten* (1868; *The Fisher Maiden*, 1869), and the stories of Guy de Maupassant, several of which Chopin translated in the 1890's. Much of the book's power, though, derives from Chopin's ability to draw on firsthand knowledge of Louisiana's Cane River country where the novel is set and, even more significantly, on her own experiences and emotions in the 1880's in Cloutierville. She could describe Edna Pontellier's quest for fulfillment and rejection of convention so convincingly because she was writing about herself.

Whereas Edna rebels against her background as well as her society to forge a life of her own, Chopin found much in her heritage to encourage independence. Even as a child, she longed to know what lay beyond the bounds of her genteel household; her father, a successful St. Louis businessman, introduced her to his riverfront world of trappers and alcoholics, poor children begging for coins, hawkers, thieves, and the homeless, a universe apart from the cloistered Sacred Heart Academy where Chopin began her education in September, 1855.

Thomas O'Flaherty may have inadvertently contributed even more to the shaping of his daughter's literary career when he died in November of that year. As a prominent St. Louis citizen, he was chosen to participate in the first train crossing of the Gasconade Bridge. The bridge collapsed, and ten of the eleven railroad cars fell thirty feet into the river below. Thirty people were killed, including Thomas. In Chopin's "The Story of an Hour" (1894), Louise Mallard learns that her husband has died in a similar accident. Far from grieving, she rejoices in her newfound freedom, only to discover that her husband is alive after all—just as in 1855 two people initially reported dead survived the train disaster. Plunged back into her former condition, Louise suffers a heart attack and dies. The onlookers believe that she could not bear the happiness of having her husband restored, but the reader knows that she has been killed by disappointment and despair. Toth suggests that the story may mirror Eliza O'Flaherty's feelings in 1855 and observes that Mrs. Mallard's first name, Louise, much resembles "Eleeza," as Kate's French-speaking relatives would have called her mother. Although there is no other evidence to support such a reading of Eliza O'Flaherty's sentiments, the similarities between the Gasconade tragedy and Chopin's story demonstrate the impression that the event made on the five-year-old girl.

Thomas' death interrupted Chopin's attendance at Sacred Heart, though she later returned to the school and was graduated in 1868. The interlude at home was, however, significant for the future writer. Her great-grandmother, Madame Victoire Verdon Charleville, assumed responsibility for the girl's education during this period, teaching her French and piano, and, more important, telling her stories about the founders of St. Louis. Among them were two of Madame Charleville's uncles who carried on affairs, one with an Osage Indian and the other with a woman of mixed blood. Madame Charleville had herself been four months pregnant when she married. She also told Kate about Marie Thérèse Bourgeois Chouteau, who left her brutal husband to live with another man, and of Elizabeth de Volsay, who lived with another man while her husband traveled on business. The husband received St. Louis' first divorce but proved no paragon of marital virtue: He left most of his fortune to an illegitimate daughter. Chopin thus became acquainted with people who flouted convention and chose freedom over traditional morality. These people would serve as models in her life and writing.

Outwardly, Chopin seemed the typical adolescent socialite. On December 31, 1868, she recorded in her diary, "I write . . . to day the first time for many months; parties, operas, concerts, skating and amusements ad infinitum have so taken up all my time that my dear reading and writing that I love so well have suffered much neglect." Much of her early reading was not unusual for the period—Sir Walter Scott's *Ivanhoe* (1820), Grace Aguilar's *The Days of Bruce* (1871), Margaret Oliphant's *Zaidee* (1856)—though Chopin would use these materials in her own way. Toth observes, for example, that Zaida in *A Night in Acadie* (1897) resembles the title character of Oliphant's novel; Isabella in Aguilar's historical romance marries the wrong man and later falls in love with someone named Robert, just as Edna Pontellier does in *The Awakening*.

Chopin's first surviving story, "Emancipation," which was written in 1869, suggests that an unusual intelligence lay behind the standard behavior and choice of books. In that piece, a caged animal enjoys a comfortable life. Then one day, the cage door is left open. After some hesitation, the creature flees, and though its life of freedom involves suffering, it never returns to captivity. Subtitling the tale "A Life Fable," Chopin already was indicating that she, too, preferred independence to security.

Yet on June 9, 1870, she married Oscar Chopin, a Louisiana cotton trader who was six years her senior. Oscar introduced her to New Orleans and the resort of Grand Isle. These places would color her fiction, though most of her work is set in the Cane River country around Cloutierville, where the Chopins lived after Oscar suffered financial losses in 1878 and 1879. Toth discusses various people in Natchitoches Parish who appear in the stories and novels. Father Jean Marie Beaulieu became Père Antoine in *At Fault* (1890) and a few short pieces. Charles Bertrand, another acquaintance, is the inspiration for the shopkeeper Chartrand in "Love on the Bon-Dieu" (1892). Most significant was Albert Sampite, who may have been Chopin's lover even before her husband's death in 1883, and almost certainly was afterwards. Sampite's daughter maintained that Kate destroyed the Sampite marriage. The handsome planter Alcée Laballière in "At the 'Cadian Ball" (1892) and "The Storm" (written in 1898, published in 1969) and Alcée Arobin and Robert Lebrun of *The Awakening* are patterned after Sampite. Toth points out that Chopin divided Albert's name to create Edna's two lovers, ALcée and RoBERT. *At Fault* thinly disguises Loca Sampite's unhappy marriage, with Kate appearing as the attractive widow, Thérèse Lafirme. *The Awakening* is even more autobiographical. Edna, like her creator, seeks escape from her boring marriage by having an affair. Eventually Edna realizes that she must rely only on herself. Shedding her clothes, the last sign of restraint, she swims out into the Gulf of Mexico and drowns.

Chopin, too, chose herself. In 1884 she left Albert to return to St. Louis. When her mother died the following year, Dr. Frederick Kolbenheyer, a family friend who had assisted at the births of two of Chopin's six children, suggested that she turn to writing to help her deal with her grief. Edna Pontellier had wished for a vocation that would give meaning to her life; Chopin was lucky enough to find hers. Toth claims that Chopin continued to wonder whether she had made the right choice. Her first published poem, "If It Might Be" (1889), suggests that she had not forgotten Albert.

> If it might be that thou didst need my life;
> Now on the instant would I end this strife
> 'Twixt hope and fear, and glad the end I'd meet
> With wonder only, to find death so sweet.

> If it might be that thou didst need my love;
> To love thee dear, my life's fond work would prove.
> All time, to tender watchfulness I'd give;
> And count it happiness, indeed, to live.

Albert was still in her thoughts three years later. In mid-June, 1892, flooding in Natchitoches Parish destroyed his crops. Later that summer, Chopin created Alcée Laballière, whose crops are ruined in a cyclone. "At the 'Cadian Ball" derives from Albert Sampite's love for Maria Normand DeLouche, with whom he had an affair after Kate left Louisiana. Maria becomes Calixta in the story, loving and loved by Alcée but married to Babinôt. Chopin's "The Storm," written six years later, portrayed Albert's relationship with Maria so passionately that the author did not try to find a publisher.

Toth indicates that there may have been other affairs in Chopin's life. One possible lover is John Alvarez Dillon. Dillon had grown up in St. Louis and was editor of the *St. Louis Post-Dispatch*, which published Chopin's second story, "A Point at Issue!" on October 27, 1889. Dillon later moved to New York to edit Joseph Pulitzer's *New York World*; Toth remarks that when Chopin went east in 1893 to find a publisher for her novel *Young Dr. Grosse* and a collection of short stories, she may also have been prompted by a desire to see Dillon again. There is no evidence that Chopin did carry on an affair with Dillon or anyone else in St. Louis, but she was popular with men.

Her work habits left her much time for socializing. Toth quotes her son Felix: " 'I have seen her go weeks and weeks without an idea, then suddenly grab her pencil and old lapboard (which was her workbench), and in a couple of hours her story was complete and off to the publisher.' " Her manuscripts confirm this statement, showing virtually no revisions, and her diary reveals periods of inactivity interrupted by frenzied writing. In January, 1892, for example, she produced three stories in two days, and all were accepted by *Harper's Young People*.

Chopin did not set out to write exclusively about Louisiana. A number of her early stories deal with Missouri, but these were hard to place in magazines, in contrast to her success with stories with a more southerly setting. As the 1890's progressed, she became less concerned with popularity than with truth. Rejecting William Dean Howells' genteel tradition, she focused on disappointment, loneliness, and the joys and sorrows of sex. These concerns culminated in *The Awakening*, a work well ahead of its time. Even those who recognized its artistry feared the novel's discussion of marital tedium, extramarital affairs, and women's search for fulfillment and independence. The *Congregationalist* wrote, "It is a brilliant piece of writing, but unwholesome in its influence. We cannot commend it." Willa Cather in the *Pittsburgh Leader* condemned the book; and the *St. Louis Post-Dispatch* commented that the book "should be labeled 'poison.' "

Many women loved the work. St. Louis' Wednesday Club, which was composed of women, honored the author, and some reviewers did praise her novel. The general reaction was, however, so negative that Chopin's daughter Lelia said that the response ended her mother's writing career. Toth explodes this myth, but shows that magazines no longer eagerly published Chopin's work even when they had paid for a story. Only five Chopin stories appeared between *The Awakening* and its author's death of a cerebral hemorrhage on August 22, 1904. For decades, her work remained neglected, but the resurrection of Chopin's reputation appears permanent. Nearly a century after her death, she is justly recognized as a leading nineteenth century American writer.

Joseph Rosenblum

Sources for Further Study

Booklist. LXXXVII, October 1, 1990, p. 248.
Boston Globe. December 9, 1990, p. 13.
Chicago Tribune. December 16, 1990, XIV, p. 6.
Library Journal. CXV, October 15, 1990, p. 89.
Los Angeles Times. November 30, 1990, p. E14.
The New York Times. November 27, 1990, p. C19.
The New York Times Book Review. December 30, 1990, p. 10.
Publishers Weekly. CCXXXVII, October 12, 1990, p. 52.
The Times-Picayune. November 18, 1990, p. E7.
The Washington Post Book World. XX, November 25, 1990, p. 3.
Washington Times. December 3, 1990, p. F1.

KILLING MISTER WATSON

Author: Peter Matthiessen (1927-   )
Publisher: Random House (New York). 372 pp. $21.95
Type of work: Novel
Time: 1892-1910
Locale: The Ten Thousand Islands off the southwest coast of Florida, between Fort Myers and Key West

E. J. Watson is the most powerful and most dangerous man on the Florida frontier until his reputation and the fear of his neighbors combine to cause his death

> *Principal characters:*
>
> EDGAR J. WATSON, a planter, merchant, family man, and murderer, liked and respected but feared by other pioneers in this wild area
>
> JANE WATSON, E. J.'s second wife and the mother of three children, Eddie, Lucius, and Carrie
>
> EDNA WATSON, E. J.'s third wife and the mother of three children
>
> HENRY THOMPSON, an employee of E. J. Watson and operator of Watson's boat
>
> JEAN CHEVELIER, a French resident of the area who hunts plume birds and searches for lost Indian treasure
>
> BILL HOUSE, the son of a local landowner, an employee of Chevelier, and a reluctant participant in the killing of E. J. Watson
>
> BIG JIM COLE, a local entrepreneur, braggart, and political force
>
> LESLEY COX, a fugitive and E. J. Watson's foreman whose killing of two other employees leads to Watson's death
>
> FRANK B. TIPPINS, the sheriff who investigates Watson's death
>
> TED SMALLWOOD, a postmaster, former poacher, and neutral observer of Watson's death

Peter Matthiessen's sixth novel is partly the history of a violent man, Edgar J. Watson, a historical figure about whom there continue to be many rumors but few facts. It is also partly a record of the way in which the prolific wildlife of southern Florida, west of the Everglades, was destroyed in a few short years in the late nineteenth and early twentieth centuries. From the sparse remaining records, Matthiessen has constructed a story that, as he says in an author's note, contains "nothing that could *not* have happened."

The story is told through the imaginary reminiscences of nine of the people who lived in the area and knew Watson during the years between his arrival in 1892 and his death in 1910, as well as through fictitious historical accounts and newspaper reports. Among the narrators are Watson's friend and employee, Henry Thompson; Bill House, a solid citizen who has worked for the French plume hunter and misanthrope, Jean Chevelier, and who is a reluctant but important participant in the shooting of Watson; and Watson's sentimental and conventional daughter, Carrie Watson Langford, whom her father married off for political reasons when she was fourteen years old.

The narrators provide various pictures of Watson and what his contemporaries thought of him. Soon after his arrival in the islands, he buys a land claim from a widow whose husband had been killed in a gunfight. Rumors about Watson's tendency to violence begin to circulate when his property is enlarged following the death of Chevelier. The Frenchman had promised in a will to leave his holdings to two young members of the Richard Hamilton family who looked after him in his final illness, but when they arrive at his home for a routine visit they find Watson, who tells them that Chevelier is dead and buried and that he had sold him a quitclaim deed to the property. No will ever surfaces. The young Hamiltons are frightened away, and the story begins to circulate that Watson helped Chevelier to his death.

Watson's reputation for violence continues to grow, even as he establishes himself more firmly as the most successful planter and trader in southwestern Florida. In an encounter with a local landowner, he uses a knife to cut the man's throat, not quite fatally; the man and his family sell out and move away. A book about the West surfaces, containing the story that Watson murdered the famous Western outlaw, Belle Starr; two cowboys who come looking for Watson to avenge Belle Starr's death are shot by another local gunman. It becomes general knowledge that Watson grew up in northern Florida but was forced to flee the area because of a murder charge. In the West, he committed at least one more murder, possibly killed Belle Starr, was jailed as a horse thief in Arkansas but escaped, and returned to northern Florida, before finding his way to Chatham Bend, the location of his plantation.

Watson's home, Chatham Bend, becomes a place for other people to avoid. Many of the fishermen and hunters refuse to pass by in their boats unless they are carrying loaded weapons. Before his wife, Jane, and their children join him there, Watson has a housekeeper who bears him a daughter, and the housekeeper's sister is also among his mistresses. Other rumors circulate—one implies that laborers on Watson's place may be killed when they ask for their wages, but because most of these men are black or Indian none of the local whites inquires too closely into the facts. When two deputies try to arrest Watson in connection with a murder, they are frightened away.

Even as the people of the area fear Watson, most of them claim to like and respect him. He is unfailingly polite to everyone, especially women; he has more education than his neighbors; he is generous when people in the area need help; he is a handsome man and the most skillful businessman in the area; he pays all of his bills promptly; and he has a vision of the potential economic expansion of the area and his role in it—the Frenchman, Chevelier, calls him "l'empereur." Many of the narrators refuse to believe the stories about him, although it is clear that they are very cautious in their dealings with him. He gains some sympathy because his genteel wife, Jane, is very ill. She moves to Fort Myers with her younger children and before long she dies.

The first half of *Killing Mister Watson* moves rather slowly. Chevelier receives much attention as an irascible man who hunts plume birds (egrets) for the market, but who at the same time is appalled at the wholesale destruction of birds, alligators, and other wildlife—first by local hunters and eventually by tourists who slaughter indiscriminately for mere pleasure. Chevelier is finally pushed over the edge when Northerners find the treasure trove of Indian artifacts he had been searching for ever since coming into the area. The priceless relics are moved north, eventually to be destroyed in a fire. When they are taken away, Chevelier is too sick and disgusted even to protest; he prepares to die.

The first half of the novel develops a picture of an essentially lawless frontier society. The people of the area are poor, hardworking, suspicious of outsiders, and resentful of the encroachment of external authority. Several game wardens appointed to protect the disappearing wildlife are murdered and no suspects are ever identified or charged. Channel markers which are put up in the dangerous inlets and bays of the area to provide navigational guidelines for visiting yachtsmen disappear as soon as they are installed—the natives know where the channels are, and they want no outsiders in their waters. Murders and other crimes are avenged by those involved or by relatives; the sheriffs are wary of intruding.

Matthiessen's horror at the ravaging of the natural resources of the area, which is comparable to the hunting to extinction of the passenger pigeon or the bison in other parts of the country, is made clear. He also shows that the dredging of rivers and creeks in and around the Everglades has ruined the area as a habitat for wildlife. The author's commitment to environmental causes, very close to the surface in this part of the novel, is given additional force by having the destruction reported by those who participated in it, only to realize what they have done to a land they love. That commitment, however, diverts attention from the story of E. J. Watson until one more violent event takes place.

Killing Mister Watson gathers momentum and dramatic force with an especially horrifying episode which takes place in 1901. A local family, the Atwells, have some claim to a piece of property, Lost Man Key, although legal claims in this frontier area are cloudy at best and are often enforced by violence. The Atwells have allowed a young man named Wally Tucker and his pregnant wife Bet to live on the land, build a house there, and raise a crop. Watson buys the claim and tells the sellers to move the squatters out. There is a mild attempt by the Atwells to soften his demand, but he is implacable; the Tuckers must go. The young husband defies Watson and says he will not leave until his crops are in; shortly thereafter, someone hears shooting. Men passing in a boat find both the Tuckers dead; Wally Tucker has been shot in the back, Bet in the head, and their bodies have been left to rot.

There are no witnesses, although the circumstantial evidence is strong that Watson was responsible; he has left Tucker's defiant note where other men can find it. Watson's son by his first marriage, Rob, who has been living at Chatham Bend with his father, is never seen again after the deaths of the Tuckers, leading to the rumor that his father forced him to kill the pregnant woman and that he has fled. Local men bury the bodies and find the evidence pointing to Watson, but no legal action is ever taken, and no sheriff or deputy is foolish enough to go into Watson's territory to try to arrest him.

Watson disappears from the area, not returning until 1906, by which time the story of the death of the Tuckers has changed and faded. In the interim Watson returned to northern Florida, where he was accused of two more murders in connection with a family feud and put on trial. Local resentment ran so high that there was a change of venue, but, since his friend Jim Cole had helped to pick the jury and the only witness against him was a black man, Watson was summarily acquitted. Back in the islands, he brings with him his third wife, Edna, a sweet young woman, and their two infant children. None of the locals seems disposed to accuse him of the murder of the Tuckers. They convince themselves that the young wife has gentled Watson and that he has reformed.

Watson's downfall coincides with a terrible hurricane which strikes southern Florida in October, 1910. He has moved his family away from Chatham Bend to avoid the storm. While he is gone, the house is occupied only by his foreman, Leslie Cox, a sinister man who evidently knew Watson earlier in his life and has some claim on him; a hired hand named Green Waller and his lover, the gigantic woman Hannah Smith; and a black field hand. The storm causes terrible destruction throughout the area, but when it is over the black man appears in the village of Chokoloskee with a wild tale. He says that Cox murdered Hannah Smith and Green Waller and forced the terrified black man to help him eviscerate the bodies, load them with metal, and sink them in the river.

Later, according to the black man, Watson's boat came up the river, carrying Watson himself and Dutchy Melvin, a former foreman who had annoyed Watson. Cox, who had hidden in a shed, shot Melvin, whereupon Watson turned the boat around and left the area. According to the black man's account, Watson had planned to have Cox kill Melvin. Under hostile questioning by Sheriff Frank B. Tippins, the frightened witness changes his story to exonerate Watson. It is clear, however, that Watson has gone to considerable trouble to create an alibi for himself.

Their nerves scraped raw by the devastation of the storm, the men of the area gather their guns and prepare to confront Watson at last. He denies all charges and says he will go and either kill Cox or bring him back. Later he returns, claiming to have shot Cox in the head and lost the body in the high water left by the hurricane. He tosses the men a hat with a hole in the crown, defiantly claiming it is Cox's.

D. D. House, a respected businessman, refuses to accept the story and tells Watson to turn over his arms. Watson refuses and there is a standoff; when Watson raises his shotgun the men fire and kill him. His body is towed by boat to a nearby key and buried in a shallow grave. Eventually his daughter Carrie has it disinterred and reburied next to her mother in Fort Myers. Sheriff Tippins carries out an investigation, but none of the men is ever arrested or tried. They maintain that in the absence of any sheriff or deputy they were trying to arrest Watson and shot only when he resisted arrest. The black man whose account implicated Watson is taken on a boat for transfer to Key West, but he vanishes overboard before the boat reaches its destination.

Matthiessen is obviously fascinated by the contradictory nature of Edgar J. Watson's character, by the combination of admirable and revolting traits found in a single individual. Yet Watson is also the vehicle Matthiessen uses to present the history of a unique area. Through Watson, the author creates a many-layered picture of a rough frontier area in which racial hatred, land hunger, and the rapid disappearance of the wildlife that provided some income combine to produce a violent and rancorous society. *Killing Mister Watson* is not always clear; the variety of narrators and characters is sometimes confusing. The force of the central character and the special nature of the locale, however, make this a memorable novel.

John M. Muste

Sources for Further Study

Booklist. LXXXVI, April 15, 1990, p. 1585.
Chicago Tribune. June 24, 1990, XIV, p. 1.
Harper's Bazaar. CXXIII, July, 1990, p. 18.
Los Angeles Times Book Review. July 8, 1990, p. 1.
The New Republic. CCIII, November 5, 1990, p. 43.
The New York Times Book Review. XCV, June 24, 1990, p. 7.
The New Yorker. LXVI, September 17, 1990, p. 108.
Newsweek. CXV, June 11, 1990, p. 63.
Publishers Weekly. CCXXXVII, April 27, 1990, p. 52.
Time. CXXXVI, July 16, 1990, p. 82.
The Times Literary Supplement. August 31, 1990, p. 916.
The Washington Post Book World. XX, June 24, 1990 p. 5.

THE KING

Author: Donald Barthelme (1931-1989)
Publisher: Harper & Row (New York). Illustrated. 158 pp. $16.95
Type of work: Novel
Time: The World War II period
Locale: King Arthur's court

King Arthur and his knights battle the Nazis in a postmodern comedy

> *Principal characters:*
> KING ARTHUR, a monarch who has lived several centuries too long
> GUINEVERE, his queen
> LAUNCELOT, Guinevere's lover
> MORDRED, Arthur's son
> WALTER THE PENNILESS, a socialist agitator
> THE BLUE KNIGHT,
> THE YELLOW KNIGHT,
> THE BROWN KNIGHT, and
> THE BLACK KNIGHT, knights of King Arthur's court

Donald Barthelme, one of the most important American fiction writers of the postwar period, died in July, 1989, at the age of fifty-eight. The author of fifteen books—ten short-story collections, four novels, and an award-winning children's book—Barthelme was not only one of the masters of the "postmodern" style but arguably one of its originators, who seemed to burst on the scene in the early 1960's with his talent fully developed. His first published collection of stories, *Come Back, Dr. Caligari* (1964), contains some of his most radical experiments with the collage technique that was to become his trademark. In one story from that collection, "The Viennese Opera Ball," such traditional and seemingly indispensable fictional elements as character, setting, and plot are completely ignored, and the reader is presented with a mosaic of clichés, platitudes, technical jargon, and advertising slogans, along with phrases lifted from such literary classics as Ernest Hemingway's "The Short Happy Life of Francis Macomber."

Barthelme's early stories—along with John Cage's music and Andy Warhol's paintings—heralded the end of the modernist period in the arts. Literary modernism, represented by such authors as Ernest Hemingway, William Faulkner, and Virginia Woolf, perfected a style of writing that avoided the omniscient narration and ornate literary language of the nineteenth century and instead stressed consistency in narrative point of view, psychological character development, and a return to a more natural, unpretentious use of language. "Make it new," was Ezra Pound's rallying cry.

By the 1950's, modernism had established itself as the dominant style, and experimental writers gradually began to turn for inspiration to the very things the modernists shunned: two-dimensional characterization, cliché-ridden dialogue, and pulp-fiction plotting. Instead of trying to "make it new," postmodernists force readers to contemplate the old.

Although Barthelme is probably best known as a short-story writer, his four novels are remarkable in their own right, and it is in the longer format that his underlying themes are most apparent.

Snow White (1967), Barthelme's first novel, is a retelling of the familiar fairy-tale standard. The appeal of the frame story for Barthelme is precisely that it is exhausted, overused, devoid of possibility. Even the book's characters are bored. Snow White laments her fate. "Well it is terrific to be anticipating a prince . . . but it is still waiting, and waiting as a mode of existence is, as Brack has noted, a darksome mode." When asked why she remains with the seven dwarfs, she replies, "It must be laid, I suppose, to a failure of the imagination." The absurdity of Snow White's fairy-tale existence is heightened by the fact that she is a thoroughly modern woman. In fact, she took courses in women's studies in college, along with Theoretical Foundations of Psychology, Personal Resources I and II, and Realism and Idealism in the Contemporary Italian Novel.

Barthelme's second novel, *The Dead Father* (1975), examines another exhausted mode of existence. Fatherhood is a role as burdensome as Snow White's. "I never wanted it, it was thrust upon me," says the title character. Fatherhood consists of a series of meaningless ritualistic actions, all form and no content. When someone asks the Dead Father what his latest edifying lecture meant, he answers, "[I]t meant I made a speech."

Halfway through the novel is a book-within-a-book, "A Manual for Sons." A survival course for children, the manual outlines methods for dealing with the oppressive presence of the father—including patricide. Against the backdrop of Barthelme's relentless parody of stock phrases and genre-fiction situations, it is impossible to avoid reading *The Dead Father* as a literary allegory. The larger-than-life father clearly represents the early-modern masters, and the sons are the disfranchised authors of the postmodern era, who must somehow learn to ignore the awesome and daunting accomplishments of their predecessors.

The King, Barthelme's fourth and final novel, is a restatement and refinement of the themes presented in his earlier work. Like *Snow White*, *The King* recycles old, familiar tales, perennial favorites in art and literature. Thomas Malory's *Le Morte D'Arthur* (written c. 1469; published 1485) was itself a retelling of stories found in Chrétien de Troyes and Geoffrey of Monmouth. In the sixteenth century, Edmund Spenser incorporated Arthurian elements in *The Fairie Queene* (1590, 1596), and in the seventeenth century John Milton contemplated an Arthurian epic (one of the most important unwritten books in English). Alfred, Lord Tennyson expressed high Victorian ideals in his *Idylls of the King* (1859-1885), while Richard Wagner's Arthurian operas were Nietzschean in outlook. Mark Twain laughed at chivalry in *A Connecticut Yankee in King Arthur's Court* (1889). T. H. White spoofed it more lovingly in *The Once and Future King* (1958), which in turn inspired Alan Jay Lerner and Frederick Loewe's Broadway musical *Camelot*, forever associated with the White House years of John F. Kennedy.

Again, it is the shopworn quality of the Arthurian material that appeals to Barthelme. The legends provide an overdetermined historical context for his characters to struggle against: The weight of their roles, the inevitability of their fates is almost too much to bear. "I'm getting sick, sore, and tired of this," complains Guinevere, echoing Snow White. The dreadful lack of surprise affects them all. When his subjects wonder who will win the current war, Arthur admits, "I'm terribly tempted to have a look at Merlin's Prophecy and see how the thing turns out."

Like Snow White and the dwarfs, Barthelme's Arthurians are trapped by their roles. The world is made up of kings and queens, knights and ladies, and various and sundry lower orders, and each class must obey its own unwritten rules. Arthur knows full well that there are as many drawbacks as rewards to kingship: "I am thinking of cutting my throat. . . . I know that this is not a course of action open to kings." Guinevere is similarly trapped by the role society expects her to play. "It's rather terrible, being a queen. One has to attend functions. One has to stand there smiling while the local fellow explains how the peat is packaged." The knights, too, sense that there is more to life than what they are permitted to experience. "I spend my whole life *hacking* at things," Launcelot complains. "Is this the best way to exist in the world?"

Indeed, the world of chivalry is ripe for extinction. The oppressed poor are ready to revolt. "We don't want the extraordinary. . . . It is a time for the unexceptional, the untalented, the ordinary, the downright maladroit. Quite a large constituency." That Arthur and his knights realize this is evidenced by their obsession with obituaries in *The Times*: who got the most column-inches, who merited a photograph. Launcelot has taken the precaution of going over the highlights of his career with the obituary editor in advance.

Barthelme's treatment of the Arthurian legends acknowledges and parodies earlier writers' belief in the ongoing relevance of the material. While others merely suggest analogies between Avalon and contemporary Britain, Barthelme insists on them. His knights are fighting the Nazis in World War II, and the Holy Grail they seek is a new atomic superweapon. Ezra Pound and Lord Haw-Haw broadcast pro-Fascist propaganda from behind enemy lines. The Americans have yet to enter the war, and the survival of the Round Table is threatened. "What is one knight on horseback, however accomplished, to six hundred aircraft engaged in precision bombing?"

Postmodernism is a postwar condition, and Barthelme grounds his book in the 1940's specifically to associate the anachronistic knights with the high-modernist period, whose artistic ideals Barthelme's own writing challenges. The aptly named Blue Knight was smothered by modernism as a child.

My mother was a very modern person—*advanced*, don't you know. Fond of Alban Berg, the *Wozzeck* man. Not only was I forced repeatedly to listen to *Wozzeck*, in the womb, but also to *Lulu*. . . . These horrors aside, there was the poetry of Wyndham Lewis, proprietor of *Blast*.

The root cause of the Blue Knight's despair is his realization that "even if Paradise were regained it would have music by Milhaud and frescoes by the Italian Futurists." Modernism has become deadly dull, part of the status quo.

While the issue of the postmodern exhaustion of roles was first investigated in

Snow White, the antiestablishment agenda of *The King* continues the argument of *The Dead Father*. The greatest threat to Arthur is not the Nazis but rather his own son Mordred, an ambitious young man who has no time for the antiquated posturings of chivalry, which he dismisses as mere "theatre." Mordred is ready to take over control of the government, but Arthur has no intention of stepping down. "The succession is not something one wants to think about. . . . I've evaded the issue so far." The longer Arthur holds on to the crown, the more patricidal Mordred becomes, and he sees his murderous designs as simple self-defense. Since Arthur is "as much a father to me as a sickle to a stand of wheat," Mordred must become "an antidote to kingliness." His coping strategy comes directly from "A Manual for Sons."

The King effortlessly draws together the major themes of Barthelme's career and restates them with elegant simplicity and abundant humor. In fact, the writing is so consistently amusing that it is difficult to believe that there is any seriousness of purpose to the book at all. Barthelme's critics have long debated whether he is primarily a philosophical writer who also happens to be funny, or a humorist who also happens to be philosophical. Interestingly, the same question has been asked of Samuel Beckett, one of Barthelme's mentors. In the 1950's, Beckett's plays and stories were considered grueling existentialist exercises. Later the same works came to be seen as hilarious comedies.

Like that of many great writers before him, Barthelme's method was to focus on two worlds, "one dead, the other powerless to be born," as Matthew Arnold put it in "Stanzas from the Grande Chartreuse" (1867). His great gift was his ability to see the merits and shortcomings of both sides in any struggle. Though a radical post-modernist himself, Barthelme never argues his position; instead, he simply offers the example of his own work as an alternative to what has come before—an antidote to modernism.

Edward St. John

Sources for Further Study

Booklist. LXXXVI, March 1, 1990, p. 1226.
Chicago Tribune. June 10, 1990, XIV, p. 3.
Kirkus Reviews. LVIII, February 15, 1990, p. 200.
Library Journal. CXV, April 1, 1990, p. 134.
Magazine of Fantasy and Science Fiction. LXXIX, December, 1990, p. 90.
The New York Times Book Review. XCV, May 27, 1990, p. 8.
The New Yorker. LXVI, July 9, 1990, p. 92.
Publishers Weekly. CCXXXVII, March 23, 1990, p. 65.
The Wall Street Journal. May 1, 1990, p. A16.
The Washington Post Book World. XX, June 3, 1990, p. 1.

KING OF THE WORLD

Author: Merrill Joan Gerber (1938-   )
Publisher: Pushcart Press (Wainscott, New York). 276 pp. $18.95
Type of work: Novel
Time: The late 1960's to the early 1980's
Locale: Mexico and California

King of the World *chronicles the creation and dissolution of the hapless marriage of Ginny and Michael Fisher*

> *Principal characters:*
> GINNY FISHER, a young woman with a crooked spine who works as a
>   hospital ward clerk
> MICHAEL FISHER, Ginny's husband
> ADAM FISHER, Ginny and Michael's adopted infant son
> AGNES FISHER, Michael's mother
> PAULA, Ginny's sister
> ANNIE, Ginny's therapist

Accounts of wife and child abuse are the daily stuff of newspaper and television reports. The most sensational of these stories have been analyzed in sociological treatises and thinly disguised in fictional accounts with graphic details. Fortunately, Merrill Joan Gerber's *King of the World* is neither of these. Although the novel examines what has come to be known in popular psychological terminology as a "dysfunctional family," Gerber generally veers away from sensationalism in favor of peering into the quirks and glitches in her characters' personalities. This is a tale of two arrested adolescents: One eventually self-destructs and the other ultimately decides to accept the responsibility of becoming an adult.

There is a fairy-tale quality to the opening segment of *King of the World*, which is set in Mexico in the late 1960's. Michael Fisher, a beautiful, golden-haired hippie, has rescued his ugly duckling lover, Ginny, from a boring hospital job in Los Angeles and carried her off to Tijuana to frolic: ". . . naked in the sun, nearly beside herself with a wild, scary joy. Michael had saved her again from her dullness, from her hopeless, small mind, from her frightened, useless way of thinking." Styling himself "King of the World," Michael crowns Ginny his queen, with a broken starfish for a crown.

The idyll is not without its dark undercurrents, however. When a sailor from Barbados propositions Ginny, offering to pay for her favors, Michael thinks it is a fine idea but allows Ginny to decline. This Fisher King is also a poor fisherman. Boasting of his skill, he rents a small boat and takes Ginny and her puppy, Whisper, onto the ocean to teach her to fish. When the motor balks, the fish refuse to bite, and Michael sticks a hook into his hand, his frustration boils over into violence. First he throws the tackle box overboard; then he throws the dog overboard. After he has calmed down, he apologizes:

"Don't go away, don't leave me, Ginny," he begged. "Don't be mad, I didn't mean it, I need you
so much. I can't live without you."
"I need you too, Michael," she said quietly.
"We'll be happy together, the rest of our lives," he said. "I promise you."
"I know we will," she told him. "I know it."

So much for the fairy tale.

When the story resumes fifteen years later, Ginny and Michael are mired in the
Wasteland. They have bounced from one city to another as Michael has lost one job
after another. Ginny again is working in a hospital, and Michael has lost his latest
job as a dental technician making gold crowns. They have no money, but Ginny is
intent on adopting a baby; a baby, Ginny believes, is her last hope for joy.

Gerber uses an omniscient narrator to shift between Michael's schizophrenic, paranoid view of the world and Ginny's growing desperation. Although this technique
helps to impart some understanding to each character, the reader ultimately sympathizes with Ginny's situation. The marriage has been sustained through mutual
neediness. Michael needs Ginny's steadiness and loyalty; he also needs her to obey
his every whim—he is, after all, the King of the World. Ginny needs the physical
adoration and edgy stimulation that Michael provides, and she is dependent on his
needing her. Catching sight of a bum in front of the bank, Ginny realizes that
Michael would be in the same situation were it not for her.

Michael is convinced he is being abused by the world. In his mind, it all started
when Eric Feldmutter was made an Eagle Scout and he was not. His mother explained to him that Eric's mother must have had some pull with the Boy Scouts. Not
being made an Eagle Scout ruined his life: "It would all have been different if they'd
picked him to be the Eagle Scout. It would have been all easy after that. Success
breeds success. The rich get rich and the good get screwed." He can conceive of no
other reason for his failure. He knows he should be a millionaire. He is brilliant and
beautiful and deserves the best.

Ginny believes that she deserves nothing. Her life has been blighted by her crooked
back. Doctors poked and prodded and X-rayed the progress of her scoliosis throughout her adolescence, finally deciding that she could cope without surgery. The X-rays,
however, left her sterile, and the examinations left her feeling ugly and unlovable.
The miracle of Michael's attraction to her was her salvation:

Michael's hands could make her whole: he drew them across her back, and her deformity disappeared. Her atrophied muscle grew strong, her hump grew flat, the fish-bone of her back ejected
the s-shaped snake which inhabited it and became an arrow, beautifully straight and strong and
perfect. . . . Like a magician her husband heaved her into the sea with his hand a rudder between
her thin buttocks. . . . She drowned, she rose, she drowned again. . . . Gladly she gave herself to
it, gladly she was submerged, covered, obliterated. She had no doubt that he had the strength and
knowledge to save her, to save them both, to bring them to some victorious conclusion, a thing she
could never do for herself in a million years.

Michael, however, can save no one—not even himself.

Ginny's determination to adopt a baby prevails. Through a private adoption that she orchestrates, they receive an infant, whom Ginny names Adam. Quickly her attention is refocused from Michael's needs to Adam's. Although his ultimate deterioration is momentarily halted by the arrival of his mother, Agnes, who swoops down on the family like a fickle fairy godmother, Michael becomes continually more paranoid and ineffectual. Gerber admits the reader into Michael's tormented mind with mixed results. Ultimately his view of the world is so skewed and his picture of himself so inflated that the reader both laughs at and recoils from him. Certainly Gerber creates some terror by implying that this character could try anything. The reader fears for the safety of Ginny and Adam. Michael cannot seem to accomplish anything, however. During his most desperate act, an attempt to rape two coeds, he conceives of the perfect weapon to use in a rape: a gun that could be worn around the forehead like a surgeon's light. "A string attached to the trigger could be held between the teeth. It was the idea of a genius!" The rape is a fiasco: Michael cannot get an erection and runs out on the coeds, threatening to return. Return he does—to apologize—but he is recognized and arrested.

As Michael falls apart, Ginny begins to take faltering steps toward independence and responsibility. At the insistence of her brother-in-law, she begins therapy and starts a course to become a court reporter. The reader sees her gradually caring less and less for and about Michael, but before she finally cuts herself off from him, she ends up in a battered women's shelter. After she emerges from their program, Michael's hold on her is broken. Ginny's story is in many ways typical of those of many single mothers in today's society. What perhaps sets Gerber's rendition of this story apart is her split focus. She lays no real blame—Michael is simply unable to cope with the world, and Ginny is finally unable to cope with Michael.

Gerber has published stories in magazines ranging from *The New Yorker* and *The Atlantic* to *Redbook*; in the latter she is the most frequently published short-story writer. Her prose moves swiftly and carries the reader along with some suspense. Gerber's intense focus on the two major characters is typical of the short-story genre, with which she is most familiar. The other characters in this novel appear in the extreme periphery of the protagonists' vision and are often caricatures. For example, Annie, Ginny's therapist, is grotesquely overweight and cannot stop eating, and Paula, Ginny's older sister, is almost too good to be true, though she appears in the novel only in telephone conversations. The entirety of Ginny's life is wrapped up first in Michael and then in Adam. Her connections with other people seem almost as unreal as Michael's fantasies and paranoid visions about the rest of the world. The unreality of Michael's world is understandable, but the disconnectedness of Ginny's world can be traced to lack of development.

Another aspect of this novel that seems to lack real development is the characters' tenuous relationship to the myth of the Wasteland and the Fisher King who guards the grail. Gerber tosses in the motifs—sterility, fishing, a search for something unattainable—but the allusions tantalize rather than resonate in an integrated symbolic system. The story of Ginny and Michael makes for good reading; it reflects the struggles of society's dislocated and lost souls. *The King of the World* may even be an exemplary novel—it may encourage some reader to take control of her life for her child's sake—but it awkwardly carries the weight of the grail legend. The curious effect at the end of the novel when Michael commits suicide is "Well, so much for the Fisher King."

Merrill Joan Gerber is an accomplished writer. Her strength lies in her insightful chronicling of the workings of twisted and stunted minds, letting the reader see the disturbing world inhabited by her characters. *The King of the World* should attract a wider audience for her work.

Jane Anderson Jones

Sources for Further Study

Belles Lettres. V, Spring, 1990, p. 19.
Booklist. LXXXVI, December 15, 1989, p. 812.
Chicago Tribune. January 19, 1990, V, p. 3.
The Christian Science Monitor. June 1, 1990, p. 9.
Kirkus Reviews. LVII, November 15, 1990, p. 1616.
Library Journal. CXV, January, 1990, p. 148.
Los Angeles Times. February 5, 1990, p. E5.
The New York Times Book Review. XCV, February 18, 1990, p. 20.
Publishers Weekly. CCXXXVI, November 24, 1989, p. 58.
The Washington Post Book World. XX, January 28, 1990, p. 9.

THE KNIGHT, DEATH, AND THE DEVIL

Author: Ella Leffland (1931-   )
Publisher: William Morrow (New York). 718 pp. $22.95
Type of work: Novel
Time: 1893-1946
Locale: Germany, Austria, Sweden, Switzerland, and France

A fictionalized account of the life of Hermann Göring, the second most powerful official in Nazi Germany, a man of many contradictions

> *Principal characters:*
> HERMANN GÖRING, a leading official in Adolf Hitler's Germany
> HEINRICH GÖRING, Hermann's father, a retired diplomat
> FRANZISKA GÖRING, Hermann's mother
> KARL GÖRING, Hermann's elder brother
> ALBERT GÖRING, Hermann's younger brother
> CARIN GÖRING, Hermann's first wife
> EMMY GÖRING, Hermann's second wife, an actress
> EDDA GÖRING, Hermann's daughter
> HERMANN VON EPENSTEIN, the wealthy benefactor of the Göring family, Franziska's lover
> THOMAS VON KANTZOW, Carin's son
> ROSE KORWAN, Emmy's best friend, a Jewish actress
> ADOLF HITLER, Führer of the National Socialist German Workers Party
> ERNST (PUTZI) HANFSTAENGL, Hitler's foreign press officer
> JOSEPH GOEBBELS, Hitler's propaganda minister
> ALBERT SPEER, Hitler's architect who becomes minister of armaments

Hermann Göring was, for most of Adolf Hitler's bloody reign of terror, the second most powerful man in Nazi Germany. A large, handsome, imposing figure, Göring loved his friends, relatives, and servants, and cared deeply for animals and art. A heroic pilot during World War I, he was a compelling public speaker. Under Hitler, he created the Luftwaffe, the Gestapo, and the concentration camps. He was also a drug addict and a generally inefficient administrator. Ella Leffland presents Göring as a good and intelligent man who allows his conception of Germany's destined greatness and belief in his homeland as a magical, mythical forest to override his better judgment. Leffland is the author of three previous novels: *Mrs. Munck* (1970), the story of an oppressed woman; *Love Out of Season* (1974), an account of a doomed love affair; and *Rumors of Peace* (1979), a portrait of small-town California during World War II. *The Knight, Death, and the Devil*, though a considerable departure from these books, confirms Leffland's skill as a storyteller attentive to the nuances of time, place, and character.

Göring's father, Heinrich, is a career diplomat, the first governor of southwest Africa, whose accomplishments are unappreciated. Expecting a promotion when he returns from Africa in 1889, he is instead appointed minister to Haiti because of his reputation for liberalism. In 1896, he retires and returns to Germany. Waiting for him is the three-year-old son he has never seen. When Franziska Göring, who is twenty-five years younger than her husband, becomes pregnant with her fourth child, she leaves Haiti for Germany and later deposits two-month-old Hermann with friends. When the family returns, the boy strikes his parents. Hermann, however, soon becomes devoted to his father but eventually transfers his affections from the weak, disillusioned Heinrich to Hermann von Epenstein, the family friend after whom he is named.

Von Epenstein, a wealthy Jewish aristocrat, is also the lover of Franziska and the father of her fifth child. These facts Heinrich ignores because his friend allows the Görings to live for free in Burg Veldenstein, an elaborate Austrian castle that becomes the center of young Hermann's life. As Leffland presents it, Göring's story is the quest for a strong father figure with Adolf Hitler eventually filling that need, and a parallel quest to recover Veldenstein after von Epenstein evicts the family when he marries a younger woman.

Growing up at Veldenstein is an idyllic experience for Hermann, who has been filled with German history and myth by von Epenstein. To his parents he writes, "I am the inheritor of all the chivalry of German knighthood." Hermann loves everything to do with the military and, after being expelled from several schools for rowdiness, spends five happy years at a military academy. He joins the army in 1912 and wins his first medal during World War I for showing initiative when he disobeys orders. Ignoring wrongheaded authority becomes a lifelong pattern of behavior, with the notable exception of his obedience to Hitler. Disabled by degenerative arthritis in his hips, Göring forges documents to become a pilot under a false name. After further heroics, he assumes command of Manfred von Richthofen's squadron after the death of the German ace. Suicidally reckless, he crash-lands after being shot and sustains injuries that lead to morphine addiction.

Göring's potential for following a dictator is evident even before he meets Hitler. He is disgraced by Germany's defeat in World War I and angered by the political maneuverings of communists:

> One can feel only outrage against people who attack those who sacrificed themselves for their country," he tells his fellow fliers, "only outrage against the revolutionary forces sweeping through Germany and bringing deepest shame upon it. The new fight for freedom and principles and morals has begun. We will fight against those forces which are seeking to enslave us. . . . The same qualities that made the Richthofen Geschwader great will prevail in peace as well as in war. Our time will come again.

In 1923, Göring meets the two most important people in his life. Carin von Kantzow, a thirty-four-year-old Swedish wife and mother, is overwhelmed by the dashing German, moves in with him a week after they meet, and soon marries him. Göring is unimpressed the first time he hears Hitler speak but finds that the politician's words stick in his mind. When they meet, Hitler is attracted by Göring's energy— "A huge, eager drive, waiting for release"—and decides to exploit it, making the war hero the head of the National Socialist party's private army. Though repelled by Hitler's racism and unmoved by his ideology, Göring is drawn by his "genius for moving the masses. . . . I want to break the Weimar government. I want to break the Versailles Treaty. I want a free and powerful Germany." Göring's romanticized idea of Germany's destiny causes him to ignore Hitler's obvious deficiencies until the middle of World War II.

As a burgeoning Nazi, Göring founds the Schutzstaffel (SS), is elected to Parliament, and becomes speaker of the German Reichstag. When Hitler is appointed chancellor in 1933, Göring is made a general and prime minister of Prussia. Carin cannot share her devoted husband's glory, having died from longtime lung problems. In her honor, Göring creates Carinhall, a substitute for the lost Veldenstein, built at state expense because it is a ministerial residence—the first of numerous abuses of power. Albert Speer, Hitler's architect, describes this country estate as "pure Göring, which is all things squashed together in one fistlump." The elaborate mausoleum Göring designs for Carin does not daunt his new wife, Emmy, an actress. Emmy learns to live with the ghost of Carin and, three years after her marriage, gives birth to Edda, Göring's only child.

Göring's relationship with Hitler and such fellow Nazis as Joseph Goebbels and Joachim von Ribbentrop is tempestuous. He creates the Luftwaffe, all the while claiming to be a pacifist who wants a strong military to prevent war. He survives infighting with the Luftwaffe staff and his opposition to the coming war to emerge as a hero for the air corps' effectiveness in the early stages of World War II. Göring, appointed Reichsmarschall by Hitler, disagrees with his Führer's unwillingness to bomb London when doing so would seem certain to demoralize the British; he also disagrees with the disastrous decision to open a second front against the Russians. As early as 1942, he decides the war is lost. Hitler blames Göring, whom he has designated his successor, for the defeat at Stalingrad and ignores him until having him arrested for treason shortly before the fall of Berlin. Göring regains some of his stature in defeat. During the war crimes trials at Nuremberg, he holds his own by displaying a quick and resolute mind. Sentenced to death, he commits suicide by ingesting a cyanide capsule hidden in his cell.

An irony in Göring's rise is that he is not anti-Semitic until forced to be so. Hitler warns him that he must be careful because "too many people know of your pro-Jewish attitude." As a youngster, Hermann had been assigned to write an essay about a great German. He chose von Epenstein but was told he could not write in praise of Jews. Badly beaten during the 1923 attempt to take over the Reichswehr barracks, he was rescued and cared for by a Jewish family, whom he helps a decade later when Jews begin to be sent to concentration camps. Emmy helps save others. Officially, Göring complains that Jews have disproportionate influence on Germany's political and economic life. Forced to justify his party's anti-Jewish policies, he resorts to such clichés as "We're not running a girls' finishing school, we're resurrecting a nation." Leffland makes clear that Göring wrestles with his conscience about the persecution of Jews, but she errs in not dramatizing this internal conflict.

The Knight, Death, and the Devil is a virtual catalog of Göring's quirks. He is grossly overweight, is an insomniac, and becomes addicted to paracodeine pills after twice being cured of his morphine problem. He bathes and changes clothes at least four times daily, delighting in ornate uniforms and costumes. In his last years, he sits around Carinhall in velvet dressing gowns, elaborate jewelry, and makeup. He plays with model trains and adopts a series of lion cubs, naming each Caesar, before handing them over, once they are grown, to the Berlin Zoo, where he visits them.

Göring's biggest failures result from assuming too many posts under Hitler: "He held so many offices that he could probably work twenty-four hours a day and still not get everything done. And sometimes he did not work at all. Sometimes he was extremely lazy, then afterward he had to catch up." As chief of the Four-Year Plan, he orders a cut in payments to the relatives of Luftwaffe personnel; then, as head of the Luftwaffe, he overrules this reduction. Most of the time, he simply ignores his responsibilities, as is indicated by the doodles of one of his Luftwaffe staff: "many little balloons on a string which was held by nobody."

Göring hides from his and his country's failures at Carinhall, spending most of the war there or at Veldenstein, which he inherits after the death of von Epenstein's widow. He devotes most of his energy to collecting plundered artworks that he says he will leave to the state, convincing himself that he is not a looter, making "honorable if small payment for every piece of art that crosses his threshold." In the end, Göring blows up Carinhall, including Carin's crypt, a day before the Russians arrive.

Leffland excels at delineating the details of Göring's life, but the man himself remains mostly enigmatic. She displays the inner thoughts of Albert Speer, Magda and Joseph Goebbels, and others but usually holds back with Göring, almost as if intimidated by him. Her novelistic skills are more in evidence with the minor characters. Thomas von Kantzow is the novel's moral conscience, trying to warn his stepfather against Hitler's excesses and working behind the scenes to attempt to prevent war with Britain. Göring's Harvard-educated friend Putzi Hanfstaengl is one of the best minds at Hitler's disposal, but the Führer is more impressed by his piano playing. Although Putzi tries "to slip a sliver of light" into Hitler's "narrow closetlike store of conviction," his advice is ignored. He gradually turns against Hitler, defecting to England with his son in one of the novel's most exciting episodes.

Emmy's best friend, Rose Korwan, also an actress, personifies the struggles of German Jews. She refuses to leave her country while the opportunity still exists and declines the help of the Görings. Rose means to endure, asserting her identity by risking arrest in appearing in public without her papers. She lives as a thief, sleeping in train stations and bombed-out buildings before she is betrayed. Like most of the characters in *The Knight, Death, and the Devil*, Rose is based on a real person, but as Leffland explains in the afterword, she invented most of Rose's actions, including the bizarre death that provides the novel with its most moving scene.

Leffland takes her title from Albrecht Dürer's 1513 engraving *Ritter, Tod, und Teufel*, a worn print of which Göring carries with him for the last thirty years of his life. Von Epenstein gives it to him during the Great War, writing, "See the chaos of jagged rock, and see that only the brave knight on his mount is shown fully, cast like a bright medallion against that chaos, the only true ideal in this, our strife-torn world." Göring interprets the engraving as representing his life: "the soldier who did his duty, the knight with his long spear frightened not by death, tempted not by the devil." Because of his romantic, simplistic conception of German values, however, Göring does allow himself to be tempted by the devil and helps cause millions of deaths. Count Galeazzo Ciano, Benito Mussolini's son-in-law, considers Göring the most human of the German leaders, and Göring's story is compelling because of the contrast between his sophistication, intelligence, and humanity and his capacity for evil.

Michael Adams

Sources for Further Study

Booklist. LXXXVI, December 1, 1989, p. 705.
Chicago Tribune. February 11, 1990, XIV, p. 1.
Kirkus Reviews. LVII, December 1, 1989, p. 1701.
Library Journal. CXV, February 1, 1990, p. 108.
Los Angeles Times Book Review. January 21, 1990, p. 12.
The Nation. CCL, June 18, 1990, p. 862.
The New York Times Book Review. XCV, February 11, 1990, p. 8.
Publishers Weekly. CCXXXVI, December 1, 1989, p. 48.
USA Today. February 9, 1990, p. D4.
The Washington Post Book World. XX, February 25, 1990, p. 1.

THE LADY OF SITUATIONS

Author: Louis Auchincloss (1917-   )
Publisher: Houghton Mifflin (Boston). 274 pp. $20.95
Type of work: Novel
Time: 1930-1966, chiefly the 1930's and 1940's
Locale: Long Island, a New England boarding school, and New York City

*A determined young woman whose once affluent family fell victim to the Great Depression
seeks a niche suited to the scope of her ambition*

> *Principal characters:*
> NATICA CHAUNCEY, the opportunistic daughter of a failed financier
> RUTH FELTON, her aunt, who chronicles Natica's career in a memoir
> TOM BARNES, a young minister and teacher at Averhill School
> RUFUS GRISWOLD, headmaster at Averhill
> STEPHEN HILL, a handsome Averhill English teacher
> ANGELICA HILL, Stephen's socially adept mother
> THAD STURGES, a partner in a New York law firm

For four decades Louis Auchincloss has averaged about a book of fiction a year—
usually a novel, occasionally a collection of closely related stories. In the 1960's and
1970's he penned several best-sellers and received his share of critical acclaim;
thereafter, his output has continued, but his popularity has reigned primarily among
a loyal readership who have come to expect a competently crafted narrative focusing
on the manners and mores of Auchincloss' world, whose axis typically runs from
the New England boys' preparatory school to the Manhattan financial district. It is a
world of conservative, autocratic headmasters and dedicated teachers at one end and
worldly corporate executives and attorneys at the other, often linked by school trust-
ees with a foot planted firmly at each end. The world also includes wives and sons
and daughters, but the protagonists are likely to be the men.

Auchincloss' readers are seldom disappointed. His eye and ear are nicely attuned
to all nuances of his well-endowed, comfortably situated characters. He shows them
dealing and double-dealing, gravitating to positions of power and trust of which they
are sometimes unworthy, often expressing their thoughts almost as articulately as
does their creator. If they act and sound a bit rarefied, they experience recognizably
universal passions and conflicts. They are never monsters—although they sometimes seems so to one another—but frail human beings largely incapable of heights
of heroism or depths of depravity.

In many respects *The Lady of Situations* continues the pattern. In the foreground
looms Averhill School, tucked away somewhere in New England. There the sons of
the rich prepare for their corporate life by studying the poetry of John Donne under
the guidance of men whose theology differs very little from Donne's seventeenth
century Anglicanism. Although Auchincloss has returned several times to the quintessential pre-World War II preparatory school which he evoked so memorably in *The
Rector of Justin* (1964), Averhill is his most thoroughgoing re-creation of Justin
Martyr. There are some significant differences. Rufus Griswold, while fully as dedi-

cated, ruthless, and tyrannical as Frank Prescott in the earlier novel, lacks the grandeur of Justin Martyr's venerable headmaster. *The Lady of Situations* does not remain at Averhill, although more than half the book is set there. Most significantly, this novel does not focus on a headmaster or a teacher or an Averhill boy but on Natica Chauncey.

Is Averhill an updated Justin Martyr, with coeds? Not at all. Natica is at the school by virtue of having married a faculty member, Tom Barnes. The novel focuses on Natica, with only brief omniscient excursions to introduce people who will become part of her life. Most of the time Auchincloss limits his omniscience to Natica; at intervals there appear extracts from a "memoir" written by Natica's Aunt Ruth, a spinsterish teacher in a New York school for girls, who, while not unaware of Natica's faults, loves her, encourages her, lives out her adventures vicariously, and finally breathes a sigh of relief that she need not share in the consequences.

At the beginning of the story Natica is fourteen. Her father has been ruined in the 1929 Stock Market Crash, and the Chauncey family are endeavoring to hold their heads high among their more fortunate neighbors in a well-to-do Long Island enclave. Natica must attend the public high school and go to parties in borrowed dresses. Later she must assume the ignominious role of tutor to a neighbor who attends the private school at which Natica's aunt teaches. She forges bravely on, for she has resources: good looks, intelligence, and a vast—though ill-defined—ambition. Too young to know better, she marries a devout young cleric of limited imagination and far less worldly aspirations and thus finds herself one of a small knot of females, mostly older faculty wives resigned to life in the male bastion presided over by Rufus Griswold.

Tom reveres Griswold; Natica finds him useful. She fills his need for a secretary with a cool proficiency that for a time delights the headmaster, who is himself intelligent enough to recognize her as the brains of her family. For a time she is stimulated by her task of balancing the headmaster's need for diplomacy and the assertion of his authority in internal and external Averhill conflicts. There are also a few souls at Averhill who enjoy gathering to read plays together—everything from Renaissance tragedies to the contemporary verse dramas of Maxwell Anderson. These sessions foster an attraction between Natica and a handsome English teacher from a prominent family. From this point Natica's penchant for "situations" estranges Griswold, humiliates Tom, and blights the academic career of Stephen Hill, the English teacher, who assists in the process.

The novel takes its title from the first section of T. S. Eliot's poem *The Waste Land* (1922): "Here is Belladonna, the Lady of the Rocks,/ The lady of situations." With its associations of poison and the numbing of sensibilities, Belladonna symbolizes the Natica known to Griswold and the inner circle at Averhill. In the context of Eliot's poem the rocks suggest inhospitability to such values as generosity, fertility, and decent family life. Natica's situation is indeed rocky. A femme fatale to Averhill generally and an insoluble mystery to poor Tom, she must leave. She constantly teeters on the brink of disaster but always seems to avoid the worst embarrassments.

Nevertheless, a stable relationship continues to elude her, and she seems destined to remain a lady of situations for much of the novel's length. "My only use for morality," she cheerfully tells her unblinking aunt at one point, "is if it makes for the good life." Because she does not know what the good life is, however, the reader tends to share Aunt Ruth's hope that Natica will outgrow her cynicism and find happiness, although clearly it can never take the form of a vine-covered cottage. She yearns for acceptance in the world her father's misfortune has always kept just beyond her reach, but she also needs a sense of accomplishment more akin to that sought by Auchincloss men.

Auchincloss quietly manipulates the point of view in such a way that the reader cannot, like the characters Natica outrages, condemn her, but neither is it possible to view her as a feminist hero battling male oppression. Despite her status as a capable woman hemmed in by a narrow range of options, she is too self-absorbed and opportunistic to serve very effectively in such a role. She is feminine enough, but her affinities are with Auchincloss' ambitious male protagonists. She faces one moral dilemma—what to do about an expected child—bravely, but for the most part her moral reflections tend to be as lamentably shallow as the one already quoted. Even allowing for her penchant for shocking people, her moral horizon is distinctly utilitarian. Natica does provoke her aunt's—and the reader's—consciences, but also the sort of grudging respect that amidst the bewildering complexities of modern life one is compelled to feel for the person who is often called a "survivor."

Auchincloss convincingly shows her at odds with Averhill's denizens and their mores but in the process calls attention to the enormous social changes of the past generation. Natica is governed by a social code that seems nearly as remote as that operating in the novels of Anthony Trollope or William Dean Howells. Both the manner of her transgressions and her stratagems for avoiding their consequences exude an antique air. The Averhill chapters in particular create a much different effect than did *The Rector of Justin* in 1964, although the period is the same. (The date of the opening entries in Brian Aspinwall's journal in the earlier novel is 1939.) In 1964 schools of the Averhill type still resembled their conformations of a quarter century previous; in the 1990's Averhill, with its unchallengeable headmaster and its cloistered young males facing homoerotic temptations, recedes before the image of a school brimming with boys *and* girls and sprinkled liberally with minorities totally ignorant of cotillions and summers in Newport. Auchincloss is undoubtedly wise to stick to the prep school he knows so well, but far fewer readers in the 1990's can recognize it as part of the formative influences upon their own generation. Thus *The Lady of Situations* is much more of a period piece than was *The Rector of Justin*, to which the book-jacket blurb invites readers to compare it, and which reached print at the beginning of an era of particularly rapid and profound social change. Auchincloss remains a fine novelist of manners, but not in this book the manners of the late twentieth century.

Like another female from *The Waste Land*, Natica is a lovely woman who "stoops to folly." Eliot's young woman, it will be recalled, behaves in sharp contrast to Oliver

Goldsmith's eighteenth century version, who can find nothing better to do than die; the 1922 model "smoothes her hair with automatic hand,/ And puts a record on the gramophone." Natica too lacks all sense of having perpetrated any enormous wrong in destroying the lives of two men who both have loved her deeply. Unlike the woman of Eliot's poem, however, Natica has ambition. She goes to work and works her way up in the world.

Rather abruptly Auchincloss qualifies her for the Wall Street end of the axis, throws her into the company of more painfully conservative people, and discloses in her a social conscience better developed than her personal one, a not entirely implausible trait in a woman who has felt the sting of social disapproval. She quickly forms an attachment to Thad Sturges, one of the conservative lawyers, who is sketched deftly in his capacity as a law partner but whose appeal for Natica seems to reside chiefly in demonstrating the truth of the theory that opposites attract. Where he is conservative, she is liberal; where he is diplomatic, she is brusque. They have little trouble setting differences aside.

The novel ends, as it begins, with a few pages from Aunt Ruth's memoir. Suddenly it is 1966, Ruth has become an octogenarian, and Natica is fifty. It is important to note that the reader now sees Natica only through Ruth's eyes. There are two main revelations. First, things have gone astonishingly right for Natica in the past twenty years. Secondly, Ruth, contemplating the human casualties of Natica's more distant past, still must apparently serve as her niece's conscience, for Natica simply does not look back. Her present mode of life can give no one cause to call her a lady of situations, but she has grown complacent. She seemingly has learned nothing about herself. Ruth has learned, or has at least decided now to report, that an unexciting life as an unmarried teacher of rich girls has the advantage of imposing no great burden of remorse such as Natica should feel. Or must feel? Perhaps Auchincloss is suggesting that even Natica cannot escape her conscience, but where is the evidence that she has developed one? Natica remains someone impossible to admire, impossible not to wonder at.

Aside from being a character study of a woman who is neither as bad as acquaintances suppose nor as good as one might hope she would become, Louis Auchincloss' *The Lady of Situations* is that rare thing in contemporary popular fiction, a literate novel about literate people. From its delightful presentation of Stephen Hill's classes' bouts with John Donne and William Butler Yeats to the Averhill readings to which Natica contributes her acumen, and on to the literary, artistic, and musical allusions that brighten conversations even in the towers of Wall Street, this novel reflects a cultivated sensibility. In an age when writers so determinedly avert their eyes from past artistic landmarks, Auchincloss' determination to endow his characters with cultural literacy is refreshing. He knows that such attainments render people no better morally, but they remind readers of the existence of human activities beyond the satisfaction of biological urges and the acquisition of material wealth.

Robert P. Ellis

Sources for Further Study

Booklist. LXXXVI, June 15, 1990, p. 1956.
Chicago Tribune. July 6, 1990, V, p. 3.
Kirkus Reviews. LVIII, May 1, 1990, p. 597.
Library Journal. CXV, July, 1990, p. 126.
Los Angeles Times Book Review. September 30, 1990, p. 2.
The New York Times Book Review. XCV, July 8, 1990, p. 11.
Publishers Weekly. CCXXXVII, May 11, 1990, p. 250.
The Washington Post Book World. XX, July 1, 1990, p. 6.

LAST THINGS

Author: Madison Jones (1925-   )
Publisher: Louisiana State University Press (Baton Rouge). 206 pp. $17.95
Type of work: Novel
Time: The late 1980's
Locale: East Alabama

A novel of the rural drug underworld in the Deep South, Last Things *gives a new perspective on the age-old question of good versus evil by making the definition of both elusive if not illusory*

> *Principal character:*
> WENDELL CORBIN, a graduate student in English literature and would-be writer

Last Things is the eighth novel by Madison Jones, professor emeritus at Auburn University. His is a distinguished body of work, and none of his novels is marked by the academic timidity or theoretical denseness one might expect from a professor of English or from a university writer-in-residence. One of Jones's earlier works, *A Cry of Absence* (1971), is a masterful exploration of morality, and anyone who reads it will not be able to forget its unyielding protagonist, Hester Cameron Glenn. She is one of the most compelling characters in twentieth century American fiction, and it is not by chance that she is named "Hester." *A Cry of Absence* tells a Faulknerian tale without the stylistic pyrotechnics and gothic trappings of much regional writing. Jones presents his narrative in a straightforward, rich prose; he is a storyteller who embellishes his tales with sparing but effective stylistic flourishes.

The narrator of *Last Things*, however, seems to be caught in the middle of an allegory difficult to describe in conventional language. His protagonist is essentially selfish, other characters sketchy and driven by artificial forces, and the action so sensational that Jones runs the risk of losing his reader back to the pulp fiction where he or she does not have to worry so much about "good writing." The comic touches are heavy-handed, darkly ironical, and, occasionally, satirical to the point that they verge on caricature. Especially from the foibles of academics does Jones draw blood. Dr. Leonard T. Rathbone, a secondary character, is a marijuana-abusing Blake scholar who wages an esoteric polemic over two lines of "The Tyger." This seemingly picayune quarrel with another Blake critic consumes Rathbone; he is an ivy-covered buffoon, his ivory tower clouded by smoke from his reefers.

Rathbone is the cause of the protagonist's return to his home town. Wendell Corbin studies English literature at the nearby state university and, because he understands how to appeal to Rathbone's vanity, is invited to rent a room in the house the professor shares with his slovenly "intellectual" mistress in Turnbull. Wendell decides that, because he is from the county and not the small town itself, he will accept the professor's offer:

Wendell Corbin's return to Bliss County, a place where he had sworn never again to set foot, was like something fated to be. Even at the time it seemed to him a little bit this way. Later, after the events of that summer, the truth of this was a kind of dark certainty in his mind. A fated thing, a mystery.

It is evil, pure but not simple, that awaits Corbin in Bliss County, an ironically named symbol for the unsettling moral apathy of this "New South" town.

Jones reveals early that his tale is an allegory with Wendell as a sort of Camus-like stranger whose emotional distance from his family and his home is not far enough to spare him pain. The moral vacuum which masquerades as his soul is equally ill-equipped to deal with the realities of malicious intent. Physical distance when he left home, the drug-induced distance he attempts from time to time, and the absence of moral values are all poor substitutes for good judgment and common sense. Wendell is not "good," in the sense that he embodies any moral certainty. What happens to him is evil, but, up to a point, he participates in it willingly. His revulsion is short-lived, predicated on self-interest, and prompted less by conscience than by egoism. His plans for a life independent of his past go awry, and he is caught up in forces too powerful to ignore, too relentless to escape, too shrewd to outwit.

Even Wendell's standing as a genuine antihero is suspect. He is too lethargic, too self-absorbed in the nonissue of himself for his ideas to become relevant to others. As the only achiever in a family of ne'er-do-wells, Wendell wants to put as much time and distance as possible between himself, his father Hap, and his brothers, Majer, Miner, and Fawbus. Too detached to become really engaged, he is diverted by the study of literature and aspires to share his own wry observations of man's nature in a "blistering comic novel" peopled by "clowns, fools, self-deceivers, serviceable knaves," and others of that ilk.

So remote is Wendell from his redneck roots, so secret and shameful to him is his past, that he apes his more polished classmates and "passes" as a middle-class collegian. He believes himself invulnerable, opaque to the scrutiny of others, ultimately alone but protected by an aura of mystery. "Together with a conviction of mental superiority that his performance as a student confirmed in him, it fed the germ of disdain or contempt for everybody around him." He chooses English literature from "his determination to define himself with as wide a margin as possible between him and the rest, including especially the sorry lot of folks he had derived from." Thus, Jones has created in Wendell an unpromising character for carrying forth his story of small-town corruption. The reader must bear with Jones. Frankly unsympathetic, Wendell gets from life just what he got from a short-lived affair: ". . . something he had not asked for, the cold shoulder." But then, he does not care all that much until the world takes too much of an interest in him and his past.

He runs into Cat Bird, an acquaintance from his penny-ante, drug-dealing past, who delivers him into the clutches of Jason Farrow, a character Jones presents as a giant toad, a creature so subterranean that he requires darkness to reveal his true nature. With comic understatement, Jones makes him a used-car salesman by day, a reptilian drug merchant by night. Farrow gives Wendell a choice of jail—to which he holds the key through the sheriff in his pocket—or a job in the "business." Wendell, at first defiant and vengeful, acquiesces more graciously when he realizes just how rich he can get with Farrow.

In the meantime, he has met his neighbor, Tricia Harker, with whom he forges a tentative alliance against boredom. Tricia is older but inexperienced, married but restless. Half educated, she turns to an unlikely source, the writings of Friedrich Nietzsche, both for stimulation of an underdeveloped imagination and as a means of resistance to an overbearing mother-in-law. Tricia longs to join the ranks of *Ubermenschen* so that she may escape the ordinariness, the routine of existence in Turnbull. Her oft-absent husband leaves her to care for his querulous, insulin-dependent mother, who is a curiously ambivalent character. She is petulant, nosy, and even mean-spirited to Tricia, but she retains the dignity and values of an earlier age when good breeding was prized. As a symbol of the old South, she too is fated to fall when she threatens the corrupting materialism of the new South. The author calculates her destruction carefully; in this tale, it is necessary that she, reliant on a woman whom she despises as trashy, must die at the even trashier hand of Wendell Corbin, the reformed redneck.

Tricia is a problematic character for Jones. His intention is unclear: Is she, true to the pulp genre, a convenient love interest for Wendell? That she is, but she is also a seriocomic invention. Deluded by Nietzsche already, she is easy prey for Wendell, to whom deception is second nature. With the Mephistophelean Farrow pulling his strings, Wendell draws the unsuspecting Tricia into a nightmare and leaves her stranded there to fight off alone the demons of guilt. Her complicity in murder, as unlikely as it is, given the satirical tone in which her character is described, is an almost casual act of manipulation, another "fated thing" that is beyond explanation.

True to its status as allegory, the novel has one mythic figure, the itinerant preacher Sears, whose fundamentalism is as opposed to situational ethics as it is contrary to Wendell's "intellectualizing." Sears wanders in and out of the novel, usually at those moments when Wendell is most compromised, and at those times, the preacher easily prods Wendell's slumbering conscience awake. Wendell fears the preacher, a large man whose physical presence in itself is intimidating but whose words are even more terrifying in their ability to pull away the layers of deceit in which the young man wraps his actions and thoughts: "It's not any secret from His eyes, Wendell. And no dark thing that won't be brought to light. That's what He sent me to tell you. To open your heart and let His light come in. Before it's too late, boy."

Sears represents the promise of redemption, not with his brand of Protestantism but as an example of an upright man. Wendell's chief sin—and the one consistent example of evil in a novel full of such iniquities as murder, betrayal, suicide, and drug-dealing—is lying, and Sears is no liar. Just what he foretells, happens. Wendell, whose life is built on denial of his past, denial of the concept of guilt, denial of any absolute truth, at last comes to realize that when he finally wants to speak truth, to give evidence of the network for which he has worked, no one can believe him.

Suspect anyway for being "old Hap Corbin's boy," he is, in addition, tainted as a liar and is now dependent on "forces of a superrational kind" to purge his present from the sins of his past, both distant and recent. "But taking things all together he found it difficult not to believe that his soul had been the object of some discarnate form of manipulation." Wendell's story is all fabrication until Sears believes it, until a really honest man blesses it with credulity:

> If there was any moment when his story appeared in a suddenly different light, it was here—as if this light had passed to him from the eyes that were fastened on him. This was what he imagined, turning his face aside. In any case it was in that one flash of experience that the word *appalling* received its final definition for Wendell. As though the gaze turned on him was his own, he saw himself but not, somehow, himself—a self too small in stature, shrunken and burnt-dry-looking and pitiless in the face, that was and was not him. The image afterwards kept no precisely fixed character in his mind. What remained entirely fixed was the feeling with which he had received it. *Hate* would have to serve to designate that feeling, though he never had felt hate like that toward any person or thing.

This passage, illustrative of Jones's direct, spare style, effectively closes the novel of ideas, but Wendell's visit to his father finishes the novel of action by allowing him a chance for reconciliation with his past and preparation for his future. He is a new man, one reformed and reborn by having experienced in life the four last things: death, judgment, heaven, and hell.

Last Things presents a disturbing picture of a society held together by treachery and subterfuge. In this novel, the fiction of morality is no match for the reality of evil, an altogether too attractive option for Wendell, who is perhaps an altogether too common character in an age confused by differences in right and wrong. Riches lure him into full participation in life, and, once engaged, he cannot disentangle from its complexities without the *ex machina* intervention of Sears. With assurance and mastery, and in spite of a quirkiness of tone and a distasteful protagonist, Madison Jones has created in *Last Things* an evocative description of the allure of evil, one, it is to be hoped, that is not prophetic.

William U. Eiland

Sources for Further Study

Atlanta Journal Constitution. December 31, 1989, p. N8.
Booklist. LXXXV, July, 1989, p. 1868.
Kirkus Reviews. LVII, July 15, 1989, p. 1019.
National Forum. LXX, Spring, 1990, p. 47.
The New York Times Book Review. XCIV, September 24, 1989, p. 48.
Publishers Weekly. CCXXXVI, July 14, 1989, p. 59.
Southern Living. XXV, February, 1990, p. 120.
The Washington Post Book World. XIX, October 15, 1989, p. 4.

A LAW UNTO ITSELF
Power, Politics, and the IRS

Author: David Burnham (1933-   )
Publisher: Random House (New York). 419 pp. $22.50
Type of work: Current history
Time: Primarily 1930-1989
Locale: The United States

An investigative reporter presents evidence of mismanagement and corruption in the Internal Revenue Service (IRS)

Principal personages:
DONALD C. ALEXANDER,
MORTIMER C. CAPLIN,
SHELDON COHEN, and
LAWRENCE B. GIBBS, IRS Commissioners
FRANKLIN D. ROOSEVELT, thirty-second president of the United States, 1933-1945
JOHN F. KENNEDY, thirty-fifth president of the United States, 1961-1963
LYNDON B. JOHNSON, thirty-sixth president of the United States, 1963-1969
RICHARD M. NIXON, thirty-seventh president of the United States, 1969-1974

One of the United States' most respected investigative journalists, David Burnham has long devoted himself to exploring the nation's most complex and powerful institutions. As a reporter for *The New York Times* in the 1970's, he exposed corruption in the New York City Police Department and thereby triggered significant reform. His subsequent probes into the nuclear industry and, in *The Rise of the Computer State* (1983), the effects of computerization on American democracy, bear witness to his ongoing concern that fundamental freedoms and rights may be threatened as bureaucracies and technologies develop to a degree unimagined in the earliest days of the nation.

Certainly the Founding Fathers could not have anticipated the tremendous growth of the Internal Revenue Service in the decades following World War II. A survey of American tax history in the opening chapter of *A Law Unto Itself: Power, Politics, and the IRS* establishes that, with few exceptions, federal taxation activity was extremely limited prior to the Civil War. In 1862 the Office of the Commissioner of Revenue, created along with the first income tax, became a fixture in the federal system. Constitutionally questionable, the tax itself flickered in and out of existence until 1913, when the Sixteenth Amendment authorized Congress "to lay and collect taxes on incomes, from whatever source derived, without apportionment among the several States, and without regard to any census or enumeration." Together with these landmark events of 1862 and 1913, Burnham suggests, the establishment of the withholding tax in 1943 was the foundation of the national taxation system of the late twentieth century.

Providing the United States with monetary muscle befitting a world power, the federal taxation system developed into a similarly powerful and well-entrenched bureaucracy: The approximately 123,000 employees on its payroll in 1989 made the IRS the largest law enforcement agency in the country. Although its agents use the catchphrase "voluntary compliance" to describe the manner in which the organization intends "to collect the proper amount of tax revenues at the least cost to the public, and in a manner that warrants the highest degree of public confidence in our integrity, efficiency and fairness," the agency's unique power creates an atmosphere in which anything but compliance would appear to be prohibitively risky. Able to level criminal suits against alleged wrongdoers, the IRS may also initiate civil suits in which the burden of proof lies with the accused. If the IRS suspects that an individual may take drastic action to evade payments, it can seize property without seeking prior authorization from a judge. It can identify delinquent taxpayers by comparing extensive data gleaned from tax returns (194 million in 1988), third-party reports (approximately one billion annually), and an information-sharing plan involving the tax agencies of every state and New York City. Officers may even order banks and other institutions to provide additional information.

Considering the manifest persuasiveness of such power, it is not surprising that Burnham finds the IRS essentially effective as a collector. In 1988, for example, the agency collected almost one trillion dollars, 90 percent of the amount the government estimated taxpayers were required to pay. Eighty percent of the tax dollars were collected using the withholding tax; in comparison, enforcement projects brought in about 2.8 percent of all 1988 tax revenue.

Burnham contends, however, that the agency's might often places citizens at a great disadvantage in defending themselves against abuses arising from the enforcement of a Byzantine tax code that confounds taxpayers, professional tax preparers, and IRS agents. Burnham presents numerous case studies to argue that the organization urgently needs reform. Yet he frequently fails to establish whether many of the problems he identifies are isolated or truly widespread.

In one example, Burnham cites a case involving two taxpayers to suggest that thousands of others have suffered grave harm because of IRS computer errors. Although Gina and Paul Husby's challenge of a 1986 IRS claim required the agency to suspend its collection activities, the couple received four more dunning notices within the following twelve months, after which the IRS began serving notices of levy on their assets. Even after a Federal District Court judge enjoined the IRS from issuing more liens and levies, the agency dispatched a notice of lien which was placed in public files. At a subsequent hearing, an attorney speaking for the IRS conceded that the incorrect claims had been generated by a faulty computer, but argued that the agency could not be held responsible for such mistakes. The court ruled in favor of the Husbys—who eventually received $22,000 in damages and court fees—but did not order the agency to repair its system or identify the individuals responsible for the computer malfunction. Burnham admits that he lacks proof that such computer errors are symptomatic of massive systemic flaws; nevertheless, he embarks on a frivolous inductive exercise suggesting that 11,835 other taxpayers were illegally defamed along with the Husbys.

Much of *A Law Unto Itself* describes ways in which the IRS seems to be distracted from its goal of raising revenue. Burnham contends, for example, that the Criminal Investigation Division sometimes opens costly criminal cases that promise relatively little financial reward, consequently neglecting the pursuit of some major tax offenders. In one instance, stockbroker David Jonsson spent six years prodding agents to investigate the questionable commodities investment scheme known as the "silver butterfly" tax straddle, which, according to *The Wall Street Journal*, cost the government more than one billion dollars annually.

Jonsson's initial forty-five minute meeting with an IRS agent in July, 1973, did not even bring about a promised follow-up a week later. It was not until 1976 that agents contacted Jonsson for more assistance, informing him that his information had been misplaced. The following year the stockbroker met with numerous investigators, who seemed unenthusiastic about pursuing the matter. In 1978 Jonsson brought his story to the attention of IRS Commissioner Jerome Kurtz and Shirley Jackewicz, a reporter for *The Wall Street Journal*. An assistant of Kurtz sent him a noncommittal note, but Jackewicz wrote an influential front-page story about the scheme. Over the following years, Jonsson was finally able to aid the IRS in efforts to expose the damages associated with the silver butterfly. For his persistence in revealing a scheme that cost the government billions of dollars, Jonsson received a substantial $220,659 "Reward for Original Information" near the end of 1983, more than ten years after he began his campaign.

Jonsson's many years of frustrating finger-pointing contrast sharply with fast-moving IRS action described elsewhere in the book. In the same year that the stockbroker first approached the IRS, Florida police officers informed IRS agent John Zahurak of the arrest of a woman named Sharon Willits. Zahurak relied on cryptic notes found in her purse to estimate her debt to the government as being $25,549; within days, the IRS served notices of levy for all of her assets. More than a year passed before the Fifth Circuit Court of Appeals determined that, because there was no evidence to substantiate Zahurak's assessment, the IRS action was "excessive, arbitrary, capricious, and without factual foundation."

The misguided zeal with which Zahurak pursued the unpromising Willits case and the puzzling disinterest with which the agency investigated the costly silver butterfly scheme illustrate the author's assertion that the IRS wields its power erratically and inefficiently. Burnham finds that one reason for the agency's misguided efforts is political pressure to widen its focus beyond raising revenue. Ever since Herbert Hoover triggered the famous IRS investigation that led to the arrest and imprisonment of Al Capone, presidents and other influential leaders have exploited their sway over the IRS for a variety of goals, including wars on organized crime and narcotics. Burnham charges that such politically motivated investigations divert the agency from collecting money efficiently: He cites the Willits case as an example of how one anti-drug campaign misfired. Even inside the agency, such activities have proven divisive.

Burnham also devotes significant portions of his text to portraying IRS vulnerability to more covert political tampering. Franklin D. Roosevelt, John F. Kennedy, and Robert F. Kennedy, are among the top government leaders Burnham accuses of such misconduct. Richard Nixon's involvement with the agency may be the best-known example of improper activity: The second article of impeachment presented by the House Judiciary Committee in 1974 charged him with unlawfully seeking to obtain confidential information contained in income tax returns and attempting to cause audits and investigations to be initiated in a discriminatory manner.

Perhaps Burnham's most troubling allegation is that the IRS itself may be rampant with serious misconduct. Besides presenting case studies in which functionaries have shown Creationist and homophobic bias in exercising their authority to grant or refuse tax-exempt status, he also offers a particularly disturbing account of IRS susceptibility to bribery. For more than twenty-five years, representatives of the prominent Saligman family of Philadelphia bribed officials in order to obtain favorable audits. Corrupt agents validated a charitable deduction exaggerated by more than 300 percent and even conducted token audits of past returns to lend credibility to the family's dubious tax history. The benefits of auditing the Saligmans were so well-known that bribe-hungry IRS agents actually competed against each other to examine the family's tax returns, according to the 1986 testimony of Saligman accountant Charles Toll.

Such revelations came about as part of an ongoing corruption investigation that, by the time *A Law Unto Itself* appeared, had resulted in convictions of ten IRS agents and ten businessmen (no charges had been brought against the Saligmans). Essential to the case was the cooperation of an IRS agent named Jude Dougherty, who reported a bribe offer in 1980 and worked as a double agent until 1984. Dougherty's integrity notwithstanding, the fact that corrupt officials conspired with Saligman representatives for more than two decades suggests that, at least on a regional basis, IRS standards for honesty and internal investigations have been distressingly low. Burnham presents evidence that in Chicago, Cincinnati, Los Angeles, and Washington, D.C., officials have also been sluggish to investigate evidence of internal corruption.

Burnham's allegations suffer from poor organization as well as insufficient substantiation. Eighteen pages of charts and figures at the back of the book might have had greater impact had they been incorporated into the main text. Furthermore, considering the length of the work, the proposals he puts forth in his conclusion are surprisingly meager. Nevertheless, his call to "audit the auditors" with an eye toward greater integrity and efficiency was particularly pertinent in 1990, when federal monetary woes consistently appeared as front-page news items. Though the IRS may appear monolithic and unassailable to many, Burnham's work supports the position of those who feel that the somewhat youthful agency could stand some improvements.

David Marc Fischer

Sources for Further Study

Business Week. February 12, 1990, p. 16.
Choice. XXVII, June, 1990, p. 1753.
The Christian Science Monitor. February 21, 1990, p. 20.
Library Journal. CXV, March 1, 1990, p. 104.
Los Angeles Times. March 7, 1990, p. E9.
The New Republic. CCII, April 9, 1990, p. 40.
The New York Times Book Review. XCV, February 11, 1990, p. 1.
Reference and Research Book News. V, June, 1990, p. 18.
Time. CXXXV, February 5, 1990, p. 67.
The Wall Street Journal. April 13, 1990, p. A9.
The Washington Post Book World. XX, February 11, 1990, p. 1.

LAWRENCE OF ARABIA
The Authorized Biography of T. E. Lawrence

Author: Jeremy Wilson
First published: 1989, in Great Britain
Publisher: Atheneum (New York). Illustrated. 1188 pp. $35.00
Type of work: Biography
Time: 1888-1935
Locale: England, France, Arabia

A panoramic, meticulously documented biography of the World War I hero of the Arab campaign and distinguished man of letters, which draws extensively upon previously embargoed government documents

Principal personages:
> T. E. LAWRENCE, the British field leader of the Arab campaign, an archaeologist, historian, and writer
> SARAH LAWRENCE, his mother
> LADY ASTOR, the American-born wife of Viscount Astor, a friend of T. E. Lawrence
> E. M. FORSTER, a British novelist and friend of Lawrence
> ROBERT GRAVES, a British poet, novelist, and biographer, a friend of Lawrence
> GENERAL SIR EDMUND ALLENBY, the commander of British forces in the Middle East from June, 1917, to the end of the war
> SIR GILBERT CLAYTON, principal British intelligence officer at Cairo, later head of the Arab Bureau
> CHARLOTTE SHAW, the wife of the playwright George Bernard Shaw, a friend and confidante of Lawrence
> SIR HUGH TRENCHARD, the "father" of the Royal Air Force, a friend and benefactor to Lawrence

When Robert Graves finished writing his 1928 biography of his friend T. E. Lawrence, Lawrence was bitterly disappointed at the result. In a letter to Graves, Lawrence lamented, "I had hoped to find someone who would retell the story of the Arab Revolt from the available eye-witnesses, leaving the "I" of *Revolt in the Desert* out of it: whereas you only turned first to third person." More than half a century later, Lawrence has at last found in Jeremy Wilson a biographer equal to the job. Wilson's *Lawrence of Arabia: The Authorized Biography of T. E. Lawrence* does the finest job yet of re-creating the complexity of the situation in the Middle East as Lawrence encountered it and of relating the viewpoints and aspirations of the many men who formed and carried out British policy in that region. Thus Wilson presents within its historical context the complex part Lawrence played in the Arab campaign during World War I. So balanced and complete is Wilson's account of this most crucial segment of Lawrence's life that it might have been authorized not by Lawrence's estate but by Lawrence himself. Wilson takes great pains to do what Lawrence reproached Graves for not doing: He uses eyewitness accounts by principal participants to document the Palestine expeditions. These accounts can no longer take the form of interviews, since all the principals are dead, but they exist vividly in letters, diaries, reports, dispatches, bulletins, newspaper articles, telegrams—and these Wilson has consulted exhaustively, and quotes extensively throughout the book.

The title of Wilson's biography underscores the centrality of Arabia in Lawrence's life. His role in the Arab campaign—despite his expressed desire to escape or move beyond that role—was the distinguishing feature of Lawrence's career. Fittingly, Wilson's biography details most fully the years of the campaign and of Lawrence's involvement in the Allies' postwar settlements with the Arabs. Drawing upon previously embargoed government papers, Wilson augments, corrects, and clarifies Lawrence's account of his part in the Arab campaign as related in *Seven Pillars of Wisdom: A Triumph* (1935). Most important, Wilson points out how Lawrence's thinking and decisions were influenced and often determined by the thinking and decisions of Allied policymakers. For example, Wilson suggests that Lawrence's anxieties in the Arab campaign were largely determined by his awareness of the terms of the secret Sykes-Picot Treaty, while his continuing hopes for Arab independence after the war were buttressed by like-minded commanding officers, such as Brigadier General Gilbert Clayton; and officials such as Ronald Storrs, the Oriental Secretary of the High Commissioner in Egypt. In this way, Wilson draws on a wide range of sources to reveal the genuine dilemma of Lawrence's position during the war, whereas Lawrence's guilt-ridden account of divided loyalties in *Seven Pillars of Wisdom*, when considered in isolation, seems quirky, grandiose, and disingenuous.

As Wilson points out, Lawrence, as adviser to Sherif Feisal, leader of the Arab Revolt, often had to make decisions that were morally and politically questionable in order to retain Feisal's trust so as to keep him firmly on the British side. Among these was his decision to reveal the terms of the secret treaty between France and Britain to Feisal so as to warn him of French ambitions in Arabia and thus incite him to extend the Revolt: Feisal would thus conquer land for the Arabs while at the same time helping Britain to defeat the Turks. His need to make many such decisions throughout the war helps to explain Lawrence's recurrent theme in *Seven Pillars of Wisdom* of "the mental tug of war between honesty and loyalty."

The Peace Settlement after the war, which favored French over Arab interests in Syria and British over Arab interests in Mesopotamia, augmented Lawrence's guilt and sense of having betrayed the Arab cause. For this reason, as Wilson suggests, Lawrence devoted himself to obtaining a just settlement for the Arabs. By accepting a job in the Middle Eastern Department of the Colonial Office, under Winston Churchill, and by devoting himself to a new settlement at the Cairo Conference in 1921, Lawrence accomplished what he had set out to do: He was instrumental in establishing the state of Iraq (formerly Mesopotamia), with Feisal on the throne; and installed Feisal's brother Abdulla as Emir in Trans-Jordan. Initially Lawrence was exultant: He called the settlement "the big achievement of my life: of which the war was a preparation." Later he had some misgivings about the first steps of the infant state:

Irak did a good deal of falling between 1916 and 1921: and since 1921, under Feisal's guidance, has done much good trying and no falling. But I don't think it yet walks very well. Nor can any hand save it from making its mess.

Subsequent history has shown that the geographical and political emendations which Lawrence effected in the Middle East were to have far-reaching consequences beyond any he could have foreseen.

While Wilson's biography pays fullest attention to Lawrence during the war years, it does not stint in examining his later life, including his years in the ranks of the Royal Air Force (RAF) and in the British Tank Corps; his achievements as a writer, book publisher, and designer of high-speed military powerboats; and his friendships with an extraordinary range of people, some obscure, many prominent, including King Hussein, of the Hejaz; Sir Winston Churchill; Lady Astor; George Bernard Shaw; E. M. Forster; Noel Coward; and Sir Hugh Trenchard, founder of the RAF.

Only the reader who seeks the most intimate details of Lawrence's life will be disappointed in this biography which is reticent about Lawrence's psychological difficulties, his masochism, and his sexuality. Wilson, preeminently a historian, is primarily concerned with accuracy, with substantiation, with demonstration, and with reasonable inference. He does not veer far from facts and common sense. Clearly, he prefers to leave in-depth psychological analysis to professional practitioners, including the psychoanalyst-biographer John E. Mack, whose analysis of Lawrence, in his 1976 study *A Prince of Our Disorder*, Wilson credits but does not attempt to expand, revise, or improve.

This is not to say, however, that Wilson's study affords no new glimpses into Lawrence's personality or provides no further insights into his behavior. Rather, these appear in Wilson's accounts of Lawrence's dealings with his friends and of his conduct as an enlisted man in the RAF and in the Tank Corps. Many of these personal qualities emerge in Wilson's account of Lawrence's relationship with Feisal. Wilson points out that Lawrence not only bolstered Feisal's frequently lagging resolve and confidence in the Arab Revolt but covered over Feisal's timidity when representing him to British officials, gave Feisal ideas for strategy which he then attributed to Feisal, and even wrote a good part of the draft of Feisal's memorandum to the Peace Conference, setting out the Arab case.

In general, Lawrence was a generous but demanding friend, who often got what he wanted through manipulation and indirection. Wilson points out these qualities in Lawrence's friendships with Robert Graves and Charlotte Shaw. Lawrence's relationship with Shaw, while confiding and intimate, was also somewhat guarded. When she gave him an expensive motorcycle as a gift, he accepted only when he could find means gradually to repay her. When she refused Graves access to Lawrence's letters to her, which Lawrence had urged Graves to obtain for writing his biography, Lawrence discouraged Graves from pursuing them further, thus tacitly acknowledging Charlotte Shaw's excessive attachment to him and the emotional inequality of their relationship.

A very important but mysterious relationship in Lawrence's life was his friendship with Janet Laurie, the only woman to whom he ever felt a romantic attachment. After she refused Lawrence's unexpected marriage proposal, she became engaged to his brother Will. After Will's death, Lawrence carried out Will's wish to help her financially. But, as Wilson points out, Lawrence carried out this obligation in an extreme way. Lawrence gave her half of his inheritance of five thousand pounds, an excessively generous gesture which Wilson does not comment upon or attempt to account for. This puzzling gesture remains a disturbing mystery in the background of Lawrence's life, as Wilson's biography goes on to document the financial difficulties which kept Lawrence in the RAF even after he felt some desire to leave.

Wilson does, however, attempt to deal with some other difficult questions about Lawrence's life. He tries, for example, to answer the thorny question of why after the war Lawrence chose to enlist in the ranks rather than follow a career more commensurate with his abilities. Wilson cites as principal reasons Lawrence's contempt for wealth and possessions and disinclination to pursue a conventional career. In addition, he notes Lawrence's continued ambition to distinguish himself as a writer and his conviction that his experience in the ranks would provide him with important material for a book. Wilson points moreover to Lawrence's fear of solitude and longing for comradeship. Finally, Wilson cites Lawrence's underlying insecurity, which stemmed from his illegitimacy and from his short stature.

Wilson also addresses the oft-repeated allegations of Lawrence's homosexuality in his relationships with his fellow servicemen, particularly with R. A. M. Guy. Wilson examines the three pieces of evidence that have been cited to support these allegations—Lawrence's observations about Guy's good looks; an affectionate letter from Lawrence to Guy, reminiscing about their closeness while together in the ranks; and Lawrence's nicknames for Guy, "Rabbit" and "Poppet." Examined in full, both Lawrence's remarks about Guy's appearance and the letter seem innocent enough—and, most tellingly, Wilson points out that "Rabbit" and "Poppet" were nicknames for Guy which not only Lawrence but also all their fellow servicemen called him, just as they in general used nicknames for each other.

At points in this biography, Wilson ventures some new and intriguing interpretations of Lawrence's life. He maintains, for example, that over time Lawrence was able to overcome the excessive guilt he felt about the part he had played in the war. Wilson bases this observation on an interpretation of the course of Lawrence's letters, in which this preoccupation diminishes as he grows older.

Not all Wilson's interpretations are positive. Wilson points out that Lawrence, who believed that unscrupulous journalists had gotten him drummed out of the RAF was, in fact, responsible for his own dismissal by repeatedly calling attention to himself and by his arrogance and insubordination. Wilson points out some of Lawrence's other limitations as well, including his essential dislike of analytical thought and his wordy style that often obscured essentially simple ideas or that masked muddled thinking.

Over the years, as is predictable for a man of his fame and following, too many biographies have been written about T. E. Lawrence. Those written in his own time were either vulgar and sensational—such as Lowell Thomas' *With Lawrence in Arabia* (1924)—or inadequate and incomplete—such as Robert Graves's *Lawrence and the Arabs* (1927) and Basil H. Liddell Hart's *"T.E. Lawrence" in Arabia and After* (1934). Inevitably, the initial adulation was followed by disillusionment and debunking—as in Richard Aldington's *Lawrence of Arabia—A Biographical Enquiry* (1955) and Philip Knightley and Colin Simpson's *The Secret Lives of Lawrence of Arabia* (1969). Fortunately, recent years have brought several efforts to set the record straight. John E. Mack's sensitive treatment of Lawrence's life offered insight and psychological understanding. Finally, Jeremy Wilson's biography provides accuracy and amplitude. The reader of this biography not only learns to assess Lawrence's achievements within the context of an entire historical period but also experiences the historian's task of wading through a plethora of facts, details, and documents in an effort to learn what is salient and true.

Biographies in recent years have tended to get bigger and bigger—not always justifiably. Wilson's study, however, builds by accretion. It rewards the reader's patience with balance and depth. Most clearly it fulfills Wilson's stated aim: "A biography such as this must not merely be accurate: it must be seen to be accurate." *Lawrence of Arabia: The Authorized Biography of T. E. Lawrence* affords the reader this rare opportunity.

Carola M. Kaplan

Sources for Further Study

Chicago Tribune. June 17, 1990, XIV, p. 6.
Contemporary Review. CCLVI, April, 1990, p. 222.
Kirkus Reviews. LVIII, April 1, 1990, p. 493.
Library Journal. CXV, June 15, 1990, p. 118.
Los Angeles Times Book Review. June 3, 1990, p. 3.
New Statesman and Society. III, February 16, 1990, p. 36.
The New York Times Book Review. XCV, June 10, 1990, p. 42.
Publishers Weekly. CCXXXVII, March 23, 1990, p. 68.
The Times Literary Supplement. June 15, 1990, p. 635.
The Washington Post Book World. XX, July 1, 1990, p. 4.

LETTERS OF KATHERINE ANNE PORTER

Author: Katherine Anne Porter (1890-1980)
Edited, with an introduction, by Isabel Bayley
Publisher: Atlantic Monthly Press (New York). Illustrated. 642 pp. $29.95
Type of work: Letters
Time: 1930-1964
Locale: New York, Mexico, Berlin, Basel, Paris, New Orleans, California, Ann Arbor, Rome, and Washington, D.C.

A comprehensive collection of Porter's letters written during her most active years as a writer and edited in a clear and thoughtful manner

> *Principal personages:*
> CYRILLY ABELS, a magazine editor and Porter's agent
> ELIZABETH AMES, the head of Yaddo, the writer's colony where Porter worked on her novel
> DONALD BRACE, Porter's publisher for much of her working life
> ALBERT ERSKINE, an editor and Porter's fourth husband
> CAROLINE GORDON, a novelist and for many years a Porter confidante
> JOSEPHINE HERBST, a novelist and close friend of Porter
> HARRISON BOONE PORTER, Porter's father
> PAUL HARRISON PORTER, a nephew whom Porter encouraged to write
> EUGENE DOVE PRESSLY, Porter's third husband
> ALAN TATE, a distinguished poet, Caroline Gordon's husband and close friend of Porter
> ROBERT PENN WARREN, a novelist and poet who befriended Porter
> EUDORA WELTY, a novelist and short-story writer encouraged by Porter's example and assistance
> GLENWAY WESCOTT, a novelist and one of Porter's most intimate friends
> MONROE WHEELER, intensely involved with the arts and a close friend of Porter and Wescott

This is one of the most comprehensive and clearly ordered collections of a major American literary figure's letters. Isabel Bayley is Katherine Anne Porter's literary executor. She has obviously spent many years pondering the letters and deciding how best to present them. In her acknowledgments she thanks, among others, Leon Edel, who advised her on the work, and it is apparent that she has profited greatly from the counsel she has sought.

One of the problems of large collections of letters is continuity. It is often difficult to sustain narrative momentum, to keep relationships between correspondents clear, and to shape a sense of the subject's life. Bayley has solved these problems by including a detailed chronology, a "who's who" section, and an incisive introduction that samples and introduces the themes of the letters. In addition, Bayley divides the book into sections, each corresponding to a phase in Porter's life—a phase that is emphasized in paragraph-long introductions that set the scene and touch on key phrases in the letters.

This careful structure would be for naught if Porter did not exhibit the characteristics of a great letter writer. Fortunately, she is always lively and engaging, writing at length about both her writing and her personal life—indeed, intertwining the two in a way that makes her phrase about herself, "a literary woman," a most apt characterization. Art and the life of the artist were never far from Porter's concerns. She was a totally dedicated writer who sometimes sorrowed over how slowly her stories came to her but who insisted that she would not rush herself. Her highly principled and loving nature comes through clearly in her letters. Certainly she had her quirks, and she was the first to regret her woeful selection of husbands, but the relish she took in sharing her life with others—such as fellow writers Glenway Wescott and Robert Penn Warren—and their devotion to her make reading the letters a stimulating and edifying experience.

Porter seems to have relied on her correspondence not merely to stay in touch with friends and family and to conduct business but also to construct a narrative, an ongoing account of her experience on which she expected friends to comment. Yet there is nothing self-conscious about the letters or anything pretentious. She has a fascinating passage in one of her letters about men being the heroes of their life stories and suggests that women "give themselves dead away." She may have been exaggerating a bit, but there is a sense in which her letters bear her out, for she is constantly admitting how vulnerable she is and confessing that she is "full of misgivings and reconsiderations." At nearly the same time, however, she recognizes that she is "fairly tough inside." She seems to be able to cope with any degree of personal disappointment and not to be shaken by the many periods in which her work is interrupted, often because of pressing financial problems.

The range of Porter's experience is impressive. She was in Berlin to see the ascension of the Nazis, in Mexico during revolutionary upheavals, a part of the Sacco-Vanzetti protest, and an inveterate traveler who lived in various parts of the United States and Europe. It is good to have her long letter about her ocean voyage to Europe, which became the basis of her novel *Ship of Fools* (1962). In the letter she delineates the atmosphere and character relationships on which she would work for more than twenty years before releasing the novel to great acclaim.

As devoted as she was to art, Porter believed that art was one thing, life another and that the two should not be confused, even though they often fed on each other. In one of her letters, she suggested that if Ezra Pound was indeed a traitor, then he should be hanged not saved because of his literary reputation. She took this position out of no animosity toward Pound. Quite the contrary, in other letters she acknowledged him as one of the greats of her period, but she saw the danger of privileging art when it came to the demands of citizenship. Pound, she believed, should be judged as any other man or woman is judged in such matters.

Although Porter cooperated with the Federal Bureau of Investigation (FBI) during what she called the "serio-comic so-called witch-hunts," she held no brief for distasteful investigative methods and told one FBI agent as much. She was deeply offended when a university president asked her to sign a loyalty oath and declined the teaching position he offered her. She was equally shocked when she learned that one of her friends was indeed a Communist, and she questioned how well she knew some of her friends. Unlike some of her colleagues, she took politics seriously. If one espoused Communist ideas, one might very well be a danger to the state. In other words, she did not indulge her fellow writers when they committed themselves to ideas or principles she despised.

As Porter well knew, young men often fell in love with her, and it is easy to see why. Not only was she a striking-looking woman (see the photograph of her at sixty-one seated at her spinet), but she was a charming raconteur, a fine cook, and an incisive thinker. She felt entirely comfortable with men half her age. Albert Erskine was one of these men, whom she continued to treat tenderly after their brief marriage failed. Other male friends, such as Glenway Wescott and Monroe Wheeler, remained devoted to her all of her life, and other writers, such as Robert Penn Warren and Eudora Welty, looked to her for advice and comfort.

To Porter art was, in some ways, more real than life, but it was life that always gave her her start. Writing to her editor Seymour Lawrence, about *Ship of Fools*, she observed:

> You know, when I begin a story I always lean down and touch the palm of my hand to the earth— that is, I begin with an incident, a situation, a place, certain persons, something in the most factual, verifiable sense *real*; and often I do not change a name, or a location, or the time of year in which something occurred that took root in my mind and became fiction; so, I have not changed the name of the real ship on which I sailed from Vera Cruz on April 22, 1931.

This one voyage became the universal story of the human voyage, the facts transmuted into enduring fiction.

One of the pleasures of reading Porter's letters is knowing that she would have approved of their publication. She almost says so in a letter that evokes her pleasure in the thousands of letters she has written and received. In another letter she remarks: "I love memoirs better than any kind of reading except somebody's else's most private letters, after they are safely dead of course. I am saving all mine and every body's just because it will make such lively reading matter for those to come after us." She urged her correspondents to save their letters, even though she was initially doubtful about keeping carbons of hers, as that seemed too calculating. Porter's spirit was irrepressible, however, and wanting to have her letters published after her death was not so much vanity on her part as a genuine belief that subsequent generations would be enlivened and perhaps even instructed by her lifetime's struggle to write and to endure as a writer without compromising her talent.

Until Porter had her great financial success with *Ship of Fools*, she was almost always in need of money. She wrote briefly for motion pictures, took on nonfiction assignments, and taught at several universities. Her letters reflect her often desperate efforts to support herself and the generosity of friends who lent her money or made it possible for her to live in quiet circumstances and complete her stories. She thought it a hard life but not one that she regretted. She could make even her complaining sound lively and interesting—probably because her values were always so forthright and her goal unswerving: "my one fixed desire: to be a good artist."

Porter did not consider herself a feminist. She disliked labels such as "woman writer." If she did not make women's rights a cause, she was nevertheless very astute about the way men had arrogated privileges for themselves. She knew how important it was for a woman to respect herself. Was it bitterness or only the sad recognition of a lifetime's experience with men that led her to remark: "I know that when a woman loves a man, she builds him up and supports him and helps him in every possible way to live. . . . I never knew a man who loved a woman enough for this."

Porter's letters are an important counterpoint to the biography by Joan Givner, which sometimes misses the wit and the sheer fun of being around Porter. In her introduction, Bayley is especially good at getting at this side of Porter. Recalling how she told Porter about what she and her husband were going to do with some honey—use it in an Italian recipe for a cake or pour it over ice cream—Porter "exclaimed with surprising joy": "Oh! Oh! . . . You don't know how I love to hear this!"

There are many instances in the letters of the infectious power of Porter's enthusiasm. Whether the letters are read for their incisive commentary on the craft of fiction, for guidance on how an artist maintains his or her equilibrium in a world that often does not value art, for instruction on how a woman maintained her dignity and sense of direction in a milieu that could easily have deflected her from her art—the overwhelming strength of Porter's will is apparent. There was nothing sentimental or self-pitying about the hardships she endured. On February 11, 1931, she wrote to her good friend and fellow novelist Josephine Herbst: "Unless writing, or painting, or whatever, is your life and nothing else will do, and unless you have the power to make this dedication effective, its [sic] no good."

Nothing else would do for Porter. Writing was her way of keeping faith with herself and her friends. Writing letters documented her life, enforced her sense of the real, of what was deeply rooted in her fiction. Writing thousands of letters helped to show how she worked at her life and her art to make them all of a piece.

Carl Rollyson

Sources for Further Study

America. CLXIII, November 3, 1990, p. 330.
Belles Lettres. V, Spring, 1990, p. 30.
Booklist. LXXXVI, March 1, 1990, p. 1257.
Chicago Tribune. April 29, 1990, p. 3.
The Houston Post. July 15, 1990, p. C6.
Kirkus Reviews. LVIII, April 1, 1990, p. 489.
Library Journal. CXV, April 15, 1990, p. 93.
The New York Times Book Review. XCV, May 27, 1990, p. 1.
Publishers Weekly. CCXXXVII, April 6, 1990, p. 106.
The Washington Post Book World. XX, April 29, 1990, p. 4.

LEWIS PERCY

Author: Anita Brookner (1938-   )
First published: 1989, in Great Britain
Publisher: Pantheon Books (New York). 261 pp. $18.95
Type of work: Novel
Time: 1959 to the 1970's
Locale: Paris and London

A novel about the life and sentimental education of the title character, a student of nineteenth century literary heroism

> *Principal characters:*
> LEWIS PERCY, the central character, a scholar and librarian
> GRACE PERCY, the sixty-two-year-old mother of Lewis, a widow
> PATRICIA (TISSY) HARPER, Lewis' wife, an agoraphobic
> MRS. BEATRICE (THEA) HARPER, Tissy's mother
> PENRY (PEN) DOUGLAS, a friend of Lewis and a fellow librarian
> EMMY DOUGLAS, the sister of Pen Douglas, a bohemian in love with Lewis
> DR. RALPH JAGO, a physician and psychiatrist to Tissy, her mother's lover

Anita Brookner's novels are noted for their wit and understatement, their literate, romantic heroines, and their nearly Jamesian portrayal of moral scrupulosity. *Latecomers* (1988) reversed this formula to some extent by offering as protagonists two male figures, Jewish immigrants to England from the war-torn Europe of the late 1930's. It was a remarkable book and represented a shift in Brookner's attention from primarily romantic plots to that great theme: the impact of the past on the present. *Lewis Percy*, as several reviewers have noted, returns to the combination of romance and psychological realism evident in Brookner's novels prior to *Latecomers*. Indeed, the title character, a student of nineteenth century literary heroism, resembles the female protagonists in such works as *The Debut* (1981), *Providence* (1982), and *Hotel du Lac* (1984). All are somewhat melancholic, highly principled characters engaged in the romantic tradition, not only as lovers but also as scholars of romantic literature or authors of romance novels. In *Lewis Percy*, Brookner seems to have deliberately reversed her usual romance plot in order to study the male ego in its search for ideal love and under the constraint of behaving well in the face of romantic defeat.

The character of Lewis Percy—whose name may be a conflation of Percy "Wyndham" Lewis, the colleague of Ezra Pound and founder of Vorticism, and C. P. (Charles Percy) Snow's Lewis Eliot—is the only son of Grace Percy, a woman who has endured the loneliness of widowhood by doting on her son. The novel opens in 1959, in a period prior to the sexual revolution of the 1960's, when Lewis is a doctoral student in Paris. There he passively seeks the protective company of women in the evening—Roberta and Cynthia, his fellow boarders, and Madame Doche, the companion and servant of his landlady—while reading romantic literature all day at the Bibliothèque Nationale.

As the novel unfolds, it is clear that Lewis is a man with nineteenth century values caught in an era of changing sexual mores. His sentimental education is of the type once suited only to women (he avidly reads his mother's favorite novels after she dies) or to nineteenth century literary figures. From the outset, in fact, Lewis identifies with various nineteenth century literary heroes and with the world of women. At the age of twenty-two he is fond of quoting Julien Sorel, the protagonist of Stendhal's *Le Rouge et le noir* (1830; *The Red and the Black*, 1898): *"Laissez-moi ma vie idéale"*—clearly calling attention to his own quest for a heroic ideal. Here and elsewhere in *Lewis Percy*, Brookner suggests both her hero's concept of life and his central dilemma: the conflict between "the life of contingencies" and "the life of the spirit"—between a life that imprisons most people (and Lewis himself after his marriage) in stultifying routine and the life of the imagination, of passion, and, ultimately, of hope. In Lewis' time in Paris, this latter life is associated not only with the literature he reads but also with the salon where he quietly enjoys the company of women, offering a piece of Camembert or a bag of cherries as his contribution to the evening. Indeed, at this point in his life, Lewis sees his "lifetime quest" as "the study of, and love for, women." He believes that women are compassionate—in his peculiar formulation, they are a "beneficent institution"—and at the salon, with the aid of literature, he hopes to acquire his "final education."

For all this romanticism and attraction to women, at this point in his life Lewis is virginal, passive, and naïve. He overlooks the shabbiness of the salon, a relic of "a long vanished bourgeois French family," and the indifference to him of the three women whose company he shares. For all his idealism, the young Lewis Percy is a pitiable character, leading a disciplined, dull, and meager life. In the romantic city of Paris, he studies the exploits of romantic heroes rather than emulating them. In the city of love and light, he is chaste and spends his days closeted in a library. While his whole life is marked by excessive hunger—for food but also for freedom and a dangerous passion—Lewis settles in after his return to London. When his mother dies, he is desperate for someone to care for him, tend his house, and cook his meals. Marriage to Tissy Harper, an agoraphobic who works in the library that his mother used, is an alternative to loneliness, a substitute for the passion he desires. Where once Lewis identified with his mother's humility, he finds himself identifying with Tissy's virginity. Yet throughout this second phase of his development, Lewis idealizes his courtship by seeing himself as an emancipator. He believes he will rescue Tissy from her agoraphobia and Tissy's mother from the duty of caring for her fearful daughter. It is, of course, he who needs liberating, but Lewis' innocent egotism does not allow him to see this or to recognize the extent of his mother's loneliness and illness before her death.

Writing in the tradition of the nineteenth century *Bildungsroman*, or novel of learning, Brookner traces Lewis' sentimental education from his student days in Paris through his return to London, his marriage, the birth of his child, and his divorce and departure for America. Significantly, in several interviews, she has acknowledged the influence on her work of such nineteenth century French writers as Stendhal, Gustave Flaubert, and Honoré de Balzac and of American author Henry James.

Her fiction also evokes the London of Charles Dickens and the middle-class Victorian world of Anthony Trollope.

Almost as homage to her literary forebears, she alludes to all these masters in *Lewis Percy*. Lewis either identifies with their characters at different stages of his development or alludes to them in some way. After his marriage, for example, he begins to model his life on that of "gentlemen in Trollope, to whom he was devoted even more than to his early heroes." When his marriage feels stultifying, he thinks of Emma Bovary. When it fails and he learns that Tissy is pregnant, Lewis envisions himself as Silas Marner, "a gray-haired old man, devoting his life to a pretty and unsuspecting little girl," his daughter. At another point, he refers to himself as a Pooterish character, a reference to the principal character of George and Weedon Grossmith's *The Diary of a Nobody* (1892), a work that may be a literary antecedent for the record of Lewis' drab existence as a librarian in London. Dickensian eccentrics keep Lewis company at the library. There is the satiric figure, Arnold Goldsborough, a deconstructionist critic and Lewis' boss: a "florid, large, shapeless" man "with rosy curls blossoming above his collar" and a "cautious eye, which was oblique, like that of a halibut." Arthur Tooth, "a long-retired librarian," helps by ranging "with crab-like slowness round the stacks" and by displacing "books requested by readers in his pursuit of ideal symmetry."

The wit and understatement captured here are characteristic of Brookner's work. Her literary allusions suit Lewis Percy, who is a scholar and author of a Ph.D. dissertation on nineteenth century literature, but at the same time they are a subtle way of depicting both Lewis' development and a central moral theme in Brookner's work: the shifting sexual code in the twentieth century and the breakup of traditional morality. Indeed, Lewis Percy is a man baffled by these changes and by women's liberation, a movement that Tissy joins after leaving him. When Emmy, the bohemian sister of his friend Pen, falls in love with Lewis and insists he sleep with her, Lewis discovers he wants marriage, was fated to be married "since birth," eventually even to Emmy. Aware that Emmy has had married lovers since she was sixteen, he will nevertheless expect her to be faithful, even though they both live in an age when "faithfulness seemed to have gone out of fashion, replaced by more aggressive, more affirmative modes." Lewis realizes that he is doomed, "obsolete, [a] relic of a forgotten species," a man who does not want affairs but must be "either married or divorced but nothing else." Yet he persists. This may, indeed, be the true source of his own heroism: that he insists on behaving well, on behaving morally in an age when doing the opposite is more convenient and practically demanded. Pen speaks prophetically for himself and for Lewis when he says, "Basically I belong to the age of the quill pen."

Brookner does not leave Lewis Percy in the nineteenth century. He matures, eventually recognizing that his sentimental education has been "faulty." Brookner writes,

> The old Lewis Percy, the Lewis Percy who had wanted to be a character in a book and who had not managed to be one, had bowed out long ago.

It is ironic that when Lewis releases himself from this ideal, he is lifted from his miserable, confining loneliness and job by the offer of a lectureship in America. As if to show this as somehow a continuation of Lewis' search for an artistic ideal, Brookner presents his rescuer, Professor Millinship from Massachusetts, as a man who, with his beautiful wife, resembles a work of art: He looks like a figure from an El Greco painting, she an icon of female beauty. Yet Lewis is able to see at this point that the woman, at least, for all her beauty, her "high accomplishment," is cold, a figure to be admired, like the ideals of beauty in art, but not loved. The one Lewis loves is the disorderly Emmy, who is the antithesis of Mrs. Millinship and Lewis' wife, Tissy. "She was not slim, careful, elegant, virginal. She was the opposite of all those things, very much the opposite." Emmy is, Lewis sees, "outrageous; but . . . also spontaneous, instinctive," the antithesis of artistic control and order. Lewis cannot identify with her looseness—he loves "domestic peace and quiet"—but by the end of the novel he has matured to the point that he can tolerate imperfection, disorder, and contrast and is willing to ask Emmy to marry him and come to America. "The essence of a sentimental education," he sees, is "that nobody lived happily ever after." To reinforce this change, moreover, Brookner has Lewis contemplating the subject of a new book: "the hero enters the twentieth century" or "what constituted heroic behaviour in those who lived in the real world and were not bound—or protected—by the conventions of literature." It is a work inspired by Emmy, a representative of twentieth century womanhood and mores and one who scorns old-fashioned chivalry.

If, as Anita Brookner said in an interview, most of her protagonists are to some extent autobiographical, then Lewis Percy embodies certain aspects of herself. Brookner published several volumes of nineteenth century art criticism prior to becoming a novelist. Like her, Lewis Percy is a scholar of nineteenth century art. He is a Victorian in the twentieth century who grew up in a dark house run by his widowed mother. Brookner too has mentioned having been reared in a Victorian household in the company of only her elderly parents. As a romantic figure, both an idealist and a student of romantic literature, Lewis takes his plight and himself quite seriously, succumbing to melancholy after his mother's death and later, after his marital separation. Although it would be impossible to say that Brookner is not serious about morality—the subjects of her fiction show otherwise—nevertheless, her style and characterizations suggest that she approaches her work at least, if not life, with wit and amused understatement.

In this she is quite different from her protagonist. A careful reader of *Lewis Percy* will find numerous nougats of humor and understatement. The descriptions of Arnold Goldsborough and Arthur Tooth (no doubt a satiric name) offer examples, but there are others. At one point Brookner mocks the forced good humor of the British themselves. Faced with drabness, they chide themselves: "'Mustn't grumble. Can't complain,'" as if, she has Lewis observe, it were "unpatriotic, an un-English activity" to complain. She mocks Lewis' somberness by describing him as having "large ears, . . . an owlish and solemn air, very far removed from the dandyism that he thought desirable." Scholars, libraries, and scholarship—which Brookner knows well from her years as lecturer in art at London's Courtauld Institute—provide the subject for several biting witticisms. She describes one library as "something of a day care center for the lonely, the naturally silent, the elderly and the reclusive." One patron, prone to napping, calls a self-rightous librarian a "silly bitch" when she clatters across the floor to awaken him. Arnold Goldsborough reminds Lewis of "an animal in a dry water course" as he navigates the library. As Brookner sardonically observes of critics like Goldsborough, "In academic life fortune favours those who have their eccentricities to speak for them."

One of the characteristics of Brookner's style, for which some critics have faulted her, is a tendency to narrate her novels largely through reportage or exposition rather than dramatization. Her focus is not on the main events of her characters' lives but on the small occurrences that define a life. Lewis' wedding, for example, and most of the details of his courtship of Tissy are not recorded. What the reader does witness is his first stammering attempt to get Tissy to walk home with him and the first afternoon he has tea with her, her mother, and Dr. Jago, Mrs. Harper's lover. This undramatic method of narration is purposeful. It captures the unheroic quality of life while also depicting the private heroism needed to endure. Moreover, Brookner captures the truth of her characters' lives and personalities in this way. Their behavior at tea, what and how they eat, the types of food they serve others—how, in effect, they live out their daily lives—are more telling than major life events, when people are likely to behave grandly or falsely. Like Henry James, whose fiction she greatly admires, Brookner is more interested in the moral impact of events on her characters' thoughts than she is in the events themselves. Ideals, motives, growth of consciousness, maturation: These are the main subjects of her work, not the scaffolding of plot.

All of this suggests that Anita Brookner is writing in the tradition of the nineteenth century novel of England, France, and America. Her novels are slowly paced and draw the reader carefully to an awareness of her protagonists' internal trials and triumphs. One might argue that, like her hero Lewis Percy, Brookner is out of place in late twentieth century literature. This seems an unnecessarily harsh judgment, however, for in insisting on substance in an age when many readers prefer the quick reading of dramatic action, Brookner is being bold, breaking new ground—much as Lewis Percy does when setting out for America at the end of the novel. *Lewis Percy* may not be Brookner's best novel to date, but it is skillfully written. Bouyant, if flawed at the end by the *deus ex machina* device, it is a thoughtful look at the male quest for romantic love and heroism.

Stella Nesanovich

Sources for Further Study

The Christian Science Monitor. April 26, 1990, p. 14.

Library Journal. CXV, March 15, 1990, p. 110.
London Review of Books. XI, September 14, 1989, p. 19.
Los Angeles Times Book Review. March 25, 1990, p. 3.
New Statesman and Society. II, August 25, 1989, p. 26.
The New York Times Book Review. XCV, March 11, 1990, p. 10.
The New Yorker. LXVI, April 23, 1990, p. 115.
Publishers Weekly. CCXXXVII, January 12, 1990, p. 46. `
Time. CXXXV, March 19, 1990, p. 83.
The Times Literary Supplement. August 25, 1990, p. 916.
The Washington Post Book World. XX, February 18, 1990, p. 3.

LIES OF SILENCE

Author: Brian Moore (1921-   )
Publisher: Doubleday (New York). 197 pp. $18.95
Type of work: Novel
Time: The 1980's
Locale: Belfast and London

A suspense novel that explores the conflicts in Northern Ireland

> *Principal characters:*
> MICHAEL DILLON, the manager of a hotel in Belfast
> MOIRA DILLON, Michael's wife
> ANDREA, a Canadian who works for the British Broadcasting Corporation
>   and is Dillon's girlfriend

Lies of Silence is a suspense novel, a study of human nature, and an examination of the conflicts in Northern Ireland. What connects all three aspects is the recognition of mystery: the mystery of a thriller, the mystery of human beings, and the mystery of political and religious conflict.

The suspense novel revolves around a plot initiated by the Irish Republican Army (IRA) to assassinate a Protestant clergyman. A group of IRA men plan to place a bomb in the car of Michael Dillon, the manager of the hotel in which the clergyman is scheduled to speak. Breaking into Dillon's house, the IRA conspirators take Dillon and his wife, Moira, hostage; they force him to drive his car to the hotel, telling him that Moira will be killed if he informs the police.

Dillon drives to the hotel, as directed, but telephones the police in time to evacuate the guests and employees. Moira is not physically hurt by the gang, but she is hurt by what she perceives as her husband's lack of concern for her welfare and, eventually, by what she learns about him—that is, he is planning to leave her for life in London with Andrea, a Canadian who works for the British Broadcasting Corporation (BBC). The conclusion of the suspense novel revolves around Dillon's departure and the relentless pursuit of the IRA to prevent him from identifying the gang that had held him and his wife hostage.

This suspense novel is also a study of human beings who are mysterious, enigmatic individuals. Michael Dillon is a middle-aged man, unhappy in his marriage and with his decision to have abandoned his earlier calling as a poet. Additionally, he is unhappy living in Northern Ireland, seeing it as a place of irreconcilable and unresolvable conflicts. What author Brian Moore has called "the fragility of the self" is apparent in Dillon: He is a vulnerable human being who sees Andrea and London as the way out of his entrapment. Unfortunately for Dillon, in this novel, as in life, there is no simple, happy ending for a complex, unhappy individual.

Dillon's wife, Moira, is another example of the fragile self. A beautiful woman fearful of losing her physical attractiveness, Moira is bulimic, a condition described by a doctor as being associated with women who "want to become a stereotype of helpless, dependent, female beauty." Additionally, according to the doctor, bulimics can be suicidal.

Moira and Dillon also exemplify Moore's interest in the moment of crisis when individuals are faced with complexities and choices that will change their lives forever. In the case of the Dillons, their captivity by the IRA gang, brief as it was, transforms them. The capture puts Dillon into the position of risking his wife's life on behalf of the many lives of people in the hotel; choosing the welfare of many over the safety of Moira complicates his life irreversibly. Similarly, Moira decides, after the capture, to proclaim the atrocities of the IRA on the airwaves, assuming a kind of Joan of Arc approach to life, as one of her friends points out. Like Dillon, she is changed by this decision, transformed from helpless, dependent beauty to self-determining, independent spokesperson.

In addition to being a suspense novel and a study of human nature, *Lies of Silence* is an examination of the ongoing and seemingly irreconcilable conflicts in Northern Ireland. The conflicts between Catholics and Protestants, Irish and British, are problematic in themselves, but at the heart of this book—and indicated by its title—are the lies that caused and perpetuate these problems. Thus Dillon reflects on the

> lies which had made this, his . . . birthplace, sick with a terminal illness of bigotry and injustice, lies told over the years to poor Protestant working people about the Catholics, lies told to poor Catholic working people about the Protestants, lies from parliaments and pulpits, lies at rallies and funeral orations, and above all, the lies of silence from those in Westminster who did not want to face the injustices of Ulster's status quo.

Dillon is eager to leave Northern Ireland and its repository of lies, while Moira refuses to leave this place of her birth, though she shares in her husband's condemnation of both the lies and the liars. Despite their differing responses to Belfast, both have a love-hate relationship with Northern Ireland, thus emphasizing the mysterious force that a place and its inhabitants exert upon individuals.

Lies of Silence is Moore's seventeenth novel, and it shares many of the qualities of his earlier books. It deals with ordinary people and the commonplace, a quality Moore's literary hero James Joyce celebrated in his books, especially *Ulysses* (1922). Dillon and Moira are such individuals, as are Moira's parents, individuals who live in an ordinary, drab home. When Moira retreats to this place, it and her parents engulf her in the grayness and ordinariness that Moore suggests is fundamental to life in Belfast. The house, with its cramped rooms and view of a rubbish dump, is described in careful detail, including its decor—or lack thereof. "As depressing as the lounge in an old people's home," this abode of the butcher and his wife contains "plastic-covered sofa and chairs, a television set which was never shut off, garish kitsch paintings, cheap statuettes of nymphs and Disney animals, ethnic rugs and tasseled cushions, all of them purchased as souvenirs on package-tour holidays to the Costa Brava, Florida and the Algarve." Though depressing, this house is nevertheless a home, a home for ordinary people who love their daughter and welcome her back to them with warmth and concern.

This attention to the details of ordinary people and the commonplace suggests that Moore's talent is cinematic—that is, he helps readers see in the way that film-makers assist their viewers. This technique may be the result of Moore's having worked with Alfred Hitchcock, for whom he wrote screenplays. Like Hitchcock, Moore rivets the attention of his viewers-readers upon details while, at the same time, moving them quickly through a plot that contains complicated actions initiated by equally complicated individuals. Compressing this plot into a short space—many of Moore's books have fewer than two hundred pages—is another modern cinematic technique, a belief that less is more, that what is not said or seen is as important as the words or images presented by the author.

Lies of Silence is a brief, powerful combination of suspense, characterization, and culture. Like Moore's first, and some say best, novel, *The Lonely Passion of Judith Hearne* (1955), this book deals with daily choices and daily losses, the mysterious forces that motivate people and movements and countries, the lies of both individuals and nations. It is, finally, about questions that cannot be answered, including the question Dillon asks himself moments before his death: "Was any country worth the price that Ireland asked, a beggar's price, demanded again and again and never paid in full?"

Marjorie Smelstor

Sources for Further Study

Books in Canada. XIX, April, 1990, p. 42.
Kirkus Reviews. LVIII, June 15, 1990, p. 828.
Listener. CXIII, April 5, 1990, p. 20.
London Review of Books. XII, May 24, 1990, p. 18.
Los Angeles Times Book Review. September 9, 1990, p. 3.
Maclean's. CIII, June 18, 1990, p. 66.
New Statesman and Society. III, April 20, 1990, p. 36.
The New York Review of Books. XXXVII, December 6, 1990, p. 22.
The New York Times Book Review. XCV, September 2, 1990, p. 1.
Newsweek. CXVI, September 17, 1990, p. 59.
Publishers Weekly. CCXXXVII, June 22, 1990, p. 47.
Punch. CCXCVIII, April 13, 1990, p. 30.
The Spectator. CCLXIV, April 21, 1990, p. 31.
The Times Literary Supplement. April 20, 1990, p. 430.
The Washington Post Book World. XX, August 26, 1990, p. 5.

LIVES OF THE SAINTS

Author: David R. Slavitt (1935-   )
Publisher: Atheneum (New York). 213 pp. $19.95
Type of work: Novel
Time: The 1980's
Locale: Florida

A bereaved writer's ironic ruminations on the destinies of victims

Principal characters:
> THE NARRATOR-PROTAGONIST, a former college professor, now a writer for a
>   tabloid
> SIDNEY LANSBERG, the narrator's managing editor
> JOHN BABCOCK, a mass murderer, interviewed by the narrator
> STEPHANIE STRATTON, the widow of one of Babcock's victims

The tone of David R. Slavitt's novel *Lives of the Saints* reflects his literary career. His novels *The Hussar* (1987) and *Salazar Blinks* (1988), his books of poetry *The Walls of Thebes* (1986) and *Equinox* (1989), and his 1990 translation *Ovid's Poetry of Exile* are, as it were, some of his credentials for such a tone. In addition, Slavitt has been a college professor and a film critic for *Newsweek*; the narrator-protagonist of *Lives of the Saints* himself is a former college teacher and writes for the *Star*, a sensationalist tabloid. As an intellectual, he philosophizes on the events and characters of the novel, punctuating his commentary with allusions to everything from the half-life of uranium to the Tang Dynasty poets Yuan Chen and Po Chu-yi.

The narrator's grief over the death of his wife Leah and his daughter Pam in a car accident caused by a drunk driver, James Macrae, moves him to ask why such a senseless tragedy should happen. Moreover, his managing editor at the *Star*, Sidney Lansberg, allows him to extend this question by assigning him to investigate six people randomly shot to death by a remorseless nobody, John Babcock, in the parking lot of a Piggly Wiggly store in Florida.

Steeped in his own loss, and fascinated by these random murders, the narrator turns to the philosophy of Nicolas de Malebranche, a late seventeenth, early eighteenth century French Catholic priest. Malebranche writes that the human world (and nature, for that matter) is not defined by cause and effect, but by destiny. No one, moreover, can predict what is going to happen to him or her; only God knows this, and no one can know God's mind.

This view of human affairs leads the narrator to juxtapose the victims in the novel to the saints of Roman Catholic hagiography. This is ironic since he is a Jew, and doubly ironic since he does not believe in God. He finds, therefore, the lives and deaths of both saints and victims absurd—indeed, in being irrational and unpredictable, fuel for his depression and his elegantly savage humor.

Lansberg complicates this similarity between saints and victims when he tells the narrator to write a series of articles on the belongings or "relics" of the latter. The point is to provide the kind of gruesome copy that the tabloid's readers feed upon.

The narrator concentrates on four of the victims who occasion the assignment: Amanda Hapgood, a divorcee; Laura Bowers, an embezzler; Roger Stratton, a poet and college English professor; and Edward Springer, a child. Nothing in these victims' lives points to their bizarre deaths, of which the narrator becomes poignantly sure when, by way of gaining access to their belongings, he interviews those who were close to the victims.

As for the saints themselves, they are a good example, in the narrator's mind, of Malebranche's philosophy; one's choices are not really choices at all, but part of an impenetrable design. That these saints' lives, like the deaths of Babcock's victims, are outlandish arouses the narrator's sense of humor.

In this vein, he mentions Saint Barbara, among other saints. According to legend, she insisted that her family's privy have three windows in it in honor of the Blessed Trinity. When she would not listen to reason, her father beheaded her, then was himself struck dead by lightning. Saint Eustace is absurdly amusing, too, as the narrator sees it. This saint was a Roman general during the reign of Trajan. He converted to Christianity, simply because he saw a cross in the configuration of a stag's antlers. At first he lost his position, and his wife and sons left him. He recovered both when the army needed him for a campaign, during which he won an important battle. He refused, however, to offer sacrifice to the gods for this victory. He was martyred for not doing so, and—to compound the absurdity—his wife and sons were executed along with him. Saint Lucy also died for her faith. The humor in her destiny arises from its circumstances. She was committed to a brothel by a suitor whom she had rejected. Her chastity actually survived this, as did she the death by fire decreed for her. It took a sword shoved down her throat to kill her.

The saints who were not martyred had absurd destinies, too, the narrator points out. Blessed Lydwina is one of the more laughable of these. She was paralyzed by an ice-skating accident when she was sixteen, and later she went blind. The legend goes that she offered up her suffering for the sins of others, had visions, and ate nothing but the Eucharist after a time. A new priest in the Dutch town where she lived suspected that she was a fake, but the townspeople threatened to get rid of him if he did not leave her alone. From a rational standpoint, her condition affected her mind, but from a religious (or irrational) standpoint, she was favored by God. Even her suffering, and what she did about it, was a blessing—that is, her destiny. That she became the patroness of ice skating is, to the narrator, the most amusing thing about her.

Like the objects or "relics" associated with saints, certain objects left behind by Babcock's victims reflect their lives without making sense of them. There is even a saint, Stephen the Younger, who lost his life defending such icons against the iconoclasm of Emperor Constantine V of the Eastern Roman Empire. The narrator believes that the price Stephen paid for doing this is absurd; on the other hand, he cannot deny the comfort that such objects give the living or the irony and sadness with which they resonate for him.

Saint Agatha's breasts signify her chastity, for they were cut off when she, like

Saint Lucy, defended it to the death. Laura Bowers, one of the murder victims, left behind several photographs of her husband and his girlfriend making love. Her bitterness, to which her sister Felicity attests, is represented by these pictures, as is Amanda Hapgood's lust by her vibrator, Roger Stratton's wish to write poetry by the pencils on his desk, and Edward Springer's need for distraction by a wooden gameboard piece with which he played.

Objects can also signify the living. When Lansberg is fired, he leaves an anthology of Chinese poetry in translation in the narrator's desk drawer. This "relic" shows that beauty is not lost on Lansberg, as well as highlights the irony of his having worked for a paper as dimwitted as the *Star*. Objects also define the irony of how William T. ("Tweedy") Harris, who was graduated from Princeton University and has published a few short stories in minor literary journals, replaces Lansberg as editor. Al Cosgrove, the moronic publisher of the tabloid, goes looking for Bostich staples in the office at one point. By chance (meaning by Malebranchean design), he finds them in Harris' desk, where he also finds Harris' list of the clothing of Hafiz Kezemi, one of Babcock's six victims. Each item on the list is preceded by a dot, or dingbat. The dingbats move Cosgrove to promote Harris to Lansberg's job. In short, a random pattern defined by objects leads—less by cause and effect, according to the narrator, than by absurd destiny—to the success of one man and the failure of another.

While mixing saints, victims, and "relics" in a kind of Malebranchean test tube, the narrator searches for what will make his own life sensible and bearable after the death of his wife and daughter. Driving on highways gives him a sense of freedom, and the people he works for or interviews, though they evoke his sympathy in varying degrees, amuse him. They also add to his evidence that life is ironic and disorderly. Harris is promoted over and then fires the narrator, who hired him in the first place. Felicity Bowers gives her sister Laura a job in her travel agency, and Laura embezzles twenty-six thousand dollars from it. Ronald, Amanda Hapgood's husband, cares more about his flashy dental work and his female conquests than he does about her. Lucy, Edward Springer's mother, has separated from her husband because their child's death has left them with no excuse to stay together. Only with Stephanie, Roger Stratton's widow, does the narrator find some measure of solace— first through intelligent conversation, then through sex, and finally when she gets him to give up numbly lying around his house and lets him move in with her.

Before this resolution, however, the narrator interviews John Babcock, the murderer, and James Macrae, the drunk driver. His meeting with the first shows him that people are merely instruments of one another's destiny, and his meeting with the second that such instruments can be unintentional and passive.

In the end, the narrator takes over the desk of Stephanie's husband, the failed poet, to write his novel. Faced with Stephanie's need to serve (especially a writer, since she had become accustomed to her husband), and unable to shake the mystery of why people have the fates they do, he can do this at least. If this means that he can play God by creating his characters' destinies, it also means that he can try to uncover the "loftier truths of coherence." "Loftier" seems intentionally ironic, given the irony that the novel finds in the lives on which it focuses. How much, that is, can the novelist believe in his work as a means of solving the Malebranchean problem? Not much, the irony suggests.

The problem of the novel itself is that its commentary overwhelms its plot. Astute and witty as it is, this commentary also recites its Malebranche to the point of tedium, and cannot say one thing without posing an alternative, usually connecting the two with the word "or."

Notwithstanding this drawback (if that is what it is), Slavitt has a knack for disclosing the personalities and feelings of characters through where they live, what gestures they make, what they look like and say, and what they own. Lucy Springer, for example, displays her coldness through her having emptied her dead son's room, her nervousness by her habit of fooling with her hair, and her irritation by the abrupt way she talks to the narrator. The reproduction of a Soutine painting of the carcass of a sheep which Harris puts up in Lansberg's office when he takes it over helps to show how inhumane he is at heart, and the stereotypically contemporary furnishings of Felicity Bowers' house suggest her superficial taste, as her red nail polish suggests her aggressiveness.

Slavitt's syntax and vocabulary are adept, too, for blending the formal and informal; they fit the novel's view that human life has neither rhyme nor reason to recommend it.

Mark McCloskey

Sources for Further Study

Booklist. LXXXVI, December 1, 1989, p. 725.
Chicago Tribune. January 2, 1990, V, p. 3.
Kirkus Reviews. LVII, November 1, 1989, p. 1559.
Library Journal. CXV, January, 1990, p. 150.
Los Angeles Times. December 21, 1989, p. E8.
The New York Times Book Review. XCV, February 11, 1990, p. 18.
The New Yorker. LXV, January 29, 1990, p. 95.
Publishers Weekly. CCXXXVI, November 10, 1989, p. 50.
The Wall Street Journal. January 30, 1990, p. A16.
The Washington Post. January 25, 1990, p. B3.

LONDON FIELDS

Author: Martin Amis (1949-   )
First published: 1989, in Great Britain
Publisher: Harmony Books (New York). 470 pp. $19.95
Type of work: Novel
Time: The 1990's
Locale: London, New York City, and Connecticut

Four lost souls come together in London in a darkly comic novel about sex, violence, wealth, poverty, crime, darts, and the role of fiction

Principal characters:
> KEITH TALENT, a small-time criminal and darts player
> NICOLA SIX, a mysterious woman
> GUY CLINCH, a well-to-do innocent
> SAMSON "SAM" YOUNG, an American writer
> KATH TALENT, Keith's neglected wife
> KIM TALENT, Keith and Kath's infant daughter
> HOPE CLINCH, Guy's unfaithful wife
> MARMADUKE CLINCH, Guy and Hope's hyperactive son
> LIZZYBOO BROADENER, Hope's sister and Sam's lover
> MARK ASPERY, a writer and former lover of Nicola

Martin Amis has rapidly become one of the leading satirists among contemporary novelists. In *The Rachel Papers* (1973), *Dead Babies* (1975), *Success* (1978), *Other People: A Mystery Story* (1981), and *Money: A Suicide Note* (1984), Amis lampoons the excesses of modern England. He writes about the banality, brutality, and loneliness of urban life, about shallow people bored with all aspects of their existence, including sex. His characters are neurotic and insecure, often question their own sanity, and are unable to communicate with one another. The son of conservative satirist Kingsley Amis, he finds humor in a violent world from a liberal perspective but is far from being didactic, often mocking his characters' moral and political pretensions. *London Fields* is the major work toward which Amis has been building, one that effectively explores all of his themes.

Set sometime in the near future, *London Fields* is a darkly comic interpretation of the ennui and decadence of Western civilization. Through examining the lives of four protagonists from different strata of society, Amis depicts the boredom, triviality, and violence of contemporary England. Samson Young, a young but dying American writer visiting London, is writing his first novel. Nicola Six, a mysterious, highly erotic, intelligent, but disturbed woman, wants to be murdered. Because Sam lacks the imagination necessary to create fiction, he relies on observing his friends and incorporating them into his novel. Nicola cooperates, keeping him informed of what transpires between her and Keith Talent, the small-time hoodlum she has selected to be her murderer, and Guy Clinch, the wealthy innocent she lures into her web of duplicity.

Nicola chooses Keith to be the catalyst in her death because he seems to have been born for the part. Keith, twenty-nine, considers himself a racketeer preying on the helpless, but he devotes too little time and effort to be a successful crook. Keith resorts to crime less from need than from an antisocial temperament. Though Amis sympathizes with the disadvantaged, he hardly sentimentalizes them; Keith represents the malaise and insensitivity of the working class. Keith marries Kath because she teaches him to read and write; he gets her pregnant and gives her a venereal disease; then he ignores her, not even allowing her to ride in his car. He names their infant daughter Kim after his hero, England's leading darts player, but neglects her as well. Kath, a victim, victimizes Kim in revenge for her husband's sins.

Sexually insatiable, Keith commits adultery numerous times each day with his stable of lovers, none of whom he regards as remotely human. He cares only for darts (more a national obsession for the working class than a pub game) and for the glamorous world of television. Keith's dream is to merge the two by playing darts on television. Keith is romantic about darts in a way he is incapable of being romantic about women, even the ostensible dream lover, Nicola. He retreats into darts because he can understand the game; perhaps it is the only thing he *can* comprehend. His only regret about darts is that he cannot cheat at it, as he does in every other aspect of life.

Keith is too stupid to understand why Nicola befriends him after wandering into the Black Cross, his home pub. He thinks she is attracted by his darts potential: "A guy like Keith—and she must have sensed this—there was nothing he couldn't do, there was nothing beyond him." The ironically named Keith Talent, however, vastly overrates himself. He is below average as a criminal and only slightly better at darts. As soon as she sees him, Nicola recognizes the inability to love, though he later decides that "he loved her as he would his own manager, in the big time." Keith is finally a pathetic, almost sympathetic figure because he recognizes his need for an identity: "He wanted her for her belief in him, because she was the other world, and if she said that Keith was real then the other world would say it too."

Though at the other social, educational, and economic extreme, Guy Clinch is as much a cipher as is Keith. Guy longs for love, any kind of love, but can elicit none from Hope, his unfaithful wife of fifteen years; Lizzyboo, her voluptuous sister; or Marmaduke, his tempestuous infant son. His inherited wealth, about which he feels guilt, and good looks offer no solace. His restlessness leads him into the Black Cross, an unlikely friendship with Keith, and an awareness of the world beyond his privileged environment: "Guy always thought it was life he was looking for. But it must have been death—or death awareness. Death candour. . . . It is mean, it is serious, it is beautiful, it is poor." Because Keith is poor, Guy "honoured him and pitied him and admired him and envied him (and, he sometimes thought, even vaguely *fancied* him)."

Guy thinks he finds what will fill the emptiness of his life when he encounters Nicola, falling in love with her at first sight. She immediately perceives him to be "an insufficiently examined self, or an insufficiently critical one." Guy is a good person who tries to be what others want him to be. He is obedient, industrious, and uncomplaining; he is faithful to Hope until Nicola comes along; he loves Marmaduke even though his son is an unlovable brat with an Oedipus complex; he even imagines "natural delicacy" on the part of the crude Keith. Guy is so naïve that he believes Nicola is a thirty-four-year-old virgin. Amis offers him as indicative of the potential for good in his class, but Guy is too shallow to act on his good intentions.

Most of the events in *London Fields* result from or are influenced by Nicola's machinations. She wants Keith—or someone—to kill her simply because she is bored with life and cannot imagine how it could ever be any different. Because of her enormous vanity, she must end her life by intricately planning her demise, choosing her birthday—also the date of the finals for Keith's national darts competition—as her "appointed deathnight." She keeps intimate diaries about her myriad sexual adventures and throws them away seemingly so that Sam will find them and become her coconspirator.

As a child, Nicola has an imaginary friend named Enola Gay who gives birth to a son called Little Boy. She tells Guy that Enola Gay and Little Boy are refugees in Southeast Asia, then gets money from him to find them and gives it to Keith. Nearing the end of her manipulations, she gives Guy a book about Hiroshima which shocks him into confusion. The atomic bomb is a metaphor both for Nicola's death wish and for her society's potential for self-destruction. She selects Guy for her plot because she sees him as the opposite of Keith, as containing "a strong potentiality of love, which she needed, because the equation she was working on unquestionably needed love in it somewhere." She also wants a second potential killer in case Keith fails her. Having had seven abortions, she delights in convincing Guy she is totally innocent about love. She goes to the other extreme with Keith, making pornographic videotapes of herself both to provoke and to weaken him. A self-professed male fantasy figure, Nicola becomes less and less real as her scheme unfolds.

Samson Young, like Guy and Keith, is sexually excited by her but lacks their illusions. Sam has only occasional qualms about the moral implications of his involvement with Nicola and even fewer illusions about his art: "I am less a novelist than a queasy cleric, taking down the minutes of real life." He is a successful observer because the other protagonists trust him: "I'm like a vampire. I can't enter unless I'm asked in over the threshold. Once there, though, I stick around." Dying of some vague ailment, cynical, dissatisfied with his affair with Lizzyboo, Sam needs life and innocence, so he falls in love with Kim, the only character in *London Fields* capable of being saved. He baby-sits for her and tries to provide the affection her parents will not. Comforting the child provides the insecure Sam with his only pleasure.

London Fields is an indictment of a society that values goods and services above all else, prefers sex to love and sometimes even pornography to sex. Amis' London is a gloomy landscape plagued by theft, vandalism, and general tawdriness. England is in rapid decline; America is slowly going insane; politics poses more problems than solutions; the world economy is uncontrollable; God is dead; and love is seriously ill. Amis presents his characters against a background of potential international crisis as tensions among the United States, the Soviet Union, and the Arab countries, together with assorted natural disasters, threaten to destroy the planet. Even physics itself is said to have died. More important is humanity's dwindling ability to love: "Love made the world go round. And the world was slowing up. The world wasn't going round." Love is disappearing because no one cares to preserve it. Western civilization at the end of the twentieth century is a place where "nobody is to blame for anything, and nothing matters, and everything is allowed."

The tone of *London Fields* is less one of anger than of disappointment. Amis is upset by society's flaws while also amused by them. Like conservative satirists such as his father, Kingsley Amis, and Evelyn Waugh, Martin Amis ridicules the deficiencies of his culture but does not expect them to change. One of the most frequent targets of his ire is the effect of television on the Keith Talents of a postliterate world that will never recover from television's influence. While Keith reads darts magazines and a tabloid newspaper, he spends most of his time away from pub and bed in front of his television set, even though the medium makes him feel like an outsider: "Television was all about everything he did not have and was full of all the people he did not know and could never be." It distorts his sense of the real world because television represents "an exemplary reality, all beautifully and gracefully interconnected, where nothing hurt much and nobody got old. It was a high trapeze, the artists all sequin and tutu . . . enacted far above the sawdust, the peanut shells and poodle droppings, up there, beyond a taut and twanging safety-net called *money.*" More even than money, Keith covets the status television confers on its celebrities. He strives to reach the darts final not so much out of his love for the sport as because it will be televised on his favorite program: "TV, he thought. It was the best he could do." Knowing Keith as she does, Nicola picks the best possible way to cast a spell on him: showing herself nude on television. Keith thinks he can control television because he can videotape it and play it at different speeds, and if he can control it, maybe he can influence the world at large. Yet when he is finally about to appear on it, he becomes bewildered: "Himself on TV: he couldn't work out how the two worlds overlapped." Keith is shocked to discover that the pub in his darts program is merely a set. The world he thought he knew so well, the one thing in life he trusted, turns out to be a false reality.

English novelists have traditionally been realists writing about the surface of society and drawing almost exclusively on their English predecessors as literary influences. Amis comes from a generation of English writers such as Julian Barnes, Angela Carter, and Ian McEwen who have been influenced by continental, American, and Latin American novelists. While there are references in *London Fields* to Charles Dickens, D. H. Lawrence, and Evelyn Waugh, and although Guy Clinch is a Waugh-like innocent, the major inflences on Amis are Americans. When Guy surveys Nicola's library, he says, "Your fiction shelves are the mirror image of mine. Apart from the Americans." Guy represents traditional society; she, a more eclectic world.

In addition to allusions to Saul Bellow, Thomas Berger, Norman Mailer, Vladimir

Nabokov, Philip Roth, and John Updike, Amis displays the infuence of writers out-side the United Kingdom in his use of a self-conscious narrator, as does Nabokov, whom Amis has called his favorite writer. Sam, who resembles Nabokov's Humbert Humbert, worries that readers of his novel will think he has invented what he is simply reporting. He takes the reader into his confidence in discussing problems facing the novelist: "When I take on Chapter 3, when I take on Guy Clinch, I'll have to do, well, not happiness, but goodness, anyway. It's going to be rough." Sam quibbles about his structure and style, regretting that he must rush through the writ-ing process because his health is declining. Although the reader has to take Sam's word that he is dying (no other character notices anything is wrong with him), Sam insists, "Man, am I a reliable narrator." He is bothered by the implications of his roles as participant and creator: "writing brings trouble with it, moral trouble, unex-amined trouble." He notes a discrepancy between the reality of art and the reality of life: "Perhaps because of their addiction to form, writers always lag behind the contemporary formlessness. They write about an old reality, in a language that's even older. It's not the words: it's the rhythms of thought. In this sense all novels are historical novels."

His narrator's neuroticism and potential unreliability are among the devices Amis employs to modify the darkness of what is essentially a comic novel. Typical of the undercutting humor is Sam's consideration of the possibility of being "in a book written by somebody else." Amis signs an introductory note "M.A.," and Nicola's diary frequently refers to an "M.A." The latter is Mark Aspery, the hack novelist and playwright in whose apartment Sam is staying. Nicola has had an affair with Aspery and destroyed his one attempt at writing a serious novel. Aspery is success-ful in life and with women in a way Sam can never be, and Sam seems intimidated by him even though Aspery is never physically present. Sam's nemesis ridicules all he does, suggesting in a note that he is wasting his time with his novel: "It doesn't matter what anyone writes any more. . . . The truth doesn't matter any more and *is not wanted.*" *London Fields* offers lively evidence that the novel—and the contem-porary English novel in particular—does matter.

Michael Adams

Sources for Further Study

Chicago Tribune. March 4, 1990, XIV, p. 1.
The Christian Science Monitor. April 11, 1990, p. 12.
London Review of Books. XI, September 28, 1989, p. 7.
Los Angeles Times Book Review. March 4, 1990, p. 3.
The Nation. CCL, April 23, 1990, p. 565.
The New Republic. CCII, April 30, 1990, p. 45.
New Statesman and Society. II, September 22, 1989, p. 34.

The New York Times Book Review. XCV, March 4, 1990, p. 1.
Newsweek. CXV, March 5, 1990, p. 62.
The Observer. September 24, 1989, p. 47.
Publishers Weekly. CCXXXVII, January 5, 1990, p. 62.
The Spectator. CCLXIII, September 23, 1989, p. 36.
Time. CXXXV, February 26, 1990, p. 71.
The Times Literary Supplement. September 29, 1989, p. 1051.
The Wall Street Journal. March 13, 1990, p. A14.
The Washington Post Book World. XX, February 18, 1990, p. 3.

LOOKING FOR A SHIP

Author: John McPhee (1931-   )
Publisher: Farrar, Straus & Giroux (New York). 242 pp. $18.95
Type of work: Travel
Time: The late 1980's
Locale: Charleston, South Carolina; New York; aboard the *Stella Lykes* on a run through the
Panama Canal and along the Pacific coast of South America

*The account of a journalist's forty-two-day voyage on one of the few remaining ships in the
American merchant fleet*

> *Principal personages:*
> JOHN MCPHEE, an adventuresome journalist, the writer of the book
> ANDY CHASE, the second mate on the *Stella Lykes*, McPhee's friend
> CAPTAIN PAUL MCHENRY WASHBURN, the highly respected skipper of the
> *Stella Lykes*

Admirers of John McPhee have noticed a common element in his many books, as
well as in his regular articles in *The New Yorker*: McPhee likes to write about people
who are confident that their work is important and are determined to do their jobs
well. The canoemaker in *The Survival of the Bark Canoe* (1975), the vegetable-
growers and the chef in *Giving Good Weight* (1979), the geologist in *Basin and
Range* (1981), and the men of the merchant marine in *Looking for a Ship* are all
enthusiastic about what they do. When McPhee moves into the various worlds where
his people live, observing their work and obtaining answers to hundreds of questions, he takes his readers along, and they find themselves fascinated by subjects
which may be extremely remote from their own natural interests.

One does not have to be a sailor, for example, to admire the men McPhee describes in *Looking for a Ship*. Their love of the sea is indicated by the very title of
the book. Since the number of American merchant ships is steadily declining, the
men who wish to go to sea must take turns. They stay on shore for months, living on
the earnings from the last voyage, until they have moved high enough in the rotation
system to be given slots on ships. Furthermore, because of the scarcity of ships
under the American flag, they sometimes have to accept jobs below their actual
rank. It is obvious that a man who is willing to live under these uncertainties in
order sometimes to get to sea must find satisfaction in his job.

Although McPhee is primarily a reporter, not an advocate, it is obvious that he
considers the loss of America's merchant fleet to foreign flags and the replacement
of American mariners by ill-trained, cheap labor, willing to work under unsafe conditions, a trend which at some point the United States will have reason to regret.

Typically, McPhee dramatizes social and economic changes by observing their
effects on the lives of individuals. In the case of the U.S. Merchant Marine, it is an
old friend, Andy Chase, who provides McPhee with his opportunity. It is time for
Chase to look for a ship. At his suggestion, McPhee comes to Charleston with him,
goes through the process with him, and when Chase is hired as second mate on the

Stella Lykes, makes arrangements to ship out with him on a run through the Panama Canal and along the west coast of South America. This voyage not only gives McPhee a perspective which research alone cannot provide but also enables him to draw his readers along from incident to incident in the manner of fiction.

There is no doubt that many of the days aboard a ship at sea are routine. In his third chapter, McPhee sums up many of those periods with the first day he chooses to describe in detail. It is the twentieth day out, and the ship is proceeding toward Valparaiso, Chile. Dramatically, McPhee describes the darkness on the bridge and the cool sea air. At first, the helmsman, Vernon McLaughlin, is only a voice. As dawn comes, however, he becomes first a vague shape, then a visible person, whose physical characteristics suggest the staunchness of his character. In this chapter, too, comes the first physical description of Andy. Although his observations have been quoted regularly in the first sections of the book, he has been as invisible as the helmsman in the dark. Now he, too, can be seen clearly, a tall, skinny man with reddish hair and beard, whose Maine cap proclaims his origins.

In this scene, the description of Captain Paul McHenry Washburn is delayed until this personality has been established. McPhee has commented on the captain's tendency to worry; his characteristic tenseness is illustrated by the fact that he is in continual motion in the bridge area. As he walks, he talks in unrelated fragments, such as those McPhee quotes, evidently sometimes directed toward himself, sometimes to anyone who cares to listen, but often to the ship, his closest companion. More important than his eccentricities thus described, more important than the physical description, still to come, is the sum of his achievement at work. He runs a happy ship; his crew have sometimes risked the loss of a job in order to sail with him. They respect him because he knows his business; they like to work for him because he also respects his crew, treats them as professionals, and leaves them to do their jobs. Even before McPhee describes Captain Washburn in his shore-leave clothes, immaculately dressed, solid-looking, with an expressive face and a firm jaw, the captain has become a person. As McPhee comments, "If he sometimes seems to prefer talking with himself, there's an obvious reason: he's the most interesting person on the ship."

In this scene, McPhee has touched on another point which he stresses throughout the book, the fact that however routine a day at sea may appear to be, it always has the potential for disaster. There is the danger of collision with another ship. A vessel with forty thousand tons of momentum cannot come to a sudden halt in the water, cannot even change course abruptly. Only continual vigilance, constant attention to radar can prevent a disaster. There is also the difficulty of docking. Although pilots are supposedly experts at this complex kind of maneuver, there are innumerable stories of ineptness, and the captain is ultimately responsible for his ship. With his command and his experience comes the knowledge that at sea and in port, a great many things can go wrong. The best the captain can do is to think ahead, so that he can prevent as many problems as possible.

Every chapter of *Looking for a Ship* points out some of the difficulties and hazards involved in the life men such as the captain and Andy have chosen. It is not the sea they love, McPhee realizes: It is their ships and the way of life associated with them. As the captain says, mariners are not sentimental about the sea; instead, they perceive it as their antagonist. When foul weather comes, the sea attacks the ships upon it, which are all relatively frail, no matter how impressive they may seem at the dock; when those ships develop weaknesses, the sea is waiting to devour them. Every day, almost every hour, Captain Washburn muses, some ship somewhere is sinking. The captain and the members of the crew have dozens of anecdotes to illustrate the dangers of their occupation: times when the winds and the seas tossed the helpless ship far off course, pitched off the deck cargo, and threw crewmen against the rails, sometimes to be rescued, sometimes to go overboard to death. Often the crew, abandoning ship, could not make it to their boats; often they perished in the icy waters, the doom of innumerable sailors in the winter North Atlantic. McPhee reiterates the point so often made by the men on board: that no matter how careful they are, they may be fated not to survive. He emphasizes this fact with a list that might seem dull in another kind of book but which has a horrible fascination here, once the people in *Looking for a Ship* have become as real as small-town neighbors. From random issues of the *Mariners Weather Log*, McPhee cites disasters for three printed pages. Often, it is clear that no human wisdom could have prevented the disaster: There is fog, lightning, a succession of waves. In other cases, there is a collision or a cargo shift, which well might be the result of human carelessness or error. The situation of the *Stella Lykes*, which at the end of the book is crippled, points up another fact that mariners must live with: Whether ships are licensed under foreign or under American flags, the shipping companies are primarily motivated by the bottom line. Sometimes, as with the *Stella Lykes*, that means that crews travel in aging ships, which are more susceptible to breakdowns; in this case, weather does not compound the difficulty, and there is no disaster. In many cases, however, the profit motive sends ships on a course too near a storm; in others, chances are taken with even the most essential safety precautions.

It is clear, however, that not all the dangers to shipping lurk at sea. While the South American run is noted for fairly decent weather, it also has a high incidence of piracy. McPhee has collected numerous stories of this kind of theft, but he really does not expect to encounter it. Then, in Guayaquil, a fast boat nudges the ship, a handful of men swarm aboard, and before anyone can stop them, they have snatched some cartons from a deck container and disappeared. This kind of thing would seem impossible, if one did not take into account the facts that the ship is huge and the crew minimal. There are not enough men to guard the deck, which, furthermore, is cluttered with containers. On the other hand, the pirates are operating out of a four-hundred-year tradition, certainly enough time to organize an efficient spy system, which scouts out the entire ship routine and even the location of cargo before the attack is made. It is true that merchant crews have grown accustomed to the thefts by longshoremen in American harbors; however, they are concerned about the increasing violence of the pirates abroad, who when encountered pull out knives and handguns and even have taken to eliminating argument by general bursts of fire from automatic weapons. They are also concerned about the financial loss from piracy, as well as from the fines associated when drugs or stowaways are smuggled on board, since the American shipping business is already in danger from bankruptcy.

Despite all of these reasons for the captain and his crew to be worried and despite the innumerable opportunities they have to be injured or killed in what is an extremely dangerous environment, all of them seem out of their element when they are on shore. When McPhee visits Captain Washburn in Jacksonville, Florida, the captain admits that despite his affection for his family and his enthusiasm for golf, he spends his shore time waiting to go back to sea. At home, he seems confused and ineffectual, dependent on his wife for directions even in his own neighborhood; at sea, he is an unchallenged expert at all the necessary skills, including navigation, and the master upon whom his men and his ship depend.

Similarly, even though he has complex real estate projects on shore, it is obvious that David Carter's most important ambitions involve his life at sea, where he hopes to become a licensed engineer. Admittedly, some mariners are motivated simply by the paycheck. To the ordinary seaman William "Peewee" Kennedy, shipping out means a chance to provide a higher standard of living for his family. Even in his case, however, there is something missing when he sits in his house, doling out pocket money to his children, while his wife runs the household. The men who go down to the sea in ships seem to diminish when they are beached.

Nevertheless, they are being beached. McPhee stresses the fact that many of the men on board the *Stella Lykes* are in late middle age. Regrettably, as more and more American ships are lost, the younger men like Andy will have less and less opportunity to be merchant mariners. As McPhee reminds his readers early in the book, in every war the nation has depended on its well-trained, disciplined, skillful merchant marine, with shippers like Captain Washburn and with crewmen like Andy, Mac, David, and Peewee. The conclusion is obvious: In peacetime, the loss of the American shipping industry is an economic, as well as a personal, disaster; in wartime, it could be a catastrophe.

Rosemary M. Canfield Reisman

Sources for Further Study

Booklist. LXXXVI, July, 1990, p. 2043.
Chicago Tribune. September 16, 1990, XIV, p. 6.
The Christian Science Monitor. September 21, 1990, p. 14.
Christianity and Crisis. L, October 22, 1990, p. 313.
Kirkus Reviews. LVIII, July 1, 1990, p. 919.
Library Journal. CXV, August, 1990, p. 128.
Los Angeles Times Book Review. August 26, 1990, p. 1.

National Review. XLII, November 19, 1990, p. 48.
The New York Times Book Review. XCV, September 23, 1990, p. 3.
Publishers Weekly. CCXXXVII, July 20, 1990, p. 43.
The Washington Post Book World. XX, September 9, 1990, p. 1.

LUCIFER UNEMPLOYED

Author: Aleksander Wat (1900-1967)
First published: Bezrobotny Lucyfer, 1927, in Poland
Translated from the Polish by Lillian Vallee
Foreword by Czesław Miłosz
Publisher: Northwestern University Press (Evanston, Illinois) 123 pp. $17.95; paperback $8.95
Type of work: Short stories

A collection of intellectually adventurous and formally experimental stories satirizing European values in the interwar period

The momentous historical events in Eastern and Central Europe which began to take shape in 1989 contain important cultural and literary aspects. In cultural terms, greater access to the intellectual life and thought of countries previously known largely, and to some degree stereotypically, as members of the Soviet bloc is becoming available. And from a strictly literary point of view, texts which might otherwise have remained suppressed or been denied translation are being published with sufficient regularity as to facilitate at least a preliminary redrawing of the artistic map of Europe. In particular, the publication of texts such as *Lucifer Unemployed* draws attention to the development and fate of European modernism at the hands of writers who were not frequenters of the salons and little magazines which provided modernist entrepreneurs in London and Paris with their impetus.

In the light of the collection of stories under review, therefore, it is possible to consider realignments and reformulations of the conception of a modernist tradition which is more wide-ranging in its effects and more problematic in its objectives than familiar contemporary academic characterizations have been inclined to allow. Thus, the Polish Futurism which Wat is credited with cofounding, and of which this volume of his stories is a representative expression, emerges as an entity quite distinctive from its better-known Italian counterpart, of which indeed it articulates a fascinating, if not necessarily intentional, critique. Moreover, Aleksander Wat's own career, sketched in his introduction by the most celebrated figure in contemporary Polish literature, the Nobel laureate Czesław Miłosz, can be seen to function as an instructive lesson in the fate of the literary artificer under totalitarian conditions: "At the end of his tumultuous life, Wat calculated that he had known fourteen prisons."

Miłosz also draws attention, however, to the attraction between intellectuals and totalitarianism which existed particularly in the interwar period, quoting to telling effect from Wat's critically important *Mój wiek* (1977; *My Century: The Odyssey of a Polish Intellectual,* 1987). One of the most significant aspects of *Lucifer Unemployed* is its embodiment of an unnervingly dehistoricized temperament which expresses itself in tones of self-mocking frustration and coldly sardonic anger. At one level, *Lucifer Unemployed* may be read as a prolonged meditation in disenchantment, as may more prominent modernist, Anglophone texts from the same period whose authors were drawn to a totalitarianism at the opposite end of the political spectrum from that of Wat. It is possible to regard the tone and temperament of

Lucifer Unemployed as the expression of youthful arrogance and a somewhat facile, stylistically self-conscious, and even intellectually pretentious literary personality. (The book was the author's first published volume of prose.) On the other hand, it seems equally valid to regard the highly mannered character of Wat's writing (captured, on the whole, with persuasive fluency by the translator), and the stories' intellectual range, as indications of cultural desperation and aesthetic impasse, conditions which are confronted from a quite different standpoint but with not altogether dissimilar results in the early stories of Samuel Beckett.

While it is important to underline the historical importance of Wat's fiction, it is also relevant to draw attention to some of its undoubted difficulties. These constitute, broadly speaking, an absence of the fundamental features of what is conventionally understood by the term "realism." In this way, also, *Lucifer Unemployed* is a product of its time. Like many of the most highly prized English, American, French, and Russian texts of the teens and twenties of the twentieth century, Wat's stories present thought—rather than, for example, social behavior—in action. The psychology of individual characters remains undeveloped. Settings are presented only when germane to a given story's overall theme. Interaction between characters is largely schematic. Events take place with bewildering swiftness, or else they fail to take place with an equally bewildering finality. Large spans of time are arbitrarily covered. The norms of coherence generally associated with the well-made literary artifact—norms drawing on such organizational principles as linearity, three-dimensionality (or illusions thereof), explicit denouement, depiction of human relationships in a recognizable social environment and representation of familiar time-space relationships—are essentially disregarded in *Lucifer Unemployed*.

The author's obvious lack of interest in documentary verisimilitude is, however, a carefully and clearly thought-out position. There is an explicit parallel between his stories' controlled disorderliness and the moral, ethical, and historical conditions upon which his stories draw. In many instances, Wat's stories concern historical processes which are out of control or which are sustained merely by their own momentum, and hence lack responsibility toward the human subjects which are their ostensible initiators and beneficiaries. But while Wat's reliance on the momentum of processes is an obvious point of contact with a key feature of Italian Futurism, his work obviates that artistic philosophy's more egregious sociopolitical naïveté and adopts a more discursive, reflective, and ultimately satirical approach.

Of the nine stories in *Lucifer Unemployed*, it is the title story which contains the clearest account of the author's preoccupations. A sense of Wat's daring can be found in the fact that, as in the case of this volume's other pieces, the title of "Lucifer Unemployed" is to be taken literally. The story deals with the fallen angel himself, who finds, on a visit to the earth, that there is no longer any call for his services. Despite making approaches to those who might be considered his natural employers—poets, policemen, editors, and stockbrokers, to name the most obvious ones—Lucifer finds that the world is quite capable of doing his work without his assistance, relegating, but at the same time, paradoxically, elevating the former fiend to the status of film star. The story ends: "Lucifer became a film artist. We all know him. He's Charlie Chaplin." This, the longest piece in the book, is the most sustained and playful display of Wat's sense of the exhaustion of old codes, his poker-faced delight in undermining and his fascination with destabilizing his readers' expectations, together with—and perhaps above all—his concept of reversal (evident in his inverting the Latin etymology of Lucifer—"light-bearer"—so as to render it the provocative synonym of the modern term "star").

These same features are to be found at different levels, and viewed from different perspectives, in the other stories in the volume. Despite the recurrence of a basic premise and a consistent philosophical orientation—Wat affects a somewhat self-regarding faith in skepticism—the stories are cunning in their range, from the frankly comic "Kings in Exile" to the almost bathetic "Tom Bill, Heavyweight Champion" to the surrealistic "Has Anyone Seen Pigeon Street?" Some of the material, however, shows a darker, or not merely playful, side to Wat's outlook. This side is particularly to the fore in "The Eternally Wandering Jew," where religious and racial stereotypes are broken down, culminating in the election to the Papacy of a Jew, an outcome which the story locates in the distant future. The frank exploitation of the putative rigidities of race and creed in this story makes it as striking an expression of the author's daring as "Lucifer Unemployed."

Categories of ordering experience such as, for example, religious faith or political principles, are no longer, in Wat's view, capable of sustaining the order of which they speak. Rather, they give rise to what is referred to as "the madness of facts" in "Has Anyone Seen Pigeon Street?" For this reason, perhaps, the author is fond of using the term "anarchism" in connection with the condition of his protagonists (in the apostrophe to Lucifer which concludes the title story, the fallen angel is told, "You will be an anarchist dancing with a machine—an ingenious metaphor for the present day"). Wat's sense of anarchism, with its emphasis on the elimination or reversal of those terms and conditions which posit and uphold order, draws attention to his stories' persistent though understated satire on history considered as a manifestation of progress. The representation of the future as an implicitly absurd zone where the seeds of contemporary dissolution and disillusion will come to fruition functions less as a warning (Wat is too mandarin a temperament to stoop to such a blatant deployment of his perceptions) than as a means of gaining a distance from, and dramatizing, the inescapable atmosphere of irresponsibility and excess so characteristic of interwar Europe. The future is presented as pointless, possessing a merely formal inevitability.

The stories which make up *Lucifer Unemployed* confirm the nature of their author's problematic themes by virtue of their form. Their experimental character largely derives from their philosophical ambition and repudiation of realism. In addition, however, their formal properties underline Wat's preoccupations. While superficially orderly—that is, presented without the innovative typefaces and layouts sometimes favored by modernist authors—the intellectual density of the author's material, his rapid changes of time period and locale, and the peculiar focus from which his concerns are viewed ("The History of the Last Revolution in England," for example, chronicles class conflict as a soccer match) all ensure a reading experience that can border on the vertiginous. The reader's difficulty in reordering the multiple levels at play in *Lucifer Unemployed* gives direct access to the author's sense of anarchism, and also reveals the subversive impetus which lies beneath—and which seems at odds with—these stories' fastidious stylistic surface. The antinomy between matter and manner is arguably the most audible hint as to his intentions which this impersonal, and self-mockingly omniscient, author gives the reader. And despite the undoubted difficulties of Wat's perceptions, subject matter, and angle of approach, it is likely that the most immediate pleasure to be had from this volume comes from the supple and sophisticated style in which it is written.

Despite its obvious interest as a historical and aesthetic document (which it is also possible to describe as its curiosity value), *Lucifer Unemployed* must ultimately be judged as a minor work. Its relation to the European artistic tendencies of its day, and its intriguing adaptation of the strain of imaginative extravagance found in other works of Polish literature, ensure its historical significance. The book's stylistic brilliance and thematic adventurousness are in key with the radical relationships of its material to such genres as the fable, the parable, and the essay: Wat is an author who looks back to Voltaire while clearly living in the same century as Franz Kafka and Bruno Schulz, to mention only two relevant contemporaries. Yet, perhaps the daring of *Lucifer Unemployed* acts ultimately as a limitation. Once its provocative and unnerving approach has been identified and assimilated, other elements of its vision— its terminal satire, for example—can seem a little facile. Nevertheless, the appearance of *Lucifer Unemployed* in English is very welcome, and is particularly apt at a time when very much more about the cultural and literary history of Eastern Europe needs to be known.

George O'Brien

Sources for Further Study

Kirkus Reviews. LVII, November 15, 1989, p. 1632.
The New York Review of Books. XXXVII, July 19, 1990, p. 23.
The New York Times Book Review. XCV, March 25, 1990, p. 23.
Publishers Weekly. CCXXXVI, December 1, 1989, p. 52.
World and I. V, April, 1990, p. 362.

LUCY

Author: Jamaica Kincaid (1949-   )
Publisher: Farrar, Straus & Giroux (New York). 164 pp. $16.95
Type of work: Novel
Time: The late 1960's
Locale: A large city (probably New York) and a summer house on the shore of one of the
  Great Lakes

*Leaving her Caribbean island home to work as a domestic for a wealthy family in New York
City, a young woman acquires a sense of self, blending influences from her childhood with her
own dreams*

Principal characters:
> LUCY JOSEPHINE POTTER, a nineteen-year-old black woman from a small
>   Caribbean island, who works as an *au pair* in New York City
> MARIAH, a wealthy white woman who employs Lucy to take care of her
>   four young daughters
> LEWIS, Mariah's husband, who leaves her for her best friend
> PEGGY, Lucy's friend in New York City
> PAUL, an artist, Lucy's lover
> ANNIE, Lucy's mother, who, although living in the Caribbean, influences
>   all that Lucy does

Born Elaine Potter Richardson in 1949 on the small Caribbean island of Antigua,
Jamaica Kincaid knows intimately the world of which she writes. Her first book, a
collection of short stories entitled *At the Bottom of the River* (1983), provides impressionistic glimpses into the life of the island. Her second book, the strongly autobiographical novel *Annie John* (1985), chronicles the growth of a young girl as she
struggles to find herself within the limits set by the island culture and by her mother,
finally opting to leave her twelve-by-eight-mile island to pursue a career in England
as a nurse. With some variations, *Lucy,* also autobiographical, continues the story of
Annie, now renamed Lucy and working in New York as a live-in baby-sitter.

The novel opens with Lucy's first day in New York (although not named, the city
is strongly suggested through the descriptions). Waking up to a sunny January day,
Lucy slips on a light madras dress unsuitable for the cold of winter. Always on her
island, sunshine meant warmth. Thus begins Lucy's introduction to New York and
the first of many adjustments. She will encounter indoor plumbing, apartments,
elevators, refrigerators, snow, and daffodils.

Although naïve when confronted with the world beyond her island, Lucy has the
clear-sightedness that comes from being an outsider. Her critical eye is focused on
the lives of Mariah and Lewis, her employers, and those of their upper-class friends.
Living in a world of privilege that includes an expensive New York apartment and a
large house on one of the Great Lakes, Lewis and Mariah never realize that their
life-style is dependent on the subjugation and oppression of people such as Lucy.
They never understand that they are the exploiters of nature and that should all
Mariah's fashionable ecological concerns be realized their possessions would be

fewer. They "made no connection between their comforts and the decline of the world that lay before them." Yet Lucy is ambivalent about their extravagant lifestyle. On the one hand she reacts with anger and bitterness because she is the servant and they the masters, repeating the colonial situation on her island home, but on the other hand she welcomes the luxuries, regretting the absence of a second bathroom when she moves into her own apartment.

Her relationship with Mariah is also complex, resembling the love-hate relationship that she has with her own mother. Lucy treats Mariah with hostility, resentful of her privilege and her picture-perfect world, repeatedly taunting her with "How do you get to be that way?" At the same time, however, Lucy is appreciative of her kindness and understanding. Mariah presents her with a book of photographs that leads her into photography; she encourages Lucy, reassuring her that women are "in society . . . in history . . . in culture . . . everywhere." She comforts Lucy during an emotional crisis: Mariah "held on to my two hands; she drew me close to her. She must have known that I was about to break apart, and what she was doing was holding me together in one piece." With her clear vision, Lucy knows that Mariah's refined and elegantly constructed world will soon shatter. She recognizes the signs of Lewis' infidelity long before Mariah, whose previous experiences do not include encounters with discord and unpleasantness.

Though young, Lucy understands the politics of race, class, and gender. Her childhood on the then British colony of Antigua (also not named, but again the descriptions indicate this island) schooled her in the nuances of subject-master relationships. She knows that her ancestors were brought to the island as unwilling slaves and that more recent generations were, and still are, servants. She knows that the culture of the ancestors of her grandmother, a Carib Indian, was obliterated as part of the systematic destruction of the indigenous cultures by the colonizers of the New World. As a young girl, Lucy rebelled, refusing to sing "Rule, Britannia." She is oppressed not only by the colonial status of her island but also by the role assigned to her gender. Her position in the male-dominated culture became clear at the birth of each of her three younger brothers, when her parents discussed plans to send the boy to a university, something that was never considered for Lucy. This disregard for her abilities precipitated the break between Lucy and her mother: "I felt a sword go through my heart, for there was no accompanying scenario in which she saw me, her only identical offspring, in a remotely similar situation . . . and I began to plan a separation from her." Even Lucy's traveling to New York is, in a way, limiting; it provides an opportunity to study to be a nurse, not a doctor. Realizing that nurses take orders rather than give them, Lucy soon rejects the plan. In New York she discovers that sexism is not limited to her island. She notices that the lives of men, but not women, are chronicled in the books shelved in the libraries and that men, not women, have the opportunity to become artists; on a more personal level, she sees that Mariah automatically assumes the guilt and responsibility for her failed marriage. Though Lucy might be ignorant of the physics of elevators, she is well versed in the dynamics of power.

Lucy envisions New York as her chance to escape not only from her island home but also from her mother. She has grown beyond her island and feels constricted by its limits, an island whose people judge her harshly because they have known her since birth, an island where Lucy's options are limited by the culture and by the available education. Lucy also must create herself as a separate being from her mother. For the first nine years of her life there was almost no separation between mother and daughter: Their dresses were sewn out of the same fabric; they bathed together. Then the birth of her brothers and the onset of puberty caused a rift between them, altering their close, symbiotic relationship. Lucy fears her mother's perceived power: "She was . . . like a god. I wondered . . . how it came to be that of all the mothers in the world mine was not an ordinary human being but something from an ancient book." She resists her mother's influence: "My mother's love for me was designed solely to make me into an echo of her." Sensing her own loss of identity and believing that "I was not like my mother—I was my mother," she flees to New York. So determined is she to sever ties with her mother that she leaves unopened her letters, including one marked urgent, knowing that if she reads them, she "would die from longing for her." The sealed letters contain the news that a family friend must bring her: the death of her elderly father. Even so Lucy does not return home, although she sends her savings to her suddenly impoverished mother. To prevent the arrival of more unwelcome letters, Lucy, upon moving to an apartment, provides her mother with an incorrect address.

Even though New York City is thousands of miles from Antigua, Lucy never leaves the island and her mother far behind. Images and memories from her childhood are ever present. Decorative plants in a Greenwich village apartment are familiar to Lucy as cassy, which she has eaten with "fungy and salt fish," and as dagger, whose fibers she has woven. Her lover's fish tank recalls the fishermen of her childhood and the day that one returned without the other as a result of a sudden squall. A walk through the woods summons up memories of the demons among the trees on her island and her mother's encounter with a possessed monkey. The island and its lore are part of Lucy, and she cannot escape. Yet that does not prevent her from acquiring a sense of self forged from her past and her own desires: "I understood that I was inventing myself." She suspects for the first time that she might be beautiful; she pursues her newfound interest in photography. She does not know who she will become, but she knows that she will not be someone's possession or afraid of life or insignificant: "By then I already knew that I wanted to have a powerful odor and would not care if it gave offense."

Jamaica Kincaid's strengths as a fiction writer are numerous. She creates a vivid sense of place with her descriptions of the island of Antigua, where dinner might be "a bowl of pink mullet and green figs cooked in coconut milk," where an obeah woman heals a sick child or curses an adulterer, and where spirits are as real as the living. Kincaid's language evokes the West Indian dialects of the Caribbean. Her lilting rhythms, repetitions, and images have led critics to call her prose poetic. Her explorations of the loneliness of childhood and of the complex mother-daughter relationship with its mixture of love and hate have introduced important but often neglected themes to fiction.

In *Lucy*, as in her earlier works, Kincaid relies on personal experience. She shares with Lucy her birth date and the events of her childhood. She had a stormy relationship with her mother, to whom she often lied. Later Kincaid would credit the falsehoods as a source for her creativity: "Lying is the beginning of fiction. It was the beginning of my writing life." In 1966, at the age of seventeen, she left Antigua to work as an au pair in Scarsdale, New York, not returning to her home for nineteen years. Jamaica Kincaid has taken these experiences, filtered them through the lens of her craft, and provided the reader with memorable fiction.

Barbara Wiedemann

Sources for Further Study

Chicago Tribune. October 28, 1990, XIV, p. 6.
The Christian Science Monitor. November 26, 1990, p. 13.
Kirkus Reviews. LVIII, August 15, 1990, p. 1120.
Library Journal. CXV, November 1, 1990, p. 125.
Los Angeles Times Book Review. October 21, 1990, p. 3.
The New York Times Book Review. XCV, October 28, 1990, p. 11.
Newsweek. CXVI, October 1, 1990, p. 68.
Publishers Weekly. CCXXXVII, August 17, 1990, p. 50.
Self. XII, October, 1990, p. 98.
The Washington Post Book World. XX, October 7, 1990, p. 7.

LUTHER
Man Between God and the Devil

Author: Heiko A. Oberman (1930-   )
First published: Luther: Mensch zwischen Gott und Teufel, 1982, in West Germany
Translated from the German by Eileen Walliser-Schwarzbart
Publisher: Yale University Press (New Haven, Connecticut). Illustrated. 380 pp. $29.95
Type of work: Historical biography
Time: 1483-1546
Locale: Saxony and the surrounding regions of the Holy Roman Empire

An analytical biography of Martin Luther organized around connected essays that describe both Luther's life and the setting out of which he and the German Reformation emerged

Principal personages:
MARTIN LUTHER, the major leader of the German Reformation to the 1540's
CATHERINE (OF BORA) LUTHER, his wife and former nun
HANS LUDER, Martin Luther's father and a successful copper miner
MARGARET (KUNHEIM) LUDER, Martin Luther's mother
CHARLES V, Holy Roman Emperor (1519-1556) and king of Spain as Charles I (1516-1556)
JOHANNES ECK, a Catholic theologian and opponent of Luther
DESIDERIUS ERASMUS, a Dutch theologian and scholar who led a reform movement within the Roman Catholic Church but rejected Luther's approach
LEO X (GIOVANNI DE MEDICI), Pope (1513-1521) during the early Reformation
PHILIPP MELANCHTHON, a colleague of Luther and a professor of Greek at Wittenberg who wrote *Loci communes* and otherwise supported and interpreted the Lutheran Reformation
JOHANNES VON STAUPITZ, Luther's confessor at Wittenberg who helped shape the Lutheran view of salvation by faith alone

One of the most incisive and readable of the many books triggered by the five hundredth anniversary of the birth of German Reformation leader Martin Luther is Heiko A. Oberman's *Luther: Man Between God and the Devil*. Unusual in both organization and approach, this book provides new insight into both Luther the man and the Reformation that he sparked.

More of a series of connected essays than a typical biography, Oberman's study focuses on the origins of the German Reformation and the shaping of young Luther's thought. Yet Oberman covers in considerable detail the major episodes of Luther's life from his birth in 1483 to his death in 1546. Sensitive to faith and values—in the tradition of Roland A. Bainton, to whom the book is dedicated—Oberman provides a penetrating view of Luther's spiritual struggles. Oberman sensed that "Luther learned to draw life from the struggle against the Devil. For the just shall *live* by faith, and 'life' does not begin in Heaven." In contrast to the prevailing medieval concept that in the midst of life human beings are surrounded by death, Oberman claims that "Luther's faith enabled him to vigorously turn this on its head: 'In the midst of death we are surrounded by life.' "

Long known for his view that Luther and the Reformation have been distorted in many rationalistic studies, Oberman finds the key to understanding Luther in his existential struggle with personified evil. The Devil was very real to Luther; that much has been widely recognized. Oberman insists, however, that this fact has not been fully understood or adequately analyzed in previous studies. The underlying current of Oberman's analysis is that Luther's view of the Devil was at once generically medieval and distinctively his own.

> Luther's world of thought is wholly distorted and apologetically misconstrued if his conception of the Devil is dismissed as a medieval phenomenon and only his faith in Christ retained as relevant or as the only decisive factor. Christ and the Devil were equally real to him: one was the perpetual intercessor for Christianity, the other a menace to mankind till the end.

To say that Luther never overcame the typical medieval belief in the Devil, according to Oberman, is not to say too much, but too little. Luther, he argues "even intensified it and lent to it additional urgency."

The first of the three major sections of Oberman's biography deals with "The Longed-For Reformation." This section begins with an account of Luther's death in February, 1546, permitting Oberman to set the tone of the book in terms of Luther's personality traits and the images of his life. He alludes to a funeral oration by Philip Melanchthon, Luther's perennial colleague and interpreter of the Lutheran Reformation. Delivered in Latin in the name of the University of Wittenberg, where both had taught, Melanchthon's eulogy was candid in recognizing Luther's flaws of temper and speech but described him as a "strict healer," who was "God's instrument for renewing the Church." This struck Oberman as a misleading characterization that contributed to a distorted image of Luther. Luther was indeed "strict"—that was a trait Melanchthon had experienced at firsthand—but he was not a "healer." Luther saw himself as "God's instrument" but " 'renewal of the Church' was something he did not envisage," Oberman claims.

What, then, was Luther's role in the Reformation, and how did he perceive himself within it? To understand these issues, insists Oberman, one must study the life of Luther "from an unconventional perspective. It is history 'sub specie aeternitatis,' in the light of eternity; not in the mild glow of constant progress toward Heaven, but in the shadow of the chaos of the Last Days and the imminence of eternity." Thus, Oberman begins his first concentrated essay on the situation that produced the Reformation.

The second major section of the book deals with "The Unexpected Reformation," in which Oberman analyzes the young Luther's intellectual and spiritual development from 1505 (when he decided to become a monk) to 1521 (the year of the Diet of Worms before Charles V). By then the German Reformation had become a cause of concern to the young emperor. Posting the *Ninety-Five Theses* in 1517 led quickly to confrontation with the papacy and Catholic leaders in Germany. In 1519 Luther was drawn into a debate at Leipzig with Johannes Eck, who skillfully maneuvered him into supporting the heretical views of John Hus. Two years later Charles V, who dreamed like Charlemagne of a vast, unified Christian realm, tried to force Luther to recant at Worms. Luther was too committed to the theology of "salvation by faith alone," however, to be deterred.

The last section focuses on "The Reformation in Peril," beginning in the 1520's and continuing to where the book began, with Luther's death in early 1546. Here Oberman is at his best in showing the Luther who constantly had to deal with problems: illness, political resistance, division in his own movement. Throughout his ordeals Luther remained a man of faith, not only in terms of theological affirmation, but also living by faith in the midst of problems aggravated by bouts of illness and depression.

By several measures, Oberman is a revisionist. He maintains throughout that the principal driving force of Luther in the Reformation was his unenviable but paradigmatic position between the Devil and God. This is not to say that Oberman underestimates the importance of Luther's political and social setting, but he suggests that it does not reveal the real Luther. For that insight, it is necessary to examine his spiritual struggles.

Oberman's analysis of the late medieval setting is generally thorough. Basic to it is his argument that the Reformation was both a "German event" and a "medieval event." He begins with a description of Frederick the Wise of Saxony, the famous Elector who protected Luther in the early critical period following 1517. Oberman also deals extensively with Emperor Charles V, who was elected to succeed Maximilian I in 1519. Both men would play significant, and opposing, roles in Luther's life and the Reformation. Frederick, whom Luther described as the "great hesitator," did not always please Luther. His theological views contradicted some of Luther's, although the famous Elector did want to be a Christian sovereign and lent Luther crucial support. Charles V, on the other hand, represented the established order of the late medieval Holy Roman Empire, a political entity that had always fallen short of uniting or ruling the German states. The heir of Spain as well as of Burgundy and the Holy Roman Empire, Charles V found the Reformation threatening to his goal of imperial unity. As a "German event," the Lutheran movement drew upon discontent among princes who rejected Charles V's authority, as well as German antipathy toward the Roman Catholic papacy.

Luther was born on November 10, 1483 and was baptized on St. Martin's Day, more than thirty-five years before Charles V's succession. His family, headed by Hans Luther (Luder), a copper miner who had been able to lease mines and rise above the economic level of his counterparts, was ambitious but subscribed to late medieval values in all other respects. Martin was planning to carry out his father's wish that he become an attorney when he experienced a spiritual crisis in 1505 that led him to become a monk. His mother, Margaret, is often described as gentler than Hans and, in works such as Erik Erikson's *Young Man Luther* (1958), contrasts sharply with Luther's strict, sometimes oppressive father. Oberman notes, however, Margaret's own tendency to be firm with young Martin. Margaret Luther, or Hanna, as she was called by the family, is not widely treated in the extant sources. It is known that she worked hard and was devoted to the Christian faith, but, Luther recalls, she could also be very strict at times. One adult memory was that she had once thrashed him to the point that her discipline "drew blood." Oberman thereby opens a door to some revisionist evaluation of the psychological forces that shaped young Luther's insecurity about life and God. Almost every other scholar focuses on the stern, ambitious father, but Oberman suggests that in its own way this incident reflects another reason for Luther's intense awareness of the Devil. "If the Devil cannot do anything against the teachings," wrote Luther, "he attacks the person." That kind of perception stayed with Luther throughout his life.

Contextual factors that influenced the Reformation included nominalism. By the sixteenth century, traditional Scholasticism, the great achievement of Thomas Aquinas in the thirteenth century, was being challenged again by the heirs of William of Occam and his dialectical nominalism. Luther referred to Occam as his "master" and "the greatest dialectician." As he became both a monk and a university professor at Wittenberg, Luther began to study more deeply not only the Bible but also the Occamist view that faith and reason are two distinct realms. Luther did not agree with Occam's view of salvation, but he applied the nominalist method to his criticism of Scholasticism, which contributed to his theology of "salvation by faith alone." Oberman also includes useful analyses of the Augustinians, the Observantines, and the Brethren of the Common Life movement in the Rhineland that influenced Desiderius Erasmus of Rotterdam, among others.

Luther's relationship with Erasmus is of particular interest. Erasmus was a seasoned scholar who produced an improved Greek New Testament and such works as *Moraie encomium* (1509; *The Praise of Folly*) and *Adagia* (1500; *Adages*). Yet he remained in the Catholic Church and persisted in his belief in the freedom of the human will and the perfectibility of man. In 1525 Luther broke with Erasmus, as he did with the extremists at Wittenberg. In December Luther published *De servo arbitrio* (*The Bondage of the Will*), a polemical tract against Erasmus' *De libro arbitrio* (*The Free Will*). For Luther more than Erasmus, man was in need of liberating grace and was unable to improve his condition with his own strength.

That same year Luther married Catherine of Bora, a converted nun. Luther married her out of compassion rather than out of romantic love, but the marriage proved to be fruitful and satisfying in many ways. Oberman discusses at length their home life, the three sons and three daughters (two of the girls died) born to the couple, their several adopted children, and Luther's attitudes toward women and marriage. By traditional Catholic standards, this union of a monk and a nun was repulsive, but Luther found it rewarding and legitimate, contrasting sharply with the bigamous relationships of Philip of Hesse and the concubines of the errant clergymen and popes of the day.

Oberman's Luther is strikingly human, wrestling with everyday challenges as if each was part of the larger struggle with Satan. His kidney stones and other ailments he took as manfestations of a battle that he could not win on his own. "Did we in our own strength confide," Luther wrote in his great hymn "A Mighty Fortress," "our striving would be losing." In the final section, Oberman shows that Luther ascribed the same dilemma to the Church as a whole. "The Reformation in Peril" begins with a thorough discussion of Luther as a man "driven"—from 1517 to the end of his life—not by his natural predisposition to reform the Church, his personal ambition, or even "divine guidance" in the usual sense.

> Luther . . . preferred a phrase drawn from the mystical tradition: "I was swept along," an expression less of a destiny guided by a remote Almighty than of the intervention of a present, all-powerful God. Man does not appear in the light of his self-determination, but in the light of his need for guidance from God's overwhelming power. Modern man shrinks from the thought of such direct divine intervention.

Oberman suggests that to modern man Luther appears to be a person who "confused his own mind with God's counsel," an impression with which Oberman disagrees. He argues that "Luther could never regard Providence as a private court of appeal or as justification for his own actions."

The intensity with which Oberman has presented Luther makes the book very readable, quotable, and thought-provoking—in that respect it has few equals. The reader encounters a real man who was beset by ordinary problems and extraordinary opposition yet remained consistent in his interpretation of life and God. Another strength of the book is its detailed treatment of internal divisions within the Reformation over sacraments, the physical symbols of religion, and the freedom of the human will. It lacks, on the other hand, a clear treatment of the social context of the Reformation: the Knights' War, the Peasants' War, or the economic foundations of German opposition to Rome. If Luther has been distorted by the humanistic, liberal Protestant interpretation, as Oberman claims, his work does much to present an alternative perspective. His focus on Satan as the key to unifying Luther's theology and personal struggles is intriguing. Oberman also presents Luther, in the final analysis, as a man who affirmed life and hope in the face of despair. In English translation, his book adds much substance to the field of Reformation scholarship.

Thomas R. Peake

Sources for Further Study

American Historical Review. XC, June, 1985, p. 709.
The Christian Science Monitor. February 9, 1990, p. 13.
Commonweal. CXVII, March 9, 1990, p. 161.
History Today. XL, March, 1990, p. 55.
London Review of Books. XII, May 10, 1990, p. 20.
The New Yorker. LXVI, February 26, 1990, p. 132.
The Times Literary Supplement. March 30, 1990, p. 348.
The Washington Post Book World. XX, May 27, 1990, p. 11.

MADNESS IN THE STREETS
How Psychiatry and the Law Abandoned the Mentally Ill

Authors: Rael Jean Isaac (1933-   ) and Virginia C. Armat (1947-   )
Publisher: Free Press (New York). 436 pp. $24.95
Type of work: Social history
Time: The 1970's and 1980's
Locale: Mostly New York City

An investigation of the political reasons behind the deinstitutionalization of mental patients during the 1970's and 1980's that points to a combination of factors involving constitutional guarantees, economics, and advances in psychoactive medications

According to Rael Jean Isaac and Virginia C. Armat, the shift in care for mentally handicapped patients during the last two decades has caused the patient's right to receive treatment to be replaced by the patient's right to refuse treatment. The result is that substantial numbers of people with varying degrees of eccentricity and derangement are living on the streets of the nation.

In 1985, Mayor Edward Koch of New York City ordered metropolitan police officers to remove such people from the streets when dangerously low winter temperatures threatened their survival. Court challenges, however, upheld the right of people to refuse mandatory shelter even in life-threatening circumstances such as freezing to death. Since the Civil Rights movements of the late 1960's, courts have generally reaffirmed the constitutional rights of all citizens, including mental patients.

The trend to deinstitutionalize surfaced at a time when a host of promising new pharmaceuticals had been developed to treat various kinds of mental disorders from schizophrenia to depression. Because of these wonder drugs, many of the older methods of treatment—mainly psychosurgery such as lobotomies and electroconvulsive therapy, the so-called shock treatment—came to be used less frequently than before. Many patients who would have faced a lifetime of confinement in mental institutions a decade earlier were pharmaceutically managed, if not completely cured, to the point that they could rejoin their families and resume their places in the community.

In many venues, led by the initiative of President John F. Kennedy, institutions that had been labeled "lunatic asylums" in literature and in common parlance were either shut down or drastically altered. During the Kennedy and Johnson Administrations, federal funding was available to patients being treated in community mental health centers and to mentally disturbed people confined to nursing homes or community residences, but not to those confined in mental hospitals.

Conventional mental hospitals emptied quickly as large numbers of mentally handicapped people found that they could have their conditions treated satisfactorily in the community mental health centers that were now springing up all over the country. Communities responded well to this method of coping with the mentally ill because it is much less costly to staff and maintain community health centers, nursing homes, and community residences than it is to maintain residential mental hospitals.

Clients in community centers suffer less social and professional stigma than people who have been confined to mental hospitals. Another immediate social benefit at the beginning of this trend seemed to be that many people who could not function productively were now able, while being treated, to hold jobs and pay taxes rather than being financial drains upon society.

Idealistic dreams about the possible benefits of having a national network of community mental health centers, however, were soon eroded. The staffs of such centers became factionalized, the major split usually coming between the clinicians, who considered it their responsibility to care on a day-to-day basis for the people who came to their centers, and the group that viewed mental illness as a broadly social problem that could be solved only by changing society through eliminating poverty, drug dependence, and other factors that contribute measurably to mental illness.

The internal squabbling within the staffs of community centers prevented many of them from accomplishing their fundamental aims. Racism became a divisive force as the community centers developed. In many communities, the mental health centers were accused of working more with neurotic or mildly psychotic patients than with the deeply psychotic. Obviously, the success rates of professionals who treat slightly ill people will be more impressive than those of professionals who treat the gravely ill. Therefore, many community centers invoked procedures that effectively discouraged seriously psychotic patients from seeking and receiving the long-term, intensive treatment that their conditions demanded. At the same time, such centers were treating substantial numbers of other patients who showed remarkable progress in short periods of time.

Although most professionals in the field applauded the idea of returning mental patients to their own communities whenever they could, many were adamant in saying that it does no good to return such people to the community unless they are assured of being able to lead good lives within it. Therefore, constant support services must be available, and those who do not come to the centers voluntarily, must be sought out and encouraged to avail themselves of the help proffered by the community.

This latter notion became a major point of controversy. How aggressive can social agencies be in pressing their services upon unwilling clients, even unwilling clients who probably cannot make rational decisions about matters that intimately and directly affect their own welfare and physical safety? Within psychiatric and legal circles, there was no agreement on an airtight definition of insanity. When does eccentricity cross the thin line into insanity? Does one not have the right to be eccentric? Does one not also have the right to be crazy? Professionals have not been able to provide categorical answers to these cogent questions.

Without such answers, the matter of individual rights assured under the Constitution had to be interpreted by the courts. In 1968, Bruce Ennis, a recent graduate of the University of Chicago School of Law, sought employment on the staff of the New York Civil Liberties Union (NYCLU). Although the NYCLU had no vacancy at the time, Ennis was told that the organization was likely to launch a special project on the rights of the mentally ill. Armed with this information, the young attorney began to read about the mentally handicapped. He found Thomas Szasz' landmark work, *The Myth of Mental Illness* (1974), particularly compelling and illuminating.

The authors describe how Ennis worked to get the NYCLU to pass a resolution in 1969 that denounced involuntary hospitalization of mental patients. Ennis attempted to hold a conference on the subject in 1971, but could not arouse sufficient interest to justify convening the meeting, so it was canceled. The next year, however, Ennis was able to publish his *Prisoners of Psychiatry*, which was a strong indictment of the psychiatric profession, and widespread interest in the matter was sparked. In 1973, a conference that Ennis helped to organize on the rights of the mentally handicapped attracted more than five hundred participants. Three other major conferences followed this one almost immediately, and advocacy groups for the mentally ill were formed across the nation.

As a result, when public interest attorneys brought to the courts cases that affected the homeless and/or the mentally ill, their arguments had more credibility than they had earlier enjoyed. The courts almost unanimously supported the contention that all American citizens have constitutional guarantees—all American citizens, not merely those who are adjudged rational by some external group of community guardians, who often find themselves in basic disagreement about the definition of sanity.

The authors argue that blaming deinstitutionalization for homelessness in the United States is overly simplistic. Although deinstitutionalization may be a substantial contributing factor, other causes lead to homelessness as well. Urban renewal has in many instances replaced affordable dwellings with aesthetically superior housing that is financially unattainable for many former slum dwellers.

Armat and Isaac also note that two deinstitutionalizations really took place during the late 1960's and early 1970's. In the first group were the chronically ill, who could receive subsidies if they were confined to nursing homes or community residences, but not if they were kept in mental hospitals. The second group was the one encouraged by public interest attorneys who argued, according to Isaac and Armat, that it is a constitutional right of United States citizens to be crazy.

The authors cite and discuss in detail more than a dozen crucial court cases in which the rights of the mentally ill have been affirmed judicially, in some cases at levels as high as the United States Supreme Court. Early in their study, they provide an in-depth review of factors that resulted in what they label the "anti-psychiatry movement" of the 1960's that continued through the next two decades.

It is clear even from the titles of a few of the book's major divisions that Isaac and Armat are far from dispassionate, disinterested researchers. Part 1 is titled "Anti-Psychiatry: Birth of a Social Delusion"; part 3, "The Law Becomes Deranged"; part 4, "The War Against Treatment"; and part 5, "Families as Mental Institutions." Their work has a distinctly conservative bias and is consistently critical of the liberal tendencies that proliferated during the 1960's and that, in their eyes, resulted in many of the social ills that they address in *Madness in the Streets*. They take to task such liberal organizations as the American Civil Liberties Union, identifying it as "left wing."

Throughout the book, and particularly in "Families as Mental Institutions," Isaac and Armat document some of the horrors that have occurred because mental health clinics treated deeply disturbed patients with medications for short periods of time and then released them as cured. The authors document cases when such patients committed horrendous crimes that resulted in the deaths of family members or in the irrational killing of large numbers of innocent strangers, such as when a deranged gunman fired on a crowd in a McDonald's restaurant in Southern California.

The greatest danger that the authors see is that of banning involuntary commitments to mental institutions on the ground that they violate the civil liberties of United States citizens. Isaac and Armat advocate changing the laws to allow family members or governmental authorities to demand the confinement of deranged persons. The authors, however, are unable to define clearly such crucial terms as "insanity," "derangement," and "mentally disturbed." Without such definitions, involuntary commitments are constitutionally questionable.

Obviously, the psychiatric profession has not agreed categorically on definitions for these crucial terms. Besides, many members of the legal profession in the United States—conservatives, liberals, and moderates alike—would predictably rush to defend people who are threatened with preventive detention, which in essence confines people for crimes not yet committed but are feared to be in danger of commission, a pernicious form of prejudgment that presumes guilt before that guilt is proved. Because the American judicial system does not recognize clairvoyance as a basis for action by the guardians of society, any attempts to move in this direction legally would be regarded as patently unconstitutional.

R. Baird Shuman

Sources for Further Study

Booklist. LXXXVII, September 15, 1990, p. 123.
The Christian Science Monitor. October 22, 1990, p. 13.
Kirkus Reviews. LVIII, August 1, 1990, p. 1061.
Library Journal. CXV, October 15, 1990, p. 97.
Los Angeles Times Book Review. September 9, 1990, p. 1.
National Review. XLII, September 17, 1990, p. 46.
The New York Times Book Review. XCV, September 16, 1990, p. 9.
Publishers Weekly. CCXXXVII, July 13, 1990, p. 48.
The Wall Street Journal. October 18, 1990, p. A14.
The Washington Post Book World. XX, August 26, 1990, p. 1.

MARIANNE MOORE
A Literary Life

Author: Charles Molesworth (1941-   )
Publisher: Atheneum (New York). Illustrated. 472 pp. $29.95
Type of work: Literary biography
Time: 1887-1972
Locale: Kirkwood, Missouri; Carlisle, Pennsylvania; Bryn Mawr, Pennsylvania; New York
City; and Brooklyn, New York

*This first full-length biography of Moore traces the life of one of the original practitioners
of American "New Poetry" and analyzes the important influences her family and poet contemporaries had on her work*

> Principal personages:
> MARIANNE CRAIG MOORE, the poet-subject
> MARY WARNER MOORE, her mother
> WARNER MOORE, her brother

On May 15, 1886, Emily Elizabeth Dickinson died. Exactly eighteen months
later, on November 15, 1887, Marianne Craig Moore was born. Both of these extraordinary women changed the direction of American poetry. Certain similarities
between them, though not remarkable in themselves, considering the era in which
they were reared and the social class from which they came, are worth noting. Both
came from Puritan stock, from families filled with ministers; both were in their own
ways reclusive, and both employed nature-related themes in their verse. Dickinson
had a close relationship, despite occasional frictions, with her father and brother.
Moore's father died legally insane before she was born, but her mother and brother
played important roles in her artistic development. Both Dickinson and Moore had
superb educations for women of their era: Dickinson at Mount Holyoke and Moore
at Bryn Mawr. Both families faced serious financial difficulties involving bankruptcy. The poetry of both women came to be accepted only in the 1920's.

Then there is this remarkable little poem, written by Moore when she was twenty-
six:

> The clouds between
> Perforce must mean
> Dissension.
>
> The broken crock's
> Condition mocks
> Prevention.

Were Lavinia Norcross Dickinson (the poet's sister) to have found it among the
1775 poems that Thomas H. Johnson published in 1955 as Dickinson's complete
oeuvre, not a critic in the world would have challenged its authorship. Even so,
Moore's poetry is distinctive. All indications, based on her college studies and lists

of personal readings, are that she had not read any of Dickinson's poetry and that she likely had barely heard of the "Queen Recluse of Amherst" in 1913. Charles Molesworth, author of this first full-length biography, mentions almost nothing about the Dickinson-Moore similarities, nor should he have done so, for his is a study based on facts. It is a welcome study, which examines carefully the heady twentieth century environment that produced an American genius and much-loved poet.

Much was against Moore's becoming an important literary figure, or for that matter much else of importance. Her mother, Mary Warner Moore, reared her and her brother Warner in the manse of John Riddle Warner, pastor of the Presbyterian church in Kirkwood, Missouri, near St. Louis. Warner was the poet's maternal grandfather and was financially secure with some private income from property in Kirkwood and in Pueblo, Colorado. For her first seven years, then, Moore and her brother lived a relatively peaceful life, not directly affected by the financial collapse and early death of her mentally unstable father. Nevertheless, her grandfather was an old man, even at Moore's birth, and he died in 1893. This left Moore's mother with two children, ages seven and eight, and virtually no family members upon whom she could depend. Their subsequent eventual move to Carlisle, Pennsylvania, came about primarily because of the Reverend Warner's previous ministerial service in Pennsylvania and the presence of a strong Presbyterian congregation there.

The three Moores remained in Carlisle for the next twenty years. Mary joined the Second Presbyterian Church of Dr. George Norcross, taught at the Metzger Institute there, and sent her children to the best schools: Warner to prepare for the ministry at Yale University, Moore to a newly founded but already excellent college for women named Bryn Mawr, after the town in which it was located.

Moore came to love Bryn Mawr, though, as often happens, she did not fully realize how much its values had influenced her until her later life. Though she wrote for *Tipyn O'Bob* (Welsh for "a bit of everything") and became a consulting editor of this Bryn Mawr literary magazine in the final years of her college career, she rarely had the unqualified support of her instructors. Indeed, one, a Miss Donnelly, advised her not to major in English. She considered Moore's logic too disjunctive for academic criticism. Ironically, Moore's reviews in *The Dial*, the influential literary publication originally founded by Ralph Waldo Emerson, are some of the most perceptive and thoughtful ever written. Instead, Moore majored in politics, continued to write verse, and adopted a socialist veneer, radical for the times and primarily based on the contemporary issue of women's suffrage.

Even as Moore continued to distinguish herself at Bryn Mawr, her brother was making his own reputation at Yale. He worked hard, with relatively little financial support from home, and determined during his years there to pursue graduate ministerial studies at Princeton Theological Seminary. Though the Moores lived apart during these college years, they remained close through relayed letters. Warner consistently restates his intention to reunite the family after his ordination, and for a time it appeared that he would succeed by his acceptance of a New Jersey pastorate. As it happened, marriage and World War I intervened. He joined the Navy as chaplain and subsequently settled with his wife in California. Still, the Moores remained close, and Moore and her mother would establish residence in Brooklyn in the mid-1930's, primarily to be closer to Warner when he subsequently worked at the Brooklyn Navy Yard.

Throughout the 1920's, though, Moore and her mother lived in Greenwich Village, during that decade a magnet for artists of all varieties. It is difficult to imagine what two essentially conservative women made of bohemian life there, but it is undeniable that Moore's residence in this lower Manhattan haven brought her into close proximity with those who would shape her career. Molesworth explores a number of these unlikely friendships, most notably with H. D. (Hilda Doolittle, a protégée of Ezra Pound) and H. D.'s companion Winifred Ellerman (who adopted the name "Bryher"). Bryher became something of a patron for Moore in these early years, and H. D. brought Moore's poetry to the attention of Ezra Pound, the famous, later infamous, arbiter of taste and maker of poets. Pound's influential magazine, *The Egoist*, would publish some of Moore's early work. This, and reviews Moore would write for *The Dial*, eventually brought her writing to the attention of another Pound protégé, Thomas Stearns Eliot. The academic realism of Eliot's writing distinguished them aesthetically, but Moore admired Eliot's detachment as well as his Christian spirituality, two elements characteristic of her own style.

Another important friend was Scofield Thayer, who with James Sibley Watson rejuvenated the influential literary magazine known as *The Dial*. Moore published more in this journal than all other similar outlets combined, and eventually became its editor. Her popular recognition in the 1920's and 1930's derives not from her relatively small output of verse, but from the perceptive reviews she wrote for it. It was Moore who first reviewed the verse of Eliot, William Carlos Williams, and Wallace Stevens, and her insightful reviews brought her closer to these poets.

Above all one remembers the patrician gentility of Moore, a quality which characterizes her verse as much as her critical writing. Moore preferred a tone that was dispassionate, objective (almost in a scientific sense), one that was as nearly devoid of emotion as possible. She believed this was the best way to scrutinize those themes most important to her. In this, she comes close to espousing the "objective correlative" of Eliot; yet, she remained wary of realism. Her poetry is academic insofar as it often introduces uncommon or exotic elements; yet, baseball, as illustrative of popular culture, was as important to her as botany and zoology. Unicorns, pangolins, mongooses, kivu lizards, basilisks, baseball, and poetry itself are legitimate subjects for her verse, and in this Moore subscribes to the modernist credo of Pound and Williams that no subject is innately poetic. A poet could, however, treat all things poetically, relying on form to create art. This comes close to literary formalism, such as that espoused by Yvor Winters, and it provides the thesis of "Poetry" (1935), the poem in which Moore describes her philosophy of composition.

There were, however, subjects toward which Moore was personally averse, primarily anything she considered "obscene." In this she included what offended taste, and in this she departed from Williams, the poet whose works most closely resemble her own. The criterion of taste, which for Moore implied refinement, caused her to make at least two controversial decisions as editor of *The Dial*. The first of these was the title change and substantial cuts she required before publication of Hart Crane's "The Wine Menagerie" (1926). The dispute which ensued provoked Crane's comment, referring to Moore and Margaret Anderson, editor of *The Little Review*, that American poetry was in the hands of two hysterical virgins.

Crane's poem ultimately appeared in its revised form in the May, 1926, issue of *The Dial* and the controversy eventually diminished, but a second editorial decision, Moore's refusal to publish the Anna Livia Plurabelle chapter of James Joyce's last novel, *Finnegans Wake* (1939), in March, 1927, had far-reaching consequences. Though Moore herself enjoyed playing with words in her poems, incorporating titles as part of first lines, breaking words between lines and even stanzas, or introducing quotations (which may or may not have been derived from external sources), she disliked obscurity for its own sake. She always had considered Joyce guilty of this fault, and she had never forgiven him for the scatology of his novel *Ulysses* (1922). She consulted Watson, one of the founding editors of *The Dial*, by mail regarding his feelings on the matter, and interpreted his ambiguous response as approval of whatever decision she made. Even so, it appears Watson would have willingly serialized the entire novel. As things happened, *Finnegans Wake* never appeared in *The Dial*, and many attacked Moore for her conservatism.

This byzantine procedure of having to consult by mail presumably retired editors regarding daily editorial decisions was apparently one Moore was willing to tolerate. Every month of her tenure, she sent a roster of articles scheduled for inclusion in the forthcoming number of *The Dial* to Thayer and Watson with room not only for their comments but also for possible substitutions of equivalent length for every item on the list. In effect, this necessitated preparing two issues for every number of *The Dial* which actually appeared. One can imagine the added work this involved, as well as the frayed nerves it caused when European mailings arrived late.

For many, however, Moore's most remembered persona is that of Brooklyn's poet-in-residence, an identification she acquired in the 1930's after *The Dial* ceased publication. Characteristically, Moore welcomed the move. Her new surroundings took her away from the center stage of Manhattan's literary scene, and the apartment, which she shared with her mother, was airy and bucolic compared to the cramped surroundings of Greenwich Village. Moore was never a recluse in the accepted sense of that word, but her poetry often alludes to the need for sanctuary. Retreat was what her home provided best of all; yet, it was only a few minutes' walk from the Brooklyn Navy Yard, at which her chaplain-brother worked.

The 1930's thus became a time of renewed family relationships with mother and brother as well as one of seclusion during which Moore produced her most distinctive poetry. Animal poems predominate, and two of her most famous, "The Jerboa" (1932) and "The Plumet Basilisk" (1932), date from this period. Moore developed as a fully formed "new poet," introducing unusual subject matter even as her process of revision became more severe and conservative. This careful conservativism, always a part of her personality, became more outspoken even in her politics. The self-proclaimed socialist of Bryn Mawr supported Herbert Hoover, even with the onset of the Depression. She would maintain this stance even into her old age. Letters to family and friends almost invariably contain anticommunist references, and in 1968 she would agree wholeheartedly with her brother's letter of commendation to then-president Lyndon Johnson on the Gulf of Tonkin resolution, which, in effect, began the Vietnam War.

Moore's last twelve years saw her return to residence in Greenwich Village. Her mother, to whom she was devoted and who likely had inspired much of her care, editorial precision, and general conservativism, had died in November, 1947. Though her most productive period of composition had concluded, the honors she deserved for a lifetime of achievement began. She received the Gold Medal of the Poetry Society of America in January, 1960; Bryn Mawr, her alma mater, in the same year gave her, along with seventy-four other alumnae, a certificate of honor to celebrate the college's seventy-fifth anniversary. Goucher College conferred an honorary degree upon her. The celebrated *Esquire* magazine article of June, 1966, declared her to be one of the few people everybody likes, and a festschrift of poems, essays, and recollections by such friends and colleagues as Conrad Aiken, Harry Levin, May Swenson, Robert Penn Warren, and Allen Ginsberg appeared in her honor. Moore was a regular guest of Joan Payson, then the owner of the New York Mets baseball team; her broad-brimmed or tricorn hats, which had become equivalent to a signet, made Moore instantly recognizable to millions who had never read a word of her poetry.

At a reception given in 1969 by the New York Public Library, Moore met Pound, her longtime friend and mentor, for the last time. Bystanders strained to eavesdrop, but the poets' conversation was virtually wordless. Looking frail but still very much alive, they held hands, gazed at each other, and spoke the other's first name. The final meeting was as moving and filled with meaning as one of Pound's haiku poems. Though nearly all the "new poets" had died, that moment had vorticized life into art.

Welcome as this first full-length study of Moore is, several shortcomings will disconcert some readers. Academic readers will object to its relatively scanty citation of sources, particularly of unpublished material such as letters and uncollected poems. These reside in a variety of locations, much in the Rosenbach Museum and Library, Philadelphia, lesser amounts in the Berg Collection of the New York Public Library, the Beinecke Manuscript Collection at Yale University, and the Cumberland Historical Society in Carlisle, Pennsylvania. Lesser flaws concern the index, which is incomplete and without cross-citations, and miscellaneous unfortunate errors in the text.

Robert J. Forman

Sources for Further Study

Booklist. LXXXVI, August, 1990, p. 2146.
Boston Globe. September 23, 1990, p. 43.
Chicago Tribune. July 22, 1990, XIV, p. 3.
Choice. XXVII, August, 1990, p. 2146.
Chronicles. XV, February, 1991, p. 22.
Kirkus Reviews. LVIII, June 1, 1990, p. 782.
Library Journal. CXV, June 15, 1990, p. 113.
The New York Times Book Review. XCV, August 26, 1990, p. 8.
Publishers Weekly. CCXXXVII, July 13, 1990, p. 45.
San Francisco Chronicle. August 26, 1990, p. REV8.
The Washington Post Book World. XX, August 19, 1990, p. 7.

MARS BECKONS
The Mysteries, the Challenges, the Expectations of
Our Next Great Adventure in Space

Author: John Noble Wilford (1933-   )
Publisher: Alfred A. Knopf (New York). Illustrated. 244 pp. $24.95
Type of work: Popular science

A science journalist provides a history of human fascination with Mars, a summation of
contemporary scientific knowledge of the planet, and a plea for American support for human
exploration of the Martian surface

This book is part history, part popular science, and part advocate for future manned exploration of Mars. Wilford begins with an episodic review of thousands of years of human curiosity about and study of the planet Mars. His presentation is concise and insightful, but limited in depth and detail. There is no original research evident in his discussion, but he has read some of the more significant contemporary historians of astronomy and summarized their views accurately. His examination of Mars in popular culture is confined primarily to Orson Welles's version of H. G. Wells's *The War of the Worlds* (1898) and the novels of Edgar Rice Burroughs. Surprisingly, he shows little interest in the images of travel to Mars that appeared in television and film. All in all, the historical chapters are the least important of the book. They contribute nothing to the literature. Wilford could easily have deleted or reduced the historical background even further without an adverse impact upon his book. History of this sort is irrelevant for his main purpose.

His review of more contemporary research is qualitatively another matter. Wilford has won two Pulitzer Prizes for his science reporting, so it is not surprising that both his account of the exploration of Mars by spacecraft and his précis of the state of scientific knowledge of the planet are outstanding. Here he is dealing with material with which he is intimately familiar and has already written about: the scientific achievements of the American and Russian space programs. Mission after mission, whether success or failure, is sketched out with a sure hand. Unlike other histories of the unmanned space program, Wilford is not concerned with celebrating technological accomplishments. Engineers are not his heroes. Instead, he focuses on the scientific knowledge gained, underscoring the unexpected or puzzling fact and the impermanent nature of scientific theories. He scrutinizes the work of the planetologists, geologists, biologists, and astronomers, balancing discussion of the geology of Mars with interest in the question of the existence of Martian life. The second section ends with a chapter summarizing the state of scientific knowledge of Mars at the conclusion of the Viking missions (approximately 1980). It is a chapter recommended to anyone without technical expertise who wishes to understand what scientists know and do not know about Mars. This is popular science writing and science journalism at its best, written by a man who understands and appreciates the excitement of scientific discovery. It establishes his credentials in a way that the first section of the book does not. At the same time, the chapter provides a sense of urgency for further exploration of Mars by emphasizing that there is no consensus yet on the question of whether life exists, or at least existed at one time on Mars. He quotes both Russian and Western scientists as insisting that the results of the Viking missions did not settle the issue once and for all.

The history and the review of science are but a prologue, however, for the final half of the book: a justification for future human expeditions to Mars and a subtle effort to influence American space and foreign policy for the next two to three decades. As the subtitle proclaims, Wilford believes that Mars will be the next great adventure in space. It is human destiny to walk on the surface of that planet. If that is so, then he believes that it would be a grave mistake on the part of American political leaders and policymakers not to have the United States take part in the exploration. This book is an effort to gain support for American participation in an international space adventure.

Wilford lays out three possible paths that humankind could follow to fulfill its destiny on Mars. Perhaps most likely is a landing by the Russians, who are already publicly committed to exploring the planet. Slowly, but surely—Wilford characterizes their program as patient and unrelenting—they are progressing toward a manned landing. The new openness to the West can only accelerate their progress. Wilford appears confident that eventually, despite their failure to send men to the Moon, they will land explorers on Mars.

Alternatively, the United States might recapture its fervor for crossing new frontiers. The Reagan years were empty of accomplishments in space science and planetology. The *Challenger* explosion in 1986 shook the nation's confidence in its space technology and forced a reexamination of many assumptions. That trauma, however, is presumably behind the country, and President George Bush has been publicly more enthusiastic about civilian-scientific exploration than was his predecessor. Perhaps an Apollo-like commitment might be made, but would the United States be willing to spend the necessary funds, especially in a political atmosphere in which the rivalry with the Russians no longer can serve as a justification?

Wilford's dream is a third path: a joint venture by the United States, the Soviet Union, and Western Europe. He envisions such a joint manned voyage to Mars as both a sign and an outgrowth of the demise of the Cold War and the dawning of a new age of international cooperation. From planning the early robotic missions to touchdown of the manned vehicle would demand up to three decades of scientific and technical collaboration. It would involve highly visible and dramatic teamwork.

To persuade readers that he is not existing in a dream world, Wilford reviews various possible scenarios for a trip to Mars. None of these scenarios depends on highly exotic technology such as nuclear propulsion. Wilford does not believe that technical problems would present insurmountable obstacles. In his descriptions of possible approaches, the technology is already present, soon to come, or at least feasible. All that is needed is the proper level of commitment. Some scenarios can be compared to sprints, growing out of a hope to land as quickly as possible. Wilford sees landings carried out based on this strategy as possible in the first few years of the twenty-first century. This is the same type of strategy developed for the Apollo missions to the Moon. Like Apollo, sprint scenarios see the landing as an end in itself and do not worry about what happens next. The danger with the sprint strategy for Mars is that the end result could also resemble that of the Apollo missions. Once the landing is achieved, there would be no plan for follow-up. Other scenarios conceptualize a stepwise process, perhaps with the establishment of a base on the Moon as the preliminary stage. These scenarios, which would take a decade or more longer to accomplish than sprint missions, see Mars exploration as a long-term endeavor. Ultimately, Mars might even become a colony of Earth. Science fiction would become reality.

There are many echoes of Wilford's arguments and descriptions in the arguments and accounts developed by the Planetary Society and in the statements of one of that organization's leaders, Carl Sagan. It is clear that Wilford is sympathetic to the goals of this organization. Sagan makes frequent appearances in the book, although the Planetary Society appears only once. It is probably less a case of a connection than the fact that there are a limited number of reasons for Martian exploration.

After reading Wilford's book, the reader must answer two questions. First, how inevitable is human exploration of the surface by Mars during the next twenty-five years? Given the huge cost involved, even if spread among a number of countries, and the many problems facing the planet Earth, might not the world's collective leadership think it would make more sense to put off the exploration a generation or two? Meanwhile, science could continue probing the planet with increasingly sophisticated robots at a fraction of the cost and without endangering human lives. In developing his concept of travel to Mars as destiny, Wilford draws heavily upon a theory of history which sees exploration as part of the cultural heritage of Western Europe. He also assumes that the United States is a participant in that culture. As the United States becomes more multicultural, however—as the Soviet Union begins to confront the fact that it is both European and Asian—there is no guarantee that Western European cultural values will dominate the Earth of the twenty-first century. Abolishing famine might take precedence over walking on another planet, at least in the near term. This would not negate Wilford's more conservative prediction that humans would walk on Mars by the end of the twenty-first century.

The second question is related to the first. Even if Europe and the Soviet Union wish to travel to Mars, should the United States participate? How important, in terms of prestige and national identity, is such participation? Does the United States always have to be at the cutting edge of developments in science and technology across the board? Would it make more sense for the United States to focus its efforts on other areas of science and technology, such as genetic engineering, or alternative forms of energy, leaving space technology to other countries?

These are questions that must be debated, at least in the United States, in the political arena. Policy should reflect the wishes of the people. Wilford's is one voice in what should be an important debate.

Marc Rothenberg

Sources for Further Study

Ad Astra. II, September, 1990, p. 39.
Booklist. LXXXVI, May 15, 1990, p. 1755.
Business Week. July 30, 1990, p. 8.
Chicago Tribune. July 18, 1990, V, p. 3.
Kirkus Reviews. LVIII, May 15, 1990, p. 721.
Library Journal. CXV, June 15, 1990, p. 130.
The New York Times Book Review. XCV, July 15, 1990, p. 1.
Newsweek. CXVI, August 6, 1990, p. 65.
Publishers Weekly. CCXXXVII, June 8, 1990, p. 39.
The Washington Post Book World. XX, August 12, 1990, p. 39.

MARY REILLY

Author: Valerie Martin
Publisher: Doubleday (New York). 263 pp. $18.95
Type of work: Novel
Time: The 1880's
Locale: London

Mary Reilly, a housemaid in Victorian London, is drawn into confidences with her "Master," Dr. Henry Jekyll, and becomes increasingly aware that he is involved in a strange, tragic relation with a sinister young man known as Edward Hyde

Principal characters:
>MARY REILLY, the narrator, a young woman from a poverty-stricken background, housemaid to Dr. Henry Jekyll
>DR. HENRY JEKYLL, a wealthy, gentlemanly, middle-aged doctor engaged in mysterious medical researches
>EDWARD HYDE, a small, sinister young man whom Dr. Jekyll introduces as his assistant and protégé
>POOLE, Dr. Jekyll's elderly butler and head of the household staff
>MRS. KENT, Dr. Jekyll's cook
>MR. UTTERSON, Dr. Jekyll's attorney
>BRADSHAW, Dr. Jekyll's footman
>ANNIE, another maid of Dr. Jekyll
>MRS. FARRADAY, Mr. Hyde's ill-reputed landlady
>DR. LANYON, a fellow physician and former classmate of Dr. Jekyll

Mary Reilly is a variation on Robert Louis Stevenson's novella *The Strange Case of Dr. Jekyll and Mr. Hyde* (1886), a classic study of good and evil. Born and reared in Calvinist Edinburgh, Stevenson rebelled against his Puritan upbringing and, as a young man, led a Bohemian life, sometimes consorting with harlots. Dr. Jekyll is a handsome, "large, well-made, smooth-faced man of fifty," but like Stevenson, he was "wild when he was young," indulging in irregular pleasures, suffering a "perennial war among my members." Thus, Dr. Jekyll "stood already committed to a profound duplicity of life" before he began the chemical experiments that enabled him to separate the good and evil elements in himself and to turn into the "wholly evil" Mr. Hyde. Jekyll equivocates that Hyde alone is guilty of the sins he commits; when he turns back into the respected doctor, Jekyll is entirely innocent. The evil in Hyde was already a part of Dr. Jekyll before being distilled into its own pure form, however, and at first, Jekyll feels an exhilarating freedom when living a double life as Hyde. After Hyde commits a series of atrocities and a murder, Jekyll's conscience takes over, as well as his sense of self-preservation, and he determines to become Hyde no more. By this time, however, his body chemistry has been so altered that he becomes transformed into Hyde without taking the formula, and it is increasingly difficult to provide the antidote. Finally, trapped forever in Hyde's body, Jekyll commits suicide as his lawyer and butler break down the door to his laboratory.

There is no point in retelling *The Strange Case of Dr. Jekyll and Mr. Hyde* only to tell it again. It has been staged, has been filmed at least eight times (most recently in

1990), and has played in Houston as a musical. By focusing on Jekyll's housemaid, however, who is mentioned only once and not given a name in Stevenson's novella, Valerie Martin tells a different story that becomes interwoven with Stevenson's. Unlike the film versions, which add a good fiancée and a wicked woman of the underworld to represent the two sides of Jekyll and Hyde and which often turn Hyde into a grotesque monster, Martin's novel is meticulously faithful to Stevenson, leaving out any sacred and profane love stories. It describes Hyde as a small, almost dwarfish young man who nevertheless has deadly strength and a terrifying aura of evil. In its general outlines, Stevenson's is one of the world's best-known stories, so that it is not necessary to read it in order to understand *Mary Reilly*, though reading Stevenson first enables one to appreciate the great skill with which Martin has appropriated Stevenson for her own ends.

Dr. Jekyll is a bachelor who associates only with male friends, and Stevenson's friend Henry James cited the novella as an example of Stevenson's "heartless independence" from the necessity of introducing female characters into his stories. By shifting the point of view to Mary Reilly, Martin offers a feminist perspective not only on Dr. Jekyll and Mr. Hyde but on the lower classes in Victorian England as well. Stevenson himself told the story indirectly, filtering information through several intermediary characters: Richard Enfield, who relates Hyde's first atrocity; Mr. Utterson, Jekyll's attorney; Dr. Lanyon, in a letter left to be read after his death; and, finally, Dr. Jekyll himself, in the written confession found after his death. Stevenson also does not present the story in chronological order; only at the end does the reader learn of Dr. Jekyll's experiments on himself. Martin retells the story in linear chronological order as Mary writes it in her daily journal. *Mary Reilly* is four times as long as *The Strange Case of Dr. Jekyll and Mr. Hyde*, of necessity because Mary is not only the title character but also the central one, and the novel is her story.

Thus, the reader sees the events exclusively from the viewpoint of a poor, young, meagerly educated but sensitive and intelligent young woman who only gradually becomes aware of what is going on. After a painful childhood, in which she was sometimes tortured by her drunken father, Mary considers herself fortunate to be working for a kind master in what Stevenson calls a house with "a great air of wealth and comfort." There is no arrogant mistress to look down her nose at Mary and no messy children for her to clean up after; in fact, five other servants help to care for Dr. Jekyll in his great house. There she is well fed, and though she shares a garret bed with Annie (another maid) and works incredibly long hours scrubbing, cleaning, doing laundry, building fires, being a chimney sweep, and doing whatever other chores are assigned for a mere twelve pounds a year, plus her room and board and half a day off a week, Mary is grateful for her position—a damning commentary on the exploitation of the servant class in Victorian England. Much of the novel is a graphic picture of the conditions of the life "downstairs," with its own hierarchy, and all of it a world removed from the "upstairs" aristocracy. Mary has no life except working and sleeping and little hope for a better future.

Mary begins unobtrusively enough, but when her employer notices the scars of what look like bites on her hands and neck, he asks her to write for him an account of how she got them. The novel opens with this account, Mary's first attempt at writing, as she recalls the horrible episode of her childhood in which her brutal father locked her in a dark cubbyhole under the stairs and then threw in a rat, which bit Mary repeatedly until she fainted.

Mary's Master (as she always calls him; the reader does not learn that he is Dr. Henry Jekyll until page 67) is surprised at the vividness of her writing—he would not expect a person with her background to be more than barely literate, if literate at all. Thereafter, he begins to take an increasing interest in her. Much of the drama of the novel is the development of the relationship between Mary and Dr. Jekyll. Aside from her sickly, ineffectual mother and the cook, Jekyll is the first person to treat Mary kindly and to pay any attention to her as an individual, though he seems to have no real understanding of the hardships of the servant class. Certainly he is the first man to show Mary kindness and consideration. Poole, the head of the household staff, is an officious martinet who resents Mary's moments of intimacy with their employer. Consequently, even more than the rest of the household, Mary becomes increasingly distressed at Dr. Jekyll's irregular hours, his driving himself to illness by obsessive, mysterious work in his laboratory. Prone to depression herself, she comes to share his worries and his sadness, though the reader understands the reason for them better than she does. It is not clear when Jekyll has effected his transformation into Mr. Hyde, though by page 40, Mary begins to hear the light, dragging footstep that comes to be identified with Mr. Hyde, who is not specifically mentioned for another forty-three pages.

From the beginning, Jekyll is intrigued by the enigmas and relationships between good and evil, and, sensing an affinity between Mary and himself, he often uses her as a sounding board for his ideas, though doing so is a bit like playing a game of cat and mouse. Mary, though the docile servant, has moments of rebellious thought, as when Dr. Jekyll expresses gratification at the fact that she learned to read at a school he helped to support. She thinks of what a rough, cruel place it was: "looking at Master across the dirt feeling all the world was standing between us and we'd no way ever to cross it, but also that somehow we was also two sides of the same coin, doing our different work in the same house and as close, without speaking, as a dog and his shadow." Thus, Mary, as well as Mr. Hyde, becomes a *Doppelgänger* for Dr. Jekyll. She, too, has light and darkness in her life, the latter often personified by nightmares of her father, whose image somewhat merges with that of Mr. Hyde, but she would not give up the darkness because it seems to her a true part of life. She feels particularly drawn to Dr. Jekyll "because we are both souls who knew this sadness and darkness inside," but she is also a foil to him because "no matter how dark I feel I would never take my own life," as he will do at the end.

The deeper he gets into his double life, the more Dr. Jekyll confides in Mary, who in turn has occasional erotic responses to him, though he is more than twice her age. Admitted once into his forbidden laboratory, she sees a mirror image of herself so that "for a moment it seemed I was looking back at myself from the edge of the world, and if I didn't step carefully I would fall off into nothing." Dr. Jekyll sends her, on her own time, to a wicked neighborhood in Soho with a letter to the vile Mrs. Farraday, who apparently runs a house of ill repute, asking her, as the reader knows, though Mary does not, to arrange accommodations for Mr. Hyde. Mary cannot understand how the good doctor could even know such a person, let alone have dealings with her. Now Mary and her Master share a secret. He has other secrets, however, that he shares with no one, and Mary wonders whether he is really in his laboratory during all the hours he is supposedly sequestered there.

Devoted to her Master, Mary becomes increasingly uneasy as the sense of some sinister mystery grows within the household. If she cannot be safe in such a great house, with such a kind and caring master, she feels she cannot be safe anywhere. Another visit to Mrs. Farraday's terrifies her, as the vicious madame forces her to look at a bedroom with blood-soaked and twisted sheets and blankets, the stains of a bloody hand dragged along the wall, and a ripped and blood-soaked night shift, apparently the murderous work of Mr. Hyde. Part of the effectiveness of *Mary Reilly* is that the narrative suggests much more than it describes, so that Hyde's evil is elusive, understated, suggested by such a detail, on their second encounter, as his breaking a teacup in his hand and then dragging his bleeding fingers across Mary's mouth. Otherwise, Mary finds him cold and sardonic, "twisted somehow," and certainly not a gentleman, but he presumes a familiarity with her that she cannot account for. "Don't you know who I am, Mary?" he taunts her. What could possibly have recommended him to the distinguished Dr. Jekyll? Mary, however, believes that she has no right ever to speak of him, though she continues to write in her journals to help clarify the darkness.

As her fears intensify, so do her Master's, though she still does not understand why. Increasingly she feels that somehow they are alike, equals despite caste. The significance of caste, however, becomes painfully acute when Mary's mother dies, and the reader sees the contrast between the death of the poor and the rich—Mrs. Reilly and Sir Danvers Carew, murdered by Mr. Hyde.

Now that Hyde is known as a murderer, Dr. Jekyll can have nothing more to do with him, and he desires to reform, believing he has learned an awful lesson. Yet Mary continues to sense Hyde's presence. Dr. Jekyll knows only a brief interlude of calm, followed by intensifying fears that he confesses to Mary, the only person with whom he feels any intimacy. Not yet understanding the horror, she vows not to leave him, though she is sorely tried when Hyde reappears and is violent toward her. "*I am your master, Mary,*" he says, but she still cannot comprehend, and even if she could, it is too late to help Dr. Jekyll. After his death, she makes a last, startling testimony of her devotion.

Not simply a retelling of Stevenson from another angle, *Mary Reilly* succeeds on its own as a subtle tale of terror similar to *The Turn of the Screw* (1898), as well as a graphic picture of the ordered world of Victorian aristocracy and the bestial sewer of the underworld that ran beneath it. It is also a sensitive character study, primarily of Mary herself but also of Dr. Jekyll in the tragic course he has set upon. The style of

Mary's first-person narrative, fast-paced yet introspective, with a slightly mannered Victorian flavor, is highly effective. The great skill Martin shows in developing mounting suspense is all the more impressive because the story is already known, so that the suspense is not in wondering what will happen but in waiting apprehensively for what the reader knows must happen. Her sixth book, *Mary Reilly* is Martin's breakthrough novel, one that is making her widely known. Margaret Atwood has called it "an astonishing tour de force which more than fulfills the expectations raised by her previous work." It is a worthy companion piece to *The Strange Case of Dr. Jekyll and Mr. Hyde*.

Robert E. Morsberger

Sources for Further Study

Booklist. LXXXVI, December 1, 1989, p. 705.
Chicago Tribune. February 4, 1990, XIV, p. 5.
Kirkus Reviews. LVII, December 1, 1989, p. 1701.
Library Journal. CXV, January, 1990, p. 149.
The New York Times Book Review. February 4, 1990, p. 7.
Newsweek. CXV, March 12, 1990, p. 90.
Publishers Weekly. CCXXXVI, December 8, 1989, p. 40.
Time. CXXXV, February 19, 1990, p. 84.
The Times Literary Supplement. June 1, 1990, p. 586.

MATERIAL DREAMS
Southern California Through the 1920s

Author: Kevin Starr (1940-   )
Publisher: Oxford University Press (New York). Illustrated. 453 pp. $24.95
Type of work: History
Time: 1880-1930
Locale: Southern California

This third installment of Starr's chronicle of California traces the growth of Los Angeles and surrounding communities from the late 1800's through the boom times of the 1920's

Principal personages:
WILLIAM HAMMOND HALL, an engineer
WILLIAM MULHOLLAND, an engineer
GEORGE CHAFFEY, a land developer
LYNDEN ELLSWORTH BEHYMER, an impresario
GEORGE WYMAN, an architect
JAMES OSBORNE CRAIG, an architect
JACOB ISRAEL ZEITLIN, a poet and bookseller
HARRY WARD RITCHIE, a graphic designer
LAWRENCE CLARK POWELL, an author and librarian
ROBINSON JEFFERS, a poet

The pre-Socratic philosopher Thales maintained that all things come from water; in Southern California he would have found support for his theory. The water from which Los Angeles and the Imperial Valley rose did not, however, appear of itself. The rain in California stays mainly in the north: Only about ten percent of the state's precipitation falls on Los Angeles and the region to its south. Like everything else about the area, therefore, water here was produced by will—Friedrich Nietzsche as well as Thales would have been pleased by the emergence of Los Angeles, Santa Barbara, Pasadena, and the rich farmlands that fed these cities. In ancient times Southern California had been submerged by the Colorado River's emptying into the Salton Sea. Tens of thousands of years ago, geological upheavals rerouted the river to the Gulf of California, leaving rich alluvial soil that turned to desert. George Chaffey envisioned returning the Colorado to its former outlet through irrigation. Unsound engineering to divert the river would cause, or at least aggravate, a series of floods in 1905-1907 that again submerged part of what Chaffey named the Imperial Valley, but a million acres came under cultivation. Starr discusses the conflict between those such as William Ellsworth Smythe, who wanted the government to control irrigation in order to create cooperative social democracy on the New Zealand model, and Chaffey and his supporters, who hoped to use a public resource—the Colorado River—for private profit. In typical American fashion, the latter view triumphed.

While Chaffey looked east for water, Los Angeles turned north to the Owens Valley, two hundred miles away. The federal government had planned to use the

Owens River to irrigate small farms in Central California, but Los Angeles won, gaining the right to drain the valley for water and electricity. This water allowed the city to grow rapidly because Los Angeles refused to share the life-giving substance with nearby communities unless they agreed to annexation.

Migration, too, fostered growth. Starr notes that in the 1920's two million Americans moved to California, most of them to the southern part of the state. Of these, 1.2 million settled in Los Angeles County, 661,375 in the city itself, helping to triple its population during the decade (576,673 people in 1920, 1,470,516 ten years later). Such expansion was fostered by the Los Angeles Chamber of Commerce, which sent idealized photographs to newspapers around the country. The discovery of oil and the rise of the film and aviation industries also fueled the great expansion of the 1920's.

One consequence of the increase in population was more traffic. The Los Angeles Railway and Pacific Electric both provided public transportation, but by 1924 some 200,000 vehicles a day were competing with the surface trains for downtown street space. In 1926, Angelenos rejected a bond issue to fund elevated or submerged tracks, thus dooming interurban rail service and making the city a motorized municipality. The freeway system therefore arose, as did the Miracle Mile along Wilshire Boulevard, whose developers bet, rightly, that people would drive to shop. To escape the traffic nightmare of downtown Los Angeles, people moved to the suburbs; just as the subways and limited land prompted Manhattan's vertical growth, so the automobile fostered Los Angeles' horizontal development, a pattern of expansion that only exacerbated the traffic problem by making suburbanites still more dependent on their vehicles.

The migrants to Los Angeles may have rejected the 1926 bond issue because they did not want to reproduce the Chicago or New York they had left behind. Just as they envisioned a different cityscape, so they dreamed of new lives for themselves, new identities. Starr shows how Edgar Rice Burroughs and L. Frank Baum turned their fictional worlds of Tarzan and Oz into reality after they moved from the Midwest to Southern California. Others skipped the step of first imagining a world on paper and simply re-created themselves. Repeatedly in this account one encounters people who went west to metamorphose, just as Europeans for three centuries had crossed the Atlantic to begin life anew.

Among those Starr discusses is Lunden Ellsworth Behymer. He had managed a general store in Dakota Territory before coming to Los Angeles in 1886. Here he rose from scalping tickets at the opera house to become general manager of the Los Angeles Philharmonic and the region's leading impresario. George Wyman is another who, Jay Gatsby-like, created himself. A self-taught architect, he designed the Bradbury Building (1893), which typified Southern California in its fusion of modern technology and sunlight. Merle Armitage, born Elmer Armitage, came to Los Angeles in 1920; he first supplanted Behymer and later discovered a talent for graphic design that led to the position of design director of *Look* after World War II.

Los Angeles imagined itself as a major American city, and by 1930 it had become the fifth largest metropolitan area in the country. Santa Barbara, too, held a vision of itself. Starr regards this self image as a fulfillment of the fiction of Zorro, an aristocratic, romantic hero more Spanish than the Spaniards of California. Significantly, one of the main streets of Santa Barbara is Anacapa, meaning mirage. To promote this dream vision, Irene and Bernhard Hoffmann hired James Osborne Craig to create El Paseo ("street" in Spanish) around a hundred-year-old adobe. Like the city itself, illusion thus grounded itself in an element of fact but greatly elaborated on the truth. El Paseo was a commercial venture, like the Miracle Mile, and like the Miracle Mile it asserted an identity: Los Angeles as entrepreneurial and automotive, Santa Barbara as Spanish and aristocratic.

When an earthquake on June 29, 1925, damaged or destroyed virtually every significant older structure in Santa Barbara, the city's Plans and Planting Committee used the disaster to refashion the area according to its Spanish image. Almost all of the two thousand new buildings were of Spanish design; the reconstruction culminated in the completion of the County Courthouse (1929), a Spanish castle with 140,000 square feet of floor tile made in Algeria. Even the jail was beautiful. Dan Sayre Groesbeck, set designer for Cecil B. De Mille, executed the murals depicting Santa Barbara's vision of its heritage. Among his paintings is one of Juan Rodriguez Cabrillo's raising the Spanish flag over the site of the city in 1542. The event never occurred—actually, Cabrillo broke his arm on one of the barrier islands. Still, the illusion, appropriately created by a leading figure of California's illusion industry, provides a fit symbol for a city that, like Los Angeles, made dream into a kind of reality.

Life was pleasant in Santa Barbara, California's version of Rhode Island's Newport. Visiting in 1928 to work on his novel *I Thought of Daisy* (1929) and pursue Margaret Canby, the critic Edmund Wilson wrote to his editor, Maxwell Perkins, "The weather is beautiful and all the days are exactly alike. The calm Pacific spaces are excellent for work—I always feel cramped in New York. But if you stayed out here very long, you would probably cease to write anything, because you would cease to think—it isn't necessary out here and the natives regard it as morbid."

However desertlike the climate, though, Southern California was no cultural Sahara. Starr devotes a quarter of his book to "Life and Letters in the Southland," and he has much to tell. While Los Angeles had a symphony and other cultural amenities, its greatest intellectual and artistic strength lay in the book. As Starr observes,

> The book provided the City of the Angels with an available and relatively inexpensive way for its intelligentsia to galvanize itself into interconnected communities. The book and its related arts served as a vehicle of enjoyment and self-identification for intellectuals who were finding themselves in a relatively unprecedented city.

Again it was a self-made transplant from the Midwest, Jacob Israel Zeitlin, who provided a focus for the rise of the rare book trade. Zeitlin had hoped to become a bard like Carl Sandburg. Arriving in Los Angeles in 1925, Zeitlin published "Gypsy

Nights" in *The Southwest Review* (1926) and followed that with *For Whispers and Chants* (1927), for which Sandburg himself wrote the foreword. Poetry provided a precarious income, though, so Zeitlin turned to selling books. As a struggling writer he had worked briefly for the great collector Estelle Doheny; a few years later as an antiquarian bookseller he was dining with her and advising her about her library. In addition to becoming a premier bookman, he turned his store into a gallery that promoted local artists such as Edward Weston (photography), Gordon Newell (sculpture), and Paul Landacre (wood-carving). In 1929, Zeitlin started a fine small press, Primavera, continuing a California tradition that had begun in the north with the Grabhorns and John Henry Nash. Zeitlin would refer to all these developments as a limited renaissance, but with such patrons as Doheny, Henry Edwards Huntington, and William Andrews Clark, Jr., the libraries of Los Angeles and San Marino would soon rival other major collections around the world.

Pasadena evolved its own intellectual ambience. Much of it was provincial, but Occidental College produced Lawrence Clark Powell and Robinson Jeffers, writers with international reputations, and Carlyle Ferren MacIntyre, poet and translator of Johann Wolfgang von Goethe, Rainer Maria Rilke, Charles Baudelaire, Paul Verlaine, and others, taught at the school. Though both Jeffers and Powell left Pasadena, neither went far; the former moved to Carmel by the Sea, the latter to the University of California at Los Angeles. Ward Ritchie, who established a fine press in Pasadena, also attended Occidental.

The 1920's were what Starr calls "the building time" for Southern California, providing the basis for future growth by transforming the physical and cultural landscape through acts of will and imagination. In his next work, *The Dream Endures: California Through the Great Depression*, Starr will explore the fate of the region in the 1930's. Meanwhile, those wishing to pursue the subjects raised in *Material Dreams* will find ample resources discussed in a lengthy bibliographical essay at the end of the volume. Another helpful feature is the portfolio of the photographs that show many of the people and places the work discusses. A few maps would help the geographically innocent, but their absence is a very small flaw in a masterfully detailed, readable account of America's most peculiar state and state of mind.

Joseph Rosenblum

Sources for Further Study

AB Bookman's Weekly. LXXXVI, August 6, 1990, p. 448.
The Atlantic. CCLXV, March, 1990, p. 108.
Boston Globe. April 1, 1990, p. 44.
Choice. XXVIII, September, 1990, p. 210.
The Christian Science Monitor. June 12, 1990, p. 12.
Library Journal. CXIV, December, 1989, p. 144.

Los Angeles Times Book Review. April 1, 1990, p. 1.
National Catholic Reporter. XXVII, November 9, 1990, p. 28.
San Francisco Chronicle. April 1, 1990, p. REV8.
The Washington Post Book World. XX, April 15, 1990, p. 11.

MEMOIRS

Author: Andrei Sakharov (1921-1989)
First published: Vospominaniya, 1990, in the Soviet Union
Translated from the Russian by Richard Lourie
Publisher: Alfred A. Knopf (New York). Illustrated. 773 pp. $29.95
Type of work: Memoir
Time: The twentieth century
Locale: The Soviet Union

A memoir by the Soviet scientist and dissident

> *Principal personages:*
> ANDREI DMITRIEVICH SAKHAROV, the nuclear physicist who developed the Soviet Union's hydrogen bomb, a Nobel Prize-winner and a leading dissident
> EKATERINA SOFIANO SAKHAROV, his mother
> DMITRI SAKHAROV, his father, a physicist and writer
> KLAVDIA "KLAVA" VIKHIREVA, first wife of Andrei Sakharov
> ELENA "LUSIA" GEORGIEVNA BONNER, pediatrician and second wife of Andrei Sakharov
> JOSEPH STALIN, successor to Vladimir Ilich Lenin as head of the Communist Party of the Soviet Union and the Soviet government from 1928 to 1953
> LEONID BREZHNEV, General Secretary of the Communist Party, 1964-1982
> IGOR TAMM, a physicist who influenced Andrei Sakharov both in his scientific training and his views on social questions
> ROY MEDVEDEV, a historian and dissident
> ZHORES MEDVEDEV, a biologist, writer, and dissident, who emigrated in 1978

At the center of Andrei Sakharov's life lies a paradox. Known for decades as the moral and intellectual leader of the liberal dissidents in the Soviet Union, he was also the "father of the Soviet hydrogen bomb." For Sakharov, developing the hydrogen bomb represented the highest kind of scientific challenge and an opportunity to do "superb physics." "The physics of atomic and thermonuclear explosions," he observed, "is a genuine theoretician's paradise."

Yet, it was more than theoretical physics that attracted Sakharov to the development of nuclear weapons. In the early phase of his research, he believed deeply in the principle of nuclear parity: he was convinced that approximate equality between the nuclear superpowers was essential for deterrence, and thus peace. In later years, he increasingly focused on the dangers of nuclear age rivalry. His 1968 book *Razmyishleniya o progresse, mirnom sosushchestvovanii i intellektuyal' noy svobode* (*Progress, Coexistence, and Intellectual Freedom*, 1970), which coincided with the liberal reform in Czechoslovakia known as the Prague Spring, called for rapprochement between the superpowers and advocated human rights and pluralistic societies.

By his own admission, Sakharov's career in nuclear physics troubled him in certain respects. He knew the risks, both to the environment and human life, that nuclear energy posed. The "appalling danger" of nuclear war was very real to him, and he thought "long and hard . . . about ways to avert it." That aspect of his work brought him the 1975 Nobel Prize for Peace; in his acceptance lecture, "Peace, Progress, Human Rights," he stated the triad of concerns that defined his later career. In several works between 1968 and the mid-1980's, Sakharov spoke out in behalf of world peace and the convergence of socialist and capitalist systems. He also founded, along with fellow physicists Andrei Tverdokhlebov and Valery Chalidze, the Human Rights Committee (1970), which was persecuted for its human rights advocacy despite its efforts to stay within the limits of Soviet law.

Sakharov carried with him through life the seminal influences of his childhood and adolescence. The son of Dmitri and Ekaterina Sofiano Sakharov, he was born on May 21, 1921, just as civil war was ending and Vladimir Ilich Lenin was implementing the liberal New Economic Policy. Andrei's father was a physicist and writer whose publications were the major source of the family's income. Sakharov long remembered his father's influence in shaping his own interest in science, as well as his values. It was from him, Sakharov notes, that he learned the value of moderation in life. His mother was also quite influential in the development of his values, particularly by her devotion and faith: but Sakharov never internalized the religious experience she exemplified. When he was writing his memoirs, he still had mixed feelings about religion: He respected sincere, believing people but was repelled by the "many instances of bigotry, hypocrisy, money-grubbing, and blatant disregard for human suffering" which he saw in some avowed believers.

Sakharov was both precocious and persistent in his educational odyssey. After learning to read at age four, he progressed through elementary and secondary schools during the difficult 1930's as Joseph Stalin consolidated his dictatorship. Like all other Soviet youth, Sakharov was taught the basics of Marxism-Leninism, but his first love was science. At the time, he had no major ideological problem with Marxist theory. "[I]t never entered my head," he wrote, "to question Marxism as the ideology best suited to liberate mankind, and materialism too seemed a reasonable philosophy." What bothered him most was "the attempt to carry over the outmoded concepts of natural philosophy into the twentieth century (the age of exact science) without amendment." He disliked what sometimes became scientific chicanery and the polemical thrust of such works as *Das Kapital* (1867; *Das Kapital*, 1909) and Lenin's *Materialism i empiriokritisism* (1920; *Materialism and Empirio-Criticism*, 1925).

When World War II began in 1939, Sakharov was in his second year of studying physics at Moscow University. The collapse of the German-Soviet Nonaggression Pact in 1941 brought the war into the Soviet Union. Adolf Hitler's Operation Barbarossa unleashed blitzkrieg attacks on Leningrad, Moscow, and the Ukraine. Sakharov's senior year was thus markedly different from the first three. Along with all Moscow University students, Sakharov was evacuated to Ashkhabad, where he finished his undergraduate studies. For the duration of the war, he was involved in the military struggle against Nazi Germany. He helped handle military equipment, used his scientific knowledge to make a magnetic probe to locate shrapnel in injured horses, and joined an air defense unit that helped extinguish fires caused by incendiary bombs. For more than two years, he worked in a munitions plant at Ulyanovsk, making cartridges and using his scientific training to improve the armor-piercing steel cores of antitank gun ammunition. During these important years, Sakharov not only continued to advance his skills but also became sharply aware of the horrors of war.

Just before the end of the war in 1945, Sakharov began his graduate work in theoretical physics at the Physics Institute of the Academy of Sciences (FIAN) in Moscow. With the help of his father, Sakharov was asked by Professor Igor Tamm to work under his supervision. Sakharov left for Moscow in January, 1945, one month before his first wife, Klava, gave birth to a daughter, Tanya. Three months later, the war ended in Europe as Nazi Germany capitulated to the Western Allies. Sakharov's career, however, was only beginning; his work would immerse him in the process of developing nuclear weapons which would become the quintessence of Cold War rivalry between the Soviet Union and the United States.

Beginning in 1948, Andrei Sakharov applied his knowledge and energy to nuclear weapons development for two decades. That he could do so despite his opposition to Stalinism was the result of his conviction that nuclear strength is essential for the Soviet Union to have the capability of deterring war. The scientific dimension was also crucial to Sakharov. Under the influence of such distinguished physicists as Tamm, Isaak Pomeranchuk, Nikolai Bogolyubov, and Yakov Zeldovich, he gradually became the leading light of Soviet nuclear weapons theory. Tamm had the greatest impact on Sakharov, especially in shaping his approach to social issues. What Sakharov would later discover by personal experience, Tamm had known for decades: There were limits even for scientists to free thought in the Soviet Union. Tamm had been arrested by the counterrevolutionary agency known as the CHEKA in the early days of Bolshevism.

Sakharov's revelations of the interior life of the "Installation," where Soviet nuclear research was carried out, are among the most graphic and important parts of his memoir. He described himself as a "soldier in this new scientific war," one that would prevent the sort of carnage that plagued the Soviet Union and many other nations during World War II. From age twenty-seven to his late forties, Sakharov labored in that perspective, but he began to see the biological and ecological dangers of nuclear weapons. He had thought relatively little about the effects of radiation and shock waves until several accidents graphically revealed them. One notable testing accident in 1955 killed a small girl and a soldier, causing Sakharov considerable distress. "I did not hold myself personally responsible for their deaths," he reflected, "but I could not escape a feeling of complicity."

The following decade brought a deepening of nuclear age tensions. By 1958 Nikita Khrushchev had completed his dramatic and somewhat tenuous five-year rise to power. Khrushchev affirmed the doctrine of "peaceful coexistence" with the United States and seemed to be initiating a thaw at home and abroad. His use of force to squelch a rebellion in Hungary in 1956 and his periodic brushes with conflict with the United States, however, clashed with his policy of détente. By 1962, he had placed nuclear missiles in Cuba, where Fidel Castro had come to power in 1959. The 1962 Cuban Missile Crisis, despite its peaceful resolution, reminded the world that nuclear war was a distinct possibility. Sakharov was concerned about the increased Soviet-American rivalry and was pleased when the Cuban crisis was followed by an atmospheric test ban treaty in 1963. He was not satisfied, however, with the abrupt halt of the work at the Installation.

By then, Sakharov's concern over genetic and other effects of nuclear radiation put him at odds with the Khrushchev regime. He began to write and speak against the pseudo-scientific genetic theories of Trofim Lysenko, as well as the growing signs that Khrushchev's thaw had its limits. Through the seventeen-year period under Leonid Brezhnev and beyond, Sakharov became more widely known for his protests against dangerous nuclear rivalry, censorship, and overt persecution of dissidents and prominent writers such as Boris Pasternak and Aleksandr Solzhenitsyn. Although Sakharov's outlook differed significantly from Solzhenitsyn's, there was mutual respect between them. Both cared about the Soviet people, world peace, and human rights, although Solzhenitsyn appeared to hope for restoration of a traditional religious and political system in Soviet Russia. More significantly, Solzhenitsyn criticized Sakharov's convergence approach to Soviet-American relations as naïve.

Sakharov's career after 1968 was largely one of leading the liberal dissident movement, campaigning for human rights and the democratization of the Soviet system and seeking to prevent nuclear war. His early commitment to peace through mutual deterrence eroded as he realized that nuclear war and even the unbridled development of nuclear energy were unacceptably risky. He saw the 1986 accident at Chernobyl as a reminder of the dangers that had receded from public awareness with the 1963 nuclear test ban treaty. As his publications vividly expressed these views, Sakharov's life became increasingly difficult. In the Brezhnev era, he was awarded the Nobel Peace Prize in 1975, and his books were read by tens of millions around the world, yet he was banished to the closed city of Gorky in 1980 after he criticized Soviet intervention in Afghanistan. Through this period, from 1980 to 1986, his second wife, Elena "Lusia" Bonner, was a source of strength and a major factor in his becoming the symbol of dissidence against the Soviet system. They had been married since January, 1972, three years after the death of Klava. Elena, a medical doctor, helped keep her exiled husband's case in the world's consciousness and endlessly sought his release. Finally, in 1986, when Mikhail Gorbachev was pursuing his early *perestroika* and *glasnost* reforms, Sakharov was given his freedom, three years before his death.

The value of Sakharov's memoir is undeniable. He has provided the first inside look at several important elements of scientific research, as well as a dramatic and moving account of his own suffering, hope, and philosophy. Much can be learned from a careful reading of his references to other people, among them his second wife Elena Bonner, fellow dissidents Roy and Zhores Medvedev, Solzhenitsyn, and numerous *samizdat* writers.

Andrei Sakharov's *Memoirs* is another significant addition to the growing body of personal and scholarly accounts of life in the Soviet Union at a time of fundamental change. It also more clearly reveals Sakharov the man. To many, he remained a media figure, a prominent but somewhat elusive hero of both science and social reform. Sakharov portrays himself as a searcher who never quite found the answers he needed, a man who was rather introspective but was drawn into public dissidence by the 1968 Czechoslovakian crisis and its effects. To the end of his life, he remained a believer in the possibility of peace in a complex world. Sakharov closed his long volume with a very personal reference. "Today, in the seventh decade of my life, my personal aspirations and my entire existence center on my beloved wife, my children and grandchildren, and all those who are dear to me." If that is not an unusual perspective for an aging man whose adult life had been extremely difficult, then it is particularly interesting coming from a man who, as much as any other, brought the Soviet Union into the nuclear age.

Thomas R. Peake

Sources for Further Study

The Atlantic. CCLXVI, September 1990, p. 123.
Chicago Tribune. July 1, 1990, XIV, p. 1.
Los Angeles Times Book Review. July 8, 1990, p. 1.
The Nation. CCLI, July 9, 1990, p. 58.
New Statesman and Society. III, August, 1990, p. 34.
The New York Review of Books. XXXVII, August 16, 1990, p. 3.
The New York Times Book Review. XCV, June 17, 1990, p. 3.
Newsweek. CXVI, July 9, 1990, p. 64.
Physics Today. XLIII, August, 1990, p. 51.
Publishers Weekly. CCXXXVII, April 6, 1990, p. 106.
The Times Literary Supplement. August 17, 1990, p. 863.
The Washington Post Book World. XX, June 24, 1990, p. 1.

THE MESSAGE TO THE PLANET

Author: Iris Murdoch (1919-   )
First published: 1989, in Great Britain
Publisher: Viking (New York). 563 pp. $22.95
Type of work: Novel
Time: The 1980's
Locale: London

The rise and fall of a contemporary magus is the center of a novel that explores moral predicaments

Principal characters:
    MARCUS VALLAR, a mathematician and philosopher
    IRINA VALLAR, the daughter of Marcus
    ALFRED LUDENS, a lecturer in history and disciple of Marcus, in love with
        Irina
    GILDAS HERNE, a failed Anglican priest
    PATRICK FENMAN, an Irish poet
    JACK SHEERWATER, a successful painter
    FRANCA SHEERWATER, Jack's wife
    ALISON MERRICK, Jack's mistress

Part of the interest of yet another novel by the prolific Iris Murdoch is charting the intense reactions it invariably provokes among reviewers. A Murdoch novel is not only wildly creative but also can be a cause of creativity in others, judging from the range of simile and metaphor used to express the satisfaction, bafflement, or exasperation of its readers. Murdoch's twenty-fourth novel, *The Message to the Planet*, is no exception. "[A]s sturdy and reliable as a well-made trench coat" observes one, while another finds in *The Message to the Planet* "the impassive force of a natural disaster, predictable but unstoppable; and a trail of broken critics, as ineffectual as a picket fence in a hurricane, lies in its wake." "Like Henry James on crack" muses another (perhaps one of the broken pickets), who confesses uncertainty as to whether *The Message to the Planet* is "a great novel, a merely interesting one, or an unclassifiable pandemonium." The latter reviewer adds, however, that "I wouldn't dream of missing one of her novels," even though Murdoch "is like one of those middle aged English walkers who take you up steep hills without a pause for breath."

That a writer as demanding as Murdoch can also be a popular novelist (in Britain her books are best-sellers) is surprising. Many have tried to isolate the specific qualities of her fiction which have earned for her an unexpectedly large following; much analysis has been devoted to her hypnotic narrative style, her uncanny plots and eccentric characters, her "superb rendering of emotional turmoil," her ability to interweave "humor with psychological and philosophic insights." Critics have attempted to classify her, to place her in a tradition—of English realism or of magical realism or of the twentieth century Continental novel of ideas—or to see her as an existentialist writer. Ultimately Murdoch eludes classification and remains like one of her novels: enigmatic and singular.

Murdoch does, however, develop recurring themes within her strange fictional world, and recurring character types—primarily upper-middle-class British intellectuals and pseudo-intellectuals. Like *The Book and the Brotherhood* (1987), *The Message to the Planet* features a powerful demonic-charismatic figure around whom much of the action and most of the other characters revolve. Marcus Vallar, a Jewish intellectual, was recognized as a mathematical genius at age nineteen for developing the Vallar Theorem. After that he became a chess champion, briefly took up philosophy "but soon 'saw through it,'" took up painting but abandoned it for Sanskrit and Japanese, and is currently on the track of "deep foundations, pure cognition, the nature of consciousness, a universal language underlying the tongues of east and west"—or so, at least, his ardent disciple Alfred Ludens believes. Ludens, who is the central consciousness of this novel, is a young lecturer in history on leave from a London college and is the most passionate of the Vallar watchers. Others in the group are Gildas Herne, a former Anglican priest who works in a Bloomsbury bookshop; Patrick Fenman, an Irish poet believed to be psychic; the painter Jack Sheerwater and his wife, Franca; and Jack's mistress, Alison Merrick.

Marcus has powerfully affected the lives of the major characters. He caused Gildas to leave the priesthood, taught Jack Sheerwater a style of painting that brought Jack great commercial success, placed a curse on Patrick that brought him to the brink of death and then miraculously resurrected him, and has Ludens believing that he, Marcus, is a god who possesses some secret, ultimate knowledge. Ludens becomes obsessed with Marcus, following him everywhere, demanding that he write down his ideas, "as if Marcus were the possessor of an intellectual secret, some master-key, talisman, password or radiant lamp of deep fundamental knowledge which, if it could be acquired, would shine through all other knowledge, utterly transforming it." Murdoch's faithful readers will recognize here that Ludens is in a state of enchantment and also in the grip of one of Murdoch's most dangerous demons: the demon of the absolute. Ludens' ultimate disenthrallment with Marcus (who finally has nothing to say and who ends as a suicide in a mental institution) is the major victory in the novel, though that seems too strong a word. In the end, Ludens has matured somewhat and is groping toward reality; he has freed himself from some illusions (the illusion that he and Irina, Marcus' daughter, are in love), but he remains a somewhat self-deluded character who has much to learn.

A difficulty with *The Message to the Planet* may be that a reader is likely to care little about what happens to Ludens, who is one of the most tiresomely immature central characters Murdoch has created. Similarly, Marcus, for all of his supposed charisma and supernatural powers, may strike the reader as a pompous bore, but as Murdoch watchers know, it is her habit to create characters who are not entirely satisfactory. It is part of her strategy to cause readers to see and think critically, and not allow them merely to lapse into fantasy and comfortable identification with her characters. It is ironic that much of Marcus' power derives from his remote, truculent personality. It seems that in his later life Marcus never really had any unusual ideas or powers but that Ludens desperately needed to believe he did. Marcus as god thus seems a creation of Ludens' imagination, except for the miraculous resuscitation of Patrick from a deathlike state.

Is this a paranormal incident or only another example of projection, this time of Patrick's imagination? Murdoch leaves the question open, but it is clear that Marcus is no holy man. Although he is capable of uttering trenchant truths (as when he denounces Jack Sheerwater as "a facile commercially-minded painter with a vile promiscuous sex life"), Marcus' own failings are obvious: He is an unfeeling, uncommunicative person. In the words of Gildas Herne, who speaks for Murdoch in this novel, Marcus is a megalomaniac, "false prophet, pseudo-scientist, pseudo-philosopher." Marcus is symptomatic of a degenerate postreligious age, an example of "the cheap quackery that dresses up power as wisdom and promises instant salvation . . . scientology and astrology and spiritualism and psychoanalysis."

Marcus is only one of many self-absorbed, self-deluded characters. A particularly grotesque example of the moral blindness that egocentricity can inspire is Jack Sheerwater. He has convinced himself that his constant adulteries are good, necessary to his creative life as a painter. Adultery is bad only if one lies about it, and he never lies to Franca. He tells her that she is a saint and that "absolute love precludes jealousy." Franca has endured his many affairs with patience and generosity, but when he moves his latest mistress, Alison Merrick, into their home, Franca finds she is not a candidate for sainthood after all. Her rejection of the role of passive victim is another small victory in the novel.

Murdoch's message in *The Message to the Planet* is one she has developed in other novels: People must resist their egocentric desires to manipulate and control others; they must try to free themselves from fantasy, enchantment, illusion, and magic—all the forms of self-delusion they prefer to the hardness of reality; they must try to leave the darkness of the cave and seek the light. In short, people must aspire to what Murdoch (following Plato) calls the Good: that real, true but undefinable and transcendent idea of which Plato speaks as the sun. As Plato says in Murdoch's *Acastos: Two Platonic Dialogues* (1987): "[T]here are different levels in the soul, only a bit of us is real and knows truth, the rest is fantasy, anxiety, resentment, envy, all selfish tricks. . . . We have to change ourselves, change what we want, what we desire, what we love, and that's difficult. But if we even *try* to love what's good our desires can improve, they can change direction. . . . Real freedom is not to be a slave of selfish desires."

People such as Ludens who hunger for magic, secret knowledge, complete explanations, and absolutes must modify their desires, must learn a humble, disciplined respect for the human "muddle" where knowledge at best is limited, fragmentary, and ambiguous. Again, Gildas speaks for Murdoch when he scorns the idea of "deep foundations" upon which some kind of absolute knowledge can be erected. He points out that human beings necessarily live with chaos, jumble, and chance. What can they do? They must rely on "empiricism, decent Western empiricism," and particularly on "honest truth-bearing ordinary language." He points out that in Shakespeare there is no "shamanistic nonsense . . . no Arthurian mysteries, no Grail—

just the beauty and the horror of the world, and love—love—love." That, it seems, is the message.

Karen A. Kildahl

Sources for Further Study

Chicago Tribune. February 18, 1990, XIV, p. 1.
Commonweal. CXVII, May 18, 1990, p. 326.
London Review of Books. XI, September 28, 1989, p. 26.
Los Angeles Times Book Review. February 18, 1990, p. 3.
The New Republic. CCII, March 5, 1990, p. 40.
The New York Times Book Review. XCV, February 4, 1990, p. 3.
Publishers Weekly. CCXXXVI, December 15, 1989, p. 55.
The Sewanee Review. XCVIII, January, 1990, p. 159.
Time. CXXXV, February 26, 1990, p. 71.
The Times Literary Supplement. October 20, 1989, p. 1149.
The Washington Post Book World. XX, March 4, 1990, p. 6.

MIDDLE PASSAGE

Author: Charles Johnson (1948-   )
Publisher: Atheneum (New York). 209 pp. $17.95
Type of work: Novel
Time: 1830
Locale: New Orleans, the Atlantic Ocean, and the west coast of Africa

A novel in the form of a ship's log about the "middle passage" from self-serving individualism to concern for and union with others

> *Principal characters:*
> RUTHERFORD CALHOUN, the narrator-protagonist, a rogue
> JACKSON CALHOUN, his altruistic brother
> RILEY CALHOUN, their father
> EBENEZER FALCON, the captain of the *Republic*
> ISADORA BAILEY, a schoolteacher
> PAPA ZERINGUE, a black patron and gangster
> NGONYAMA, one of the Allmuseri, an African tribe

Like so many of the best contemporary American novels, including his own *Oxherding Tale* (1982), Charles Johnson's *Middle Passage*—winner of the National Book Award for fiction—is at once wildly original and self-consciously derivative. Read one way, the novel is an allegory of the African-American's struggle for freedom and identity; read another it is a pastiche of its own literary past: slave narrative, Robert Hayden's poem "Middle Passage," Edgar Allan Poe's *The Narrative of Arthur Gordon Pym* (1838), Herman Melville's *Moby Dick* (1851) and "Benito Cereno" (1855), Jack London's *The Sea Wolf* (1904), Samuel Taylor Coleridge's *The Rime of the Ancient Mariner* (1798), John Gardner's novella *The King's Indian* (1974, itself a pastiche of these same works; Gardner was Johnson's teacher at Southern Illinois University), and Leslie Fiedler's *Love and Death in the American Novel* (1960), whose thesis Johnson adopts as a point of departure. Freed by his slavery-hating master, a minister and biblical scholar, in 1829, Rutherford Calhoun, also known as "Illinois," arrives in New Orleans; there this petty thief and teller of tall tales (of which *Middle Passage* may be one), meets Isadora Bailey, a schoolteacher from Boston and collector of stray and maimed animals, including Calhoun. A man "drawn to extremes," he finds this plain-looking woman intellectually and spiritually attractive, but when she arranges to pay his debts to Papa Zeringue, a black gangster and entrepreneur, in effect blackmailing him into reform, respectability, and marriage, Calhoun flees. As anyone familiar with Fiedler's book knows, Calhoun fears marriage just as much as he fears Santos, Papa Zeringue's 280-pound goon, who suffers from "that rare disease—gaposis—where nothing fits right."

In *Middle Passage*, on the other hand, almost everything fits just fine, narratively speaking. Scenes may shift, plots and characters proliferate, but not without yielding to a sense of an unfolding, densely parallel whole. Fleeing from Isadora, for example, Calhoun reenacts his father's escape from both slavery and family in 1811, when Calhoun was three years old. His ambivalence toward the father he admires as a free man and despises as a traitor and deserter is understandable, for Riley is, as the son imagines him, the "possible-me that lived my life's alternate options, the me I fled. Me. Yet not me. Me if I let go. Me if I gave in." This ambivalence is complicated still further by Calhoun's distaste for his older brother Jackson's willingness to be everything that their father apparently was not: patient, fair, devoted, responsible, altruistic. Against Jackson's commitment to "plodding reform," Calhoun posits the self-serving "sedition" of lies, petty thievery, and flight, first from Jackson and southern Illinois and now, one year later, from Isadora and New Orleans. Turning away from marriage, he turns toward the sea, stowing away, ironically enough, aboard a slave-ship aptly, and ironically, named the *Republic*, captained by a tyrant, Ebenezer Falcon, and manned by a crew of misfits, "refugees from responsibility," who may discern in the aged, drunken, polygamous cook, Josiah Squibb, an image of themselves as they eventually will be.

Squibb is one of Calhoun's several surrogate fathers. Falcon is another. Polymath, perfectionist, and pederast, the dwarfish captain is one of Charles Johnson's finest creations, the comically horrific embodiment or caricature of Franklinesque self-improvement and Emersonian self-reliance. He is a Wolf Larsen-like variation on the Melvillean theme of the isolato, one whose survivalist mentality and anti-affirmative action rhetoric resonate with the peculiarly contemporary Americanness which characterizes so much of this mock-nineteenth century novel. "A creature of preposterous and volatile contradictions"—son of a minister who was himself one of the American Revolution's rabid Sons of Liberty and of a doting mother who filled his head with visions of faraway places—Falcon is the Faust of *Middle Passage*, who bewitches and tyrannizes his crew: "In a sense we were all ringed to the sharper in cruel wedlock." Although he pities Falcon for his incompleteness, Calhoun also feels, upon reading the captain's journal, as if he "had fallen into another man's nightmare." Against Falcon's tyranny and nightmarish vision, the sensitive, Starbuck-like first mate, Cringle, spokesman for civilized values over "formless Naught," can only offer his reluctant participation in a planned mutiny which Calhoun will betray and a slave revolt will make unnecessary, and his own nightmarish vision of the future: homeless people, viral infections, venereal complaints, the blurring of racial and sexual distinctions, urban riots, exotic religious practices, feminism, the buying of America by Orientals, worship of entertainers as cult figures, and "Hottentots spouting Hegel."

If Cringle's nightmare looks ahead in time, the Allmuseri, the *Republic*'s human cargo, its black gold, look back to Johnson's *Oxherding Tale* and to several stories in his 1986 collection, *The Sorcerer's Apprentice*, and further still to some prehistoric stage, some primal unity of being from which all Europeans as well as European-ized blacks, including Calhoun, have fallen. With their reverence for life, language of fluid wholes rather than static substances, opposition to private property, and ignorance of empirical science, the Allmuseri represent man in his original state. As Calhoun comes to realize, his brother Jackson might have been one of the Allmuseri, who "seemed less a biological tribe than a clan held together by values" — values which the Allmuseri, originally seafarers and explorers, may well have spread throughout the world. Melville's Ishmael rhetorically asks, "Who ain't a slave?" *Middle Passage* implies a similar question: "Who ain't an Allmuseri?" Who is not black, at least in part, in his very origin, his deepest being? Not even the Allmuseri, however, are wholly or purely Allmuseri any longer. Not merely dispersed (by choice in the case of the explorers; by force in the case of the slaves aboard the *Republic*), they are also divided among and within themselves (just as Calhoun and his brother are and just as the United States was in 1830 and still is in 1990). After the slaves' shipboard revolt, Ngonyama, representing the Allmuseri in their best and purest state, gradually loses influence as the cowardly, vengeful Diamelo gains control, killing the whites and eventually, although accidently, destroying the *Republic* and all aboard except Calhoun, Squibb, and three of the Allmuseri children, who will be rescued by a passing ship, the *Juno*.

Mishaps, mayhem, and mysteries abound in the first three-quarters of *Middle Passage*, supplanted by the revelations and reconciliations of the novel's final pages. The first of these revelations and reconciliations occurs when the Allmuseri god — Falcon's prized secret cargo — reveals itself to Calhoun in the form of "the one man with whom I had bloody, unfinished business," his father. Only now does Calhoun learn (if it is indeed a revelation and not a hallucination or a trick, the god's or Calhoun's as narrator) that his father never returned to free his family because he was shot and killed shortly after his escape. The father's death raises at least the possibility that Riley might have intended to return to buy his family's freedom or, failing that, to help them escape. Calhoun's ambiguous vision of "devastating father and divine monster" leads him, and therefore the reader as well, to understand the error in viewing the world as anything less than an open, interconnected (Allmuseri) whole whose very essence is the process of its own becoming. The Allmuseri god unfolds itself not in the distinct form of Riley Calhoun but instead in "a seriality of images"; it "could not bring forth one man's life without delivering as well the complete content of the antecedent universe to which my father, as a single thread, belonged." Compare that vision of a wholly interconnected world with what "Captain Falcon and his species of world conqueror thrive upon, the desire to be fascinating objects in the eyes of others."

Papa Zeringue is another of the novel's "fascinating" characters. Owner of the *Juno* and therefore in a sense Calhoun's savior, he is also part owner of the *Republic* and therefore Calhoun's as well as the Allmuseri's oppressor who rationalizes his trafficking in slaves by claiming to serve the greater good of the entire race as patron and as role model (the successful black businessman). It is an argument that Calhoun does not accept any more than Isadora, playing the patient Penelope to Calhoun's wandering Odysseus, weaving and unweaving sweaters for her cats, accepts Papa's offer of marriage. Instead, Calhoun uses the *Republic*'s logbook to blackmail Zeringue, who, fearing exposure and scandal, agrees to leave the couple alone and to support the three surviving Allmuseri. Here the novel ends where it might very nearly have begun had Calhoun not initially confused escape with freedom, self-centeredness with responsibility. Even now, however, Calhoun faces a new problem. Fending off Isadora's strained attempt at passion, he realizes that it is not sex he craves but "fullness,"

> our bodies blended, not our limbs, our histories perfectly twined for all time, not our flesh. Desire was too much of a wound, a rip of insufficiency and incompleteness with an identical charge. . . . Rather, what she and I wanted after so many adventures was the incandescence, very chaste, of an embrace that would outlast the Atlantic's bone-chilling cold.

The ending is poetic, apt, yet nonetheless disappointing in that it lacks the wild energy and Captain Falcon-like fascination of the endings of *Faith and the Good Thing* (1974) and *Oxherding Tale* and of *Middle Passage*'s earlier pages: the excessive, exuberantly fantastical, and at times nearly hallucinogenic quality of Johnson's comically grotesque prose. At novel's end, the reader may well wonder whether the problem that Calhoun raises midway through the novel—"how to win without defeating the other person"—might not apply equally well to Johnson as author, for the conclusion of *Middle Passage* signals just such a defeat, or perverse validation of, the very forces which Johnson claims to want to control—a control which only leads to self-contradiction and its own deconstruction. Calhoun and Isadora may wed, but Johnson's wild narrative energy and "chaste" vision do not. The novel, composed in the form of a ship's log which Calhoun claims to have written in order to free himself from the voices he hears and to "transcribe and therefore transfigure" experience and thereby make peace with the past, and which he addresses to a reader who may very well be Jackson, the brother with whom he now longs to be reconciled, cannot be the book it purports to be. Johnson's text proves at once something less (it does not include all that Calhoun claims to have written) and something more as well (an edited version and therefore akin both to narrative art and to the false log Falcon drew from the true one in order to deceive the ship's owners concerning the captain's own private dealings and profits). *Middle Passage* forms just such an indecidable whole: less the deceptive reconciliation it pretends to be and more a self-deconstructing text which ends not in self-willed transcendence and transfiguration but instead in the complex and compelling intertextuality of its conflicting, intersecting voices, its "warring forces of signification," as deconstructionist Barbara Johnson would say.

Robert A. Morace

Sources for Further Study

Booklist. LXXXVI, June 1, 1990, p. 1878.
Chicago Tribune. July 8, 1990, XIV, p. 6.
Essence. XXI, August, 1990, p. 50.

Kirkus Reviews. LVIII, April 1, 1990, p. 451.
Library Journal. CXV, May 1, 1990, p. 112.
Los Angeles Times Book Review. June 24, 1990, p. 1.
The New York Times Book Review. XCV, July 1, 1990, p. 8.
Publishers Weekly. CCXXXVII, April 6, 1990, p. 103.
The Washington Post Book World. XX, July 15, 1990, p. 6.
Washington Times. July 23, 1990. p. F1.

A MIDWIFE'S TALE
The Life of Martha Ballard
Based on Her Diary, 1785-1812

Author: Laurel Thatcher Ulrich (1938-   )
Publisher: Alfred A. Knopf (New York). Illustrated. 444 pp. $24.95
Type of work: Social history
Time: 1750-1820
Locale: Maine, along the Kennebec River

The reconstructed diary of a middle-aged Maine frontier midwife, giving a complete social history of a community in the early years of the American republic

Principal personages: *
  MARTHA BALLARD (1735-1812), a housewife and midwife in the Kennebec River Valley, Maine, at the end of the eighteenth century
  EPHRAIM BALLARD, her husband, a surveyor for the province of Maine and state of Massachusetts
  HANNAH AND DOLLY BALLARD, their daughters
  PARTHENIA BARTON, a niece who lives with and works for the Ballards until her marriage
  REBECCA FOSTER, the wife of ousted minister Isaac Foster; she brings rape charges against Colonel North, who is acquitted
  JAMES PURRINTON, a neighbor, heavily in debt, who murders his wife and six children before committing suicide in 1806
  HENRY SEWALL, the town clerk

Martha Ballard's twenty-seven-year diary, covering 9,965 days, is a unique record of a midwife's life in frontier Maine on the Kennebec River, brought to life by veteran women's history professor Laurel Thatcher Ulrich. The diary, long available to researchers, was not thought worthy of reprinting by earlier historians despite its being one of the few documents in this period from the hand of a woman and the only one by a midwife.

Martha Ballard (1735-1812) was a midwife—and more. Her record, together with the fascinating context developed by Ulrich, gives readers a "social web" of the daily life and relations of the town of Hallowell (near present-day Augusta, Maine). Both health care and textile production (linen and wool) were primarily in the hands of women. From the growing and harvesting of the flax to the weaving of finished cloth and its distribution and exchange in the community, linen production was totally a female occupation. Weaving is used as a central metaphor throughout the book, as Ulrich images the gendered social relations of the community in terms of the weaving of a piece of indigo-and-white-checked linen homespun. The white threads are women's activities—weaving, gardening, midwifery and healing, neighborly visits, child and animal care, sewing. The indigo threads are men's activities— town meetings, surveys, land transfers, religious controversies, trade, milling and lumbering—the "public" side of life. Men's endeavors show up in town records; they are the "indigo squares" of the cloth. Women's activities, however, are represented not only by the white squares, but also by the mixed blue and white ones, for women participate in men's activities (such as religion and trade), but invisibly. Women's professions do not show up in town records. As Ulrich says, "There were no Committees to Inspect the Kitchens and Gardens of Hallowell, no Packers of Candles or Cullers of Linen Thread, nor was there a Sealer of Reels and Sleighs." Women's invisibility reflects not only the patriarchal organization of society but also the perishable nature of their work. Land endures; butter, chickens, ashes (for soap), herbs, and linen simply disappear.

Henry Sewall, the town clerk, kept a diary from 1776 to 1842, covering the same period as Martha. But his diary does not impart any daily living detail, even about his own family. Martha Ballard's diary tells the reader more about Sewall's wife and children than he does. As Ulrich says, Henry Sewall "leaped from indigo square to indigo square, from courtroom to town meeting to the gathering of saints with little awareness of the finespun fibers between. . . . Martha's world was a web without a selvage, a shuttle perpetually in motion." The reader learns more about war and politics from Martha Ballard than about women's world of medicine, textiles, gardening, and visiting from Henry Sewall.

In structure, the book is divided into chapters, based on topics and sections of the diary. Ulrich quotes a piece of the diary, usually the short daily entries for two or three weeks, then picks an important incident or topic and fills in the social, historical background—the birthing process, health care, death, the legal system, sexual division of labor, crime and justice, marriage, trade and barter, daily and seasonal life on the Kennebec River. Ulrich wisely does not reprint the whole diary, admittedly a dry, elliptical, and sparse work. A typical entry goes like this: "Clear. Mr. Voce & Parmer Laying Shingles on our house. We Brewed. I went to see wido Williams. Shee is Better. Dolly winding the warp for Check." Instead, Ulrich overlays this material with description, narrative, and explanation, drawing on a wealth of external documents: other diaries, court records, census surveys, information about Colonial and early republican frontier life. Still, it is in its very "dailiness" that the diary is unique, and the long passages quoted verbatim help the reader to experience the rhythm of Martha's life.

The information provided about medical care during the period is some of the fullest and most interesting. The midwife was a key element in the healthcare "system" of the time. She cared for women in their pregnancies and births, looked after them at other times, and did most of the nursing and healing of children. "Midwives and nurses," says Ulrich, "mediated the mysteries of birth, procreation, illness, and death. They touched the untouchable, handled excrement and vomit as well as milk, swaddled the dead as well as the newborn. They brewed medicines from plants and roots, and presided over neighborhood gatherings of women." The town also had male doctors, but nurses were more in demand. Martha Ballard and the other women who nursed were constantly on the go, since more than two-thirds of the population was either female or under the age of ten. In 1795, she spent more than sixty nights away from home, attending the sick and those giving birth, "sitting with laboring women or coiled in wakefulness in unfamiliar beds," more nights than the fifty-nine her husband Ephraim, a surveyor for the state of Massachusetts and province of Maine, spent in the woods on surveying expeditions. In 1795, Ballard was sixty-one, and her husband seventy. By the end of that year, she had delivered 608 babies in less than twenty years. By the end of her life in 1812, she had delivered 816 babies.

The section dealing with Ballard's attendance at an autopsy is fascinating. Her medical work in Maine coincided with a movement to bring standardization and licensing to health care. Midwives were being forced out by the new requirements for medical school training (for which women, because of their sex, could not qualify). Midwives from early times had always been present at autopsies, but a shift occurred around this time and by 1820, Harvard Medical School authorities were arguing against women's training in dissection—it was simply not "fitting." Women healers were increasingly being put in a double bind: They could not be certified without dissection and general medicine (which medical school would provide), but learning anatomy would disqualify them *as women* and therefore as midwives. In the case narrated here, Martha Ballard is present for the autopsy of Parthenia Pitts. As a traditional midwife, Ballard connected illness and death with life; her diary records all the ways she was connected to Parthenia (niece, servant, neighbor, patient, friend), how long Parthenia had been ill, the religious state of her soul, and details about the autopsy.

Chapter 5 treats the birthing process and the centrality of the midwife to the process during Martha Ballard's lifetime. Most women gave birth about every two years; among the women of the early Republican period there was little wet nursing. This contrasts with the European practice; one is reminded of European women castigated by Mary Wollstonecraft in 1793 for refusing to breast-feed their own babies. In Ballard's community in contrast to urban communities, few women died of childbed (puerpural) fever—only five in all the years of her practice.

As evidenced in Martha Ballard's diary, the childbirth process had three stages: first, the calling of the midwife, either with the onset of labor or the expectation of labor (especially in times of snowstorms or the breakup of ice on the river); this stage might last from several hours to several days. The transition to the second stage was marked by the calling of "the women": the midwife required at least two assistants, as the actual birthing usually took place literally in the arms of a female friend or relative. Often there were more, up to ten women in attendance; most were neighbors. These women stayed until delivery and traditionally partook of a celebratory meal afterward. Some would remain until the afternurse (often a teenage girl or older woman) arrived to help out in the "lying-in" period. Actually, very few new mothers stayed in bed, but the afternurse helped with household chores until the mother could "return to the kitchen" fulltime. During this period, the midwife would visit once or twice, more if necessary.

Ballard kept very clear records of the births she attended, and noted when her fee was paid. The equivalent of 6 shillings ($2.50) was always paid by the husband (often several months later), sometimes in barter or trade. The length of labor did not affect the fee. Martha Ballard sometimes stayed with a laboring woman several days.

The midwife was a necessary official in the town, especially in the case of illegitimate births. Her testimony as to the identity of the father—the midwife was supposed to ask the laboring mother the name of the father during the birthing process—was always accepted by the legal system in determining who was responsible for the child's support. Premarital sexual intercourse was fairly common, although more often than not the couple married before the child was born. Both Ballard's diary and court records indicate that births often occurred months before the couple had been married nine months.

The most important step in the several-month-long marriage process—which included betrothal and "publication" or written notice at church, a simple civil ceremony, and setting up housekeeping—was the last, when the couple went to their own physical space. This often took place several months after the actual wedding ceremony, the couple in the meantime residing separately with their respective parents. Getting a new household ready was time-consuming and expensive; besides, the young woman was still needed in her mother's household. For Martha Ballard, the day when her daughter was "gone to housekeeping" was much more memorable than the actual wedding day.

The presence of daughters in her household enabled Martha to continue her midwifery. In fact, the family labor system in New England was premised on both the sexual division of labor and large families. The mix of boys and girls in a family and their order shaped a family's life as surely as any other factor. Routine housework, weaving, gardening, and childcare was done by daughters, supervised by the mother. Fieldwork—including clearing, plowing, and fencing—was done by fathers and sons. Women helped out at peak times outside, but men never did "women's work." Both before her daughters were old enough to take charge and after they married, Ballard's ability to continue in midwifery was precarious when she could not get household help. Her preferred role was that of manager only, except for the care of the garden and animals. Housework, weaving, and cooking she routinely left to others. As Ulrich comments in studying the complete diary, "Her spirits rose and fell with the presence of a maid." During the one and a half years her husband spent in debtors' prison, Ballard was often reduced to near freezing because she had no fuel: Getting wood from the forest was the man's task. Her husband was in jail, and she refused to ask her son, with whom she did not get along.

Violence was very much a part of this society, and it was violence perpetrated by men, sometimes on women. Rape was not uncommon (usually what is now called "acquaintance rape"), as in the Foster case for which Martha Ballard gave court testimony. Multiple murder and suicide of a neighbor's family—Captain James Purrinton slit the throats of his wife and six children before killing himself in 1806—also disturbed the peace of the small town. Several ministers preached on the event, saying that Purrinton's Dissenter's belief in universal salvation (instead of the orthodoxy of the doctrine of the elect) contributed to the motive for the multiple murder.

The explanation was that Purrinton's extreme indebtedness caused his suicide; his belief in universal salvation caused him to decide to "take his family with him."

Martha Ballard's garden was always a joy to her; she records when and what she planted, unusual varieties raised, saving and selling of seeds, harvesting and drying of herbs for her practice. Thus the reader learns the length of the growing season, that new wild greens and vinegar were an early spring treat, that she planted several varieties of squash, and that she harvested new peas before the first of July. An appendix listing all the medicinal ingredients noted in the diary and their uses is an interesting addition to Ulrich's account.

That the diary was saved at all is miraculous. Ballard's great-great-granddaughter Mary Hobart (1851-1930) became one of the first fully licensed female physicians, a graduate of Dr. Elizabeth Blackwell's Woman's Medical College of the New York Infirmary in 1884 who later worked at the New England Hospital for Women and Children. Given the manuscript diary by her great-aunts when she finished medical school, Hobart ultimately donated it to the Maine State Library. Another descendant, Clara Barton, became famous during the Civil War as the woman who made nursing an acceptable female profession. She too may have received inspiration from Martha Ballard's pioneering medical work for women.

A Midwife's Tale is, finally, a true "gendered" social history, coming close to what historian Gerda Lerner has called for: a new universal history which tells what everyone was doing in the new American society, what life for all was like—female and male, poor and wealthy, educated and illiterate, not just life as lived by the well-known white males usually noted in the history books.

Margaret McFadden

Sources for Further Study

Booklist. LXXXVI, March 1, 1990, p. 1262.
The Christian Science Monitor. April 24, 1990, p. 14.
Kirkus Reviews. LVIII, January 15, 1990, p. 98.
Library Journal. CXV, March 15, 1990, p. 102.
The New England Journal of Medicine. CCCXXIII, August 16, 1990, p. 492.
The New York Times Book Review. XCV, March 4, 1990, p. 12.
Publishers Weekly. CCXXXVII, January 26, 1990, p. 409.
The Washington Post. March 5, 1990, p. D3.

MISSING MEASURES
Modern Poetry and the Revolt Against Meter

Author: Timothy Steele (1948-   )
Publisher: University of Arkansas Press (Fayetteville). 340 pp. $22.95; paperback $12.95
Type of work: Literary criticism

The various arguments for a poetry freed from meter are, from Steele's perspective, at best sincere and misguided, at worst insincere rationalizations for an unwillingness to master a highly demanding discipline

Over the last few decades, there have been several attempts to explain the diminishing status of poetry and its shrinking audience. Timothy Steele's exploration contributes to this discussion and raises it to a new level of sophistication. One precursor is Paul Fussell's influential text on prosodic analysis, *Poetic Meter and Poetic Form* (1965), designed to teach a liberated generation raised on free verse how to be responsive to the expressive values of meter, fixed forms, and stanzaic composition. Central to Fussell's demonstrations is the conservative argument that great monuments of poetry were founded in mastery of prosodic craft, though craft was never sufficient in itself. Fussell seems to hope that if readers' ears can be awakened, poets will be obliged to make fruitful accommodations to tradition. Fussell's first edition contains no material on free verse. His 1979 revised edition adds such a chapter, but it reads like a concession to the marketplace: Fussell's heart is not in it.

In *The Place of Poetry: Two Centuries of an Art in Crisis* (1981), Christopher Clausen argues that aesthetic formalism had much to do with the alienation of audiences. He calls for a "recovery of the balance between thought, feeling, and form, and for a more fruitful sense of subjects and purposes." Clausen worries about such notions as "the autonomous poem," which divorced the artwork from the surrounding world. Although Clausen does not focus his arguments upon the abandonment of meter, he feels that the insistent rejection of the past has done more harm than good.

Another precursor is Stephen Fredman's *Poet's Prose: The Crisis in American Verse* (1983), a study that acquiesces to and even celebrates the changes it describes. Fredman observes "how deeply the impulse toward prose is embedded in the larger issues of the character of American poetry and the crisis of modernity" while striving to discover the causes and outcomes of this impulse.

Timothy Steele's *Missing Measures* places "the revolt against meter" in both its immediate cultural setting and in the larger context of poetic revolutions across Western history. His patient, scholarly discussion clarifies the elements in this latest revolution, tracks down causes, and exposes some of the hollow arguments and fraudulent, or at least misguided, appeals to authority that have been used to justify the abandonment of meter. It is a bold book, perhaps the most significant offering to date in the gradual emergence of a conservative force in contemporary poetic thought. Not for the casual reader, Steele's arguments might stir up enough poets and academics (since both groups live uneasily together on our nation's campuses) to make a difference in the teaching and in the writing of poetry.

Steele is concerned with what makes the modern revolution in poetry unique. He observes that earlier revolts against tradition were motivated by the desire to rid poetry of what, for any "contemporary" period, was considered artificial or archaic diction in favor of a colloquial idiom. Steele presents relevant passages from John Dryden, William Wordsworth, and other premodern reformers that attest this common thread. The revolution spearheaded by Ford Madox Ford, Ezra Pound, and T. S. Eliot, however, was simultaneously a revolt against meter. For these men, Victorian diction and traditional meter were inseparably linked. The overthrow of the former demanded the overthrow of the latter.

Steele argues that this revolution was detrimental to the further development of poetry, and in fact that the literature that has emerged under the rubric of "free verse" may not be poetry at all. He agrees with earlier reformers who believed that shifts in diction (as well as other elements of poetry) could and should be accomplished without undermining the metrical basis of poetic art. Steele reviews and documents the history of attitudes toward the relationship between poetry and meter. He considers the theory and practice of writers from classical antiquity, the Middle Ages, the Renaissance, and the more recent periods. Throughout his study, the findings are illuminating and puzzling. He notes, for example, that the prose writers of the past looked to poetry for the formal means to enhance their art, while the modern situation has turned that relationship around.

Moreover, through the faulty transmission of classical theory and the conflation into a uniform view of the diverse views of ancient writers, fundamental distortions of emphasis occurred on key issues. While Aristotle considered imitation fundamental to the character of poetry, he nowhere discredited verse. Later commentators found ways of asserting a secondary status to measure, and still others managed to divorce the categories altogether. That is, they developed the argument that one could have verse that was not poetry—an acceptable view if one considers verse as necessary but not sufficient. More recently, the extension of that distinction has led to the modern dictum that one could have poetry without verse (meter), and that, indeed, one should.

As Steele traces various strands leading up to the modern situation, he considers the historic conditions during which various shifts in the relationship between poetry and meter took place. He examines, for example, how during the late eighteenth and throughout the nineteenth century, the novel usurped the roles and status of poetry, relegating poetic effort to its shorter and less discursive forms. He reviews the contours of poetry's long and positive relationship with fiction, its more recent opposition to fiction, and its paradoxical alignment with prose forms in our own era. Steele discusses the ways in which the yearnings of prose writers and poets coalesce in the middle ground of a grace based on rhythm: a dimension of language whose semblance of order and musicality hovers between chaos and the confinement of meter.

Over and over again, Steele returns to misrepresentations of Aristotle, at one point taking apart Marjorie Perloff's slipshod translation and use of the ancient master. Perloff invokes Aristotle to hold the transcriptions of David Antin's extemporaneous "talk poems" above the achievement of such metrical poets as Robert Wells. Steele, returning to the source, destroys Perloff's argument. After so doing, he concludes:

> Whether one agrees or disagrees with Aristotle's contention that poetry can be properly defined as mimetic, and whether one agrees or disagrees with his contention that it is wrong to identify poetry simply with meter, one should remember that the rhythms of prose and the meters of poetry are givens in Aristotle's view of literary composition. If we forget this in reading the *Poetics*, we do so to our own confusion.

Yet Steele is not primarily concerned with rescuing Aristotle from so many centuries of misrepresentation. After all, the misrepresentations are in the service of a credo that justifies a poetry divorced from and even opposed to meter. By exposing the distortions in self-seeking appeals to authority, Steele raises questions about the motives of free verse proponents, asking why they cannot argue fairly. If their arguments are corrupt, perhaps the whole free verse enterprise is similarly corrupt.

The various arguments for a poetry freed from meter are, from Steele's perspective, at best sincere and misguided, at worst insincere rationalizations for an unwillingness to master a highly demanding discipline. The modern concept of the autonomous poem, a central concern in Clausen's book, is one such rationalization to which Steele pays special attention. His chapter on "Free Verse and Aestheticism" traces the history of the autonomous art concept, particularly as it developed in the works of Immanuel Kant, Friedrich von Schelling, and Samuel Taylor Coleridge. By Coleridge's time, the aesthetic faculty was understood as gaining its value and status as a mediating force between understanding and reason. Later writers went further, considering that faculty to be less a mediating force than a separate and superior one. Thus, artworks could be said to remove themselves from the demands of the other, lower, nonaesthetic faculties and from one another.

In an incomplete appeal to nature, Coleridge and other aesthetic thinkers in the Romantic tradition articulated the concept of organic form, a concept that insisted on each artwork's total individuality. Its unique form would be generated from within, according to its own rules. The related notions of the autonomous artwork and organic form in the twentieth century were claimed by those—Charles Olson and William Carlos Williams in particular—who argued for the abandonment of meter. No such denial of meter's centrality to poetic art was prompted by Coleridge, however, who felt that "meter beneficially links will . . . with feeling" and "insists that it is meter that enables genius to speak comprehensively."

Closely related to the defense of free verse through the autonomous art argument is the argument that claims or espouses certain parallels between poetry and music. Those who value autonomy as essential to artworks raise music, the most nonreferential art, to the highest place. Instrumental music, which has no story to tell, does not—according to the influential aestheticians—represent phenomena so much as the inner nature of things. It is the most purely affective of the arts.

In seeking a similar autonomy for poetry, modern thinkers aspired to the model of instrumental music, valuing not regular musical measures as substitutes for or supporters of prosody, but rather the indefiniteness of meaning and form that they found in such music. Steele quotes passages from Williams, Eliot, and others to substantiate this thread of the free verse enigma, and then proceeds to expose the limitations of the language/music analogy. Steele has even less patience with those free verse modes that depend on typography as if it were an equivalent to written or printed musical notation. He considers these trends signs of desperation: "Much modern poetry expresses the anxiety that all the great poems have been written, and that there is nothing more for poets to do." Nothing, that is, except to put the greatest possible distance between themselves and the medium of that greatness: meter.

The appeals to notions of progress and to science—especially evolution—are the final modern arguments with which Steele contends. The simpleminded "newer is better" sloganeering needs little attention. Steele is at pains to dismantle the weak analogy between the new scentific instruments that led to new discoveries and the new instrumentation (prosody) called for by the modern poet-theorists. He observes, also, that the path of evolution is not characterized by abrupt junctures but rather by gradual change in which fundamental attributes of kinds remain recognizable. The various appeals to science, Steele rightly observes, are attempts to gain for poetry (indeed, all the arts) the status that science achieved in the post-Renaissance centuries. The particular arguments and analogies, such as the asserted parallel between free verse and the principle of indeterminacy, he finds intellectually unsound.

By setting the free verse phenomenon in its historical context and by engaging the arguments of its proponents, Steele has cleared the ground for "an assessment of free verse" that he calls for in his conclusion. Steele is convinced that the modern revolt has led nowhere; the free verse medium "has no positive principles for its proponents to defend" and allows no basis for meaningful comparative judgment. Steele urgently pleads for a poetry of our time that will not only "elevate and console us" but also will enable, at some later time, "some reader somewhere . . . [to] be moved by lines that bear witness to us and . . . commit our words to heart and mind that we may live again." For Steele, this poetry will have to be a poetry grounded in meter. He makes the case with skillful logic, with passion, and with eloquence.

Philip K. Jason

Sources for Further Study

Choice. XXVIII, November, 1990, p. 489.
The Christian Science Monitor. May 2, 1990, p. 12.
Chronicles. XV, February, 1991, p. 22.

The Hudson Review. XLIII, Winter, 1991, p. 549.
Library Journal. CXV, April 1, 1990, p. 117.
The New Criterion. IX, November, 1990, p. 41.
The Southern Review. XXVI, Summer, 1990, p. 708.
The Times Literary Supplement. February 1, 1991, p. 19.

MOZART IN VIENNA, 1781-1791

Author: Volkmar Braunbehrens (1941-   )
First published: Mozart in Wien, 1986
Translated from the German by Timothy Bell
Publisher: Grove Weidenfeld (New York). Illustrated. 481 pp. $25.95
Type of work: Historical biography
Time: 1781-1791
Locale: Vienna

Dispelling the numerous myths that have surrounded Mozart since the first biography about him appeared in 1798, Braunbehrens presents a clear and accurate portrait of the composer and his world

> *Principal personages:*
> WOLFGANG AMADÉ MOZART, a composer
> CONSTANZE WEBER MOZART, his wife
> LEOPOLD MOZART, his father
> JOSEPH II, the Emperor of Austria
> LEOPOLD II, the successor to Joseph II (reigned 1790-1792)
> COUNT HIERONYMUS COLLOREDO, the archbishop of Salzburg, the employer
>   of Leopold and Wolfgang Mozart
> EMANUEL SCHIKANEDER, a Viennese impresario, actor, and librettist
> LORENZO DA PONTE, Mozart's best librettist
> MICHAEL PUCHBERG, Mozart's chief creditor

Great figures attract myths. Every child knows the story of George Washington and the cherry tree. Mention Edgar Allan Poe, and people at once envision a slightly mad drunk and drug addict. Thanks to Percy Bysshe Shelley's *Adonais* (1821), Keats has been seen as a pale, sensitive youth too frail to survive a bad book review. One would have to go far, however, to find anyone whose life has been more distorted than Mozart's. Everyone knows the story. Ignored by an obtuse Austrian court and an indifferent public, he struggled with poverty throughout his decade in Vienna. His wife, Constanze appreciated his genius no more than any other of her compatriots. Concerned only with her own comfort, despite the family's financial difficulties she insisted on expensive vacations at Baden, where she carried on an affair with Mozart's pupil Franz Xaver Süssmayr. What little support Mozart received came from his fellow Freemasons, but after he exposed their secrets in *Die Zauberflöte* (*The Magic Flute*) in 1791, they too abandoned him. Antonio Salieri, kapellmeister to the emperor, recognized but feared Mozart's great abilities and therefore blocked every avenue of advancement. Driven by envy, Salieri finally poisoned his rival, who was buried in an unmarked pauper's grave; Mozart was so obscure by the end of 1791 that no one attended the funeral. After his death, Constanze, knowing and caring nothing about her husband's compositions, sold off his manuscripts by the sheet to the highest bidders, thus dispersing his work.

Such are the outlines of the received life of Mozart, presented most egregiously in Peter Shaffer's *Amadeus* (1979) but available in purportedly nonfictional accounts as well. Unhappily for lovers of romantic tales about neglected genius, this version of the biography is utterly without foundation. In his new book, a successor to his biography of Salieri, Braunbehrens has set out "to remove the patina, encrustations, and later deposits from Mozart's monument." The character that emerges from Braunbehrens' pages is not a melodramatic hero but a fascinating, resourceful, and often enigmatic human being.

Among the misconceptions this study removes is that of Mozart's poverty. As court organist for Count Hieronymus Colloredo, Archbishop of Salzburg, Mozart was earning 450 florins a year in 1780. The sum was not generous, but it was more than a schoolteacher would have earned. In 1790, Friedrich Schiller received less (400 florins) as a professor. A number of factors influenced Mozart's decision to leave the archbishop's service and remain in Vienna. Mozart wanted to write operas, but Salzburg had no opera house. He was in love with Constanze Weber, who was living in Vienna. He sought independence from a demanding employer, and, much as he loved his father, at twenty-five the young composer may well have wanted to put some distance between himself and Leopold. High on any list of reasons was also the desire to earn more money. Even in 1781, when he had only one student for most of the year and initially lacked important contacts (he had not been to the Austrian capital since 1773), he earned at least 962 florins. A detailed account of his income thereafter shows that except for 1786, he never made less than a thousand florins. All the sources of his income are not known; he might have earned far more, perhaps as much as two or three thousand florins a year. He was far from impoverished at his death; indeed, 1791 was financially his most successful year: He received at least 3,725 florins and possibly as much as 5,000.

Why, then, did Mozart toward the end of his life borrow heavily from Michael Puchberg—some fifteen hundred florins between 1788 and 1790? Braunbehrens notes that Mozart never saved money, and, considering the unreliability of banks in the eighteenth century, his extravagance was not altogether foolish. The frugal composer Franz Joseph Haydn amassed a fortune that was rendered worthless by the inflation that struck Napoleonic Europe in the early nineteenth century. Still, without money in reserve, Mozart had no resources to fall back on if his income fell or if unexpected expenses arose. In 1788, both occurred. The previous year had been quite successful, producing at least 3,216 florins. Then the Turkish War disrupted Vienna's economy; Mozart's income fell by two-thirds. At the same time, Constanze became ill and required expensive treatments. By 1791, Mozart's income had risen again, and he had begun to repay Puchberg, though he still owed a thousand florins at his death. Obscure references in Mozart's letters suggest that gambling and business speculations may also have contributed to his lack of money despite more than respectable earnings.

Earning as much as he did, Mozart must have enjoyed wide support. Joseph II has been accused of neglecting the greatest musical genius in his kingdom, and Mozart accused the emperor of stinginess. Braunbehrens agrees that Joseph's successor, Leopold II, was indifferent to Mozart, but Joseph II, though a frugal monarch, was fairly helpful. When Mozart came to Vienna in 1781, the most lucrative court positions were occupied; in 1787, when a vacancy occurred, the emperor appointed Mozart to the post of *Kammerkompositeur*, a sinecure that paid 800 florins a year and demanded nothing. Even in 1781, Mozart had received a commission for an opera to celebrate the visit of Paul, Crown Prince of Russia. The request came from Count Franz Xaver Wolf Rosenberg-Orsini, director of the Hoftheater, but Braunbehrens believes that the idea came from the emperor. The opera was not ready in time for the visit, but it was performed the following year, and Mozart received 426 florins for it. Thereafter the emperor requested an opera about once every three years; for each he paid 900 florins. Braunbehrens cites other instances of royal patronage as well. For example, in 1781, Joseph invited Mozart to play against Muzio Clementi in a piano competition, for which Mozart received 225 florins.

Joseph II's musical taste, though sometimes maligned, was good. He appreciated Mozart's work, and in this attitude he was hardly alone. In the composer's lifetime his operas were performed all over Europe (Mozart received no royalties from these productions). Bohemia commissioned *La Clemenza di Tito* (*The Clemency of Titus*, 1930) for Leopold's coronation in Prague in 1791 and paid 1,125 florins for it. The emperor did not care for the piece, but it enjoyed much popularity among the populace. In 1790, Mozart had received a lucrative offer to come to England to compose two operas, and he received pensions from The Netherlands and Hungary (1791). The absence of graveside mourners when Mozart was interred in the cemetery of St. Mark's resulted from Viennese burial practices: The body was taken to the cemetery at night and buried the next morning. No stone marked his grave because regulations forbade the practice. Mozart's death did not, however, pass unnoticed. His funeral, in a small chapel of St. Stephen's Cathedral, attracted a number of people, though it is impossible to say how many. In Prague, where he had always been popular, more than four thousand attended a memorial service for him shortly after his death. The *Wiener Zeitung* reported the event on December 24, concluding the account with praise for Mozart's music.

As Braunbehrens shatters the myth of neglected genius, of a pauper's grave, of a mysterious death (rheumatic fever and the treatment for it were the culprits), he also dispels the received opinion about Constanze. Mozart's first biographer, Franz Xaver Niemetschek, claimed that "Mozart never acted without consulting his wife"; in 1790, when he went to Frankfurt, he entrusted sensitive business matters to her. Throughout their married life he showed the greatest affection for Constanze, and she demonstrated true appreciation for his music. The soprano solo in the unfinished C Minor Mass (K. 427) probably was composed for her, and she probably performed it at the work's premiere in Salzburg in 1783. In 1829, she told Mary Novello that Mozart always sought her opinion of his operas; the fugues that he wrote for two pianos or four hands were most likely meant for himself and Constanze. After Mozart's death, Constanze preferred to withhold manuscripts from publication rather than have them appear in doubtful condition, even though such scrupulousness cost her money. Instead of trying to find the highest bidder for each piece, she dealt only with two publishers, thus ensuring that the compositions would not be dispersed.

As Braunbehrens illuminates the life of Mozart, he presents a vivid panorama of Josephine Vienna. Not all the information is relevant to understanding Mozart's music, but much of it sets the man and his work in context. For example, political considerations explain Joseph's decision to ban performances of Pierre Augustin Caron de Beaumarchais' *Le mariage de Figaro* (1784) but to order the staging of *Le nozze de Figaro* (1786), Mozart's opera based on the French play, at the Hofoper. This site guaranteed an aristocratic audience impervious to the more revolutionary aspects of the work; at the same time, the attacks on aristocratic privilege supported Josephine reforms.

The only flaws in this well-researched, well-written book lie in the apparatus. The scanty index provides no entries for individual works, nor does it provide subheadings. The researcher seeking Leopold Mozart's reaction to his son's marriage, for example, must search each page listed under Leopold's name. The bibliography has been taken directly from the German original of the work. Hence, the entries reflect none of the work published on Mozart since 1986—and the approaching bicentennial of Mozart's death has prompted some useful books and articles. One wonders, too, whether those reading the book in English will be able to get—or understand—the items listed. Although Braunbehrens' book will not be the final word on the last decade of Mozart's life, no one seeking to understand the composer can ignore this work. A better index and bibliography would make the text more useful to those who will need to refer to it.

Joseph Rosenblum

Sources for Further Study

The Atlantic. CCLXV, June, 1990, p. 121.
Booklist. LXXXVI, September 1, 1989, p. 22.
Choice. XXVIII, September, 1990, p. 127.
Library Journal. CXIV, September 1, 1989, p. 191.
National Review. XLI, December 22, 1989, p. 47.
The New York Times Book Review. XCV, February 25, 1990, p. 7.
The Observer. June 17, 1990, p. 58.
Publishers Weekly. CCXXXVI, July 28, 1989, p. 212.
The Times Literary Supplement. November 16, 1990, p. 1238.
Wilson Quarterly. XIV, Summer, 1990, p. 95.

THE MUSIC ROOM

Author: Dennis McFarland (1949-   )
Publisher: Houghton Mifflin (Boston). 275 pp. $19.95
Type of work: Novel
Time: August, 1976, with flashbacks to prior years
Locale: Manhattan, New York; Norfolk, Virginia; Newport, Rhode Island; and San Francisco, California

A search into the causes of his brother's suicide draws Martin Lambert into a confrontation with his family's past

> *Principal characters:*
> MARTIN LAMBERT, the twenty-nine-year-old narrator of the novel, a former cellist and owner of a small record company, recently separated from his wife
> PERRY LAMBERT, Martin's younger brother, a gifted pianist, who has just committed suicide as the novel opens
> RUDY LAMBERT, their father, a failed musician who drank himself to death ten years earlier
> HELEN LAMBERT, their mother, a former Las Vegas show girl, who is also an alcoholic, in and out of sobriety
> JANE OWLCASTER, Perry's girlfriend
> RAYMOND, the Lamberts' houseboy
> MADELINE LAMBERT, Marty's wife
> FELICIA SNOW AND LITTLE TEDDY, drinking buddies of Helen
> MAX DOLOTOV, a semifamous composer and old family friend, also Perry's teacher
> FAYE BARRYMORE, minister of the church to which Perry donates his estate

In the novel's opening scene, Marty Lambert vacuums the hundred self-adhesive glow-in-the-dark stars from the ceiling of the nursery that would have belonged to his firstborn child. Months earlier his wife suffered a second miscarriage, and he and his wife are now separated. The phone rings and a New York detective informs him that his brother Perry is dead, having thrown himself off the twenty-third floor of a midtown hotel. In the general wash of his own marital failures and disappointments, Marty's first impulse is to feel sorry for himself. It is a self-pity which, on the way to New York to claim his brother's body, gradually dissolves to be replaced by a single focusing purpose: to discover why his brother, in neither apparent crisis nor despair, would take his own life.

Yet *The Music Room* is both more—and less—than a simple mystery novel. Perry's suicide is a riddle that is never completely resolved. Marty's initial search through the effects of his brother's life turns up no pat answers and few clues. Family memories prove far more telling. The real subject of the novel is the Lambert family's haunted past, full of characters whose motives, like Perry's, are never completely knowable, though they become, in the course of the novel, somehow understandable.

The literal "music room" of the title plays a small role in the novel's action. In the present tense it does not even exist, having been destroyed in a fire caused by a careless cigarette smoker years before. Yet it functions figuratively as an emblem for the collective family closet, where dysfunction breeds further dysfunction. Marty's investigation into Perry's death draws him to uncover the secrets in his family's closet, where a legacy of alcoholism, untimely death, and musical talent and its betrayal draws a complex portrait of lives spent searching for some kind of redemption. The promise of their future has dried up like the glue on Marty's glow-in-the-dark stars.

At the center of the family mystery are the parents, Helen and Rudy Lambert. A Las Vegas show girl, Helen is rescued from a cheap and inconsequential life when Rudy, the son of a coal and tobacco heiress, impulsively marries her. When the spark of passion that ignited the union fades, it is replaced by a glue that proves to be puzzling in its strength. Helen and Rudy are adversarial and childish, yet bound together. One night, while Marty and Perry watch unobserved, their parents drunkenly dance and wrestle in the window: "Mother, whirling, collapses onto a sofa, Father jerks her erect, they both fall against a desk, sending a lamp crashing to the floor, and their immense shadows break across the library ceiling." Helen and Rudy make colorful but fragile guardians; they throw a quality of broken glass into the family center. Yet their dance scene, which Marty finds "spectacular" and "vaguely frightening," seems to please Perry.

Two seeds from the same broken source, the brothers develop along different routes, with Perry choosing suicide and Marty not sure what he has chosen until the novel's end. One childhood incident in particular crystallizes the difference between them. The boys are at a summer party in New Jersey when Perry is fifteen and Marty is nineteen. Without Marty's knowledge, Perry has volunteered their father's Lincoln as the central piece in a daredevil game in which the players drive the car—with its headlights off—toward a ditch, the object being to stop the car closest to the edge of the gully without falling in. Perry drives the car into the ditch. Rather than feeling fear or remorse about what he has done, however, Perry feels an incredible wonder, an almost religious sense of awe. This moment, echoed years later by another daredevil leap Perry takes from a cliff in Corfu, seems to foreshadow the suicide jump and suggests that Perry was driven by something far more mysterious and engaging than either sheer recklessness or despair. Yet it is this riddle at the center of Perry's character which Marty is never quite able to solve. At the party, when Marty admonishes his brother for the trouble he has just gotten into, Perry is disappointed; his brother has failed to understand the moment. "At least *I* know what kind of trouble I'm in, Martin," he says.

In trying to pin down the elusive character trait that throws Perry into suicide, Marty inadvertently learns more about himself. Numb to his own pain, he finds one blind alley after another, blaming his mother, Perry's teacher, Perry's girlfriend, and the church to which Perry bequeaths his inheritance. At the same time, Marty blindly seeks some kind of salvation in a love affair with his brother's girlfriend and in alcohol. He has always been ignorant of his own motives; his life before Perry's death was equally haphazard and blind. Victim to the same hazy denial that has cursed his family for years, Marty gradually begins to recognize the truth.

As Marty unravels the family secrets, he finds that Perry had always known more about the family than he did. One of the secrets Perry learns first is the cause of their grandparents' death. Shortly after Rudy and Helen's marriage, the airplane that Rudy's father was piloting crashed into the side of a mountain, killing both him and his wife—an event which Rudy then blamed as the single greatest cause for his own failed career as a concert pianist. Yet, Marty learns, the crash occurred not because of his grandfather's age or the inclement weather, but because his grandfather was drunk. Further, his father's recital career was not cut short because of an incapacitating grief over the loss of his mother, but rather because Helen threatened to take his sons from him if he continued to embarrass the family with his second-rate musical gifts.

Yet despite all the failures and mistakes, no clear hero or villain emerges from the Lambert family portrait. If anything, they are all very much alike; each in his own way is an escape artist. For a short period of time, Perry was the single element that seemed to hold the family together. To Marty, it seems that his childhood began when Perry was born. Fascinated with Perry in a way they never were with Marty, Rudy and Helen briefly became attentive parents. Yet the glue did not hold; inevitably, the family splintered. A recurrent memory Marty has of one September afternoon is telling. Rudy is drunkenly playing a Beethoven sonata in the music room while Perry and his nurse listen and watch. Marty has come home from his first day of first grade. Seeing Marty, Perry squeals and wriggles out of his nurse's arms, hitting his chin on the hardwood floor with a scream that threatens to wake the dead. Rudy knocks over a tumbler of whiskey, sending shattered glass flying across the floor. Helen appears in the doorway, and soon everyone is struggling for possession of Perry. Marty is able to steal his brother from everyone else's grip and run with him, out of the room, out of the house, down to the end of the yard. The family center will not hold; eventually, everyone's solution is to run.

Unable to live their lives fully, each member of the Lambert family develops a strategy to flee it. Helen spends long afternoons in the library, drinking with friends Felicia and Teddy and occasionally taunting her husband. Rudy briefly attempts sobriety, rededicating himself to his music, then quietly drinks himself to death. Perhaps the only difference between Perry's death and the deaths of both his father and grandfather is that his is an intentional suicide; the others kill themselves less consciously. Marty might have been heading for a similar fate had Perry's suicide not awakened him. One last secret that Perry knows first is that Marty also has a drinking problem. Toward the end of the novel, Marty stops drinking.

Becoming sober brings clarity, but not redemption. Not until the closing scene does Marty release Perry's ghost and achieve a sense of salvation. Marty finally consents to visit the institution to which Perry has bequeathed his estate, a church school for disadvantaged children. To the relief of the minister, Marty no longer plans to contest Perry's will. Marty sells his business and is without any significant romantic relationship; it is as though the slate of his life has been wiped clean, ready for some new beginning. Exploring the school, Marty finds a thirteen-year-old boy struggling to play a Bach sonata on the cello. He later learns that the boy has an abusive father. When Marty, who has not played his own cello in years, decides to tutor the boy, his—and his family's—real healing begins.

It is not surprising that redemption comes through Marty's music and through a child: Both require going beyond the family legacy. To be able to teach and nurture a child means no longer being a broken child, a fate his parents could never escape. The child is also an image of creativity successfully expressed. The two miscarriages in Marty's marriage symbolize the family legacy of artistic failure, an inability to create. Both boys initially follow in their father's footsteps, though for different reasons. Perry throws away his musical talent because the burden of its genius frightens him. Marty throws it away because his own gifts do not seem like genius at all, but bland mediocrity. Ultimately, however, talent—like a child—is not something to discard; it is something to be responsible to, whatever degree of greatness or mere adequacy it holds. Years earlier Marty dropped out of school because he could not stand the thought of being a music teacher for the rest of his life; like his father, he could not bear to face himself. Now, as he commits to tutoring this child, he knows for the first time who he is. His brother's suicide has been the doorway into a new music room.

The Music Room is Dennis McFarland's first novel. In a remarkable sleight of hand unusual for a first effort, McFarland leaves the story's central mystery— Perry's suicide—unresolved, yet the work is nevertheless satisfying. If anything, this lack of resolution makes the novel more true to life. The novel asks the questions: "Does one ever really know why someone else takes his life?" and "Should one even try to find out?" McFarland has drawn his characters as people are in real life; they can be known but not pinned down. McFarland's lyrical prose blends dream, memory, and present-tense action into a single center of consciousness that gradually awakens to healing self-knowledge.

Dana Gerhardt

Sources for Further Study

Booklist. LXXXVI, March 15, 1990, p. 1417.
Kirkus Reviews. LVIII, February 15, 1990, p. 212.
Library Journal. CXV, April 1, 1990, p. 138.
Los Angeles Times Book Review. April 8, 1990, p. 8.
The New York Review of Books. XXXVII, August 16, 1990, p. 45.
The New York Times Book Review. XCV, May 6, 1990, p. 11.
Newsweek. CXV, May 28, 1990, p. 74.
Publishers Weekly. CCXXXVII, February 16, 1990, p. 67.
The Times Literary Supplement. August 31, 1990, p. 916.
The Washington Post. May 9, 1990, p. B2.

MY FATHER'S ISLAND
A Galapagos Quest

Author: Johanna Angermeyer (1948-   )
Publisher: Viking (New York). Illustrated. 303 pp. $19.95
Type of work: Autobiography
Time: 1958-1966
Locale: California, Ecuador, and the Galapagos Islands

The odyssey of a girl in search of her heritage

> *Principal personages:*
> JOHANNA ANGERMEYER, the author
> EMMA ANGERMEYER, her mother
> JOHANNES (HANS) ANGERMEYER, her father—deceased but a continuing presence in her life
> TONY AGUIRRE, her half-brother
> MARY ANGERMEYER, her sister
> JOHNNY ANGERMEYER, Mary's son out of wedlock
> GUS ANGERMEYER, Johanna's uncle, "King" of Galapagos
> CARL ANGERMEYER, another uncle, "Duke" of Galapagos
> FRITZ ANGERMEYER, another uncle

The Galapagos Islands owe their fame to two nineteenth century giants, one scientific and one literary. In 1835 a young naturalist aboard the British surveying ship *Beagle* spent a month in these volcanic islands astride the equator some six hundred miles west of Ecuador. Charles Darwin's observations of the flora and fauna there suggested to him the theory of evolution that he finally set forth in *On the Origin of Species* (1859). In the early 1840's a similarly youthful seaman, Herman Melville, visited the islands twice and made them the basis of a group of sketches called *The Encantadas, or Enchanted Isles* (1854).

Subsequently, other scientists and travelers and a novelist as well known as Kurt Vonnegut have written of the islands, but few, if any, inhabitants of the Enchanted Isles have ventured into print. A 1958 *Argosy* magazine article purported to be the work of Carl Angermeyer, one of the few hundred inhabitants of the relatively livable Santa Cruz, but his sister-in-law in the United States recognized the article as ghostwritten. The locale is not one to attract literati, and the English name for Santa Cruz, Indefatigable, describes a trait much more crucial to a colonist than literary talent. Carl Angermeyer's niece has now produced an account of life in this remote paradise—to use a word that Johanna Angermeyer employs not as a cliché but with attention to its implications. Many of her relatives live there, but she went there in search of a father who had spent only a few months in the islands and had died in her infancy. She supplies the rather complicated background of her "quest" through a variety of techniques that collectively re-create the impression of a girl discovering both her cosmopolitan ancestry and the motivations and doings of her forebears.

Johanna Angermeyer was born about as far from the ocean as one can get on the North American continent. Her mother's Russian-born family had emigrated to

Lincoln, Nebraska, early in this century and enacted their version of the American success story. Emma, Johanna's mother, fell in love with a dashing young Ecuadorian who was enrolled in the Charles Lindbergh School of Aviation in the 1930's. They married and moved to Quito, the Ecuadorian capital, but shortly after the birth of their son the flyer crashed in the Andes. Eventually the boy would inherit property in Ecuador, but in the meantime the young widow married a refugee from Hitler's Germany. Johannes Angermeyer (usually called "Hans") and three of his brothers had gravitated to this South American nation with dreams of beginning life anew in the Ecuadorian island possessions in the Pacific, but Emma's pregnancy kept the couple in Quito. Two months before their daughter Mary was born, the Japanese bombed Pearl Harbor; the American government insisted that Emma return home as soon as the child could stand the trip, but her German husband was denied entry.

After the war the couple finally managed to join Gus, Carl, and Fritz Angermeyer in the islands, but with Emma expecting another child, Hans refused to risk the birth in an archipelago barren of medical resources, so the rest of the family went back to Nebraska while Hans, by then seriously ill with tuberculosis, petitioned unavailingly for entry to the United States. He died in Quito in 1948 without ever seeing his second daughter. Later the family moved to California, and the book begins with the ten-year-old Johanna girding herself for her first crack at show-and-tell in her classroom. Having seen her Galapagos relatives featured on a television program called *Travel to Adventure*, she truthfully, although unconvincingly, relates her discovery to Miss Bean, who is skeptical of the existence of islands that do not appear on the big world map, and classmates who chortle at her account of the "Gallopin' Islands." The narrative proceeds from this point to the time when the eighteen-year-old Johanna learns to ride a half-broken stallion over the crusted lava of Santa Cruz.

The islands entranced her from the beginning, and the reader is invited to participate in the unwinding of the long process which finally takes her there at the age of fourteen for a summer visit. The author intersperses stories that the twice-widowed Emma tells her three children, letters, diary entries, and information pried from relatives in her attempt to discover the full Angermeyer saga and particularly her father's role in it. The mystery of her father gradually but never completely unfolds for her. To the very end she is denied so much as a glimpse of his final resting place, for when, as a young woman, she visits the cemetery in Quito, she finds that his grave has been "reoccupied" for the lack of anyone to pay an annual maintenance fee. The book becomes a testament to her unknown father; Santa Cruz is not the island where her uncles have flourished; it is "my father's island."

Nevertheless, the uncles, especially "King Gus" and "Duke Carl," as they are styled, emerge as remarkably vital persons, as do a number of the author's other relatives, male and female. Fourteen-year-old Johanna finds Gus to be the sort of man who, stranded in a small boat with its engine dead off dangerous rocks, decides to take a nap. When he and his brothers had first settled in the islands, Gus had been gored by a wild boar. Deciding on the need for a boat in emergencies, they ignored the other islanders' arguments that, even if they were fortunate enough to find suitable timber, they would never find a way to convey it to the shore or, even if accomplishing that feat, had no rivets, nails, or screws with which to fasten members together. Somehow they built and floated the boat anyway. Now, years later, Gus could not be bothered by a defective engine; as he pointed out to his niece, they could always row home if necessary. The even more flamboyant Carl had once been induced to travel to Hollywood by a man "called Howard something or other" for a screen test; told that he should stay and become a star, Carl opted for Santa Cruz instead. It was simply more fun to amaze visiting scientists with his tame iguanas, which would come at his call to eat the dog's leftovers.

The Angermeyers clearly loved the role of hosts. The *Argosy* article quotes Carl: "Why don't you come and see us? We'd welcome your visit. . . . But don't plan on staying unless you're ready to accept life on a lonely, abandoned, sunbaked bit of lavaland." If anything worried the brothers, it was the specter of Santa Cruz as a routine tourist attraction. Their island may have looked like paradise, but it was one in some peril of being lost. It is interesting to contrast their view with Melville's nineteenth century one. Contemplating the wave-lashed, rocky coast, the largely reptilian and entomological life, the dense thickets inland, the arid weather, and the ubiquitous lava, Melville concluded that "in no world but a fallen one could such lands exist." The Angermeyers knew that only the hardiest could live in paradise but paradoxically felt the urge to share it even while they guarded it against the inevitable corruption from outsiders. Carl's penchant for publicity—he had even managed a trip back to Germany during which he had been interviewed by virtually every possible journalist—could become the instrument of their own undoing. His niece expresses their fear thus: "There were many people out there still searching for paradise. How long before the world caught up with and trampled Eden to death?" This appears to be the Galapagueños' dilemma: wanting to recede from a world of television, shopping malls, and vast highways, they awaited like children each invasion of that world's representatives.

The author noted that although the population was sparse, it was diverse, and settlers from many nations appeared to live together quite amiably. She found music and dancing to be the favorite entertainment of her German relatives, who always had an eye peeled for another fiddler or accordionist. Storytelling too was popular. Johanna was regaled with the tale of a woman called "the Baroness" who came from Australia, attracted an entourage of lovers, and proclaimed herself "Empress of the Pacific," thus outboasting Gus and Carl. Stories of the marauding pirates who found convenient lurking places on some of the larger islands also abounded. To attend an evening of society, Johanna sometimes had to walk (barefoot, to save precious shoes) over perilous, rock-strewn paths in the dark. Like everything else in the Galapagos, entertainment exacted its price, but she was (and is—for as the wife of the curator of Wordsworth House in the English Lake Country, she continues to maintain a home there) the kind of person willing, even eager, to pay that price.

Despite its charm in revealing day-to-day existence on one of the Enchanted Isles, Angermeyer's book is primarily her own story. Caught up early in the romance of "this stalwart Swiss Family Robinson," as the *True Adventure* television program described her kinfolk, she yearned for a taste of this life. Although the reality often surprised and sometimes pained the girl, she exuded a rock-ribbed determination to savor it in all its ruggedness.

Not so polished a writer as, say, Annie Dillard, Angermeyer nevertheless approximates Dillard's evocation of the sights, sounds, and feelings of the girl she was a quarter century ago in *An American Childhood* (see *Magill's Literary Annual 1988*). Angermeyer adroitly communicates not only the clumsiness, the ineptness, the self-consciousness, but also the alertness, the honesty, the sympathy of her juvenile years. She is especially adept at conveying the frustration of discovery that can find no adequate audience with whom to share it. When she returned to school on the mainland following her first summer on Santa Cruz, for example, she could not relate her experience to her classmates because "our geography professor had pronounced the islands fit only for reptiles and hardened criminals."

Her style is relatively simple and colloquial but metaphorically vigorous. A young Ecuadorian woman has "glossy braids and a keyboard smile," her own mother "weighed her words out and placed them in small parcels labelled Handle With Care," their island home's "back door opened on a glob of lava so large that in the moonlight it looked like a wild beast with gleaming obsidian fangs." After a swim in the surf, the "sun dried us like three happy fried eggs on a sidewalk." In the final chapter she describes her arrival at the point of pondering the significance of her quest for not just an island but a father:

> Hans had never escaped the war. Hitler had follwed him all the way. The debris of my father's life lay scattered halfway across the world *en route* to paradise. But Father hadn't really been searching for paradise. All he wanted was a house on a beach big enough for us all, with windows wide enough to let in the moonlight. Was it so much to ask?

She interprets her largely unknown father as distinctly different from her relaxed, well-adjusted uncles. They had had decades to forget the Nazi oppression which circumstances had allowed to shadow their brother far longer and which a fatal illness left him no opportunity to forget. Although Hans lived only briefly and never securely in the Galapagos with his family, the island was, in his daughter's eyes, peculiarly his—his perhaps to appreciate beyond the power of his more fortunate brothers.

The generous selection of excellent photographs in the book is divided between black-and-white family snapshots and color reproductions of such famous Galapagos denizens as the huge tortoises, sea lions, marine iguanas, and the like. The text does not concern itself with these creatures except for occasional confrontations. Johanna Angermeyer and her family found themselves dealing primarily with those fittest of survivors everywhere, roaches, rats, and ants, although the Galapagos versions of familiar creatures are sometimes vexatiously exotic, as for instance the ten-inch centipede that became involved with the author's hair.

During her adolescence Angermeyer's life on the island encompassed chiefly vacation time. She has promised an account of adult experiences. Readers of these engaging reminiscences will no doubt look forward to the sequel.

Robert P. Ellis

Sources for Further Study

Booklist. LXXXVI, January 15, 1990, p. 969.
Chicago Tribune. March 13, 1990, V, p. 3.
Kirkus Reviews. LVII, November 1, 1989, p. 1569.
Library Journal. CXIV, November 15, 1989, p. 90.
Los Angeles Times Book Review. January 28, 1990, p. 2.
New Woman. XX, January, 1990, p. 28.
Publishers Weekly. CCXXXVI, November 10, 1989, p. 53.
San Francisco Chronicle. February 21, 1990, p. E4.
The Times Literary Supplement. August 24, 1990, p. 905.
The Washington Post Book World. XX, February 4, 1990, p. 13.

MY SON'S STORY

Author: Nadine Gordimer (1923-   )
Publisher: Farrar, Straus & Giroux (New York). 277 pp. $19.95
Type of work: Novel
Time: The 1970's and 1980's
Locale: Johannesburg, Pretoria, and Rustenburg, South Africa

A novel describing the family tensions that result from a black man's involvement in the South African struggle for freedom

> *Principal characters:*
> SONNY, a black schoolteacher, later an activist
> AILA, his wife
> BABY, their daughter, who eventually becomes a revolutionary
> WILLIAM (WILL), their son, a student
> HANNAH PLOWMAN, a white human-rights worker, Sonny's mistress

Both in her works and in interviews, Nadine Gordimer has made it clear that she disapproves of apartheid; it was her sympathy with blacks that caused South Africa to ban three of her novels, *A World of Strangers* (1958), *The Late Bourgeois World* (1966), and *Burger's Daughter* (1979). As some of her more perceptive critics have pointed out, however, Gordimer herself is in two ways an outsider in the movement with which she sympathizes: She is white and she is a woman. It may well be that it is this sense of alienation, or at least of difference, that enables Gordimer to write novels with such a sense of the complexity of life. In *My Son's Story*, for example, she shows how difficult it is in a time of social change to choose wisely between conflicting duties, to understand the motives for making those choices, and to accept the negative effects from even those decisions that seemed most clearly right.

The title *My Son's Story* suggests that there will be a single narrator in the novel, perhaps with an introductory passage by the father. In fact, the novel incorporates several points of view. Some of the story is told through the eyes of the father, a black schoolteacher who has been called Sonny since his own childhood. Some of it is told by his son, William (Will), a student. Some of it is told by Sonny's white mistress, Hannah Plowman, a human-rights worker who first became acquainted with Sonny when he was jailed for opposing the white South African regime. The point is that the story involves all three of these characters, and in addition, Aila, Sonny's wife, and Baby, their daughter, whose points of view, however, are not explored except through their comments and their actions.

At the beginning of the novel, Gordimer establishes the kind of life Sonny and Aila are leading before Sonny becomes committed to the black struggle: a happy, tranquil life to which Will and Aila later look back as being almost a lost paradise. Sonny is a respected schoolteacher, who loves his wife Aila very much, and whose greatest commitment, apart from his profession, is to ensure the social and intellectual development of his beloved children. Then there is a demonstration near his school; driven by an emotional necessity, Sonny leads the students who have been entrusted to him into the demonstration. Their parents are horrified. As a result, Sonny is fired from his job and, without ever really choosing to become an activist, is incorporated into the movement for black liberation.

Ironically, as Gordimer makes clear, what Sonny finds in the movement is the opposite of freedom. He is ordered to leave the home where he and his family have been so happy and to move into a neighborhood that is becoming increasingly racially mixed. Aila protests, but it does no good. Like the parents of his students, Sonny's own family believe that they have been betrayed, that they have been used for the sake of the movement to which Sonny is now committed.

Dedicated mother that she is, Aila attempts to make the new home and the new life seem normal, to accept the new responsibilities her husband has, which take him away from home and even into prison, as merely another kind of job, not unlike that of a schoolteacher. What she cannot or will not realize is that the movement, unlike his previous profession, regards him as a pawn, who can be sent to danger and to death should such a course seem beneficial to the movement. The fact that she does not understand his new life creates a gulf between Aila and Sonny. Yet neither of them realizes how far apart they are until Sonny becomes involved with Hannah Plowman.

At first it appears that Hannah, though white, is synonymous with the cause of black freedom. A representative of an international human-rights organization, she gets to know Sonny when she visits him in prison, and soon he sees her as his contact with the real world outside, the world of the movement. Because of her experience, Hannah understands Sonny's needs and his concerns as Aila can never do. Instead of news of the children's doings, Hannah can bring Sonny coded news of the movement's activities. Instead of a puzzled sympathy, Hannah can give him real support; she can discuss problems of organization with him, as well as empathizing with his fears and uncertainties. Unlike Aila, Hannah is Sonny's comrade; it is not surprising when she becomes his mistress. To Sonny, the relationship is essential. He needs Hannah to talk to him of their common concerns; he also needs Hannah to give him strength and release from his fears. Indeed, he believes that only his relationship with her enables him to function effectively as a revolutionary.

Yet the relationship between Hannah and Sonny is more complex than it might appear, for it has elements of selfishness. At one point, Sonny is present when one of his comrades is shot in a riot. In such a situation, he is expected to remain with the man who fell. Unfortunately, Hannah is present, unguarded, and Sonny ignores his duty, leaves the fallen man, and gets her to safety. The incident troubles Sonny, for he now realizes that Hannah is more to him than a help in his work. He needs her for himself, not merely as an aid to his work in the movement. In most situations, lovers recognize their own selfishness and forgive themselves because it is merely evidence that they are human. Unfortunately, the standards for revolutionaries are more exacting. Sonny's leaders would see his action in saving Hannah as a betrayal of the cause.

To William, it is very clear that Sonny's relationship with Hannah also involves betrayals of Aila, of Baby, and of himself. It is perhaps not surprising that after he has become Hannah's lover, Sonny changes toward Aila. Though still polite, he is secretive, distant, and cold. He even finds it distasteful to make love to his wife. Clearly, Aila is disturbed, but she fulfills her wifely functions, cooking the meals and tending to the children, perhaps assuming that it is merely the cause that has taken away her husband. Yet Sonny also distances himself from the children. He is often absent, ostensibly on missions but actually luxuriating in Hannah's bed, and when he is at home he is preoccupied, clearly no longer interested in guiding them.

For Baby, the loss of her father is devastating. Her orientation has always been social; unlike Will, she has never been studious. Therefore, without the father she depended on, she turns to unsavory peers and promiscuity. Eventually, in an obvious cry for attention, she cuts her wrists and nearly dies. When Baby most needs him, however, Sonny is unavailable, not because he is involved in a political intrigue but because he is having one of his clandestine meetings with Hannah. After he returns to his home and finds out what happened in his absence, Sonny decides to make sure that such an episode cannot be repeated. He is not prepared to give up Hannah; the best he can do is to make sure that someone will always be able to find him when he is with her. He cannot tell his leaders; they would order him to dissolve the relationship. The only person he can depend on is his son. Now, having betrayed Aila by his infidelity and deceit and having abandoned Baby, Sonny is ready to betray the third member of his family by making him an accessory to adultery.

Bribed with a motorbike, Will seems contented with the arrangement. He remains studious; he stays out of trouble. It is clear, however, that the damage to Will is as serious as the damage to Baby. Will has no perception of the real love that Sonny feels for Hannah; he sees only a middle-aged man who is trying to prove his virility, and in his adolescent dreams, Will himself takes his father's place in bed with the blonde woman and then shares his father's guilt as the betrayer of Aila.

Eventually, Aila rebels, and she follows Baby into an extremist group. When she returns, Sonny once again disappears for an idyllic weekend with Hannah, and once again, a family disaster occurs, this time Aila's arrest for possessing weapons of terrorism. Her political position makes Sonny's seem conservative.

Some readers might misinterpret *My Son's Story* as being simply a description of the results of adultery or, more broadly, of the results of choosing a political responsibility over one's family responsibilities. Neither of these fairly represents Gordimer's intention. She is above all a realist. As in *July's People* (1981), she is simply exploring the complex relationships between the personal and the political. Probably, given his environment, when he joined the movement Sonny made the only choice he could make. As a realist, however, Gordimer must point out the consequences of his choice and leave it to her readers to decide difficult questions such as whether those consequences were the inevitable result of his choice or the result of a personal involvement that could and should have been avoided.

My Son's Story is also the story of three women who must deny their instincts because they live in a society in turmoil. By nature, Aila is happy in her traditional role; although she works hard to complete her education, she likes being in her home, caring for her husband and her children. There is great courage in her quiet struggle to preserve some semblance of family life, even after her husband has turned away from her and abandoned his responsibilities for his children. Nevertheless, Aila cannot be patient forever. When she cuts her hair, she is symbolically rejecting her traditional role, and she eventually joins the terrorists.

Baby, too, finds it difficult to be a woman in a turbulent society. At first, her promiscuity is a reaction to her father's indifference. Eventually, however, she turns to political action. Fleeing the country with her extremist husband, she proceeds to begin rearing their baby in a camp where young people are trained as revolutionaries.

Ironically, Sonny is troubled when his wife and daughter abandon their traditional roles, though it is the fact that Hannah is not traditional that has attracted him to her. While Aila represented order, even in her housekeeping, Hannah represents the chaos, the excitement, and the disruption of the revolution itself. At the end of the novel, however, Sonny must pay the price women have so often had to pay for loving men. It is Hannah, not Sonny, who is offered an exciting job and must move; Sonny is left behind, out of power because he has compromised himself at the request of Hannah, while the three women in his life, all of whom have freed themselves from traditional roles, take his place in leading the struggle for political freedom.

My Son's Story illustrates the fact that while Gordimer is dedicated to the defeat of racism, she rejects the easy answers that make many works with a political dimension essentially dishonest. Whether her protagonists are whites coming to understand and to change their own deep-seated attitudes, as in *The Lying Days* (1953) and *The Conservationist* (1974), or blacks similarly learning to examine their own roles and motivations, as in *My Son's Story*, they may be expected to suffer, but also to develop as human beings, in proportion to their own sensitivity and complexity. It is Gordimer's honesty in creating her characters and in reflecting life as she sees it that makes her a major contemporary novelist.

Rosemary M. Canfield Reisman

Sources for Further Study

Booklist. LXXXVII, September 15, 1990, p. 99.
Chicago Tribune. October 14, 1990, XIV, p. 3.
Kirkus Reviews. LVIII, August 15, 1990, p. 1115.
Library Journal. CXV, November 1, 1990, p. 123.
London Review of Books. XII, September 13, 1990, p. 17.
Los Angeles Times Book Review. October 28, 1990, p. 3.
New Statesman and Society. III, September 21, 1990, p. 40.
The New York Review of Books. XXXVII, November 8, 1990, p. 8.

The New York Times Book Review. XCV, October 21, 1990, p. 1.
Newsweek. CXVI, October 1, 1990, p. 68.
Publishers Weekly. CCXXXVII, August 17, 1990, p. 53.
Time. CXXXVI, October 29, 1990, p. CT12.
The Times Literary Supplement. September 28, 1990, p. 1037.

MY TRAITOR'S HEART
A South African Exile Returns to Face His Country, His Tribe, and His Conscience

Author: Rian Malan (1954-   )
Publisher: Atlantic Monthly Press (New York). 349 pp. $19.95
Type of work: Autobiography/contemporary political and social history
Time: The 1950's to 1980's
Locale: South Africa

An Afrikaner attempts to come to terms with the racial dilemmas of South Africa by delving deep into his own psyche and by chronicling the murder and mayhem that disfigure his country

> *Principal personage:*
> RIAN MALAN, an Afrikaner, scion of a family that settled South Africa
> more than three hundred years ago

There was a telling moment during Nelson Mandela's conquering-hero tour of the United States in 1990: President Bush, standing together with Mandela on the White House lawn, called on him to follow Dr. Martin Luther King's example of pursuing change through nonviolent means. Mandela coolly replied that the President did not understand the situation in South Africa. It was a remarkable incident: the leader of black South Africa telling the President of the United States that as far as South Africa was concerned, he did not know what he was talking about. Rian Malan's compelling and harrowing book, *My Traitor's Heart: A South African Exile Returns to Face His Country, His Tribe, and His Conscience,* tends to confirm what that moment on the White House lawn implied: Only a South African can understand South Africa—and then only after much soul-searching and ruthlessly honest thinking. Malan is well suited to the task. He possesses a relentless introspection reminiscent of Leo Tolstoy; he writes with a novelist's storytelling skill; and he pursues his inquiries with the dogged persistence of an investigative reporter. His anger—the anger of a decent, moral, and intelligent man forced to contemplate a horrible situation in which he is inextricably bound up—is sometimes barely under control. *My Traitor's Heart* is the kind of book which leaves the reader feeling drained: shocked, horrified, yet also humble. It also gives brilliant insight into the dilemma which faces white South Africans today.

Rian Malan is a member of a prominent Afrikaner family which has played a significant role in the last three centuries of South Africa's turbulent history. His ancestor was Jacques Malan, a Huguenot refugee who in the seventeenth century was deported to the Dutch colony at the Cape of Good Hope. The Malans were present at all the most critical moments in South African history: They fought in the Zulu wars, and in both wars against the British. Rian Malan is related to Daniel François Malan, who became one of the chief architects of apartheid when the Afrikaner National Party came to power in 1948. Another relative, General Magnus

Malan, was South African Minister of Defense during the black uprising in 1976.

Even as a young boy, however, Rian Malan never embraced the Afrikaner attitude that (as he puts it) the blacks must be kept down lest they rise up and slit white throats: "I was never much of a Boer," he comments. He describes growing up in a wealthy white suburban home in Johannesburg in the 1950's and 1960's. As a teenager, much of his life was not greatly different from that of his counterparts in the United States: drugs, alcohol, long hair, rock music, left-wing politics. Rebellion against the harsh and narrow-minded ideology of Afrikanerdom came easily to him. At the age of thirteen, he became, in his own eyes, the Just White Man, champion of the oppressed. He found that he spontaneously loved blacks (who were still known as natives in those days), and he embraced African culture, organizing fund drives for black education.

In the early 1970's, during the heyday of what Malan calls the "imperial Calvinist tyranny" of South Africa, Malan secured a job on *The Star*, a liberal English-language newspaper in Johannesburg. As a magistrates'-court reporter, and later a crime reporter during the Soweto uprising in 1976, he received firsthand insight into the muggings, murder, and violent rebellion that became part of everyday life in the township. Armageddon seemed to be hovering in the air, and Malan came face-to-face with so many horrific crimes, including voodoo killings, that in his mind Soweto came to resemble Europe in the Dark Ages. Although he wrote a number of op-ed pieces attributing the crime to bad social conditions, he realized, in opposition to some white assumptions about innate black criminality, that the matter was not as simple as that.

One of the great merits of *My Traitor's Heart* is that Malan has the honesty and intelligence to look deep inside his own heart, and to confess that the picture he liked to present of himself as the Just White Man was not the entire truth. In examining his own "secret racist heart" he succeeds in illuminating the complexity of race relations in South Africa, the frightening collision of two alien cultures. At the core of the book lies a paradox, which Malan identifies but can never fully resolve. During his years as a reporter, he began to realize that although he had always loved blacks, he had always been scared of them as well; he hated the injustices which had been done to them, but was horrified by the violence they were capable of, both against whites and against themselves. Fear gripped him whenever he ventured into Soweto, and he began to question whether he was really on the side of the blacks. Seeing only nihilism and rage in the Soweto uprising, he feared that the violence might eventually swallow him up too, simply because his skin was white. Civil war broke out in his own brain.

In 1977 Malan left South Africa, partly to avoid the military draft (he decided he was not going to carry a gun for apartheid), but mainly because he was afraid of what the future held for South Africa. Unable to choose one side or the other, and aware that there seemed to be no middle ground, he ran away from the paradox. After traveling through Europe for a few years he ended up in Los Angeles in 1979, writing rock and roll reviews for a small music magazine. During the time Malan

was in the United States, Steve Biko, the leader of the Black Consciousness movement in South Africa, died in police custody; Pieter Botha came to power and in-
stituted some liberalizing reforms, which were followed in 1984 by a fresh outbreak
of violence and black rebellion. As more and more whites fled the country, Malan
began to feel himself a traitor to everyone—to his black friends on *The Star*, to the
Afrikaners, and to himself. Feeling that he was not facing up to the situation in
which history had placed him, he returned to South Africa, to resume work as a
crime reporter and to resolve the paradox "in tales of the way we killed one another."

In part 2 of *My Traitor's Heart*, Malan traces the lives and deaths of many different types of South African individuals, black and white, who were caught up in
the tragedy of the times. Malan's vivid narrative produces some moving human stories; a recurring theme is that nothing has really changed from the days of frontier
violence between Boer and black in the early period of white colonization ("Once
frontier, still frontier.")

Many of the stories are both heartbreaking and horrifying, and Malan does not
spare his reader the grisly details. One example is of a black man named Dennis
Mosheshwe, who made the mistake of being "cheeky" to his wife's Boer employer.
Mosheshwe was kidnapped and taken to a group of Boers—men, women, and children—who were enjoying a traditional *braaivleis* (an open-air barbecue). Just to
teach him a lesson, the black man was beaten, tied up, and subjected to a barbaric
torture which finally killed him. The white man responsible for his death later received a seven-year prison term. On the same day he was sentenced, a member of
the banned African National Congress, who had been caught in possession of revolutionary pamphlets, received a ten-year term.

Then there was the story of young Moses Mope, told to Malan by his father.
Moses was a church-going teenager from a black township outside Pretoria. He took
no part in politics, but one night he and some of his companions were mistaken by
the police for "comrades" (black activists). In the chase that followed, Moses Mope
was set upon and beaten to death by a white policeman. A police constable was later
charged with culpable homicide, but was acquitted. Mope was only one of 750
blacks to die in thirteen months of violence which began in 1984.

But there is another side to the violence: For example, an idealistic, white, foreign
doctor who worked in a black hospital in Soweto, was knocked off his motorcycle
and attacked by a mob wielding steel fence poles—a victim of what Malan calls the
"law of genetic complicity," under which any white person, whether they sympathized with the black cause or not, might become a target for murder. One of the
most harrowing tales is of a murderer known as the Hammerman, who bludgeoned
four whites to death with a hammer while they slept in their beds at night in the town
of Empangeni, ninety miles north of Durban. Malan uses the story as a symbol of
the fear and sense of guilt under which white South Africans live. The Hammerman,
who turned out to be a thirty-five-year-old black named Simon Mpungose, became a
hero to the local Zulus. Malan calls him a black Everyman, a classic case of a man

warped by apartheid. Following a hopelessly deprived childhood, the Hammerman had ended up in Barberton Prison, the most notorious in the country, where he tried several times to commit suicide. During his incarceration he had a prophetic dream in which he killed a white person with the hammer that he used to break rocks. Given that he was a Zulu, he interpreted the dream as a message from his ancestors which revealed his destiny. Fulfilling it would relieve him of his torment. Although he tried hard to resist the command, he eventually accepted his destiny, and at his trial he frequently said that he was now at peace and ready to die.

Malan uses the story to exemplify the clash of irreconcilable cultures in South Africa—a recurring theme of the book. Beliefs and practices that are difficult for the Western mind to understand flourish among black South Africans. Many of them, for example, put their beds on stacks of bricks to thwart a ground-hugging night gremlin called the *tokoloshe*; in 1985, there were 10,000 *sangomas* and *inyangas* (witch doctors, or traditional healers) practicing in greater Johannesburg, who were consulted by 85 percent of all black households. In one violent industrial dispute, a witch doctor promised that his medicine could turn the white man's bullets into water, and this accounted for the lack of fear shown by black workers when confronted with a water cannon. For Malan, this brings out a curious paradox: White liberals in South Africa tend to ignore these cultural differences, because to acknowledge them would seem to play into the hands of one of apartheid's underlying tenets—that there are immutable distinctions between races. Malan also believes that the picture of South Africa presented in the American media is a false one, consisting mostly of "caricatural white villains and black victims," and largely ignoring the horrific black-on-black violence (people having their ears lopped off for breaking boycotts, for example, or being forced to drink detergent for violating "don't buy white" campaigns, not to mention the unspeakably vicious internecine warfare, much of it conducted by teenagers, between the Black Consciousness movement and the combined African National Congress and United Democratic Front).

Having carefully guided his reader through this modern-day hell, Malan does his best to conclude on a note of hope. He tells the extraordinary story of a courageous white couple, Neil and Creina Alcock, who chose to settle in the barren district of Msinga, in one of the self-governing Zulu homelands. For twenty years they lived like black Africans, sharing their privations and learning to see African problems through African eyes. Neil Alcock pioneered agricultural development projects in the most unpromising places, using African methods and African technologies. For a time these projects met with considerable success, before the inhospitable climate defeated their best efforts. Even though the story ended in betrayal—Neil Alcock met a violent death, caught in the crossfire between rival Zulu factions—the Zulus venerated his memory almost as one of their own, and Malan believes that the Alcocks' "investment of love" in this forgotten part of Africa possesses permanent significance. It offers a glimpse of "light beyond the darkness—a tiny pinprick of dawning possibilities, casting just enough of a glow to show the rest of us the way." Although this seems more like the visionary hope of the poet than the reasoned optimism of the political analyst, the reader will be grateful for the tranquility it offers as the conclusion to a book which for the most part burns in the mind like angry fire.

Bryan Aubrey

Sources for Further Study

Foreign Affairs. LXIX, Summer, 1990, p. 191
London Review of Books. XII, April 19, 1990, p. 9.
Los Angeles Times Book Review. February 4, 1990, p. 1.
Maclean's. CIII, February 5, 1990, p. 65.
The Nation. CCLI, July 30, 1990, p. 134.
New York. XXIII, January 15, 1990, p. 59.
The New York Times Book Review. XCV, January 21, 1990, p. 3.
The New Yorker. LXVI, May 7, 1990, p. 110.
Newsweek. CXV, January 22, 1990, p. 63.
Publishers Weekly. CCXXXVI, November 10, 1989, p. 52.
Time. CXXXV, April 16, 1990, p. 79.
The Times Literary Supplement. May 4, 1990, p. 482.
The Washington Post Book World. XX, January 21, 1990, p. 3.

NO LAUGHING MATTER
The Life and Times of Flann O'Brien

Author: Anthony Cronin (1926-   )
First published: 1989, in Great Britain
Publisher: Grafton Books (London). Distributed by Trafalgar Square/David & Charles (North Pomfret, Vermont). Illustrated. 260 pp. $39.95
Type of work: Literary biography
Time: 1911-1966
Locale: Ireland, principally Dublin

This full-length biography of the Irish satiric novelist and columnist emphasizes his accomplishment in the novel while accounting for the influence of Irish place and intellectual environment

> *Principal personages:*
> BRIAN O'NOLAN, also known as FLANN O'BRIEN and MYLES NA GOPALEEN, Irish novelist and newspaper columnist
> MICHAEL O'NOLAN, his father
> AGNES O'NOLAN, his mother
> EVELYN O'NOLAN, his wife

Flann O'Brien was a novelist; Myles na Gopaleen (properly na gCopaleen) was a newspaper columnist and author of one short novel in Irish; Brian O'Nolan (sometimes Nolan, sometimes O Nualláin) was, for more than eighteen years, a civil servant in the Local Government Office of the Irish government. All three were the same person—Brian O'Nolan, to give him his birth name. Anthony Cronin has well handled both the combinations of the three and the distinctions among the three.

Cronin's choice of the name Flann O'Brien for his subtitle clearly suggests the emphasis of the book—on the novelist. While by no means neglecting the other personas, Cronin is clear that the significance of this many-faced writer is to be found principally in his accomplishment in the novel, an accomplishment based on only four novels: *At Swim-Two-Birds* (1939)—the title is a literal translation of the place-name Snámh Da Ean, a resting place of King Sweeney in Irish mythology; *The Third Policeman* (1967), written by 1940 but rejected by the publisher and not published until after O'Brien's death; and *The Hard Life* (1961) and *The Dalkey Archive* (1964), both of which were written in his last years while he suffered various physical maladies exacerbated by drink.

Though all these novels differ widely in their ostensible subjects (from Irish mythology to a Dublin man's desire to provide public conveniences for women), they have a number of similar characteristics. The most notable is that all are fantastic or wildly impossible. Also—unusual for "modern" novels—they are almost entirely devoid of sex and have little place for women at all. In addition, as Cronin points out, while they may be witty in parts, they are not very good at dialogue; this was a weakness that asserted itself in latter years when O'Brien, in need of money, attempted to write scripts for Irish television comedies. In a deeper vein, all the novels are characterized by Cronin as postmodern, suggesting a grim universe, an avoidance of the traditional methods of novel construction, and a generally existential view. For example, it is not at all uncommon in contemporary novels to see the writer using the ploy of basing his story on a writer who is writing a novel about a writer who is writing a novel and whose characters take on lives of their own. Yet this technique was certainly something new and different in 1939, when O'Brien published *At Swim-Two-Birds*. In a sense, just as Laurence Sterne's *Tristram Shandy* (1759-1767) prefigured many of the devices of James Joyce's *Ulysses* (1922), so O'Brien created for his novels structures and a worldview that it would take other modern novelists thirty years and more to catch up with.

The very organization of Cronin's biography makes a pointed and ironic comment on the life of its subject. There are four sections to the work, of which the first, "Origins," is a fairly straightforward account of O'Brien's antecedents and upbringing. The second chapter, "The Brilliant Beginning," is by far the longest, covering O'Brien's life from his entry into University College, Dublin, to age thirty-five, at the end of World War II. This chapter is longer than any two other chapters put together and is just under half of the whole text. The third chapter, "The Dubliner," is heavily anecdotal, filled with Dublin names, among them that of Anthony Cronin. The final chapter, "The Close," is short and sad, as O'Brien's health declines and his drinking and need for money grow. This organization indicates, as indeed Cronin's text makes clear, that after the brilliant beginning there was, sadly, little development and no glorious close.

Flann O'Brien was born (as Brian O'Nolan) in 1911 in Strabane, County Tyrone, now in Northern Ireland. His father was a civil servant in the Customs and Excise, and the family moved several times, finally settling in Dublin. From his father, who died in 1937, O'Brien seems to have inherited his own spirit of exactness and even pedantry. His father also was a dedicated Irish speaker and transmitted his love for and skill in that language to his son; Irish was the language of the household for many years. His father's disapproval of schools conducted in English led him to keep his three eldest sons (Brian was the third) at home until they had moved to Dublin, where the three were finally sent to an English-speaking school; apparently the father did not object by this time.

O'Brien attended University College, Dublin (UCD), obtaining his B.A. in 1932 in Irish and German. He went on to take an M.A. with a thesis entitled "Nature in Irish Poetry." He was well known at UCD for his efforts in student debating societies and for his contributions to college publications. In 1935 he also applied to, and was accepted by, the Irish Civil Service. He spent the next eighteen years rising through the ranks of civil servants in the Local Government Office. He was, until near the end of his career, a conscientious and able official, achieving regular promotion and good recommendations from his superiors.

With the death of his father, O'Brien, as the eldest son living at home and the only one bringing in a steady income, became the main support of his mother and his nine younger brothers and sisters. It is from this time that money worries began to plague him. Though his salary from the Civil Service was quite sufficient for a bachelor living at home, it did not go all that far toward keeping up a house and providing for a large family. It must be said, however, that this was a responsibility that O'Brien clearly accepted and did not try to escape.

His career as novelist was now under way (*At Swim-Two-Birds* would be published in 1939 by the English firm of Longman's upon the advice of its reader, Graham Greene); he continued to be the proper and meticulous civil servant; and in 1940 he took a new name, Myles na Gopaleen, for a sometimes daily newspaper column entitled "Cruiskeen Lawn" for the *Irish Times*. A rough translation of the title would be "The Little Full Jug." It was a humorous, often satiric production in which the author aimed his darts at a wide variety of Dublin and Irish topics and foibles. The columns were between five and six hundred words long and were first published in Irish; for a time they alternated Irish and English and eventually came to be almost entirely in English. O'Brien continued with the column until the very last years of his life. Na Gopaleen's common topics in the column included the follies and foolishness of the romantic, peasant-worshiping, Gaelic League mentality of many Irish nationalists; the doings and sayings of "The Brother"; collections of clichés; the proper running of the Irish railways; the doings and splendid puns of the resurrected poets Keats and Chapman. These and other running topics made the name of Myles na Gopaleen current in the Dublin of the 1940's and 1950's. In his own day and time, O'Brien was best known for his *Irish Times* columns, so much so that among his acquaintances in the many pubs he frequented he was commonly known and addressed as Myles. Ultimately, a succession of columns to which a government minister took exception caused the forced retirement of Brian O'Nolan in 1953.

In 1940 occurred one of the stranger incidents in O'Brien's life. He had completed the manuscript of a second novel, *The Third Policeman*, which was rejected by the publisher of his first novel and could not be placed elsewhere by his literary agents. O'Brien squirreled the manuscript away, put about rumors that it had been lost or destroyed in various ways, and never tried again to publish it, even later in life when his reputation as a novelist had begun to grow. It was not published until 1967, after his death. It was common for O'Brien for the last twenty years or so of his life to detest, or at least to affect to detest, both his first novels, denigrating them as juvenilia. Meanwhile, in 1941, Myles na Gopaleen published a short novel in Irish, *An Béal Bocht* (translated in 1973 as *The Poor Mouth*). This was a hilarious and often sharp satire of those Irish who romanticized the language and culture of the peasantry of the West of Ireland.

In 1948, Brian O'Nolan married Evelyn McDonnell, to the great astonishment of his friends; they had come to regard him as a natural bachelor. It is one of the small lacks in Cronin's book that she never becomes more than a shadowy figure. Not much is said of her, though by what accounts there are she was strongly supportive of him while remaining much of a homebody. She put up with the vagaries of his later years, at least in public, with patience and calm.

Through the 1940's and 1950's, Myles na Gopaleen was at the height of his powers; Brian O'Nolan was becoming less and less attentive to his duties as a civil servant; and Flann O'Brien was mostly silent. There were only two novels left to come during O'Brien's lifetime: *The Hard Life* and *The Dalkey Archive*. The first is a wildly improbable tale of a group of Dublin folk, led by Mr. Collopy, to attempt to get the Irish government (and eventually the Vatican) to supply public conveniences for women. It is short, satiric, and highly entertaining, but does not, in Cronin's view, advance the reputation of O'Brien much. The second work is probably O'Brien's least successful work. It borrows from the then still unpublished *The Third Policeman*, its structure is even more confusing than usual for O'Brien, and the characters seem more symbols and mouthpieces than interesting people. O'Brien died, ironically enough to some, on All Fools' Day, 1966.

Throughout the work, Cronin makes it clear that autobiographical statements from Brian O'Nolan, Myles na Gopaleen, and Flann O'Brien are often to be viewed with considerable suspicion. O'Brien liked to spread stories about himself and make claims. For example, Cronin investigates O'Brien's claim to have spent several months in Germany, studying the language and literature; in fact, the best that Cronin is able to discover is that O'Brien spent no more than two weeks, if that, on a sort of tour. Cronin finds the claim that O'Brien was at one time one of the many authors of the popular Sexton Blake books highly unlikely and almost certainly not true. O'Brien's claim to have spent several months in hard research in the Reading Room of the British Museum is clearly false.

O'Brien was, at least at his best, a satiric writer of genius. He had a hatred of cant and, like all great comic writers, was ultimately deadly serious. He was a bit of a loner, surprisingly shy, and not a great conversationalist, except when he had taken sufficient drink. He had a basic irreverence and cynicism that, as he grew older, came to appear as a bitter, sarcastic denigrating of almost everything. His humor was highly intellectual and verbal, and no doubt became more and more of a shield against a basic insecurity and an increasing need of reassurance. He found himself an intellectual and sophisticated writer, trapped, partly by his own decisions, in a narrow and isolated city and country; at the most critical time in his career he was cut off from the outside world by economic boycott, by World War II, and, most of all, by the dulling peasant and bourgeois values that he saw about him.

Several themes recur throughout Cronin's book. The most important is the novel *At Swim-Two-Birds*. Comments about the novel appear again and again, not only where the publication of the book is dealt with. This is certainly for Cronin O'Brien's major work (as many another critic would agree). To some extent it was a millstone around O'Brien's neck, as he could never quite manage to match it or to seek new directions. It is the cornerstone of O'Brien's achievement, and Cronin refers all other works to it.

On the more strictly biographical level, money was a consuming topic in O'Brien's life. Drink is also mentioned repeatedly on the pages of the book. By the 1940's, O'Brien was a confirmed whiskey drinker, and after his resignation from the Civil Service he was never seen to be sober past the afternoon. No doubt, some of his money problems could be traced to the outlay for large quantities of drink. Cronin also asserts often how O'Brien, in spite of his cynicism and personal failings, was born and remained a quite straightforward Roman Catholic, admittedly with Manichaean tendencies, tendencies not uncommon in the Ireland and the Irish church of the day. Finally, Cronin is at pains to assure the reader that O'Brien's lengthy bachelorhood was not the result of some sexual problem but a common and even natural condition supported by traditional Irish customs and life-styles.

Cronin makes it clear that this is not a book of literary criticism; it is a biography, and the life of O'Brien remains paramount. Cronin does examine the main themes and structures of O'Brien's works and judges their quality, but he does not supply lengthy analyses. In his preface, Cronin specifically points out that his work is a "life *and* times," as the subtitle makes clear. While Cronin does not supply lengthy descriptions of background of place and time, he certainly gives sufficient space to necessary topics. He is excellent at supplying brief, often simply two- or four-paragraph, treatments of such topics as Ireland during World War II, wartime Dublin, the ideas and conduct of the Gaelic Leaguers, and the attitudes to marriage of that time and place.

This is a fine biography of an interesting and important figure in twentieth century Irish letters, done with great understanding and even sympathy by an author who knew his subject personally but is in no way blinded to his faults. It is exceptionally well written by one who is himself a considerable figure in current Irish letters.

Gordon N. Bergquist

Sources for Further Study

Booklist. LXXXVI, July, 1990, p. 2061.
Boston Globe. July 10, 1990, p. 24.
Kirkus Review. LVIII, May 15, 1990, p. 703.
Listener. CXXII, October 26, 1989, p. 34.
New Statesman and Society. II, November 3, 1989, p. 38.
The Observer. October 22, 1989, p. 48.
Publishers Weekly. CCXXXVII, May 25, 1990, p. 47.
Punch. CCXCVII, November 17, 1989, p. 44.
The Spectator. CCLXIII, October 28, 1989, p. 35.
The Times Literary Supplement. October 27, 1989, p. 1171.

NOTES OF A HANGING JUDGE
Essays and Reviews, 1979-1989

Author: Stanley Crouch (1945-   )
Publisher: Oxford University Press (New York). 275 pp. $22.95
Type of work: Social criticism

A collection of searching, piercing essays and reviews that deal with the ambivalence and profound ambiguities of being an African American at the end of the Civil Rights movement

Public discussions of emotionally charged issues such as civil rights or affirmative action typically descend into an exchange of clichés, of "politically correct" statements that mask the absence of a deeper consideration of what is at stake for the future of a common and united American experience and culture. Too often, such discussions merely generate a tense uneasiness for most in the audience and a resignation to the damning fact that all has been heard and that the only task left is simply the assigning of blame for a certain state of affairs. To assume otherwise is to belabor the obvious and to wander in naïve and errant optimism. Rare is the thinker who can penetrate to the heart of race-related issues in order to move beyond stereotypes and intractable generalizations.

In this collection of thirty-seven disparate essays and reviews written between 1979-1989, Stanley Crouch, former jazz columnist and itinerant social critic for New York City's *The Village Voice*, proves he is exactly such a thinker. *Notes of a Hanging Judge* brings together an eclectic set of pieces that nevertheless emanate from a single, piercing vision that refuses to accept the received wisdom about race and class in contemporary America. They chronicle a decade of Crouch's nonconformist musings on what he calls "the Age of Redefinition," by which he means an age in which both disillusionment with and confusion about the recent past and its meaning dominate our society, placing the African American in particular historical peril and perplexity. The Civil Rights movement, Crouch avers, helped in many ways to transform a fossilized, comfortably racist America and to make it possible to envision a new kind of community in which both dominant and dissenting cultures could thrive and even merge in peace and harmony.

Yet, the opportunity for such a society has been lost, Crouch believes, because the black community has largely accepted the dogma of racial preferentialism, forgetting the emphasis that Martin Luther King, Jr. placed on developing a society in which people are judged as individuals, "by the content of their character rather than the color of their skin." Relinquishing this quest for equality, Crouch argues, has bred an ideology of blood guilt and a reliance on unproductive sloganeering that reduces rather than enlarges black character.

The phrase "by the content of their character" in many ways encoded the ethos of the Civil Rights movement and recalls the ideal, as expressed in the 1960's, of a "color-blind" society. In reading Crouch, one can look back on that period with some nostalgia as well as some alarm, as the color-blind society has not, apparently, been achieved and now is seldom even sought let alone held up as a rallying metaphor. This is the case partly, some would argue, because of the dubious success of the Civil Rights movement in making the ethnicity of racism's victims such a prominent feature of the proffered solutions offered by both white and black political leaders. The result is ever-increasing race consciousness and racial bickering.

To such an assessment, Crouch would say "Amen." Believing that he is part of an "undeclared lost generation," Crouch searches for the key that will rescue his contemporaries in the larger dominant culture and his peers in the black community from a noble cause that has now "gone loco." He seeks nothing less than an end to what he regards as a debilitating politics of victimhood that serves to promote only the twin evils of racial warfare and self-segregation. In this posture, Crouch writes courageously and courts alienation from mainstream black activists who, perhaps, most need to hear his contrary opinions of their exploits. Against seasoned politicos such as Jesse Jackson or pop culture avatars such as Spike Lee, Crouch mounts a convincing argument that they are too comfortable in fomenting stereotypes of both white and black culture that engender the breakdown of a once hoped-for community of shared values between the two groups.

Like his fellow dissenting black writers and social commentators Shelby Steele, Thomas Sowell, and Anne Wortham, Crouch is hard to classify politically; is he, as the *National Review's* Brad Miner wonders, a "liberal, neo-liberal, neo-conservative, or what?" Whereas it is unlikely that Crouch would be happy being labeled a "conservative," much of his criticism of the legacy of the Civil Rights movement—as well as his depiction of the more elusive problems of black family life—sounds the familiar themes of self-help and the appeal to color-blind justice associated with Reagan-era policymaking.

Merely to categorize the focus of Crouch's cumulative wisdom on these matters as politically to the left or to the right is to misconstrue both his intent and the nature of these essays. Crouch is writing not only to or for minorities, but for all Americans— trapped as they are in the morass of their own history and failed attempts to bring equal rights before law to all citizens. For non-black readers, Crouch provides an uncommonly incisive entry point into the world of black culture for the ignorant outsider. In essay after essay, Crouch's unblinking eye guides the naïve, uninitiated reader into the labyrinthine experience of minorities more skillfully than perhaps any other writer since James Baldwin. Rather than stacking up familiar indictments about racism and bigotry among whites, Crouch prefers to contemplate and champion the epic nature of African-American experience, and thereby to register the hope that Americans can unlearn from the past and recent history as much as they may have learned.

Crouch's subject matter is varied. He heads the collection with his most recent piece, a profile of Jesse Jackson on the campaign stump in the 1988 presidential campaign, and he expends many pages on the vicissitudes of black political culture. His last piece is a dazzling tour de force that captures the ambience and aura of an Italian jazz festival. Throughout the collection, Crouch authoritatively addresses aesthetic issues within and without black culture, as well as the interactions between the black community and various subcultures such as the feminist and homosexual liberation movements in their appropriation of the tactics of the 1960's Civil Rights establishment. The index catalogs a breathtaking scope of personages, books, and ideas on which Crouch has offered a refreshingly wry assessment or comparison. In his own words, Crouch is "primarily interested in those affirmations of human value that have brought about reconsiderations of history, the arts, and heavy-handed, demeaning, or soppy media images." As a consequence, Crouch has little patience with lazy or propagandistic aesthetics.

This passion is a particular feature of his redoubtably effective film and fiction criticism. With estimable skill, Crouch pronounces some devastating judgments on the aesthetics of several prominent black artists, including in his collection two particularly scathing reviews of the work of filmmaker Spike Lee and novelist Toni Morrison. Writing of Spike Lee's *Do the Right Thing* (1989), Crouch first praises Lee's technical skill as a director and his gift for comedy and then does not equivocate in accusing him of prostituting his art to exploit racial aggression. In the slashing climax to his unabashedly negative review, Crouch ponders Lee's success with critics, particularly white liberals:

> It is precisely because Lee can make audiences laugh that the fascist aesthetic he follows with such irresponsible deliberation slips the critical noose. Intellectually, he is like John Wayne Gacy in his clown suit, entertaining those who cannot believe the bodies buried under his house.

For Crouch, Lee's films try to wish away the "unarguable persistence of a declining racism"; the result is cinema that panders to "[i]ntellectual cowardice, opportunism, and the itch for riches by almost any means necessary," that is, propaganda in the service of personal wealth and glory.

Compared with his decimation of Spike Lee, Crouch's treatment of Toni Morrison's prizewinning *Beloved* (1987), a brutal chronicle of slavery and its effects on the black psyche, is almost charitable. In citing Morrison's skill, he nevertheless proceeds to undermine the reader's confidence in it: "Morrison, unlike Alice Walker, has real talent . . . but she perpetually interrupts her narrative with maudlin ideological commercials." Doctrinaire ideology is the enemy, Crouch pleads, of artistic achievement and of black advancement in particular, and he proclaims that *Beloved* was written to placate feminists who earnestly desire "that the vision of black woman as the most scorned and rebuked of the victims doesn't weaken." Art that attempts to sentimentalize atrocity thus demeans the artist and the people she seeks to redeem. Crouch's summary comment is lit up by mordant wit:

> *Beloved*, above all else, is a blackface holocaust novel. It seems to have been written in order to enter American slavery into the big-time martyr ratings contest, a contest usually won by references to, and works about, the experience of Jews at the hands of Nazis.

Perhaps Crouch's most daring piece is his coverage of the Bernhard Goetz case about the subway avenger who shot four black teenagers who allegedly attempted to extort money from him. Here Crouch finds not simply another example of white racism, but an essential insight into white fear about the real and imagined threats posed by a black underclass. Crouch suggests that whites "aren't troubled by Negroes per se. Their nemesis is the violent criminal who is too often construed as emblematic of the black underclass. I would suggest that their anger isn't so different from that of anyone humiliated by a person inferior in every way other than his ruthless willingness to intimidate or assault."

The major contribution of this collection remains Crouch's searing indictment of the self-styled messiahs of the black oppressed. The title of the collection is drawn from a line in his introduction to the collection in which he confesses he has outlived and outgrown many of his earlier allegiances and associations, and has come to reject many of the politically correct notions most black intellectuals are supposed to accept: "I have become something of a hanging judge, much like Henry Morgan, who sent many of his former pirate buddies to the gallows, certain that they deserved what they got." In Crouch's estimation, black activism has been wallowing in a "xenophobic darkness" and has retreated from the vision of universal humanism that animated the original Civil Rights movement.

In its place has come what Crouch calls an "ethnic nationalism," which strategically rejects the concept of universal equality commonly associated with the Judeo-Christian tradition and liberal Jeffersonian democracy. This concept views each individual as a unique creature of God who, bearing His image, inhabits a society of persons created equal and endowed with inalienable rights. The ethnic nationalist offers a progressive extrapolation of the individual from himself as a unique person. In this stratagem, personal identity is reallocated to an abstract class, race, or tribe; personhood is merged into the vagaries of a stereotyped, collectivist group-identity. Life becomes one grand class action against Western culture on behalf of the oppressed.

The marshaling of political forces behind racially based hiring and promotion procedures helps to create the notion that no individual as such exists, and that there is no universal personhood requisite to a man or woman except that which can be buttressed with the statistical credentials of the victimized minority. The fruit of this dissociation of individual uniqueness, character, and merit from the meaning of personhood is an antinomianism that dismisses the concept of equality before the law while flaunting it in the pursuit of power. The results, Crouch observes, can be seen in the disintegration of the black family.

Crouch is thus unsparing in his criticism of the "base opportunism" which he believes is at the heart of much contemporary racial activism: "[A]fter all these years of asserting that whites should vocally separate themselves from racists, demagogues, and hysterics in their midst, few black people in positions of responsibility are willing to do what they demand of others." Crouch is anxious to get on with the difficult business of learning how to live together as one multicultural people; yet, he is not blinded to its current impossibility. *Notes of a Hanging Judge* is his manifesto for declaring it possible even to imagine such a promise again.

Bruce L. Edwards

Sources for Further Study

American Spectator. XXIII, September, 1990, p. 35.
Booklist. LXXXVI, February 1, 1990, p. 1055.
Library Journal. CXV, February 15, 1990, p. 204.
Los Angeles Times. May 21, 1990, V, p. 1.
The Nation. CCL, May 21, 1990, p. 710.
National Review. XLII, June 11, 1990, p. 56.
The New York Times Book Review. XCV, March 11, 1990, p. 9.
Time. CXXXV, April 9, 1990, p. 92.
The Washington Post Book World. XX, April 8, 1990, p. 5.
Wilson Library Bulletin. LXV, September, 1990, p. 117.

NOTHING EVER HAPPENS TO THE BRAVE
The Story of Martha Gellhorn

Author: Carl Rollyson (1948-   )
Publisher: St. Martin's Press (New York). Illustrated. 398 pp. $24.95
Type of work: Biography
Time: 1908-1990
Locale: St. Louis, Missouri; New York; Florida, Cuba, Europe, Mexico; Africa; England

A comprehensive and sensitive biography of one of the leading women writers in twentieth century America, whose fiction and journalism were well received and influential, especially during America's years at war

> *Principal personages:*
> MARTHA GELLHORN, a journalist and fiction writer
> ERNEST HEMINGWAY, one of America's major voices in fiction in the twentieth century, Gellhorn's second husband
> ELEANOR ROOSEVELT, the wife of American president Franklin D. Roosevelt and a personal friend of Gellhorn
> BERTRAND DE JOUVENEL, a French writer and critic, Gellhorn's first husband
> DAVID GUREWITSCH, a prominent American physician, friend of Eleanor Roosevelt, and Gellhorn's lover
> T. S. MATTHEWS, a longtime editor of *Time* magazine, Gellhorn's third husband

Ask any well-read student of American literature who Martha Gellhorn is and the response will surely be, "One of Hemingway's wives." That, of course, is true. Gellhorn met Hemingway in Florida in 1936, struck up an intimate relationship almost immediately, and soon supplanted the novelist's second wife Pauline both in Hemingway's affections and then in his household. Those familiar with Hemingway's life know of Gellhorn's travels with him to Spain to cover the civil war there in the late 1930's, and of their separate ventures throughout the European war zone during the 1940's. Some might even recall that she was a journalist.

In some ways those stormy years with Hemingway, and the bitterness which each harbored for the other after their divorce, have colored perceptions of Gellhorn and obscured her contributions to America's understanding of the people and places ravaged by war throughout the world during this century. It will probably astonish the uninformed to discover exactly how prolific Gellhorn has been, and how respected she has been by fellow professionals. During her long career, she has published nearly 120 articles and stories, supporting herself through her writing (even during the four years when she was dallying with Hemingway before their marriage, and for some time afterward, too). These pieces appeared in the best periodicals in America: *Collier's* (for whom she worked during the years of the Spanish Civil War and during World War II), *The Saturday Evening Post*, *The New Republic*, *The Atlantic Monthly*, *Harper's*, the *Guardian*, *Story*, the *Paris Review*, *The Observer*, *The New Statesman*. Dozens of these pieces have been collected, and added to, in six volumes of short stories and three of nonfiction. Additionally, Gellhorn produced six novels, which, though not universally lauded, were nevertheless received quite well by many contemporary reviewers. That none has found its way into the canon of twentieth century American literature may in part be attributed to the fact that she has been considered too close to Hemingway to be truly original. Since most information about Gellhorn is generally gleaned from biographies about Hemingway or works that focus on his close male associates, it may be some time before the link is broken and Gellhorn is allowed to emerge in her own right among the literary figures who have shaped America's image of itself.

Carl Rollyson's *Nothing Ever Happens to the Brave: The Story of Martha Gellhorn* is a major step forward in helping to correct Gellhorn's damaged image. Though significant attention is given to Gellhorn's years with Hemingway, this biography covers her entire life. Beginning his narrative with a brief discussion of Gellhorn's grandparents and parents, Rollyson gives careful attention to all of Martha's hectic life: from her childhood as the only daughter of prominent St. Louis activist Edna Gellhorn to her years as a working journalist and world traveler. He tries to capture the independent spirit of the young woman who bent (or broke) rules at school, who spoke up for what she believed in even before she struck out on her own, and who left Bryn Mawr before graduation to seek a career in New York (much to the chagrin of her anguished father). Without question, Rollyson finds much to write about when dealing with the years after Gellhorn had established herself as a journalist and novelist and before she separated from Hemingway and began a life that might be described as semirecluse; from the beginning of the 1930's until after World War II she flitted across America and all over the globe, writing about what she saw and making headlines in her affairs with America's most notable living novelist. Rollyson devotes the last third of the work, however, to a discussion of Gellhorn's career after she and Hemingway separated, focusing on her growing involvement in social issues that pose threats to world peace and world prosperity.

To paraphrase Ralph Waldo Emerson, Gellhorn emerges as a Representative Woman—representative, certainly, of twentieth century women, independent, willing to take chances (even in life-threatening situations), interested in making a contribution to society outside the home. One gets a sense that Gellhorn may have been born too soon. Restless throughout all her four marriages, she seems out of place in the early and middle decades of the century. Her behavior and her sympathies would have made her a sister to the women of the 1970's and 1980's, who have been able to balance marriage, family, and career with less difficulty, largely because they have the support of public opinion. Though Gellhorn was not always concerned about public opinion, it is still apparent that she had to contend with significant disapproval from family, friends, associates, and the public at large.

Because of Gellhorn's wide circle of acquaintances, Rollyson's biography becomes more than simply biography. Through Gellhorn's eyes the reader sees many of the major political events of the century. Important people crossed her path, and with some of them she had more than a passing acquaintance. This is especially true of her relationship with Eleanor Roosevelt, who first befriended the youthful Gellhorn as a favor to Martha's mother. The two developed a close friendship and exchanged correspondence routinely for years; only when Martha began to be serious with David Gurewitsch, the handsome doctor for whom Mrs. Roosevelt felt a special fondness, did that friendship suffer any sign of strain. There are, too, the portraits of Gellhorn's three husbands, men successful in their own professions and in varying degrees famous outside their relationship with Gellhorn. Her years of courtship and marriage to Hemingway have been well documented, and Rollyson presents little that is new. What he does well, however, is to describe the Hemingway-Gellhorn relationship from Gellhorn's point of view. The same can be said of his handling of the story of Gellhorn's other marriages: Readers come to understand why a woman so independent-spirited as Martha could be drawn to marry repeatedly, then succumb repeatedly to the disappointments that inevitably followed pronouncement of the marriage vows.

Because Gellhorn made her living as a writer, Rollyson finds many opportunities to engage in literary criticism, discussing each of his subject's major works in the context of her life. Predictably, he gives most of her fiction an autobiographical interpretation; in most instances, though, such a reading seems justified by the text. Though the criticism only scratches the surface of Gellhorn's literary productions, what appears in *Nothing Ever Happens to the Brave* seems to be a good start toward an assessment of Gellhorn's merits as an author.

Rollyson tries hard to present a balanced portrait of his subject. He does not make more of Gellhorn than he should, or become too fulsome an apologist for her weaknesses. Generally, Rollyson's work is full of strengths: comprehensiveness, honesty, a balance between what Gellhorn had to say about events in her life and what others have observed about her. One gets a sense of Gellhorn's passion for activism, her intense need to get involved in various causes and to speak out both in print and in person whenever given the opportunity.

As a consequence, the weaknesses of this biography may not be apparent, but a careful review of the notes, bibliography, introduction, and supplementary materials suggests that Rollyson may not have been able to get as close to his subject as he would have liked. By his own admission, he was unable to meet with Gellhorn, and therefore was not able to give the text the personal touch that such an interview may have provided. He relies heavily on the spadework of others (though this is not to suggest that he has not dug deeply into the archives where the letters and other unpublished materials of those who knew Gellhorn and her friends and family are stored). He also seems to assume that those who were friends of Hemingway and who made unkind or disparaging remarks for Gellhorn had obviously done so because they were under Hemingway's spell. There is a strong possibility, not often admitted by Rollyson, that these people had formed independent opinions about Gellhorn—and that they simply were not taken with her. The overall sense one gets is that Rollyson's Gellhorn is a lot nicer than the person vilified by many who knew her.

None of these personal biases—either favorable or unfavorable—should detract from an appreciation of the professional accomplishments of this remarkably energetic and resourceful woman. Her contributions to American journalism, her ability to convey to her readers the horrors of war (especially the suffering of its innocent victims), and her achievements as a writer of fiction—all these merit recognition. Rollyson has filled that need with considerable scholarly skill and in a style that is readable and unobtrusive.

Laurence W. Mazzeno

Sources for Further Study

Booklist. LXXXVII, December 1, 1990, p. 694.
Kirkus Reviews. LVIII, October 15, 1990, p. 1443.
Library Journal. CXV, November 15, 1990, p. 76.
Los Angeles Times Book Review. December 16, 1990, p. 2.
The New York Times Book Review. XCV, December 30, 1990, p. 6.
Publishers Weekly. CCXXXVII, October 26, 1990, p. 61.
The Washington Post Book World. XXI, January 6, 1991, p. 3.

OMEROS

Author: Derek Walcott (1930-   )
Publisher: Farrar, Straus & Giroux (New York). 325 pp. $25.00
Type of work: Poetry
Time: The present as informed by the past through myth, history, and memory
Locale: St. Lucia, West Indies

This contemporary epic uses the timeless structure of myth to define history as a wound from which humanity strives continually to recover

> Principal characters:
>   OMEROS, the Homeric narrative voice of the poem present in various archetypal figures such as the blind sailor Seven Seas
>   ACHILLE, a fisherman whose life bears mythic similarities to that of the Greek hero Achilles
>   HECTOR, a fisherman turned taxicab driver; rival of Achille for Helen
>   HELEN, a domestic servant turned waitress, then shopkeeper; mistress of Hector
>   PHILOCTETE, a fisherman unable to work because of a festering leg wound; recalls the wounded Philoctetes of Greek myth
>   MAJOR DENNIS PLUNKETT, former British officer turned émigré pig farmer on St. Lucia
>   MAUD PLUNKETT, his Irish-born wife who commercially cultivates orchids

Modern poets have often relied on classical imagery to present their theories of history. William Butler Yeats saw history as a series of cycles, repetitions with variations to which only the poet-artist remained sensitive. Indeed, the poet-artist of Yeats is an adept in the mystical sense who rebuilds civilizations through art after those charged with safeguarding culture, the politicians and diplomats, have helped destroy old ways of life through their failures. In Yeats's poem "Leda and the Swan" (1923), the poet queries whether the raped Leda could have foreseen that the ultimate consequence of Helen's birth would be the death and destruction caused by the Trojan War. T. S. Eliot notes the spiritual failures of history, considering it a series of cunning passages and corridors, a labyrinth which deceives even as it informs. Like Tiresias, the title figure of his poem "Gerontion" (1920) has insight in blindness but prophesies to an unheeding world. This need to prophesy is the futile compulsion of Eliot's poet-artist. Nikos Kazantzakis, attempting to redirect positively the philosophy of Friedrich Nietzsche, which had been perverted by Nazism, extended the myth of Odysseus in his epic *Odyssia* (1938; *The Odyssey: A Modern Sequel*, 1958) to show that the history of human achievement is bound up with the will to endure and embrace challenge with enthusiasm. It is against this background that Derek Walcott, the distinguished poet born on the Caribbean island of St. Lucia, has written his epic *Omeros*, a poem worthy of the company of any of the above masterpieces.

Walcott's verse has a contemporary tone which recalls that of Kazantzakis; it also displays a predisposition toward wordplay, rather like the latter prose of James Joyce. Even so, Walcott is entirely his own master, and his poem functions simultaneously on three levels: mythic, historical, and contemporary. True to epic convention, *Omeros* opens in mid-action, the fishermen felling cedar trees to make new boats. The process is age-old, and the tree-gods willingly surrender themselves to the axes. The armada the boats form is not bound for Troy, but it does allow the fishermen continued subsistence. The blind seer Seven Seas functions as a contemporary Homer, recalling the indefinite identity of the blind ancient Greek poet. The name Seven Seas corresponds to Homer's own universality and emphasizes the universal application of human experience.

In Greek mythology, preparations for the Trojan War begin when the Trojan Paris, whom Homer calls Alexandros, convinces Helen, wife of the Spartan king Menelaos, to leave her husband and return with him to Troy. Pledged to defend Helen's marriage, Menelaos' brother Agamemnon recruits a massive armada of forces from various regions of the Greek world. These sail for Troy, and a ten-year war begins before Troy ultimately falls, ironically not through military might but through the strategy of the wooden horse. Walcott's Helen is variously seductive, inconstant, and sympathetic, just as she is in Greek myth; even so, she is an entirely contemporary figure, a poor native of St. Lucia, extremely proud and the object of much male attention because of her striking beauty. When given a yellow velvet dress by Maud Plunkett, the Anglo-Irish woman for whom she has worked as a domestic servant, Helen fittingly resembles a monarch butterfly. She regally flits along the beach, attracting the silent admiration of many men, including that of Maud's husband, Major Dennis Plunkett, a former British officer turned émigré pig farmer on St. Lucia.

In Walcott's epic, just as in those of Homer, Helen provides the impetus for conflict, though Walcott decidedly shifts the emphasis which the *Iliad* outlines. In Homer's poem Hector is a Trojan, and his marriage to Andromache is idealized as a happy one. Hector's farewell to Andromache and their son Astyanax is, indeed, one of the most poignant scenes of the *Iliad*. Hector's combat with Achilles and the fated death of the Trojan hero constitute the climax of the *Iliad* and anticipate the fall of Troy itself. Walcott's Helen inspires the conflict of two young St. Lucians, both bachelors, Hector and Achille, the Greek name of the latter appropriately altered to its Franco-Antillean form. It is Helen who causes Hector to abandon the independent but unremunerative trade of fisherman for the compromising job of taxiing tourists to the local airport. In the short term his fight with Achille is successful, for he wins Helen, but the price he pays is high, and their relationship is ultimately tragic.

Achille, on the other hand, responds to his loss of Helen by making both a literal and a psychic sea journey in search of his origins. Though logic dictates that his hollowed-out wooden boat could not survive a journey to the coast of Africa, he nevertheless finds himself there, and it is there that he meets Afolabe, a tribal chieftain who is apparently his father, though, more significantly, Afolabe is also the spirit of Achille's ancestors. Such a journey to recover the past is regularly a part of the mythic hero's prospectus, and readers of Walcott's poem will likely recall that a crucial element of Odysseus' return to his native island of Ithaca is that hero's journey to the Underworld, the realm of the dead in which he hears the prophecy of Tiresias and meets the shade of his mother Antikleia.

Walcott's Achille similarly encounters a parental ghost and in a sense witnesses a prophecy as well, for Achille is present when enemy warriors stage a surprise raid on the village to capture slaves to be shipped to America. He, therefore, not only witnesses the past that has shaped his own life on St. Lucia but also experiences the psychological wound that history causes. That he had christened his boat, the very one which had brought him to his African past and in which he earns his living, *In God We Troust* shows the irony with which Achille optimistically accepts the American premise of his life on St. Lucia. His misspelling of "trust" implies his childlike naïveté and his confidence in fate. It is only after his journey that Achille recognizes the continuity of sights he had unquestioningly accepted since his birth. Slavery remains in the form of European passenger liners and tourist hotels, small boys who dive for coins tourists toss, domestic service in the homes of comparatively wealthy Europeans, and even in the form of cast-off gifts such as Helen's dress. What is worse, native St. Lucians attempt to correct social inequities through ultimately divisive political forms such as capitalism and communism; these merely polarize, never unite, its population. Obviously, Achille is not an intellectual and so never articulates these arguments, but he does acquire some sense of the damage history does and how difficult it is to alter it radically.

The Plunketts have their own psychic wounds, and these are similarly private and unarticulated. Economic reality forced their emigration from Britain. Maud looks wistfully back upon her youth in Ireland and silently wonders about the remote possibility of her return. Like Achille, Major Plunkett wonders about his origins and undertakes genealogical research which ties his own background to St. Lucia. He discovers an ancestor peripherally involved in the wars between the British and French which ultimately made St. Lucia part of the British West Indies. Major Plunkett's genealogical research is the counterpart of Achille's extraordinary voyage, though it yields no more in the way of tangible results. The Plunketts, too, are slaves to the past, and their traditionally antagonistic European backgrounds complicate their estrangement, between themselves as well as among their fellow St. Lucians. Though they did decide to emigrate to St. Lucia, they did so only from necessity; though their situation appears ideal to most black St. Lucians, the Plunketts have neither the financial resources nor the intellectual capacity to return to a wholly Europeanized way of life. Even if able to make the journey physically, their own differences would be magnified by greater proximity to England and Ireland. Fate has placed them on St. Lucia, and their history has left its scars.

History has clearly wounded all the characters of Walcott's *Omeros*, and the wound thus becomes the poem's exponential symbol. In the case of Philoctete, a fisherman unable to practice his trade effectively because of a festering sore on his thigh, the wound is literal as well as psychological. Philoctete recalls the Philoctetes of Greek myth. Philoctetes, son of Poias and prince of the Malians, had inherited the bow and arrows of Heracles and was to have led seven ships against the Trojans, but was bitten by a snake on the island of Lemnos. His wound became infected, and because its stench became so intolerable the Greeks abandoned him there. Philoctetes spent ten years on Lemnos suffering miserably with his wound. He could not die, nor could he live normally. Even so, when the Greeks learned that Troy would fall only by the arrows of Heracles, Odysseus and Diomedes journeyed to Lemnos and begged Philoctetes to accompany them back to Troy. The Greek myth is a telling commentary on toleration, which is all too often based on expediency rather than liberality.

Walcott's Philoctete bears a wound from a rusty anchor, and Philoctete is also left behind, by the fishermen of St. Lucia. He does not make the African journey with Achille, yet he bears the wound of history externally as well as within. Reduced to showing tourists how the fishermen carve their boats and to smiling for photographs as the stereotype of a happy islander, he unwittingly holds the key to his people's future. Philoctetes was cured only when he participates in the conflict at Troy. Philoctete, whose situation most closely resembles that of the majority of humanity, can be cured only by comparable involvement in the events that surround him.

Omeros, though clearly Walcott's most comprehensive and ambitious work, reflects the themes of many of his earlier poems. Because of his origins as a black man born on St. Lucia but one who was educated in the classical British tradition, he acutely recognizes his divided allegiance; his poems regularly deal with the resulting sense of isolation, estrangement, and rootlessness. Even so, he recognizes that these feelings apply universally to the human condition, and he sees them as a consequence of history. Walcott offers no easy cure for the wound each human being bears, but he does suggest that living life is the best means of dulling history's pain.

Robert J. Forman

Sources for Further Study

The Christian Science Monitor. October 31, 1990, p. 14.
The Economist. CCCXVII, October 27, 1990, p. 97.
The Guardian. October 25, 1990, p. 24.
The Listener. CXXIV, September 27, 1990, p. 30.
The New Republic. CCIII, October 29, 1990, p. 36.
New Statesman and Society. III, October 5, 1990, p. 36.
The New York Review of Books. XXXVIII, March 7, 1991, p. 3.
The New York Times Book Review. XCV, October 7, 1990, p. 1.
Publishers Weekly. CCXXXVII, May 25, 1990, p. 46.
The Times Literary Supplement. September 14, 1990, p. 977.
The Washington Post Book World. XX, November 11, 1990, p. 1.

ORDINARY MONEY

Author: Louis B. Jones
Publisher: Viking (New York). 345 pp. $18.95
Type of work: Novel
Time: c. 1990
Locale: Marin County, California

A comic first novel exploring the interweaving of the real and the fake in the values, dreams, and life-styles of two suburban California families

> *Principal characters:*
> WAYNE PASCHKE, a family man and unemployed housepainter
> LAURA PASCHKE, his wife, a waitress at Denny's
> KIM PASCHKE, their part-plastic fifteen-year-old daughter
> RANDY POTTS, Wayne's buddy, an unemployed carpenter
> MARY POTTS, Randy's former wife, a feminist
> CYNTHIA (CINDY) POTTS, their fifteen-year-old daughter, best friends with
>   Kim
> BIM AUCTOR, a phony plastic surgeon and crazy counterfeiter
> ERIC DEBONO, Kim's high school boyfriend
> BUDDY, Wayne's supervisor in a pyramid-sales scheme
> FORTINBRAS ARMSTRONG, father of the pyramid-sales scheme
> DAN MCBRIDE, Randy's hotshot blind lawyer
> BOB LUDEX, a Secret Service lawyer
> FRANK HODGES, a Treasury Department investigator
> RALPH CONLIN, a State Department representative
> EDDIE MENSINGER, an expert on monetary systems
> ARTHUR VAN SICHLYN, Randy's neighbor, an English aristocrat
> KEVIN VAN SICHLYN, his artist son, creator of instillations
> TINA, a lonely woman at a bar

Few first novels have been both as entertaining and as artistically controlled as Louis B. Jones's *Ordinary Money*. Jones's comic theme is the stagy California life-style, with its irresolvable mix of the real and the fake. Satire of the Californian culture can be traced at least as far as Evelyn Waugh's *The Loved One* (1948). Compared with Waugh's savage fun, Jones's satire of Californians is much kinder, gentler, and more forgiving, perhaps because he speaks as one of their own. Jones was graduated from the M.F.A. program at the University of California, Irvine, and resides in Mill Valley, California.

For a novel satirizing phoniness, *Ordinary Money* has one glaring fault: its contrived plot. Are readers to believe that two temporarily unemployed Marin County workmen come into possession of twenty million dollars in perfect counterfeit bills and that the counterfeiter then conveniently dies of an infected fingernail? These key events form the basis of the plot of *Ordinary Money*. Jones manages to hide the starkness of these events by spreading them over the novel and surrounding them with a smoke screen of believable detail. Perhaps the joke is on the readers, who are conditioned to accept the contrivances of the media as reality. More sophisticated readers can also enjoy the joke, joining the author in a festival of tongue-in-cheek metafiction; as the novel's characters themselves occasionally say, "This is fiction."

The contrived basis of the plot is no overwhelming obstacle, and, despite any metafictional elements, Jones moves the story along in an old-fashioned way reminiscent of Charles Dickens, with multiple subplots generating many caricatures and much suspense.

The main plot concerns two beer-drinking buddies, Wayne Paschke and Randy Potts. Since they dropped out of high school, Wayne has developed into a solid family man, complete with paunch. Randy has become an older version of his foot-loose high-school days: He "still wore the same size jeans as in high school . . . had divorced Mary neatly and with good humor . . . and in the same swift motion bought a convertible Camaro." When a smooth-talking counterfeiter named Bim Auctor places an advertisement for a " 'general secretary/handy man, w/some financial savvy,' " Randy answers it and is groomed by Auctor to launder the fake money. In return, Randy gets supposedly foolproof and fail-safe legal protection and freedom to spend as much as he wants.

Randy soon involves the even more gullible Wayne, who is conned into sending a sample counterfeit bill twice to the Secret Service for testing: The bill is certified to be genuine both times. Randy also hides a wooden box containing two million dollars in Wayne's garage. By the time Randy has finished depositing nine other such boxes in various banks, Auctor has mysteriously disappeared and the FBI begins looking for Randy. Before the plot ends, Randy has moved to an elegant neighborhood; the Secret Service, the Treasury Department, and the State Department have become involved; and the international monetary system almost collapses. Along the way, the author caricatures federal agents, lawyers, plastic surgeons, English aristocrats, avant-garde artists, and academic experts; in this world, the perfect counterfeit bills seem a proper emblem.

In a secondary parallel plot satirizing business organizations and their special language, Wayne Paschke also answers an advertisement, for employment as a phone salesman. The advertisement is actually a slick sales technique, tricking desperate and/or stupid people into buying large quantities of a useless product to sell. Wayne qualifies splendidly on both counts. In his quiet desperation, he daydreams of being a homeowner, "a tiny stick figure in this origami condominium," but lies awake at night "upon the breathing balloon of debt" from his daughter's many operations. Even though Wayne detects "the obvious fishiness" of the pyramid sales scheme, trendily called Marketrend, he signs on. It is painful to read how Wayne soaks up every drop of propaganda; how he polishes his phone image before the mirror hour after hour, without results; and how, in a last-ditch effort to recoup his losses, he sinks his wife's inherited money market fund into the scheme.

In another secondary plot, the two teenage daughters mirror the relationship of their fathers. Kim Paschke is shy, conventional, and self-conscious about her plastic ear and nipple, implanted in a series of operations to correct birth defects. She is easily led by the flamboyant Cindy Potts, whose own mind is a hothouse of steamy melodrama. Cindy has a Kermit the Frog stuffed with "her collection of suicide notes," and she runs away from home but gets only as far as the local pizza parlor. When her father actually does spirit her away, Cindy calls the hotline for missing children to check if she is listed. She tells every student at her high school that her father is a counterfeiter. In the same vein, Cindy takes Kim in hand and molds her into sexy jailbait.

In this tale of two families, both families dance around the real and the artificial. The Pottses are comic victims of the American Dream, pursuing shallow fantasies fed by the consumer culture and the media. Cindy's mother Mary is inspired by books and magazines featuring such articles as "Why Men Fear Intimacy" to turn her husband into "a textbook illustration of her feminism." Now a successful divorcée and career woman with a Porsche, Mary seeks authenticity by sleeping with Tom, Dick, and Harry (the actual names of her boyfriends in the novel).

On the other hand, the solid Paschkes are solidly anchored in loving relationships. They have already achieved authenticity as human beings by being their simple, honest, loving selves. Evidence of their genuine substance is abundant: their commitment to Kim's operations, their aversion to the counterfeit money, and even Wayne's misguided faith in the phone sales scheme. The pillar of strength in the family seems to be the nurturing Laura, who shows excellent judgment about people and about everything that happens in the novel. Moreover, she appears to have handed on her good sense to Kim.

Yet, in America, even the salt of the earth can be tempted. In part of the novel's climactic chapter, Wayne tries to adopt the persona of his pal Randy. Wearing Randy's fancy sport coat stuffed with two thousand dollars in counterfeit bills, he heads for a bar called Rumplestiltskins. He gets slightly drunk and meets a lonely big-bosomed woman name Tina, who takes him home with her. All the opposing values of the novel are evoked in the encounter and embodied in the two women, Tina and Laura, tugging at Wayne. The encounter is never consummated. Instead, Wayne drives home to Laura's meat loaf in this delightful novel that should please both family counselors and Hollywood.

Harold Branam

Sources for Further Study

Booklist. LXXXVI, December 1, 1989, p. 724.
Chicago Tribune. February 13, 1990, V, p. 3.
Kirkus Reviews. LVII, November 1, 1989, p. 1551.
Library Journal. CXIV, December, 1989, p. 169.
Los Angeles Times Book Review. January 7, 1990, p. 3.
The New York Times Book Review. XCV, January 14, 1990, p. 7.

The New Yorker. LXVI, February 26, 1990, p. 131.
Publishers Weekly. CCXXXVI, October 27, 1989, p. 57.
The Wall Street Journal. February 28, 1990, p. A12.
The Washington Post Book World. XX, January 14, 1990, p. 3.

PASSING ON

Author: Penelope Lively (1933-   )
Publisher: Grove Weidenfeld (New York). 210 pp. $17.95
Type of work: Novel
Time: The 1980's
Locale: Long Sydenham, a village in the Cotswolds, England

A novel tracing the attempts of a middle-aged brother and sister to find meaningful lives after the death of their destructive and dictatorial mother

> *Principal characters:*
> HELEN GLOVER, a part-time librarian
> EDWARD GLOVER, Helen's younger brother, a teacher in a private girls' school and an ardent conservationist
> LOUISE GLOVER DYSON, their younger sister, a designer who lives in London
> TIM DYSON, Louise's husband
> PHIL DYSON, Louise's teenage son
> GILES CARNABY, a widower, the Glovers' solicitor
> RON PAGET, an unscrupulous developer

Since she left the juvenile field and began publishing novels for adults in the late 1970's, Penelope Lively has gained a distinguished reputation for her penetrating character studies and thematic preoccupation, the relation between individuals and what is generally called history. In *According to Mark* (1984), she followed a biographer as he sought the truth about his subject and himself and was changed in the process. In *Moon Tiger* (1988), winner of the Booker Prize, Lively followed the mind of a dying woman as she re-created her own life against the background of her tumultuous world. In *Passing On* (1989), Lively's focus is far more private, involving neither an imagined subject for biography nor a real World War II. Except for the minor theme of the destruction of nature by developers, the emphasis in the book is on personal history, the attempt of two middle-aged children to shake off the destructive influence of their mother, now dead.

The youngest of the three Glover offspring, Louise Glover Dyson, escaped early. In childhood, she had dared to bite her mother; at seventeen, she had run away from home. When she returns for the funeral, she is largely free of her mother's influence and therefore both concerned and impatient because her older sister and brother still obey the dead Dorothy Glover as if she were present.

The son of the family, Edward Glover, had taken refuge in passivity. Spurned by his cold and spiteful mother, he found his only affection in his relationship with his sister, herself a child though three years older than Edward. Although he was later attracted to young men and boys, Edward realized that this possible outlet was interdicted by his society and by the demands of his profession. After an unfortunate episode at the boys' school where he was teaching, Edward realized that he must avoid male companionship and, obviously, male love. His passivity, then, is willed. In order to avoid temptation, Edward avoids looking at anyone; he teaches at a girls' school, the only male on the faculty. Although he has always genuinely loved nature, there is an additional reason he so loves the Britches, the private, overgrown woods owned by the Glovers. There he need not fear any accidental encounters that might prompt him to approach a boy, as he had done at a school where he taught, with disastrous results. Living with Dorothy Glover, Edward, though taunted and minimized, felt safer from his own impulses. When she is gone, he is afraid of what he may do with his freedom.

The protagonist, Helen Glover, is the most complex and sympathetic of the three siblings. Like Louise, she made an attempt to get away, but she returned. After her mother's death, she feels compelled to search her soul for the reason. When she thinks about it, Helen admits that the need to be with her dependent younger brother was merely her excuse, not her real motive. She concludes that her difficulty must have been a kind of apathy, a lack of will or resolution. The fact that she lacks the ruthlessness shown by Dorothy and by Louise in her defiance of Dorothy, without being weak like Edward, makes Helen an interesting and appealing character.

Instead of devoting long passages to psychological analysis, Lively prefers to put her characters into situations in which their internal conflicts can be dramatized. These situations may seem trivial. For example, one of the most touching episodes in the novel is Helen Glover's attempt to buy a becoming blue sweater. At fifty-two, she has long accepted her mother's assessment of her. Her color is brown, she hears her mother saying. It takes courage for her to purchase the blue sweater; indeed, after Helen returns home, the mocking voice of her mother becomes overpowering, and Helen puts away the sweater, planning to give it for the next church "jumble" or rummage sale.

A memorable chapter in the novel illustrates Lively's fascination with the themes of time and history, as well as her skill in revealing character through action. Because Louise's husband, Tim Dyson, has suggested that they consult someone about investments, Helen and Edward go up to London for the first time in twenty years. There they discover that their remembered world with moderate price tags and familiar, friendly restaurants has vanished. They feel like Rip van Winkles. Lost and alone in a foreign city, they cling to each other like children, and when they are separated from each other in a department store, Helen feels as she did when five-year-old Edward got lost. This chapter emphasizes the fact that Dorothy Glover robbed these two children of more than their confidence and self-respect; she robbed them of the entire thirty years they lived with her in Long Sydenham. During that time, the world developed and they did not. Now, with Dorothy's death, they are not equipped to live in the world which lies beyond their door. This, then, is Lively's variation on her usual theme of history: She explores a kind of time-warp experience in which middle-aged children are propelled into an alien environment. Accustomed to their surroundings, which Dorothy has decreed must never change, they are naturally terrified.

Helen's relationship with Dorothy was more complex than those of the other two offspring. Like Cassandra, the legendary daughter of King Priam who was given the ability to foresee the future but fated never to be believed, Helen could see what was going on but was unable to resist it. Her mother's psychological strategies were evident to Helen. Unfortunately, her own reaction—almost total capitulation—was also predictable. Unlike her self-centered sister, Helen was too kind, too gentle, too understanding to intimidate her mother, much less to resist her. As a result, she came to accept Dorothy's assessment of her as a failure in every area of life. Dorothy made it clear that she considered Helen's job as part-time librarian proof of her lack of initiative and intelligence. She sneered at every young man Helen dated, convincing her daughter that only a very poor catch would ever take an interest in someone as stupid and ugly as Helen. The only defiance in which Helen succeeded was one that Dorothy was too ignorant to understand: Because Dorothy hated books, Helen worked in a library. It is interesting that Helen perceives this minor rebellion only after her mother's death; while Dorothy is alive, Helen can see through her mother, but she cannot see her own virtues or small successes.

The structure of *Passing On* is much like that of *According to Mark* and *Moon Tiger*, in that although the period covered is fairly brief, the protagonists range far into the past in search of the truth. While Lively herself emphasizes the similarity to historical research in her works, it is evident that she also owes a debt to the conventional mystery story. As each novel proceeds, past events are discovered, and these events provide the clues that help the protagonist to unravel the mystery.

In *Passing On*, there is even an unexpected bequest that casts new light on Dorothy's motivations. To everyone's amazement, Dorothy leaves her house to her grandson, Phil Dyson, instead of to Helen and Edward, who have lived there with her for thirty years. The most uncharitable construction of her action is probably the true one: Because Helen and Edward have no other property except the Britches, which Dorothy did indeed leave to them, they will not have the money to leave Long Sydenham but must stay there, taking advantage of their lifetime tenancy. Thus, they imagine, Dorothy will continue to control them, whispering rebukes if they consider even changing the draperies, much less discarding a lifetime of accumulated rags and rubbish.

It is when Helen defiantly begins to sort through the rubbish, however, that she finds the clues to her own wasted life and the proof of her mother's malevolence. First she finds hidden away the only becoming dress she ever owned, a gift from her godmother, which after one wearing her mother insisted had been ruined by the cleaner. Then she finds letters from the man who had been most serious about her, begging her to reply, so that they could make up a quarrel. These discoveries convince Helen that she could be physically attractive to a man. As a result, she permits herself to telephone Giles Carnaby, the solicitor, who has been paying her some attention, and eventually tells him that she has fallen in love with him. Although the romance comes to nothing when Giles admits that he is by nature sentimental and has misled her, Helen at least comes to realize that her loneliness was not primarily the result of her own unworthiness but, rather, of her mother's machinations.

As the novel proceeds, Helen ceases to hear her mother's voice. Dorothy's influence has not, however, ended. The very fact that she is absent removes Edward's inhibitions, and he makes advances to the son of Ron Paget. As a result, Helen has to make a major decision: Will she sell Paget the Britches so that he will spare her brother prosecution or disgrace, or will she preserve the woods that she and Edward feel so strongly must not be violated? When Helen refuses to give in to Paget, it is evident that despite her disappointing romance, she has developed a new self-respect.

The trap in a novel with so sympathetic a protagonist would have been to reward her with clear proof of the physical attractiveness her mother had denied. Lively does not, however, permit Helen either an ecstatic physical relationship or a passion-motivated marriage. More important is that she takes Helen to a new assertiveness, which enables her to break off the relationship with Giles rather than accepting his humiliating offer of "friendship" and flirtation in exchange for her love.

The brightest hope at the end of the novel, however, comes from an unlikely source: the leather-garbed adolescent heir, Phil. From the time he appears on their doorstep seeking refuge from his own mother, Phil brings a surprising amount of pleasure to Helen and Edward. Practical, resourceful, and considerate, Phil makes many of the small decisions that the hag-ridden Helen and Edward no longer have the resolution to make. In a crisis, Phil proves to be as steady as a rock: It is he who finds Edward and drags him home so that his suicide attempt can be foiled.

More important, however, Phil's affection for Helen is more significant for her than a proposal from the womanizer Giles would have been. Once she has realized that Phil is a young man of some substance, Helen can see herself through his eyes — as a woman who is interesting, intelligent, and worthy of love. It is this change in Helen, brought about not by the practiced compliments of Giles but by the honest affection of an adolescent nephew, that makes possible what is a happy ending for the novel. In the final chapter, it is clear that Helen is now free enough of her mother to make changes. She will buy appliances. She will sell the clock her mother doted on and buy some trees for Edward. Above all, she will venture out; unhesitatingly, she and Edward accept an invitation from Louise to go back to that alien city, London, for Christmas. Lively's conclusion sums up the change in the Glovers and the real, if restricted, hopes which that change has made possible: "They saw that there is nothing to be done, but that something can be retrieved. Both sniffed the air; each, gingerly, made resolutions." This is the final revelation which comes to Edward and Helen: Although the wasted years cannot be regained and the future is circumscribed, there can still be something saved from their dead mother's tyranny.

Rosemary M. Canfield Reisman

Sources for Further Study

Chicago Tribune. March 4, 1990, XIV, p. 7.
Library Journal. CXV, March 1, 1990, p. 117.

London Review of Books. XI, April 29, 1989, p. 20.
Los Angeles Times. May 21, 1990, p. E5.
New Statesman and Society. II, April 7, 1989, p. 37.
The New York Times Book Review. XCV, February 11, 1990, p. 12.
The New Yorker. LXVI, March 19, 1990, p. 109.
Publishers Weekly. CCXXXVI, December 1, 1989, p. 48.
The Times Literary Supplement. April 7, 1989, p. 363.
The Washington Post Book World. XX, February 4, 1990, p. 3.

THE PENCIL
A History of Design and Circumstance

Author: Henry Petroski (1942-   )
Publisher: Alfred A. Knopf (New York). Illustrated. 434 pp. $25.00
Type of work: History
Time: The sixteenth century to the present
Locale: Great Britain, France, and the United States

This exhaustive history of the pencil relates, on a metaphoric level, the wonders of engineering in meeting human needs in ways whose details are often lost to those who take commonplace implements for granted

Henry Petroski's main point in writing *The Pencil* is to sharpen his readers' awareness of the fact that common implements used in daily life—implements that are often taken for granted—reveal much about the social fiber of humankind. Petroski's approach to history should erase forever the notion that its study necessarily emphasizes considerations of wars and treaties, of despots and those who topple them, of royal genealogies and palace intrigue—if, indeed, such notions still lurk in the public mind.

Near the turn of the century, Marcel Proust was launched on a creative endeavor that eventuated in the six volumes of *À la recherche du temps perdu* (1913-1927; *Remembrance of Things Past*, 1922-1931) when the taste of a madeleine dipped in tea unlocked his unconscious and catapulted him into vivid reflections of his early childhood. Petroski, who, until he was forty, used but never meditated profoundly on pencils, had a Proustian experience of sorts when in 1983 he read an article in the *Journal of Applied Mechanics* on the physics of broken-off pencil points. A Duke University professor of civil engineering, Petroski was fascinated to learn that lead pencil points nearly always break at an angle rather than straight across.

Pursuing this arcane tack, Petroski wrote a specialized scholarly article to explain the phenomenon. In so doing, he launched himself on a research course that has resulted in this 434-page book on the history of the pencil and has elevated the most common writing device to a position of public appreciation that it has never previously enjoyed, despite the fact that fourteen billion of the slender implements are produced worldwide each year. Fifteen percent of the world's pencils, some two billion, are produced annually in the United States.

Petroski, who writes with the kind of gentle wit required to sustain for 434 pages a discourse as narrowly defined and focused as this one, strays from his point (breaking slantwise) whenever it seems appropriate to lead his readers along byways and over well-calculated, carefully marked detours that are connected to the main discourse but which offer interesting, readable sidelights on it. The author also anticipates the major questions that puzzle readers and cause some of them to chew on their pencils in frustration.

Perhaps the most significant of his explanations has to do with how manufacturers get lead into the wooden grooves of pencils. The select and stalwart minority that has puzzled over this problem at all has probably concluded that the long, hexagonal shaft somehow has a narrow hole drilled in it and that this narrow hole is then filled with lead that flows under pressure from some sort of extruding machine. The wood then is assumed to be coated with its characteristic yellow paint, the color of most wooden pencils. In reality, pencils are not made that way.

The best pencils are made from red cedar, though other woods are used as well, and other materials have been tried by some manufacturers. The wood is carefully cut into long, narrow slats, both flat, and one side is grooved. The thin cylinder of lead is laid into the groove, and the corresponding, mirror-image part of the shaft is glued and placed on top of the bottom piece. The long, slender shafts are then painted, cut to a specified size, stamped with the legend that is to appear on them, and adorned with an eraser bound to the pencil by a ferrule. The best ferrules are said to be brass and to have painted bands around them.

This whole process may sound noncontroversial if not exactly simple. Petroski, however, informs his readers of the politics of pencil making, thereby thickening the plot in the convoluted story his research has uncovered. He tells of how wadd, officially designated graphite in 1789, a year of social discontent, first was discovered at Seatoller Fell near Borrowdale, not far from Keswick in England. Graphite was mentioned in print as early as 1565 in a book Konrad Gesner wrote on fossils. Gesner offers an annotated drawing of graphite secured in a wood holder to be used for writing. Wadd, or a substance much like it, had by that time already been used widely by Cumberland farmers to mark their herds and was called black lead by some, plumbago—the Latin word for "that which acts like lead"—by those with a classical bent.

Borrowdale remained the chief source of graphite for many years, and pencils not unlike the ones most people use every day were made by securing strips of the mineral in wood or other materials. Despite efforts to conserve the Borrowdale supply of graphite, it was exhausted before the middle of the nineteenth century, and other sources had to be found or substitutes devised. Before the supply was exhausted, however, the French had begun to explore how to make pencils; during the last decade of the eighteenth century, France, at war with Great Britain, had its graphite supply cut off. As pencils came to be only a memory in many precincts of Paris and other French cities, government services were impaired, schools were unable to function effectively, and commerce was impeded.

The French began what Petroski labels a "Manhattan Project" sort of thrust to find a way to make pencils, placing Nicolas-Jacques Conté in charge of the project. Conté found that by mixing clay and water with graphite of inferior quality and letting it harden in molds, he could produce a lead much like the kind used in pencils today merely by firing the hardened compound at high temperatures.

Conté's method was used quite generally and is still in widespread use today. With the depletion of the Borrowdale mines, however, the search accelerated for a graphite as fine as those mines had produced. A rich vein was struck in 1847 in Siberia virtually on the Sino-Russian border. The German company of A. W. Faber, which survives as A. W. Faber-Castell, held exclusive rights to this mother lode and was soon turning substantial profits by selling pencils made from what it advertised as the finest graphite from the Far East.

As interlopers began to imitate Faber, they tried to lure customers by producing pencils with such Oriental-sounding names as Mongol and Mikado. To emphasize that their graphite was from the Orient, these companies painted their pencils an Oriental yellow, the color of most of the pencils produced around the world today. When Asian names became a liability to American pencil manufacturers after the Japanese attack on Pearl Harbor, the names were changed, the Mikado quickly being renamed the Mirado on December 8, 1941, the day after the United States was drawn into World War II.

The characteristic hexagonal shape of most pencils evolved because it was economical to make them in that shape. More pencils could be made from the wood available if pencils were hexagonal rather than round. The trick was to create a pencil that fit the hand well and that could be held easily but to conserve materials as much as possible in manufacturing them. It was also necessary to make sure that the lead in each pencil was centered exactly in its groove, because if it were off center, it could not be sharpened to a satisfactory point and often the lead would break in the sharpening process.

Adding erasers to the pencil's slender shaft led to a political controversy, especially among educators. Many purists said that the presence of an eraser was an invitation to make errors. Some contemporary elementary and secondary schools will not allow their students to use pocket calculators in mathematics classes; similarly, in the nineteenth century, many schools forbade students to use pencils with erasers, reasoning that doing so would make them less careful about their writing. The eraser, fixed in place by a gleaming brass ferrule, tops most contemporary pencils, emphasizing and advertising the pencil's main advantage over the pen: Graphite is more forgiving than ink.

The etymology of the word "pencil" derives from Latin *peniculus*, which is the word for "brush." The original Latin word is a diminutive form of *penis*, the Latin word for "tail." In Roman times, most writing was done with fine brushes, as the original word suggests. The Romans, Petroski tells his readers, also wrote with an implement called a *stylus*, which was made from lead or a lead alloy. It, unlike the *peniculus*, wrote dry, but its marks were faint and hard to read.

Henry David Thoreau (whose name, Petroski informs the reader, was David Henry until his graduation from Harvard) was the son of a pencil maker credited with making the first high-quality pencils in the United States. The younger Thoreau himself made a venture into pencil manufacturing, devising a compound of graphite and clay, much like Conté's, of which pencils could be made. Thoreau found that by varying the quantity of clay used in the compound, he could adjust the hardness of the lead. He assigned numbers and/or letters to pencils to designate their hardness, as Conté had done in France.

The young Armand Hammer, recently out of medical school and hobnobbing in

Russia with Vladimir Ilich Lenin shortly after the Russian Revolution, began his entrepreneurial ventures in the Soviet Union by moving an entire German pencil factory—workers and all—to Russia. It flourished, aided by Russian laborers, in a village made to seem as German as possible so that the transplanted workers would not feel homesick. When the Soviets confiscated the plant in 1930, it was renamed the Sacco and Vanzetti Pencil Factory. Its pencils bore as their logo an impression of the Statue of Liberty.

For all of its lore about the invention and development of the pencil as it is currently known, Petroski's book goes far beyond the narrow limitations that its title might suggest. Rather than wear his readers down to nubs by inundating them with specialized details about his subject, Petroski light-handedly demonstrates how engineering functions in society to affect the lives of all humans, sometimes in large, apparent ways, but more often in small, barely perceptible ones. After reading Petroski, one begins to appreciate many commonplace items that he does not specifically mention: safety pins, can openers, stapling machines, staples, incandescent light bulbs, aluminum cans, bridges, rubber bands, and a host of other impressive things that have been made possible by engineering.

In two of his earlier books, *Beyond Engineering: Essays and Other Attempts to Figure Without Equations* (1986) and *To Engineer Is Human: The Role of Failure in Successful Design* (1985), Petroski has revealed a vision that undergirds his broad view of the field in which he teaches. *The Pencil* advances the author's basic thesis—one that runs through all of his recent work—that engineering is a humane discipline, often with humane outcomes. The book espouses a philosophy that makes engineering a handmaiden to human beings, not human beings pawns to the industrialization that engineering has made possible. This approach has resulted in a book that might have been more scientifically specialized and more oriented to specialists in engineering rather than a book that has delighted the vast general audience it has reached.

R. Baird Shuman

Sources for Further Study

The Atlantic. CCLXV, January, 1990, p. 94.
Booklist. LXXXVI, January 15, 1990, p. 961.
Chicago Tribune. February 25, 1990, XIV, p. 6.
Kirkus Reviews. LVII, December 1, 1989, p. 1732.
Library Journal. CXV, March 1, 1990, p. 112.
Los Angeles Times Book Review. March 4, 1990, p. 2.
Nature. CCCXLIV, April 26, 1990, p. 897.
The New York Times Book Review. XCV, February 4, 1990, p. 21.
The New Yorker. LXVI, June 4, 1990, p. 99.

Publishers Weekly. CCXXXVI, November 24, 1989, p. 63.
Science. CCXLVIII, May 18, 1990, p. 894.
U.S. News and World Report. CVIII, January 22, 1990, p. 63.
The Wall Street Journal. February 23, 1990, p. A9.
The Washington Post Book World. XX, January 28, 1990, p. 3.

PHILADELPHIA FIRE

Author: John Edgar Wideman (1941-   )
Publisher: Henry Holt (New York). 199 pp. $18.95
Type of work: Novel
Time: 1985
Locale: Philadelphia

Philadelphia Fire *is a dark kaleidoscope of characters and incidents arising from the narrator's confrontation with the bombing of the MOVE house on Osage Avenue in Philadelphia on May 13, 1985*

> *Principal characters:*
> CUDJOE, an expatriate Philadelphian who returns home from Greece to search for the lone survivor of the MOVE bombing
> MARGARET JONES, a former member of MOVE
> SIMBA MUNTU, "THE LION," the boy who survived the MOVE bombing
> SAM, Cudjoe's editor
> TIMBO, a cultural attaché to the mayor
> JAMES "J. B." BROWN, a Philadelphia street dweller
> THE NARRATOR

On May 13, 1985, in West Philadelphia, after bullets, water cannon and high explosives had failed to dislodge the occupants of 6221 Osage Avenue, a bomb was dropped from a state police helicopter and exploded atop the besieged row house. In the ensuing fire fifty-three houses were destroyed, 262 people left homeless. The occupants of the row house on Osage were said to be members of an organization called MOVE. Eleven of them, six adults and five children, were killed in the assault that commenced when they refused to obey a police order to leave their home. A grand jury subsequently determined that no criminal charges should be brought against the public officials who planned and perpetrated the assault.

The conflagration on Osage Street is the literal fire of John Edgar Wideman's *Philadelphia Fire*; it is a metaphor for the destruction of the social fabric that this novel presents. Wideman has elsewhere declared himself a pessimist; the vision he presents in *Philadelphia Fire* is an extremely dark one.

Cudjoe, the protagonist of much of the novel, is an expatriate African-American novelist who has lived on Mykonos for several years. Driven into looking for the "story of a fire and a lost boy," he returns to Philadelphia, his hometown. Yet his quest is also for a city that might allow people to live in "brotherly love." What he finds are the fragments of a civilization: alienation, squalor, violence, and the total absence of innocence—a city of "brothelly love."

Cudjoe's initial search is for a child, called Simba Muntu, "the Lion," who supposedly ran, burning, from the house on Osage Street, the lone survivor of the bombing. He interviews a former member of MOVE, Margaret Jones, who recalls the fascinated revulsion she felt for King, also known as John Africa, the leader of the group. Despite his excesses, she says, he spoke the truth; "he's right even if he did things wrong sometimes, he's still right cause ain't nothing, nowhere any better."

MOVE offered an Edenic, if dirty, island for one trying to stay alive in a hostile ocean. Yet the ocean inevitably swept the island away. Margaret knew the people who had been taking care of Simba, nursing him back to health: Cudjoe thought he had a path to the child, to the story of the fire. One day, however, Simba got on a bicycle and rode away. No one could find him; he simply disappeared—another lost fragment.

In the city to which Cudjoe returns, even the possibility of childhood seems to have been lost. The omnipresent graffiti spells out "*Kid's Krusade. Kaliban's Kiddie Korps.* MPT . . . *Money Power Things.*" Cudjoe's friend Timbo, a former college classmate, now the mayor's cultural attaché, translates the message: "Kids today are a bitch. . . . Now they kill anybody. Anything. . . . Ice water in their veins. . . . They want to take over, man. . . . Claim the only difference between them and grown-ups is grown-ups hold the money, power and things." Yet Timbo also lists atrocities that reveal adult indifference to the fate of children. The system not only has failed children in the schools, courts, hospitals, and streets but also has ignored them except to exploit their salability: "lack of legal rights, child abuse, kiddie porn, kid's bodies used to sell shit on TV." This is not a place where childhood can survive or nurturance can be passed on from one generation to the next.

The break in the chain of nurturance that Cudjoe witnesses is reflected in his own life. The house to which he returns in Philadelphia is full of the memories of the summer he spent caring for his dying grandmother. "He learned the parts of a woman's body caring for her. . . . He loved her. Shared her secrets. If he sat in the rocker keeping watch while she slept, she would not die." Yet she did die, and her death seems to have broken the link of responsible caring for Cudjoe.

He is divorced and has no contact with his children. Sam, the editor who nurtured his talent, is dead. He lunches with Timbo and encounters the younger brother of his childhood friend Darnell on a city basketball court. Darnell is in jail for dealing drugs. None of the connections holds. In one segment of the novel, Cudjoe recalls a time he spent teaching when he directed a production of *The Tempest*.

It was an improbable feat. He barely convinced himself that he could pull it off—teaching black inner-city kids to speak blank verse, to pull together to create a production: "To catch a conscience. To prick pride and dignity and say, Hey, we're alive over here. That was Shakespeare youall just saw performed. And we did it." Yet they did not. It rained the two days the production was scheduled for the park, and the sets were washed away. They had to start all over again, but they had lost steam. Cudjoe quit teaching, feeling guilty for not doing enough and knowing that he could never do enough. The dreams dissolve.

Wideman's answer to Langston Hughes' haunting question, "What happens to a dream deferred?" is that the dream turns to ashes: ashes in the mouth, ashes in the air, ashes ground into the skin of one's being. Both John Africa's dream of a return to a natural paradise and the black mayor's dream of a new Philadelphia are consumed by the ashes of the bombing on Osage Street. Darnell Thompson's dream of basketball ends in a jail cell. Timbo's dream of using politics to effect change is consumed by expensive lunches paid for with the perks of office. Cudjoe's dreams of teaching children, of finding the child Simba Muntu, are discarded. Still he dreams, however, of the child that might have been saved—a kid hanging from the rim of a basketball hoop.

> It's me and every black boy I've ever seen running up and down playing ball. . . . I don't know how I remember it's just a nightmare and cut him down. . . . Grateful almost to realize he's just a child. That his body is small and I can bear the weight of it as I back down the ladder.

Cudjoe's nightmare is a reflection of Wideman's own. Interspersed throughout the novel are letters to and conversations with his son Jacob, sentenced to life imprisonment for inexplicably stabbing a friend on a camping trip. Wideman lays bare his own agony, his inexpressible sadness, and his frustration in being unable to help his son. At one point he asks, "What is the word for a parent who's lost a child? I have no word, no place to begin." Even with education, material success, and escape from the inner city, Wideman was unable to protect his child, or himself, from the curse long ago laid.

J. B., the homeless Job of Philadelphia's streets, is the survivor. He panhandles and feasts on the contents of the dumpsters behind fast-food restaurants. He survives only because he hoards the scraps of existence and tenaciously hangs on—hangs on for no particular reason except out of habit. His dreams are haunted with images of men warring against men throughout history and across the globe.

On receiving an honorary degree from the University of Philadelphia in May, 1986, Wideman said, "And so my notion is not—not that we dream in order to become something, but we dream because when we dream, we *are* our better selves. And that's why I write—because I have that ideal in front of me. . . . You need to put your dreams in a pot." *Philadelphia Fire* is a potful of nightmares. It ends with Cudjoe's hearing a mob screaming for blood; this time he refuses to run. "He turns to face whatever it is rumbling over the stones of Independence Square."

Philadelphia Fire is a difficult book. The narrative is fragmented, and the focus on characters shifts without warning. Wideman's language leaps from lyrical prose to stream of consciousness to the rap of the street, and his style is densely allusive. Yet it is the questions that Wideman leaves with the reader that are the most difficult.

Jane Anderson Jones

Sources for Further Study

Booklist. LXXXVI, August, 1990, p. 2124.
Chicago Tribune. October 28, 1990, XIV, p. 1.
The Christian Science Monitor. October 23, 1990, p. 15.
Esquire. CXII, August, 1989, p. 122.
Kirkus Reviews. LVIII, August 1, 1990, p. 1042.
Los Angeles Times Book Review. September 30, 1990, p. 3.

New York. XXIII, October 1, 1990, p. 66.
The New York Times Book Review. XCV, September 30, 1990, p. 7.
Newsweek. CXVI, October 1, 1990, p. 67.
Publishers Weekly. CCXXXVII, August 17, 1990, p. 53.
Time. CXXXVI, October 1, 1990, p. 90.
U.S. News and World Report. CIX, October 15, 1990, p. 92.
The Washington Post Book World. XX, October 7, 1990, p. 6.

PICTURING WILL

Author: Ann Beattie (1947-   )
Publisher: Random House (New York). 230 pp. $18.95
Type of work: Novel
Time: 1989
Locale: Charlottesville, Virginia; New York City; and Florida

A novel of fragments centering on five-year-old Will and the adults connected variously to him

Principal characters:
 JODY, Will's mother and Wayne's former wife, a talented photographer
 WILL, Jody and Wayne's five-year-old son
 WAYNE, Jody's first husband, a self-centered and irresponsible man
 MEL ANTHIS, Jody's lover and later her husband
 MARY VICKERS, Jody's best friend in Charlottesville
 WAGONER, Mary's son and Will's best friend
 D. B. HAVERFORD, a New York art gallery owner, nicknamed "Haveabud" by Jody
 SPENCER, the seven-year-old son of Haverford's former client
 CORKY, Wayne's third wife

When *Picturing Will* opens, Jody has established herself as a successful wedding photographer and is living comfortably as a single parent four or five years after her short, disastrous marriage to Wayne. Will, now beginning to create himself as an independent being, has been essential to her emotional survival. She is a loving and attentive mother, worried that she is too protective, aware that Will sometimes does not like her. She is also a standoffish lover, wary of committing herself to Mel, cognizant that by freely offering physical love yet not committing herself, she makes Mel desire her all the more. However much she would like them to, things cannot stay poised in this way for much longer because Jody now stands on the verge of a new career as an art photographer. Fearful of leaving what she has created and un-certain of her feelings for Mel, she hesitates to commit herself either to him or to the slim possibilities of success in New York City. Decisions that seem to be hers are made for her, however: Mel engineers a showing of her work in New York by mak-ing it a condition of his working for D. B. Haverford, and Haverford's promise to launch her career forces Jody to move to New York. Shortly thereafter, it appears, she marries Mel, and he takes over the rearing of Will.

These same events that precipitate Jody's move and marriage send Will on a brief trip to Florida to visit his father and Corky while Jody establishes herself in New York. This trip introduces a new cast of characters and provides glimpses into some the reader has already met. "Haveabud," the opportunistic gallery owner, seduces the seven-year-old boy-genius Spencer. The main focus of this section, however, is on irresponsible, philandering Wayne, already considering leaving Corky after only eighteen months. Like Jody, he finds that events have a logic and momentum of their own, as a quick, passionate affair with Kate leads unexpectedly to his arrest on drug charges. Corky, Wayne's third wife, emerges as a loving but deluded woman who clings to hopes that Wayne will soon want children and who meanwhile shows her talents for motherhood by caring expertly for Will.

The third section, a one-chapter coda entitled "Child," depicts Will twenty years after these events of 1989, a successful art historian at Columbia University with a wife and young child of his own. Here, too, the author gathers the loose ends from parts 1 and 2, sketching in a few details about Wayne (last heard of in Mexico City), Corky (now a nurse's aid), and Haveabud (something of a celebrity in Paris). It is also in this last chapter that the reader learns that the essays on childhood and child rearing irregularly placed among the chapters of narrative are not by Jody or the omniscient author but by Mel, who, after Jody's rapid rise in the New York art world, took over the task of rearing the boy.

In typical postmodern fashion, *Picturing Will* is less a narrative with a plot than a series of scenes or snapshots. Whether this method of constructing a novel succeeds or fails for the reader will depend on what one expects a novel to do or say. Those with few demands about the conventional devices of plot and character will find much to please them. The writing is witty, insightful, and stylish. Beattie meticulously lavishes attention on each sentence, shearing it of anything superfluous or showy. It is a style often called "minimalist," an intense, nervous, pared-down prose that aims primarily at a precise depiction of contemporary reality, disclaiming the suggestiveness and symbolic resonances of the twentieth century's earlier writers. Minimalism has affinities with what Jody learned from Wayne's wordless departure: "It had been a rude awakening, but later a relief, to find that saying nothing could be the strongest way of communicating." In Beattie's skillful hands, this style is compelling, for even without a continuous narrative thread, the novel pulls one along by the sheer power of each individual incident to engage the attention and reveal something important about present-day life.

Beattie's great strength as a writer is her ability to convey a scene without rhetorical flourishes or overwriting. The key to her art may well lie in an analogy with photography, for like successful pictures, Beattie's best scenes "transcend expectations." Like a photograph emerging from the developing fluid, Beattie's incidents vibrate with the life imparted by some unexpected detail, some turn of phrase, bit of psychological insight, or emotional truth. These powers of selection and observation reach their height in this novel in the chapter describing a Halloween party and its aftermath. Perhaps the kaleidoscopic and surreal events of the party lend themselves especially well to Beattie's sensibilities, for her prose embraces the contradictions of mask and reality, child and adult, humor and terror, innocence and foreboding that the occasion holds. The party culminates in the nightmarish scene of Mary's automobile accident, in which the death of a deer matter-of-factly throws into sharp relief the silliness and pathos of the costumed partiers as they come on the scene.

Few episodes in the book achieve such dramatic intensity, but others have equally memorable qualities. The rise and fall of Haverford's first client, Luther, is entertaining in itself and perhaps a moral interlude on the pitfalls and temptations that await Jody as she climbs the slippery and precipitous slope to fame in New York's fickle art world. Jody's first interview with the slick and conniving Haverford is delicious in portraying the country hick getting the better of the supposedly streetwise city slicker. The book's most disturbing scene takes place in the motel where Haverford, Mel, Will, and Spencer stop for the night. Haverford at first seems a figure of innocent fun when he smears his and the boys' lips with lipstick, but this turns into pederasty when, to Will's uncomprehending eyes, Haverford seduces Spencer in the bathroom. There are tender moments too, however, as when Corky fondly packs Will's suitcase, hoping that Wayne will notice her skill with children and agree to have a child.

Beattie is in like manner highly effective in the introspective essays that comment, sometimes directly and sometimes indirectly, on the narrative incidents. These, as we learn in the last chapter, are written by Mel as a kind of diary or journal on Will's childhood. One essay asserts that, in the parent's memory, the child is always two years old. Another is written from a child's perspective, particularly about time but also about continuity and the arbitrary actions of adults. A third is about a child's nighttime fears, and the fourth is Mel's personal account of rearing Will, ending with a series of questions directed to him. There is a sense in which these essays are unfair to the reader, as their author is presumed to be Jody or the omniscient narrator until the last moment. To put them into proper perspective, the reader must reread the book. It is difficult to say why Beattie chose to play this particular game with the reader, unless to make the metafictional point that fiction is, after all, fiction—an artifice not to be confused with reality or even verisimilitude. This said, it must also be acknowledged that these essays contain some of Beattie's most intense and insightful writing, as well as revealing an enviable imagination. Her ability to see the world simultaneously from the perspectives of children and adults makes these essays at once thoughtful handbooks on child rearing and splendid, introspective essays in their own right.

Less effective than the incidents and essays are the characters, and here the criticism grows directly from the method Beattie has chosen. For this method—effective as it is in shining its light into many dark corners of the contemporary psyche—is not one that lends itself to the development of character. Jody holds center stage long enough to become interesting and then disappears from view, to return only briefly as a celebrity with a reputation. Mel, who could have been the most interesting and complex character in the book, is barely introduced in the narrative portions and only slightly developed in the essays. Considering that he coped with Jody's fame, reared Will from age six onward, composed compelling essays on the joys and pains of parenting, and created an atmosphere in which both mother and son could thrive, his neglect is particularly unfortunate. Perhaps this is the ultimate feminist irony: that the tasks of homemaking, even when accomplished by men, are still not worth reporting. Wayne, all ego and sex drive, takes up more space than he deserves, particularly in the gratuitous copulations with Elliott, the bored woman of nearly fifty who interests Wayne simply as an easy conquest. Haverford is delightfully slimy and disturbingly predatory, but his appearances, too, are relatively brief. The boy-genius Spencer has an eerie appeal, but he also comes and goes too quickly. Finally, there is Will, who in spite of the title is not pictured at all but barely glimpsed from several points of view. His appearance in the last chapter as a successful and well-adjusted adult is a tremendous non sequitur, not because the reader would have predicted disaster for the boy, but because the information the author provided makes any ending possible.

Perhaps the non sequitur of Will's adulthood is the point of the book. Certainly one of the recurring themes is that events have a logic of their own—that choice, though not entirely a delusion, is also less decisive than we often assume. Another such idea is the contrast between adult and child, epitomized in one sense by the Halloween party in which adults behave like children, and discussed at some length in Mel's essays. Jody's thoughts also occasionally reflect this theme. Contrast, however, is not connection, and here again the structure frustrates the sense. What have any of these episodes done to shape Will the man out of Will the boy? If the answer is nothing, then Beattie has at least been internally consistent, denying causality in human affairs generally. Philosophically, this may be a rational and defensible position; morally and aesthetically, however, it is less than satisfying, at least to readers accustomed to the notion that the novel has something to say. The last chapter is particularly unsatisfactory, for it simply snatches "endings" for the various stories from thin air, incidentally reporting probable but not compelling last pieces of information about the various characters. It reminds one of the last scene of an eighteenth century play, in which mysteries are solved and marriages arranged in wholly arbitrary and unpredictable ways.

In an entirely different context, the late scientist and historian of science Jacob Bronowski once claimed that facts are useless without theories to bind them into a satisfying unity. That admonition might well apply to Beattie's novel. It is full of facts—the everyday facts of people's daily existences, from brand-names and place-names to the peculiar manners and mores of the last decade of the second millennium. There is a highly satisfying surface reality here and enough incidental insights to more than justify reading this genuinely entertaining and accomplished novel. Perhaps it is wrong to criticize an author for not accomplishing what she has not attempted, but it will be a rare reader who feels that *Picturing Will* has provided genuine enlightenment and not mere information.

Dean Baldwin

Sources for Further Study

Booklist. LXXXVI, December 1, 1989, p. 705.
Chicago Tribune. January 28, 1990, XIV, p. 3.
The Christian Science Monitor. February 5, 1990, p. 12.

Commonweal. CXVII, May 18, 1990, p. 322.
Kirkus Reviews. LVII, November 15, 1989, p. 1610.
Library Journal. CXV, January, 1990, p. 145.
Los Angeles Times Book Review. January 21, 1990, p. 3.
The New York Review of Books. XXXVII, May 31, 1990, p. 33.
The New York Times Book Review. XCV, January 7, 1990, p. 1.
Publishers Weekly. CCXXXVI, December 1, 1989, p. 46.
Time. CXXXV, January 22, 1990, p. 68.
The Wall Street Journal. January 31, 1990, p. A16.
The Washington Post Book World. XX, January 28, 1990, p. 5.

A PLACE I'VE NEVER BEEN

Author: David Leavitt (1961-   )
Publisher: Viking (New York). 194 pp. $18.95
Type of work: Short stories
Time: The 1980's
Locale: New York, Paris, rural Italy, and American suburbia

Leavitt's second collection of stories focuses primarily on conflicts associated with the gay life-style

David Leavitt's first collection of stories, *Family Dancing* (1984), published when he was twenty-three years old, consisted of nine stories that mostly dealt with the tensions that strain the delicate fabric of family relationships—sex, divorce, illness, death. A central tension was that of a young gay male trying to come to terms with his homosexuality or trying to find acceptance within his family. In *A Place I've Never Been*, Leavitt's second collection, eight of the ten stories focus on conflicts arising out of the gay life-style. In this book, however, Leavitt's homosexual charac-ters, both male and female, have pushed beyond the problem of psychological self-acceptance or social acceptance by others; they now either confront the further im-plications of living with their sexual orientation or deal with homosexual versions of the problems that face the heterosexual mainstream.

The clearest indication of Leavitt's shift from adolescent to more adult ramifica-tions of the gay life can be seen in the title piece of the collection, which features two characters introduced in the story "Dedicated" in *Family Dancing*: Nathan, a young homosexual, and Celia, his female friend. In the early story, Celia was an ungainly and unattractive twenty-three-year-old in love with a young homosexual man named Andrew and good friends with Nathan, Andrew's lover. In "Dedicated," Celia envied the gay men and admired them for their romantic difference; she yearned to put aside her fleshiness and put on their sleekness. In the opening story of *A Place I've Never Been*, Celia has lost weight and is trying to find her female identity. Nathan, on the other hand, is putting on weight and suffering from a phobic anxiety about catching the AIDS virus after his former lover has been tested positive. The reunion of the two friends reveals how far both have developed and diverged since the period of the early story.

The character Celia is rejoined in the eighth story in the collection, "I See Lon-don, I See France." She is in rural Italy with her new heterosexual lover, Seth, who has "saved" her from her dreary previous existence. The emphasis of the story is on Celia's desire to be someone else, to deny her ordinary past and be like the wealthy and glamorous expatriate family she and Seth are visiting. Yet the romantic "dif-ference" of the couple is similar to that which Celia perceived in her gay friends earlier in her life. By the end of the story, Celia recognizes this and understands the falseness and play-acting of her romance with Seth. She accepts her past, yet knows that she will become a different person from the one she formerly was. For Leavitt, the process of growing up means rejecting the façade of romance and accepting oneself for who one is.

A similar theme informs the story "Ayor." The word is an acronym for "at your own risk," used in *The Spartacus Guide for Gay Men* to designate bars and bathhouses where there are dangers. The protagonist is a young male homosexual, similar to the young men introduced in Leavitt's first collection. When a long-time gay friend, Craig, is raped, the protagonist realizes that he has used Craig to live the many dangers of the gay life-style by proxy, experiencing those dangers only from the perimeter with Craig to protect him. As Craig sinks lower into degradation, the protagonist manages to remain aloof and untouched by the underworld of the gay man's inevitable double life. At the conclusion of the story, the gay protagonist moves toward an understanding of his earlier fascination with the dangerous or "ayor" zones of life and develops a more mature acceptance of himself, as he returns to his regular and simple relationship with his lover Laurent.

As shown in *Family Dancing* and the two Celia stories in *A Place I've Never Been*, Leavitt is quite capable of assuming a female point of view. In "My Marriage to Vengeance," Ellen, a homosexual woman, receives an invitation to her former lover's heterosexual wedding and fantasizes going to the ceremony with a shotgun and shooting herself in front of the celebrants. Nothing quite so drastic occurs. It is not Ellen's action or realization that constitutes the story's denouement but rather the confession of her former lover, Diana, who admits that she is marrying because she wants a "normal" life instead of one as a "social freak." The story ends with Ellen trying to deal with her grief at the loss of Diana, yet consoling herself with the knowledge that Diana will face a life of mistakes resulting from her one act of compromise, having preferred a life of easy mistakes to one that was harder but better.

Two of the stories that focus on homosexual orientation and the gay life-style are, if not parodies, at least gay versions of two typical heterosexual concerns: the great American dream of a home of one's own and the American nightmare of the fragmentation caused by adultery. "Houses" centers on a male homosexual real-estate agent who has recently returned to his wife after having lived three months with a man. Although he tries to accept a heterosexual life-style, he becomes involved with a man to whom he has taken the family dog for grooming. The center of his conflict between a heterosexual life with his wife and a homosexual relationship with his new love interest is an ordinary little house that he fantasizes about as the dream house he will share with Ted, referring to it as their "love nest" and their "cottage." By the end of the story, however, neither relationship has worked out, and the uprooted protagonist secretly sleeps in the many empty houses that he has listed for sale. He relishes most of all the one night a week he stays in the "dream house," feeling when he arrives there as if he has somehow come home.

The story "When You Grow to Adultery" is based on the pun in the title, with its implications of the shift away from childhood to the adult world in which adultery is a real possibility. The story deals with the relationship between Andrew (the lover of

Nathan in the story "Dedicated" in *Family Dancing*) and Allen—a relationship that is complicated by Andrew's adulterous love affair with Jack. Just as in a heterosexual marriage, Andrew's illicit relationship with Jack is much more fascinating than his everyday quasi-marital relationship with Allen, with its boredom, disagreements, competitions, and disapprovals. The result is the pattern so familiar to heterosexual relationships: lies, secret meetings, guilt, and self-loathing. The conflict faced by Andrew, because he knows that he does not want to leave Allen yet still does not want to lose Jack, reaches symbolic intensification when the couple visits Allen's family. As the two young men lie in bed, Allen drifts off to sleep with sighs of pleasure and gratitude as Andrew caresses him by writing with his fingers "I love Jack Selden" on his back.

Only two of the stories, "Chips Is Here" and "Spouse Night," deal with issues unrelated to homosexuality. The former is an atypical satiric piece about a man who plots the murder of his neighbor because the neighbor's dog killed his cat. "Spouse Night," however, focuses on a more common Leavitt theme, the death of a family member. The story deals with a man and woman who continue to attend the "spouse night" meeting of a support group for people with incurable illnesses, even after their husband and wife are dead. The focus is on the conflicts and guilt they feel when they become lovers and must cope with the disapproval of their families and the sense of betrayal of their lost partners. Death in the family has been a concern of Leavitt's from the beginning of his career, as clearly shown by two poignant stories in his earlier collection *Family Dancing* that deal with characters dying of cancer. In his second collection, he continues to show his understanding of the pains and tensions such a lingering death creates; however, whereas cancer was the metaphor for death in the earlier work, here AIDS becomes the central symbol.

The book's shortest story, "Gravity," because of its lyrical and symbolic quality, is the most intense of the stories that deal with the implications of homosexuality. Theo is a young homosexual with AIDS who has chosen to take a drug that would save his sight rather than one that would keep him alive. Because he is dying, he comes to live with his mother. On a shopping trip to buy an engagement gift for a cousin, Theo's mother chooses an expensive crystal bowl; while examining it, she literally tosses it through the air to her feeble son. The fact that the bowl is heavy and yet fragile, combined with the fact that the son is able to catch it and hold on to it, constitutes a symbolic moment that provides both mother and son with a small but sustaining victory.

"Roads to Rome," the final story in *A Place I've Never Been*, is the most complex of the ten pieces in the collection. It centers on Fulvia, the ninety-six-year-old matriarchal head of an Italian family, who is dying. The story does not concern her death, however, but rather the resurrection of the past which this impending event prompts. Among the many who have come to say good-bye to the "dying queen" are her best friend Rosa, Rosa's son Marco, and Marco's American lover Nicholas. The most important element of the past which Fulvia's impending death resurrects is a story of Fulvia and Rosa's meeting two young American soldiers during World

War II. Whereas Rosa married her soldier and went to live with him in Kansas, Fulvia stayed in Rome and became an important cultural critic. Rosa could tolerate the blandness of the American Midwest for less than a year before she returned to Italy and ultimately to Fulvia. "Roads to Rome" really has to do with decisions of the past that impinge on the present. At the end, although Fulvia has been celebrated as a glamorous and romantic cultural queen, she recalls a time when she went to New York and called the soldier she had met during the war. Although the man was an Iowa car salesman who barely remembered the young Italian girl he called "La Glamorosa," Fulvia feels sad for roads not taken, for the inevitable loss of the past and all of its romantic promise.

Family Dancing was a top contender for the prestigious National Book Critics' Circle Award and the PEN/Faulkner prize. Leavitt later won a John Simon Guggenheim Foundation Fellowship and has been a writer-in-residence at the Institute of Catalan Letters in Barcelona, Spain. His novels *The Lost Language of Cranes* (1986) and *Equal Affections* (1989) have received favorable critical attention and a small but discriminating readership. *A Place I've Never Been* further affirms his emerging position as a powerful and poetic voice of middle-class gay life. All these stories deal with universal human themes of self-discovery, divided allegiances, and the search for acceptance. It is simply that in the fictional world of David Leavitt such universal needs and conflicts primarily derive from the biological and social reality of homosexuality.

Charles E. May

Sources for Further Study

Belles Lettres. LXXXVII, September 15, 1990, p. 138.
Booklist. LXXXVII, September 15, 1990, p. 140.
Chicago Tribune. July 15, 1990, XIV, p. 4.
Kirkus Reviews. LVIII, July 15, 1990, p. 954.
Library Journal. CXV, August, 1990, p. 143.
Los Angeles Times. September 21, 1990, p. E12.
The New York Times Book Review. XCV, August 26, 1990, p. 11.
Newsweek. CXVI, September 3, 1990, p. 66.
Publishers Weekly. CCXXXVII, July 13, 1990, p. 40.
San Francisco Chronicle. September 23, 1990, p. E1.
The Washington Post Book World. XX, October 7, 1990, p. 7.

THE POLITICS OF RICH AND POOR
Wealth and the American Electorate in the Reagan Aftermath

Author: Kevin Phillips (1940-   )
Publisher: Random House (New York). 263 pp. $19.95
Type of work: Current history
Time: Primarily the 1980's
Locale: The United States

Phillips explores how wealth in the United States concentrated in the hands of a few during the Reagan years and argues that these economic developments have produced watershed changes in American life

The Great Depression of the early 1930's is in the past, but in the early 1990's the United States again faces depression aplenty. In late 1990, for example, Saddam Hussein's invasion of Kuwait and the United States' Operation Desert Shield meant a long-term American presence in the Middle East while oil prices soared. The American economy was headed for recession in the midst of a savings and loan fiasco, the costs of which may never be fully known, and a protracted federal budget debacle. The latter fiscal mess resulted from the equally problematic leadership of a Democrat-controlled Congress and a Republican-controlled White House. George Bush's sarcastic "Read my hips" is the sequel to his "Read my lips: no new taxes." That vow's hollow promise buried American heads in economic sand while budget deficits climbed higher than Middle Eastern crude.

Events happen faster than books can be written about them. *The Politics of Rich and Poor*, Kevin Phillips' brilliant critique of American life in the 1980's, appeared before some of the aforementioned events took place. Yet none could have surprised him completely. They continue the saga of what Phillips' subtitle calls "wealth and the American electorate in the Reagan aftermath."

Irony riddles that story. The world seemed to be going America's way. The Berlin Wall came down. Much of Eastern Europe rejected communism, embraced democracy, and invested hope in capitalism. The Soviet Union became more friend than foe. Self-congratulation, however, was premature. Enthralled by international developments that appeared to vindicate the United States, the nation's leaders underestimated socioeconomic distress at home, and it threatened to turn the American Dream nightmarish.

By the end of the 1980's, homeownership, long a basic ingredient in the American Dream, was becoming only a dream for more and more Americans—especially those in their twenties and thirties. That example is one of many that Phillips had in mind when he began his first chapter—"The Best of Times, the Worst of Times: The Critical Duality of the Reagan Years"—with an apt quotation from *The Wall Street Journal* of March 31, 1989: "Statistical evidence already suggests that the American dream is fading." Not everyone, of course, felt so gloomy. For many Americans, the Reagan years and even their immediate aftermath would be the best of times—or so they were led to believe.

Whatever the beliefs, Phillips' revisionist appraisal shows that the Reagan era produced an immense redistribution of wealth. In that redistribution the poor and working middle class lost ground and the rich—especially the richest of the rich—gained it. If Ronald Reagan's appeal subdued that intention at first, Phillips further shows how it eventually became dominant.

Very late in the day, Phillips contends, the nation is starting to face the economic devastation that comprises the Reagan aftermath. A 1980's sea change took the United States from being the world's largest creditor to being the world's leading debtor. During the decade, the national debt tripled to more than $3.1 trillion. The "Great Communicator" will be remembered for many things, but few of his accomplishments will be more important than the toll taken by Reaganomics. Phillips' tally is that it will sap the nation's strength and standard of living for years to come.

Contrary to the conventional wisdom of Reagan's most trusted economic gurus—George Gilder, Arthur Laffer, and Milton Friedman, to name a few of these capitalist theologians, as Phillips dubs them—debts and deficits mattered mightily and would not disappear, as their theories predicted. No chorus of hosannas to laissez-faire could change that, nor could the tax cuts and tight monetary policies that were hailed as tickets to prosperity. Some tickets to prosperity there were, but most went to a favored few. Charitably, Phillips thinks philosophy and policy, more than greed, dictated that outcome. Nevertheless, he says, "the American dream was beginning to crumble not just in inner-city ghettos and farm townships but in blue-collar centers and even middle-class suburbs." That realization portends political upheaval. Most Americans do not resent wealth per se, but they do resent its accumulation through favoritism.

Phillips' credentials make his deep concern about these results all the more telling. No Marxist or socialist, he is not even a Democrat. This keen observer and astute journalist was the chief political analyst for the 1968 Republican presidential campaign. His conservative identity is as solid as it is long-standing. Appraising the Reagan-Bush 1980's, Phillips' voice is that of the responsible critic-from-within.

While focusing on contemporary American politics, *The Politics of Rich and Poor* has added interest because it includes three important historical dimensions. First, stressing what even American political parties often overlook, Phillips sees conflict over the distribution of wealth at the heart of the American political process. "[T]he genius of American politics," he says, "has been to manage through ballot boxes and electoral votes the problems that less fluid societies resolve with party structures geared to class warfare and even with barricades." In the United States, politics is civil war by other means. Power clashes—singly or in combination, they include regional, cultural, ideological, and especially economic interests—produce revolutionary results. Typically these clashes are between economic classes. The wealthy, the poor, and the middle classes may all be American and may all want greater wealth, but these shared realities also keep them at odds.

The stakes in American elections are high. "Since the American Revolution," Phillips argues, "the distribution of American wealth has depended significantly on *who controlled the federal government, for what policies, and in behalf of which constituencies."* Putting that point in a more colloquial way, Phillips quotes blues singer Ray Charles, "Them that's got is them that gets, and I ain't got nothing yet."

Billionaires and the homeless—not by accident the United States got a lot more of both during the Reagan years. Phillips notes that Ronald Reagan had a personal antipathy toward income taxes. He was far from alone, and there was enthusiasm for his tax reduction program. Its most significant component—a key to the "trickle down" component of Reaganomics—involved reducing the top personal tax bracket from 70 to 28 percent before his second term ended. By Phillips' reckoning, however, that measure produced precious little trickling down. "[T]he top 1 to 5 percent of the population," claims Phillips, got the lion's share of the benefits. For the vast majority of Americans, Reaganomics cost them. If enterprise grew, much of it focused on leveraged buyouts, junk bonds, and other forms of paper entrepreneurship, rather than on more productive forms of investment. Meanwhile, economic inequality also grew while increasing amounts of American property—to say nothing of jobs—left American hands.

As trade balances shifted in their favor, debt-servicing interest receipts boomed, and the dollar's value fell, investors from Japan, England, and Germany found America selling itself at bargain basement prices. The Reagan aftermath finds less and less of the country owned and controlled by Americans themselves. Downtown commercial real estate illustrates the point. According to Phillips, by early 1988, foreign owners held 21 percent of such property in Manhattan, 32 percent in Minneapolis, 39 percent in Houston, and 46 percent in Los Angeles. In one industry after another, foreign firms have been increasing their global leadership by acquiring American companies.

The selling of America made some people rich, and Ronald Reagan helped the rich get richer. They won the 1980's economic battle in American politics. Phillips thinks, however, that victory cost far too much because it squandered the nation's future. "[I]n terms of international purchasing power," he laments, "the United States is now only the ninth wealthiest country in the world in terms of per capita GNP. We have been surpassed by Austria, Switzerland, the Netherlands, West Germany, Denmark, Sweden, Norway, and Japan."

What has happened is unprecedented—but not entirely, which leads to a second historical component of major importance in Phillips' analysis. If American politics consists of power clashes often rooted in economically based class disparities, he believes it also has a distinctively cyclical quality. Dating from Thomas Jefferson's election to the presidency in 1800, Phillips discerns "a series of twenty-eight to thirty-six-year waves" inaugurated by watershed elections that change the nation's direction. Invariably these elections target an elite that is considered to have gone too far. The pattern is as follows: One party takes power from another through voter rebellion against an entrenched elite that has lost touch with a broadly based constituency. Within two or three decades, however, the party that took power gets similarly trapped. Empowering its own elite excessively, it becomes "a target for a new round of populist outsidership and reform." If Phillips is correct, the present Republican jig might be up in 1992.

Phillips sees Ronald Reagan as pivotal in what is the third cycle of a Republican version of the pattern described above. Abraham Lincoln's election in 1860, William McKinley's in 1896, and Richard Nixon's in 1968—in these watershed cases a broadly based appeal for national unity, far more than commercial interests, led to a victory for populism Republican-style. Before these Republican cycles ended, however, economic interests endemic to Republican ideology took over.

"Beyond its emphasis on the politics of national unity," surmises Phillips, "dynamic capitalism, market economics and the concentration of wealth are what the Republican party is all about." Ronald Reagan put it more simply when he said, "What I want to see above all is that this remains a country where someone can always get rich." In any case, the Republican pattern that Phillips discerns entails a "shift from broad middle-class 'nationalism' into 'capitalist overdrive.'" Disinflation, limits on business regulation and government alike, tax reduction, high interest rates—these are among the traditional Republican measures that take effect. If they appeal widely for a time, their success creates disillusionment: Not only does the gap widen between the haves and have-nots, it also tends to make increasingly disproportionate the favored few and the much less favored many.

Phillips believes Ronald Reagan won election with an appeal to a Republican version of populism. With him in the White House, it would be morning in America again. Both government spending and taxes would be cut, the budget deficit would be pared, and military spending would rise to keep the nation's defenses strong. Some of these things did happen, and Phillips finds some cause for celebration. On the whole, however, his cheer is muted and not least, ironically, because of the Democrats' sorry opposition.

That showing is not entirely surprising, for Phillips points out that the Democrats are "history's second most enthusiastic capitalist party. They do not interfere much with capitalist momentum, but wait for excesses and the inevitable populist reactions." Phillips is particularly critical of the disastrous 1988 campaign Michael Dukakis waged against George Bush. The Democrats refused to understand that the contest was fundamentally about economically based class differences. They did not mobilize their traditional constituency: lower- and middle-class Americans. Those groups had good reason to be fed up with the intentionally pro-rich policies that Reagan bequeathed to George Bush, his more patrician heir. The Democrats' "metooism" about "heyday capitalism," as Phillips calls it, may have cost them the election. If they can find good leadership, which is not to be taken for granted, the Democrats may come to their senses in 1992, when economic discontent with the Reagan aftermath could make the White House theirs for the taking.

Does Phillips want a Democratic victory in 1992? Not likely, but clearly he does want economic reform. In the final analysis— and this is the third historical point to note—his book retains a traditional optimism about the American people. Phillips counts on them to do the right thing. He senses they will not tolerate excess for too long, whether the excess is that of too much government control and too many taxes or too much wealth in the hands of a few and too many others left out and hurt.

Yet, if Phillips retains elements of an optimistic American populism, he also senses that the cycles of American politics may not recover and revitalize all that needs reclaiming. His closing remarks observe that "by 1989 concentration of wealth, mounting debt and financial recklessness" increasingly caused Americans to approach the future with foreboding. No less than the many Americans for whom he speaks, Phillips displays that mood too. Unfortunately, little to justify changing it has happened as the Reagan aftermath still shadows the 1990's.

John K. Roth

Sources for Further Study

Business Week. July 16, 1990, p. 13.
The Christian Science Monitor. July 23, 1990, p. 13.
Los Angeles Times Book Review. June 10, 1990, p. 1.
The Nation. CCLI, August 13, 1990, p. 175.
The New Republic. CCIII, July 30, 1990, p. 35.
The New York Times Book Review. XCV, June 24, 1990, p. 1.
Newsweek. CXVI, July 9, 1990, p. 19.
Publishers Weekly. CCXXXVII, April 13, 1990, p. 53.
Time. CXXXV, June 25, 1990, p. 69.
The Wall Street Journal. June 14, 1990, p. A12.
The Washington Post Book World. XX, July 8, 1990, p. 1.

POSSESSION

Author: A. S. Byatt (1936-   )
Publisher: Random House (New York). 555 pp. $22.95
Type of work: Novel
Time: 1825-1987
Locale: England and France

The discovery of love letters between two Victorian poets sets two modern scholars off in pursuit of history, truth, and romance

Principal characters:
>ROLAND MICHELL, a young English scholar, an expert on Randolph Henry Ash
>MAUD BAILEY, another young scholar, an expert on Christabel LaMotte
>RANDOLPH HENRY ASH, a prominent Victorian poet
>ELLEN BEST ASH, his wife
>CHRISTABEL MADELEINE LaMOTTE, his lover, a poet
>BLANCHE GLOVER, her companion, a painter
>VAL, Roland's lover
>JAMES BLACKADDER, Roland's mentor
>MORTIMER CROPPER, the leading American expert on Ash
>LEONORA STERN, the leading American expert on Christabel
>FERGUS WOLFF, Maud's former lover
>SIR GEORGE BAILEY, Christabel's descendant
>LADY JOAN BAILEY, his wife
>SABINE LUCRÈCE CHARLOTTE DE KERCOZ, Christabel's French cousin
>RAOUL DE KERCOZ, Sabine's father
>HILDEBRAND ASH, the last in the Ash line
>MAIA (MAY) THOMASINE BAILEY, the illegitimate daughter of Christabel and Ash

Author of four previous novels, A. S. Byatt was known primarily as acclaimed novelist Margaret Drabble's older sister before *Possession* won the Booker Prize, Great Britain's most prestigious literary award, as well as the Irish Times-Aer Lingus International Fiction award. Byatt's earlier novels, *The Shadow of a Sun* (1964), *The Game* (1967), *The Virgin in the Garden* (1978), and *Still Life* (1985), received favorable reviews for their insights into the domestic lives of middle-class Britons. They have also been criticized for being too difficult and too verbose, with a narrating sensibility too willing to intrude and explain. *Possession*, an ingenious blend of history, literary criticism, mystery, and gothic romance, fortunately has none of these flaws.

Roland Michell is a twenty-nine-year-old Ph.D. in English literature who, having been unable to obtain a teaching position, works for his mentor, James Blackadder, who is editing the poems of the Victorian Randolph Henry Ash in a basement room of the British Museum known as the Ash Factory. Doing research at the London Library, Roland stumbles upon the drafts of two letters Ash wrote to an unknown woman. He steals the letters and keeps their existence secret from Blackadder. Ash is thought to have had a happy forty-four-year marriage to his devoted Ellen. The possibility of adultery will alter the poet's image and invite reinterpretation of his works.

Further research identifies the woman as the poet Christabel LaMotte, relatively unappreciated during her lifetime but recently embraced by feminist literary critics. The discovery will also change LaMotte scholarship, since she is thought to have been a lesbian, having lived with the painter Blanche Glover until the latter's mysterious suicide. Roland takes his find to the leading British expert on Christabel, Maud Bailey, who runs the Women's Resource Centre in Lincoln and is descended from Christabel's sister.

At Seal Court, the Bailey family estate where Christabel lived with her sister's family after Blanche's death, Maud and Roland discover the complete Ash-LaMotte correspondence. The letters appear to be the property of the current resident of Seal Court, the hostile, suspicious, and rather seedy Sir George Bailey. Only because Roland is kind to the wheelchair-bound Lady Joan Bailey are they even allowed onto the estate. Roland and Maud decide to keep what they know from Blackadder and from the leading American authorities on the poets, the flamboyant lesbian Leonora Stern and the crudely acquisitive Mortimer Cropper. They want to find out as much as they can about the Ash-Christabel relationship before making it public. Roland is daunted by the beautiful but austere Maud, uncertain if she is his partner or opponent.

Roland and Maud learn that the jealous Blanche stole some of Ash's letters to Christabel, destroyed them, and informed Ellen Ash of the affair. Maud's former lover Fergus Wolff, another Ash scholar, finds out about the letters and tells Blackadder, Cropper, and Roland's unhappy lover, Val, who has been supporting him for years. Cropper offers Sir George a large sum for the letters, and Sir George accuses Maud of deceit.

A clue leads the critic-detectives to Brittany, where they read the journal kept by Christabel's young French cousin Sabine de Kercoz, in 1859-1860, when Christabel sought sanctuary with Sabine and her father, Raoul. It gradually becomes clear to Sabine that Christabel is pregnant, but the poet never acknowledges this fact. When she disappears for several days and then returns without an infant, Raoul is unable to discover the child's fate. Twenty-eight years after her pregnancy, Christabel writes to the dying Ash about their child, but Ellen, to whom he had confessed his affair years earlier, will not let him read the letter and buries it with him.

Cropper reveals the letters' existence, and a national debate begins over their import and the need to keep them in England. Cropper and Hildebrand Ash, last of the Ash line, decide to dig up the poet's grave and solve the last piece of the mystery. After finding the box containing the letter, Cropper and Ash are almost killed in a storm. As the storm ends, they are confronted by the other Ash-LaMotte scholars. Maud is given the honor of reading the letter, which reveals that the child, Maia, also known as May, lived and was reared as the daughter of Christabel's sister, making her Maud's great-great-great-grandmother. Maud and Roland finally confess their love.

Byatt's method of presenting her twin stories is as noteworthy as the other elements of *Possession*. She has created not only Christabel and Ash but their works as well. Her narrative consists of the modern story told from several points of view, flashbacks to the nineteenth century, the poems (some rather extensive) and letters of Christabel and Ash, Christabel's prose fables, the journals of Ellen, Blanche, and Sabine (the latter the most stylish and enthralling of the narratives), Blanche's suicide note, and commentaries by others on the works of the Victorian writers. These commentaries include those by fictional characters as well as those of real-life writers such as Algernon Charles Swinburne and F. R. Leavis.

The most admirable of Byatt's many achievements is her ability to create a distinctive voice and style for each of her writers. Christabel and Ash write appropriately dense, allusive Victorian poetry; Leonora writes in an equally difficult structuralist-feminist style.

A genre Byatt exploits is the mystery or detective novel. Maud says, "Literary critics make natural detectives," and she and Roland painstakingly track down clues that will unlock the complicated secrets of the past. Byatt drops numerous hints— and some red herrings—to force the reader to participate in the unraveling. At the beginning of the novel, Roland thinks that he knows and understands Ash but recognizes in the portrait of the poet by Édouard Manet "an almost teasing aspect, a challenge: 'So you think you know me?'" Sabine's journal ends with Christabel receiving a letter but not opening it, and Byatt allows the reader to decide what it is. Christabel tells Ash, "You have made a murderess of me," one of many suggestions that her baby is dead. (Actually, she is referring to Blanche's suicide.)

The unreliability of the apparent truth is one of the themes of *Possession*. Ellen edits her journal to prevent the "ghouls and vultures" from uncovering matters she wants left unknown. She does not know that other sources provide the details that she chooses to exclude. Maud articulates Byatt's point that everything, finally, is connected: "I suppose one studies . . . literature because all these connections seem both endlessly exciting and then in some sense dangerously powerful—as though we held a clue to the true nature of things."

One of the virtues of *Possession* is the strength of its characterizations. Roland has the potential to be a good scholar but fails in most other areas of his life. He is so obsessed with Ash and literature in general that he is blind to Val's needs, to his exploitation of her. He acts without thinking, getting so involved in the pursuit of the correspondence that he loses Val and his job in the Ash Factory. While Maud considers him "a gentle and unthreatening being," Byatt bemoans a world in which such qualities are not considered virtues. Roland changes gradually over the course of his investigation, becoming less self-centered, going from hating his landlady's fifteen cats to caring for them when she becomes ill. He experiences a sort of epiphany, deciding that he can become a poet and create his own art rather than attempt to possess another's.

Maud is presented as aloof and untouchable, using her work as an escape from the messy details of life. Like her ancestor, she is often compared to a princess and resembles the otherworldly women in pre-Raphaelite paintings. She covers her luxurious hair as if she feared her sexuality. In pursuing the truth about Christabel, she is for the first time taking a chance on something she cannot control. She is drawn to Roland because she realizes that they share deficiencies.

Randolph and Ellen Ash illustrate how people hide their inner lives. There is a contrast between "the ferocious vitality" of Ash's poetry and the guarded dullness of his non-Christabel letters, the only apparent record of the private man. As the truth about him and Christabel is revealed, Ash evolves from icon to man, from lofty observer of the intellectual life of his time to understandably flawed human. He would not be the poet he is without the influence of Christabel, whom he calls his muse. He is attracted to her because she refuses to fit the Victorian mold of the compliant female. Ellen has allowed herself to play this role in part to make up to Ash for never consummating their marriage because of her fear of sex (one of several facts withheld from the twentieth century characters). She admits to herself that her life is a lie, that Christabel is "in one sense his true wife."

Like Ash, Christabel is thought not to have had a life beyond her work. She recalls Samuel Taylor Coleridge's unfinished "Christabel" (1816), for the complete truth can never be known about her: "I am my own riddle." Enigmatic on one level and transparent on another, she resembles the mythical half-woman, half-snake Melusina, who marries a mortal to gain a soul only to be betrayed. Yet she is the one to abandon Ash. Sabine perceives some of Christabel's complexity, comparing her with "the romantic Jane Eyre, so powerful, so passionate, so observant beneath her sober exterior." Christabel, like Maud, discovers an unexpected need to take risks. According to Blanche, "Independent women must expect more of themselves, since neither men nor other more conventionally domesticated women will hope for anything, or expect any result other than utter failure." In the context of the complicated events in *Possession*, such an observation is both true and oversimplified.

The novel's ironic title refers to the subplot about the battle over the legal ownership of the Ash-LaMotte correspondence, the loss of self-control through sexual passion, and, more important, the futile efforts of one person to possess another. Ash recognizes this: "He would teach her that she was not his possession, he would show her she was free." Keeping their child a secret is an attempt to assure her freedom. Christabel gives up May, in part, for this same reason, only to endure the pain of watching the girl grow up as her indifferent niece. Roland eventually sees that neither he nor anyone else has a right to the letters and their secrets: "Ash had not written the letters for Roland or for anyone else but Christabel LaMotte. Roland's find had turned out to be a sort of loss." No one, finally, comes close to possessing the truth. A postscript reveals that Ash knew of May's existence and even met her once. In slowly peeling back layer upon layer of her complex, romantic tale, Byatt dramatizes the mysterious hold of the past on the present.

Michael Adams

Sources for Further Study

Booklist. LXXXVII, September 11, 1990, p. 138.
The Christian Science Monitor. November 16, 1990, p. 13.
Kirkus Reviews. LVIII, August 15, 1990, p. 1107.
London Review of Books. XII, March 8, 1990, p. 17.
Los Angeles Times Book Review. October 28, 1990, p. 2.
New Statesman and Society. III, March 16, 1990, p. 38.
The New York Times. CXL, October 25, 1990, p. C24.
The New York Times Book Review. XCV, October 21, 1990, p. 9.
The New Yorker. LXVI, November 19, 1990, p. 151.
The Observer. March 11, 1990, p. 68.
Publishers Weekly. CCXXXVII, August 24, 1990, p. 54.
Punch. CCXCVIII, March 23, 1990, p. 41.
Time. CXXXVI, November 5, 1990, p. 94.
The Times Literary Supplement. March 2, 1990, p. 213.
Vogue. CLXXX, November, 1990, p. 274.
The Wall Street Journal. December 6, 1990, p. A16.
The Washington Post Book World. XX, October 17, 1990, p. 1.

THE QUEST FOR EL CID

Author: Richard Fletcher
First published: 1989, in Great Britain
Publisher: Alfred A. Knopf (New York). Illustrated. 218 pp. $24.95
Type of work: Historical biography
Time: The eleventh century
Locale: Spain

A *study of the life and times of Rodrigo Díaz, an adventurous medieval soldier of fortune who was immortalized as El Cid*

Principal personages:
RODRIGO DÍAZ, the aristocratic mercenary warrior known as El Cid, whose remarkable career culminated as ruler of Valencia
SANCHO II, king of Castile (1065-1072) and Rodrigo's first patron
ALFONSO VI, king of León (1065-1102) and later of Castile (1072-1109)
BERENGUER RAMÓN, Count of Barcelona (1092-1131) and Rodrigo's principal competitor in the conquest of Valencia
YŪSUF IBN TĀSHUFĪN, king of the Almoravides (1061-1106) and governor of Morocco

Like Barbara Tuchman's *A Distant Mirror* (1978), this biography is essentially the history of an era with the heroic career of an interesting and important individual thrust into the foreground to establish continuity and context. Like Tuchman, Richard Fletcher believes in the utility and propriety of popular history written with beauty and distinction. Fletcher also resembles Tuchman in that he is not afraid to take on the academic establishment—in this case, the school of Spanish patriotic history as personified by Ramón Menéndez Pidal, whose 1929 book, *La España del Cid*, has formed much of the modern understanding of the culture and politics of eleventh century Spain. Unlike Tuchman, Fletcher is thoroughly familiar with his subject—the multiethnic civilization of the Iberian peninsula at the time that the Christian rulers of Castile and León began their drive south to seize lands ruled by the Moors.

Fletcher could hardly have written a traditional biography for several reasons: First, very little is known about El Cid personally; second, what is known is in the form of a medieval epic, which was not intended as a source for modern scholarly research; and, finally, Fletcher is a storyteller. "In the summer of the year 1099," Fletcher begins, "there died in the city of Valencia, on the eastern seaboard of Spain, a man whose name was Rodrigo Díaz but who is better known to posterity as El Cid." These words provide a marvelous beginning for his tale, and are almost as memorable as the first lines of the subsequent chapter: "Long ago, in the early years of the seventh century of the Christian era, there lived a middle-aged businessman who started to behave rather oddly." This sentence is a powerful reminder of the continuity of the Spanish culture from the age of El Cid to that of Miguel Cervantes' *Don Quixote de La Mancha* (1605-1615). Though Fletcher fails to sustain this quality throughout his essays on the Spanish past and reverts to the style of the professional historian, his repeated use of quotations from Moorish and Christian poets reflects his love of poetry and epics and his admiration of a well-told story.

Rodrigo Díaz (c. 1043-1099) was a knight from an aristocratic house in Vivar and a vassal of the king of Castile. He participated in his first campaign in 1063 under the king's son, Sancho II. When his patron ascended the throne of Castile, Rodrigo became the commander of the royal forces. Sancho met a violent death in 1072, and sweeping changes in the administrative offices were carried out by his successor, Alfonso VI. Men such as Rodrigo, who only shortly before had driven the new king from León into exile among the Moors, were replaced en masse. Fortunately, the new king had the makings of greatness: Although Alfonso would not award Rodrigo with a high office, he did assist Rodrigo in private lawsuits and in arranging his marriage to a woman from a prominent family. This patronage proved to be less than the ambitious Rodrigo demanded, however; in 1081, after quarreling with the king, he went into exile.

For five years, Rodrigo served as a mercenary of the Muslim ruler of Zaragoza, fighting against the princes of nearby petty Moorish states. In the course of these operations he gathered together a private army, which would sustain him throughout the remainder of his complex military career. In the political chaos of these years, the only dependable forces were those that a charismatic and successful warrior could raise privately. The vulnerability of the Moorish states attracted the attention of outsiders. When Alfonso took Toledo, the Almoravides crossed the straits from Morocco, hoping to recover the city and impose their stern puritan interpretation of the faith on the more tolerant Moors. The first clash of crusade and jihad—at Sagrajas in 1086—resulted in an overwhelming Almoravide victory. With Rodrigo now unemployed and Alfonso frightened by his new enemies, the way was open for their reconciliation.

Rodrigo drove a hard bargain with Alfonso. He obtained a promise of hereditary possession of any and all lands he could conquer from the enemy. While Alfonso concerned himself with the defense of Toledo, Rodrigo moved southeast toward Valencia. The immediate problem facing the Christians was disunity in their own ranks. In particular, Count Berenguer Ramón refused to subordinate Catalan ambitions completely to Castilian leadership and abandon his own plans to annex Valencia and put his armies at the disposal of Rodrigo. Even after Rodrigo had defeated the count, however, Berenguer failed to become the loyal vassal Alfonso wanted but sought to make himself independent of Castile. Rodrigo collected tribute from the local Muslim princes, made alliances with more distant Moorish rulers, and appointed Jews to administer his government. In the ensuing years, Rodrigo defeated both Alfonso and the Almoravides, and in 1094, he captured the city of Valencia. Rodrigo's death in 1099 brought to an end his plans to establish a dynasty; within three years, the city was besieged by a powerful Almoravide army. Alfonso responded to the call for help from Rodrigo's widow; upon viewing the situation, however, he declared himself unwilling to commit troops permanently to the defense of a city so far from his domains. The king abandoned the burning city to the

Almoravides but carefully brought Rodrigo's body back to Castile.

An unknown poet (or poets) took this story as the basis for the great *Poema de Mio Cid* (c. 1140; *The Poem of the Cid*). The historical knight was absorbed into an epic hero. In contrast to the real Rodrigo, El Cid of the poem was emphatically Castilian, Christian, and loyal to his lord, King Alfonso VI. Although this fictional character was calculated to appeal to thirteenth century Spaniards, it was so far removed from reality that eventually someone had to perceive the discrepancy. It was Reinhart Dozy, a Dutch Arabist and historian, who in 1849 described the Cid as "more Muslim than Catholic." A persuasive Spanish reaction to Dozy's hostile portrait was not forthcoming until Ramón Menéndez Pidal's 1929 biography reconciled the apparent contradictions of literature and history. At a time when national unity was threatened, Menéndez' scholarship gave a foundation to patriotic arguments that Castile must provide the leadership in unifying Spain and that Castilians alone could personify Spanish virtues. Menéndez' Cid was subsequently used by Francisco Franco's propagandists and the Nationalists who dominated his military dictatorship to justify their most barbaric acts in the name of the Catholic church and Spain—a development which pained the politically moderate Menéndez. That the Falangist portrayal of the Spanish past had less to do with the historical Rodrigo Díaz than even the Cid of Charleton Heston (Menéndez was the technical adviser to the film) should not be surprising: History has been the handmaiden of politics before and will be so again. In any case, Fletcher's Rodrigo Díaz is heroic enough to satisfy all but the most extreme fanatics and human enough for the skeptics—in a complex world of deadly enemies and unreliable friends, he rose by sheer skill and bravery to previously unimagined heights. If in the end he was unable to provide for the defense of his conquests, Díaz left an example for posterity which was worthy of epic poetry. In a world that needs heroes made of more common clay than Menéndez' paragon, Fletcher's Cid is preferable for his very plausibility.

The remainder of Fletcher's book—arguably the better half—describes the society of this age, particularly its art, poetry, arms, and attitudes. This teeming scene would be incomprehensible if the author intended his readers to remember the individual rulers, generals, and poets he presents. Instead, his aim is to render intelligible the beautiful but cruel and complex world of El Cid.

William Urban

Sources for Further Study

The Atlantic. CCLXV, May, 1990, p. 139.
Booklist. LXXXVI, March 15, 1990, p. 1414.
The Economist. CCCXIII, November 4, 1989, p. 111.
History Today. XL, April, 1990, p. 57.
Kirkus Reviews. LVIII, February 15, 1990, p. 237.

Library Journal. CXV, March 1, 1990, p. 98.
Los Angeles Times Book Review. September 9, 1990, p. 2.
New York Times Book Review. XCV, April 8, 1990, p. 35.
The Observer. October 1, 1989, p. 49.
Publishers Weekly. CCXXXVII, February 2, 1990, p. 72.
The Times Literary Supplement. October 6, 1989, p. 1098.

RABBIT AT REST

Author: John Updike (1932-   )
Publisher: Alfred A. Knopf (New York). 512 pp. $21.95
Type of work: Novel
Time: 1988-1989
Locale: Southeastern Pennsylvania and southwestern Florida

The fourth, and final, volume in Updike's thirty-year attempt to record the life and times of Harry "Rabbit" Angstrom

Principal characters:
> HARRY "RABBIT" ANGSTROM, a fifty-five-year-old former basketball star and Toyota dealer
> JANICE ANGSTROM, his increasingly independent wife
> NELSON ANGSTROM, his wayward son and steward of the Toyota franchise
> TERESA "PRU" ANGSTROM, Nelson's wife
> JUDY ANGSTROM, Harry's eight-year-old granddaughter
> ROY ANGSTROM, Harry's four-year-old grandson
> THELMA HARRISON, Harry's clandestine lover
> RON HARRISON, Thelma's husband and Harry's childhood classmate
> CHARLIE STAVROS, a retired car salesman

"You might say it's a depressed book about a depressed man, written by a depressed man," said John Updike cheerfully to the American Booksellers Association convention in Las Vegas three months before the publication of *Rabbit at Rest*. The first draft of his book, which Updike described as "a kind of dying for me," was completed ten days before the death of his mother, his last personal link to the corner of Pennsylvania that Rabbit inhabits. *Rabbit at Rest* is the ultimate installment in the tetralogy that began with *Rabbit Run* (1960) and continued with *Rabbit Redux* (1971) and *Rabbit Is Rich* (1981). "Enough," concludes the latest volume, and Harry "Rabbit" Angstrom, one of the most widely followed characters in contemporary American fiction, seems to have had his final run.

Rabbit at Rest is the culmination of Updike's thirty-year attempt to record the life and times of the high school basketball star of Brewer, Pennsylvania. The book begins with premonitions of death as Harry awaits the arrival of his son Nelson and his family at the Southwest Florida Regional Airport, and it ends in the intensive-care ward, where the fifty-six-year-old has been hospitalized following a massive heart attack. As in the previous Rabbit books, Updike employs a flexible third-person technique that allows him to represent the observations, memories, expectations, and fantasies of his characters, primarily Harry Angstrom.

The author echoes the opening of *Rabbit Run* with a late scene in *Rabbit at Rest* in which his aging, overweight former athlete challenges youthful hotshots at a playground hoop. Harry "has time left only for truth," and, despite its 512 pages, making it the longest book in the Rabbit series, the novel compels attention with the sense of fundamental truths about American society during the waning months of the 1980's, years that, as much as the 1930's of W. H. Auden's "September 1,

1939," appear "a low dishonest decade." Written in the present tense that Updike pioneered in the first volume, *Rabbit at Rest* engages the reader with a sense of immediacy and urgency.

Leaving management of the family Toyota franchise to Nelson, Harry and his wife, Janice, spend half the year in a condominium in Deleon, Florida. Rabbit's rest is disturbed, however, by revelation that his son is a cocaine addict who has bilked their business of more than $200,000 in order to support his habit. Despite recent angioplasty following a boating mishap with granddaughter Judy, Harry returns to run Springer Motors, the dealership created by Janice's late father, while Nelson undergoes rehabilitation at a clinic in Philadelphia. In an episode verging on ethnic caricature ("Toyota agency must be a prace of disciprine, a prace of order," declares Mr. Shimada), a Japanese executive from the corporation visits Harry to inform him that Toyota has decided to withdraw authorization for Springer Motors to sell its automobiles. Harry revisits his lover Thelma Harrison, now smelling of urine and dying of lupus, and ignites an explosive relationship with his daughter-in-law Pru. When pressures become too oppressive, he again takes to the road.

Throughout the tetralogy, Updike has used Harry as a unit of measurement for calculating transformations in the United States during each of four decades. Harry was bred to be a member of the species *Homo mediocris americanus*, a "middle American" who, despite coming into some money at the death of his father-in-law, is demographically, intellectually, and spiritually unremarkable. He is a hero for a shabby time that lacks authentic heroes. One of the challenges that Updike does not always master is to avoid the role of ventriloquist, of projecting into his often un-couth character the more sophisticated insights of his author. Yet the novel has also been faulted for the banality of its observations, a charge that is itself an indirect tribute to Updike's success in capturing the mental and emotional life of *l'homme moyen sensuel*. In his nonfiction, Updike has expressed intellectually unfashionable sentiments of patriotism, but never in the vulgar terms in which Harry conceives his love of country—"all in all this is the happiest fucking country the world has ever seen." The novel's melancholy, its rueful sense of social entropy, belies such occa-sional bursts of smugness.

Rabbit at Rest, in which Harry dresses up as Uncle Sam for a Fourth of July parade in Pennsylvania, records a world in which acquired immune deficiency syndrome and drug abuse are rampant and young people, much more than 230-pound Harry, a compulsive gobbler of junk food, are obsessed with their diets. Women are more as-sertive and independent than they were in Harry's youth, and, while he becomes in-capacitated, Janice joins a women's group and takes classes on real estate. The Ang-stroms' practice of television-channel surfing and the montage of radio stations that Harry tunes into and out of as he travels the nation's highways make the novel a time capsule of popular music, advertising, and current events for the end of the twentieth century. *Rabbit at Rest* is deftly attentive to the knowing detail, and a denizen of the twenty-first could do worse than read the book to find out how it was.

The novel is a fitting extension and culmination of its three predecessors, but it is also self-sufficient. A reader need not have read the other Rabbit books in order to understand and savor Harry's final months, to be moved by, for example, the grandfather's developing relationship with his granddaughter. Still, *Rabbit at Rest* does offer richer resonances to a reader familiar with its prehistory, who has lived with Harry, Janice, Thelma, and the others almost as long as they have lived with one another. When Harry reads a newspaper headline about renovations to a circus museum—"Circus Redux"—he cringes at a term that has grown familiar and dear to most of his readers: "He hates that word, you see it everywhere, and he doesn't know how to pronounce it." While that intertextual jest is apparent to anyone who has merely heard the title of the second Rabbit book, other references to leporine lore add lusher complexities to the reading experience for those conversant with the earlier books.

Although Harry, Janice, and the new volume remain haunted by parental responsibility for the bathtub drowning of the Angstroms' infant daughter, readers of *Rabbit Run* are best equipped to see parallels to the incident in *Rabbit at Rest* in which Harry desperately struggles to save his granddaughter Judy after their Sunfish capsizes off Florida's Gulf Coast. The mutual resentment of Harry and Nelson is best understood by those who have examined the full record of paternal neglect and filial disappointment. When Harry is aroused from angioplasty in a Brewer hospital, he finds himself attended to by a nurse named Annabelle, who proves to be the daughter of Ruth Byer, the kindly local whore with whom Harry had a fling long enough ago for Annabelle to be his daughter. That possibility troubles and tantalizes Harry and will most intrigue those readers who have earlier met Ruth, who remains offstage throughout *Rabbit at Rest*. Some of the parallels, symmetries, and recurrences seem contrived, but most serve to create a fictional continuum in which Rabbit, ever eager to evade the consequences of past mistakes, can run but not hide.

Harry is more adept at selling cars than formulating philosophy, but, reflecting on the radical transformations to which he has been forced to adjust during an untidy lifetime, he ruminates on the insubstantiality of earthly existence: "Rabbit realized the world was not solid and benign, it was a shabby set of temporary arrangements rigged up for the time being, all for the sake of the money." The form that *Rabbit at Rest* and the entire tetralogy take—deliberate, sober, and cumulative—is at odds with that observation, except that the spectacle of one man's frenetic race through his brief appointed time is a reminder of the vanity of human wishes. The Rabbit series is an enduring monument to evanescence.

"There is just no end to it, no end of information," muses Harry over news of Tiananmen Square, First Dog Millie, the Lockerbie plane crash, ozone depletion, elections in Poland, and Mike Schmidt's retirement. Yet Updike's Rabbit habit has an apparent end. While Harry is recovering from coronary surgery, his sister Mim phones from Las Vegas. Recalling their dead parents, Mim declares: "I suppose their hearts failed in the end but so does everybody's, because that's what life is, a strain on the heart." A valediction to the end of an era and of an obnoxious, libidinous, and endearing character as distinctive and representative as Sinclair Lewis'

Babbitt, *Rabbit at Rest* strains the heart without failure.

Because of the critical and commercial success of its three predecessors, the appearance of *Rabbit at Rest* was a major publishing event. Updike's stature, acquired largely by means of the Rabbit books, as perhaps the most serious popular novelist or the most popular serious novelist in the United States in his day guarantees widespread attention to anything he produces. *Rabbit at Rest* immediately leaped onto the best-seller lists, and it elicited a spectrum of impassioned reactions from critics. Garry Wills, surveying the entire tetralogy in *The New York Review of Books*, finds the series increasingly implausible and vacuous. He is particularly harsh toward *Rabbit at Rest*, faulting it for an elaborate and clever camouflage of its own emptiness: "Description makes up for analysis; detail for design; inclusiveness for rigor; and mere length for moral heft or grip." By contrast, *Newsweek* critic Peter S. Prescott provides this verdict on the Rabbit series: "It's been a grand trip, and this finale is one of Updike's best books." Writing in *The Washington Post*, Jonathan Raban hails Updike's book as a masterpiece: "*Rabbit at Rest* is one of the very few modern novels in English (Bellow's *Herzog* is another) that one can set beside the work of Dickens, Thackeray, George Eliot, Joyce and not feel the draft."

Windy pronouncements about Updike's achievement have filled scholarly and popular publications for decades. What is probably safe to conclude is that *Rabbit at Rest*, an autopsy and a requiem for the 1980's and for a character who is as much an emblem of it as Roseanne Barr, Donald Trump, and Marion Barry, will continue to be read and discussed for many decades to come.

Steven G. Kellman

Sources for Further Study

Chicago Tribune. September 30, 1990, XIV, p. 1.
Los Angeles Times Book Review. October 7, 1990, p. 3.
The New Criterion. IX, October, 1990, p. 30.
New Statesman and Society. III, October 26, 1990, p. 33.
The New York Review of Books. XXXVII, October 25, 1990, p. 11.
The New York Times Book Review. XCV, September 30, 1990, p. 1.
The New Yorker. LXVI, October 22, 1990, p. 143.
Newsweek. CXV, October 1, 1990, p. 66.
Publishers Weekly. CCXXXVII, August 10, 1990, p. 433.
Time. CXXXVI, October 15, 1990, p. 84.
The Times Literary Supplement. October 26, 1990, p. 1145.
The Washington Post Book World. XX, September 30, 1990, p. 1.

RACE AND SLAVERY IN THE MIDDLE EAST
An Historical Enquiry

Author: Bernard Lewis (1916-   )
Publisher: Oxford University Press (New York). Illustrated. 184 pp. $24.95
Type of work: History
Time: 600-1900
Locale: The Middle East

An interpretive history of slavery and race in the Islamic world

Throughout much of history, human bondage has been an acceptable institution to a large part of mankind. It was not until the mid-nineteenth century that the world-wide movement for abolition began slavery's long and sometimes painful decline to the status of a generally recognized evil. Racism, particularly that directed toward black Africans, is not as ancient as slavery, but, by the nineteenth century, these two unsavory features of human existence had become inexorably coupled. It is almost impossible to discuss one completely without, in some way, coming to grips with the other. Slavery, racism, and the relationship between the two have become favorite subjects of inquiry for historians and social scientists, and hundreds of books have been produced examining the problem from almost every conceivable angle. One surprising area of scholarly neglect, however, is the long and complex history of slavery and race in the world of Islam—the Middle East. Bernard Lewis, Dodge Professor of Near Eastern Studies emeritus at Princeton University, attempts to begin the process of filling in this unusual gap in the historical record with his brief "historical enquiry."

The explanation for the lack of hard data about Middle Eastern slavery and racial attitudes, according to Lewis, is "the extreme sensitivity of the subject." Neither scholars inside nor outside the world of Islam have found such questions open for thorough and objective examination. Middle Eastern governments as well as the general populace often see such research from Western scholars as an attack upon their religion and culture, and Muslim scholars simply do not have the same freedom of inquiry as their American and European counterparts. This is particularly regrettable since it has led to a confused and inaccurate image fostered by Western scholars as well-known as Arnold Toynbee. According to this distorted view, the Islamic world was largely color-blind, and Islamic slavery was somehow less repugnant than the Western variety. While Lewis warns his readers not to make the assumption that Muslim racial attitudes mirror those of South Africa or that Islamic slavery was a replica of the plantation system in the American South, he makes it clear that slavery was a crucial element in Middle Eastern society for much of its history and, like slavery everywhere, produced human suffering. Morever, it was also accompanied by various forms of prejudice and discrimination against black Africans.

Historians generally agree that racial distinction played no appreciable role in the systems of bondage in antiquity, such as Greece and Rome. While most ancient societies did assume that outsiders were inferior, using descriptive terms such as "barbarian," and foreignness was generally sufficient justification for enslavement, nowhere in the ancient world did this almost universal ethnocentrism take on the characteristics of what is termed racism in the eighteenth, nineteenth, and twentieth centuries. Modern racism places primary emphasis on supposedly inherent characteristics, which can never be changed, while prejudice against foreigners in the ancient world was largely an expression of cultural difference. This meant, in effect, that anyone might be a slave, regardless of physical characteristics, and that once free an individual found it easier to become part of the general population.

The three great religions of the Middle East—Judaism, Christianity, and Islam—originated in an era in which slavery was the accepted norm, and all three contained instructions to believers intended to soften the lot of the slave. In Lewis' estimation, Islam, the youngest of the three, contained the strongest bias toward freedom. Still, slavery was an accepted institution, and the rapid expansion of Islam through conquest brought the Arab peoples into contact with thousands of potential candidates for enslavement. As a result, human bondage became a very important part of Islamic society, and while it never played as crucial a role as plantation slavery in European expansion centuries later, it did have significant impact on the Middle Eastern economy.

Ironically, the efforts of Jewish, Christian, and Muslim theologians and jurists to regulate the treatment of slaves in the spirit of their religious beliefs left a body of law and custom that would eventually act as support for slavery when it was attacked from outside. In 1855, for example, the Ottoman government, in response to British pressure, attempted to halt the traffic in slaves within the Turkish Empire. The Arab leaders of the Al-Hijaz province, who were responsible for protecting the holy cities of Mecca and Medina, rose in revolt citing the ban on the slave trade as an excuse. Such an action, they claimed, was a violation of the holy law of Islam. The Turks were able to put down the rebels, but were ultimately forced to exempt Al-Hijaz from the empirewide decree banning commerce in human beings. Regrettably, this commerce would continue in Arabia at least until the mid-twentieth century.

By the time of the revolt against the Turks, the vast majority of slaves sold in Al-Hijaz were black, and there is little doubt that they occupied a lower position than white slaves. Such discrimination based on color, as Lewis makes clear, runs counter to the spirit of the Koran. Both Christianity and Islam began as universalist religions opening their ranks to all. Such an attitude would certainly act as a counterforce against the development of modern racism, but, as is so often the case, these ideals were quickly overwhelmed by social reality. Lewis finds evidence that, by the late seventh century, black skin was becoming a mark of inferiority. Part of his argument is based on the apparent necessity for Arab writers to reaffirm continually the principle of equality under God, implying the presence of prejudice. Particularly significant is the repeated use of blackness in an Arabic rhetorical device which seeks to emphasize a positive principle by carrying it to an absurd extreme. For example, good Muslims were instructed to select their wives for piety, not beauty or wealth, and told that "a slit-nosed black slave-woman, if pious, is preferable." The implication is clear; while piety is most important, black skin is somehow less acceptable than light skin. A similar kind of evidence comes from the works of Arabic poets of African descent who used their own blackness metaphorically, lamenting the failure of society to see beyond skin color. Lewis' arguments are similar to those used by students of slavery and racism in the Americas, such as Winthrop D. Jordan who, in his well-known study *White Over Black: American Attitudes Toward the Negro, 1550-1812* (1968), stresses the general antipathy that existed toward blackness in the English language and culture before the development of slavery in British colonies.

In the Islamic world, as in the Americas, this basic negative attitude toward blackness ultimately led to what would be called in the modern context "racial stereotyping." Arabs developed a mind-set toward the people of sub-Saharan Africa that saw them as somehow uniquely suited for slavery. This was particularly true of the so-called Zanj, an Arabic term which inevitably became pejorative, used to refer to the Bantu-speaking peoples south of Ethiopia. Even as noted a scholar as Ibn Khaldūn, who was certainly one of the most outstanding observers of human culture in the Middle Ages, contributed to the adverse image. While he placed the blame for African inferiority on climate rather than genetics, he believed that the Zanj had little that was "human" about them. Instead they had "attributes" that were "quite similar to dumb animals." In the multicolored world of Islamic slavery, the Zanj eventually came to be associated with the most degrading forms of labor. With the passage of time even the original Arabic word for slave, *abd*, evolved to mean only a black slave or in some areas any black, even if free.

Lewis illustrates how close the Arab stereotype came to resemble the well-known stereotype in the West by using examples from perhaps the best-known work of Arabic literature, *The Book of a Thousand and One Nights* or *Arabian Nights*, made famous in the Victorian era by Sir Richard Burton's translation (1885-1888). Several of the stories deal with what is clearly seen as distasteful sexual contact between white women and lascivious black male slaves. In addition to such typical white male sexual nightmares, Lewis draws on numerous other Arabic sources to outline a view that pictured blacks as foulsmelling, stupid, incurably frivolous, dishonest, and unusually gifted with a sense of rhythm. The image would fit well with the ideas of nineteenth century defenders of slavery in the American South or twentieth century members of the Ku Klux Klan.

In spite of the similarities between slavery and racism in the Islamic world and the Americas, Lewis is careful to remind his readers of essential differences which would clearly have an impact on racial attitudes as well as the lot of the individual slave. Probably most important for the actual structure of the institution, bondage in the Middle East was never involved in an expanding commercial society such as that of the Americas. With some important exceptions, such as a brief period of cotton growing in Egypt or gang labor used in draining the tidal marshes of southern Iraq, Islamic slavery did not typically produce the same sort of regimented labor that was so much a part of the European plantation system in the colonies. In fact, while little is known about the actual status of slaves in rural areas of the Middle East, it is reasonable to assume that slavery was much more of an urban institution in the Islamic world than it was in European colonies. As a result, a much larger percentage of Muslim slaves were probably involved in domestic service. Moreover, the cultural differences between Europe and the Middle East produced considerable variation in the actual use of slaves. European colonial slavery never produced institutions such as harems and never made extensive use of eunuchs. In addition, there was no real parallel in European experience to the Muslim use of slaves in military units such as the famous Egyptian Mamluks. Such differences are as important as the similarities in understanding slavery.

From the perspective of racial attitudes, it is important to remember that slavery in Muslim societies was not restricted to one race. White Europeans as well as other ethnic groups made up part of the slave population. This fact, along with the impact of Islamic values, probably meant that the degree of actual racial antipathy between master and slave was never as deep in the Middle East as in European societies such as the American South. Still, as time progressed, blacks were restricted to the more menial tasks and an obvious hierarchy developed among the slaves which worked to the advantage of those with light skin. Whether such attitudes should be classed as the same kind of racism that existed in the West is simply a matter of semantics.

Bernard Lewis clearly intends his short treatment of Islamic slavery and race as the beginning of a badly needed examination rather than as a definitive conclusion. He would be the first to admit that his arguments are provisional and may well be revised by more extensive research. To aid those who would follow his lead, he adds an appendix which includes some of the most important available documents. Inevitably, future studies of this important and still obscure part of the human past will owe a debt of gratitude to his pioneering work.

David Warren Bowen

Sources for Further Study

The New York Review of Books. XXXVII, October 11, 1990, p. 35.
The New York Times Book Review. XCV, August 5, 1990, p. 20.
The Times Literary Supplement. December 21, 1990, p. 1371.
Washington Times. August 20, 1990, p. F3.

RANDALL JARRELL
A Literary Life

Author: William H. Pritchard (1932-   )
Publisher: Farrar, Straus & Giroux (New York). 338 pp. $25.00
Type of work: Literary biography
Time: 1914-1965
Locale: The United States

This biography of twentieth century American poet Randall Jarrell finds in his life and work the unifying theme of real and imagined losses

> *Principal personages:*
> RANDALL JARRELL, the American poet
> OWEN JARRELL, his father
> ANNA CAMPBELL JARRELL, his mother
> MACKIE LANGHAM JARRELL, his first wife
> MARY VON SCHRADER JARRELL, his second wife
> KITTEN, his cat
> ROBERT PENN WARREN,
> JOHN CROWE RANSOM,
> ROBERT FROST,
> CONRAD AIKEN,
> ALLEN TATE, and
> W. H. AUDEN, American poets

"Back in Los Angeles, we missed/ Los Angeles," says the torn and baffled speaker of "Thinking of the Lost World," the title poem of Randall Jarrell's posthumous collection. In Jarrell's translucent, elegiac poems, the real places are those in the mind and heart; those in the world are only disappointing approximations, even frauds. William Pritchard's biography skillfully links events of the poet's life with his work in an absorbing narrative that shows the development of this intensely lyrical and passionate voice.

Pritchard is known for his other literary biographies, particularly *Frost: A Literary Life Reconsidered* (1984), which reevaluates Frost in the wake of Lawrance Thompson's highly uncomplimentary biography. The Pritchard book is a convincing rehabilitation, partly because of the subtlety and complexity of the analysis. There is no such controversy over Jarrell, the facts of his life being hidden behind no myth. The only debatable issue here is the value of Jarrell's work to the postmodern era, with accusations of sentimentality balanced by praise for the fine edge of his anguished lyricism. Here too Pritchard argues for the affirmative. His biography provides links between poetry and life which aid in understanding the poems and contribute to appreciation of them.

The "losses" that were to characterize Jarrell's poems began early. Born in 1914 to an attractive Tennessee photographer and his delicate and somewhat hypochondriacal wife, Anna, Jarrell had his childhood idyll shattered by the divorce of his parents and his mother's ensuing financial problems. He lived then for a time with his paternal grandparents in California, but this period of relative peace and pleasure was terminated by his grandparents' inability (or perhaps unwillingness) to support him further. Pritchard notes that it was the rediscovery near the end of his life of his childhood letters written to his mother from California that informed "the remarkable poems—'The Lost World' and 'Thinking of the Lost World'—which crown his work as a poet."

Jarrell's sense of alienation and of not belonging persisted throughout his years at Vanderbilt University, during which he perceived of himself as a Romantic poet and a misunderstood outsider. In actuality, however, the reigning literary giants— John Crowe Ransom, Allen Tate, and Robert Penn Warren—supported and encouraged him from the start. At a time when most writers his age were lucky to get polite rejection slips, Pritchard comments, Jarrell was being published in *The Southern Review* and *The New Republic*. He played the role of the *enfant terrible*, criticizing his mentors and often disregarding their suggestions; nevertheless, they continued to advance his career, as apparently did the many others who found him mysteriously attractive as a poet and as a person.

From 1937 to 1939, Jarrell taught at Kenyon College and then at the University of Texas. Pritchard's account shows how neither Jarrell's marriage to Mackie Langham, a colleague in the English Department at Texas, nor his growing reputation was enough to mitigate his sense of alienation and deprivation. His poetry, however, grew in force as he set aside romantic clichés and deliberate obscurity for an attempt to create character and voice. Pritchard identifies "90 North," published in *The New Republic* in 1941, as the first poem in Jarrell's mature style that captures his most enduring characteristics:

> The attempt to be "rather like speech" instead of "false or rhetorical" (in the words of a December 1940 letter to Tate); the impulse, concurrently, to speak in a gravely authoritative way about human experience; and the sense that somehow the child is importantly connected to that way of speaking come together in the . . . poem, "90 North."

This poem, exploring "the difference between childish illusion and adult disenchantment," introduces the essential Jarrell

His first collection, *Blood from a Stranger* (1942), was for the most part a nostalgic/ romantic collection of poems of pathos. It was not until Jarrell experienced the war first hand that he found his true voice. His enlistment in the Army Air Corps and his experiences as a celestial navigator tower operator working with B-29 crews formed the basis for many of his best-known poems. His two books of war poems, *Little Friend, Little Friend* (1945) and *Losses* (1948), include many widely anthologized pieces including the ubiquitous "The Death of the Ball Turret Gunner." The chapter "In Service" is one of the most enjoyable of the biography; its detail makes Jarrell's service experience come alive as well as showing how in his poetry, as in his letters home, it is often "the army rather than the war" that is his true subject.

What characterizes the army poems, however, is the sense of baffled desire, of devastating loss. Tragedy mingles with pathos and irony in lines such as those that open the poem "Losses":

> We read our mail and counted up our missions—
> In bombers named for girls, we burned
> The cities we had learned about in school—

Jarrell has clearly established his theme, the collision between youthful idealism and adult disillusion, and it remains the same throughout the poems of his life until the anguish of personal and universal loss crescendoes in his last collection, *The Lost World*.

Pritchard's account of life and literature does not stint Jarrell's impassioned, opinionated criticism, which generated fires in his classrooms besides providing memorable capsule commentaries on many major figures. The account describes the love-hate relationship Jarrell had with the New Critics, his guides and mentors, who found the work's meaning within the text and rejected concerns external to the text such as history, biography, and theory. In Jarrell's criticism there are no rigid boundaries; biography and history and psychology and even his own students' random comments turn up in his analyses. His judgments are quirky; he often takes up for unpopular figures and dispraises the favorites, but his most throwaway comments often have the ring of truth, as when he said in a mostly favorable critique of Robert Frost that here was "the public figure's relishing consciousness of himself" and of Walt Whitman's "I am a habitan of Vienna" that "one has an immediate vision of him as a sort of French-Canadian halfbreed to whom the Viennese are offering, with trepidation, little mounds of whipped cream."

The biography also examines the novel and the children's books, both of which show Jarrell's meticulous attention to detail and his identification with children and outsiders. The novel, a caustic satire on academe based on his experiences teaching at Sarah Lawrence College, is more of interest for his random and devastating observations than for its expertise *qua* novel. *Pictures from an Institution* (1954) is, as its title implies, closer to a series of observations than to a well-made story, and the key to its appreciation is partly in recognition of the figures it fictionalizes. The president of Sarah Lawrence, Harold Taylor, becomes Dwight Robbins, president of Benton College. As Pritchard comments parenthetically, "Taylor would also figure in [Mary] McCarthy's novel *The Groves of Academe*, causing him—as he put it years later—to think twice before appointing visiting 'novelist-teachers with a predisposition to carve people up.'" The novel contains characters with whom professors are cozily familiar and presents slices of academic life in such a way as to cause an explosion of flashes of recognition. It is not in the strictest sense, however, a novel.

The more successful children's stories, illustrated by Maurice Sendak, show that the childless poet Jarrell had nevertheless an intense understanding of the child's vision. *The Bat-Poet* (1964) and the two other stories completed near the end of the poet's life take a sympathetic view of idiosyncrasy and isolation and weave poetic tales of what it means to watch the mainstream flow by from some distance not quite far enough for detachment.

Pritchard's biography concentrates more on the interior world for the second half, though it does describe the end of Jarrell's first marriage, the friendship (affair?) with Elizabeth Eisler, and the second marriage with Mary Jarrell—a woman clearly more appropriate a wife for Jarrell than was Mackie, as Mary was willing to give up her own potential achievements to be the supportive mother/wife Jarrell demanded. Lively anecdotes represent Jarrell as professor at Princeton University and Greensboro College, throwing out to his students the same sort of literary witticism that enlivened his criticism. Much of the focus here, however, is on the development of his poetic gift as he approached his last phase, marked in his life by depression and instability and in his work by the unbalanced intensity of *The Lost World*.

If there is a controversy regarding the facts of Jarrell's life, it concerns his death: He was struck by a car while recovering from a suicide attempt. Pritchard skirts the controversy, not taking a decisive stand as to whether this end was indeed a suicide or simply an ironic accident. "My own impulse is to believe that Jarrell's death was unintentional," he says; "that—however slowly—he was recovering from his madness of that previous spring; that his forward looking plans, professional and artistic, revealed a will to live." Offered as indirect support of this position are the points of optimism or transcendence in his last and perhaps most powerful poems, published posthumously in *The Lost World*. "Perhaps the deepest impulse in 'Thinking of the Lost World' and in the other poems Jarrell wrote near the end of his life was the will to believe that there was more to life than the disillusionment granted the child-grownup in '90 North,'" Pritchard reflects. These poems to him indicate a coming to terms:

> I hold in my own hands, in happiness,
> Nothing: the nothing for which there is no reward.

This is "rueful acceptance mixed with real elation at what imagining the past has made available"; it is a bittersweet epiphany. The poems, however, can be read as a welcoming of death. Finally, this kind of speculation can never be anything but air-castle construction.

Overall, this book achieves a fine balance between biography and criticism, tracing the exterior events as they imprint the interior world and leave their mark on the poetry, fiction, and criticism. The "literary life" promised by the subtitle is double; not only is the book a literary life, but Jarrell lived a literary life, experienced most intensely through letters, poems, words. (The book's one drawback is that it does not lend itself so easily to the scholar as to the enthusiastic reader: Its index is confusing and incomplete, its notes noncommittal.) Through the interweaving of biography and analysis the reader gets a clear picture of the difficult, self-absorbed, and alienated man for whom a transcendent nostalgia is the hallmark of all his work. Perhaps even more persuasive, this apparently evenhanded treatment is nevertheless a convincing argument that Randall Jarrell's poetry is well worth the reader's serious attention.

Janet McCann

Sources for Further Study

Booklist. LXXXVI, February 1, 1990, p. 1063.
Chicago Tribune. June 24, 1990, XIV, p. 4.
Choice. XXVIII, September, 1990, p. 114
Kirkus Reviews. LVII, December 15, 1989, p. 1811.
Library Journal. CXV, February 1, 1990, p. 86.
National Review. XLII, September 17, 1990, p. 48.
The New Leader. LXXIII, May 14, 1990, p. 13.
The New Republic. CCIII, July 23, 1990, p. 32.
The New York Times Book Review. XCV, May 6, 1990, p. 3.
Publishers Weekly. CCXXXVII, March 2, 1990, p. 70.
The Washington Post Book World. XX, April 15, 1990, p. 4.

RECALCITRANCE, FAULKNER, AND THE PROFESSORS
A Critical Fiction

Author: Austin M. Wright (1922-   )
Publisher: University of Iowa Press (Iowa City). 242 pp. $25.00; paperback $12.95
Type of work: Literary theory

An exploration, within the context of a fable, of recalcitrance as a means of resolving formalist/anti-formalist conflict in literary theory

> Principal characters:
> CHARLIE MERCER, an untenured English professor
> BILL TUTTLE, a formalist critic and professor
> JAKE JACKSON, an anti-formalist critic and professor
> OLGA WING, a feminist/political critic and professor
> ARTHUR BIRDSONG, a philanthropist, founder of an ideal English department
> EVE BIRDSONG, Arthur's daughter, an initially confused student

Austin M. Wright has written a rare work of literary theory, a readable and entertaining study of a major theoretical problem that can be understood by a thoughtful reader who is generally unfamiliar with literary theory. The key to his success is his use of the dialectical approach which he adopts from Plato. Wright discusses this method at the end of the book, when he has two of his characters, Charlie Mercer and Eve Birdsong, discuss how their experience of a four-day roundtable can be written up most effectively. There are good theoretical and practical reasons for presenting the ideas they have discovered in the way they discovered them rather than as conclusions based on discussions, but Charlie acknowledges that such an approach will be less efficient than a direct presentation. This approach, however, is what makes the book accessible perhaps even to undergraduates.

In Arthur Birdsong's ideal English department, a disturbing rivalry has developed between Bill Tuttle and Jake Jackson. Because they are friendly in public, this rivalry is not easily apparent, but their students notice it in the classroom, because what they learn from Tuttle is contradicted and scorned by Jackson and vice versa. Student Eve Birdsong takes this problem to her friendly junior professor, Charlie. Both go to her father, and the result is one of his favorite activities, a department roundtable. The interested parties gather and agree that Tuttle and Jackson will present their positions and defend them in debate. They will use William Faulkner's *As I Lay Dying* (1930) as an exemplary text, because all the participants are familiar with it. Eve is to decide the winner; his prize will be her hand in marriage.

The conflict between Tuttle and Jackson is one of the ancient problems of literary studies as well as of philosophy. William Blake embodies this conflict when he characterizes the two impulses of the poetic imagination as the prolific and the devourer in *The Marriage of Heaven and Hell* (1793). In *Die Geburt der Tragödie aus dem Geiste der Musik* (1872; The Birth of Tragedy Out of the Spirit of Music, 1909), Friedrich Nietzsche describes the two great opposing forces of culture as

Dionysian and Apollonian. Continuing this perennial debate, Jackson speaks for the forces of indeterminacy and for the joys of tearing down ideas of order to find contradictions and plurality of meaning. He argues that wholeness is not a characteristic of literary works and that attempts to describe their wholeness are wrong on multiple grounds. (One of the more important objections to formalism is that it imposes the critic's view upon the work and attempts to silence other points of view.) On the other side, Tuttle speaks for the primacy of order and wholeness in literary works, and protests against the notion that literary works are without determinate forms and meanings. He argues that novels cannot be made or read without some governing idea or plot to guide the writer and the reader.

The roundtable at Phil's Pub lasts four days and moves through twelve chapters. People prepare for the debate by reading a set of student papers from Charlie Mercer's class on *As I Lay Dying*. Acknowledging that the novel presents reading problems, Charlie asks his students to write about one or more of the problems they have. These papers help to expose a number of ways in which the novel resists any easy description of how it works, in its parts and in its possible wholeness.

In chapters 2 through 4, which cover the first evening, the two senior professors present their papers. Tuttle argues that *As I Lay Dying*, despite the oddity of its narration by multiple narrators (many of whom do not speak their parts in their own normal voices), is nevertheless unified by a comic plot in which the rural Bundren family, as a multiple protagonist, is tested and found wanting by the quest imposed upon them by their dead mother's wish to be buried in town. Jackson's reply begins by searching for the failures in Tuttle's analysis. Jackson denies and argues against the validity of a number of Tuttle's critical concepts such as implied reader, plot, and wholeness. This exchange illustrates the value of the dialectic method, for it helps ensure that the few specialized terms in the book receive fairly clear definitions. Jackson distrusts what he sees as an authoritarian purpose behind Tuttle's approach, and he suggests there is a kind of moral cowardice there as well, a wish to gloss over the difficulties of art and life with pretty pictures of the way Tuttle wants things to be. Jackson then states his own position. The force of a work, he believes, depends on its resistance to attempts to make it fit into a form, or a description of wholeness. The reader's job is to resist whatever in the work leads one to desire a final resolution. He sees potentially dozens of meanings in *As I Lay Dying*, and chooses one to share, an allegory in which Addie Bundren, the dead mother, represents the novel, a dead genre that continues to live as long as it can hold readers' attention. These two papers are followed by a discussion that questions the assumptions and intentions of both sides. Afterward, as Charlie visits with Eve about the debate, he decides he may have a paper of his own to give, a way of reconciling the two points of view they have heard.

The second day—chapters 5 and 6—includes two more presentations. Olga Wing argues that both Tuttle and Jackson are ignoring the truly important aspects of literature. How a work holds together or fails to is of little interest next to two other aspects of the experience of reading: the moment-by-moment experience of the details and parts of the story and the sociopolitical meanings that arise from this experience. Wing points out that even though she is caught up pleasurably in the experience of reading *As I Lay Dying*, when she steps back from the experience, she finds Faulkner's misogyny disguised but not absent in the work. Moreover, she is morally offended by what she and Tuttle see as Faulkner's condescension to his characters in making poor white Southern farmers the butt of his humor. Charlie follows her with his attempt to reconcile Tuttle and Jackson, but he is unprepared at this point to respond adequately to Wing.

Charlie's presentation is the heart of the book. He offers the idea that there are two opposing forces operating in any act of reading: form and recalcitrance. Form may be described as the reader's desire to understand how the whole story fits together. The reader experiences this quest for an appropriate order at virtually every moment of the reading experience. It begins with picking up the book, when it might be about anything at all, and gradually narrows to a series of increasingly informed guesses about how the elements that have been read will fit together with those yet remaining to be seen. Recalcitrance may be described as all those elements in the work that prevent or at least delay the reader from forming a final idea of how the work fits together. Recalcitrance, too, is present at every moment of the reading experience. In *As I Lay Dying*, and probably in virtually all interesting fiction, recalcitrance remains at the end of the reading and even after rereading and considerable postreading activity. This point is illustrated by the fact that rarely does anyone write the definitive, never-to-be-challenged description of the form of a novel.

While presenting his view, Charlie offers a new interpretation of *As I Lay Dying* that is more satisfying than either Tuttle's or Jackson's. He argues that the clash of form and recalcitrance in this novel leads the characters and the reader to astonishment or wonder. The novel is not so comic as Tuttle argues, nor is it ultimately discontinuous as Jackson argues. Instead, it seems designed to evoke the reader's wonder at the mysterious integrity of the Bundrens on their absurd and painful quest.

The third long day, chapters 7 through 10, covers challenges to Charlie's new theory from Jackson, Tuttle, and Wing, and a number of interesting questions and problems from other participants. These chapters are the most difficult part of the book; yet in the process of testing Charlie's ideas and raising a variety of questions, this section greatly enriches the concept of recalcitrance. Jackson's challenge draws out Charlie's thinking, locating different kinds of recalcitrance in different places in reading: in the written text, in the fictional world, in the narrative presentation, and in its suggestions of form. Jackson leads Charlie through the terminology of a number of modern theorists, such as Roland Barthes, Jonathan Culler, Gérard Genette, and Wolfgang Iser, to show how they also seem to have attended to the form/recalcitrance opposition. Although Jackson finds Charlie's thinking attractive, he is unwilling to surrender his stance that what is truly interesting in fiction is its failure to achieve form.

Tuttle's challenge also amounts to an exploration of Charlie's ideas that ends with Tuttle still preferring to do formal analysis. Tuttle points out that the form/recalcitrance opposition leads the critic to a dialectical method in which each side of the opposition speaks alternately, offering the reader a possible form that will realize the whole of the work and then offering a discovery that makes the imagined form inadequate. He finally justifies his own approach by pointing out that those critics who are most interested in recalcitrance as a literary effect need inventors of ideas of form in order to exist and have work.

Wing's challenge differs from those of Tuttle and Jackson because she sees Charlie's conceptions of the novel and of criticism as useful to them, but not to her. She is interested in the value of the literary experience to real, flawed people in a flawed and unjust society. Charlie agrees with her and argues eloquently that while fiction offers pleasure in the short run, this pleasure is a means to a higher end that could be called truth. Reading and analyzing fiction makes people more civilized by educating their imaginations to understanding, sympathy, and constructive activity. He also argues that the kind of dialectical analysis he and Tuttle have come upon is a major tool for describing with some precision what ideas and values are expressed in a literary work. Wing also is unwilling to give up her preferred mode of reading and teaching, though she too sees value in Charlie's ideas.

The fourth and final night, chapters 11 and 12, include several short discussions initiated by various participants. Arthur Birdsong opens a discussion about the kinds of recalcitrance writers experience and the barriers they encounter, avoid, or overcome. This discussion helps bring to a head the problem of aesthetic judgment that returns periodically in the discussion. Contrivance and banality emerge as two fatal weaknesses in fiction. Contrivance occurs when the writer fails to handle a writing problem and produces fiction that seems unfinished or finally incoherent; that is, there is too much recalcitrance. Banality occurs when the author makes something too easy, so that the reader becomes convinced before finishing the work, or soon after, that there is little of value to be gained from the reading; in other words, there is too little recalcitrance. Birdsong's questions also lead to a discussion of how knowledge about the implied author, the actual author, and the composing process can contribute to one's experience of literature. This discussion is followed by discussions of how length, from short stories through *War and Peace* (1886), affects the recalcitrance of fiction and of how to understand the differences between fantasy and realism in terms of the recalcitrance that the writer feels in the act of composing.

Wright's critical fiction has an appropriate novelistic ending, as Eve makes her decision about who wins the debate and whom she will marry. Her decision illustrates well the student's position in debate on literary theory. Participation increases the fun for all and the sophistication of the student, but does not resolve the debate. Everyone wins, and no one wins. In Birdsong's ideal English department, there are no losers except, perhaps, those who did not participate. In this respect, the book's final position is to offer Birdsong's English department as a model for modern literary studies of the kind Wayne C. Booth describes in *Critical Understanding: The Powers and Limits of Pluralism* (1979). Repeatedly the participants recognize that while there might be some personal satisfaction in reducing the opposing party to silence by one's brilliance, the deepest human value of talk about literature remains in the process of talking. While absolute truth or form may threaten to end this talk, one can always depend upon the recalcitrance of every aspect of human existence to keep the final solution at bay. Like Socrates in Athens, literature has two important functions: to stimulate dreams of order and to prevent the terror of their full realization.

Terry Heller

Source for Further Study

Choice. XXVIII, January, 1991, p. 782.

ROBERT GRAVES
The Years with Laura, 1926-1940

Author: Richard Perceval Graves (1945-   )
Publisher: Viking (New York). Illustrated. 380 pp. $24.95
Type of work: Literary biography
Time: 1926-1940
Locale: Egypt, England, Spain, and the United States

A detailed biography of the years 1926-1940, the years of Graves's passionate devotion to the American poet Laura Riding, their relationship to members of an "inner circle" of poets and artists, and finally, the end of the Graves-Riding liaison

> *Principal personages:*
> ROBERT VON RANKE GRAVES, an English poet and novelist who also wrote literary criticism, autobiography, biography, and biblical and mythological commentary
> LAURA RIDING GOTTSCHALK, the American poet who became Graves's literary collaborator and partner
> ANNIE MARY "NANCY" NICHOLSON, Graves's first wife and mother of Jenny, John David, Catherine, and Samuel Graves, their children
> GEOFFREY PHIBBS, an Irish poet who along with Nancy, Robert, and Laura became part of the "four-life"

Robert Graves: The Years with Laura, 1926-1940 is the second volume of a meticulously detailed biography by his nephew Richard Perceval Graves. When John Graves (Robert's younger brother) died in 1980, Richard inherited the substantial family archives, consisting of "thousands of items dating from the 1790s onwards: chiefly letters, but also diaries, personal memoirs, family trees, portraits, and photographs." In addition to reviewing this voluminous material, Richard Graves studied collections of papers in Spain, England, and the United States and corresponded with still-living members of the Graves-Riding drama, including Laura.

This wealth of written and eyewitness account gives this biography a journalistic flavor. It almost seems that at any given moment in the lives of Robert and Laura someone was looking in the window. In addition to the diaries and letters of the extensive Graves clan—all of whom commented on the unorthodoxy of Robert's life—the many friends who made up the "inner circle" had much to say about the personalities of Robert Graves and Laura Riding.

One of the great strengths of this biography is that the author prefers to allow the participants to comment on the who and why of the events rather than rely on his own interpretation. This approach gives the work immediacy, impact, and credibility.

What emerges is a portrait of Robert Graves as a man who sought and needed approval and direction from intense personal relationships. The wife of George Mallory (a friend of Robert who was later killed climbing Mount Everest) observed that even in his student years at Charterhouse (1909-1919) Robert seemed happiest when he found someone he admired who could give him direction. Robert seems especially to have craved the support and direction of women.

As was observed in the first volume, *Robert Graves: The Assault Heroic, 1895-1926*, the principal influence on Robert's early life was his mother, Amalie (Amy) von Ranke Graves, who brought up her son in a blend of idealism, sexual embarrassment, and religious orthodoxy—which Graves later rejected.

Robert had married the independent-minded feminist Nancy Nicholson in 1918. Nancy insisted on wearing corduroys, retaining her own name, and passing it on to her two daughters, Jenny and Catherine, as well as attempting to achieve "judicial equality of the sexes." Although they were happy at first, living in the peaceful village of Islip, Robert had to abandon his academic work because of recurring bouts of shell shock, and his continuing failure to support the family by writing was beginning to alienate him from Nancy—whose word was law. Robert's relationship with Nancy provides a model of dominance by the woman and submission on Robert's part; he was ready to accept Nancy's ideas simply because they were Nancy's. For example, in 1919, Robert commented, "Nancy's crude summary of the Christian religion: 'God is man, so it must be all rot,' took a load off my shoulders." Already Robert had begun to reject the religious and sexual orthodoxy of his upbringing. The pattern would repeat itself with a vengeance with Laura Riding.

Laura Riding, born Laura Reichenthal in 1901 in New York of Jewish parents, was reared in an idealistic and impoverished house. Because of an older sister's generosity, Laura was able to spend all four years at the Girls' High School in Brooklyn, where her "formidable intelligence" asserted itself; after she was graduated, having been offered three scholarships, she enrolled at Cornell University. At Cornell, she fell in love with Louis Gottschalk, a graduate student; they were married in 1920. By 1923 the marriage was failing, and Laura dedicated herself to writing poetry and fiction. Judging that "Laura Reichenthal Gottschalk" was too weighty for editors and readers, she changed the Reichenthal to Riding. Later, she would drop the Gottschalk as well.

One of her poems, "Dimensions," appeared in the August/September, 1923, issue of *The Fugitive*, the house magazine of a group of poets at Vanderbilt University that included John Crowe Ransom, Allen Tate, and Donald Davidson. They were impressed with her work, and in November, 1924, they awarded her the Nashville Prize for Poetry. Yet Laura soon tried to dominate the group with her ideas, and some "bitterly resented the arrogant manner in which she expected everyone else to fall in with her own views." This need for domination would later characterize her relationship with Robert and members of their circle. Laura gradually became disillusioned with her American fellow-poets, so when the invitation came at the end of 1925 to go to Europe to collaborate on a book with Robert Graves, she accepted.

By the end of 1925, Nancy had become ill, and the doctor advised that she should spend the winter in a warm, dry climate. Robert was recommended by many influential friends for a professorship of English Literature at Cairo University—a conventional and official way of life he knew he would detest, but he took it anyway. Earlier, Robert had been attracted to Laura Riding's poetry and had corresponded briefly with her. He and Nancy invited her to come with them to Cairo. Although

Robert was soon to take a new (and well-paid) position in Cairo, he was later to reflect that a personal disintegration was under way. "Now," writes Richard Graves, "as he set sail for Egypt, he was in serious need of a strong and self-reliant person upon whose judgement he could rely, and in whose affection he could feel secure." Laura Riding was that person.

Given Robert's state of mind, it would have been surprising if he and Laura had not fallen in love. Although he loved Nancy and certainly accepted her ideas, she was never his intellectual equal, as Laura certainly was; nor could Nancy give Robert the literary direction that the controlling and domineering Laura would do. Later, the Graves family asserted that Laura had "vampirised him from the first." At the end of March, 1926, after only three months of being with Laura, Robert wrote an astonishing letter to Siegfried Sassoon, saying, "It is extremely unlikely that Nancy, Laura and I will ever disband, now we've survived this odd meeting and continue to take everything for granted as before."

Thus what Alfred Perceval Graves would later call the "Trinity" was born. Yet they did eventually "disband," and for obvious reasons: Nancy simply could no longer tolerate the bizarre life she was leading with Robert, Laura, and others. Although Nancy and Robert remained married, by May of 1927 Nancy was permanently settled in Cumberland with the children, and Robert and Laura were living openly as lovers in Hammersmith, London. Still, for the time the Trinity held. In July, Nancy brought the children to stay for three weeks, which pleased Robert because it proved that the arrangement was working.

Things were going well. Robert, at T. E. Lawrence's insistence, had written *Lawrence and the Arabs*, and by November of 1927 the money was rolling in. With it, Laura and Robert purchased a printing press, hoping to circumvent the publishing world that they had come to despise, and they also bought the barge *Avoca*, which they planned to convert into a houseboat for Robert's children and keep on the nearby Thames. As it turned out, Nancy herself joined the children and by December, 1928, had decided to sell the goats and goods in Cumberland and move permanently to London.

The Graves family was mortified. Robert's sister Clarissa had written to Amy that it was wisest

> to lay low until a far more favourable opportunity of helping them occurs . . . After all, we are, like the chorus in a Greek tragedy, not responsible for the action of the principal figures, an action which must work itself out by its own inherent laws.

In 1929, those "laws" asserted themselves with an incident that not only precipitated the final break between Robert and Nancy but, perhaps more important, also reveals a pattern in Laura and Robert's lives that was to continue until their final break in 1940. Laura and Robert had adopted the custom of including those who shared Laura's ideas about poetry and literature into a sort of "inner circle" of poets and artists. One such poet was an Irishman named Geoffrey Phibbs. In October, 1928, Robert had traveled to Ireland to interview Geoffrey as a possible candidate for inclusion. Although Geoffrey was married, to the beautiful illustrator Norah McGuiness, the *ménage à trois* of Laura, Robert, and Nancy soon turned into a *ménage à quatre* of Laura, Robert, Nancy, and Geoffrey. In Laura's words, the "three-life" had become a "four-life." A devastated Norah, having been left out in the cold, fled to Paris, where she took up her painting. Laura ruled the flat at 35(A) Hammersmith, where she lived with Geoffrey and Robert; Nancy ruled the *Avoca* on the Thames.

What is important is the extent to which Laura was able to dominate the men, and the exalted view she began to have of herself. Laura had begun to think of herself as a goddess, as a figure of destiny; as she herself said, she embodied "Finality." Robert unhesitatingly accepted this view, and Geoffrey made some notes "about time and history being either 'a projection from Laura,' or 'necessitated by Laura.' " Geoffrey, however, was not the devoted acolyte that Robert was and began to turn to Nancy, who seemed the most emotionally healthy member of the group. On April 1, 1929, Geoffrey left without a word for Paris and Norah. Laura dispatched both Nancy and Robert to fetch him back, and at length he came but refused to live with or near Laura.

On April 27, Laura could take no more. She drank some Lysol, in imitation of a young woman poet who had committed suicide some time earlier, but evidently did not drink enough. To the horror of Robert, Nancy, and Geoffrey, she then threw herself out the fourth-floor window of the flat. Robert began running downstairs; by the time he got to the third floor, having realized that Laura was probably dead, he forced open a window and threw himself out as well. Much to the astonishment of Nancy and Geoffrey, both Robert and Laura were alive. Miraculously, Robert was only bruised and winded, but Laura had four broken vertebrae, her pelvis was broken in three pieces, and her spinal cord was badly bent. Thanks to Robert's sister Rosaleen, who was working at Charing Cross Hospital, the best of care was secured for Laura, who eventually recovered.

The police investigated the incident, and the details of the "four-life" were revealed. A scandal ensued, and at the end of October, 1929, Robert and Laura left England for Majorca, Spain, never to return, except for brief visits. Nancy and Geoffrey lived together for a time at Islip, Nancy's break with Robert was now permanent.

This brief glimpse into the early years of the Riding-Graves relationship is telling. Wherever Robert and Laura were, they were surrounded by an inner circle of admirers who allowed themselves to be dominated by Laura and her ideas. Robert was her utterly devoted champion. As other members of the circle noted, Robert seemed happiest when he was satisfying her slightest whim. In 1936 they were forced to flee Majorca because of the Spanish Civil War; their path eventually led to the United States, where Laura abandoned Robert for the American poet Schuyler Jackson.

Despite the intense emotional atmosphere that inevitably surrounded Robert, Laura, and their circle, Robert produced some of his most important works during these years, notably *And Goodbye to All That* (1929), *I, Claudius* (1934), *Claudius the God* (1934), *Collected Poems* (1938), and *Count Belisarius* (1938). There is no question that Laura Riding deeply influenced Robert Graves and his writing. During these years he wrote some of the most exquisite love poetry of the twentieth century. Yet it was chiefly as a formidable literary critic that Laura influenced his thinking and writing.

At the beginning of the book, Richard Perceval Graves asserts that the focus is the drama of personal relationships. At times the reader is angry at Laura, disgusted at Robert for his submissiveness, puzzled and haunted by his longing for love and acceptance. Sometimes the reader is simply exhausted from the emotional intensity and the detail of the presentation, but in the end, one cannot help but be enchanted and fascinated by this passionate story. Richard Graves closes this biography by hinting that there may be a third volume, detailing Robert Graves's life after 1940.

Dean Davies

Sources for Further Study

The Atlantic. CCLXVI, December, 1990, p. 131.
Booklist. LXXXVII, October 15, 1990, p. 412.
Kirkus Reviews. LVIII, September 1, 1990, p. 1223.
Library Journal. CXV, November 1, 1990, p. 100.
The Listener. CXXIII, March 29, 1990, p. 30.
London Review of Books. XII, April 5, 1990, p. 10.
The New York Times Book Review. XCV, November 11, 1990, p. 95.
Publishers Weekly. CCXXXVII, October 5, 1990, p. 88.
The Spectator. CCLXIV, April 14, 1990, p. 32.
The Times Literary Supplement. August 3, 1990, p. 820.

SCHOPENHAUER AND THE WILD YEARS OF PHILOSOPHY

Author: Rüdiger Safranski (1945-   )
First published: Schopenhauer und die wilden Jahre der Philosophie, 1987
Translated from the German by Ewald Osers
Publisher: Harvard University Press (Cambridge, Massachusetts). 385 pp. $30.00
Type of work: Biography
Time: 1788-1860
Locale: Central Europe, primarily Germany

> *Recounting Schopenhauer's life, Safranski places him within his intellectual, political, and historical milieus*

Principal personages:
ARTHUR SCHOPENHAUER, a German philosopher
JOHANNA SCHOPENHAUER, his mother, a novelist
HEINRICH SCHOPENHAUER, his father
ADELE SCHOPENHAUER, the philosopher's sister
G. W. F. HEGEL, a German philosopher, Schopenhauer's rival
J. W. VON GOETHE, a German romantic writer and friend of Johanna Schopenhauer

Arthur Schopenhauer, the philosopher of pessimism, published the first edition of his magnum opus, *Die Welt als Wille und Vorstellung*, in 1818, though it was not until the 1850's that he achieved widespread recognition. Several generations of readers have known that work in English translation as *The World as Will and Idea* (1883-1886). In 1958, however, E. F. J. Payne published a superior modern translation under the title *The World as Will and Representation*; Payne has also translated *Parerga und Paralipomena* (1851; *Parerga and Paralipomena*, 1974), the collection of miscellaneous essays that first brought Schopenhauer fame.

Payne's translations have contributed significantly to a revival of scholarly interest in Schopenhauer in Great Britain and the United States. Scholars in Germany, Schopenhauer's native land, have produced an almost constant stream of monographs since his death, but to English readers the renewed scholarly interest is best reflected in several important analyses. Among these are Christopher Janaway's *Self and World in Schopenhauer's Philosophy* (1989) and Brian Magee's more general survey, *The Philosophy of Schopenhauer* (1983). Rüdiger Safranski's clearly written biography represents a welcome addition to the scholarly titles available in English that attempt to explain Schopenhauer's somewhat loosely constructed system.

The causes for Schopenhauer's revival are perhaps related to those that initially brought him attention following long neglect during most of his lifetime. First, unlike other German followers of Immanuel Kant, he writes in a pellucid, fluent style, with clarity and grace, qualities that survive translation. Second, he stands in stark opposition to the historical and rational optimism of G. W. F. Hegel; in times like the present, when the Hegelian tradition appears on the decline, Schopenhauer might well be expected to be revived. Third, his philosophy of the will, as Safranski points out, bears a close resemblance to the existential movement prominent since World

War II. Finally, more than any other modern philosopher, his system has appealed to creative artists, notably in literature and music, beginning with Richard Wagner and extending through Thomas Mann. One can name many writers beyond the borders of Germany who are heavily in his debt: Guy de Maupassant and Marcel Proust in France, Leo Tolstoy in Russia, and Joseph Conrad and W. Somerset Maugham in England, to list a few. Since critical interest in these creative artists has been intense, Schopenhauer's name and system have often been cited as contributing sources of their work.

Drawing on numerous contemporary accounts, Safranski has produced the most comprehensive biography of Schopenhauer available in English. To be sure, the known facts about the philosopher's life are somewhat limited, largely because of his manner of living. Essentially a loner following a careful daily routine, he lived in boardinghouses for most of his adult life. Because of his father's early death, probably by his own hand, Schopenhauer possessed a legacy that enabled him to live comfortably without working and to devote all of his energy to study and writing. Yet from his father he also inherited a tendency toward depression that afflicted him periodically. He had a deep aversion to noise, and any prospect of civil violence and disorder terrified him. He suffered from a morbid fear of disease that caused him to break off courtship of two of the three women he might have married, fearing they had tuberculosis. A third marriage prospect, a girl of seventeen, found him quite unappealing. He found it difficult to maintain any harmonious human relationships, largely because he did not restrain his tongue or pen and seemed to delight in disconcerting the company at the Englisher Hof Hotel in Frankfurt, where he dined regularly during his later years. His caustic comments about contemporary philosophers had the effect of limiting dissemination of his own works, for he was fond of applying terms such as "charlatan," "quack," "windbag," and "monkey" to prominent contemporaries such as Hegel and J. G. Fichte.

With a financial independence that enabled him to sponsor private publication of his own works, Schopenhauer felt no need to curb his truculent nature, though, as Safranski demonstrates, age mellowed him somewhat, particularly his misogyny. From the welter of largely unpleasant biographical detail, however, Safranski identifies the factors that account for Schopenhauer's development. In addition to his depression, he was influenced by a lack of love as a child; his mother, highly romantic by nature, had entered into a loveless marriage with an affluent older merchant. From numerous letters it is obvious that both parents took the welfare of their children seriously and provided for them. Yet it remains true that the closest resemblance to normal family life Schopenhauer experienced was in the home of a French merchant of Le Havre, where he was sent as a boy to learn the language. As a young man, he delighted in climbing mountains and looking down on all below; from this experience he derived a kind of exultation not uncommon in those who have shared it—but not conducive to warmth or benignity toward others. Safranski relates this emotion to a kind of verticality in Schopenhauer's nature. He set himself above others and seemed to prize genius above all other human qualities, while remaining convinced that civilization normally produces only one true genius each century.

A further value of the biographical portions of the book lies in Safranski's clarifying the setting in which Schopenhauer lived. His early life was spent against the backdrop of the Napoleonic Wars, which affected Germany profoundly, though he carefully avoided military service. Drawing on contemporary accounts, primarily journals and letters, Safranski describes the cities in which Schopenhauer lived during the early and mid-nineteenth century: Danzig, Berlin, Dresden, Frankfurt. From a biographical standpoint, the historical and physical settings are amply clarified.

The biography divides into two books, the first concerning the philosopher's early life and education, with an account of his formative influences. In this part, Safranski explores the all-important impact of Plato and Kant, two philosophers recommended by Schopenhauer's *Gymnasium* teacher. When he was able to turn to a formal education after the death of his father, Schopenhauer chose medicine; but in his first year in the university, he changed to philosophy, convinced that human life is so complex that one should spend a lifetime learning about it. He viewed himself as a follower of Kantian philosophy and identified the "thing-in-itself" as the *will*, a term that must be understood in its broadest possible sense in Schopenhauer. A blind and imperious driving force, the will includes conscious and unconscious drives, as well as biochemically controlled, totally unconscious systems of human beings and other organisms. It also includes what Aristotle meant by teleology, the development of an organism toward some end or purpose. Through the mental categories of time, space, and causality, individuals comprehend that the outside world exists. Yet all one possesses of that world is perceptions and thoughts—not, as Kant pointed out, the world as it really is. The fundamental being, the thing-in-itself, is the individual will that comprehends the existence of other objects and other wills.

In addition to the continuation of biography, Safranksi's "second" book provides an account of Schopenhauer's writings. Safranski is especially valuable in explicating the lesser-known works, including Schopenhauer's University of Jena dissertation, *Über die vierfache Wurzel des Satzes vom zureichende Grunde* (1813; On the Fourfold Root of the Principle of Sufficient Reason, 1889), and *Die beiden Grundprobleme der Ethik* (1841; *The Basis of Morality*, 1903). Safranski clearly relates these works to the major achievement of the philosopher, *The World as Will and Idea*, though the explication of this work is somewhat brief. Even less attention is given to the miscellaneous collected essays, *Parerga and Paralipomena*, which Safranski considers interesting primarily for the appended "Aphorisms."

Schopenhauer can hardly be said to have a metaphysics; his thought has psychological importance, but the major areas of emphasis are epistemology, aesthetics, and ethics. Safranski's analysis concentrates on these three elements and goes far toward clarifying them for those who have never read the original texts. In the pessimistic and skeptical traditions of David Hume and Kant, Schopenhauer explored epistemology through his concept of will, though he left the relationship of aesthetics and ethics to each other and to the will somewhat vague.

In Schopenhauer's thought, aesthetics is related to "idea" in Plato. Through arresting time, freezing it in one scene, a painter delivers the mind from the web of causes and effects that perplexes the will. The viewer's involvement is contemplative, reflective; the experience of viewing art suspends the will and silences its constant, restless struggle. Thus, art leads the participant into the realm of contemplation of ideas.

Suspending the will is related to Schopenhauer's ethical thought, though it seems odd that a philosopher who emphatically denies freedom of the will should concern himself with ethics. Yet Schopenhauer argues that the will can be tamed, all to the good as far as he is concerned, for the unbridled egoism of the human will represents evil. Hindu asceticism, self-denial, is for him the most ethical course, though, as Safranski points out, Schopenhauer did not himself follow it. That an individual can choose to tame the will seems contradictory in the ethics, since Schopenhauer denies freedom of volition, yet he suggests how it can be done. In a passage on government, he argues that the role of law should be to restrain human excesses, to provide a counterweight of punishment against people's natural rapacity. Thus, an individual can take the possibility of punishment into account before acting, and fear becomes an effective deterrent to the will.

Elsewhere, he argues that character does not change throughout life. Once a person has stolen, that person is a thief because the action is an index to the character. Yet the person may not steal again because he fears punishment, because he understands that stealing inflicts harm on others or on himself, or because he does not wish to suffer in reputation. Thus, Schopenhauer acknowledges that reason and understanding can furnish the will with countermotives that influence its actions. As art enables an individual to suspend the demands of the will temporarily, reason or understanding furnishes motives the effects of which can tame the will into a kind of asceticism.

Here Schopenhauer's thought confronts another problem. He adamantly rejects all influences on the mind that are untrue or undemonstrable. As he assumes that reason originates motives that become causes, he quite logically should acknowledge that codes, myths, religions, ideals—insofar as they are embraced and accepted rationally by individuals—also supply motives to the will. For providing this kind of motivation, illusion may serve as well as truth; and this Schopenhauer was unwilling to acknowledge.

Safranski's book, however, is perhaps most valuable for the way it clarifies Schopenhauer's place in the philosophical currents of his time, described as the "Wild Years" during the Romantic movement, when philosophers, following Kant, explored the place, value, and purpose of the individual ego in an unfriendly universe. Among the followers of Kant, Schopenhauer alone showed that rationalism, positivism, and historical optimism represented illusory paths—that the individual ego, such as it was, stood alone in an indifferent world sustained only by the will.

The summations of the philosophies of Hegel, Fichte, Karl Marx, and others are inviting accounts in themselves, so riveting that Safranski seems momentarily to lose sight of his subject. At the moment when he appears to be on an interesting but digressive tangent, however, Safranski draws the discussion back to Schopenhauer to demonstrate the major differences between his work and that of his contemporaries. All scholars acknowledge Schopenhauer's originality as a follower of Kant, but no other study readily available goes so far in clarifying his place in the philosophical milieu of nineteenth century Germany.

Stanley Archer

Sources for Further Study

Choice. XXVIII, October, 1990, p. 324.
The Guardian. October 5, 1989, p. 22.
Library Journal. CXV, March 15, 1990, p. 93.
The New Republic. CCIV, March 4, 1991, p. 38.
The Observer. November 19, 1989, p. 46.
The Spectator. CCLXIII, December 2, 1989, p. 41.
Thought. LXV, June, 1990, p. 215.
Washington Times. August 6, 1990, p. F2.

THE SEARCH FOR MODERN CHINA

Author: Jonathan D. Spence (1936-   )
Publisher: W. W. Norton (New York) Illustrated. 876 pp. $29.95
Type of work: History
Time: 1600-1989
Locale: China

A broad yet detailed interpretive historical synthesis, this study by a distinguished Sinologist explores a wide range of factors that have precluded China, the world's largest and oldest civilization, from achieving degrees of reform that by general criteria, past or present, define "modernity"

The Search for Modern China encompasses nearly four centuries of China's unique, complex development politically, economically, culturally and socially. During these years, torques and tensions among its peoples have variously—as much of the Ming dynasty (1368-1644) evinced—brought it temporarily to levels of achievement exceeding, or at least matching, those characterizing Europe, indeed any other extensive culture. And this was despite—sometimes because of—an almost unbroken sequence of authoritarian traditions and regimes.

Just as persistently, however, authoritarian beliefs and practices have been subject both to recondite forces that tended to refashion them, as well as to populist and intellectual challenges—peaceful on some occasions, violent on others. Over much of the previous four centuries challenges to authority, or insistence upon reforms, have been internal in origin. Since the latter eighteenth century, however, they have been hastened and inspired frequently by Western and by other foreign incursions and influences—Japanese and by Russian, for example.

Thus, embedded within China's authoritarian traditions, whether they emanated from within the provinces, in Nanking, in Shanghai, or in Peking, there have always been Chinese who were eager, often desperate, for what they regarded as vital reforms. Their demands over time have taken many forms: factional conflicts within dynastic establishments from the days of the Ming to the Qing (1644-1911), opposition to warlordism as well as to landlords, peasant revolts, and from 1911 until 1989 conflict between and within Chiang Kai-shek's Kuomintang (Nationalist Party) and the Communist Party of Mao Zedong or Deng Xiaoping.

After his thirty years of Chinese studies, resulting in publication of seven major books centered upon important facets of changes in China's development, inclusive of exemplary personalities, Yale historian Jonathan Spence centers his attention in *The Search for Modern China* on cycles of real and attempted reforms directed toward modernizing China. These often intertwined cycles characterized by the collapse or fragmentation of authority as well as by strategies designed to sustain reconsolidation and, while maintaining traditional cultural and emotional values, to unfetter progressive initiatives, Spence believes, can best be understood in their historical contexts. The glories of the Ming and their subsequent decline, that is, a grasp of what historical factors undergirt or undermined the Ming dynasty—and subsequent regimes—therefore enhance more accurate perceptions of present-day China. In the aggregate, they are links in a continuing chain of events.

While the meaning of the term "modern" has itself undergone significant historical evolution, certain generalized criteria for defining "modern," Spence observes, have proven relevant through the past several centuries. One essential qualification for being designated as modern is the presence of a tolerably well-integrated polity or state. Another that underlies such political and administrative integration is a notably secure and widespread sense of self-identity—a sense, in this instance, of Chinese-ness. Furthermore, flowing from this emotional and cultural awareness is a receptiveness to cooperative behavior in relation to other states and peoples, a willingness to join them broadly and at several levels on a presumptively equal footing, and, even though selectively, to exchange markets, technologies, and, by no means least, ideas.

Evaluating Chinese performance by these standards over the course of nearly four hundred years—a period covering nearly all of white American history—what tentative assessments can reasonably be offered? Certainly until 1949, marked by the flight of Chiang Kai-shek's Nationalists to Taiwan and establishment on the mainland of Mao Zedong's Communist Peoples' Republic, the Chinese had rarely delineated a well-integrated polity or nation state for themselves. Both the Ming and Qing eras, for example, witnessed rapid expansions and equally swift contractions of their several kingdoms, each seeking dominance over the others. In addition, although Chinese governments generally claimed hegemony over Outer Mongolia, Inner Mongolia, Sinkiang, Tibet, Korea, Laos, Cambodia, and Annam, these areas, most of them of vast extent, manifestly were not under Peking's direct authority. Even by the late nineteenth century, precisely what China was, politically and administratively, continued to be unclear, mooted. This was a picture further complicated by foreigners' assertions of their rights to extraterritoriality, spheres of influence, and effective influence in many respects over national finances. The collapse of the Qing dynasty and the proclamation of Sun Yat-sen's Republic of China (1911-1912), while auguring a new era, still left the country fragmented. Local bosses, gangs, and regional warlords temporarily filled the breaches through the 1920's, indeed into the 1930's.

Increasingly extensive clashes from the 1920's until 1949 between Nationalists and Communists, further complicated by massive Japanese incursions, first into Manchuria, then after 1937 into China's major ports, river valleys, and heartland, produced a real political vacuum. Anomalously, during World War II, major Western belligerents, which only a few decades earlier were charged with contributing to the disintegration of China, tried frantically—and at considerable expenditure in lives and money—to transform wartime and postwar China into the semblance of a consolidated nation-state. The United States even went so far, to the bemusement of its British and Soviet allies, as to insist that China be treated as a world power. But rhetoric proved a poor substitute for reality. Not until Mao's Communists successfully swept aside Nationalist elements on the mainland in 1949 did it appear that the Chinese had at last achieved political and ideological consolidation, although the United States refused recognition of the regime until "normalization" of relations began with President Richard M. Nixon's initiatives in 1972. Yet responding to Nixon's flattery that Mao had created a nation and altered the world, Mao rejoined that he had only been able to change a few things in the areas around Peking—this almost a quarter of a century after the Communists' victory.

Doubtless Mao exaggerated. Certainly, however, during the mid-1950's, in order to win adherents throughout the country's other precincts, his Socialist visions were revised. Intellectuals, students, and other actual or potential dissidents were encouraged to vent their alternative suggestions or grievances under the slogan of letting a hundred flowers bloom. But the relaxation of internal tensions was brief: The springtime of hundreds of flowers blooming was Arctic. By his own admission nearly 25 million Chinese, plus another million or more Tibetans who ostensibly menaced his regime had been exterminated before Mao's death in 1976. In the interim, as if they were mere commodities, hundreds of millions of urban Chinese were effectually deported to the countryside better to conform to Peking's ideological swings and subsequently—years after the shattering of their personal and familial lives—relocated into urban areas once again. Similarly, the rupture of Sino-Soviet relations in 1960, accompanied by the swift withdrawal of Soviet economic and technical assistance, persuaded the Communists to augment massive rural collectivization with their own industrial Five Year Plan. Simultaneously, through fanatical actions by Red Guards who were designated as the vanguard of the Cultural Revolution, a complete realignment of the existing social system was launched. Disasters of a magnitude possible only in China were the results: Rural collectivization, the heart of the Socialist dream failed; the Five Year Plan directed toward domestic industrialization failed; and the Cultural Revolution essentially erased centuries of Chinese attainments in arts, letters, sciences, in vigorous intellectual life, as well as in urgently needed sustenance for education that everywhere has been prerequisite to advances toward modernization. Such were some of the scenarios that were to script development of the Peoples' Republic.

Thus if a secure emotional sense of self-identity—the notion that China's culture has been and continues to be inherently superior to others—exists among most Chinese, Mao's regime and its successors through 1989 clearly have left untold millions of them befuddled, dizzied, cynically passive, suspicious, and skeptical of both the integrity and wisdom of their authorities. It has likewise caused those possessing some knowledge of the international scene to ponder where they stand in reference to the developed world surrounding them—not only in the West, but also in the Soviet Union and in many other parts of Asia: notably in Japan, Taiwan, South Korea, Singapore, and Hong Kong. Consequently ambivalence has marked cries originating within China for change and for progressive reforms. Quite conscious and proud on the one hand of their past glories, they have in Spence's view, on the other hand yet to come to terms with fitting themselves into the increasingly open, increasingly diversified congeries of nations.

Though Spence's study begins with the decline of the Ming dynasty commencing in the late eighteenth century, patterns apparent then persistently and discernibly projected themselves right into the twentieth century. That is Spence's rationale for tracing the characteristics of these cycles through two-thirds of this volume as they have reappeared—to be sure with variations—from 1911 to 1989. This is quite evident in China's almost invariably bewildering reactions toward foreign ideas and technologies. Remarkable as were Ming achievements in the mastery of techniques from which sprang superb craftsmanship and arts—porcelains, silks, and printing, to note only a few—there were only jejune attempts by Chinese to enter them into exchange. At the same time, Western Europeans were launching and sustaining explorations that opened many of the most distant places on the earth to multilateral commerce, in the process laying the deep foundations on which they raised a global economy. Such relative openness simultaneously brought before them a vast store of novel techniques, along with an immense fund and variety of fresh knowledge that rapidly transformed and modernized Western civilization. On the contrary, Ming emperors—and therefore their subjects—shrank from overseas enterprises and from exposure to foreign knowledge or ideas, inevitably losing opportunities to maintain pace with the leading Western societies.

The developed countries, whether Western or Asian, have long been aware of China's potential. Especially that has been true of China's prospective impacts upon the global economy (profitable trade and investment) and on international relations. Prevalent views, however, continue to be that Chinese potentialities remain substantially underdeveloped. Despite establishment of new economic zones and rhetoric about "one country, two systems," the authoritarian state, smiling sporadically for the rest of the world, is accurately portrayed by Spence as generally prickly, turbulent, and, weighed in the balance, unprofitable. Neither its age-old curse of horrendous bureaucratization nor the flourishing corruptions attending it, have been ameliorated, let alone exorcised. More important, China's Communist rulers have yet to devise a politico-economic strategy happily accommodating the genuinely democratic pluralism—of the sort called for in Peking's Tiananmen Square in 1989—which nearly everywhere else eventually has proven essential to modernization. Nor have four centuries of omnipresent authoritarianism yielded principles or ideals which peoples of other nations are prepared to live by.

Spence's depiction is understandably filled with admiration for those capacities that the Chinese have demonstrated for coping with sheer survival—for their extraordinary endurance over lengthy periods and on an immense scale. Notwithstanding, his well-substantiated conclusion is that China has yet to attain great power status or to warrant designation as a modern society.

Clifton K. Yearley

Sources for Further Study

America. CLXIII, September 29, 1990, p. 190.
Commonweal. CXVII, August 10, 1990, p. 462.
Los Angeles Times Book Review. May 27, 1990, p. 1.
National Review. XLII, August 6, 1990, p. 43.
The New Republic. CCIII, July 30, 1990, p. 30.
The New York Review of Books. XXXVII, May 31, 1990, p. 16.
The New York Times Book Review. XCV, May 13, 1990, p. 1.
Publishers Weekly. CCXXXVII, March 16, 1990, p. 56.
The Times Literary Supplement. July 27, 1990, p. 795.
The Washington Post Book World. XX, April 22, 1990, p. 1.

THE SECOND WORLD WAR

Author: John Keegan (1934-   )
First published: 1989, in Great Britain
Publisher: Viking (New York). Illustrated. 607 pp. $29.95
Type of work: Military history
Time: 1919-1945
Locale: Europe, North Africa, Asia

A complete but fast-moving history of World War II which combines a general survey of the entire combat with more in-depth analysis of the situations and strategies of the major participants

> Principal personages:
> WINSTON CHURCHILL, Prime Minister of Great Britain, 1940-1945
> FRANKLIN D. ROOSEVELT, President of the United States, 1933-1945
> JOSEPH STALIN, Premier of the Soviet Union, 1941-1953
> GENERAL GEORGE C. MARSHALL, Chief of Staff, United States Army
> GENERAL DOUGLAS MACARTHUR, Commander of Allied Forces, Southwest Pacific Theater
> GENERAL DWIGHT D. EISENHOWER, Commander of Allied Forces, North Africa, later in Europe
> GENERAL HIDEKI TOJO, Prime Minister of Japan
> ADMIRAL ISORUKU YAMAMOTO, Commander of the Japanese Combined Fleet
> ADOLF HITLER, Chancellor and Führer of Nazi Germany, 1933-1945

John Keegan is the premier military historian of the second half of the twentieth century. He has a sure command of both the broad concepts of strategy and the intricate nuances of tactics; his appreciation of the essential role of logistics and supply is keen and incisive; and his understanding of the psychology of the individual fighting man, whether general or private, is as acute and penetrating as that of any novelist. Uniting all this is Keegan's unsurpassed talent in presenting the terrible facts of war to his reader clearly and vividly, without false glory or cheap sentiment.

In his stunning and original study of men at war, *The Face of Battle* (1976), Keegan introduced to the general public (and even to many military historians and their more specialized readership) an entirely new way of looking at warfare. Instead of the traditional battle piece, which presents armies as massive, homogeneous units moving and wheeling obediently to their generals' commands, *The Face of Battle* took a common-sense look at the common soldier and his leaders, in order to reconstruct what must have been possible in the actual chaos of battle.

Two examples illustrate Keegan's technique. The famous English victory at Agincourt was caused by many factors, but the French knights in the front ranks were so tightly packed and strongly pushed forward by their comrades behind that they could neither fight nor flee—and that was just as important as the bravery of Henry V and his band of brothers who fought together on St. Crispin's Day. In much the same way, the fabled British squares at Waterloo were not broken by the French cavalry charges partially because of the discipline of Wellington's troops, but also because horses will almost never run headlong into human bodies if they can possibly avoid doing so. Keegan's underlying theme is clear: There is more to battle than many historians have considered and much of it is mundane—except that it causes unimaginable pain, suffering, and death, as well as the famous victories and defeats which are the stuff of most military history.

There have been other studies of individual fighting men in the cauldron of battle, most notably those done by the United States Army examining the dynamics of small groups in combat, but none had shown the breadth and insight of Keegan's book. *The Face of Battle* was a truly original synthesis that presented, in a sharp and unforgettable style, the closest approach the average reader can make to the experience of combat. It also reminded the student of a fact that more traditional military history tends to forget: In a very real sense, it is men, and not armies, which fight battles, and win or lose them.

Keegan's examination of battle on the front lines was counterpointed in 1987 with another, equally impressive book, *The Mask of Command*, in which he turned his gaze on those who lead others into war. Alexander the Great, the Duke of Wellington, Ulysses S. Grant, and Adolf Hitler were his chosen examples, and he deftly moved among them, highlighting the different aspects of command which make not only for military but—in certain men—moral greatness. Keegan went beyond the conventional criteria used to judge a successful war leader, simply that of winning battles, to standards more intangible but perhaps more important: why a commander chose to fight at a certain place and at a certain time, for what reasons, and what casualties he was willing to endure.

In Keegan's hands, these are subtle and telling guides, and they lead his readers to understand why Wellington avoided more battles than he fought, and why Grant believed that both the military situation and national goals of his war demanded his dogged, apparently callous hammer blows of attack. On the other hand, Keegan reveals that Alexander was probably incapable, culturally and psychologically, of refusing battle, while Hitler justified worldwide war and the death of millions solely in terms of himself.

Keegan has thus reintroduced into the study of warfare a long neglected aspect, that of morality. It is not a simple or easy morality—such as all war is bad, all warriors evil—but a careful and discriminating one, which recognizes that so long as war remains a part of the human condition, there are standards by which it should be waged, and limits which must be observed. Given the inherently terrible nature of war—and Keegan never glorifies, never romanticizes its intractable brutality—the truly great commander is the one who adheres to those elusive but essential standards, and still wins battles.

These are the two aspects of war: the common soldier and his commander; how they interact in actual combat is the core of Keegan's impressive study of the Allied invasion of France in 1944, *Six Armies in Normandy* (1984), and now his most ambitious work to date, *The Second World War*, a sweeping study that covers the whole of that global conflict. These are works that show Keegan operating brilliantly as a practicing historian: marshaling facts, compiling figures, following the chronological and thematic lines of his subject to present the particular events, the actual battles. Yet, at the same time, this approach is undergirded by Keegan's insight that the universal exists somewhere in the particular.

In order to impose "a little order for the reader on the chaos and tragedy of the events" of World War II, Keegan uses a two-part structure. The first is chronological and geographical, studying the combat as it progressed in western Europe, on the Russian front, and across the broad Pacific. The second part is thematic and exemplary: strategic analysis of the situations, examination of a particular "theme of war," such as supply, bombing, secret weapons, and so forth, and a "battle piece," to present a concentrated expression of how these various elements actually emerged in combat. It is a framework which serves Keegan remarkably well, imposing order without unduly simplifying the complexities he recounts. Above all, it helps the reader understand what happened—and, as much as anyone can understand such a thing, why it all happened.

As others before Keegan have pointed out, World War II was actually three interrelated struggles: the Axis against the Allies in the west; Germany against the Soviet Union in the east; and the Chinese, British, and especially Americans against the Japanese in the Pacific. The conduct of these various wars within a world war were determined by many factors—available troops and shipping, supplies and materiel, the ebb and flow of battle—but most of all by the leaders involved.

Hitler, Stalin, Churchill, Roosevelt, and Tojo were fighting for vastly different aims, but their personalities and character were just as important—if not more important—than either their goals or their immediate situation. Harking back to *The Mask of Command*, Keegan is able to elucidate such crucial points as the different types of stubbornness exhibited by Hitler and Churchill, for example; or the reason why Roosevelt's seeming indecision on so many occasions was actually an appropriate, if characteristically masked, flexibility. Each leader faced what Keegan calls strategic dilemmas; the Allied leaders resolved theirs successfully, while the Axis leaders failed. The difference, Keegan's work suggests, was not simply a variance of military acumen, but a contrast in moral character. This contrast becomes, in an implied but powerful sense, a central theme of Keegan's study.

Keegan is most concise and impressive in the study of actual battles and the lessons they convey. The airborne battle of Crete, for example, was not determined by the German use of a new technology—paratroops—so much as by a breakdown in a basic need for the British defenders, communications. In other words, apparent innovation was clearly secondary to age-old military essentials. By contrast, the American victory at Midway was achieved because the Japanese did not fully comprehend (or, comprehending, did not accept and practice) the new methods available and necessary in carrier battles, while the American navy did, and put these methods into use, fatally crippling the Japanese fleet in a matter of minutes. Crete was a sideshow, deciding little and having relatively small impact beyond the moment; on the other hand, Midway marked a decisive turn for America's inexorable march through the island chains of the Pacific toward the Japanese homeland.

Presenting such battles and illuminating their lessons is one of Keegan's strongest features, in this and his other books. He combines the best of traditional military history, the fast-paced account of action and the heroics and terror of combat, with his own unique view of what battle must be like, why certain decisions are made and how they are executed, and how these combine to bring about the terrible conclusion. War is probably too awful and too chaotic for full meaning to be brought to it, but John Keegan musters as much understanding and comprehension as can be found.

No doubt because it was so widespread and diverse, because it was actually three wars in one, there was no single turning point, no one decisive battle in World War II. Pearl Harbor, Stalingrad, El Alamein, Midway, Normandy, Kursk, Okinawa, even the fall of France in 1940—all of these marked stages in the war, but none was in itself sufficient to end the fighting. As a military historian, Keegan is well aware of the irony of this, and while he rightly and skillfully recounts each of these actions, he reserves his main emphasis for a point noted earlier: the vital strategic decisions made by the war leaders, of which these battles and so many others were only the terrible but inescapable results.

It is here that Keegan's history of World War II is tied together most strongly, touching on those intangible factors such as moral character, a theme which he explored overtly in *The Mask of Command*. Most specifically, Keegan follows the paired decisions of Hitler to invade the Soviet Union before finishing off Great Britain, with the commitment by Roosevelt to "Europe first" strategy. These were crucial to the outcome of the war. As Keegan notes, three out of four German troops killed during World War II died fighting the Russians. The Wehrmacht bled to death on the Eastern Front. The American emphasis on Europe, while important in terms of actual numbers of troops, and tons of supplies, was much more important as an expression of moral support for a Great Britain that found itself alone and all but defeated, but still defiant. An American concentration on the Pacific, understandable enough in the aftermath of Pearl Harbor, and urged by many military thinkers of the time, might have had fatal results for Churchill's government, and possibly Britain's survival—even the eventual outcome of the entire war. Hitler's decision was wrong; Roosevelt's was right.

Hitler, that self-anointed military genius, oversaw the conduct of campaigns down to the most minute (and ultimately unimportant) detail; Roosevelt, by contrast, "directed American strategy as he had directed the New Deal—by lofty rhetoric and by rare but decisive strikes at the conjunctions of power." Keegan implies that the difference went beyond temperament and leadership: It involved moral character.

It was more than that, however. Hitler had Mussolini for a partner; Roosevelt had Churchill, with Stalin as an enigmatic ally but a determined enemy of Germany. There was also the enormous industrial and economic might of the United States, and the presence of such brilliant military minds as George Marshall and Dwight Eisenhower. There was a large amount of what might be called luck, or perhaps, as one American admiral termed it, the "definite prejudice of divine providence." It was a complex and complicated mixture, difficult to understand and almost impossible to describe, but both the understanding and the description are to be found in John Keegan's extraordinary study, *The Second World War.*

Michael Witkoski

Sources for Further Study

American History Illustrated. XXV, July, 1990, p. 15.
The Economist. CCCXII, September 2, 1989, p. 83.
History Today. XL, July, 1990, p. 52.
Library Journal. CXIV, November 1, 1989, p. 102.
London Review of Books. XI, October 12, 1989, p. 10.
Los Angeles Times Book Review. December 24, 1989, p. 1.
National Review. XLII, April 1, 1990, p. 49.
The New York Times Book Review. XCV, December 31, 1989, p. 10.
Newsweek. CXV, January 29, 1990, p. 68.
Publishers Weekly. CCXXXVI, November 10, 1989, p. 52.
The Times Literary Supplement. September 1, 1989, p. 935.
The Wall Street Journal. February 7, 1990, p. A16.
The Washington Post Book World. XIX, December 10, 1989, p. 1.

THE SELECTED LETTERS OF GEORGE OPPEN

Author: George Oppen (1908-1984)
Edited, with an introduction, by Rachel Blau DuPlessis
Publisher: Duke University Press (Durham, North Carolina). Illustrated. 436 pages. $37.50;
    paperback $17.95
Type of work: Letters
Time: 1931-1934 and 1958-1981

*A pioneering presentation, with extensive annotation and critical commentary, of the letters
of George Oppen, one of the principal poets of the Objectivist group*

During the decades 1960-1990, the great modernist poets William Carlos Williams, Ezra Pound, and Marianne Moore, who had been shunted into temporary obscurity by the ascendancy of the academic New Critics, were gradually restored to a position of prominence. Yet another group, small but quite important, remained in obscurity. A generation younger than Williams and Pound, the Objectivists Louis Zukofsky, Charles Reznikoff, and George Oppen—joined in a loose association by Basil Bunting, Carl Rakosi, and Lorine Niedecker—were never able to command an audience even as limited as the one Pound and Williams found. While other such temporarily neglected writers as Robinson Jeffers and H. D. (Hilda Doolittle) were "rediscovered," they continued to exist beyond the reach of anthologies and even most small journals.

Part of the problem, at least in Zukofsky's case, was the challenging and unconventional nature of the work. For Oppen, however, a twenty-five-year hiatus in mid-career and a paucity of essays in which the poet discussed his ideas and theories about literature were also significant factors. Now, with the culmination of a twenty-five-year project begun by Rachel Blau DuPlessis in 1965 when she sent Oppen a graduate school essay on Williams' *Paterson* (1946-1958), a lost chapter of American literary experience has been rescued from oblivion. DuPlessis' selection of Oppen's letters, accompanied by interpretive notes and other relevant material, provides an excellent introduction to the singular thinking of a fascinating man and important figure in American literature.

The brief but vivid biography in the introductory chapter establishes the general outlines of Oppen's life, framing the letters within the larger concerns that dominated Oppen's thinking. Born in 1908 into a prosperous, thoroughly assimilated German-Jewish family, Oppen was confronted with an amalgam of the opportunities available to the privileged. His life was continually compounded by wrenching emotional occasions, including an automobile accident in which a friend was killed, his mother's suicide, his expulsion from college, his decision to join the Communist Party to fight for social justice, his immediate disappointment with Party politics, his decision to stop writing to avoid compromising either art or politics, his severe wound in action in World War II, his postwar exile in Mexico to avoid persecution by McCarthyist Red-baiters, and his continued harassment by the Federal Bureau of

Investigation. Yet these trials were balanced by his lifelong love for Mary Colby, whom he married at eighteen; the pleasures of a semibohemian existence as a traveler, amateur sailor, and nascent artist; the excitement of founding his own press, To Publishers, which briefly published Zukofsky, Pound, and Williams in the early 1930's; his own first work, *Discrete Series*, in 1934; the satisfaction of sticking to his political beliefs through the Depression, the war years, and the Cold War years; and then, astonishingly, the rebirth of his writing life in 1958 and the three decades of productivity that are the subject of the letters in the book.

While DuPlessis recognizes that the relatively few readers familiar with Oppen's poetry will welcome her work, she correctly construes her basic audience as those literate people interested in modern American poetry who are generally unaware of what Oppen has done. Speaking of necessity as an advocate for an essentially invisible group, she describes the "Objectivist" cohort as "under-read and shockingly under-anthologized" and argues for the importance of Oppen's letters as the only extant record of his critical thinking. The letters, she says, reveal Oppen as he formed and developed ideas and concepts in the process of conversations with friends and with himself. Like Robert Creeley, who spoke of "a leaderless Robin Hood band" of supportive peers, Oppen relished "the pleasure of companionship" after his separation of a quarter-century from the world of literature and affirmed that for a writer, "the only possible hope is in the conversation with one's peers."

In selecting and presenting the letters, DuPlessis faced a series of intriguing challenges. Her basic plan is to establish a dialogic engagement between the letters and her astute, informative commentary, with Oppen's poems forming the third leg of a triangle of interchange. Thus, while it is possible to read the letters without consulting the notes, the almost constant references to various people and works make this a frustrating and unrewarding approach. DuPlessis might have considered placing the letters and the notes on facing pages, but this would have diminished the emphasis on the primary material, and since Oppen, like Charles Olson, was very inventive in his use of typography and shape, depending "on space and organization on the page" for effect, she has chosen to avoid interfering within the text of the letters, preserving their integrity as complete entities. Her "compromised editorial humility" with respect to the reproduction of Oppen's idiosyncratic use of hyphens and dashes ("There is also a long dash—anywhere from three to eight or nine hyphens joined—these make an interior code of extension and connection throughout letters") is an indication of her command of and care for the material. Her explanations and interpretations, combining intelligence, insight, and respect for the people and issues of Oppen's life, are an assurance that Oppen has been rewarded for his confidence in DuPlessis as, effectively, the curator of his literary legacy.

The object of the enterprise, finally, is to re-create the conditions of the mind and heart that produced the poetry and to permit the reader to understand the sensibility and character of the man. The self-drawn portrait of Oppen that emerges through his letters is of a man whose personal warmth, keen intelligence, and obsession with language and form coalesced to generate what DuPlessis describes as a "sustained, elegant, perceptive body of critical and aesthetic thinking." What is also evident is his passionate conviction that political action is at least as important as artistic endeavor. Aside from the costs of his quarter-century of poetic silence, one can understand why Oppen dismissed Wallace Stevens' "little elegances" or labeled the political positions of Pound, T. S. Eliot, and William Butler Yeats as "reactionary to the point of insanity or freakishness" in the light of his belief that the "directly political" is crucial because it is "something one wants to do and without which he will not possess his own life." Oppen calls "the failure to act" a "retreat from decency." In typically arch commentary, he described Richard M. Nixon after Watergate as a "mangled rat," referred to the moon shot as a "display of para-military apoplexy," saw student activists of the late 1960's as "zealots of catastrophe" (who in this resembled poets), and, in a wonderfully bizarre analysis, compared the Warren Commission Report to *Ulysses* (1922), with Jack Ruby as a parallel to James Joyce's Bloom.

Yet his political convictions never dulled his poetic perceptions: He lamented ruefully that Carl Sandburg, politically admirable, ought to be a better poet than the crew of reactionaries but "just so obviously is not" because of his "destructive sentimentality." During his twenty-five-year silence, he notes proudly, he was "not Yeatsing on the green, nor Pounding, nor Eliotizing in the middle thirties." Still, if Pound was symptomatic of an infection in the body politic and Oppen indicative of the antidote, Oppen was able to move beyond the narrow strictures of dogma to write to Pound in 1962:

> I suppose if we should take to talking politics to each other I would disagree even more actively than all those others who have disagreed, but there has been no one living during my life time who has been as generous or as pure as you toward literature and toward writers. Nor anyone less generously thanked.
>   I know of no one who does not owe you a debt.

Beyond this, describing a meeting with Pound in 1969, Oppen wrote:

> I began to weep Pound began to weep   We cried all over each other - - by that time neither of us could speak,   so I took the book, and left. I don't know, perhaps neither of us knew what we were crying about - - - - or, of course, I do know. Every sincere or serious poet who ever met Pound has reason to have loved him.

In one of his most successful homages to Pound's spirit, Oppen responded with encouragement to everyone who sent his or her work for his comments. Writing to contemporaries who had achieved some stature as well as to embryonic would-be poets, Oppen managed to combine the kind of praise that is necessary for the exposure any poet risks with the sharpest of critical suggestions. Acting on the conviction that for a poet "to have spoken and not been heard" was a kind of death by neglect, and justifying his strong opinions by asserting that poetry was "the only field in which I might be imagined to possess competence," he could support an accomplished poet such as Williams with pure praise ("I have thought the Asphodel one of the beautiful poems of the language since I first saw it") while complimenting Dan Gerber on many details before concluding in a postscript, "(((good poems   even very good   Not good enough))."

Oppen did not have to struggle to see his work in print, and he was fortunate enough to share the great visionary publisher of New Directions, James Laughlin, with Pound, Williams, and others, but he did experience the frustration of having the British press Fulcrum sit on an edition of his collected poems for some time in the early 1970's. He knew enough of the disappointments an artist faces to warn John Crawford about a friend, "I hope to god she does not sit at a desk and mail innumerable envelopes to innumerable little magazines." In a moment of typically rueful modesty he also called himself "the oldest promising young poet in America," but generally he was more acerbic, as in his comment that it would be nice if most publishers thought of literature as a "process of thought" instead of "part of the entertainment industry."

Oppen's claims to competence in the area of poetic excellence are supported by his responses to inquiries about the early ventures of the Objectivists. His insights into the themes, subjects, and styles of Zukovsky, Reznikoff, and Rakosi, in particular, pull separate particles of information through his plane of vision into literary history. As DuPlessis puts it, Oppen's explanations ("the word 'Objectivist' indicated the contributors' objective attitude to reality. It meant, of course, the poets' recognition of the necessity of form, the objectification of the poem") lead to "an enriched sense of the poetics of modernism." Oppen's "objectivist meditations," including his basic personal credo that "a poem has got to be written into the future" and "a poem is a part of the process of thought, the means of thought," anticipate some of the theoretical and practical work of Robert Creeley and draw the poetry of people such as Robert Duncan and Cid Corman into an evolving tradition that is more continuous than had been previously thought. Even Oppen's frequent references to the linguistic philosophy of Martin Heidegger, which seemed somewhat arcane in his lifetime, have become further evidence of his ability to anticipate the concerns of the latter part of the century.

As rich and vital as the book is, it is more an invitation to look deeper into Oppen's life and work than a concluding or summary statement. As astute as Du Plessis has been in selecting letters for inclusion, others that were not included contain additional information about some of the intriguing questions of Oppen's life that have been raised. His relationship with his half-sister June Oppen Degnan, the recipient of many of these letters, a political activist (involved in the presidental campaigns of Eugene McCarthy and George McGovern) and publisher, has not been fully explored; nor has his relationship with his wife, who is mentioned glowingly but not directly addressed, or his daughter. His feelings about his father, mother, and stepmother are cryptically hinted at. The book is an "opening of the field" (to use Robert Duncan's phrase).

Oppen said to Michael Cuddihy in 1975, "The meaning of the book, the value of the book, is your own love of poetry." His words apply to DuPlessis' efforts in preparing this exemplary volume. She has made possible the launching of the critical scrutiny Oppen's poetry requires.

Leon Lewis

Source for Further Study

Choice. XXVIII, February, 1991, p. 933.

SELVES
New Poems by Philip Booth

Author: Philip Booth (1925-   )
Publisher: Viking (New York). 75 pp. $17.95
Type of work: Poetry

A collection of poems about the people, places, and questions that engage Philip Booth

Philip Booth's voice is neither strident nor trendy. His first volume, *Letter from a Distant Land* (1956), set the perimeters for both his poetic approach and his subject matter. His poetic technique has always been characterized by reticence; his subject matter has always dealt with his personal journey, however submerged; his work has always exhibited empathy with the New England landscape and seascape and with his neighbors. Over the years Booth has not veered from the course he set for himself, but he has made several discoveries along the way. The most notable additions to his original methods began with his fifth book, *Available Light* (1976). In this volume, Booth included his first dream poem, which he indicated represents a new source for his work. *Selves*, his eighth volume, continues these trends as he probes more deeply into the lives of his neighbors, the lives of the elderly in nursing homes, and his personal reaction to his own mortality.

Booth begins this volume with an introductory poem addressed to readers. "Reaching In" acknowledges that the process of making a poem is incomplete until it is read by someone. He tells the reader, "Weigh each word before you believe me./ However you read me you enter the story." Booth's self needs the selves of readers, and both are mysteriously and inextricably linked.

This opening poem describes his regard for his audience, and the epigraphs delineate the other subjects he is considering. Booth uses quotations from Anton Chekhov, Gerard Manley Hopkins, and Wallace Stevens. The Chekhov quotation, from the short story "Gooseberries," asserts that "What is terrible in life goes on somewhere behind the scenes. . . ." The quotation from Hopkins begins with the line from his poem "Binsey Poplars": "After-comers cannot guess the beauty been." The lines from Stevens sum up what Booth is trying to convey in this work: "And out of what one sees and hears and out/ Of what one feels, who could have thought to make/ So many selves. . . ."

Booth has seen and experienced Chekhov's "terrible," or he knows those who have; he is as acutely conscious of the beauty of the life he is living and of the natural surroundings which he loves. The terror and beauty of it all splinter him, divide him; bits of him appear in others, and he sees pieces of himself in his neighbors and family. Although he cites Chekhov and Hopkins, Booth's philosophy comes from the democracy of Walt Whitman. While Booth admires the poetic techniques of Wallace Stevens, whom he also cites, much of his technique seems to be influenced by William Carlos Williams. Like Whitman's, Booth's work is inclusive; it says, as Whitman did in his "Song of Myself," "I am the man, I suffer'd, I was there." In technique, his most pervasive line is, like Williams', the short line made up of only a few syllables, often only four or five. Like Williams, he insists on the rhythms of everyday speech. Unlike Williams, however, Booth uses rhyme in some poems— some end rhyme and some internal rhyme. Most of the time his rhyme is carefully hidden, a technique that reminds one of Marianne Moore's deceptive rhymes.

Reticence, however, is the key word to describe the overwhelming element in his poetic technique. Although in the volumes since the publication of *Available Light* he has loosened his hold on the actual, Booth does not let emotions spill over the page. He carefully controls the shape of the poem, and like the good sailor that he is, he has studied the charts and planned the voyage. If an unknown island or idea appears, he does not reject it but, rather, uses what the sea and the Muse proffer. One major result of his reticence is that the poems are laconic, similar to the speech of Maine people about whom he writes. Booth never uses words carelessly. In this volume, not one word could be excised without changing both rhythm and meaning.

A second result is that this extreme contraction forces the poet to find precisely the right word for each place. Booth's vocabulary seems conversational, but what appears simple on the surface is teeming with meaning underneath. In "Short Day," the poet is trying to find a nut that will fit an engine mount stud. He finally discovers that he does not have the right size and has to go into town to get one. As he drives toward the store, he lets his imagination fly ". . . beyond/ loons or mallards or// islands . . ." and gives himself "leave to/ be out there, far// offshore where,/ over the labyrin-// thine waves, a seabird/ without a name// circles, her wings quieting/ to calm the sea// as she comes in/ to light." What happens is that during an ordinary day when Booth is taking care of ordinary chores, he is lifted by his imagination as he observes the wildlife around him. Moreover, the bird quieting the waves cannot help but recall Christ quieting the waters of Galilee; though in this existentialist poem it is not mentioned, nevertheless, it is there, right below the surface. Evocative images such as these stretch the words that Booth does use, making them do more than double duty. He accepts the current miracle, as well as the recurring miracle of imagination.

Another important influence—especially in subject matter—is Henry David Thoreau. Booth admires the simplicity of Thoreau's life, his ability to do practical things, and, above all, his Yankee philosophy, high-minded but workable. He has Thoreau's regard for tools too, and a sense of humor about their perversity.

Booth is observant of the animal life around him and records it as meticulously as did Thoreau. In "Watching Out," he describes how each spring his cat catches a chipmunk and plays a deadly game with it. "Whenever// he runs, she swipes him back,/ showing off to the house/ her soft cat mouth." In "Sea Level," he finds the most exact, though common, words to evoke the sounds seals make: ". . . the snuffle and low yelp of seals"; in "Words Made from Letters," he speaks of ". . . How foxes greet/ by *gekkering*. . . ." In "Short Day," he brings together tools and animals, commending the final fitting of two engine parts—"clean as the whistle/ of two pairs of loons."

Selves is divided into four parts. As with the four panes of a window, it is necessary to look through all of them to perceive the entire view. The first part is about his
Maine neighbors: common people, working people, poor people. In the book's first
poem, "Garden," the neighbor Booth visits because the man's idiot sister and his
dog died the same day, says of the dog, ". . . *she was/ parallel from// the waist
down.*" Booth does not despise this lack of knowledge or make fun of it; rather, he
participates in the old fellow's pain: "His old eyes// wanted tears; mine/ felt them
come."

Not all Booth's neighbors are pathetic in this way, however. Even for the shiftless
ones Booth has understanding and sympathy. In "Poor," he writes about Moose
Coombs, who never seemed to get wood cut so it could cure ahead of time. Moose
is the Maine version of William Faulkner's Anse Bundren in *As I Lay Dying* (1930).
He is as annoying and as appealing as Anse. As a result of his laziness or ineptitude,
his wife had to burn green wood, which caked the stovepipe with creosote, leading
to a fire that burned down the house. Booth knows all the excuses. The man's saw or
"his back or his truck/ keeps giving out./ Or his woman's got// herself pregnant
again,/ or deer season's on, or/ he had to fix his boat."

In this section of the volume, Booth is doing more than presenting brilliant, sharp-
edged images of the people he knows. The closing poem for this part, entitled "United
States," is a condemnation of what has happened to make this country, in the parlance of sociology, two nations. In this way, Booth relates his concerns for his neighbors to national concerns and to larger issues.

The second section of the volume illustrates Hopkins' lines about the past. Here
the main characters are elderly people in a nursing home, which Booth calls, metaphorically, Farview. In "Fallback," he pictures an aging couple, perhaps Booth's
parents, spending their last days. The woman is a victim of osteoporosis, ". . . her
backbone so thin/ the doctor jokes that X-rays can't find it." The old woman and her
husband had been avid bird watchers, and now she finds that she is also a bird, "a
wren of a woman looking out/ from her cover," and that "the night girl looks like a
grebe." Several of the poems in this section are about this couple, the bedridden
woman whose mind is alert and remembering the fine past and her husband whose
body is healthy but whose mind is gone. The young women who take care of them
have no concept of the rich life they have led or the devotion of their love. This
section ends with "Rule One," the last four lines boring in on Booth's major thesis.

> Who hurts
>   and why.
>   Why we guess we know.
>   How much we never.

The third section is related to the Chekhov epigraph. Behind the façade of happy
homes there is often great sadness, or great discrepancies between appearance and
reality, or alternating emotions. "Argument" begins with Chekhov's image: "Looked
in on through the kitchen window—/ who'd doubt that we were happy?" As it turns

out, this couple argues over a single subject: "who brought the other down, down/ to this gray leveling, this daily/ burdening, and trading off, of guilt." "So," the poem that follows, is another kind of argument, one with an invisible interlocutor about death. Booth, modernist that he is, will not risk claiming immortality, but he does insist on another redeeming quality: love. He ends the poem this way:

> . . . Between what we were, and
> are going to be, is who and how we best love.

The fourth section is a series of poems that address the central question of existence: Why are we here? In "Sea Level," a poem with a multimeaning title, Booth explores some of the differences between the magical and the actual. He starts with images of a foggy morning in Maine and three seals out on a rock. Were it not for several fences, Booth says, ". . . I might walk out/ among them, pull down the fogged sun// for my halo, and—when the tide came—/ simply keep walking across. But I'm here, who I am, given// this day. . . ." The last poem in the book follows logically and emotionally. In "Presence," Booth insists that "we see near and far we own nothing:// it's us who belong to all else. . . ."

If the reader finds that Booth's subject matter is often too similar, that his reticence sometimes seems to block narrative, that his locales are almost always Maine, plain, rock-rimmed, and lonely—the reader needs to keep perspective and observe the entire window's scenes. In seemingly simple language, Booth is addressing the most cosmopolitan questions of all: the past and present; existence or extinction; how to love one's neighbor. He does this with a granite integrity, with humor, and with contractility, which Marianne Moore insisted was the first grace of style. Booth's work has that and more.

Ann Struthers

Sources for Further Study

Atlanta Journal Constitution. April 1, 1990, p. N10.
Booklist. LXXXVI, February 15, 1990, p. 1136.
Detroit News and Free Press. March 25, 1990, p. L7.
Library Journal. CXV, January, 1990, p. 114.
Poetry. CLVI, September, 1990, p. 348.
Publishers Weekly. CCXXXVII, January 19, 1990, p. 94.
The Washington Post Book World. XX, June 17, 1990, p. 10.
Washington Times. July 30, 1990, p. F3.

SEXING THE CHERRY

Author: Jeanette Winterson (1959-   )
First published: 1989, in Great Britain
Publisher: Atlantic Monthly Press (New York). 167 pp. $19.95
Type of work: Novel
Time: The seventeenth century and 1990
Locale: London

Jordan, as a child and as a young man, travels in the real world and in his mind, making fantastic discoveries

Principal characters:
JORDAN, a foundling adopted by the Dog-Woman
THE DOG-WOMAN, a giantess, a Royalist, and the fond mother of Jordan
JOHN TRADESCANT, the gardener to King Charles I
FORTUNATA, one of twelve dancing princesses and Jordan's beloved
PREACHER SCROGGS AND NEIGHBOR FIREBRACE, Puritans
JACK, Jordan's friend in the twentieth century

Sexing the Cherry is Jeanette Winterson's third novel, following *Oranges Are Not the Only Fruit* (1985) and *The Passion* (1988). A fantasy on the theme of discovery and renewal, it centers on a foundling, Jordan, who searchs with his mentor, John Tradescant, for new and exotic fruits and plants to bring back to the England of King Charles I. Jordan also embarks on more exotic voyages of the imagination.

Jordan's name comes from the fact that his foster mother, the Dog-Woman, fished him out of the Thames, as the Pharaoh's daughter rescued Moses from the Nile. The Dog-Woman wants to name him for a river, and it would be unthinkable to name a baby "Thames," or "Nile," so he becomes Jordan. The Dog-Woman has forgotten whatever name she was given, and is content to be known by the term which identi fies her as a trainer of fighting dogs. She is the character who gives *Sexing the Cherry* its firmest grounding in reality, while Jordan embarks on his real and imaginary travels, searching for the new and for himself. During most of the action of *Sexing the Cherry* (the term refers to a botanical procedure involved in hybridiza- tion) these two characters alternate narratives.

The "real" of the early part of the novel is the disordered world of London during the Puritan Revolution, which began in 1641 and ended with the beheading of King Charles I in 1649. The gigantic Dog-Woman is a Royalist, loyal to the King, and despises the Puritans, whom she sees as taking all the joy from life. She makes her living preparing dogs for the fights which provide London's poor with amusement and the occasion for gambling.

She is a lusty, vigorous person, extremely strong, but her experience has been some- what limited. Much of the comedy in *Sexing the Cherry* results from her ignorance of human anatomy and sex, and from her naïve comments on the world around her. She is certain that Jordan has sailed off the edge of the world in his voyages to far places. She is capable of drastic action; after the Restoration in 1661, she joyfully witnesses the execution of the regicides who condemned King Charles I and does her own part by beheading her grim Puritan acquaintances, Preacher Scroggs and Neighbor Firebrace.

The Dog-Woman also provides a secure place to which Jordan may return in order to rest between voyages, as well as someone to whom he can talk about his discoveries. While he was still a boy, Jordan's ability to build model boats had attracted the attention of John Tradescant, gardener to the King. At Tradescant's invitation, Jordan and the Dog-Woman had moved into the Royal Gardens while the scientist trained Jordan in botany and other fields as preparation for accompanying Tradescant on his voyages. When Jordan was little more than an infant, the Dog-Woman had taken him to witness the first appearance of a banana in England, an occasion on which the Londoners were shocked and amused by the sexual appearance of the fruit; later Jordan and Tradescant bring back another fruit with sexual overtones, the pineapple. Along with the banana, it becomes a central symbol in the novel. After the Restoration, with Tradescant dead, Jordan continues his voyages of discovery.

Jordan's emotional life, however, is rooted in the voyages he makes in his imagination. He goes to far and unrecognizable places, meeting fantastic people and seeing unbelieveable things. His narratives are filled with speculations about the nature of time, space, love, and reality. In one of his flights, he disguises himself as a girl and is shocked when a woman shows him what women think of men. In another, he lists speculations about objects and time and concludes with what are labeled lies about what people can know. He visits fantastic places, including one city whose inhabitants are subject to the plague of love; when they fall in love, they die of it. Jordan's playing of a disused guitar threatens to bring on a new outbreak. To save the city, the rulers, an old monk and an old whore, have decreed that love is forbidden. Later, Jordan learns that the plague had returned and everyone in the city except the monk and the whore were killed.

One of his trips ends with Jordan spending the night with a beautiful woman named Zillah, who has been exiled to a tower. The experience leads him to search for a dancer, one of Zillah's eleven sisters. His vision takes him to the castle of the Twelve Dancing Princesses, eleven of whom tell him the story of their marriages. The stories compose a sermon on the dangers of marriage for women. As the oldest tells Jordan, the sisters lived happily, magically flying from their castle at night to visit a place where everyone danced and returning in the morning before they could be discovered, until a clever young prince found out their secret. "He had eleven brothers and we were all given in marriage, one to each brother, and as its says lived happily ever after. We did, but not with our husbands."

Each of the princesses has had a disappointing marriage. A few of them loved other women. Others loved husbands who did not return that love. One loved a husband who loved a boy; another husband married only to disguise his multiple affairs with other women. In the end each of the princesses disposed of her husband; some simply left, others killed their spouses. When they discovered that their common fate was to have marriages that failed, they decided to live together once more.

When the sisters' stories have been told, Jordan realizes that there have been only eleven tales and only eleven princesses. The youngest, the others tell him, is Fortunata, who has never lived with them. She was the best dancer, the most agile, the lightest, the one who escaped her prince on her wedding day. "She didn't burn in secret with a passion she could not express; she shone." She must now, they fear, be old and stiff.

Jordan finds Fortunata, who has not aged but who now teaches others to dance. Fortunata then becomes a narrator, telling Jordan the story of the sisters' lives. Her story is much like theirs, although the version of her escape on her wedding day is much less romantic and magical than theirs. The center of the story is a city which, following an apparent earthquake, had lost its gravity; when a child fell into a pit, she floated, unharmed. When the citizens began to dance, they found that they were no longer bound to earth.

Eventually the city itself floated, drifting around the world and finding itself over the castle of the sisters, who allowed themselves to be drawn up to it to dance with the residents and with the city itself. The sisters decided to live permanently in the city, but before they could do so, the clever prince discovered them and they were given in marriage. Only Fortunata escaped. The city she describes is a symbolic counterweight to Jordan's city where love had been a plague and music a symptom of illness. Jordan stays with Fortunata for a time and then goes back to his ship, promising to return; both know he will not.

The final quarter of *Sexing the Cherry* takes place partly in 1990, partly in the 1660's. Jordan's modern avatar, like his seventeenth century counterpart, grows up loving to make and play with boats, much to the disgust of his friend Jack. Jordan's earlier self is evidenced in the later time in his attraction to a painting of the pineapple being presented to King Charles II and in his fascination with a book of heroes, which includes such seagoing adventurers as Christopher Columbus, Francis Drake, and Lord Nelson, as well as William the Conqueror. John Tradescant appears occasionally to Jordan wearing the same clothing he wore three hundred years earlier, yet although Jordan knows his name, he never realizes who Tradescant has been.

In this life, Jordan's parents are ordinary people. His father spends most of his time watching action movies on television. His mother saves mementos of Jordan's childhood. When he grows up, Jordan joins the British Navy, in the aftermath of the Falkland Islands conflict. He has dreams of heroism similar to those his earlier self had known. At the same time, the Dog-Woman (who does not appear in the twentieth century episodes) is telling the story of Jordan's triumphant return to London in the 1660's, the illness he suffered when the plague struck England, and the Great Fire which destroyed much of London in 1666, in the aftermath of the plague. Jordan recounts to his mother the story Fortunata had told him of Artemis and her rape by Orion.

This interpolated story, a variation on the Greek myth of Artemis, the immortal virgin goddess, seems intended to explain Fortunata's reluctance to marry. In Fortunata's tale, Artemis is raped by Orion, an event which is not part of the original myth in which Artemis killed Orion accidentally. In this version, Artemis buries Orion (in the original she set him as a constellation in the sky), but cannot truly bury her resentment of men or the pain of her violation. Fortunata's devotion to Artemis does not seem to prevent her from loving Jordan.

The other narrator in this final segment is a woman scientist, highly trained and disgusted by what human beings have done to the planet. She is not named, but she is clearly the modern version of Fortunata. She dreams of going to the World Bank and the Pentagon, kidnapping the financiers, the military men, and the world leaders, and teaching them the error of their ways. Her program is simple: "I force all the fat ones to go on a diet, and all the men line up for compulsory training in feminism and ecology. Then they start on the food surpluses, packing it with their own hands, distributing it in a great human chain of what used to be power and is now co-operation."

In reality, she camps beside a badly polluted river, calling attention to the effects of industrial waste. She is regarded as a troublemaker, but as she says, who can truly believe she prefers to live where she does instead of in comfort and ease? Jordan reads about her activity and is drawn to seek her out. They recognize that they have somehow been connected before. The woman's suggestion that they burn down a factory echoes the Dog-Woman's desire for a purifying fire which will burn down London; both wishes are fulfilled by the Great Fire. Jordan and the Dog-Woman leave on a seventeenth century ship; they will not return to London. Fortunata appears at Jordan's side and then is gone, presumably to return from time to time, as she does in the twentieth century.

The power of *Sexing the Cherry* is in its unadorned but enchanting prose and in Winterson's success in melding the elements of fantasy and reality of which the novel is made. Dreams and speculations which seem to be tangential eventually come to be essential elements of the story. Some of the symbolic elements are never entirely clear, and some of the digressions do not seem integral to the story or to Jordan's search, but the central theme of searching for the self in new experiences and finding it in others is never in doubt. The three principal characters, while they are dreamlike figures out of a fairy tale world, are nevertheless distinctive and interesting on a human level.

John M. Muste

Sources for Further Study

Booklist. LXVI, March, 15, 1990, p. 1417.
Library Journal. CXV, February 15, 1990, p. 214.
London Review of Books. XI, September 14, 1989, p. 19.
Los Angeles Times. May 3, 1990, p. E6.
The Nation. CCLI, July 9, 1990, p. 64.

New Statesman and Society. III, October 12, 1990, p. 44.
The New York Times Book Review. XCV, April 29, 1990, p. 24.
The New Yorker. LXVI, May 21, 1990, p. 95.
Publishers Weekly. CCXXXVII, February 23, 1990, p. 204.
The Times Literary Supplement. September 15, 1989, p. 1006.
The Washington Post Book World. XX, May 13, 1990, p. 9.

SIMONE DE BEAUVOIR
A Biography

Author: Deirdre Bair (1935-   )
Publisher: Summit Books (New York). Illustrated. 718 pp. $24.95
Type of work: Biography
Time: 1908-1986
Locale: Principally France

A comprehensive, vivid portrait of one of the twentieth century's most influential women

Principal personages:
SIMONE DE BEAUVOIR, a writer, feminist, and companion of Jean-Paul
   Sartre
GEORGES DE BEAUVOIR, her father
FRANCOISE BRASSEUR DE BEAUVOIR, her mother
HÉLÈNE DE BEAUVOIR, her sister
JEAN-PAUL SARTRE, her lifelong partner and friend
JACQUES-LAURENT BOST, her close friend
DOLORES VANETTI EHRENREICH, Sartre's mistress for several years
NELSON ALGREN, a writer and sometime lover of Beauvoir
CLAUDE LANZMANN, a lover and friend of Beauvoir
ARLETTE ELKAÏM-SARTRE, an adopted daughter of Sartre
SYLVIE LE BON DE BEAUVOIR, Beauvoir's close friend, whom she eventually
   adopted

Deirdre Bair has specialized in massive, comprehensive, painstakingly researched biographies of important modern writers. Her portrait of Samuel Beckett, the first full treatment of this reclusive man's life, took six years, spans 736 pages, and won a National Book Award in 1981. Bair's study of Simone de Beauvoir took nine years, covers 718 pages, and is at least an equally distinguished achievement. The text can be faulted for long-windedness and careless repetitions, pedestrian prose, and perhaps Bair's inability to comprehend fully the intricacy of her subject's opaque personality.

The book's virtues, however, far transcend its flaws: Bair has rendered a vivid, admiring, yet persuasively balanced exploration of the life of a brilliant intellectual who chose to serve as loyal subordinate to a man who never fully appreciated her worth; a woman who preferred ideas and friendships to marriage and children; the author of a famous treatise on feminism and about twenty other books, of whom it could nevertheless be said that her life was more significant than her work; a generous, affectionate, honest, charming, and remarkably courageous person who could also be abrasive, brusque, haughty, and intimidating.

Simone Lucie Ernestine Marie Bertrand de Beauvoir was born into the *haute bourgeoisie*, to one of France's most illustrious but no longer prosperous families. Her mother, Francoise, was a pious, straitlaced Catholic whose father had been unable to pay her dowry. Simone's father, Georges, was a self-indulgent, impractical atheist who failed as a lawyer and in a succession of business ventures. Simone and her younger sister, Hélène, had lonely as well as impoverished childhoods, constrained by social customs to guard themselves against possibly unsuitable connections; they could not even befriend classmates until Francoise had paid a formal call upon their mothers. The girls attended a prestigious Catholic private school, spent hours at their devotions daily, and were rigidly disciplined by the austere and obsessively orderly Francoise. As Simone changed from a pretty, plump little blue-eyed girl to an awkward adolescent, her father pronounced her "ugly" and became indifferent toward her. From an early age Simone retreated into omnivorous reading, forming her role models from such literary characters as George Eliot's Maggie Tolliver, a forceful, intelligent individualist at odds with a rigidly unsympathetic society.

In 1927 Simone began studying at the Sorbonne, sometimes attending bars and cheap nightclubs with girlfriends but remaining both a virgin and a first-rate student. Her class ranking in 1928 was second, behind only Simone Weil and just ahead of Maurice Merleau-Ponty. One group of students at the Sorbonne, enrolled in the École Normale Supérieure, had a particularly bad reputation, attending lectures only when they liked the professor; it included René Maheu, Paul Nizan, and Jean-Paul Sartre.

Sartre stood just under five feet and had a lumpy complexion, thinning hair, teeth and fingers stained by tobacco, and a right eye disfigured by strabismus. His voice was melodious, however, his mind dazzled all, and many young women found him fascinating. Simone and he met quite naturally, as members of an organized study group preparing for the comprehensive oral examinations. Because of her prodigious work habits, Maheu had awarded her the nickname by which she became known for the rest of her life—Castor, meaning "Beaver." Castor and Sartre began their association by expounding G. W. Leibniz' theories, then Jean-Jacques Rousseau's. "I was intelligent, certainly," she was to insist, over and over, "but Sartre was a genius." Bair registers her disapproval of such a subordination, preferring Sartre's assessment in a 1975 interview: "She was the only one at my level of knowledge of myself, of what I wanted to do. . . . What is unique between Simone de Beauvoir und me is the equality of our relationship." Both Castor and Sartre passed the *agré gation* examinations with brilliance; he barely edged her for first place.

They did not become lovers until the following summer, in the country town of Meyrignac. From the beginning, their romance was at least as verbal-intellectual as it was physical: Each poured out floods of words, words, words upon the other. After Simone's parents had become aware of their relationship, Sartre politely offered to marry her. Later, recalled Beauvoir, "we were both embarrassed that we had even briefly considered the most bourgeois of institutions, marriage, to be the answer." Instead, they initially decided on a "two-year lease" for their liaison, then renewed it for their lives. For the first two years they agreed to forgo other sexual involvements, even though in principle they regarded themselves as entitled to a multiplicity of sexual partners. In the second of her series of memoirs, *La force de l'âge* (1960; *The Prime of Life*, 1962), Beauvoir recalls Sartre's definitions and distinctions:

> "What we have," he said, "is an *essential* love; but it is a good idea for us also to experience *contingent* love affairs." We were two of a kind, and our relationship would endure as long as we did; but it could not make up entirely for the fleeting riches to be had from encounters with different people. How could we deliberately forgo that gamut of emotions—astonishment, regret, pleasure, nostalgia—which we were as capable of sustaining as anyone else?

Moreover, they promised neither to lie to each other nor to conceal anything from the other.

Beauvoir took no other lovers for many years; not so Sartre. Every woman was fair game for his considerable charm, including other men's wives and Simone's students. While Sartre made Simone his sexual partner on fewer and fewer occasions as the years passed, she remained his trusted confidante, even in erotic activities. Beauvoir was never comfortable in this role of complicity imposed on her, even though Sartre would usually conclude the accounts of his sexual peccadilloes by proclaiming the transcendent superiority of their intimacy.

Bair is unable to understand Simone's role, reluctant as it was, as voyeuse. The best explanation she manages is that "Beauvoir's ultimate need remained to be in agreement with him, which resulted in the constant denial of her true feelings." Sartre additionally demeaned Beauvoir by assigning her the task of a shielder or rescuer who would ration or totally reject the attentions of women when he became tired of them; alternatively, he would dilute a relationship by alleging that "Castor" would not want him to do this or that with the woman. Beauvoir's rationalization to Bair was that "Sartre had to be protected from himself. He would never have written had I not accepted to be his screen before the world." Throughout her life, Beauvoir would insist that her relationship with Sartre had never frustrated or otherwise disappointed her. While Bair clearly considers this assertion somewhat disingenuous, she does not analyze Beauvoir's motivation for making it.

From the mid-1930's to the rest of their lives, Beauvoir and Sartre were the reigning couple of a group they termed "the Family." The unchanging core of this unit consisted of the Kosakievicz sisters, Olga and Wanda (both of whom Sartre bedded), and Jacques-Laurent Bost, a brilliant journalist who married the moody Olga, and whom Beauvoir closely befriended and, in later years, occasionally but never passionately bedded. She and Sartre would congratulate themselves for having originated a new social network, a chosen rather than genetic family. As Sarte found a new woman she would, sometimes briefly but occasionally for years, join "the Family." Sometimes Simone would enter into a friendship with the mistress—never an overtly lesbian one—and even console her while Sartre devoted himself to another amorous adventure.

Dutifully, Bair devotes many pages to a description—never a profoundly probing interpretation—of Beauvoir's prodigious production as a writer. She was, after all, the author of seven novels, one play, two philosophical texts, four volumes of memoirs, half a dozen volumes of serious essays, two travel diaries, numerous periodical articles, and many introductions to books by others. She insisted that she mattered primarily as a writer, not as a feminist or "La Grande Sartreuse." Yet her novels are unimaginative, self-conscious *romans à clef*, and her philosophical works lack originality, while her autobiographies, often eloquent, mythicize a heroic career. Her chief contributions are, then, not to literature but to life: Her style of experientially voracious female existence supersedes her works, with the possible exception of *Le Deuxième Sexe* (1949; *The Second Sex*, 1952). This is her only book that has a life of its own.

The treatise has two parts. Book 1 is a historical outline of what Beauvoir regards as women's oppression throughout history, from early nomadic societies to the surprisingly late achievement of French suffrage in 1947. Book 2 examines various expressions of sexuality and love, emphasizing the ways in which women have, often willingly, assumed the roles of objects in patriarchal societies, living within the strictures of male fantasies. She concludes that all theories of human history are unfairly biased, because women have been considered as the other, inferior (hence "second") sex since the beginning of time. Only in the final chapter does she offer some suggestions toward what has since become known as women's liberation. They are rather vague, expressing the central hope that socialism would replace capitalism, which would enable women to gain their economic freedom, which would in turn give them a self-reliant female identity—providing they avoided the traps of marriage and motherhood. While *The Second Sex* received mixed reviews (Elizabeth Hardwick, for example, called it "madly sensible and brilliantly confused"), it sold over a million copies in its first year of publication alone, became an inspirational text for hundreds of thousands of women, and may well be the most important feminist tract of the twentieth century.

Beauvoir wrote *The Second Sex* during her celebrated though intermittent liaison with the Chicago novelist Nelson Algren, who suggested that she study the lives of black American women as examples of victimization by a male-dominated society. Algren and she met in 1947, two years after Sartre had begun an intense involvement with Dolores Vanetti Ehrenreich, a French woman married to a wealthy American physician. Beauvoir and Ehrenreich detested each other; Beauvoir was, thus, open to a consoling Algren on a visit to the United States, and found him a passionately virile lover; with him she had her first orgasm, at the age of thirty-nine.

For several years Algren and Beauvoir exchanged transatlantic visits. She wrote him effusive, rapturous letters; he gave her a silver-banded ring that she wore the rest of her life, and he pleaded with her to relocate in Chicago. Yet both she and Sartre were at the center of a wholly French intellectual and literary tradition that, they knew, was not transportable. Nor could Algren realistically imagine himself flourishing as a writer in Paris; all of his fiction was Chicago-centered. Moreover, there was that paramount pact between Sartre and Beauvoir, fidelity to which superseded even the most romantic passions. By the late 1940's, Ehrenreich knew herself defeated and gave up on Sartre. Algren fought harder for Beauvoir's allegiance, but also lost and became embittered, particularly after she had unmistakably rendered their affair in *Les Mandarins* (1954; *The Mandarins*, 1956), a novel of ideas that she dedicated to Algren.

In 1950, after Beauvoir and Algren had renounced their romance (though they occasionally met until his death in 1981), she began an affair with Claude Lanzmann, seventeen years her junior. Lanzmann was an ambitious journalist who befriended both Beauvoir and Sartre, fell deeply in love with Beauvoir, and even shared an apartment with her from 1952 to 1959. Yet their bond was never as strong as that between her and Algren; it therefore survived after their separation as a friendship, with Lanzmann, by then married, making the funeral arrangements after Beauvoir's death.

While no tensions troubled the Lanzmann-Beauvoir-Sartre friendship, plenty of turmoil resulted from Sartre's decision to make a young Algerian student, Arlette Elkaïm, his legally adopted daughter in 1965. Sartre undertook this act without having first consulted Beauvoir. While he thereby conferred French citizenship on Arlette and made her immune to deportation, he also made her the legal owner of all of his possessions, including his writings. Beauvoir felt enraged as well as humiliated; "the Family" was outraged. Arlette remained deferential to Beauvoir as long as Sartre remained in good health. Once it began to fail, in the mid-1970's, Arlette became increasingly assertive and hostile. After his death, on April 15, 1980, she and Beauvoir fought bitterly, with Arlette going so far as to send a letter to the journal *Libération* in which she disparaged Beauvoir's relationship with Sartre. The two women engaged in publishing duels over Sartre's notebooks (edited by Arlette) and his letters to Beauvoir (issued by Beauvoir).

Beauvoir devoted the few years left her after Sartre's death largely to traveling with her closest woman friend, Sylvie le Bon, and to writing memoirs of the last ten years of Sartre's life, which she called *La cérémonie des adieux* (1981; *Adieux: A Farewell to Sartre*, 1984). Over and over, even against evidence to the contrary, Beauvoir would insist on the primacy of her and Sartre's relationship as the successful couple, loving, like-minded coconspirators against the conventions of bourgeois society.

On March 20, 1986, Beauvoir was hospitalized, suffering from cirrhosis of the liver, pulmonary edema, and pneumonia. On April 15, she died, virtually six years to the day after Sartre's death. Bair sums up Beauvoir as an immensely complex, often contradictory woman. Was her alliance with Sartre an open marriage of true minds and free spirits, or did Beauvoir place herself as a pedestal beneath him, serving his wishes at an exorbitant cost to her own needs? This question will probably divide biographers for generations to come. Bair clearly believes that Sartre treated Beauvoir badly, and that the saint of feminism did not sufficiently liberate herself from the spell cast by a magisterial but macho man of letters.

Gerhard Brand

Sources for Further Study

America. CLXII, May 12, 1990, p. 479.
Booklist. LXXVI, January 1, 1990, p. 866.
Chicago Tribune. April 8, 1990, XIV, p. 3.
Kirkus Reviews. LVIII, February 15, 1990, p. 232.
London Review of Books. XII, June 14, 1990, p. 6.
Los Angeles Times Book Review. April 15, 1990, p. 3.
The New Republic. CCII, June 11, 1990, p. 27.
New Statesman and Society. III, June 8, 1990, p. 35.
The New York Times Book Review. XCV, April 15, 1990, p. 1.
Publishers Weekly. CCXXXVII, April 13, 1990, p. 47.
The Washington Post Book World. XX, April 15, 1990, p. 5.

SKEPTICISM AND MODERN ENMITY
Before and After Eliot

Author: Jeffrey M. Perl (1952-   )
Publisher: The Johns Hopkins University Press (Baltimore, Maryland). 231 pp. $29.95
Type of work: Cultural history and literary criticism

An analysis of the enmities characteristic of modern thought, particularly those surrounding the thought and critical reception of T. S. Eliot, and how they derive not from disagreement but from the need to avoid consensus

In his first book, *The Tradition of Return* (1984), Jeffrey Perl argued that forward-looking "progress" and backward-looking "return" may not be opposite phenomena but, rather, components of a single cultural process. He concluded that the dynamic interaction between dedication to social change and devotion to original sources has conditioned much of modern cultural history. Perl's new book—a more focused study of the enmity created by the tension between liberal and conservative perspectives on the career of T. S. Eliot—is characterized as a "preliminary case study" for a comprehensive history of such enmities in literary culture, enmities that Perl says have blocked what is really consensus.

Perl argues specifically here that although Eliot was often criticized as a classicist, he was as radical a skeptic as those who criticized him. Perl's basic support for his conviction that critics have misread Eliot because they saw his similarity to them as differences are Eliot's unpublished notebooks in philosophy—manuscripts, typescripts, and class notes of the poet/critic's undergraduate years at Harvard—and the published essays that derive from them.

The first chapter is a general introduction both to this book-length analysis of Eliot from the perspective of skepticism and to the multivolume study of ambivalence in literary culture of which Perl says this is the first offering. The most general thesis of the book is that the established order is a myth; the modern paradigms that seem to compete and exclude each other—such seeming dichotomies as classic versus romantic, modern versus postmodern, liberal versus conservative—do not reflect an inability to agree but, rather, a deeply ambivalent need to avoid consensus. Using as his basic example the ritual of how authors and works get admitted to the literary canon, Perl traces the critical reception of William Shakespeare's *Hamlet* (c. 1600-1601) as a play that was accepted into the canon despite its violations of the classical rules of drama; as a result, it altered and expanded those rules.

Much of Perl's argument about the shifting critical reception of Shakespeare's great tragedy reflects the familiar practice of literary critics' redefining a literary work in terms of their own critical predispositions and thus claiming every great work and every great literary movement as their own. His thesis cuts deeper than that, however. As Perl points out, modernism is the restitution of tradition for its adherents and the interruption of tradition for those who scorn the term. As a result, there is no canon that ensures continuity and coherence. Instead, the history of modernism is a pattern of anomalies resulting from an ambivalence that is never really faced. Perl's basic rationale thus springs from his conviction that such pernicious ambivalence can be resolved and overcome only when its victims are made to see it. Eliot, a writer in whom—like Shakespeare, Johann Wolfgang von Goethe, and James Joyce—everything can be found, reflects this ambivalence, which Perl takes as his task to lay bare.

The difficulty in understanding Eliot, Perl argues in a chapter entitled, paradox-ically, "One Multiple Reception," lies in trying to understand how he was accepted into the canon so quickly despite being disliked by many influential artists and crit-ics. Perl then makes a gesture toward solving the puzzle by showing how Eliot was made canonical by his opponents rather than by his supporters. Perl points out, for example, how William Butler Yeats made space for Eliot's work in the Oxford an-thology so that he could declare him unacceptable in the preface. More recently, he notes, the current so-called Yale critics have rejected Eliot as firmly as their own precursors at Yale, the so-called New Critics, embraced him.

Perl's theories about these shifting alliances and enmities seem primarily derived from Harold Bloom's basic notion of the "anxiety of influence," a theory that ac-counts for how one generation rebels against the parent generation by purposely "misreading" it. Perl's position is that Eliot, who once wrote that error or misread-ing is an essential part of all interpretation, is the forerunner of Bloom's argument. More central to Perl's analysis is Eliot's observation that contrariety signifies agree-ment rather than opposition—a notion which, Perl argues, illumines Eliot's para-doxically critical position in the literary canon.

The heart of Perl's study lies in the three chapters in the section entitled "Dif-ference." These chapters unearth the origins of Eliot's philosophic perspective in his Harvard studies of Eastern religious thought, clarify his philosophic perspectivism in his "relative poetics," and outline the skepticism of his social and political views. The most basic ideas that Eliot took from Indian philosophy, Perl reminds his readers, are the notion that reality is the result of human creation, the theory that every concept and doctrine about reality is self-contradictory, and the concept that there is no real distinction between appearance and reality.

According to Perl, the commonplace notion that Eliot is a great defender of tradi-tion is erroneous. Eliot's affirmation of tradition and convention is not absolutist but, rather, the expression of a radical skepticism in regard to any philosophic per-spective. Consequently, Eliot's conversion to religious faith was not the embracing of an absolute belief system but, according to Eliot himself, the pursuit of skepticism to its utmost limit. Although such an assertion may sound contradictory to funda-mentalist Christian believers, it is actually the expression of the kind of difficult faith maintained by such theistic existentialists as Søren Kierkegaard and Paul Tillich, as well as indicative of the kind of skepticism Eliot says is reflected by Voltaire and Bertrand Russell.

Perl's discussion of Eliot's critique of philosophy, drawn from his graduate note-books and class papers, further indicates Eliot's relativism and contextualism. The real world is a contextual fabric of presuppositions, implicit theories that people have agreed to call facts, claims Eliot. There is no real distinction between a successful theory and the real world, for the real world is indeed the network of theories that enables people to experience it. Reality is a convention, Eliot argues, created by language and tacit assumptions. It was because of this theory of reality as a language construct that Eliot gave up philosophy and moved to poetry. According to Perl, Eliot realized that theoretical language manufactured truth. Because most theorists denied this process of construction and argued that they were discovering reality, Eliot wanted no more to do with them. The poet, conversely, uses language to show how truth is manufactured, Eliot believed. The symbolist poem in particular lays bare the rules by which language creates reality, showing how reality depends on the perspective of the perceiver and the conventional nature of language use.

These are crucial concepts central to postmodern philosophy and literary theory. Although Perl does not attempt to relate Eliot's theories to such poststructuralist thinkers as Roland Barthes and Jacques Derrida, Eliot's thought, as Perl describes it, also characterizes much of that brand of European phenomenological theory which underlies postmodern thought. Particularly postmodernist is the idea that the artwork lays bare the fictional process whereby everyday reality itself is created, for such a view provides the basis for much literary theory since the Russian Formalists established the concept of "literariness" in the 1920's. It is one of the striking anomalies of modern literary thought that formalists such as Eliot and the New Critics shared so many concepts with their contemporaries the Russian Formalists, despite the fact that they knew nothing of each other's work.

Perl argues in his chapter on Eliot's politics that there is no inconsistency between Eliot's relativist philosophic position and his antiliberal political views, for Eliot himself believed that the connection between skepticism and liberalism so often drawn by liberals and conservatives was nonexistent. In fact, Eliot believed that each of the great modern skepticisms, such as Marxism, pragmatism, and psychoanalysis, had degenerated into belief systems of absolutism. Eliot was opposed not to democracy, says Perl, but to the notion that a majority should determine for all; Eliot believed that every political philosophy should be allowed to have its influence. Much of Perl's argument about Eliot's political convictions reflects his defense earlier in the book of Eliot's religious conversion as actually being an affirmation of his skepticism rather than an absolute belief.

There is no contradiction between Eliot's skepticism and his seemingly conservative religious and political beliefs, argues Perl, for skepticism is not a belief or a position but a meta-belief or meta-position; skepticism is an attitude toward holding beliefs or taking positions. Although the skeptic may have opinions and believe that they are true, what sets him apart from other believers is what he means by truth. For the skeptic, truth is coherence within a field of discourse. For Eliot, every belief is valid within some context. Eliot's replacement for absolute truth is subjective truth believed absolutely. Eliot could maintain a religious belief, knowing all along that it was subjective, for subjectivity is all there is.

Although the evidence of Eliot's best-known criticism and poetry would seem to support Perl's arguments, much of his discussion sounds like special pleading to convince the critical world that Eliot was neither a Christian absolutist nor a political conservative—a case that hardly needs such arguing. What gives *Skepticism and Modern Enmity* its most basic underpinning is the general thesis of postmodern thought that reality is a fictional construct and that fiction provides a privileged means by which that process can be analyzed. Such an approach, at least as old as European phenomenology and Russian Formalism, compels modern readers to go substantially beyond the New Critics of the 1920's and thus focus on the process of fictional meaning rather than the thematic product of that meaning.

Furthermore, Perl's thesis, taken largely from Harold Bloom, that the way cultural history develops is by writers reacting against their precursors and thus misreading them, is also largely derived from the Russian Formalists, who argued that literature and culture develop through time by means of current writers parodying and satirizing their precursors and thus cutting themselves loose from early influences even as they simultaneously make use of that influence. Eliot's influential essay on tradition and the individual talent is crucially important in making clear that tradition—that is, the clusters of literary conventions that make literary communication possible—is the predominant factor in the development of the literary canon.

Although this is a small book, it is a thickly textured book, as its sixty pages of endnotes suggest. *Skepticism and Modern Enmity* is, as is customary for much modern criticism, pitched at a relatively high level of abstraction and generality. There are few discussions of individual works here to ground the reader with some sense of concreteness. Moreover, many of Perl's assertions are—perhaps inevitably, given the nature of his argument—contradictory and paradoxical. Although one might accept Eliot's view that such a book as Bertrand Russell's *Why I Am Not a Christian* (1927) is a Christian document, it is somewhat harder to accept Perl's own assertion that it is precisely because such polar terms as "classic" and "romantic" are one that they are consequently irreconcilable. The reader is often likely to lose his or her place in the undergrowth of Perl's abstract argument. If readers are willing to pick their way gingerly through this book, however, they will be rewarded with a number of important insights into Eliot's contribution to postmodern thought, not the least of which is Eliot's position—so ubiquitous in contemporary culture—that there is no unitary truth or meaning.

Charles E. May

Sources for Further Study

Essays in Criticism. XL, July, 1990, p. 263.
The Sewanee Review. XCVIII, Spring, 1990, p. 305.
University Press Book News. II, June, 1990, p. 34.

SMALL VICTORIES
The Real World of a Teacher, Her Students, and Their High School

Author: Samuel G. Freedman (1955-   )
Publisher: Harper & Row (New York). 431 pp. $22.95
Type of work: Education
Time: 1987-1988
Locale: The Lower East Side of New York City

This novelistic, nonfiction narrative describes the life and work during one school year of Jessica Siegel, an award-winning New York City high school teacher

> *Principal personage:*
> JESSICA SIEGEL, a high school English and journalism teacher

"I'm really tired. I work all the time. I have no life. And I just can't take it any more. . . . I have to do this. To survive." These are the words Jessica Siegel uses to explain to her friends why she cannot continue teaching English and journalism at Seward Park High School on the Lower East Side of New York City.

In *Small Victories: The Real World of a Teacher, Her Students, and Their High School*, Samuel G. Freedman follows Siegel through her last year at Seward. He conveys the texture of her life and work with portraits and histories of some of her students and colleagues and with narratives of typical incidents in the routine of the school year. Siegel emerges from his portrayal as a true American heroine who performs secular miracles of education. Her success seems miraculous, because it occurs despite tremendous odds against her. This book approaches the form of classical tragedy, as it shows a great teacher forced out of teaching by the overwhelming dissonance between the system within which she must work and her own idealism. Seward Park High School is shown strangling in overcrowding, bureaucratic indifference, and underfunding in the chaos of a virtually abandoned inner-city community. Siegel's almost tragic flaw is her drive to serve and to do what is right and good no matter what the cost to her personal life and health.

Born in 1949 and educated at the University of Chicago, Siegel began a career in journalism, working for a left-wing collective news agency. She learned the skills that led her to advise the *Seward World*, where a number of her students won city and national awards for their pieces. After working for several years at Covenant House, a residence for troubled teenagers, Siegel became a paraprofessional at Seward in 1976, partly to gain a $650 raise in salary. While working at Seward, Siegel completed her master's degree at Teachers College and eventually became a licensed full-time teacher.

Though talented, she was not a natural teacher, and therefore had to learn the art from her own best teachers, from the best at Seward, and by dedicated practice. Freedman's accounts of her teaching in advanced English and in journalism show her nurturing her students' intelligence, challenging them to read closely, to think carefully, and to strive to connect what they read to their own experience of the world. He shows her giving away her home hours reading the piles of essays she assigns to her 140 students. These essays tell her who her students are, so that her teaching becomes increasingly individualized during the term, while simultaneously teaching the students to write in English, which for many of them is a second language.

Though she has weaknesses and failures, Siegel is a master teacher, and she is not the only master educator at Seward. Freedman fills out the portrait of the school and of teaching there with sketches of other dedicated people. John McNamara is a highly educated and gifted history teacher who cannot support his family on his $25,000 salary and who, therefore, moonlights at a "wedding palace," hosting receptions most weekends and holidays. Bruce Baskind is another fine history teacher who concentrates his efforts on helping ghetto children build their identity and spirit of pride. There are portraits of the principal, a truant officer, and other officials who care about the school and the children it serves. All of these people fight for small victories against immense odds.

The problems facing these dedicated people are unimaginable to outsiders. They range from the individual needs and problems of the students themselves through almost every aspect of the school, the community, the city system, the teachers union, the state and federal bureaucracies, and finally to America's sense of itself as a nation. In his treatise, "The Subjection of Women" (1869), John Stuart Mill defines the character of a modern democratic society and aptly expresses the ideal that motivates Siegel: "Human beings are no longer born to their place in life, and chained down by an inexorable bond to the place they are born to, but are free to employ their faculties, and such favorable chances as offer, to achieve the lot which may appear to them most desirable." Siegel and the other heroes that Freedman describes want their students to participate in this liberty. At every level, the central message from system and society is the same: The will to give these children a chance at liberty is lacking; for a variety of reasons, America as a whole does not care about these children.

When students walk into her classroom, Siegel can see the results of this indifference. Her students know that they are insignificant and are expected to fail. Freedman explains in detail how most students arrive at Seward Park. New York City's system is designed to draw into special schools all the clearly talented children in the city who manage to find the will to complete secondary school. Those students remaining go to neighborhood schools such as Seward Park, which carry out the obligation of offering free public education to all who want it. A student at Seward Park, then, is almost by definition lacking any special worth in the school system. The first barrier a good teacher must overcome is each student's sense of hopelessness concerning his or her future.

This selection process gives Seward Park not only the least successful students, but also all the problems that produce unsuccessful students: language barriers, broken and dysfunctional homes, poverty, street crime and violence, gangs, drugs, and racial conflict. Freedman's portraits of individual students and of Siegel's interactions with them remind the reader repeatedly that these students often deal daily with responsibilities equal to those of any adult member of the middle class while burdened with all the normal immaturity and emotional needs of adolescence. They have children of their own, hold jobs that help parents meet soaring rent payments, and work beside their mothers in garment factories, where they can earn at most about two dollars an hour. Before coming to school, they must accompany younger siblings to other schools to ensure their safe passage through streets populated by rival gangs, drug dealers, and addicts, where gunfire, knife fights, or beatings may erupt at any moment. Because welfare has placed them across town, some students must commute an hour or more to get to school. With such responsibilities, they still must find the time and the motivation to learn, harboring only the slimmest hope that a college will accept them and that tuition money will be available.

Siegel tries to overcome their hopelessness by helping them to know themselves and by developing their skills and confidence. While teaching them, she works continuously to prod them in the directions that will get them into college programs with financial aid, and she tirelessly builds connections between the students and colleges that are likely to accept them. She prepares them for college, and she gets them admitted. To do so, she engages in a constant struggle with their community and the school system. Thus, her work engages all of her time and energy, leaving her without a social life and without hope of marriage.

The community's influence is clear in student backgrounds. It extends from the dangerous streets around Seward High to the attitude of distrustful indifference toward the urban poor that has radiated from Washington, D.C., since 1980. Freedman devotes several segments to brief histories of the development of local neighborhoods. From these histories emerges a picture of successive waves of immigration, especially from China and the Dominican Republic. These immigrants have flooded the Lower East Side with new cultural influences and the schools with students who do not speak English. At the same time New York is sinking into bankruptcy and the federal government is backing away from programs encouraging low-cost housing and living wage employment in the inner cities. The numbers of the poor and almost poor continue to increase while services designed to help them avoid or escape poverty decrease.

The school system is one of those services, and it offers barriers to good teaching at almost every conceivable level. Seward Park is overcrowded by 50 percent. The two buildings are in continual and long-standing disrepair. When a nearby school building becomes vacant, the Seward Park administration's efforts to secure it are brushed aside. Twenty-five English teachers share a 160-square-foot office, where individual student conferences must always be public and where no one has adequate work space. There is money to buy video equipment but not books. The photocopier is locked in an administrator's office, and the teachers must use an ancient and barely functioning mimeograph machine that destroys each master it uses; as a result, teachers who want to introduce new texts in their classes must retype them each time they use them, pay for printing out of their own pocket, or go out on their own, begging for free copies. To help some of her students get into college, Siegel drives them at her own expense to interviews. The teachers' union, fighting for fairness city-wide, runs over, obstructs, and repeatedly defeats individual teachers who are trying to do good work without being continuously hampered by petty restrictions. The city bureaucracy is little different. For example, it takes the licensing bureau two to four years to grade an examination that grants a trained teacher a license.

Freedman characterizes the general operation of the New York City school system as triage at several levels. Triage is the practice in medical emergencies of treating first among the seriously injured those most likely to survive. Seward Park receives the students least likely to survive. It must serve them in an inadequate building with an inadequate number of teachers. Its budget within the city is kept to a minimum, so that basic necessities are always in short supply. Almost every inducement in the system draws good teachers away from Seward and encourages the worst teachers to stay where they are not really expected to succeed. For example, teachers' salaries are better and living costs lower outside the city. At the state level, the process occurs again. New York City, with by far the greatest need for education funding in the state, is systematically given no more than its per pupil share of state funds. Triage became official policy at the federal level in the 1980's, when all programs to benefit the poorest communities were officially defined as failures and were to be discontinued as soon as possible.

It is not surprising that some teachers give up in the face of this monolithic message to accept defeat. Freedman mixes contempt and pity for the many teachers at Seward who see their work, in one way or another, as superintending failures and then giving them passing grades. Some teachers become despairing managers who present their material, give tests and grades, and stay as far away from their students as possible. Some teachers try to move into administration or union positions in search of the power to change things for the better. Many of the best teachers despair, burn out, and give up, as does Jessica Siegel. The rewards of success are great, but the price for Siegel is every waking moment of her life from September to June of each year. Every child who makes it through this system and into college is more than a small victory. These success stories, however, do not give rest to the Jessica Siegels, nor do they raise their salaries, or give them comfortable homes, adequate workplaces, respect from politicians and the public, and time for development and contemplation while on the job. Instead, Siegel's reward is a brief moment of satisfaction and a summer to restore herself before the next group of abandoned students enters the classroom.

Freedman's absorbing, moving narrative has an unquestionably polemical intent. America must manage to care, even moderately, about what happens to its poor, to learn what schools are trying to do and how they are trying, to re-create a common vision of what is good for the nation. If the country rises above its indifference to the poor, then it can have Jessica Siegels teaching in its classrooms, and it can see the American Dream realized again in the images of poor, immigrant children becoming independent Americans. Without such concern, the Siegels gradually will be driven away, and more children will be wasted in the crumbling streets of decaying cities.

Terry Heller

Sources for Further Study

Booklist. LXXXVI, March 15, 1990, p. 1398.
Commentary. XC, August, 1990, p. 61.
Kirkus Reviews. LVIII, April 1, 1990, p. 477.
Library Journal. CXV, May 1, 1990, p. 97.
Los Angeles Times Book Review. May 20, 1990, p. 2.
The New York Times Book Review. XCV, May 20, 1990, p. 3.
The New Yorker. LXVI, September 24, 1990, p. 113.
Newsweek. CXV, May 21, 1990, p. 94.
Publishers Weekly. CCXXXVII, March 16, 1990, p. 56.
Time. CXXXV, June 4, 1990, p. 84.
The Washington Post Book World. XX, May 6, 1990, p. 1.

SOLOMON GURSKY WAS HERE

Author: Mordecai Richler (1931-   )
Publisher: Alfred A. Knopf (New York). 413 pp. $19.95
Type of work: Novel
Time: The 1840's to the 1980's
Locale: Northern Canada and Montreal

The search for and discovery of the elusive Solomon Gursky by Moses Berger

> *Principal characters:*
> SOLOMON GURSKY, the leader of a family liquor business who escapes from the conflicted world of his family
> MOSES BERGER, a failed writer who tries to fulfill a lifelong ambition to discover and tell Solomon's story
> BERNARD GURSKY, the greedy and duplicitous older brother of Solomon Gursky
> MORRIE GURSKY, the younger and weaker brother of Solomon who only emerges at the end of the novel

Solomon Gursky Was Here, Mordecai Richler's ninth novel, is very different from his earlier works; it does not focus on the contemporary scene in Montreal but ranges over the last two centuries to tell an absorbing tale of a Canadian Jewish family. The Gurskys are involved in the liquor trade, and there are many hints that this is a *roman à clef*; the story of the Gurskys is similar to that of the Bronfman family, who controlled Seagrams. Richler stresses not only the triumph of a Jewish family but also the costs and conflicts that come out of that struggle to succeed.

Richler begins with the founder of the family, Ephraim Gursky; Ephraim is the only survivor of an ill-fated British expedition to find the Northwest Passage led by Lord Franklin. How he survived and the details of his earlier life are revealed only gradually throughout the novel. In fact, his story (which includes some time in jail, transportation to Australia, and a period as the head of a religious sect) is told piece by piece in reverse chronological order. Ephraim is not a passive character but a trickster who succeeds in deceiving many of the people he meets. These qualities are passed down to his grandsons.

The central section of the novel deals with the three grandsons of Ephraim. The oldest, Bernard, and the middle one, Solomon, are the most important characters. Solomon has ease, grace, and the ability to win people over to his side while his older brother, Bernard, is greedy, grasping, and predatory. Ephraim singles out Solomon as most like himself when Solomon is very young and takes him on a trip to the far north, initiating him into the hardships of the world and teaching him how to cope with difficulties. He advises Solomon to deal with Bernard as he would with a wolf, to leave a knife smeared with honey so the wolf will lick it and cut himself to death. The conflict between the two brothers is made clear very early in the novel, but the results of that conflict are not revealed until much later.

The main narrative begins in 1973; Bernard is now an old man and, as the head of an empire based on liquor, is immensely wealthy and powerful. It is his seventy-fifth birthday and he is surrounded by toadies and weaklings. He rages at others and takes pleasure in tormenting those who are dependent upon him, including his brother Morrie. Morrie is younger and weaker and seems incapable of doing anything right. Bernard's naked greed and need to degrade others can be amusing and some of his observations on people can be hilarious, but he is a most unattractive character. Solomon, the true leader of the family, has supposedly died in the 1930's, but the conflict between him and Bernard and his true fate are slowly revealed in the novel, primarily through interviews and journals.

The early life of the Gurskys in the wastes of western Canada was not very prosperous; Ephraim's sons owned a dry goods store and struggled to buy more property. Their prosperity comes from Solomon, who steals the money in the store and wins a hotel, a boarding house, and most of the rest of the town in a poker game. Bernard concentrates on expanding the fortunes of the family by purchasing other hotels, but Solomon is never caught by the need to possess things. He gambles, enjoys an enormous number of women, and does what he thinks most interesting and important. For example, he joins the British Air Force in World War I because it is a meaningful experience; he does not expect to profit from it financially.

The family becomes involved in bootlegging as prohibition begins in the United States and their empire is expanded. The conflict between Bernard and Solomon increases as a result; Solomon is engaged in meaningful things, such as trying to persuade the Canadian government to allow more Jewish emigration as World War II nears, while Bernard grinds away at the business. A crisis occurs when Bernard wishes to marry a respectable Jewish girl, but her parents oppose the match because Bernard's future is not secure—he does not have a partnership contract with his brothers. He writes a contract that gives him fifty-one-percent, Solomon, thirty percent, and Morrie nineteen percent, but Solomon laughs at this: He does not take Bernard's attempt to dominate the family or become respectable in WASP terms seriously. The conflict is intensified when a customs official refuses to accept a bribe or the advice of his superiors and brings the Gursky family to court. In a meeting with the judge, Bernard agrees to allow his brother, Solomon, to be convicted to appease public opinion and to pave the way for his marriage and control over the family's affairs. Escaping before the trial is completed, Solomon goes north, as his grandfather did, and apparently dies when his plane explodes. Yet it is uncertain whether he is really dead or has escaped into a larger world.

Much of the story of the Gursky family is told through the eyes of a Canadian Jewish writer, Moses Berger. Moses has his own conflict with his father L. B., a socialist poet who compromises his integrity by agreeing to write speeches for Bernard Gursky. L. B. is not very successful in publishing his works, and when his Rhodes Scholar son, Moses, has a story accepted by *The New Yorker*, L. B. intercepts it and sends a letter to the magazine declining the offer. Moses has been taken to the Gursky's palatial home by his father as a child, but instead of playing with Bernard's children, he gravitates to the despised children of Solomon. Eventually Moses forms the ambition to write a book on the Gurskys, especially the true story of Solomon. Moses seems to be seeking a surrogate father to replace his own envious and disgraced one. Moses is incapacitated by the earlier Oedipal struggle and his alcoholism, and has not succeeded in anything despite his great promise. A surrogate father may restore him to his rightful place.

While at Oxford as a Rhodes Scholar, Moses is invited to catalog the Arctic books of a wealthy Englishman, Sir Hyman Kaplansky. Moses discovers more about the Franklin expedition and about Ephraim in some of Kaplansky's documents. He also begins an affair with Lucy Gursky, the daughter of Solomon, through the help of Kaplansky. After a series of curious incidents, he makes the connection between Solomon and Kaplansky and discovers that this is the man he has been searching for. When he tries to speak to Solomon/Kaplansky, however, the object of his quest has vanished. Moses does receive some of Solomon's journals and his legacy, but Solomon is always one step ahead of him. As the quest continues, Moses finds documents containing evidence of Solomon in Berlin during World War II, and later at Entebbe when the Israelis freed hostages from Idi Amin. Finally, he hears that Solomon is in the Arctic and pursues him. Once more, he is moments too late, and Solomon leaves a note and more of his journals so that Moses might understand him better.

The narrative shifts from Moses' quest when Bernard dies and more family trouble begins. Bernard's son Lionel wants to take over the business and tries to acquire the shares of Solomon's children. Henry and Lucy resist Lionel, but Henry has an Oedipal problem of his own. His son, Isaac, does not wish to live in the Arctic or to follow Henry's strict religious ways. Isaac is fascinated by the wealth of the Gurskys in New York and wants to be part of it. There is, however, a takeover bid coming from an unidentified source; shares in the Gursky empire are being bought mysteriously by someone named Corvu, the word for raven—a sign used by both Ephraim and Solomon. Votes for and against Lionel are being sought by the two factions and suddenly Morrie becomes a force in the novel. With the help of the Corvu shares, he gains enough votes to expel Lionel and to place his son, Barney, and Isaac on the board. He has undone the earlier betrayal of Bernard, given Solomon's children a new place, and asserted his own worth. Corvu is Solomon. When his children are threatened, he acts to defend them and to restore the balance in the family. He returns to the north as Ephraim did, and he gives a signal to Moses by waving the wings of the plane he takes to the Arctic. He repeats his earlier trip, but this time without the need to fake his own death.

Solomon Gursky Was Here uses some basic myths for its power. The struggle between Bernard and Solomon is similar to the Cain and Abel story in the Bible, except that this Abel does not die but resurrects himself to live a fuller life and to displace finally the son of his antagonist. In addition, the Oedipal conflicts between Moses and L. B. Berger and Henry and Isaac Gursky are other examples of essential problems within the family structure. These conflicts, in contrast to the one between Solomon and Bernard, are not completely overcome. Moses is still an alcoholic and has not written his book on the Gurskys, although he has come closer to understanding Solomon. Isaac acquires a seat on the Gursky board, but he is a greedy and grasping character who is far less worthy than his religious father. Solomon also becomes a mythic character; he leaves the world of wealth to become a hero who is always there to help or defend the Jews in difficult times. He seems also to have escaped death in this ageless and all-powerful characterization.

This novel covers a larger historical range than Richler's previous works and has a complex but effective structure. Richler uses Moses' quest for a surrogate father to tell the saga of a extraordinary family in a highly original fashion. Richler possesses an exceptional ability to create dramatic scenes and to reveal character. His portrayal of Bernard's seventy-fifth birthday is hilarious and chilling; his description of Solomon in court calmly and wittily dealing with the forces of respectability is wonderful; and Richler's use of dialogue is one of the most effective elements in the novel. The give-and-take between characters in an Arctic bar and between Solomon and Bernard is also very fine. *Solomon Gursky Was Here* may be the best novel yet by Mordecai Richler.

James Sullivan

Sources for Further Study

Booklist. LXXXVI, February 15, 1990, p. 1122.
Chicago Tribune. April 8, 1990, XIV, p. 6.
Kirkus Reviews. LVIII, February 15, 1990, p. 215.
Library Journal. CXV, April 1, 1990, p. 138.
Los Angeles Times Book Review. June 17, 1990, p. 4.
Maclean's. CII, November 13, 1989, p. 64.
The New Republic. CCII, May 7, 1990, p. 42.
The New York Times Book Review. April 8, 1990, p. 7.
Publishers Weekly. CCXXXVII, February 16, 1990, p. 67.
Time. CXXXV, May 14, 1990, p. 92.
The Times Literary Supplement. June 15, 1990, p. 653.
The Wall Street Journal. March 27, 1990, p. A18.

SOUND, SPEECH, AND MUSIC

Author: David Burrows (1930-   )
Publisher: University of Massachusetts Press (Amherst). 138 pp. $20.00
Type of work: Aesthetics

Using observations on the phenomenology of inarticulate sound, informal and formal speech, musical sound, and song, the author traces the relationships among these methods of communication and views these connections as fundamental to human development

Sound, by its very nature, is intrusive. Even as the writer writes this review or the reader reads it, myriad uninvited sounds form a backdrop to the intellectual process involved in comprehending the written words or coherently paraphrasing another writer's ideas. Its intrusiveness does not, however, necessarily mean that extraneous sounds destroy the intellectual process involved. The Bach partita fortuitously playing on the radio may help mask backfiring cars, low-flying jets, or noisy neighbors, in effect allowing people to hear themselves think. Paradoxically, it is often difficult to work in windowless, completely soundproof rooms; their ambience feels unnatural, too estranged from the living world.

It is, therefore, more than mere semantics to speak of hearing thought. Johann Sebastian Bach's music was not intended to facilitate the reading or writing of a book review, but for some at least it is anodynic and it or its like may even be necessary. David Burrows, a professor of music at New York University, examines these connections in his short but challenging book. He is not the first to posit three fields of human action. Georg Wilhelm Friedrich Hegel and Edmund Husserl recognized similar phenomenological spheres, but Burrows grounds his three fields in aesthetic experience, and rather than presenting them hierarchically demonstrates the surprising number of ways in which they interpenetrate.

Field 1 is physical space, that which a body occupies and through which a body moves. Because of its physicality, it is the most sense-related of the three, and vision thus necessarily dominates it. The very state of physical existence, environment, separation, or conjunction constitutes its domain, and accordingly every sentient creation is aware of itself functioning within its setting. The center of this field is the body, which accordingly perceives itself as central but influenced by that which surrounds it. All that surrounds the body thus assumes a unidirectional, dynamic character pulled tight to the ground level of the body. This is as true of a perceived distant object (for example, a star) as of one close at hand (a book). While content of the field constantly changes with the body's mobility, the topological coordinates are constant since the body always perceives in relation to itself.

Field 2 is invisible, intangible, intellectual space, the Cartesian *res cogitans* (the thinking process). Individuals have their own distinctive intellectual domains in memory, but these broaden, theoretically infinitely, through conjecture, hypothesis, and synthesis. Precincts within these domains may fall into disuse, though they may be perfectly (or imperfectly) recalled. It follows that Field 2 is concurrently collective, even though individuals who draw on the common treasury may be unaware that they do so. Hence, a carpenter may never have studied the Pythagorean theorem, yet may use it when constructing a staircase. Cognition, often an ancillary element in Field 1, thus becomes the focus of Field 2, for it is this that allows the patterns of associative thought that produce knowledge. Artifacts, institutions, and human works of any kind from codes of law to administrative procedures to a set of pliers function as a protective zone between individuals, groups, and their other. Field 2 is thus more associative and far-ranging than Field 1, though intelligibility as well as plausibility constrains it. Field 2 is consequently the domain of reason, but also of madness and violence.

Field 3 is the realm of the spirit, whose center is everywhere and whose periphery is nowhere. This is mystic more than theological spirituality; it is like Sigmund Freud's "oceanic feeling," the oneness of ensemble, or ritual celebration. Its visual depiction is the hologram. Burrows theorizes that because sound is constantly elaborating intellectual activity and concurrent with the spiritual, it plays a crucial role in human development. Vocal sound, ranging from inarticulate utterance to speech to versified language to sung words, is nonhierarchic but interpenetrative; each facet, often in combination, utilizes one or more of the three fields of human action. The fields themselves often overlap and include communications that range from fortuitous to purposeful.

Voice and appearance are the two means of establishing presence, though voice is more intimately social. They are discrete in the sense that the one can function without the other. Ideally, however, they are complementary. The perceiver in Field 1 instinctively seeks an appropriate pairing of the two, for example by imagining the appearance of a never-seen radio personality or by expecting that a large man will necessarily have a deep voice. The surprise when reality, as it sometimes does, betrays these expectations is often considerable. Reaction to this peculiar kind of surprise may be an unguarded and socially embarrassing exclamation, a primitive music that results from an inner dialogue between force and resistance. Expression combined with a chance monosyllable upon being introduced to an individual with incompatible voice and frame also conveys an unintended message to those who witness the introduction. Those who ghoulishly expect such a reaction will likely be able to control their own and maintain a neutral silence, but it is entirely possible that some will betray their own embarrassment through a smile or exclamation, thus compounding the awkwardness of the meeting.

Speech, however, allows a vocalizer's control. The words of a speaker expand centrifugally to incorporate an audience, thus crossing over into Field 2. This is potentially dangerous, for intellectual perceptions are even more tentative than the visual perceptions of Field 1; yet they also represent progress beyond the here and now. To underscore its distinctive character, one need only note the preadaptive process of speech: Teeth, tongue, jaws, and lips, all of which evolved for the eating process, are utilized to produce phonemes rather than consume food. Speech therefore shares the aggressive character of eating, though it reverses the process, dominating an environment, and is sustained, theoretically infinitely if synthetically reduplicated, by the medium of air that carries it.

A single phoneme, such as a scream, a simple exclamation, or the word "fire" or "thief," has an immediate influence upon those who hear it. A casual suggestion to have lunch makes another individual an associate and suggests another setting into which present action may flow. Physical direction, such as taking the person by the arm or pointing to a restaurant, supplements the Field 2 suggestion and often follows it. Moreover, both persons involved will likely have thoughts about the lunch which may or may not be articulated. Clearly, then, Field 1 and Field 2 interpenetrate, and the conversation forms a nexus of potential movements of approach and evasion. This emerges most obviously at a conversation's beginning, especially if there is no agenda for discussion. A speaker essentially pulls a neutral topic from the verbal vacuum, usually a unique and unrepeatable remark that points the dialogue along its trajectory.

The process is formalized in rhetoric and stylized in vocal music. Almost everyone has heard a brilliant speaker deliver a particularly effective speech. The centrifugal effect noted above operates in this instance too, though it likely involves the audience to an even greater degree and more universally than does formal conversation. The setting generally limits opportunities for response to the extremes of approval (applause) or disapproval (booing or heckling). Almost always the pressure toward approval is greater, evidenced by the general desire to allow the speaker to continue. Paradoxically, though, the speaker is almost always in control. Even when not allowed to continue, the audience senses unfairness, and in the greatest number of instances, a skilled rhetorician can reestablish harmony and prevail.

When such harmony prevails the scene of action enters Field 3. The very auditorium and all of those in it become the thesis of the words spoken. At this point there is no center of focus, only the idea. Clearly, Field 3 is the most fragile of all spheres of human action, but it manifests itself more often than one might imagine. It frequently occurs when the audience knows the script beforehand, as in the performance of a play or in the realm of music.

Burrows focuses closely in this connection on vocal music, specifically the song by English composer Henry Purcell known as "Music for a While" (1692). Were the song's verses declaimed, they would likely move through a continuously variable flow of pitch; still, Purcell's music indicates a single pitch throughout. Similarly, Purcell's setting requires approximately two seconds for the sung word "music" whenever it appears. The vowels of the song are consistently pure. Imagine the lugubrious effect of declaiming the song as verse with uniform pitch and intonation, emphasized pure vowels, and as long as two seconds to pronounce certain key words. Even so, speech and song are the two major ways people influence one another through the use of sound. Lyric verse and poetry that depends extensively upon aural devices such as alliteration, assonance, and onomatopoeia often approach the genre of music, though, with the exceptions of *Sprechgesang* (sung speech) and recitative, the distinction between speech and music usually remains clear.

The lyrics of Purcell's song are also a poem by John Dryden. The song was commissioned for insertion in a revival of *Oedipus* (pr. 1678), the play itself by Dryden and Nathaniel Lee. Dryden wrote the first two acts; Lee wrote most of the remainder, though not the section that contains the song. It is likely that Burrows chose the Purcell song because of this complex origin, for once it is taken out of the context of the play one could never guess it had any relevance to the Oedipus myth. Dryden's poem is literally about music's effect. Thus, when one analyzes the song it is natural to question whether the poetic voice is Dryden's, Purcell's, the 1692 singer's, the contemporary singer's, or the interpreting listener's. The most nearly correct answer is that it is to some degree all of these simultaneously.

Paradoxically, when words reach the realm of art they lose their center, or rather their center is everywhere and nowhere (Field 3). A work of verbal art acquires something through every interpretation. Possibly what it acquires in a given instance is undesirable, but the alternative, that it remain stored in a book or score waiting to be realized as read or sung text, is entirely unsatisfactory. To use the analogy of the American writer Washington Irving, a library is a charnel house. The text or score is thus essentially bones waiting eternally for their resurrection and alive only at times of use.

Burrows concludes with some intriguing observations on instruments. From the perspective of Field 1, they are furniture; yet they also form extensions of the human ability to speak. As such, woodwind instruments function as extensions of the larynx. Their reeds vibrate like vocal cords and produce sounds similarly from hidden recesses. Clearly, many musicians personify their best instruments, frequently naming them, and the positions required to play many stringed instruments (bass, cello, and violin, for example) approximate an embrace or caress. A virtuoso performance makes one question whether the sound produced is more that of performer or that of instrument, or whether the performer is, in effect, the instrument.

Sound, Speech, and Music contains myriad observations on the semiotics of verbal and musical sound and their connections and interpenetrations, as well as the gray areas that one could call both speech and music. It is a small book, but also a tightly written hypothesis on the origin of knowledge and aesthetic enrichment. Burrows provides almost no extended illustrations of the principles he enunciates, apart from his general discussion of Purcell's song. Even so, the reader can summon these up from personal experience, and perhaps this collaboration of author and reader is firm proof of the individuated power of Burrows' words.

Robert J. Forman

Sources for Further Study

Choice. XXVII, December, 1990, p. 639.
University Press Book News. II, June, 1990, p. 27.

SOURCES OF THE SELF
The Making of the Modern Identity

Author: Charles Taylor (1931-   )
Publisher: Harvard University Press (Cambridge, Massachusetts). 601 pp. $37.50
Type of work: Philosophy

A careful analysis of the philosophical ideas that have shaped the experience of individuality in the modern, Western world, and that have empowered the pursuit of freedom, universal justice, and benevolence

Charles Taylor, a professor of political science and philosophy at McGill University in Montreal, maintains that a person's sense of self and of how that self may be related to other selves, to nature, and to God is fundamental to an understanding of what Taylor calls "hypergoods." These are life-orienting moral goods that have captured one's allegiance. The modern hypergoods of "justice for all" or "benevolent treatment of all" for many men and women in the twentieth century are unquestioned and unquestionable. It is with reference to these or other hypergoods that a person is able to construct a life narrative, the story that gives meaning to everyday moral choices in the context of larger human goods. Such stories differ from person to person, but all invoke what Taylor describes as "strong evaluation."

Evaluation is part of the human enterprise; hypergoods "command our awe, respect, or admiration" because they "stand independent of our own desires, inclinations, or choices" and in fact "represent standards by which these desires and choices are judged." They are not independent of the human person, but they are more than mere accidents of one's personality. Thus, any exploration into the self which attempts to comprehend human moral life apart from or in denial of the significance of this strong evaluation is, at the very least, deficient. The first part of *Sources of the Self* takes issue with the "naturalist" temper, which seeks to reduce one's sense of a moral hierarchy (in which some goods are seen to be incomparably higher than others) to mere emotional expression—or, as in the case of some forms of utilitarianism, to reduce all qualitative moral distinctions to quantifiable responses to pleasure or pain.

The naturalist, as Taylor uses the term, believes progress in the human sciences can come only as those sciences transcend any moral framework, frameworks that in the past—be they the honor ethic, Plato's life of ordered reason, or the modern life of self-mastery—have compelled human beings to moral and artistic achievement but which are now seen as imperiling scientific objectivity. Qualitative distinctions among goods, and the supreme place of a hypergood in a person's life-narrative, the naturalist takes to be elitist. What the naturalist requires is the "affirmation of ordinary life" that is both antielitist and tolerant or even supportive of the manifold ways in which people choose to structure their lives. This affirmation of the ordinary Taylor identifies as one of the strongest attractions to the modern mind, but it continues to coexist in the self with the strong sense of moral hierarchy (some exploits are more to be praised than others; some vocations are more admirable than others).

Yet naturalism fails at its own project; as Taylor points out, "the affirmation of ordinary life, while necessarily denouncing certain distinctions, itself amounts to one; else it has no meaning at all."

Taylor takes as his task the articulation of the complex interactions of ancient Greek, medieval Judeo-Christian, and eighteenth century Enlightenment ideas that are part of the modern sense of self. He finds that the moral sources of the modern self are multiple and in conflict, that hypergoods may themselves conflict or that their pursuit may end in mutilation. "Proponents of subjective fulfillment" he writes, "allow nothing to stand against 'liberation'"; "the demands of benevolence can exact a high cost in self-love and self-fulfillment"; and the outworking of Christianity has been seen by many in the modern world as conducive to injustice visited on others and a stifling of inner freedom. "From all these examples," says Taylor, "in my view, a general truth emerges, which is that the highest spiritual ideas and aspirations also threaten to lay the most crushing burdens on humankind." This is as true of the many varieties of high-minded secularism as it is of Christianity.

The first part of the book establishes the moral framework within which Taylor's analysis takes place. The framework is derived in part from the familiar Socratic formula that the unexamined life is not worth living; more specifically, that by clarifying by examination the nature of the particular hypergoods to which individuals give regard, those hypergoods found adequate as a basis for moral life also become the motivators of that life. The articulation of moral sources may well reveal their conflicting demands within the self, but Taylor is convinced that the revelation of the self's moral sources will make available to the self new sources of moral energy. In turn, that energy will be needed by the self for a project of reconciling the "moral conflicts of modern culture" that "rage within each of us." Ultimately, says Taylor, "We have to search for a way in which our strongest aspirations towards hypergoods do not exact a price of self-mutilation."

The three central parts of *Sources of the Self* are narratives unpacking what Taylor sees as the main, and often antagonistic, constituents of modern self-awareness. He is careful to stress that his is not a study of cause and effect, and that there is no simple linear account possible of the effect of one philosophical idea on another. The study is not meant as an answer to "what caused the modern identity"; rather, its purpose is to provide an interpretation of what in the streams of philosophic thought—especially from the eighteenth century onward—the modern mind has found so attractive. These include what Taylor characterizes as "inwardness," "the affirmation of ordinary life," and "the voice of nature."

For many moderns, Plato's conception of a human being situated within a pre-existing cosmic order, called by reason to conform to that order (thus fulfilling the highest human good in love and contemplation of that order), is unavailable as a live moral option. It has been replaced by what Taylor calls "internalization . . . in which the order involved in the paramountcy of reason is *made*, not found." The exemplar is René Descartes, who also sought to be free of the destructive passions that lead to error, as the ancients had taught. By Descartes' time (the seventeenth century), however, reason no longer discovered a cosmic moral order; rather, Descartes looked inward to find something sure. He found, he said, an immaterial self the existence of which could not be coherently denied (for who would do the denying?). Just as clear in Descartes' mind was God's existence, a God who would not allow his creatures to live in illusion. It followed that Descartes' perception of the existence of the physical universe must also be correct. Yet it was a very different moral universe Descartes looked on when compared with that of the ancient philosophers. For Plato, as well as for Aristotle, the use of right reason was itself a commitment to a universe ordered by the Good; for Descartes, reason was disengaged and instrumental. That is, reason saw the universe, and the physicality of humans within it, as morally neutral. This disengaged reason could then in essence create a narrative of one's place in the "scheme of things," the scheme itself the product of human rationality. The human being "goes within" to construct ideas useful in controlling the natural world.

John Locke, born a generation after Descartes, denied the notion of innate ideas and a mind naturally attuned to truth. Rather, Locke asserted, one's understanding came from the mind's putting together simple ideas; with the will, a human being, following procedures of obtaining evidence (procedures developed by instrumental reason), could decide what constituted the greatest good and could choose to move in that direction. The self, by the use of "procedural reason," had objectified not only its surroundings but itself as well. Reason was not substantive, forming the connection between the person and the cosmic order, but methodological, endorsing a kind of self-construction. There is no goal or *telos* of nature, as Aristotle would have it; rather, as we take the inward turn, "we become constructors of our own character."

Another component of the modern self is the affirmation of ordinary life, supremely a product of Puritan theology, which rejected earlier Christian conceptions of a higher life or calling through the renunciation of this world. Instead, one's daily life was hallowed, and what was important was how one conducted one's life, not what life one led (this observation, of course, was not absolute). As this stream of influential thinking flowed on into the eighteenth century Enlightenment, it mingled with the philosophy of Locke to produce a forceful number of tributaries that emphasized the dignity of the individual. Instrumental reason—the genius of science— was to be used to preserve one's ordinary life; nature itself could be seen as a vast, interlocking system designed by the Creator to perpetuate itself. The human being had great dignity because he or she was an autonomous agent participating in the order of nature through disengaged reason, free of traditional authoritarian constraint. The idea of grace, something superadded by God to fulfill what nature had provided only in part or deficiently, was becoming unfashionable.

A Lockean kind of deism, with its emphasis on disengaged reason, was not the only tributary that emphasized the dignity of the person. The theorists of moral sentiments (and here Taylor focuses on Francis Hutcheson) also affirmed such dignity, though for a different reason. Hutcheson maintained that what gave moral power to human beings was the discovery of the good within, which amounted to feelings or sentiments of benevolence (the ultimate source of which was God). The practice of universal benevolence was an acknowledgment of the dignity of its recipient. One's sentiments became one's access to the order of nature; not as the ancients saw it, as a cosmic hierarchy to be loved by the man of right reason, but nature as simply the fount of moral sentiments. Nature became the voice within.

Less and less is a theistic framework needed to provide a moral impetus. Moral sources lie with disengaged reason, with human dignity itself, or with the impulses of nature within. In fact, Taylor maintains that modern notions of dignity, universal benevolence, and individual freedom came, in the last two centuries, to be perceived as undermined by adherence to Christian faith, which the disengaged self began to see as a rival. The utilitarianism of Jeremy Bentham and his heirs ushered in a kind of naturalism (not to be confused with the position espoused by Jean-Jacques Rousseau) which concealed its incoherence by remaining inarticulate about its moral sources. Utilitarianism reduced the good to pleasure but could not provide an answer to why one ought to seek the optimally benevolent society as opposed to the egoism of a Marquis de Sade. Any basis for strong evaluation had been lost.

With Rousseau, the voice of nature called for the human will to be transformed, and nature itself was seen as a strong moral source, in some sense actually defining the good. One must find nature within in order truly to pursue the good life, in the face of the chains of a society that had shackled human autonomy. Immanuel Kant also called for a transformed will, conformed to the moral law within, but Immanuel Kant broke with Rousseau (though both condemned utilitarianism). The moral law had as it source neither an external cosmic order nor an internal order of nature; rather, it was a product of procedural reason which itself lacked content.

Taylor's analysis is completed with his consideration of another form of the inward turn, that of "expressivism," or the Romantic movement. By the late eighteenth century, this expressivism was not merely an acknowledgment of nature as a moral source; rather, "each individual is different and original, and . . . this originality determines how he or she ought to live." This emphasis on creative individualism is one source constituting the modern self, but Taylor points out that it is in tension with another source, that of the disengaged reason of the Enlightenment.

By the Victorian period, various forms of unbelief had become genuine sources of moral motivation competing with Christianity. In the early twentieth century, art itself lay claim as a source of moral epiphany (a perceived contact with a moral source). This art sought to capture "lived experience," but with a twist: The modernist plunged not into a universe of cosmic order, even interior order, as had his Enlightenment or Romantic brother, but one of flux. The unitary self gave way to fragmentation in order to be at one with that flux; the poetry of Ezra Pound and T. S. Eliot relied on juxtaposition of fragments to produce its epiphany, not within what is written, as it were, but between the stanzas. This was no longer the expressivism of the individual self, but words or images driving the reader inward into a kind of multilevel consciousness. Nothing seemed to fit together neatly, but that realization itself was an empowering force against the instrumental reason that had endeavored to remake nature to suit man's own will to power.

Such moral sources, as Taylor understands them, are not simply subjectivist; they intend to capture something very deep in human life, accessible only through "personal . . . resonance." He wants to see the modernist impulse as a positive force unleashed against destructive naturalism and faulty religious authoritarianisms. The human spirit, he says, is being stifled. Yet having traced the lineaments of the modern self, Taylor implicitly acknowledges that none of its moral sources is adequate to adjudicate between conflicting hypergoods, or to order those hypergoods in a hierarchy. A proponent of strong evaluation, the author characterizes disengaged reason as technologically productive but morally barren; yet the inward sources of nature and art, because they are ultimately human constructs, do not seem to offer the kind of evaluation and reordering of the hypergoods for which Taylor is searching. In the final chapter, he dispenses with analysis and instead delivers what he calls the hunch on which he bases his optimism: "There is a large element of hope. It is a hope that I see implicit in Judaeo-Christian theism (however terrible the record of its adherents in history), and in its central promise of a divine affirmation of the human, more total than humans can ever attain unaided."

Sources of the Self—meticulous, subtle, and clearly articulated—is a magisterial study of the history of ideas which affirms the human necessity of strong (moral) evaluation, and which suggests that a true understanding of the goods that empower human beings must come ultimately from a source both other than, and morally greater than, the self.

Dan Barnett

Sources for Further Study

Chicago Tribune. May 23, 1990, V, p. 3.
Choice. XXVII, February, 1990, p. 964.
The Christian Century. CVI, November 15, 1989, p. 1066.
Dissent. XXXVII, Fall, 1990, p. 534.
Library Journal. CXIV, August, 1989, p. 136.
The New Republic. CCII, April 9, 1990, p. 27.
The New York Review of Books. XXXVII, November 8, 1990, p. 45.
Society. XXVII March, 1990, p. 92.
The Times Literary Supplement. March 23, 1990, p. 325.
Washington Times. October 30, 1989, p. E9.

SPINOZA AND OTHER HERETICS
Volume I: The Marrano of Reason
Volume II: The Adventures of Immanence

Author: Yirmiyahu Yovel
Publisher: Princeton University Press (Princeton, New Jersey). 2 volumes. Volume I: 244 pp. $24.50; Volume II: 225 pp. $29.50. $45.00, the set
Type of work: Intellectual history and philosophy

An effort to ground much of what is most distinctive in Baruch Spinoza's thought—and the modern naturalist and secular perspective—in Marrano experience and culture

Principal personage:
BARUCH (BENEDICT DE) SPINOZA, a seventeenth-century philosopher

Much of this two-volume work seeks to vindicate the nineteenth century poet Heinrich Heine's claim that "All of our contemporary philosophers, perhaps without knowing it, are looking through eyeglasses that Baruch Spinoza polished." If Yirmiyahu Yovel is right, much the same could be said of twentieth century thinkers. Such claims are justified, despite their seeming hyperbole, because it was Baruch Spinoza (1632-1677) who ushered in the revolution in thought that Yovel terms the "philosophy of immanence."

The "philosophy of immanence" is a perspective shared by many in the modern world. Some notable commitments of this perspective are the claim that all there is, is of this world; that whatever order is found in this world, whether causal or moral, is not to be explained by appeal to facts beyond this world in some transcendent realm; and, in particular, that this world is not to be explained by appeal to the free acts of will of some transcendent God. Since there is no transcendent realm, whatever salvation or liberation a human being can aspire to must be found within this world.

All of this Spinoza can, perhaps, be said to embrace in his assertion that all that there is, is "Deus sive Natura"—God or Nature, the one eternal and infinite substance; and for Spinoza human salvation amounts, in complex ways, to coming to understand this God or Nature. There can be little doubt that in Spinoza's work one encounters an unabashedly naturalistic voice. Spinoza embraced mechanistic explanation, argued for mind/body monism, rejected revealed religion as a source of knowledge, and advocated political tolerance. Rejecting the transcendent, he was a harbinger of modernity.

Yovel is here writing against a particular interpretive background. Spinoza has long been viewed as leading an isolated and solitary life. Though commentators have been quick to note that he was, for example, familiar with the works of René Descartes, the ancient Stoics, and Jewish medieval philosophers, as well as the revolutionary work in the sciences of his day, this has not done much to undermine the suspicion that Friedrich Nietzsche was right when he called Spinoza a "sick hermit." Indeed, Spinoza has seemed to many to have led the quintessentially philosophical life, a life of pure reflection led in isolation from his contemporaries. Still, the very great difficulty of Spinoza's own writings has added to the importance of the task of trying to come to grips with the man in the hopes that an understanding of his life might aid in the comprehension of his work.

A little more than twenty years ago Alasdair MacIntyre wrote in his essay on Spinoza for the *Encyclopedia of Philosophy* that Spinoza is "of all philosophers the one whose life has the least apparent connection to his work." What is most important about *Spinoza and Other Heretics* is that it seeks to refute this judgment. Much of the work—especially *The Marrano of Reason*—is an effort to show how the history and experience of the Marranos played a central part in Spinoza's life and philosophical work.

Marranos were Jews living on the Iberian peninsula who were forcibly converted to Christianity by the armies of the Inquisition. Spinoza was himself the descendent of Marranos who had left Portugal for the relative freedom of Holland. He was excommunicated for heresy by Amsterdam's Jewish community in 1656.

Yovel's account of Spinoza, then, is an effort to display certain aspects of Marrano experience within Spinoza's life and work. These crucial aspects of Marranism emerged in response to the complex and contradictory demands made on the Jewish community during this period. Indeed, some of the most successful and compelling portions of *Spinoza and Other Heretics* are concerned with the identification and discussion of these patterns of Marrano experience.

Nevertheless, intellectual history is always a delicate and vexed matter. It is alarmingly easy to make claims about why a particular thinker came, on the basis of his life or cultural milieu, to think as he did. Too often such claims add little to an understanding of the work of the thinker. What Yovel has to say about the experience of the Marranos does add to an understanding of the life of Spinoza; whether it also adds to an understanding of his work is a more difficult question to answer.

The responses of the Jews of Iberia to the pressures of the Inquisition were varied. Some were secret Judaizers; that is, they remained inwardly and surreptitiously faithful to their own traditions in the midst of an oppressive Christian majority. Thus, Judaizing Marranos took themselves to be Jews while they outwardly professed allegiance to Catholicism. Unsurprisingly, perhaps, their own religious practices and beliefs were often neither Jewish nor Christian but an amalgam of both. Some Marranos (the Inquisitor Torquemada and St. Teresa of Avila among them) were, however, conversos; they became devout Christians. Even here Yovel argues that there was something distinctive to the Marrano conversos, something peculiarly messianic and spiritualist: an emphasis upon the inner world of devotion rather than on the external elements of the faith. Most important for Yovel's portrait of Spinoza, however, are those Marranos who, as a result of the confusion of Judaism and Christianity, and as a result of living in a setting in which religious beliefs of one kind were affirmed inwardly but denied outwardly, were neither Jewish nor Christian but rather became skeptical rationalists. What such Marranos rejected was precisely the promise of the transcendent in favor of a this-worldly outlook in which reason replaces superstition as the mechanism whereby a human being achieves something like salvation.

Thus, the patterns which emerged from the situation of the Marrano in its various guises include a rejection of revealed religion, a need and willingness to cloak one's meaning in language which will be understood in one way by the unlearned multitude and in another way by those who are learned, an associated split within oneself between the inner truth and the outer surface, and, perhaps most important, an emphasis on immanent or this-worldly routes to salvation and an allied conviction that one knows the correct route to salvation—which, for many reasons, must remain hidden to the many.

Yovel's development of these aspects of Marranism is fascinating. His discussion of the sad story of Uriel Da Costa—a Marrano excommunicated by the Amsterdam Jewish community who committed suicide when Spinoza was a young boy—convincingly details the split between the inner and the outer that characterized the experience of the Marrano. Yovel's reading of the Marrano Fernando de Rojas' masterwork of Spanish fiction, *La Celestina* (1502; English translation, 1634), displays with great sensitivity the this-worldliness and equivocal use of language which are key themes in this account of Marranism and Spinoza. In short, Yovel's portrait of the Marrano is compelling, and there can be little doubt that it adds to an understanding of the pressures which served to shape the world in which Spinoza worked and thought. It was as a Marrano of reason that, in 1677, Spinoza refused to accept an offer of a professorship at the University of Heidelberg. In responding to the invitation, Spinoza noted that religious quarrels bring men to condemn much that is truly said; he added: "I have experienced these effects in my private and secluded station; how much more should I have to fear them after my elevation to this post of honor." In apparent and striking ways this statement recapitulates the crucial elements of Marranism.

But what is the reader to make of these patterns of Marrano existence when approaching Spinoza's philosophical works? Yovel, it seems, would seek to point directly to them in Spinoza's work. Thus in his religious heterodoxy, his use of equivocal language, his rejection of the transcendent, his effort to seek a kind of secular salvation which is beyond the capacity of the multitude, in all of these, Spinoza, according to Yovel, makes apparent his Marranism.

It is difficult to evaluate these claims. Spinoza's posthumously published *Ethica* (1677; *Ethics*, 1870) is an immensely difficult and spare work. It is, then, no real surprise that Yovel's discussion of Marrano characteristics remains somehow isolated from the particularities of Spinoza's philosophical writings. It is true that it is not the aim of *Spinoza and Other Heretics* to engage in the detailed interpretation of Spinoza's philosophy. Still, any effort to show how it is that Spinoza's philosophical work is the product of a distinctively Marrano outlook must seek to display that indebtedness in the texts themselves.

Some aspects of this enterprise are more successful than others. In particular, what Yovel has to say about the Marrano roots of Spinoza's third kind of knowledge (*scientia intuitiva*) as making for a kind of secular salvation rings true. Yovel writes:

> Like the Marranos, Spinoza was looking for an alternative road to salvation, in defiance of the one traditionally accepted in his established culture. But whereas Marranos sought it in a substitute historical religion (the Law of Moses replacing Christ's) Spinoza looked for it beyond all historical religions.

This does serve to explain what is otherwise something of a puzzle: the semi-religious and indeed quasi-mystical quality to Spinoza's discussion of *scientia intuitiva*. Thus Spinoza writes: "Our mind, insofar as it knows itself and the body under the form of eternity, necessarily has a knowledge of God, and knows that it is in God and is conceived through him." In possession of the third kind of knowledge one comes to learn that one is essentially a part of nature, an expression of the necessary laws of nature. What is here left behind is precisely one's own subjective perspective in a kind of mystic union with God or Nature.

There is some reason to be less certain about Yovel's other claims. Thus, for example, we should be suspicious of the claim that there is something distinctively Marranist about rejection of the transcendent. The English philosopher Thomas Hobbes apparently rejected the transcendent in a thoroughgoing fashion, yet he was surely not a Marrano. Much the same might be said of the use of equivocal language and the wary relation to the unlearned multitude which, Yovel argues, are central to Marrano experience. These problems are virtually endemic to philosophy, for the philosopher, insofar as he or she is not bound by the constraints of tradition, is very likely to run up against the superstitions and prejudices of the nonphilosophical multitude. Similar issues have confronted not only the Marrano Spinoza but also Plato, Descartes, and David Hume, to name but a few. Perhaps for Spinoza these issues assumed greater salience, but one cannot, in any case, regard them as peculiarly Marrano.

The second volume of the work, *The Adventures of Immanence*, takes up the development of the philosophy of immanence in later thinkers, thereby seeking to display Spinoza's great influence in the history of European thought. Among the other thinkers whom Yovel takes to be "heretics," apostles of "dark enlightenment," are Immanuel Kant, G. W. F. Hegel, Heinrich Heine, Karl Marx, Nietzsche, and Sigmund Freud. What these thinkers have in common is a rejection of the transcendent and a commitment to the pursuit of naturalist forms of liberation or salvation. In short, these are thinkers who have undermined the religious and metaphysical illusions of the multitude. That a good number of such thinkers are Jews may, according to Yovel, be no coincidence. Like the Marrano Spinoza, such a thinker, precisely because he is at home neither in the Gentile mainstream nor in the faith of his fathers, may be "better placed to uncover the hidden layers of life and mind which other persons, better integrated in the ruling culture, will be prone to miss."

That these thinkers, and many others who might have been named, have much in common is not a matter of serious doubt, but it is not only this claim that Yovel seeks to substantiate. More than this, Yovel's aim is to demonstrate these thinkers' indebtedness to Spinoza the Marrano, the philosopher of immanence. Yovel's discussions of Hegel and Heine are impressive and convincing. Still, these are thinkers whose conscious reliance upon Spinoza is manifest. In the case of thinkers such as Nietzsche and Freud, the connections to Spinoza are tenuous at best.

Indeed, to know that a given thinker is a "philosopher of immanence" is not thereby to know much about that thinker's views. It is, at best, to know only that he does not think that there is any world beyond this world, and that, as a result, one cannot look to that world for explanations or values. This surely provides only the barest of constraints. It should come as no surprise, then, that when Yovel considers the relation between, for example, Spinoza and Freud, he is forced to admit that the differences which separate them are at least as fundamental as that which unites them. It is true that for both Spinoza and Freud a kind of self-knowledge is fundamental for a kind of human freedom, but it is there that the similarity ends, for "self-knowledge" and "freedom" mean something quite different from Spinoza's conception when seen in the context of Freudian thought.

Nevertheless, Yovel's careful and learned account of the philosophy of immanence conclusively shows that Spinoza has exerted enormous influence on the history of European thought. What is not as apparent is whether this influence is the result of the idea of Spinoza or Spinoza's ideas. Readers are, in any case, in Yovel's debt for shedding much light on both.

Dion Scott-Kakures

Sources for Further Study

Commonweal. CXVII, April 6, 1990, p. 227.
Library Journal. CXV, January, 1990, p. 114.
London Review of Books. XII, April 19, 1990, p. 13.
The New Republic. CCII, May 21, 1990, p. 35.
The New York Book Review. XCV, March 18, 1990, p. 26.
The New York Review of Books. XXXVII, May 17, 1990, p. 40.
The Times Literary Supplement. August 17, 1990, p. 880.

THE STATE OF THE LANGUAGE

Editors: Christopher Ricks (1933-   ) and Leonard Michaels (1933-   )
Publisher: University of California Press (Berkeley). 531 pp. $25.00
Type of work: Linguistics

A sequel to the 1980 volume of the same title, this collection of essays by writers from many different fields offers a popular overview of the state of the English language in 1990

The State of the Language is not primarily a historical linguistic survey of how English has "drifted," in terms of pronunciation or meanings of words or even usage. It is more concerned with English as it is situated in its present social contexts. The titles of some of the sections give an idea of this—for example, "The Body Politic," "Practices," "Art," "Rectitudes." But the underlying (and sometimes overlapping) categories are even more revealing. A cursory look through the pages reveals at least four articles on feminist issues in language use, three each on the language of AIDS, pornography and censorship, and regional dialects, and two each on the language of public policy, advertising, Afro-English, the law, and computers. Some articles are hard to place within any framework, but what they all have in common is that they seem to capture a slice of how English and certain social contexts are interacting in 1990.

There are also two different kinds of interludes in this book, both very welcome. One kind takes the form of poems scattered throughout as actual entries under the section headings. The other interludes are to be found at the beginning of each section, in the form of epigraphs, sometimes obtuse, much of the time delightful. The book is large enough and diverse enough, in spite of the general trends noted above, that the appeal of the major articles themselves will vary greatly depending on the interests and values of the individual reader.

The first section contains mainstay articles on British English versus American and other versions (e.g., Australian). It also contains comments on the social depth in Black and Jewish versions of the language as well as its regional breadth. It looks from these articles as if the contributors are genuinely open-minded toward pluralism on both social and geographical planes. This comes as something of a surprise, since until recent times language scholars have traditionally been both conservative and prescriptive. Perhaps this change in itself tells us something about the state of the language.

Randolph Quirk ("Further Thoughts: Sound Barrier—Ten Years On") and Richard Bailey ("English at Its Twilight") contribute two of the volume's handful of "survey" articles describing English in relation to changing demographics and political and cultural realities in various parts of the world. These short pieces conclude that, contrary to popular intuitions about the matter, English use as a unifying force or even a *lingua franca* is quickly eroding in two ways: It is continually being spoken by a lesser percentage of the world's population as regional (and especially Third World) identities come into play, and it is being spoken in increasingly disparate ways in local situations (e.g., Nigeria and in the Afro-American culture of New York

City). These articles are fascinating for their challenge to the widely held notion that English will become the new *koine*. Apparently, if English was ever to have that role, it has already passed its zenith.

Roger Scruton ("Ideologically Speaking") has written a brave, clear article on feminist language, though he seems naïve linguistically speaking. Rather than appealing to sociolinguistics as such, he stakes his case (or the first part of it) on his readers' intuitions about the difference between "person" and "man." When he complains of the bad style produced by strict enforcement of feminist ideology in writing, however, he is on better ground. Finally, his major philosophical point about the dangers of subordinating language to ideology, if not decisively proven, will certainly resonate with many readers' experience.

Sandra M. Gilbert ("Reflections on a (Feminist) Discourse of Discourse, or Look, Ma, I'm Talking!") makes the sensible, pragmatic case that ordinary, clear, simple speech belongs to women as much as to men. This may seem obvious, but she makes her point in the face of anarchistic tendencies in contemporary feminist criticism. In the work of some feminists she sees an arcane jargon, appealing only to a small group of like-minded intellectuals, alienated from the real world of their mothers and sisters and daughters. Ironically, for Gilbert—who is herself a committed feminist—this kind of esoteric speech resembles much male language in its domination of others through the restriction of access to privileged areas of knowledge.

Seymour Chatman ("The Pajama Man: Idyll Without Words") examines the issue (touched upon by several others in the book) of the power of visual images in advertising, both commercial and political, to subvert the style of reasoning fostered by print-consciousness. Chatman shows how visual association, or, as he calls it, metonymy, can evoke narratives in the beholder that are at the same time subtle and compelling—narratives that lend themselves to Machiavellian manipulation. The other article on advertising (Suzanne Romaine, "Pidgin English Advertising") really has more to do with the difficulties of translation across cultural as well as linguistic boundaries. She shows how lack of knowledge of a local language and culture can lead to disastrous results, pointing out, for example, that "Biscuit advertisers would benefit from knowing that Tok Pisin *switbisket* (from English *sweet biscuit*) and *draibisket* (from English *dry biscuit*) have metaphorical meanings," the former signifying "a sexually attractive woman" and the latter "a woman past her prime."

Kathleen Odean ("Bear Hugs and Bo Dereks on Wall Street") examines figures of speech among financial traders, or stock market slang. Not very surprisingly, it is full of figurative sex and violence. But Odean, as well as some of the other contributors, goes too far at times in finding sexual innuendo. It is more likely the case that many terms will have several different meanings according to the different contexts in which they occur, and that one of these will invariably be sexual (one is reminded of junior high school, when everything that was said was somehow "dirty"). That this is so is no doubt because metaphors so completely infiltrate the way we talk about virtually everything (as George Lakoff has pointed out in *Metaphors We Live By*, 1980). It may also reflect the fact that there are at any one moment in any one person's active vocabulary only a finite set of terms, literal or figurative, with which to describe his or her reality.

Byron A. Garner ("The Missing Common-Law Words") offers a practical, well-argued apologetic for his own lexical project—a new historical law dictionary (the *Oxford Law Dictionary*) modeled on the *Oxford English Dictionary*. Neologisms (recently invented words) are the area in which he hopes to make the greatest contribution. Martha Minow's essay, ("The Case of Legal Language"), on the other hand, is a theoretical/philosophical treatise on the strengths and weaknesses of legal language. Ultimately she finds it cold, impersonal, and inadequate for the realms in which it operates. It provides "toe holds" and "guide rails" to accomplish its limited tasks, but rarely understands or expresses the depth of human experience.

William Lutz ("The World of Doublespeak") has written one of the best articles in the lot: clear, straightforward, even shocking while not really surprising for any but the extremely naïve reader. The depth of cynicism in public discourse is not always evident, since it is simply too much work to question everything we read or hear or see. We often forget that even our information sources are selling us the information—that is, they hope we like it enough to keep coming back—as well as the products and people they advertise. The examples Lutz uses at times are chilling, and the most chilling invariably are where political power and economic reality meet. David Reid ("Public Eloquence") also writes on speech in the public arena, and while rather obviously ideological, his article is nonetheless interesting and insightful. He rails against the bad style of most speechwriters, and especially the famous ones, or perhaps better said the ones who work for famous people. But his best points are in concert with the main point of Lutz's and Chatman's articles— that language is in trouble when people are successful, through their use of language, at convincing other people that the world is somehow different from the way it actually is. Frederic Raphael ("Further Thoughts: The Executives Take Over"), in a brief article, echoes some of the same fears expressed by Chatman, but (reminiscent of Marshall McLuhan) from the perspective of the media. His major point, however, is about who controls the media. Writing in the context of the BBC and Margaret Thatcher's aggressive "privatization" of broadcasting, he worries that the commercialization of television coupled with government control of the airwaves will cost the public audience its best programming, and that in fact, it already has.

The novelist Alison Lurie's article ("The Language of Poststructuralism") echoes the article on feminist writing by Sandra Gilbert. Lurie criticizes much of poststructuralist criticism as "medieval scholasticism," consisting of "infinitely retreating and dimming reflections in opposing mirrors." Her call (if her article can be interpreted as such) for a recovery of writing as a vehicle for something more, be it entertainment or instruction or almost anything else other than the text looking at itself, will come to many as a welcome relief from endless introspection.

There are two articles on computers and how they will affect language and writing. The first one is optimistic, the second one guarded. Interestingly enough, however, both articles are considerably more optimistic on the whole about the electronic age and its effect on language than are the random comments of the other contributors to this volume. This may simply be a function of knowledge and experience. These two writers, who seem to be more acquainted with the new technology, are less afraid of it.

The most explicitly prescriptive articles are in the last section, scolding in tone but not very convincing. Yet some of the best have also been saved until last. John Algeo's study ("It's a Myth, Innit?"), focusing on a seemingly narrow linguistic topic—the social use of the tag question in British English—is amusing as well as informative. Throughout the volume it is clear that the linguistic and sociolinguistic knowledge of the contributors varies widely, and this is particularly evident in the last section.

Most readers will want to use this diverse collection as a reference, dipping into certain articles in the volume, stopping to drink deeply from others. The resulting encounters will in themselves constitute a direct experience of the state of the language.

Robert A. Bascom

Sources for Further Study

Booklist. LXXXVI, January 1, 1990, p. 873.
Choice. XXVII, May, 1990, p. 1496.
Comparative Literature. XLII, Winter, 1990, p. 93.
The Economist. CCCXV, May 26, 1990, p. 98.
Los Angeles Times. January 18, 1990, p. E10.
New Statesman and Society. III, January 12, 1990, p. 33.
The Observer. January 7, 1990, p. 40.
Punch. CXCVIII, January 12, 1990, p. 34.
The Times Literary Supplement. February 2, 1990, p. 113.
The Washington Post Book World. XX, February 25, 1990, p. 6.

STONE JUNCTION
An Alchemical Potboiler

Author: Jim Dodge (1945-   )
Publisher: Atlantic Monthly Press (New York). 355 pp. $19.95
Type of work: Novel
Time: 1966-1987
Locale: The United States

This long, rambling story contains elements of quest narrative, tall tale, fairy tale, fantasy, and popular suspense thriller

> *Principal characters:*
> DANIEL PEARSE, the protagonist
> ANNALEE PEARSE, his mother
> JACK "SMILING JACK" EBBETTS, an entertainer and agent for AMO
> SHAMUS MALLOY, a revolutionary thief
> JESSAL "VOLTA" VOLTRANO, a magician and agent for AMO
> BILL "WILD BILL" WEBER, a teacher
> MOTT STOCKER, a drug grower
> ROBERT "BAD BOBBY" SLOANE, a gambler
> JEAN BLUER, a master of disguise
> WILLIAM CLINTON, a safecracker
> GURRY DEBRITTO, a CIA assassin
> JENNIFER RAINE, Daniel's lover

This rambling story of the education, exploits, and apotheosis of an adolescent hero is built on the framework of traditional quest fiction. It also contains elements of tall tale and fairy tale, science fiction and fantasy, and, as suggested by the "potboiler" of the subtitle, popular adventure. *Stone Junction* is vividly imagined, rich in incident and character, full of intriguing, offbeat information. More problematic are its moral assumptions, structure, and tone: the degree to which it comes together to form a satisfying whole.

Heroes of myth and legend typically are born under extraordinary circumstances, their births attended by portents, and Daniel Pearse is no exception. His sixteen-year-old mother, Annalee, is a ward of a Catholic home for girls in Iowa; shortly before his birth, she breaks a nun's jaw with a single roundhouse punch, then escapes with her new baby and heads west. Daniel's father, never known to him, is any one of seven men. The traditional hero's mysterious paternity is thus presented here in contemporary dress, suggesting something of the rootlessness and ambivalence of purpose which pervade the novel.

In quest and in fairy tale, the hero is assisted, tested, and sometimes tempted from his true path by strangers he encounters along the way. In *Stone Junction*, such strangers make up the majority of the characters. The first of these is "Smiling Jack" Ebbetts, the Singing Truck Driver, a free spirit who travels around the country entertaining in bars and nightclubs and who gives a ride to the hitchhiking Annalee and her baby. Smiling Jack offers them an isolated cabin he owns 150 miles north of

San Francisco, and there they settle for the next several years. When Smiling Jack returns, he offers Annalee a business deal: to run the place as a safe house for people in hiding from the authorities. She assumes he means criminals—and is about to agree anyway—but he tells her they are outlaws and that there is a vital distinction: "Outlaws only do wrong when they feel it's right; criminals only feel right when they're doing wrong." The novel, then, centers on the lives of outlaws, so defined, and treats them simply and unambiguously as good; the equally straightforward evil against which they are pitted consists almost entirely of law enforcement agencies and the federal government.

A young outlaw-in-training naturally would not be enrolled in a public school, which, according to Smiling Jack, teaches nothing "but how to get along with other kids under completely weird conditions" (and, though this is not spelled out, reinforces traditional values). Annalee teaches Daniel to read, and together they investigate such subjects of mutual interest as astronomy, meteorology, and botany. His education goes far beyond conventional home schooling, however: He studies penmanship with "a forger of considerable renown," "the delicate arts of subversion and sabotage" with "a revolutionary witch," and so on. Under this regimen, Daniel blooms; the cabin, with its parade of wise and kindhearted outlaws, is his Eden.

What brings this idyllic way of life to an end is, strikingly enough, Annalee's falling in love: as if to suggest that stable happiness is possible only at the cost of emotional distance, an idea reinforced by the consequences, much later, of Daniel's own brief romance. Annalee's love is Shamus Malloy, "a professional smuggler, an alchemical metallurgist, a revolutionary thief" who had recently attempted to steal uranium with a view to blackmailing the government into giving up nuclear power. With the authorities close behind, they flee Daniel's Eden. The fugitives are now aided by a shadowy, loose-knit organization that comes to play a central role. AMO, standing variously for Alliance of Magicians and Outlaws or Alchemists, Magicians, and Outlaws, is "a historical alliance of the mildly felonious, misfits, anarchists, shamans, earth mystics, gypsies, magicians, mad scientists, dreamers, and other socially marginal souls." It is, in effect, an intensely romantic wish-fulfillment fantasy, a home and a source of power for (in society's restrictively conventional view) perpetual children.

Daniel's own childhood ends suddenly when his mother, planting a diversionary bomb in aid of another attempt to steal plutonium, is blown up; he himself, struck by a sliver of metal, spends nine weeks in a coma. He wakes in the presence of "Volta," a high-ranking member of AMO and a master magician who learned (though he fears to try it now, lest he be unable to return) to dematerialize his body: literally to vanish. Volta consigns him to the care of AMO.

The warning Annalee shouted to Daniel just before she died suggests that the bomb was sabotaged and his mother murdered; the purpose of the education he now receives, according to conventional narrative logic, would be to prepare him to discover and execute the killer. Such a quest would also give the novel a sense of direction, which, to sensibilities trained on traditional fiction, it sorely lacks. In fact, the issue of vengeance, though much on Daniel's mind, becomes peripheral. Daniel is instructed in meditation and wilderness survival, the illegal drug business, gambling, lockpicking, disguise—and incidentally discovers his inability to make love to any woman more than once. Volta now takes him in hand and teaches him to vanish, for a compelling reason of his own: Volta had once had a vision of a huge spherical diamond, which he has learned is now owned by the government and held under heavy guard. He wants Daniel to turn invisible and steal the diamond for him; gazing into it will lead him to ultimate self-discovery. The plot now dissolves into the stuff of ordinary suspense fiction: Daniel, after elaborate preparation, does steal the jewel, but a code has been broken and the authorities pursue him. In addition, he has become obsessed with it and refuses to turn it over to Volta. In the course of his wanderings, he crosses paths with Jennifer Raine, a young woman who, like his mother, has escaped from an institution. He falls in love and is cured of his peculiar sexual dysfunction, but shortly thereafter, immediately following his twenty-first birthday and for reasons that remain obscure, he vanishes permanently into the diamond. He "had learned what he was meant to know. He was a god. He was Hermes, Thoth, Mercury; the prophet Hermes Trismegistos. He had accepted birth to refresh his compassion for the human soul."

To assess the aesthetic value of *Stone Junction* is strikingly difficult. What does it offer in place of the conventional expectations it fails to fulfill? "Reading *Stone Junction* is like being at a nonstop party in celebration of everything that matters," according to Thomas Pynchon; clearly, however, that is the hyperbolic view of an unusual sensibility. The novel does not celebrate, or even present as an optional path to self-realization, order, stability, or lasting human relationships. Certainly it is audacious, lively, broader than deep: The reader will learn a little about a number of arcane subjects and be entertained in the process. Of the four sections—entitled "Air," "Earth," "Water," "Fire"—probably the most enjoyable is the second, in which Daniel completes his education; the section about high-stakes poker-playing, for example, is humorously suspenseful and exuberantly American in its evocation of life on the edge.

As long as it remains in the realm of the tall tale, *Stone Junction* works—given the difficulties of spinning that subgenre out for several hundred pages—surprisingly well. It is the nature of tall tale, as of any type of humorous oral literature, to ramble along inconclusively, its rewards lying more in loosely connected, richly imagined scenes than in an incremental whole. Taken more seriously, however, or seriously in a different way, the novel runs into trouble. In fairy tales and quest narratives (the King Arthur cycle, for example), the moral order is straightforward. Heroes may be deceived by appearances and villains cleverly disguised, but ultimately it is possible to tell one from the other; anyone entering into the spirit of the story identifies with Cinderella against the wicked stepsisters. In the contemporary world, and the literature that reflects it, moral issues are not usually so simple. Here, however, at a heavy cost in psychological depth and verisimilitude, everything is black or white. The CIA is bad, the AMO is good—a viewpoint not set forth in convincing dramatic detail but simply presented as a given: To participate vicariously in the story, the reader must accept it. Yet near the beginning, one of the outlaws, a bank robber, offhandedly remarks that "we did have to hurt a few people." One of Daniel's mentors is a humorous, lusty, larger-than-life drug grower. If the real-life harm done by illegal drugs has no more significance than, say, the extravagant but harmless violence in cartoons, then the novel becomes difficult to see as more than a cartoon, despite its sporadic pretensions to seriousness.

The most enduringly interesting fantasy—J. R. R. Tolkien's Ring cycle, for example—rings true because it is firmly grounded in reality; copious attention to everyday detail brings Tolkien's hobbits to life. In *Stone Junction*, no one is ever shown— at least not in sufficient detail to matter—doing anything ordinary. Thus, the world of the novel seems to exist in parallel with the world of experience: never quite touching, and therefore never deeply moving, the reader. This psychic distancing makes it difficult to identify with the hero. Yet the issue of how well and appealingly Daniel comes across is crucial; whatever sort of book one takes *Stone Junction* to be, it stands or falls with its central figure.

Daniel, as befits a quest hero, in some ways is larger than life—generally the aptest pupil in his various teachers' experience and the only one Volta has been able to teach to vanish. He could become a successful burglar or confidence man, but clearly, as he himself realizes, that is not enough. What truly heroic action—not merely skillfully and courageously carried out, but selfless, subsumed to a noble end—does this story offer him scope to undertake?

His exceptional talents aside, Daniel develops the emotional maturity one might expect of a sensitive adolescent. Beyond that, his youthful rashness and energy make him potentially likable. His humanity is never put fully on display, however, except to some extent in his relationship with his mother; when she dies, he is cast adrift, never in close contact with anyone long enough to develop important, moving relationships. Nor is he given a quest worthy of him. The significance of the diamond, which seems intended as a central symbol, remains shadowy—this is no twentieth century Holy Grail. The Grail quest at heart was not only spiritual but also social, conducted for the good of all Christendom; the effect of the diamond, conversely, is to tempt the individual ego, thus dangerously, and at last fatally, to isolate the quester.

This leads to the troubling question of Daniel's fate. If he is really to be taken as a god in human form, he disappears prematurely—on the verge of manhood before achieving either great deeds or great wisdom. Finally, unable to live fully in the world, he withdraws—commits suicide—when he is offered and experiences love. So if *Stone Junction* is to be seen in part as a parable of the rootlessness, the affective failures, the disintegration of personality so prevalent in the late twentieth century, it is a sad one indeed: a vivid evocation of sickness, lacking any corresponding hope for healing. In that, at least, the novel is typical of much of the literature of its time.

Edwin Moses

Sources for Further Study

Atlanta Journal Constitution. February 25, 1990, p. N9.
Booklist. LXXXVI, March 15, 1990, p. 1416.
The Denver Post. March 25, 1990, p. D8.
Kirkus Reviews. LVII, November 15, 1989, p. 1615.
Library Journal. CXV, January, 1990, p. 146.
The New York Times Book Review. XCV, February 4, 1990, p. 13.
Publishers Weekly. CCXXXVI, November 24, 1989, p. 58.
San Francisco Chronicle. January 31, 1990, p. E5.

A SUMMER LIFE

Author: Gary Soto (1952-   )
Publisher: University Press of New England (Hanover, New Hampshire). 115 pp. $16.95
Type of work: Autobiographical essays
Time: The 1950's and 1960's
Locale: Fresno, California

Gary Soto describes a pastoral yet impoverished childhood in central California

"Fresno," Gary Soto writes, "was made with what was left over after God made hell." That remark comes near the end of this collection of short pieces, and its placement is significant. *A Summer Life* is no anger-laden attack on a hellhole of a birthplace. In fact, Soto's remark will take many readers by surprise, so benign has been his vision of Fresno and the central San Joaquin Valley. Anyone who has spent time, to say nothing of eighteen years of growing-up time, in the valley, has recollections of a place which defies yet welcomes human habitation. Fogs dwell there in the winter, so dense as to make the white lines on highways unseeable for a month. Schools close. Cars and trains smash together. The populace is a mix of Teutonic farmers, uprooted Oklahomans and Arkansans, Hispanic field workers, and blacks in flight from Los Angeles. Summers begin in late April with temperatures above one hundred degrees. Still, people thrive. Things grow there as they do few places in the world. Snow at thirteen thousand feet, only fifty miles to the east in the Sierra Nevada mountains, melts and replenishes the aquifer supplying row crops. A man with land can with resort to chemicals grow a lifetime's income in cotton, potatoes, grapes, peaches, pistachios, tomatoes, and apples. If the valley is a hell, it is a hell of milk and honey.

Soto, however, is not much interested in the external environment except insofar as it shaped his private, little-boy consciousness. A look through several of Soto's other books, both poetry and prose, suggests that childhood is his favorite topic. In "The Rhino," one of the pieces in *A Summer Life*, Soto says "I was four and already at night thinking of the past."

A Summer Life is a book of nostalgia for child-consciousness. Yet the touch is light and poetic in the bright adjective-to-every-noun mode which both brings Soto close to his early sensibility and renders it artificial. The target his writerly style tries to hit is the fresh first sensation a boy had of every new thing, whether ants, a blimp, taps on his shoes, or an uncle's unwashed shirt. The pieces are short, two to three pages each, as prepared for publication in *The World*, a Sunday supplement to *The San Francisco Chronicle*, and similar magazines. Soto's lower-middle-class Hispanic life in the 1950's and 1960's seems to have been relatively idyllic. His aesthetic is based on a nonaggression pact with reality. Each reader will be left to decide how successful the aesthetic is. Where it does not sentimentalize its subject, as it occasionally does, it serves.

For example, this treaty with the past declares hands-off a stepfather who is not what the dead father was. He is neither a useful presence nor a menace. He is what time happened to give little Gary, a man who emptied his pockets to the boy when coming in the door after work, drunk, naturally. What else would a man working eight hours stapling raisin boxes be at the end of the day? He would give the young Soto a fingernail clipper, and minutes later say, on seeing the tool: "I have one like that."

These pieces are nostalgic not for people and places but for the blessed sensation of innocent transaction with the world. Uncles home from Korea were embedded in the flow of phenomena: "The Korean War was over, and after a year in Japan, our uncle was discharged. He returned with a porcelain Buddha, a tattoo of blue panther with red claws, and an army blanket for sleeping on our screened porch." No deeper than this does Soto reach to probe the uncle's being. He remains safe from his life in the boy's bright apprehension. Issues of America using him, then discarding him to wander Fresno looking for old copper to sell, do not intrude. "We won't," Soto's snapshot pieces say, "get sociological and mess up the art." Certain kinds of pain are off limits.

Soto's summer life is a continuum of relations with bric-a-brac—grandfathers, uncles, smiling statues of Buddha, tattoos, bicycle brake cables, catfish. Here memory is itself a kind of fishing for things in the depthless past; Soto's retrieval of remote significances will stir readers who have their own store of erector sets, dolls, baseball gloves, and old shoes. Soto is after associations, evocations, the unsealed container holding thirty-year-old asphalt and almonds. He is also after the fiction of little Gary who walked innocently through the pastoral junkyard.

What, asks the nursery rhyme, is a little boy made of? Little Gary thinks a penny placed on a train track will derail the train. He wraps the rusty bicycle brake cable around his waist and runs around the yard using it to slow himself down. He tells another little boy to run over his ankle with a tricycle. It won't hurt. It does. His ankle turns blue and swells. A little boy is a system of beliefs tested and found mostly wanting. Yet the projections of his innocent mind invest the world with a vitality such as it will never again possess. The piece titled "The Rhino" is Soto's manifesto of the supremacy and originality of childhood knowledge. A charging rhino painted on the sign of a tire company suggests to the boy that rhino hides are used to make tires.

> It scared me to think that tires were being made from rhinoceros hides. So many things were possible. We were eating cows, I knew, and drinking goats milk in cans. Pigs feet came stuffed into cloudy jars. Cheese came in blocks from an animal that ate something very orange or very yellow. The Molinas stirred bony pigeons in pots of boiling water, and a pig's happy grin showed up on the bacon wrapper. Hop-Along Cassidy was a face that appeared on milk cartons, his hand on his pistol, and what I noticed was that his horse didn't have any feet. I imagined that someone had cut off his hooves and the horse had to lay down for the rest of his life.

The pose of innocent sensibility is also a good filter through which the writer can preserve the quirkiness of others. Around Gary were illiterate grandparents, Mexican-born, whose mentality and survival were vintage 1930's. They loved the color of money—grandfather the green of dollars and grandmother the shine of coins. Such forebears become fairy-tale emblems, assortments of colorful gesture. No need to establish the relationship or lack of same, the wisdom provided, the suffering from their passing. Such may have never occurred, and if any of it did, it is not the subject.

The subject is the poetry of living when young, and occasionally Soto's language fails, perhaps under the need to meet deadlines for those weeklies. At worst he offers diet reading, low-calorie poetry: "I took a big bite, waved a hand over my tongue, and ran for the garden hose gurgling in the rose bushes. I drank long and deep, and later ate the smile from an ice cold watermelon." Readers will resist this game, or give in to that "gurgling hose." There was a life, and then much later there was a transcription into sounds derived from the habits of writing about "experience." Were phenomena orchestrated that way in fact, or did writing retrospectively orchestrate them? Did the rose bush come at the signal of the "gurgling" hose, or was a real hose by a real rosebush? And where but from literature came the cadence of "I drank long and deep"? That long and deep drink, the smile-eating of ice cold watermelon—such is the cozy, jazzy flow which stands in for what, given time to write them, might have been more arresting lines about a specific childhood.

Yet the successes outnumber the lapses. "The first time I confessed, I admitted throwing bubble gum into a bush." Gurgling hoses give way to original mundane facts. These latter ring true. A reader does not remember drinking "long and deep" very often in childhood, but does recall a host of slightly off-center experiences which Soto's bubble-gum confession parallels. As well, Soto gets the reader's vote when emphasizing the losses of childhood, the unfairness of not looking good enough or running fast enough or thinking clearly enough. Little Gary had some chicks, but the cat methodically picked them off. Gary's cousin, Isaac, was a proficient gymnast, good at cartwheels and back-flips on the lawn while wearing professional-style gear. Gary manufactured his own gymnast costume and flopped around incompetently on the grass. Later, in high school, "it hurt to be pinned in twelve seconds in a non-league wrestling match." His opponent bore the fateful name Bloodworth; like Isaac, this boy had something rare and fine.

Pervasive as such losses were, these essays testify to an even greater loss, an all-encompassing defeat: the demise of the child, the boy, and the teenager. The freshness of consciousness itself fades, but a few people keep turning over the chaff of the innocent self. Soto admits that as early as elementary school he realized he had a way with language. Words were easy. His blood-worth was writing. In a poem, he writes about trying to tell his daughter about his childhood. She seems bored—she has her own life—but his need to tell remains. It is he who wants to hear the stories, but he knows that his daughter, when grown, will also turn to these slender mementos.

Thus, *A Summer Life* is mortar for his past, and a gift which will one day be appreciated by the girl-turned-grownup. Yet it is the sheer sadness of life, finally, that haunts these seemingly facile pieces. Where else can one find the brightness of the senses amidst a phantasmagoria which was life in a Fresno Hispanic community but in this written record? Fueled by the age-old impulse to steal from time, it is the record of a boy like a million others who decided, unlike the other million, to get it all down, to say that it amounted to something.

Bruce Wiebe

Sources for Further Study

Booklist. LXXXVII, September 1, 1990, p. 21.
Kirkus Reviews. LVIII, May 1, 1990, p. 639.
Library Journal. CXV, July, 1990, p. 97.
Los Angeles Times Book Review. August 5, 1990, p. 1.
Publishers Weekly. CCXXXVII, June 8, 1990, p. 40.
San Francisco Chronicle. July 15, 1990, p. REV6.
The Washington Post Book World. XX, September 9, 1990, p. 10.

SWEET TALK

Author: Stephanie Vaughn
Publisher: Random House (New York). 194 pp. $16.95
Type of work: Short stories
Time: The 1960's to the 1980's
Locale: Ohio, New York, California, and other sites in the United States

Stories told from the point of view of an adolescent girl or a young woman, focusing on relationships with parents, grandparents, spouses, or friends and their reactions to moments of significance in everyday living

> *Principal characters:*
> GEMMA JACKSON, a young woman who reminisces about her childhood years growing up as the daughter of a career Army officer
> ZACHARY JACKSON, her father, a career Army officer
> RACHEL JACKSON, her mother, a native Ohioan who rears a family as they move from Army post to Army post
> GEMMA'S MATERNAL GRANDMOTHER, uprooted from her Ohio home and now a member of Zachary Jackson's household
> MACARTHUR JACKSON, Gemma's brother

Stephanie Vaughn's first collection of short stories comes with a lot of sweet talk right on the dust jacket of Random House's hardbound edition. Sophisticated readers are prone to discount dust-jacket blurbs prepared by advertising specialists, whose habitual hyperbole is evident in the claim that this collection "boldly redefines the subtle art of short-story writing." It is harder, however, to ignore the remarks that adorn the back of the jacket. There, the publisher has assembled endorsements from several prominent members of the literary community, all of whom offer glowing praise for these "wonderful stories." Sheila Ballantyne finds Vaughn's stories to be infused with "deep intelligence" and "subtle humor." These are *"beautiful stories,"* Bobbie Ann Mason insists—the emphasis is hers—"some of the most honest and true stories about growing up and family life that I recall reading." Even Scott Turow, whose works about crime and intrigue are about as far away thematically as one can get from Vaughn's, has proclaimed this collection "remarkable," with a tone "extraordinary, simple, clear and defined like the ringing of a bell" (intended as genuine praise, although the clichéd comparison may cause some to wonder about the sincerity of the remark).

The pantheon of literary dignitaries offering testimonial to the merits of the collection is rounded out by two of America's grand old men of letters, Joseph Heller and Wallace Stegner, who seemingly try to outdo each other in hyping Vaughn's ability. Heller calls her a writer of "extraordinary talent." Stegner—using the same encomium "extraordinary"—says "There aren't five writers in the United States who could have written these stories"; "maybe," he continues, "only one." In a second snippet Stegner announces that Vaughn "is not a comer; she is there." All this is remarkable praise for a writer bringing out her first book, yet the plaudits are well deserved; this slim volume is a first-rate collection.

At first glance, these stories appear to be the kind found in popular women's magazines (and indeed some were first published in sources such as *Redbook*). All ten feature female protagonists. Half of the stories relate events in the lives of a single American family, the Jacksons: Zachary, his wife Rachel, her mother, and the Jacksons' children, Gemma and MacArthur. Their peripatetic life-style, the result of Zachary Jackson's military career, provides numerous opportunities for change and conflict in the lives of all five members of the clan. A soldier who becomes the victim of a system in which a small mistake in peacetime can mean the end of a career that included admirable service in war, Zachary Jackson finds continual solace in drink. Dealing with an alcoholic husband, father, and son-in-law who is nevertheless the family's breadwinner consumes the three women in these tales.

Gemma (certainly in part an autobiographical creation, as Vaughn herself was an Army brat) serves as protagonist and narrator in each of the five stories that chronicle the Jackson family history. A central issue in virtually all five involves Gemma trying to understand her father. The problems she faces in dealing with her father's alcoholism are particularly acute; she has deep feelings of love and affection for him, and Zachary reciprocates in many significant ways his daughter's devotion. As readers learn in "Able, Baker, Charlie, Dog," the first story in the collection, Jackson *père* can be a demanding teacher (he drills Gemma constantly on schoolwork); but he always maintains genuine respect for his daughter. As Gemma the narrator comes to realize when reflecting on her childhood, her father always knew that his daughter would one day be an adult, and he tried to prepare her for an independent life. Readers learn without being told directly that Zachary dies (presumably from the effects of alcoholism) before Gemma reaches womanhood, and some of the stories focus on the family's ability to adjust to life without the stern, paternalistic former soldier in their midst. In one particularly poignant episode, an adult Gemma must deal with her mother's refusal to recognize that she has developed cancer; in another, she must confront her now-grown brother, who, scarred from service in Vietnam, has chosen to withdraw from the community and live a hermit's life on a farm. Certainly, Vaughn has accomplished much in the limited space of the five Gemma Jackson stories; readers are treated to the emotional impact of a novel, a kind of feminine American *Bildungsroman* that is in some ways a paradigm for the American experience of growing up in the later twentieth century.

The other stories maintain the tone of the Gemma Jackson tales, focusing on a female protagonist's reaction to crises great and small. In one, a young woman whose husband is afflicted with a mild hygiene problem discovers that he contracted the disease as a result of an affair with her best friend. In a second, a teacher on her way home across an icy bridge slides her car into a police vehicle stopped beside the road, thereby achieving rather dubious temporary notoriety. In a third, a homemaker with two small children must manage the stress of dealing with the dozens of little annoyances such a life brings when her husband is stranded—comfortably—at a neighbor's during a snowstorm. Vaughn's particular gift is her ability to make readers empathize with her protagonists, to suggest that there is an element of universality about their predicaments that invests their lives with significance.

Vaughn's techniques of presentation also deserve mention. Several of the stories are loosely structured; though she usually starts with a crucial event on which the story turns, Vaughn frequently moves back into the past or foward into the future to provide explanations for the significance of that central action. Usually this is successful because her primary interest is in the characters she creates rather than in the action. Suspense is often subordinated to an exploration of characters' attitudes toward the everyday occurrences that make up the central activity in each of these stories. Even in those which do not feature the Jackson family, Vaughn seldom looks at the "momentous event"—at least in the way such events are traditionally defined. Instead, she is concerned with events that are significant in the lives of the ordinary people whose lives she creates and chronicles. Recent critics have noted that the best "women's fiction" does exactly that, and Vaughn may be pleased to have her work identified with the high-quality examples of that genre. To do so, however, may be to suggest a limitation that would be inappropriate. Like Joanne Greenberg, an older contemporary whose best fiction deals with similar incidents, Vaughn elevates the commonplace occurrences of life into miniature works of art.

Vaughn's style is reminiscent of that of another American writer who often deals with the same subjects she does, usually with the same sensitivity and compassion and always with similar mastery of language: John Updike. Reading Vaughn's narratives, one gets a sense—as one does in reading collections such as Updike's *Trust Me* (1987) and *The Music School* (1966)—that the author understands how to make language work to evoke human emotions. Like Updike, Vaughn displays exceptional evocative powers in describing the situations of everyday life. Unlike so many writers of popular literature, who spend their time telling readers how to feel and what to think, Vaughn keeps her readers' attention focused on the complex relationship between a character and his or her environment—especially the social environment. If one laughs or cries, it is because one is moved by the protagonist's attempts to deal with crises great and small. There is no overt moralizing; hence, these stories contain a ring of authenticity missing from the overwritten romances and domestic novels that so often find their way onto the shelves of libraries and paperback book racks.

The comparison with Updike should not suggest, however, that Vaughn may have intentionally copied either style or substance from someone who had preceded her in the genre. The stories in *Sweet Talk* can stand on their own; their vision is unique to this talented short-story writer, who is potentially, in her own way, an important voice in American fiction. It is a tribute to the editors at Random House that they have chosen to make her work available in book form.

Laurence W. Mazzeno

Sources for Further Study

Antioch Review. XLVIII, Winter, 1990, p. 122.
Booklist. LXXXVI, January 1, 1990, p. 894.
Chicago Tribune. January 28, 1990, XIV, p. 6.
Kirkus Reviews. LVII, December 1, 1989, p. 1705.
Library Journal. CXV, February 1, 1990, p. 109.
Los Angeles Times Book Review. February 4, 1990, p. 3.
The New York Times Book Review. XCV, February 4, 1990, p. 27.
Publishers Weekly. CCXXXVI, December 8, 1989, p. 40.
The Wall Street Journal. February 13, 1990, p. A18.
The Washington Post Book World. XX, January 28, 1990, p. 6.

SYMPOSIUM

Author: Muriel Spark (1918-   )
Publisher: Houghton Mifflin (New York). 192 pp. $18.95
Type of work: Novel
Time: The 1980's
Locale: London, Scotland

Ten well-to-do friends enjoy a dinner together, unaware of the evil that circulates among them

> *Principal characters:*
> MARGARET DAMIEN, a young newlywed with a suspicious history
> WILLIAM DAMIEN, Margaret's naïve husband
> HILDA DAMIEN, William's mother, a wealthy media mogul
> CHRIS HENDERSON, the hostess of the dinner party that is central to the novel
> HURLEY REED, Chris's longtime live-in companion, an established artist and host of the dinner party
> ERNST UNTZINGER, a diplomat, a guest at the party
> ELLA UNTZINGER, Ernst's wife, also a guest
> LUKE, a graduate student, a friend of the Untzingers, and a server at the dinner party
> MAGNUS MURCHIE, Margaret's Scottish uncle, who, though insane, oversees the family affairs
> DAN MURCHIE, Margaret's father

Muriel Spark employs a quotation from Plato's *Symposium* (388-366 B.C.) as one of the epigraphs to her own *Symposium*, her nineteenth novel. "The genius of comedy," Plato suggests, is "the same with that of tragedy." This is precisely what Spark demonstrates in her tightly plotted and witty novel. She does not, however, merely blur the comic and the tragic together into a kind of black comedy. What is tragic from one perspective does not suddenly become comic from another. Rather, Spark weaves together the threads of tragedy and those of comedy, allowing them to exist side by side, each retaining its own integrity as either comedy or tragedy.

The novel is composed of several separate story lines spanning a period of time anywhere from a few weeks to a few years. In the final pages of the novel, these various story lines arrive at the same point in time—the evening during which Hilda Damien is murdered. Furthermore, the narrator jumps from one story to another, back and forth in time, giving the fairly simple plot a complex, even erratic, structure. In the principal story line, concerning the mysterious Margaret Damien, the narrator seems almost not to know where to begin. We meet Margaret at the beginning of the novel on the night of Hilda's murder. In chapter 3, we find her on her honeymoon with William Damien, two weeks before. In order to develop some of the suspicious circumstances surrounding this recent marriage, the narrator takes us back a few weeks more in chapter 5 to the meeting between Hilda, William's mother, and Margaret's parents, Dan and Greta Murchie. This is apparently not far enough back in time, for immediately we are taken back another month to Hilda's first meeting with Margaret, during which Hilda immediately begins to suspect that Margaret is hiding something. Hilda is dead before she learns anything that might confirm her suspicions; the reader, however, privy to the narrator's backward reach into time, is allowed to learn precisely what is so suspicious about Margaret. This attempt by the narrator to establish a line of causality through a constant movement back in time ends in irony. Though we learn that indeed Margaret wishes to murder Hilda, a desire which Hilda intuitively knows, the actual cause of Hilda's murder comes from an entirely different direction—from one of the other story lines which the narrator has been developing alongside the one concerning Margaret.

Nevertheless, although Margaret has no hand in the murder, her story provides the central focus of the novel. For reasons apparent only to her eccentric uncle, Magnus Murchie, she has a proclivity for being near the scene of accidental and suspicious deaths. Uncle Magnus, who lives in an insane asylum, is a caricature of the Scottish highlander: deeply superstitious, a constant singer of ancient Scots ballads—especially the ones concerning murder and enmity—and a loud dresser. He feels a deep affinity for Lady Macbeth. Judged wise by Margaret and her family, he presides over all family decisions, pushing the Murchies to act in the most unethical, though practical, ways imaginable. His principal concern is Margaret. He sees untapped potentials in her—the makings of a great and noble woman. Unfortunately, her immediate family, though not exactly poor, does not have the kind of fabulous wealth necessary as a backdrop to the kind of woman he would like to see Margaret become. Thus, he sets about making her rich. First, he gets Margaret to convince his ailing mother to rewrite her will, leaving the bulk of her money to his brother Dan Murchie, Margaret's father, cutting out himself and his sisters. Within a week, the mother is murdered, strangled by a maniac who escaped from the same asylum in which Uncle Magnus lives. Though the police finally conclude that there is no evidence of wrongdoing, a scandal erupts; but Uncle Magnus performs damage control with expertly staged press interviews and soon has the situation in hand.

This is not the first time that Margaret has been linked with a suspicious death. As a girl, a playmate had drowned at the edge of a lake while Margaret ran for help. Several years later, while Margaret was having tea in a restaurant with a favorite teacher, the teacher disappeared, having gone to use the restroom, and was never seen again. Margaret, understandably distraught at having been apparently connected with a third such death—her grandmother's—enters a nunnery. For a while, Margaret is at peace. She assists the ailing in a nearby hospital and, when a television station decides to do a program on the nunnery, she poses photogenically with her patients. Inevitably, though, death follows her there: A young nun is found strangled in the convent's courtyard a few days after the camera crews have departed. The murderer is not Margaret; she has a firm alibi. But again, she has been implicated, however indirectly, in a death.

Because of the scandal, the convent collapses, and Margaret returns home, also near collapse. Her already high-strung sisters refuse to talk to her, not because they believe she is responsible for the deaths, but simply because the whole situation is too distressing for them to contemplate. Her father finds himself wondering whether somehow his daughter actually did deviously mastermind all four deaths. During her discussions with Uncle Magnus, Margaret decides that, if she is to be an agent of death, she would prefer to take a more active role; no more of this second-handedness for her. Uncle Magnus, always practical, directs Margaret to marry a rich man—even an heir to large fortune would do—and *then* act upon her new resolve. He presents her with a list of prospectives compiled from the pages of society magazines. After failing with the top two names, Margaret trails William Damien, sole heir to Hilda's massive wealth, into the fruit section of Marks & Spencer's. Commenting that the grapefruit look bruised, she catches William's eye and he falls headlong in love. All that remains is to do away with Hilda—which, as Margaret tells Uncle Magnus, merely necessitates a little walk by a lake. Before the right circumstances present themselves, though, Hilda is dead, murdered by a burglar.

On the evening of the murder, Margaret and William are at a dinner party given by Chris Henderson and her live-in companion, Hurley Reed. Among the eight guests are the aging Lord Suzy and his young wife and Ella and Ernst Untzinger. The dinner conversation revolves around Lord Suzy's recent burglary and the contradictions between romantic love and marriage. Helping the butler with the service is Luke, a young American graduate student and also a friend of the Untzingers. The development of this friendship comprises another of the novel's story lines. Both Ella and Ernst have a repressed sexual interest in Luke intermingled with a parental concern for his future. They are impressed that he is willing, unlike so many of his peers, to work his way through school; consequently, they refer him to their many rich acquaintances to work as a server at parties. One day, they see Luke wearing an extremely expensive watch. Projecting their own sexual interest, they assume Luke has been given the watch in return for sexual favors. Certainly, they think, he cannot be making that much money bearing platters at parties. What they do not know is that Luke provides lists of party guests to a ring of thieves who break into the guests' empty homes on the night of the party. On the night of Chris and Hurley's party, the burglars break into William and Margaret's apartment just as Hilda arrives, carrying a Monet she had thought to leave there as a surprise wedding gift. Instead, she ends up smothered beneath the weight of one of the burglars.

Thus, *Symposium* is composed of two principal story lines, one—the farce revolving around Margaret—which is essentially comic, the other—comprising the events leading to Hilda's death—which is tragic. Although some tragic elements are introduced into Margaret's story, namely the four deaths, the reader assumes that these elements, though necessary to Margaret's story, are not in themselves meant to be comic. The narrator manages to keep the tragic elements of the novel separate from the comic ones, although this separation is not accomplished simply by shifts in narrative tone. The narrator, adopting the typical Spark voice, remains straightforward and factual throughout, allowing the events to speak for themselves, employing the utmost economy in language with few overt witticisms or stylistic jewels. It is this economy itself which allows the reader to sense either the horror or the farce of what is being described. Thus, Hilda's murder is summed up in a few joined clauses: "She is smothered, her head held down hard and firm on the sofa, the man with one knee on her body, until she is dead." Nothing could be more simply stated than that last "until she is dead"; a more developed description is needless and would be distracting. The same holds true for the death of Margaret's schoolgirl friend, who "had jumped into a lake in the school grounds, had swum for it, got caught in some reeds and had drowned." The terseness of these descriptions allows the reader to dwell in the horror and finality of the events themselves, rather than in the verbiage attached to them.

The same goes for the comic elements. Indeed, the opening lines of the novel emblematize the disparity between verbiage and reality. Upon discovering his house has been burglarized (by the same group, it later turns out, to whom Luke has been supplying information), Lord Suzy cries "This is rape!", his voice "reaching a pitch it had never reached before." The narrator immediately steps in and undercuts Suzy's stylistic excesses with the matter-of-fact statement, "It was not rape, it was a robbery."

Spark's brand of tragedy has a modern, which is to say, sentimental flavor—that of lost opportunity and of random and meaningless death. Her comedy is timeless; it is a comedy of manners, of humours, and of intrigue. Spark successfully weaves the comic and the tragic together in *Symposium*, demonstrating her genius in both.

Peter Crawford

Sources for Further Study

Library Journal. CXV, December, 1990, p. 166.
The Literary Review. September, 1990, p. 16.
London Review of Books. XII, September 13, 1990, p. 15.
Los Angeles Times Book Review. December 2, 1990, p. 3.
New Statesman and Society. III, September 28, 1990, p. 36.
The New York Review of Books. XXXVII, December 20, 1990, p. 22.
The New York Times Book Review. XCV, November 25, 1990, p. 8.
Publishers Weekly. CCXXXVII, October 26, 1990, p. 55.
Time. CXXXVI, November 26, 1990, p. CT6.
The Times Literary Supplement. September 21, 1990, p. 998.
The Washington Post Book World. XX, November 25, 1990, p. 1.

TEHANU
The Last Book of Earthsea

Author: Ursula K. Le Guin (1929-   )
Publisher: Atheneum (New York). 240 pp. $15.95
Type of work: Fantasy

Tenar, protagonist of the second Earthsea volume, witnesses the painful end of the old order and the beginning of a new and puzzling world

> *Principal characters:*
> TENAR (GOHA FLINT), a widow farmer in her forties
> GED (SPARROWHAWK or HAWK), the former Archmage of Earthsea
> THERRU (TEHANU), a terribly scarred girl of about eight, whom Tenar adopts
> MOSS, a witch healer
> OGION, an aged mage and a friend and teacher of Ged and Tenar
> ASPEN, a wizard who still hopes to carry out the evil intentions of Cob, the villain of the third Earthsea volume
> LEBANNEN, the King of Earthsea

Ursula K. Le Guin's *Tehanu* is her fourth book to take place in the fantasy world of Earthsea, a large group of islands in a primarily oceanic world. In *A Wizard of Earthsea* (1968), Ged learns the magic arts of his world through error and suffering. In *The Tombs of Atuan* (1971), Tenar is persuaded by Ged to abandon her service to the nameless gods of nonbeing on the island of Atuan. In *The Farthest Shore* (1972) Ged, now Archmage of Earthsea, finds and defeats Cob, a renegade mage who has found a way to become immortal at the cost of destroying creation. *Tehanu* begins about the time Ged is fighting Cob, with Tenar as the protagonist.

On the island of Gont, Tenar has lived for twenty-five years since Ged persuaded her to leave Atuan. Though Ogion, Ged's friend and teacher, befriended her and attempted to teach her magic, she rejected this teaching for what she felt was her woman's power and destiny, to marry and bear children. Now, after her children have grown and left home and her husband has died, she finds her function in life at an end. She has learned, however, that such endings are not final, that there is always a new beginning in every ending. This beginning comes to her from two directions: a child snatched from death and a man who is also at an ending.

The child is Therru, a little girl whom, Tenar believes, her parents and uncle raped and beat nearly to death and then threw into a fire to destroy the evidence of their crimes. Tenar takes Therru into her home when it appears that she will survive her wounds and burns. Therru's face is severely scarred, one eye is lost, her voice damaged so she can only whisper, and one hand is reduced to a thumb and a finger. The relationship between Tenar and Therru grows closer as Tenar's love learns to transcend pity and as Therru learns trust and love. Tenar, however, becomes increasingly aware of the limits of love, which cannot heal Therru, restore her outward beauty, or protect her from more harm.

The man who is also at an ending in his life is Ged. He has been the Archmage of Earthsea, the most powerful man in his world. He has heroically sacrificed all of his magical power in a successful struggle to defeat Cob. *The Farthest Shore* ends with his victory over Cob and his rescue from death by Lebannen, who is destined to unite all Earthsea under his kingship.

The novel opens with Tenar taking in the wounded Therru. When the girl has nearly recovered, Tenar is summoned to Ogion's deathbed. There she learns that Therru has a special destiny and that everything has changed. Wise Ogion has sensed that Ged has overcome Cob, and he has glimpsed the form of the new age to come. He asks her to wait at his home. This waiting ends when Kalessin, the dragon who carried Ged and Lebannen away from the island of Selidor at the end of *The Farthest Shore*, brings a badly wounded Ged to Ogion's home. Tenar nurses him back to health with the help of Moss, the kindly and eccentric local witch.

Having lost his mage's power, Ged is in despair about how to live. When Lebannen sends a delegation to invite Ged to crown him, Ged flees to avoid contact with his old associates. Tenar protects him, sending him back to her farm, where he begins to heal spiritually in a long period of isolation as a goatherd in the mountains. Aspen, a wizard corrupted by Cob and the local lord, drives Tenar away from Ogion's cottage. Trying to return to her farm, she encounters one of the men who hurt Therru. She is rescued by Lebannen, who has come in search of his old friend, Ged. Lebannen travels in the company of a master of the Roke school of wizards, who is seeking the new Archmage.

Having returned home, Tenar begins to teach Therru the history of Earthsea, following Ogion's injunction to teach her everything. Threatened again by the family of Therru, she is helped by Ged, who had returned from his isolation with renewed self-confidence. He is now ready to make a new life, and Tenar becomes his teacher. He enters into the family, becoming Tenar's partner and lover and one of Therru's teachers. When their life seems to have settled into happiness and order, Tenar's son, Spark, returns from the sea to claim his father's farm. Tenar finds that she cannot live with him once he is master of the farm.

In the meantime, Aspen has been gathering power to oppose the new order. Planning to dispose of Tenar and Therru, he draws them back to Ogion's home. Having discovered her identity, Therru is able to rescue Tenar and Ged from Aspen's trap. The novel ends with the family making a new start in Ogion's old home.

The central theme of the novel concerns how to enter a new age. Ged, for example, does not know how to find a new beginning in his ending. From Tenar's point of view, which eventually becomes his own, he ceased growing when he became a mage. All mages are men; only men are taught the "high arts" of magic that can be used to manipulate the world on a large scale. Women's magic is considered weak and is relegated to witches, who serve mainly in domestic affairs such as minor healing and spells for the home. Thus, men and women are strictly separated with regard to magic, and mages never marry or take lovers.

Ged, therefore, does not know how to begin again because he does not know women, for whom beginning again is enforced learning. As Moss says, men are enclosed within themselves, like nuts in shells, while women do not know where they begin or end, where their boundaries are. When a man loses his work in the world, as Ged has, he is no longer alive. When a woman loses her work, she moves into another of her sets of connections and begins again. By learning to know Tenar, Ged learns how to be a new kind of masculine self and shows men the way into the new age. Ged learns to be strong in human weakness, unprotected by super power, and to be dependent upon others.

Ged's personal problem exemplifies the problem of Earthsea, which has come through a long age of disunity and decay. During this time, it was mainly male heroes such as Ged who, through great actions and sacrifice, could preserve order and being. As a result, a strong division was created between male and female power and the latter, which sustains the world almost invisibly by maintaining the daily process of producing and caring for families was devalued. The culture has thus grown to fear the deep, mysterious, almost forgotten sources of that power in nonbeing. Nonbeing, which is the potential to be, has seemed threatening during the age of declining order, but must become one foundation of a new age of creative and dynamic order.

Ged's final heroic struggle against Cob has resulted in a new age of political unity in Earthsea. When the mage masters on their island of Roke try to discover who should be their new Archmage for the beginning of the new time, they are cryptically sent to Gont in search of a woman. Because they are caught up in the old order, they assume that this woman will lead them to the Archmage. They are unable to see that the political king, who rules benevolently over all, must be balanced by a female mage who will be the voice of creative spirit in their world.

The new age of Earthsea, then, seems destined to restore a lost balance between masculine and feminine powers. Just as Ged must return to his youth to learn to relate with women, so must his world open itself now to understanding and accepting the importance of feminine power.

Le Guin connects this power with dragons. In the beginning of creation, humans and dragons were one. Gradually, those who preferred doing to being developed into humans; dragons became wild embodiments of creative potential. One of the important differences between dragons and humans in the present is that the dragons speak only the absolute language of the creation, in which names are the same as the things they name. Humans speak other languages that are not absolute, languages that have helped to imprison women in their domestic roles and make them invisible. Tenar encounters her invisible status every time she deals with the powers of the old order. Only Ged and the new king really listen to her.

Feminine power, in the world of Earthsea, is associated with the fundamental categories of nonbeing and being, with the roots of being in nonbeing. This association derives at least in part from a woman's power to bear children, to actualize potential by acting as a window between nonbeing and being. Women's experience of bearing children is a foundation for an understanding of endings and beginnings that males deny themselves when they set themselves apart and impose silence upon women. The most extreme expression of this masculine stance is Cob, who nearly destroys creation in attempting to escape nonbeing. The most extreme expression of female power is the maze of the tombs of Atuan, where self may be surrendered utterly to darkness and where creation is denied. In the dynamic balance between these two is the promised human order of peace and comparative fulfillment.

Though subtitled *The Last Book of Earthsea*, *Tehanu* is by no means the last story that can be told in this acclaimed fantasy series. This book makes the reader wish for more, to understand more fully the world Le Guin envisions to follow the end of the age of the exclusively male mages in Earthsea.

Terry Heller

Sources for Further Study

Booklist. LXXXVI, March 1, 1990, p. 1277.
Chicago Tribune. July 8, 1990, XIV, p. 6.
The Horn Book Magazine. LXVI, May, 1990, p. 338.
The New York Times Book Review. XCV, May 20, 1990, p. 38.
The New Yorker. LXVI, July 23, 1990, p. 88.
Publishers Weekly. CCXXXVII, January 19, 1990, p. 110.
School Library Journal. XXXVI, April, 1990, p. 142.
The Washington Post Book World. XX, February 25, 1990, p. 1.
Wilson Library Bulletin. LXIV, June, 1990, p. 124.
Women's Review of Books. VII, July, 1990, p. 40.

THEODORE DREISER
An American Journey, 1908-1945

Author: Richard Lingeman (1931-   )
Publisher: G. P. Putnam's Sons (New York). Illustrated. 544 pp. $29.95
Type of work: Literary biography
Time: 1908-1945
Locale: New York and California

The second and concluding volume of a major biography of one of America's most important novelists, distinguished for the social scope of his work and his efforts to bring more candor to fiction than was the case in previous generations of writers

> *Principal personages:*
> THEODORE DREISER, a major American novelist
> SARA (JUGS) DREISER, his first wife
> HELEN DREISER, the novelist's second wife
> H. L. MENCKEN, a Baltimore newspaperman, a Dreiser supporter and confidant
> MARGUERITE HARRIS, one of several important women in Dreiser's life who helped him to complete one of his last novels, *The Bulwark*
> HORACE LIVERIGHT, Dreiser's publisher for many years
> KIRAM MARKHAM, an actress who was Dreiser's mistress for several years
> GRANT RICHARDS, an English publisher who backed Dreiser's efforts to support himself as a writer

In the second volume of his magnificent biography of Theodore Dreiser, Richard Lingeman picks up at that point in his subject's life when he was contemplating a return to fiction. After the fierce reception of *Sister Carrie* (1900), a ground-breaking novel that was attacked for its emphasis on the place of sexuality in American society, Dreiser was reluctant to write more fiction. Although his novel had been hailed by his fellow writers, many of whom treated him as a towering new figure in American literature, he had suffered greatly from his publisher's suppression of *Sister Carrie* and from its small sale. He took to editing a women's magazine and to earning a comfortable living.

Recognizing that Dreiser's talents were being wasted in such mundane activities, H. L. Mencken and others besieged the novelist with requests for another novel. Mencken, then a very young newspaperman, sat in Dreiser's editor's office and brashly encouraged him to resume the great work that had begun with *Sister Carrie*. Mencken enthusiastically assured Dreiser that he would indeed be able to make a living as a novelist, given adequate promotion by a supportive publisher. Similarly, Grant Richards, an English publisher, wooed Dreiser back to fiction, paid for a trip to Europe, and convinced the novelist that contracts would be available to sustain his writing career.

Although these allies were important, it was characteristic of Dreiser to make a change in his life based on deeply personal and private reasons. He had fallen in love with a young girl, Thelma Cudlipp. Shamelessly courting her in defiance of his wife and against the admonitions of his employer, Dreiser invited disaster. Fired from his position and thrown back upon his own resources, he began to write fiction at a great rate, producing *Jennie Gerhardt* (1911) and *The "Genius"* (1915) as well as many other pieces of short fiction and nonfiction. Mencken's prediction that Dreiser would make money writing proved too optimistic. Although he did earn some income from fiction, he was often in debt, living in poor lodgings, and depending upon the generosity of the many women in his life.

During most of his career Dreiser was involved in torrid affairs with women— sometimes with several women at the same time. Sara, his long-suffering wife, held on to him as long as she could, and Dreiser, valuing her sensible presence, was reluctant to give her up entirely, finding it useful to fend off other women when they became too importunate by falling back upon his marriage and Sara's refusal to divorce him. After affairs with several beautiful women—usually much younger than himself—he settled for a stormy but long-term relationship with Helen Richardson, whom he would marry in his last years. A beautiful woman who ceased to interest him sexually after their first intensely romantic years, she stayed by him to the end, raging against the other women in his life, leaving him, but always coming back— assured by him that he would never abandon her even though he could not resist the attractions of other women.

Dreiser's almost helplessly passionate involvement with women was of a piece with his fiction, in which characters were driven by forces beyond their control. Like Frank Cowperwood, the great hero in *The Financier* (1912), *The Titan* (1914), and *The Stoic* (1947), Dreiser was a powerful, charismatic man, attracting men and women who saw in him a figure who embodied the contradictions of the culture. Indeed, in some ways Dreiser was an even greater figure than Cowperwood, for Dreiser had an enormous sympathy for all classes of society. A man who openly wept at poverty and the tragedy of the human condition, Dreiser suffered from periods of intense loneliness and despair as well as enjoying tremendous periods of great success.

Although Dreiser never recognized it, he was uncommonly fortunate in having Horace Liveright as a publisher. Liveright carried Dreiser financially for years, amending contracts and catering to Dreiser's almost incessant demands. Dreiser's deep suspicion of publishers, stemming from his belief that they did little to promote his books, drove him to goad Liveright and to accuse the publisher of reneging on deals. Usually, Liveright was blameless and put up with his author's insults. Indeed, he gave Dreiser the cushion he needed to write *An American Tragedy* (1925), a novel that was long overdue and indeed taken up after Dreiser had abandoned other fiction promised to Liveright.

Lingeman's tone throughout the biography is flawless. Since Dreiser was a large figure who provoked deep feelings in people, Lingeman wisely presents the wide range of private and public reactions to the man and the novelist. Lingeman is especially careful in tracing Dreiser's connections to the Communist Party, showing that on his first trip to the Soviet Union, Dreiser was a stern critic of the government's ideology and doubted that the Soviets could truly create a classless society. At the same time, it was natural for Dreiser, at home in his own country, to criticize America by the standard the Soviet Union had set; that is, he was both a fierce believer in and critic of American individualism, believing that all great movements depended on great individuals and yet recognizing that a society based only on the individual endangered itself by promoting self-aggrandizement and greed. Dreiser was widely read in the Soviet Union, and that may help to account for his tardy recognition that Joseph Stalin had deeply perverted the ideals of the revolution and had created a police state.

If Dreiser was attracted to the secular materialism of the Communist state, he was equally captivated by the spiritual truths of religion. He studied the Quakers for years and labored to complete a novel, *The Bulwark* (1946), that expressed his yearning to find the transcendant principle of life. He spent time with scientists, visiting their laboratories and quizzing them about their philosophical and religious beliefs. He sorely wanted, somehow, to unite materialism and idealism, individualism and collectivism, in one grand view of the universe, and his novels swing in emphasis from one form of belief to another.

An American Tragedy is generally regarded as Dreiser's masterpiece. The book changed his life. On the one hand, it gave him an enormous sense of security. Profits from book sales, a dramatization, and movie rights, provided most of his income and renown. On the other hand, Dreiser found it hard thereafter to find a subject as compelling or as comprehensive and spent much of his time capitalizing on his fame by writing ephemeral magazine and newspaper articles. Only toward the end of his life, when it was really too late to recapture his novelistic powers, did Dreiser struggle to complete his last two novels, which are decidedly inferior to his earlier work. It is to Lingeman's credit that he presents this last part of Dreiser's life compassionately, making it easy to identify with a great writer who wanted to complete his legacy and to remain true to his plans for novels he conceived in his prime.

Lingeman has written an intellectual, social, and psychological biography of Dreiser. He carefully details the background of the novels, dwelling (as he must) on *An American Tragedy* and on how Dreiser slowly and expertly transformed an actual murder case and the murderer, Chester Gilette, into Clyde Griffiths, a young man who expresses the American dream of success as well as Dreiser's own terrible hunger for status and recognition. Thus Lingeman shrewdly shows the convergence of autobiographical and objective fact in Dreiser's greatest work. Dreiser did much more than simply work up articles on the Gilette case. He thoroughly reimagined the background of Clyde Griffiths and wrote a brilliant murder scene, court scenes, and a devastating account of death row without visiting a prison until after he had drafted the novel.

What Lingeman's biography does not provide is extensive literary analysis. While there is discussion of Dreiser's novels, Lingeman does not analyze their style or structure. Instead, he shows how the fiction arose out of Dreiser's life and how it was received by reviewers and critics. This method is standard in biographies, although the consequence is that the reader cannot have a deep feeling for the fiction, for how Dreiser forged his style and point of view. There is much discussion, for example, of how much editing Dreiser's fiction needed, but there are no instances in which Lingeman shows what the editing was like. In other words, the biographer tells about the process without giving a real feel for it. To do so, however, would have made a long biography even longer. Like W. A. Swanberg, whose *Dreiser* (1965) is one of the significant predecessors of this new biography, Lingeman is content to have readers turn to other sources for literary criticism of Dreiser's work.

In his acknowledgments, Lingeman recognizes Swanberg, Robert Elias, and other biographers of Dreiser and says that his book has been built on theirs as well as on his own interviews and on papers in the Dreiser archive at the University of Pennsylvania. Clearly, Lingeman was careful to consult all of the important sources. His biography does not supersede previous ones so much as it completes and extends them, carrying forward the dialogue on Dreiser, ensuring that he will remain not merely a historically important figure in American literature but a novelist still worthy of being read for his relevance today.

Lingeman has also presented Dreiser as a great American character. Dreiser's fights against censorship, his attacks on the manners and morality of the time, his willingness to engage in political issues—not only in the Communist Party but in his visit to the striking miners in Harlan County, Kentucky—show how he wanted to integrate literature and life. The vigor of Dreiser's mind and body had to find an outlet in public action. His words had to be tied to actions. His mistress, and then his wife, Helen, called him a "great man." She had in mind, it seems, his ability to move people, to make them suffer with his characters and himself. There was something very appealing about Dreiser, for he could be at one and the same time very vulnerable and absolutely resolute. He was not a handsome man, but he had a hold over many women because there was something in him that needed mothering and nurturing even as he evinced a power that controlled the lives of his lovers. He empathized with both the "little" or the "common" man and the tycoon, Charles Yerkes, on whom he based his Frank Cowperwood. There is a relentlessness in Dreiser's fiction that is parallel to his passionate life. He amasses mountains of detail when describing his characters, providing a dense individual and social fabric for their lives that meshes with his keen awareness of how his own character had been caught up with the fate of his country. By packing his biography with a similar set of particulars, Lingeman does homage to a writer who remains important in American fiction's effort to encompass and to appraise the American identity.

Carl Rollyson

Sources for Further Study

Booklist. LXXXVII, September 15, 1990, p. 135.

Boston Globe. September 30, 1990, p. 43.
Chicago Tribune. September 16, 1990, XIV, p. 1.
Kirkus Reviews. LVIII, August 1, 1990, p. 1064.
Library Journal. CXV, August, 1990, p. 111.
The New Republic. CCIII, November 12, 1990, p. 34.
The New York Times Book Review. XCV, September 30, 1990, p. 1.
Publishers Weekly. CCXXXVII, August 3, 1990, p. 70.
USA Today. November 2, 1990, p. D4.
The Washington Post Book World. XX, September 30, 1990, p. 3.

THE THINGS THEY CARRIED

Author: Tim O'Brien (1946-   )
Publisher: Houghton Mifflin/Seymour Lawrence (Boston). 273 pp. $19.95
Type of work: Novel
Time: 1968-1990
Locale: Vietnam and the United States

A work about the need to tell the story of Vietnam and about the difficulty of telling that story

Principal characters:
TIM O'BRIEN, a soldier and the narrator-writer
JIMMY CROSS, the First Lieutenant of Alpha Company
HENRY DOBBINS,
DAVE JENSEN,
TED LAVENDER,
MITCHELL SANDERS,
NORMAN BOWKER,
LEE STRUNK,
CURT LEMON,
AZAR,
MORTY PHILLIPS, and
KIOWA, some of the men of Alpha Company
BOB "RAT" KILEY, a medic
BOBBY JORGENSEN, Kiley's replacement
MARTHA, the girl whose picture Jimmy Cross carries
MARY ANNE BELL, the "sweetheart of the Song Tra Bong"
KATHLEEN, O'Brien's daughter

Early in *The Things They Carried*—Tim O'Brien's third book about American soldiers in Vietnam, and his fifth overall—early, that is in all the shuffling back and forth between past and present, between Quang Ngai Province in 1968 and the time of the telling in 1990, ten-year-old Kathleen asks her forty-three-year-old father, "Tim O'Brien," why he continues to write war stories. She wants to know why he is so "obsessed." The cynical reader—and many American readers are cynical in the aftermath of American involvement in Vietnam—may believe that he or she already knows the answer. Following the critical success of *Going After Cacciato* (1978), winner of the National Book Award, O'Brien had claimed that he was not a writer of Vietnam War fiction. After his second non-Vietnam novel, *The Nuclear Age* (1985), was drubbed by reviewers and he had seen the popular interest in the war increase with each new commercial film and television series, however, that is exactly what he became. The same cynical reader may find the author's record of a visit paid by a former lieutenant—one of the recurring characters in *The Things They Carried* and also one of the members of Alpha Company singled out in the book's dedication—as well as the printing of a letter from another grunt/character/dedicatee, Norman Bowker, not so much sincere as self-serving.

The cynical reader would be wrong. *The Things They Carried* is not self-serving;

it is self-examining in ways and to the extent that no work on the same subject has been. The praise and prizes bestowed on *Going After Cacciato* notwithstanding, O'Brien's latest book may well be his best. Neither polemical nor sentimental (the twin pitfalls of films and fiction about what has come to be known synecdochically and rather imperialistically as "Vietnam"), it is a brilliantly and disturbingly obsessive work whose actual subject is not the war but the difficulty of writing about it. "Things happened, things came to an end. There was no sense of developing drama. All that remained was debris" and "all I am left with are simple, unprofound scraps of truth," O'Brien reports in *If I Die in a Combat Zone, Box Me Up and Ship Me Home* (1973), a book whose structure is as fragmentary and discontinuous as its genre is uncertain (fiction or memoir). The discontinuity of the war experience and of the narrative situation increases in *Going After Cacciato*, as Paul Berlin's memory and imagination spin separately on, the one chronologically jumbled, the other chronologically and geographically straightforward. Neither work, however, quite prepares the reader for the displacements of *The Things They Carried*; the "simple, unprofound scraps of truth" now seem less apparent and the "debris" more pervasive, reaching beyond the characters, the men of Alpha Company, to include the narrator-writer and the reader as well.

In *Anything Can Happen*, a book of interviews edited by Tom Le Clair and Larry McCaffery (1983), O'Brien explained that "the true core of fiction" is "the exploration of substantive, important human values." Yet when the narrator returns to Vietnam to affirm one of them by stripping off his clothes, immersing himself in the foul waters of a rice paddy/village latrine, and placing Kiowa's hatchet-talisman at what he hopes is the very spot where his friend died, neither of the two people who witness his strangely sacramental act of remembrance seems able to approve of or even understand what he has done. His daughter is incredulous, and the old Vietnamese farmer who stands some distance away appears to be angry. The isolation and uncertainty evident in this scene typify the entire book; they extend out into every narrative action and every act of narration and, therefore, into the reader's experience of both. The first of the book's nineteen chapters (if it is a novel) or stories (if it is a collection) or, simply, parts (if it is something generically "other") is made in the image of the larger text (or perhaps vice versa). Either origin or offspring, *The Things They Carried* takes the form of a list struggling to become a litany, a secular enumeration yearning for wholeness and spiritual redemption. Artfully contrived yet following no clearly discernible pattern, it catalogs the "things" the men of Alpha Company carried, everything from flak jackets to fear; above all they carried the knowledge "that they would never be at a loss for things to carry" and the opposing dream of "lightness," of being "purely borne" (a punning condensation of their twin desires of being carried and being reborn).

Like O'Brien's act of remembrance, the dream stands apart. Instead of either fulfillment or even a "sense of developing drama," the reader finds what the characters do, chapters/stories/parts oscillating back and forth in time and space. The repetition of information from one section to another creates a sense of stalled action and Sisyphean doom or, more optimistically, the need to go over the same ground again and again in the faint hope of finding the missing link that will allow the action to develop dramatically, to imagine a different end. Lacking this sense of developing drama, individual stories tend to dissolve, leaving the reader with an apparently random collection of individual images: Rat Kiley and Curt Lemon playing catch with a smoke grenade, until the latter steps on a booby-trapped artillery round; or Azar detonating the Claymore mine to which he had strapped a puppy and then responding to the others' horror with a line that rings all too true: "I'm just a boy." There is Norman Bowker, mustered out and back home, driving around and around a lake, the village they burn because Ted Lavender has been shot, the dancing of the fourteen-year-old girl whose entire family has been killed in an air attack, and the triple-canopied jungle, mist-filled and ominously silent. The starkness of these and other images parallels the simple fact that as the stories progress and the number of casualties increases, the sense of causality declines.

As O'Brien wrote in *If I Die in a Combat Zone*, "things happen," and even in the narratively more complex *Going After Cacciato*, the reader can take a certain comfort in being able to distinguish recollections from imaginings. In *The Things They Carried*, the very nature of these things, their ontological status as well as their ethical value and thematic meaning, are in doubt, strangely so given O'Brien's choice of epigraph, a passage from John L. Ransom's *Andersonville Diary* (1881):

> This book is essentially different from any other that has been published concerning the "late war" or any of its incidents. Those who have had any such experience as the author will see its truthfulness at once, and to all other readers it is commended as a statement of actual things by one who experienced them to the fullest.

The passage makes plain what most readers of war fiction assume: that such fiction is not only essentially realistic, and referential, but that it is as well autobiographically revealing, whether the text be Leo Tolstoy's realistic *Sebastopol* (1887), Stephen Crane's impressionist *The Red Badge of Courage* (1895), Ernest Hemingway's modernist *A Farewell to Arms* (1929), Norman Mailer's epic *The Naked and the Dead* (1948), or Joseph Heller's absurdist *Catch-22* (1961). While it was possible for *Andersonville Diary* to claim to be different from other books about the Civil War by virtue of its greater truthfulness, meaning its factual accuracy and historical verifiability, however, *The Things They Carried* differs from other books about Vietnam by laying claim to a very different "greater truthfulness"—by insisting upon its status as fiction, O'Brien problematizes the connection between word and world and, indeed connections of all kinds. Both essay and fiction, "How to Tell a War Story" insists: "This is true," and another generically ambiguous chapter, "Good Form," begins:

> It's time to be blunt.
> I'm forty-three years old, true, and I'm a writer now, and a long time ago I walked through Quang Ngai Province as a foot soldier.
> Almost everything else is invented.

> But it's not a game. It's a form. Right here, now, as I invent myself, I'm thinking of all I want to tell you about why this book is written as it is. For instance, I want to tell you this: twenty years ago I watched a man die on a trail near the village of My Khe. I did not kill him. But I was present, you see, and my presence was guilt enough. I remember his face, which was not a pretty face, because his jaw was in his throat, and I remember feeling the burden of responsibility and grief. I blamed myself. And rightly so, because I was present.
>
> But listen. Even *that* story is made up.

Teasingly ambiguous and indeterminate, the words "almost everything" transform this war fiction into a Borgesian garden of forking paths, a funhouse of distorting mirrors. It is a rather odd narrative turn for a writer who has spoken against experimental writing—odd but nevertheless appropriate to his aim of distinguishing between "happening-truth" and "story-truth" and forcing the reader to carry a measure of that burden of uncertainty and self-doubt which the men of Alpha Company had to carry and, in these pages, continue to carry.

It is also unsettling to find a writer who has dismissed films such as *Apocalypse Now* (1979) as "Simplistic and stupid" and "garishly overdrawn rhetorical statements" now writing his own equally fantastic version of Joseph Conrad's novel, *Heart of Darkness* (1902). One of the collection's longest stories, "Sweetheart of the Song Tra Bong," is also one of its most effective and, in its premise, certainly the most ludicrous: a soldier at a remote medical station smuggles in his girlfriend from Cleveland Heights. Mary Anne Bell is seventeen, pretty, and innocent, but also vulnerable, drawn to the seductiveness not of sex but of the violence within. She goes on ambush with six Green Berets, is later seen wearing a necklace of human tongues, and eventually disappears into the jungle, another Colonel Kurtz: "She had crossed to the other side. She was part of the land. She was wearing her culottes, her pink sweater, and a necklace of human tongues. She was dangerous. She was ready for the kill." The ending is frightening but also strangely, melodramatically comic, and trying to gauge the story's authentic register is difficult, perhaps impossible. Is "Sweetheart of the Song Tra Bong" a retelling of *Heart of Darkness* or a parody of *Apocalypse Now?* Is it even about Mary Anne and all she represents (America's loss of innocence in Vietnam, for example) or, even more than in Conrad or Francis Ford Coppola's film, is it about its own telling? "O'Brien" narrates the story through Rat Kiley, who claims to have been a witness to all but the end, which he learned (as a story) from still another narrator. This narrator also claims to have been a witness, but learned of Mary Anne's final fate (the lines quoted above) from the Green Berets, whose own version depends as much on imagination as it does on observation. The strangeness does not end there:

> Whenever he told the story, Rat had a tendency to stop now and then, interrupting the flow, inserting little clarifications or bits of analysis and personal opinion. It was a bad habit, Mitchell Sanders said, because all that matters is the raw material, the stuff itself, and you can't clutter it up with your own half-baked commentary. That just breaks the spell. It destroys the magic. What you have to do, Sanders said, is trust your own story. Get the hell out of the way and let it tell itself.
>
> But Rat Kiley couldn't help it. He wanted to bracket the full range of meaning.

Curiously, it is precisely this kind of commentary which O'Brien deleted from *If I Die in a Combat Zone* for its republication in 1979 and that he has said he will remove from *Northern Lights* (1975) should it ever be reissued. In *The Things They Carried*, this and similar passages seem at once intrusive and integral. Even as they serve "to bracket the full range of meaning," the commentaries fail to satisfy; they are explanations which do not explain. They do not so much "bracket" (explore and clarify) meaning as defer it.

This deferral process becomes especially apparent in the sequence of five sections beginning with "Speaking of Courage," whose main character, Norman Bowker, is representative of all the members of Alpha Company in his need to speak and thus to share his burden of guilt and uncertainty. Back home, however, his girlfriend is married, his best friend has drowned, and his father has withdrawn into the world of televised baseball. The only person interested in listening to him is the voice which comes over the intercom at the local A & W drive-in restaurant. Embarrassed, Norman leaves, spending the rest of his ironic Fourth of July driving around and around the lake, telling himself what he would have said to his father, had his father been willing to listen. "Notes" immediately follows, adding a number of biographical details, including his letter to O'Brien and news of his suicide. The suicide in a sense completes, or "brackets," the previous story, which in turn explains Norman's suicide. "Notes" ends, however, with O'Brien claiming that it was he, not Norman, who watched as Kiowa died. "Good Form" puts this autobiographical disclosure in question, as well as the events depicted in the sections which immediately precede ("In the Field") and follow it ("Field Trip"). The reader must proceed—as the narrator-writer does and as the men of Alpha Company did—without the consolation that Hemingway believed his writing could provide in an earlier age of disillusionment, that of "getting things right."

The Things They Carried does not offer the quick fix provided by the Vietnam War Memorial; it offers, instead, the most thorough examination yet to appear of the failure not simply to understand but even to find an appropriate means for depicting what has been insufficiently described as the American experience in Vietnam— that burden of guilt, confusion, and silence carried then, carried still.

Robert A. Morace

Sources for Further Study

Booklist. LXXXVI, March 15, 1990, p. 1395.
Chicago Tribune. March 11, 1990, XIV, p. 5.
Kirkus Reviews. LVIII, February 1, 1990, p. 132.
Library Journal. CXV, February 15, 1990, p. 212.
Los Angeles Times Book Review. April 1, 1990, p. 3.
New Statesman and Society. III, May 18, 1990, p. 38.

The New York Times Book Review. XCV, March 11, 1990, p. 8.
The New Yorker. LXVI, June 4, 1990, p. 102.
Newsweek. CXV, April 2, 1990, p. 57.
Publishers Weekly. CCXXXVII, January 26, 1990, p. 404.
Time. CXXXV, March 19, 1990, p. 84.
The Wall Street Journal. March 23, 1990, p. A13.

THOMAS JEFFERSON
Statesman of Science

Author: Silvio A. Bedini (1917-   )
Publisher: Macmillan (New York). Illustrated. 616 pp. $29.95
Type of work: Scientific biography
Time: 1700-1827
Locale: The United States, France, and England

Thomas Jefferson's lifelong obsession with the sciences is clear from his work as a surveyor, inventor, paleontologist, educator, and designer of scientific instruments, but it was as an American statesman that he made his most significant contributions, by promoting government support of science and by showing how science could support a democratic government

> *Principal personages:*
> THOMAS JEFFERSON, the author of the Declaration of Independence, third president of the United States (1801-1809), and founder of the University of Virginia
> GEORGE WASHINGTON, the Commander in Chief of the Continental Army during the American Revolution and the first president of the United States (1789-1797)
> BENJAMIN FRANKLIN, an American statesman and scientist
> GEORGES LOUIS LECLERC, COMTE DE BUFFON, a French naturalist

At a dinner for American Nobel laureates, President John F. Kennedy remarked that he was with "the most extraordinary collection of talent" ever assembled at the White House, "with the possible exception of when Thomas Jefferson dined alone." This widely circulated anecdote testifies to the reputation of Jefferson as the American Renaissance man par excellence, a reputation that Bedini's book seeks to enhance by calling the attention of scholars to Jefferson's achievements in science and technology. The previous neglect of his scientific contributions may have been the result of his status as an amateur, and it is certainly true that he engaged in science as a pastime rather than as a profession, but he was an amateur in the original French sense of the term: He was a lover and enthusiast of the sciences. Toward the end of his illustrious life he stated: "Science is my passion, politics my duty."

In the past two hundred years Jefferson has stimulated the production of writings notable for their immensity and variety but, surprisingly, the subject that he most loved has been largely ignored. Scholars have extensively analyzed him as a lawyer, architect, politician, and diplomat, but they have only cursorily treated his zealous pursuit of scientific knowledge. This vast literature about Jefferson has been accumulating for so long that even revisionist works have further revisers and reconstructions have their deconstructionists. Because of the many revelations about his private and public lives, the idealized picture of Jefferson as the humanistic revolutionary and statesman has been tarnished. On the other hand, as Silvio A. Bedini's work makes clear, Jefferson did have a genuine talent for science, and Bedini's purpose is to reinstate him as the political father of American science.

Bedini claims that his book is not a biography, but this must be taken with a grain of salt, since his work contains all the biographical trappings, from his chapter on Jefferson's family history through the chapters that chronologically trace the main elements of Jefferson's career to those detailing his retirement and death. It is more accurate to say that Bedini has written a biography that seeks to remedy previous scholars' disregard of Jefferson's important achievements in science.

Jefferson was an enlightened man in an unenlightened world. Reared in a primitive environment, he became attached, mainly through his reading, to the ideals of the European Enlightenment, especially the belief that humanity can achieve progress only by applying scientific knowledge to human artifacts and activities. On his father's plantation, Shadwell, near the Virginian frontier, he absorbed from his sylvan surroundings a deep love of nature. Gradually, science would provide him with a key to the mysteries of this natural world, but because of the immaturity of American civilization, he had to struggle to obtain this knowledge. Despite his isolation from city and culture, he came to believe that science was the way to truth and the basis for democracy. Science could lead to truth because careful observation and experiment were the basic ways that truth could be found. Science was the foundation for democracy because it flourished only in a climate of free inquiry and was consequently an ally of political freedom.

Jefferson's early education in science came from his father, a farmer and surveyor, who satisfied his young son's curiosity about how the natural world and various farm machines worked. His father also taught him how he could bring order to the wilderness through surveying instruments (the provenance of his fascination with scientific devices). Unfortunately, his father, who had helped to shape his son's scientific identity, died, at age fifty, in 1757. Thomas Jefferson, who was only fourteen, found himself the nominal owner of a large plantation with many slaves (he became the legal owner when he turned twenty-one).

Under the guidance of his guardians, who sent him to skilled tutors and teachers, Jefferson acquired facility in Latin and Greek, and in 1760 he began attending the College of William and Mary, the South's only institution of higher learning. There he enjoyed the study of mathematics and obtained his first formal knowledge of science. He was particularly impressed by how the systematic sciences brought understanding to his random knowledge of the natural world. While at this college (which had a staff of six professors and 115 students), Jefferson decided to become a lawyer. Yet the evidence that Bedini presents reveals that Jefferson found his three years of legal studies and seven years of legal practice burdensome and boring. Would not his inquisitive mind have found greater fulfillment in science? Law, it appears, was a practical choice: It would permit him to make a good living in a growing frontier community. Still, this pragmatic rationale is unsatisfying, and Jefferson's choice of vocation remains a mystery. A consequence of his choice quickly becomes obvious: Science would be his obsessive avocation, pursued with great relish.

Jefferson seems to have absorbed great strength from the land, and he loved working it and building on it. He enjoyed experimenting with ways to improve agriculture; he developed ways to make a river near his plantation navigable; and he began the construction of a house—eventually called Monticello—that became an outlet for much of his ingenious inventiveness. Despite his joys in building Monticello, circumstances always seemed to force him to perform other tasks. During the 1770's, for example, his marriage and the movement of the colonies toward independence consumed much of his energy. He understood that revolution was the extraordinary event needed to enable ordinary events to continue on a new level. He became one of the youngest members of the Continental Congress, and while in Philadelphia in 1776, he found himself a member of the committee appointed to compose a declaration of independence. Using a laptop desk of his own design, he agonized for seventeen days in writing the words that two hundred years of American history have made seem inevitable.

According to Bedini, *Notes on the State of Virginia* (1784), written at the request of the French government for information about the new nation, was Jefferson's major scientific accomplishment. From his student days, Jefferson had been making notes about the flora, fauna, climate, and geology of Virginia, and when, toward the end of the Revolutionary War, an opportunity arose for putting his knowledge into published form, he leaped at the chance. He particularly wanted to refute the theories of Georges Louis Leclerc, Comte de Buffon, the French naturalist who had asserted that America's animals were smaller in size and fewer in number than Old World animals. Jefferson had evidence to refute these claims; he also disputed Buffon's contention that New World animals were degenerate forms of Old World animals.

One of the important results of Jefferson's work on *Notes on the State of Virginia* was the growth of his interest in fossils, which he began collecting by himself and through others. He was critical of the widely accepted theory that fossils found in mountains were deposited during the Great Flood described in the Bible. As an Enlightenment rationalist, he found it reasonable to believe that these shells embedded in mountain strata were the consequence of an upheaval of an ancient ocean bed. Yet the most important part of his book is his report of an excavation of an Indian mound. Employing a technique that did not become standard practice until a century later, Jefferson systematically made careful sections of the mound and described in detail the bones and artifacts that he found.

During his years in Europe (1784-1789), Jefferson was able to indulge his passion for collecting scientific books and instruments. He also became fascinated with ballooning, which was then the rage of Paris. More relevant to his political post was his investigation of the work of the French gunsmith Honoré Blanc, who had devised a method of manufacturing musket locks with interchangeable parts. Jefferson tried in vain to convince government officials to institute similar methods of production in the United States. While in France, he finally met Buffon, who tried to convince his American critic that the moose was a degenerate animal. Jefferson, a staunch defender of this behemoth of the New England forests, arranged to have a disemboweled corpse of a New Hampshire moose sent to France. Though badly decayed, it finally arrived in Paris, where it buttressed Jefferson's arguments about its great size and where, once mounted, it amazed the king and members of his court.

Jefferson was in France for two revolutions: the creation of the modern science of chemistry and the foundation of a French republic. Because of his poor understanding of chemistry, he was unable to appreciate the significance of Antoine Lavoisier's activities in science. For example, he objected to Lavoisier's reform of chemical nomenclature because he thought that it was premature, since chemists knew nothing about what was really going on beneath their reactions (for him, chemistry was closer to cooking than to physics). Jefferson and his daughter Maria were in Paris when the Bastille fell and the French Revolution began. Initially sympathetic, like many other Americans, he eventually turned against this revolution because he believed that it had failed.

On his return to the United States at the end of 1789, Jefferson learned that President Washington had chosen him as his secretary of state. Jefferson was able to use his expertise in science in this position by establishing a rational system of weights and measures, by playing a pivotal role in setting up the American patent system, and by his invention of the wheel cipher to encode diplomatic messages. Bedini is especially impressed by this cryptographic device, since the American military was unable to put another like it into service until 1922 (when, ironically, the plans of Jefferson's invention were discovered after a long limbo in a library).

Throughout his political career, Jefferson kept returning to Monticello, where he hoped to live as a self-reliant farmer, but he was never able to maintain his arcadian existence for long, because he was constantly cajoled back into political office (as vice president in 1797 and president in 1801). Even in these powerful positions, he still found time for his scientific pursuits. As vice president, he published a work on a fossil animal that he called *Megalonyx*, or "Great Claw," and today it is known as the *Megalonyx jeffersonii* in his honor. As president, he became interested in a copying device that allowed a person to write, simultaneously, several copies of the same letter (the reluctance of businessmen to replace clerks with a strange machine doomed the device to oblivion).

With his presidential power, Jefferson was able to concretize his ideas about science through political action. For example, he was able to convince Congress to provide a modest appropriation for a mission of exploration through the Western regions of America. Jefferson's expertise in science played a role in readying the expedition for its tasks: He showed Meriwether Lewis and William Clark how to use various scientific instruments to map precisely all the rivers they would encounter, so that a direct and practicable water route across the continent could be found. From Jefferson's point of view, this enterprise was essential for the United States to set up an "empire of liberty" in the spacious lands of the Midwest and West, to ensure that, despite a steadily growing population, a predominantly agricultural society could be sustained. Jefferson's modern critics point out that in obtaining these lands he acted more like an enlightened despot than a democratic statesman; for them, Jefferson's actions represent a highly principled man performing a deeply unprincipled act. On the other hand, Bedini praises Jefferson for setting an important precedent by which government supported science for the first time.

The calamities of Jefferson's second term as president have often been commented on—the Aaron Burr conspiracy, the British impressment of American sailors, the ill-fated embargo of 1807-1809, the devastation of American commercial life, and the violation of civil liberties. Amid such political disasters it is easy to see how such successes as Jefferson's popularization of smallpox vaccinations were forgotten. At the end of his presidency, he felt great relief at leaving his position of power: "Nature intended me for the tranquil pursuits of science, by rendering them my supreme delight."

Despite a massive correspondence and the invasions of numerous visitors, Jefferson found time, during his years of retirement at Monticello, to read Euclid and Sir Isaac Newton and to pursue his interests in scientific instruments. After the British burned the Library of Congress during the War of 1812, he made his personal library of more than six thousand volumes available for purchase by the government, even though it meant a ruinous financial loss for him. He then went on to build up another large personal library. Unfortunately, this and yet another library eventually ended in ashes because of other fires in the institutions where his beloved books had found a resting place.

During his final years, the project that was closest to his heart—the establishment of an institution of higher learning in Virginia—came to fruition. For a long time he had contemplated the foundation of a national university, but such a venture proved to be politically unattainable. The University of Virginia, he happily discovered, was attainable. He became the guiding spirit behind all aspects of the university's creation: He chose the site, laid out the grounds, supervised the construction of the buildings, and determined what would be taught (a curriculum dominated by science and mathematics). In 1825 he saw his dream fulfilled when the first students were enrolled. After his death on July 4, 1826 (on a day he seems to have willed), the gravestone he designed named him the "Father of the University of Virginia."

Jefferson was not a great scientist. His significance in the history of American science consists in his promotion of science during the important formative period of the United States. A disciple of the Enlightenment, he believed that applied science could improve the health and happiness of the citizens of the new republic. Such inventions as his improved moldboard for the wooden plow illustrate the useful purpose he believed mathematics and science should serve. He never achieved the political eminence of Washington or the scientific eminence of Franklin, and his enemies attacked him, the philosopher president, for what they perceived as his indecisiveness. Nevertheless, he did bequeath to succeeding generations important political and scientific achievements. This writer, revolutionary, governor, ambassador, president, and amateur scientist proved to be, in Bedini's characterization, a peerless statesman of science. In this role he helped make science an integral part of the fabric of a great nation.

Robert J. Paradowski

Sources for Further Study

Choice. XXVIII, September, 1990, p. 204.
Scientific American. CCLXIII, October, 1990, p. 130.
The Washington Post Book World. XX, April 22, 1990, p. 17.

THREE RIVAL VERSIONS OF MORAL ENQUIRY
Encyclopaedia, Genealogy, and Tradition

Author: Alasdair MacIntyre (1929-   )
Publisher: University of Notre Dame Press (Notre Dame, Indiana). 241 pp. $24.95
Type of work: Moral philosophy

A historical and philosophical examination of contending traditions of rationality and their implications for debates over moral and political issues

In *Three Rival Versions of Moral Enquiry: Encyclopaedia, Genealogy, and Tradition*, Alasdair MacIntyre continues the line of investigation which he developed in *Whose Justice? Which Rationality?* (1988; see *Magill's Literary Annual*, 1989), exploring the historical roots of the West's inability to arrive at a consensus on the underlying moral principles by which it is going to rule. Current debates over abortion, preferential treatment programs, and the justice of gross inequalities of income are only the most obvious indicators of a breakdown of rational discussion among conflicting positions.

MacIntyre begins his historical analysis with the dominant tradition of moral enquiry in the nineteenth century and its crowning work, the ninth edition of the *Encyclopaedia Britannica*. The thesis which supported this work was that a comprehensive scientific synthesis of all knowledge, moral and theological included, was near at hand. The editors' confidence was based on three assumptions. First, the editors assumed that the history of Western civilization, at least from the Enlightenment onward, exhibited continual progress in moral and intellectual endeavors. On that basis they made a second fundamental assumption, that there was a unified and rationally incontestable scientific understanding of the whole universe. Finally, they assumed that all educated persons who examined the data objectively would assent to this soon to be finalized view of the universe, and hence, there would be a single substantive conception of rationality, namely, assent to the truths contained in their encyclopaedia.

MacIntyre does not share the rather complacent assumptions of these nineteenth century editors. The breakdown in moral arguments so characteristic of the late twentieth century clearly refutes the encyclopaedists' optimism. The eleventh edition of the *Britannica* acknowledges as much in its preface. The assumption of the current editors is that their encyclopaedia embodies no more than "faith in the unity of knowledge," and as MacIntyre says, that faith "increasingly flies in the face of contemporary realities."

And what are those contemporary realities? The interminable and increasingly acrimonious debate over fundamental moral and political issues is only the surface manifestation of a more fundamental problem. The deeper issue concerns the very notion of rationality. Even as the encyclopaedists were putting what they thought would be the finishing touches on their project, a disgruntled German professor, Friedrich Nietzsche, resigned his chair of philology and began to cry that the encyclopaedists' alleged objectivity was no more than a disguised attempt to sustain their own dominance in their culture. His cry was only faintly heard by his contemporaries, but it has been taken up by twentieth century university professors with a persistence which makes it impossible to picture the modern university as a place where knowledge of the True, the Good, and the Beautiful is impartially pursued by all involved.

According to Nietzsche, "truths are illusions which we have forgotten are illusions." His genealogical project was to write the social and psychological history of movements and traditions which pretentiously claimed insight into the truth. After making clear the multiplicity of perspectives and idioms from which truth is viewed, he went on to explain the persistence and pervasiveness of this illusion in terms of unrecognized psychological motivation, especially the will to power by the inferior masses to escape domination by the superior few whose own will to power exhibits an aristocratic nobility.

It was no accident, says MacIntyre, that Nietzsche gave up his academic position. His very mode of argument was alien to the encyclopaedists who dominated the nineteenth century university. The inability of Nietzsche's academic peers to understand his work illustrates one of MacIntrye's major themes, namely, the incommensurability of rival traditions. Nietzsche's peers could not, or would not, expend the time and effort necessary to understand him on his own terms. Instead, they read him with only enough understanding to be able to translate his theses and arguments into their terms. To be sure, his peers thought they were translating Nietzsche into a neutral idiom, a sort of metalanguage which impartially and objectively mirrored reality. The fact that this is what those in the encyclopaedist tradition thought they were doing is strong evidence that they did not understand Nietzsche. If they had understood him, they would have seen that they simply begged the question. After all, at the heart of Nietzsche's project was the contention that there is no impartial metalanguage which speaks the truth and nothing but the truth. On this point at least, MacIntyre sides with Nietzsche against the encyclopaedists.

Clearly the encyclopaedists and the genealogists hold opposing views of what constitutes rationality. The former holds that reason is impersonal, universal, and disinterested. The latter holds that reason is nothing more than the unwitting expression of particular interests hiding behind the mask of an impartial pursuit of the truth. MacIntyre's contention is that there is a third alternative, one which outside Catholic circles was only faintly heard in the nineteenth century, but which, according to MacIntyre, is now emerging as superior to the other two in dialectic conflict. This is the synthesis of Aristotelian and Augustinian traditions which was first formulated by Thomas Aquinas in the thirteenth century, misunderstood by his few followers during the Enlightenment, and finally canonized by Pope Leo XIII in his encyclical letter, *Aeterni Patris* (1879; *Scholastic Philosophy*, 1879).

In the Thomistic tradition, reason is understood as neither the disinterested pursuit of truth nor the self-interested pursuit of power. Instead, rationality is understood as the willingness to make one's most deeply and strongly held moral and theological beliefs vulnerable to dialectic refutation. Truth is in turn understood as the limit toward which we can move if we are willing to be rational. The Thomist thus agrees with the genealogist that there is no impartial and neutral starting point from which to begin moral enquiry. In fact, the Thomist argues that prior moral commitment to a community of enquirers and a willingness to submit one's un-tutored judgment to its authority on fundamental moral and theological issues is a necessary precondition of fruitful enquiry in these matters. While this previous com-mitment is at first arbitrary, it need not, as the genealogist maintains, remain an arbitrary commitment, and it does not remain such so long as one is willing to make oneself vulnerable to dialectic refutation. In short, good moral reasoning presup-poses moral virtue, and moral virtue requires good moral reasoning.

MacIntyre acknowledges the circularity of the above position but argues that it is no different from that found in Plato's *Meno* (388-366 B.C.)—the search for truth presupposes that one, in some sense, already knows the truth, otherwise one could not recognize truth when it was discovered. Furthermore, he argues that, like Socra-tes, the Thomistic tradition is able to break the circle.

How exactly is this accomplished? Following Plato and Aristotle, the Thomistic tradition likens philosophy, both theoretical and moral, to a craft. In teaching a craft a master can only work with apprentices who come to him with a talent waiting to be developed. Similarly, the Doctor of Philosophy can only work with students who come to him with a potential that allows them to follow their initial theoretical and moral reasoning. Second, the apprentice, in placing himself under the tutelage of a master, implicitly acknowledges the authority of the master. When the master says, "You attach the leg of the chair like this," the apprentice does not retort, "But I think it would be better to do it like this," or at least, not in the beginning. Similar authority is assumed in the student/teacher relationship.

Finally, while both the master craftsman and the Doctor of Philosophy are au-thorities from whom to learn, their authority is not self-assumed; rather, it is con-ferred upon them by the community in which they are working. The community in which the master carpenter works sets the goal for his work—in this case, sturdy, functional, and attractive chairs. The master's authority is the result of his histor-ically demonstrated ability to produce chairs which meet the given standards of the community. As noted above, the apprentice does not initially question the authority of his master, but as the apprentice demonstrates his ability in little matters, there comes a time when the master says, "Try attaching the legs your way." Now there is no way to know in advance if the apprentice's new technique will work. Given the standards set by the community, however, retrospectively it will be clear if the ap-prentice's technique moved the craft nearer or farther from the community's own ideal of what a chair should be.

The analogy with philosophy and moral enquiry is clear in Augustine's case. His life as a Christian began as a novice under the instruction of others, but in time it became clear that Augustine was able to elucidate the Scriptures and resolve appar-ent difficulties in a way which retrospectively was understood by the Christian com-munity to have moved them nearer to their own ideal of what it meant to understand

God's revelation. It was only then that Augustine's teaching became authoritative for those in the Christian tradition.

At this point, an obvious difficulty arises for the Augustinian tradition, at least, insofar as it claims rational superiority to other traditions. If Augustine's work is in effect judged solely by the standards of his own community, how can his tradition pretend to be rationally superior to the Aristotelian traditions? MacIntyre's response is that it can rightfully make the claim of rational superiority only because it is willing to make itself maximally vulnerable to refutation by submitting itself to examination from other traditions. Admittedly, the other traditions are not allowed to judge the Augustinian tradition by their standards of rationality, but this does not guarantee that the Augustinian tradition would win the debate. First, within all living traditions there is an internally defined set of unsolved problems. Second, all traditions which make claims to rational superiority are committed to the negative thesis that no other systematic account of the world can sustain its own position.

Even if Augustinians are willing to make their position dialectically vulnerable to refutation, the question remains, "Who makes the judgment as to the winner of the debate?" There are three logically possible answers. First, there is the answer of the encyclopaedist—we could leave the judgment to a neutral third party. According to both MacIntyre and the genealogists, however, there are no neutral third parties when it is a systematic account of the whole of reality and rationality itself that is at issue. Second, there is the answer of the genealogist—we could let the Augustinian make the judgment for the Aristotelian and vice versa, in which case the discussion will soon degenerate to a mere test of wills. MacIntyre finds this solution overly pessimistic. The third possibility, and the one MacIntyre favors, is that we allow each side to judge the relative merits of their own case.

MacIntyre understands well the difficulties with such a conception of rationality, but he argues that these difficulties are no greater than those involved in the other two options. Furthermore, historical investigation demonstrates that traditions which make themselves vulnerable to dialectic refutation, contrary to what one might first believe, do in fact willingly acknowledge the rational superiority, either in whole or part, of other traditions. His prime example is the debate which took place at the University of Paris in the twelfth and thirteenth centuries between followers of Augustine and followers of Aristotle. It became evident to both Aristotelians and Augustinians that only by incorporating elements of the other could either side continue their own research project. This grand synthesis of two seemingly incommensurable traditions was the work of Thomas Aquinas, and it won for him the title of Angelic Doctor.

Third, and most important, the obvious problem of allowing traditions to be the judge in their own case makes clear the inextricable linkage between theoretical enquiry concerning the nature of rationality and moral enquiry. At two crucial points, the Thomistic tradition requires that humility be taught as a virtue. We have already seen that a student working in the Thomistic tradition must humbly submit herself to the authority of a master. We can now add that she must have the humility necessary to acknowledge willingly the superiority of her foe's position when bested in dialectic argument. Without such humility the debate will soon degenerate into a test of wills, just as the genealogists predicted.

It would appear that we have reached an impasse. After all, the genealogist will never admit that humility is a virtue. Consider the section headings of Nietzsche's *Ecce Homo* (1908; English translation, 1911): "Why I am so wise. Why I am so intelligent. Why I write such good books. Why I am a destiny." How then can we proceed, given MacIntyre's fundamental thesis that each tradition must be judged in its own terms and by its own standards? MacIntyre does so by asking the genealogist about the nature of this "I" which is so wise, intelligent, and good. Clearly there is something of a self-congratulatory nature in the genealogist's works. Yet it is also clear, according to the genealogist's own arguments, that all narratives and texts ultimately flow from a historically conditioned and contingent perspective. Even the genealogists' own works, Michel Foucault has asserted, are nothing more than the perspectives of one wearing a particular mask which is to be discarded at will. It is this claim, MacIntyre argues, which creates an insuperable problem for the genealogists. All their works, he says, are

> of avowed achievement, achievements not of the masks but of their wearer. All such genealogical utterance contains a strain of what is not quite boastfulness because it rests upon a rejection of any table of the virtues in which humility is accounted a virtue. But the achievement of the narrator behind the masks in the continuity of this rejection requires a stable and continuing referent for the 'I'—the 'I', for example, of the section headings of Nietzsche's *Ecce Homo*.

Thus, by its own standards, and in its own terms, the genealogist's project can be shown to be incoherent.

Ric Machuga

Sources for Further Study

Library Journal. CXV, May 1, 1990, p. 90.
New Statesman and Society. III, August 17, 1990, p. 37.
The New York Times Book Review. XCV, August 12, 1990, p. 14.

TO *HERLAND* AND BEYOND
The Life and Work of Charlotte Perkins Gilman

Author: Ann J. Lane (1931-   )
Publisher: Pantheon Books (New York). Illustrated. 413 pp. $19.95
Type of work: Literary biography
Time: 1860-1935
Locale: New England, New York, and California

Describes the cultural, social, and political contexts that shaped the life and work of the feminist writer, lecturer, journalist, and social critic

> *Principal personages:*
> CHARLOTTE PERKINS GILMAN, a feminist, writer, and lecturer
> WALTER STETSON, her first husband
> SILAS WEIR MITCHELL, her neurologist and the model for the physician/ husband in "The Yellow Wall-Paper" (1892)
> HOUGHTON "HO" GILMAN, her second husband
> KATHARINE CHAMBERLIN, her daughter

The subtitle of this biography of Charlotte Perkins Gilman reflects Ann J. Lane's twin focus on the life and work of her subject, but Lane's approach is hardly conventional. From her perspective, Gilman's life is also a "work," a product "created," consciously and unconsciously (for Lane is Freudian in her reading of Gilman's life and art), by an early feminist. Moreover, Lane does not narrowly define Gilman's "work" as literary, though she was a prolific writer, but as the total contribution of a woman whose life and work were one. Lane departs from biographical norms in her style; rather than simply relating Gilman's life, she forces her readers to participate in what she calls "dialogues" between the author and the subject, between the subject's life and the subject's work—usually glossed with biographical data—and between the reader and the biographer, who periodically queries or "chats" with her audience. In fact, while many of her beliefs about Gilman are implicit, Lane does raise questions (such as the nature of her subject's sexuality) without attempting to resolve them.

Primarily because Gilman's life and work were so intertwined, Lane wisely rejects a strict chronological approach that would involve rapid switching from one focus to another. Instead, she uses a biographical account of Gilman's life until 1900, when Gilman was married to her first cousin, Houghton "Ho" Gilman. Lane then devotes two chapters to "Work" (Gilman's journals, books, and lectures), and then resumes the biographical narrative with chapters on Gilman and her daughter, Katharine. Though Lane's title implies that she regards *Herland* (serialized in 1915) as the pivotal point in Gilman's career, the turning point actually occurred in 1900, when Gilman succeeded in resolving the domestic and familial problems that plagued her early life.

Lane has structured her biography "around the central relationships in Charlotte Gilman's life," those with her parents, three intimate women friends, two husbands,

the neurologist who treated her, and her daughter. Rather than being separate relationships, they reflect recurrent psychological and behavioral patterns in Gilman's
life. Lane seems particularly intent on stressing how her parents' individual be-
haviors shaped not only her own parenting behavior, but also her relationships with
her husbands, doctor, and women friends, as well as her work habits.

The primary influence on Gilman's life, according to Lane, was her father, Frederick Beecher Perkins, whom Lane describes as "talented but undisciplined, erratic,
and unfocused." Despite her father's ties to the famous Beecher family, he had little
money and provided little stability for his own family, which he regularly deposited
with various relatives: Charlotte, her brother, and her mother moved nineteen times
in eighteen years. After Charlotte's birth, her father left the family, perhaps because
the attending physician said that the birth of another child might cause the mother's
death. From that point on, Gilman had little contact with her father, whom she
depicts as an occasional visitor. Lane's analysis of Fredrick Perkins' short stories
stresses his contradictory views of home and family, views with which Gilman herself contended throughout her life; but the similarity between daughter and father is,
for Lane, more extensive: Gilman also "abandoned" her daughter to her spouse, and
both father and daughter were more comfortable dealing with their personal problems at a distance, whether in letters, books, or in thinly veiled fiction.

Perhaps because of her tenuous relationship with her father, Gilman's fictional
fathers are usually, according to Lane, "explosive, tyrannical, self-centered, suffocating, arrogant, and unloving." Those characters modeled on her mother, Mary
Perkins, were similarly treated with contempt. Both parents were distant, emotionally stunted people, who were unable to communicate affection. Perhaps because of
her emotionally isolated situation—her mother refused to allow her to have intimate
friends—Gilman escaped into imaginative literature. Lane's psychoanalytic reading
of Gilman's early fictional fairy tales reveals Gilman's methods of "coping with
despair, danger, sexuality, and separation" and "establishing a world of hope and
success with the support of a powerful woman who befriends her." In a sense, the
fairy tales explain her mother's failure and her later attachments to women friends.
The options for the adolescent Gilman were unappealing: Her mother's restrictive
private world of women or her father's irresponsible public world of men. Mary Perkins was the easier parent to defy, and Lane supports Gilman's notion that her confrontation (at the age of fifteen) with her mother "opened up an entire new world"
to her.

Before her unsuccessful marriage to Walter Stetson, Gilman became close friends
with Martha Luther, and Lane uses their relationship to introduce and discuss nineteenth century love relationships between women, relationships that were to play an
important part in Gilman's life. In her autobiography, Gilman recognized the ambiguous nature of the relationship and denied that it had any "Freudian taint"; Lane,
however, seems unwilling to accept her subject's words on the matter.

Though Walter Stetson fathered Gilman's only child, his importance is confined
to rearing Katharine and to serving as an unsatisfying model for a feminist's hus-

band. In a sense, Walter symbolizes the well-intentioned nineteenth century husband who sees his wife not as an individual but as a type, and, in this case, one to be worshiped. Lane believes that "Walter's conventional ideas about pure womanhood" prompted him to ignore Charlotte's explicit comments about rejecting the traditional domestic role. After Katharine's birth, Gilman became depressed and only improved when she was "outside the domestic sphere." As wife and mother, she was constantly fatigued and unable to care for herself or her child. After a short visit to California without her family, she rallied; yet upon her return to domestic duties, she again suffered from hysteria, incompetence, and paralysis.

At this crucial point in her life Gilman was treated for neurasthenia by noted neurologist Silas Weir Mitchell, whose own childhood accounts for his "moral medication." The treatment, "enforced rest, enforced passivity, acceptance of the commands of male authority," was essentially "an extreme version of the cultural norms that operated outside his sanitarium." It was, in short, the process of infantilization for women and was exactly the wrong treatment for Gilman. In her story "The Yellow Wall-Paper," which Lane sees as Gilman's only genuinely literary work untouched by ideology, Gilman presents a fictionalized account of her rebellion against her husband and doctor, who represent the foundations of patriarchal society. When she discusses the culture that produced Gilman's "sickness" and analyzes the short story, Lane provides her reader with an invaluable dissection of male/female relationships in nineteenth century America.

After leaving Mitchell's care, Gilman moved to California, where she eventually was divorced from Walter. Walter was subsequently married to Grace Channing, Gilman's second close female friend. Like her father, Gilman abandoned her child to her spouse, though she remained friends with Walter and Grace. In fact, Lane examines the relationship between Gilman and Grace in some detail and concludes that "it was possible for Charlotte to have unrecognized sexual feelings for Grace and feel free to express them without fully realizing their erotic nature." Lane is more explicit about Gilman's relationship with Adeline Knapp, who succeeded Grace in Gilman's affections: "It is possible, but not certain, that Charlotte and Delle were lovers." Freed of domestic cares, Gilman began to lecture and to write extensively, but her relationship with the domineering Adeline began to deteriorate. Lane suggests that the end of their alliance completed Gilman's self-actualization: "Just as Charlotte had earlier taken on her father in the person of Silas Weir Mitchell, so now, perhaps, she faced her mother through Adeline Knapp."

Similarly, Gilman "took on" her failed marriage to Walter through her marriage to her younger first cousin Houghton, who seems not to have shared Walter's conventional ideas about women and marriage and who did understand Gilman's dictates about the life she was determined to lead. Lane discusses Gilman's "ambivalence," more feigned than real, about having another child, her insistence on separate bedrooms, though with visitation privileges, and her refusal to accept domestic "duties." Lane's thesis about Gilman reconciling the two sides of herself—her mother's insularity and her father's reaching out to the real world—through her marriage to

Houghton seems a bit forced, since it rests on Gilman's power over her younger, somewhat dependent, and passive spouse.

During her engagement and marriage to Houghton, Gilman was free to pursue her public career; in chapters 9 and 10, Lane summarizes her subject's lecturing, journalism, and nonfiction work and analyzes her realistic and utopian fiction. Readers familiar with Gilman know her primarily through her popular feminist short story "The Yellow Wall-Paper" and her novel *Herland*. Lane effectively establishes Gilman as an internationally recognized major theorist and social commentator of the early twentieth century. Almost all of Gilman's work is of a piece, partly because she worked through her ideas in her lectures, then reworked the ideas in her journal articles, and finally published them in book form. Charles Darwin, Thorstein Veblen, and Edward Bellamy were significant influences on her work; her theories about work and gender were also related to Lester Ward's Gynaecentric Theory and to contemporary architectural ideas. Gilman emerges not as an original thinker but a synthetic one, whose own eclectic ideas are built on the blocks of other theorists.

After summarizing the theses in Gilman's first three influential books—*Women and Economics* (1898), *Concerning Children* (1900), and *The Home* (1903)—Lane analyzes Gilman's realistic and utopian literature, which she finds thesis-ridden and propagandistic. For Lane, the fiction significantly focuses on mother-daughter relationships, reflecting the recurrent problem between Gilman and both her mother and her daughter. Even in *Herland*, which depicts a world without men, Gilman does not discuss, according to Lane, woman-to-woman friendships.

After discussing Gilman's work, Lane returns to Gilman herself, whose popularity declined after World War I, despite her own promotional efforts and her unflagging energy. After Houghton's death in 1934, Gilman returned to California and lived with her daughter. Despite having breast cancer, Gilman continued her work, especially lecturing and writing her autobiography, until she committed suicide on August 17, 1935.

Lane considers Gilman's autobiography, *The Living of Charlotte Perkins Gilman* (1935), "in many ways her mask," containing much "self-deception" and "purposeful misleading." For Lane, this book "does not have the author's heart in it," presumably because it was written when its author was in her seventies. Lane is not consistent, however, in evaluating an elderly person's memories, for she is much less skeptical about the disclosures made by the ninety-three-year-old Katharine, whom Lane interviewed in a nursing home in 1978. Katharine's comments serve Lane's theses and reinforce the patterns Lane creates; Gilman's often do not.

Lane's reservations about Gilman's autobiography also apply to her own biography of Gilman. Gilman accumulated a large amount of material; she wrote countless letters, most of which seem to have been saved, and wrote every word of *Forerunner*, a journal she published from 1909 to 1916. Given the sheer volume of documentation, Lane can hardly be criticized for imposing ordering patterns upon Gilman's work; those patterns, however, result in a Charlotte Perkins Gilman who is Lane's creation. Nowhere is this more obvious than in Lane's treatment of Gilman's sexuality. In spite of Gilman's often stated commitment to heterosexual monogamy, Lane consistently implies Gilman's lesbianism and even suggests that Gilman's insistence on heterosexuality "inevitably arouses one's suspicions."

Although her interpretation of Gilman may not be definitive, Lane has given her readers an engaging, thorough biography of an early feminist, whose reputation rests on a fraction of her work and life. Drawing heavily on primary sources, especially Gilman's letters, Lane provides an intimate reading of her subject, placing her within the political, social, economic, and intellectual context of her times.

Thomas L. Erskine

Sources for Further Study

Booklist. LXXXVI, March 15, 1990, p. 1412.
Choice. XXVIII, October, 1990, p. 308.
Kirkus Reviews. LVIII, March 15, 1990, p. 403.
The New York Times Book Review. XCV, July 15, 1990, p. 10.
The New Yorker. LXVI, June 4, 1990, p. 104.
Publishers Weekly. CCXXXVII, February 23, 1990, p. 208.
San Francisco Chronicle. April 29, 1990, p. REV7.
The Washington Post Book World. XX, April 22, 1990, p. 8.

THE TRANSPARENT MAN

Author: Anthony Hecht (1923-   )
Publisher: Alfred A. Knopf (New York). 75 pp. $18.95
Type of work: Poetry

A Pulitzer Prize-winning poet continues to expand and refine the range of his subjects and the poise of his craft

For thirty-five years Anthony Hecht has been writing and publishing poems of impeccable grace without sacrificing an iota of honest observation. Indeed with the years it has become quite clear that the real purpose of the high polish of his phrasing, meter, and verbal wit is to make bearable the harsh grain of human experience to his poet's touch. Quite possibly his formalism has enabled him to look more directly into the eye of the modern storm than many of his peers who have relied on the expressive intensity of free verse to rise to what they saw as the demands of modern life. If Robert Lowell and John Berryman departed from formalism and embraced free verse to do justice to the storms raging within them, Anthony Hecht has stiffened his resolve, sharpened his wit, and perfected his meters to ride out the storm all around us.

As in *The Venetian Vespers* (1979; see *Magill's Literary Annual*, 1980), Hecht intersperses longer narrative poems with translations, meditations, and elegies. In the former work two narratives, "The Short End" and "The Venetian Vespers," dominate the collection. This time Hecht's shorter pieces are as impressive as the longer ones, and the reader has difficulty finding a platform from which to view the splendid terrain with a clear sense of its range and meaning. Nevertheless, there is no doubt that this is a collection with a distinct point of view. Its title is taken from a monologue very near the end of the collection, in which a patient dying of leukemia assures his silent visitor, a Mr. Curtis (pun for courtesy?), that all is well despite the fact that chemotherapy has caused the speaker to lose her hair and made it difficult for her to "read through any of your books these days." Instead she has been studying the trees outside her window:

> One by one,
> They stand there like magnificent enlargements
> Of the vascular system of the human brain.
> I see them there like huge discarnate minds,
> Lost in their meditative silences.
> The trunks, branches and twigs compose the vessels
> That feed and nourish vast immortal thoughts.

She assigns various trees the brains of great minds: "Beethoven . . . and Kepler." It all brings to mind a "birthday toy" called "The Transparent Man" that she and a childhood friend loved to play with: "It was made of plastic, with different colored organs,/ And the circulatory system all mapped out/ In rivers of red and blue."

Just as the dying patient remains perplexed by "the tousled snarl of intersecting limbs" beckoning from the woods beyond the trees closest to her window, Hecht lets us know his problem in hers:

> If there is order in all that anarchy
> Of granite mezzotint, that wilderness,
> It takes a better eye than mine to see it.
> It set me on to wondering how to deal
> With such a thickness of particulars

In other words, Anthony Hecht's poetic vision in this collection is dedicated to the discovery of those rivers of being that rush through man and nature. Reality must yield to the poet's power and become, even if only fleetingly, "transparent."

In the first section of this volume Hecht looks through several sheets of glass. First comes childhood: a haunting image of children up at winter's dawn, their faces glued to the window of a school bus in a network of images that recall Ezra Pound's famous "In a Station of the Metro" ("The apparition of these faces in the crowd;/ Petals on a wet, black bough"):

> And are themselves the ghosts, file cabinet gray,
> Of some departed us,
> Signing our lives away
> On ferned and parslied windows of a bus.

The dying woman's trees in "The Transparent Man" have yielded to the intricate leaflike patterns ("ferned and parslied") of the frost to which schoolchildren are pressing their faces. Transparencies of youth and age reveal the same challenge: "a thickness of particulars." Hecht continues in this opening section with awe and bemused awareness to look through the meaning of the sea's surface ("Water is touched with a light case of hives/ Or wandering gooseflesh"); the vanity of longevity in a translation from Oedipus at Colonos; the universality of the painter's subject ("I am enamored of the pale chalk dust/ Of the moth's wing, and the dark moldering gold/ Of rust"); and in a strange little story of a perpetually exploited man, the timeless and comic spectacle of the cuckold. To look through things does not necessarily mean to understand them.

"See Naples and Die" is the ironic title of the long narrative poem that constitutes the entirety of the second section of the collection. The poem records the breakup of a marriage, but its real subject is the transparence of happiness *and* despair and the eerie way the former can yield to the latter; happiness is less a vanity than it is an illusion. The subtlety of this distinction is realized with brilliant allusions to the art, history, and aura of Naples and its bay. These observations reach their climax in a tour of the Elysian Fields, which turn out to be "a vacant wilderness of weeds . . . acres of desolation." But most stunning of all is the way this long meditation comes to closure. Hecht uses his classical learning to enlarge feelings of emptiness and despair until they spill over into vision. The poem's speaker, the husband who has drifted away from his wife, imagines the Elder Pliny standing at the same spot and carefully observing the terrifying eruption of Vesuvius:

> Of all those strange sights the most ominous
> Was perhaps the sudden vision of the sea
> Sucked out and drained away by the earthquake
> That was part of the eruption, leaving a sea-bed
> Of naked horrors lighted now and then
> By jets of fire and sheet-lightning flares,
> Only to be folded back into the dark.
> One could make out in such brief intervals . . .
> Giant sea-worms bright with glittering slime,
> Crabs limping in their rheumatoid pavane.

After luxuriating throughout most of the poem in images of Naple's beauty—very much in the spirit of Percy Bysshe Shelley's Italian rhapsodies—Hecht ends with a clear allusion to T. S. Eliot's refrain in "The Love Song of J. Alfred Prufrock": "I should have been a pair of ragged claws/ Scuttling across the floors of silent seas."

The melancholy speaker of "See Naples and Die" is followed in the third section of the volume by the witty musical tones of "A Love For Four Voices." Each voice is one of four musical instruments. Together, in "Hommage to Franz Joseph Haydn," they orchestrate a masque of love, an impudent and humorous entertainment, introduced by the "First Violin" (Hermia), who announces "Here we have fallen transposingly in love." She is encouraged by the "Second Violin" (Lysander), who feels "the fickle fingering" and must "confess/ It's already getting late. "Second Violin" (Helena), astonished by the power of love, answers in counterpoint with brazenly contemporary diction and rhythms:

> In an inventory of post-Freudian sex
> Called "Civilization and its Discotheques."
>   In a lingua franca phrase
> Of body language at last you've understood
>   What gauds and gilds your days.

It is now left to the "Cello" (Demetrius) to drown them all in the mellow lubricity of his self-regard:

> I am Narcissus, she simply the pool,
> Obliging, selfless, bright, wherein I see
> Intoxicating images of Me,
> Classical, isolate, withdrawn and cool.

Rarely have poetry and music interpenetrated as successfully. What Hecht does here is really beyond paraphrase. Poetry becomes music in a kind of mimicry that outsmarts itself and achieves the sublime.

Sections 4 and 5 are devoted largely to humor and elegy. The connecting theme here is personalized memory. The humor is centered on the comedy of naming, the irony of concretion; the elegies are grounded in the obscure and trivial detail of precious and irreducible moments of loving recollection.

We have come full circle to "The Transparent Man." A palimpsest for history, music, the divine power of naming—to see through a human being is to see into these things. What stands out in Anthony Hecht's poems is his recovery of characterization—what fiction had once claimed as its forte but gave up for allegory, fantasy, and minimalism. Hecht's monologues give us back Robert Browning's *Men and Women* (1855, 2 volumes). It is curious that a poet so richly identified with the decorum of polished meter and traditional form should be one of our most important sources of the realistic portrayal of human identity.

Peter Brier

Sources for Further Study

Atlanta Journal Constitution. August 19, 1990, p. N8.
Booklist. LXXXVI, May 15, 1990, p. 1773.
Library Journal. CXV, June 15, 1990, p. 115.
The New Leader. LXXIII, October 1, 1990, p. 19.
The New York Times Book Review. XCV, July 22, 1990, p. 26.
Poetry. CLVII, October, 1990, p. 34.
The Southern Review. XXVII, Winter, 1991, p. 235.
The Washington Post Book World. XX, July 8, 1990, p. 1.
Washington Times. August 20, 1990, p. F1.

TRIPHAMMER

Author: Dan McCall (1940-   )
Publisher: Atlantic Monthly Press (New York) 237 pp. $18.95
Type of work: Novel
Time: The late 1980's
Locale: Ithaca, New York

A present-tense narrative spanning several months in the life of an alcoholic, middle-aged policeman

> *Principal characters:*
> OLIVER "TRIPHAMMER" BODLEY, a policeman
> DICK BODLEY, his seventeen-year-old son
> SYDNEY, a college professor who falls in love with Triphammer

With *Triphammer*, Dan McCall returns to territory covered more routinely in an earlier novel, *Bluebird Canyon* (1983), and reintroduces a character from that work. The character's nickname gives the reader of this eponymous novel an immediate clue to the type of story about to unfold: gritty, minimalist, hard-edged.

The opening chapter leaves no doubts. Triphammer, a veteran middle-aged cop in Ithaca, New York, receives a call from a local attorney distraught over his missing twelve-year-old son. Triphammer immediately begins to worry about the case even though police procedure requires a twenty-four-hour wait before filing a missing-person report. In the morning, a patrol officer tells him that a body has been found at the bottom of Buttermilk Falls, and Triphammer reveals his inability to distance himself from a case: "When we get out on the bridge and look over the side, my heart skips a beat." Triphammer suffers from the same lack of detachment, the same emotional identification with all victims, that defines the "heroes" of most modern police procedurals. Yet he is no stereotype, and McCall's novel is no lengthy cliché. It is precisely because of the protagonist, eloquent in his misery, and McCall's skillful characterizations that *Triphammer* is memorable and original. Otherwise the thin plot and, at first glance, contrived love story would render the novel ordinary.

The child in the opening chapter is indeed dead, and a less gifted writer might well have left the story there. McCall's purpose, however, is to allow Triphammer to explain his virtues and failings as a policeman. He muddles painfully through the scene in which he has to explain to the family that the boy is dead. It is an excruciating experience, both for the reader and for Triphammer, who must return a second time to tell the family that the death was a suicide.

Such is the working life of an undistinguished but good cop in Ithaca, New York, a city that in its gray ordinariness provides the perfect locale for the crimes of murder, child abuse, and domestic violence with which Triphammer must contend daily. The weather offers no solace; it too is a symbolic backdrop for Triphammer's bleak views: "When it gets as cold as this, it reminds you of death, the trees barren, their skeleton arms all frantic in the wind. The whole wide world itself seems utterly hopeless and forbidding."

No wonder then that he is an alcoholic. He knows the rules; he tries to follow them and fails. He explains, "When you're working, you put on a suit of armor. Nothing leaks in and nothing leaks out. Every day you check to make sure all the leaks are stopped up. If you didn't, your emotions would drive you crazy." In fact, Triphammer violates his cardinal rule, "Don't let any of your emotions out," twice in the opening chapters. First he assaults a man suspected of child abuse, then he gets personally involved with an attractive victim of domestic violence.

Sydney, an intelligent graduate student of film history, is the woman who saves Triphammer—the character and the novel—from drifting into unrelieved self-pity. She is his opposite: educated, yet ill-equipped to deal with an abusive relationship; self-confident, yet timorous in the face of a new entanglement. Sydney's moral questions are complicated by the academician's tendency to qualify. Triphammer, who feels inferior to anyone who has finished college, is more direct but equally rigid in his moral concerns: "I try to treat everybody the same, but I realize I have gut feelings, not knowledge." He is ashamed of the way he has treated another woman with whom he has had an affair. She loved him but in a manipulative way, and Triphammer, completely aware of her ruses, still feels guilty: "It always upsets you when you fail to reciprocate strong feelings like that. It puts you in a bind."

It is a measure of McCall's effectiveness that Triphammer's self-descriptions, or his descriptions of others, explain motivation and, ultimately, events without being obvious or heavy-handed. What appears to be direct and simple is actually complicated and anything but straightforward. Sydney gives Triphammer's deadening routine a jolt. He falls gradually in love, and the novelist takes great care in making the subsequent events convincing, "right" for the characters he has created.

"Happily ever after" must await the resolution of a series of problems, all of which could be critical for the relationship. Sex, which for both has been joyous and fulfilling, must be set aside when Triphammer develops a medical condition that requires immediate attention and several weeks of convalescence. It is such an unattractive complaint, an impaction of the intestinal tract—serving both as a plot advancer and as a symbol for Triphammer's blocked life—that it is to Sydney's credit that she is not thoroughly put off the whole affair. It is an unlovely technical device for the novelist but an effective one to make the changes in Triphammer all the more powerful.

Other problems are equally serious, or more so in the case of Triphammer's alcoholism and his relationship with his son, Dick. Leaky to begin with, the armor of professional life is totally inadequate to deal with the exigencies of personal life. Yet the daily routine continues, and no glamorous "case" presents itself to take Triphammer's attention away from Sydney or Dick. Work does not involve Triphammer so much as it inures him. He feels sympathy for the victims, but the paperwork, the boredom, the occasional emergency have only the continuity of routine and none of the satisfaction. Even the death of an elderly, rich widow becomes merely sordid, an ending for a drawn-out series of missed chances to avert tragedy. Triphammer knows his job, however, and though he cannot seem to pass a written examination, this failing is attributable more to disinterest and inertia than to ignorance or inability. Nevertheless, he is not unambitious. When he has a chance to interview for the job of police chief, he becomes anxious to succeed, and his responses to the board betray a commitment to the job that his earlier statements seem to have denied.

Dan McCall, a professor of American studies at Cornell University, has done his homework on police procedures. He never romanticizes what is, after all, a job, and when he allows Triphammer to defend the police, it is a not-so-subtle indictment of those critics who offer no better solutions: "The police are society's arm, not its head. Police do what the society says it wants done." Because the reader admires his protagonist, McCall can "preach" a message to which some might turn a deaf ear. "If you are going to be the garbage man of society, then society should at least pay you a decent wage as a sign that they respect you and need you. Most people could not put up with the stress and aggravation of this job. Policemen are human beings and they give up a lot of their lives to serve their communities. We get very little in return."

Precisely how much Triphammer has given up of his life is illustrated in what is happening to him away from the job. His past haunts him both through memories of his former wife and girlfriends and through his inability to cope with his son's refusal to go to college. Believing that education is salvation from an existence similar to his own, he mishandles his son, not from malice or indifference but from a wrongheaded conviction that the course he sees for the future is the correct one. He also continues to drink.

Sydney, however, sides with Dick in his desire to chart his own course, and without telling Triphammer, they both join associate programs of Alcoholics Anonymous. Resentful at first, Triphammer finally accepts the challenge of their actions and realizes that it is concern for him, and for themselves, that motivates them. He joins AA, and once again what could be an easy solution for the author and his narrator is complicated by Triphammer's dislike of other members of the group and his distaste for the confessional. In fact, his rationale for drinking has been too clear-eyed, too successful an escape for abstinence to appear immediately as a cure-all. Alcohol had allowed this decent, confused man to get at "the assumptions behind everything, to the guiding principles." Take away his alcohol, even though he knows "it's bullshit," and you take away his "way of holding all [his] feelings together," his "kind of oneness" with himself.

As baldly sentimental as it appears, it is Triphammer's love for Sydney and his son that restores the "oneness." He is, in spite of everything, an unrepentant romantic. He believes in the power of education, in the basic goodness of even the most devious person—or at least in a kind of fatalistic neutrality in the face of random evil—and in the redemptive force of old-fashioned, conventions-be-damned love. His armor has been a façade, and when he succumbs wholeheartedly, he may as well discard it altogether. Sydney is his Juliet, and though he is too realistic to see himself as Romeo, he affirms that love, even with Juliet, need not be tragic or selfish: ". . . there's nothing I wouldn't do for her. . . . And how, if I truly love her, can I not want her to have that? I mean, children are the one thing that makes me believe God wasn't a complete fool."

McCall's first-person narrative makes for compelling reading. Triphammer's words are no less reflective and vigorous for being routed through a man who is wise only to the grind of life. The style works as a device to ensnare the reader into what could otherwise be a mundane account of self-help. The use of the present tense, often problematic and self-defeating in promoting immediacy, allows McCall to develop character without limiting it, but it also gives the novel a one-sidedness and self-consciousness that require getting accustomed to. The pleasures of *Triphammer* as writing are in the artful storytelling, where author and narrator are self-effacing enough to make an unremarkable story a memorable one.

William U. Eiland

Sources for Further Study

Booklist. LXXXVI, January 1, 1990, p. 892.
Kirkus Reviews. LVII, November 15, 1989, p. 1623.
Library Journal. CXIV, November 15, 1989, p. 106.
The New York Times Book Review. XCV, February 4, 1990, p. 14.
Publishers Weekly. CCXXXVI, October 27, 1989, p. 57.
The Washington Post Book World. XX, February 4, 1990, p. 10.

UNDER BRIGGFLATTS
A History of Poetry in Great Britain, 1960-1988

Author: Donald Davie (1922-   )
Publisher: University of Chicago Press (Chicago). 261 pp. $17.95
Type of work: Literary history

An analytic history of poetry in the British Isles by an accomplished poet and distinguished literary critic, ostensibly covering the years 1960 to 1988 but actually ranging selectively over the entire twentieth century

Any detailed report from an explorer who is sensitive to and aware of prominent features in the terrain, who is keenly intelligent and eloquent in expression, and who has had considerable experience in the field will be greeted with high expectations, especially when it is a pioneering venture, covering ground previously mostly uncharted. Yet if the explorer is apparently blind to certain prominent features in the landscape, almost repulsed by others, and of a very strong mind about the value of what he examines, the result of his explorations will be a map of an uneven character, vivid and precise in some regions, blurred in others, deceptive or inaccurate in still others. Donald Davie's version of the history of poetry in the British Isles, claiming as its province the three decades from 1960 to the year of its publication, is just such a map, a report loaded with insight and opinion backed up by erudition and a powerful sense of poetic excellence, but also a report directed by Davie's particular tastes. In several previous books he has made them clear enough—they include a favorable estimate of familiar forms, a commitment to the preservation of an unspoiled English countryside, a sense of approval of the self-sufficient values of the shire, and an emphasis on the importance of continuing cultural traditions.

From the perspective of these values, Davie has written "an essay in literary history" that seeks to "commemorate, or keep in memory" both well-known and slighted poets who share and express Davie's concerns, but one that undervalues or ignores a considerable number of poets whom other commentators have seen as masters of poetic art as accomplished and as crucial to the history of British poetry as the ones Davie champions. His book recalls the publication of the Donald Hall/ Robert Pack/Louis Simpson *New Poets of 1957*, an influential anthology featuring poets esteemed by the "New Critics" which was followed three years later by Donald Allen's *The New American Poetry* (1960), a book that offered selections from forty poets with no duplication of the contents of the first book. The retrospect of history has indicated the merits of the work of many people in each anthology, but the schism in sensibility that led to the mutual exclusion by the editors is repeated to an extent by Davie's choices and explanations. This in no way diminishes interest in the book, and, indeed, by choosing a definite point of view, Davie's arguments have the necessary bracing vigor of a man who knows his mind and his field and is confident of the validity of his position. As Davie provocatively puts it, "If this book seems to promote certain British authors as, however modestly, canonical, it is on the understanding that these judgments are disputable and ought to be disputed."

There is no hidden agenda here, only one that is not only disputable but also boldly assertive, and if it is a "history," it will surely draw counterhistories and revisions that will confront all of its major assumptions and nearly every one of its conclusions. As a matter of fact, Robert Richman in *The New Criterion* has already published an attack on Davie from an extreme position beyond the generally conservative stance Davie has taken, an attack from what might be called the American intellectual right wing of the academy that Davie actually joins with this text.

As a matter of organization, Davie divides what he calls his historical "narrative" into "three chapters" (for the three decades under scrutiny) of "one unfolding story," but cautions that there is no "single story-line" so that his book does not become a "polemic." His overarching title, *Under Briggflatts*, is an appropriate recognition of the importance of Basil Bunting, a friend of Ezra Pound whose work was not noticed until the end of his life. While Davie respects Bunting and admires certain aspects of his poetry, however, his praise is almost always qualified ("This suggests that all Bunting's poetry is, for good or ill, a poetry of what Dissenters have always called the 'inner voice'"), and many of the poets working today in the British Isles who owe the most to Bunting's sense of language and rhythm are not among those often praised or even mentioned by Davie. The reason he has chosen Bunting as a figure of consequence, a fixture in the poetic firmament, is revealed by his comment in the third chapter that "*Briggflatts* is most truly seen as, on the grand scale, a monument of . . . modern classicism," and by his observation that "Bunting did have, as every great poet must have, a politics, and a philosophy of history."

Davie shows no reluctance here or elsewhere to express his carefully developed theories about what constitutes poetic excellence, but in the interest of avoiding the impression that he is writing a "polemic," he has introduced his most profound criteria in a gradual fashion throughout the text. In a subtle and possibly more effective method of presentation, he introduces his fundamental precepts amid commentary, criticism, and informative observation, so that he has not fully accounted for his emphasis on a particular poet until the book is concluded, the principles behind the choices becoming clear essentially after the choices have been made. In addition to admiration of Bunting's "modern classicism," his political commitment, and his "philosophy of history," crucial elements in Davie's formulation include a fondness for the pastoral, which leads to his approval of Austin Clarke's only slightly sardonic lament for the disappearance of the horse as "man's workmate" — a real loss for Davie, who believes that "the rhythms beaten out by horses' hooves" are "so insistent that one may indeed wonder whether they are not imprinted on man's nervous system." Tom Gunn is celebrated for using "purely formal means" in defiance of the "vulgar modernism" that has "declared illegitimate" the pentameter, and for having "dug back further than any of his contemporaries . . . to recover that phase of English" that could register "the sleazy and squalid," but also, even more important, "the frankly heroic."

C. H. Sisson is admired for expressing in his poetry a political "allegiance to the nation, and to the Crown as embodying the nation," as well as for his commitment to

Christianity in the manner of John Dryden. Davie also cites with deep approval Sisson's belief that "poetry, like all the arts, is necessarily elitist" and likens Sisson to Thomas Hardy, the ultimate compliment Davie can offer. One of Davie's most ambitious books is his study *Thomas Hardy and British Poetry* (1972), and when he says of Sisson's "Burrington Combe," "The concluding section is exceptionally beautiful and moving, worthy of Thomas Hardy," he is thinking of Sisson (like Hardy) as a "patriot" because of his connection to a "larger identity called 'England,'" a patriotism that is rare and "not to be attained (by intellectuals) except through studious labor." In summarizing his claims for Sisson as a major poet, he is also summarizing his elemental criteria for poetic worth, suggesting that Sisson's rhetoric "depends upon assumptions of continuity between the English of poems, the English of prose, and the English of considered and heartfelt speech." Along these lines, the younger poet Jeremy Hooker is complimented for being "untypically in earnest," while Ted Hughes is noted for being an unalienated poet who is not modern but "Lawrentian," and Michael Hamburger is cited as an "admirable example" of the "modern classicism" Davie found in *Briggflatts*.

In almost every case, there is a historical aspect to the poetry Davie extols. This leads him to devote sections of chapters to Austin Clarke, Jack Clemo, Sylvia Townsend Warner, Ivor Gurney, Edwin Muir, Edward Thomas, and others who completed their work or died decades before the period supposedly covered in the book. In a chapter on the critic Kenneth Cox, Davie stresses the importance of making "contact with poets distant and past," and for Davie, the life of poetry in Great Britain in the decades 1960-1990 is at its most vital when it is in reciprocal interlinkage with centuries of poetry by antique masters. While the centenary of an earlier poet or the first real collection of all of his work is an important literary event, Davie's reliance on these rather contrived occasions strongly directs the attention of the book to a particular kind of poetry at the expense of other possibilities. Some of these possibilities draw a strong antipathy from Davie, who implicitly defends his exclusions by noting what he considers negative influences and trends in the latter half of the twentieth century. Foremost among these are what he calls "consumer-friendly" poems that are a part of a "service industry," and even Seamus Heaney, whom Davie grudgingly admires to an extent, is attacked for being "nimble . . . in manipulating the poetry market and the poetry-reading circuit." This is a mild critique compared to Davie's almost incoherent rage at Louis Zukovsky, who is blamed for an Americanized disregard of sacred "form" and for being a lamentable example of "the wilder shores, or the lunatic fringe, of the American avant-garde."

Going further back, Davie locates the source of many problems with William Carlos Williams, whose "The Red Wheelbarrow" he dismisses as "the little squib (for it is nothing more)," and whom he blames for being a poet who "takes for granted the absence of any agreed hierarchies." This leads to a general calumny directed at popular culture in Great Britain, and a section called "The Gurus" that savages Herbert Marcuse, Norman O. Brown, and Marshall McLuhan for espousing "an unreflecting primitivism." Summarizing in the section called "1968," Davie condemns style based on "costumes and accoutrements" which turned poetry from the serious and significant (likened to a "manufacturing industry") to the frivolous and theatrical (likened to the previously mentioned "service industry"), and he lambastes the modern reader for expecting "heat and feeling" and for not making the effort to meet the poem halfway, "where his own sympathies must go out to meet it."

For Davie, all these manifestations of intellectual decline, literary careerism, and a persistent blindness to history have led to poetry that does not carry the profound weight of "the old eternal England" and is thus a distraction at best, inferior and dismissable (like Stevie Smith, who gets a two-word description, "endearingly eccentric") or not worth noting at all. Thus, while Davie is often enlightening on the poets he admires, even if they range over the entire century rather than the period the book is supposedly examining, he is also responsible for producing a map with some enormous black holes—areas of matter so dense as to exert pressure on everything around them but invisible to the instruments that Davie uses. Where, for example, is Eric Mottram, editor in the 1970's of *Poetry Review*, venue for most of the best poetry of what is known as the British Poetry Renaissance? Poets such as Lee Harwood, Tom Raworth, Ian Hamilton Finley, Gael Turnbull, Ian Sinclair, and Allen Fisher rate no mention at all, as if Davie had not seen the edition of *The New British Poetry* compiled by Mottram and Ken Edwards which includes these poets and many others Davie ignores.

Can it be that Elaine Feinstein is the only woman among all the poets in Great Britain whose work merits discussion? The chapter called "Elaine Feinstein and Women's Poetry" suggests that Davie actually believes that there is something called "women's poetry" which that sex alone produces. Perhaps this misguided inclination accounts for the absence of even such traditional craftswomen as Penelope Shuttle, Ruth Fainlight, and Val Warner, not to mention some of the more radical, postmodern poets such as Kate Ruse-Glason, Wendy Mulford, Denise Riley, and the Irish poet Medbe McGuckian, who is included in the relatively conservative anthology edited by Andrew Motion and Blake Morrison, *The Penguin Book of Contemporary British Poetry* (1983).

The point is not that certain poets are absent, because every student of the era will have particular favorites whom others regard as nonentities (Robert Richman complains about the absence of Craig Raine and Andrew Motion, as befits his ultraconservative bias), but that an entire generation has been systematically excluded. This is hardly an act of ill will on Davie's part, but a consequence of his convictions about what constitutes good poetry, and a result of the company he associates with in the literary cosmos. His seeming lack of awareness of many small-press enterprises in Great Britain, such as Asa Benveniste's Trigram Press, Allen Fisher's Spanner Books, and William David Sherman's Branch Redd series, places emphasis on those figures published by established firms. In a dangerous extension of this insularity, the fact that a poet is not mentioned in this book may contribute to further difficulties in placing work in the future. For an American reader, probably not familiar at all with poets such as Barry MacSweeney, Norman Nicholson (who is briefly mentioned but not discussed as one of the outstanding poets to work in the Lake Country), John Fuller (son of the better-known Roy Fuller), Jeremy Reed, Bill Griffiths, and many others, the omission of lesser-known poets writing in unfamiliar modes seriously distorts what is already an idiosyncratic arrangement. In reality, a diverse grouping of younger British poets has been left out. As Davie indicates in an inadequate afterword, he is not at all comfortable with the whole enterprise roughly covered by the term "postmodern." While this does not detract from the book's virtues, it undermines any claims that the book might have to being a complete history of the period it purports to cover.

Still, *Under Briggflatts: A History of Poetry in Great Britain, 1960-1988* is consistently interesting—even chatty in its many short sections (which the publisher insists are not merely "miscellanies of reviews")—and Davie's inclination to discuss writers from the outer isles such as Sorley Maclean and Norman MacCaig at least acknowledges that England is not the entire universe of British poetry. Even with the strong feelings that Davie possesses about many subjects (royalty, religion, and the like), one can sense a determined effort, if not always a successful one, to be open. With typical grace, Davie also modestly omits any mention of his own poetry, although it is surely an important element of the tradition he believes in. He was also the man who, when head of the literature department at the University of Essex in the early 1960's, hired the gifted American poet Ed Dorn, whose work is closer to that of the American lunatics Davie despises than to that of the poets he praises. It is in this spirit of fairness that his book should be received—a map of a fascinating, complex, and still largely uncharted domain that can contribute to an understanding of the landscape.

Leon Lewis

Sources for Further Study

Chicago Tribune. April 10, 1990, V, p. 3.
Choice. XXVIII, September, 1990, p. 104.
Listener. CXXII, November 2, 1989, p. 34.
The New Criterion. IX, June, 1990, p. 81.
New Statesman and Society. II, October 13, 1989, p. 32.
The Observer. October 22, 1989, p. 49.
The Spectator. CCLXIII, December 16, 1989, p. 33.
The Times Literary Supplement. November 24, 1989, p. 1291.
The Virginia Quarterly Review. LXVI, Summer, 1990, p. 101.

UTOPIAN PESSIMIST
The Life and Thought of Simone Weil

Author: David McLellan
Publisher: Poseidon Press/Simon & Schuster (New York). 316 pp. $22.95
Type of work: Intellectual biography
Time: 1909-1943
Locale: France, New York, and London

A lucid treatment of the biography and ideas of a French teacher of philosophy who evolved from a revolutionary syndicalist into one of the twentieth century's most important Catholic spiritual writers

> *Principal personages:*
> SIMONE WEIL, a teacher, syndicalist organizer, theorist of industrial society, and Roman Catholic mystic
> ALAIN (EMILE CHARTIER), her chief philosophic mentor
> JOSEPH-MARIE PERRIN, a Dominican priest who was influential in directing her migration toward the Church
> SIMONE PETREMENT, her friend and biographer
> BORIS SOUVARINE, the founder of the Democratic Communist Circle, an important figure on the French Left, and a political mentor of Weil
> BERNARD and SELMA WEIL, her parents

David McLellan's excellent study of Simone Weil swells to nearly tidal proportions the wave of contemporary writings about this remarkable woman. In 1987, Robert Coles and Gabriella Fiori both published major interpretations of Weil's life. The year 1988 witnessed Janet Settle's *Simone Weil: Waiting on Truth* and Bernard Saint-Sernin's work on her theory of political action. British philosopher Peter Winch's *Simone Weil: "The Just Balance"* arrived in 1989, as did Mary Dietz's study of Weil's social and political thought. In the same year Lawrence Blum and Victor Seidler published *A Truer Liberty: Simone Weil and Marxism*. Also in 1989 an English translation of Fiori's 1981 intellectual biography became available. This same brief period has seen the publication of more translations of Weil's writings—notably *Formative Writing, 1929-1941* (1987; edited and translated by Dorothy Tuck McFarland and Wilhelmina Van Ness). Van Ness points out that the translation process is still incomplete.

Why this outpouring? Most know part of the answer. At first the odd shape of the biographical story is what draws one. A brilliant Parisian Jewish girl comes of age during the early years of the Depression. From her postings as a philosophy instructor in various *lyceé*, she ventures out to make contact with factory workers, peasants, the unemployed. An anarcho-syndicalist, she gains a reputation as an agitator and revolutionary—"the red virgin." On a journalistic trip to Berlin in 1932 she receives a suitcase of Leon Trotsky's papers and smuggles them into France. Later Trotsky uses her parents' apartment to hold discussions on the founding of a Fourth International. Soon, however, Weil breaks with both syndicalists and Communists, disillusioned by party bureaucracies and the direction of socialism in the Soviet

Union. In 1934, she writes *Oppression et liberté* (1953; *Oppression and Liberty*, 1958), a prescient critique of Marxism suggestive of both Reinhold Niebuhr and C. Wright Mills.

Though physically maladroit and frail, she does factory work for a year in order to experience at first hand the sufferings of the laboring classes. Her diary from this period is later described by Hannah Arendt as "the only book in the huge literature on the labour question which deals with the problem without prejudice and sentimentality." One month after the Spanish Civil War begins, Weil joins an international commando group operating alongside anarchist militia units. She is removed from action after her clumsiness results in serious burns to her left leg. In the spring of 1937, while touring the art treasures of Italy, she undergoes a profound turning of spirit toward Catholic Christianity. An Easter pilgrimage to the Benedictine abbey of Solesmes in northwest France brings her—in the midst of one of her terrible headaches—a moment of transcending lucidity when "the thought of the passion of Christ entered into my being once and for all."

From this point, Weil develops rapidly into a mystical theologian and philosopher. While never submitting to baptism—"nothing gives me more pain than the idea of separating myself from the immense and unfortunate multitude of believers"—she centers her life on the Cross and the sacraments. Her tempestuous debates with Catholic intellectuals are now undertaken from the viewpoint of an insider. At the same time, she continues to write on politics (renouncing pacifism), Greek literature, the nature of mathematical knowledge, Platonism, and the humanization of the industrial workplace. Her Jewish identity requires her to leave Paris for Vichy-ruled Marseilles in 1940. In 1942 she and her parents move first to Morocco and then to New York, but by December she is in London working in the Free French effort. During the four months of her engagement "she produced what amounts to about eight hundred pages of printed material," including the renowned *L'Enracinement* (1949; *The Need for Roots*, 1952). Her various schemes for suicidal missions with the Resistance in occupied France are rejected. The extraordinary physical abuse to which she had subjected herself for a decade now begins to weaken her irremediably. In sympathy with those who are starving in France, she refuses to eat enough to combat tuberculosis. The coroner rules her death in August of 1943 a suicide. For fifteen years her grave bore no inscription and was considered by local inhabitants to be that of a pauper. T. S. Eliot ultimately paid for a simple engraved headstone.

Yet biographical fascination is not what finally sustains interest in Weil. Indeed, one is as often repulsed as attracted by accounts of her life and personality. No hagiographer, McLellan allows the reader abundant glimpses of Weil's arrogance, hyperintellectualism, social awkwardness, and tiresomely dogged manner. Her indifference to niceties of dress and grooming became legendary. Her self-righteousness led to her being described as "the categorical imperative in skirts." Gustave Thibon observed that "the way she mounted guard around her void still paid witness to a terrible preoccupation with herself." Fernand Vidal found in her "something crude, rigid, and intransigent." Trotsky jeered at her for being a "revolutionary melancholic" and observed: "Having fallen into despair over the unsuccessful experiments of the dictatorship of the proletariat, Simone Weil has found solace in a new vocation: the defense of her personality against society." Cruel portraits of Weil exist in novels by Georges Bataille and Simone de Beauvoir.

The lure of Weil lies rather in the reader's suspicion that the enigmas of her thought and behavior point to something new and profound. In her failing, final days she wrote: "I have a sort of growing inner certainty that there is within me a deposit of pure gold which must be handed on." A thorough reading of Weil makes one anxious to seek for that deposit. So breathtaking are her mystical utterances, so stunning her Christocentric "notes," that one is forced to ask whether they link organically to views and positions that otherwise might seem wildly indefensible or crankily heterodox.

"Two prisoners whose cells adjoin communicate with each other by knocking on the wall. The wall is the thing which separates them but is also their means of communication. It is the same with us and God. Every separation is a link." What Christian can resist such images, aphorisms, metaphysics? How can one's *attention*—one of Weil's great philosophic themes—drift from a passage such as this?

> I cannot conceive the necessity for God to love me, when I feel so clearly that even with human beings affection for me can only be a mistake. But I can easily imagine that He loves that perspective of creation which can only be seen from the point where I am. But I act as a screen. I must withdraw so that He may see it.

Yet the very same voice could proclaim that "throughout twenty centuries of Christianity, the Romans and the Hebrews have been admired, read, imitated, both in deed and work; their masterpieces have yielded an appropriate quotation every time anybody had a crime he wanted to justify." Weil devoted her soul to the Church but glibly traced the sectarian spirit of European political parties to the persecuting Church of the Middle Ages. A seasoned political organizer, she nevertheless could not see the value of the church as a social organism with independent power. Nor was her much-discussed anti-Judaism simply a speculative matter. During the war she advised that in France "the existence of such a [Jewish] minority does not represent a good thing; thus the objective must be to bring about its disappearance, and any *modus vivendi* must be a transition toward this objective." McLellan tries to show that Weil seriously wrestled with philosophical pacifism, but the reader cannot help but notice that Weil consistently opted for forceful solutions—especially when she could be involved in them directly.

For all of her "realism" and "pessimism," Weil was a dangerous political romantic, reminiscent of those 1960's radicals who displayed an unquenchable desire for any sort of "action." The Weil who suddenly abandoned pacifism to become an anarchist commando in Spain seems little different from the Weil who, in 1939, devised a scheme to parachute troops and arms into Czechoslovakia. She dreamed of personally leading this effort. Her premature death seems partly explicable by the repeated rejection of her plan for a front-line nurses' corps, which would be exposed to all the hazards of battle. Charles de Gaulle responded to this idea with the words: "Mais elle est folle." From the standpoint of military strategy and prudence, he was right.

There are other sources of discomfort. McLellan works hard to defend Weil from the charge that her Christianity is Gnostic. He shows that while she often pictured the world as alien to the human essence and as ruled by a pitiless blind necessity, "the world was not something to be fled but something to be experienced in all its plenitude, however painful that might be." For Weil, work, art, science, and (especially) mathematics function as bridges to the divine, eliciting an attention that forms the soul in a godly way. Moreover, the Gnostic denial of the human reality of Jesus finds no echo in Weil. Indeed, Weil's entire theological vision rests on the fullness of the incarnation. McLellan wishes therefore to read Weil as primarily a Christian mystic, whose thought merely contains Gnostic elements.

Yet the issue cannot be left there. McLellan skillfully elucidates the Cartesian influence on Weil, but he fails to connect this affinity with the issue of Gnosticism. Yet René Descartes' sundering of the thinking self from the world of extension has strongly Gnostic features; McLellan is thus obligated to show that what is forbidden admittance through the theological entrance of Weil's house does not come in through the philosophical back door. Yet there is plenty of reason to believe that this is exactly what happens.

Both Weil's theology and social thought persistently enshrine the isolated, abstract individual of the Cartesian tradition. Her disgust with party politics parallels her abhorrence of the Catholic church as a flawed, thickly historical institution with its own "party politics." Her overweening interest in the reign of "mechanical necessity" distracted her from the world of the contingent and the particular. One of her teachers observed perceptively that Weil regarded herself as "above history." Weil's refusal to allow herself to be baptized and her distressing numbness toward her own Jewish identity point to a deep underlying commitment to the ahistorical rationalism of the Enlightenment.

Cultivating a curious detachment from all forms of belonging, she displayed an unsettling tendency toward dilettantism even after her conversion. At exactly the time when the Church and the Resistance required all of her energies, she turned to the study of Sanskrit, Buddhism, ancient Egyptian religion, and the classics of Hinduism. Thus, though she claimed to admire the work of Jacques Maritain and other French neo-Thomists, she seems guilty of the very Cartesian "angel-mindedness" that Maritain so roundly critiqued. Speaking of her *Cahiers* (1951-1956; *The Notebooks of Simone Weil*, 1956) and her interpretation of Plato, McLellan says, "The contingent and the historical have no place in this scheme of things: the historicity of the Christian religion and in particular of the Incarnation seem to be eclipsed."

McLellan's careful study may therefore point to new methodologies in Weil scholarship. Instead of looking for the "pure gold" that unifies her life and thought, Weil interpreters should read Weil as significantly—but irreducibly—contradictory. When a thoroughgoing individualist writes passionately of the "need for roots" and con-

nectedness; when a woman of the most daunting independence has nothing whatever to say about the condition of women; when a great theorist of friendship "ab-
hor[s] all physical contact with her fellows"; when a secular Jew becomes one of
this century's most quoted Catholic mystics—then certainly contradiction suggests
itself. Weil's thought developed extremely rapidly in a period of extraordinary upheaval; she died at the age of thirty-four. It cannot be expected that she offers posterity a harmonious vision of social renewal, the Christian faith, or metaphysics.

Rather, her broken, precious spirit and her remarkable textual legacy are gifts to
several contemporary communities. Weil now is the possession of feminists, leftist
radicals, rightist conservatives, syndicalists, French intellectual historians, and Simone Weil societies. In the end, the Church is her proper home and theologians her
rightful company. As Diogenes Allen has observed, however, the theological establishment pays her scant attention. Her presence is most deeply felt among wor-
shipers, as more and more material from Weil's spiritual writing appears in devo-
tional texts. For example, in a 1980's Protestant guide to prayer, eleven selections
from Weil are included—exactly the number as from Saint Teresa of Avila. In the
years just before the fiftieth anniversary of Weil's death, this coincidence takes on
unusual significance.

Leslie E. Gerber

Sources for Further Study

Commonweal. CXVII, September 28, 1990, p. 555.
Los Angeles Times Book Review. April 15, 1990, p. 3.
National Review. XLII, June 25, 1990, p. 49.
The New Republic. CCII, June 18, 1990, p. 40.
New Statesman and Society. III, February 2, 1990, p. 34.
The Observer. February 4, 1990, p. 61.
Publishers Weekly. CCXXXVI, December 15, 1989, p. 51.
The Times Literary Supplement. July 13, 1990, p. 747.
The Virginia Quarterly Review. LXVI, Summer, 1990, p. 93.
The Washington Post Book World. XX, April 8, 1990, p. 6.

VAN GOGH
His Life and His Art

Author: David Sweetman
Publisher: Crown (New York). Illustrated. 391 pp. $30.00
Type of work: Historical biography
Time: c. 1853-1890
Locale: The Netherlands, France, and England

Published on the centenary of van Gogh's death, this superbly written and thoroughly engrossing biography situates this famous and influential painter firmly in the cultural life of the nineteenth century

Principal personages:
VINCENT VAN GOGH, one of the most self-tormented, famous, and influential painters of the modern age
THEODORUS VAN GOGH, his father, a Protestant pastor
ANNA CORNELIA (NÉE CARBENTUS) VAN GOGH, his mother
THEODORUS (THEO) VAN GOGH, the painter's youngest and most intimate sibling, a successful art dealer
VINCENT WILLEM (UNCLE CENT) VAN GOGH, the painter's uncle, an influential art dealer
PAUL GAUGUIN, the famous nineteenth century painter who lived for a short time with Vincent, and was physically attacked by him

According to David Sweetman, gloom and depression are not the primary characteristics found in the paintings of Vincent van Gogh. Nor does Sweetman believe, despite the fact that van Gogh committed suicide, that despair was a dominant element in the artist's thoughts. Sweetman portrays van Gogh as an intense lover of life, growth, change, and renewal. Whatever aberrant behavior or mental disturbances he exhibited resulted from his family's long history of mental illness, epilepsy, and nervous breakdowns or from alcoholism, digitalis poisoning from an excessive consumption of absinthe, syphilis, poor nutrition, long periods of obsessive work, and too much solitude. In other words, by blaming all of the artist's bizarre behavior on heredity, environment, chemicals, or disease, Sweetman seems needlessly intent upon exempting van Gogh the artist from being responsible for what van Gogh the man did. Ultimately, neither Sweetman nor anyone else will be able to explain van Gogh's irrational behavior. Sweetman discusses the famous incident when van Gogh attacked Paul Gauguin with a razor; after being dissuaded from the attack, van Gogh later mutilated himself by slicing off his left ear. Perhaps he was drunk, Sweetman suggests; or perhaps

A classic schizophrenic act?—having failed to harm Gauguin had he then turned his violence on himself? Or was he simply filled with self-loathing at the way he had precipitated the thing he most feared, the alienation of his much needed companion? The explanations multiply. It was later discovered that he was tormented by voices; had these hallucinations begun that night, and had he attempted to silence them by cutting away the offending organ? He always said it was poor circulation which lay at the root of his physical weaknesses; had he sought blood-letting as some sort of remedy?

While all such speculation is endlessly moot, testifying to the extent to which van Gogh shall remain enigmatic, Sweetman succeeds in situating the artist in his society, in re-creating the artist's quotidian existence and artistic development, in explaining how that development progressed in relation to nineteenth century artistic movements and standards, and in describing beautifully many of van Gogh's paintings—from early drafts to finished masterpieces.

Born March 30, 1853, to Anna (née Carbentus) and Theodorus van Gogh, Vincent was the first of six children. Because Theodorus van Gogh was a Dutch Reformed pastor, his famly was relatively scholarly and of high standing in the community of Zundert, Holland. Vincent began his formal education when he was eight, attending his village's day school for one year, thereafter being educated at home for two years until 1864, at which time he was sent to a boarding school that specialized in teaching languages. He remained at the latter until 1866, when he was thirteen, having become fluent in French and English (he would later develop a sound knowledge of German). For the next year and a half, until he was fifteen, he attended a secondary school in Tilburg, Holland, but left abruptly in the middle of his second year. His sudden departure remains shrouded in mystery, since he was an excellent student and his family did not appear to be suffering any financial difficulties. Sweetman asserts that this abrupt ending of the artist's formal education "remains one of the great mysteries of his life and is possibly the lost key to much of his subsequent behavior." Van Gogh's life entered a hiatus for fifteen months, during which he lived with his family, had no work, apparently nothing to occupy his time, and no plans for his future. What emerged from this fallow period, however, was a young man longing "to dedicate his life to something, to be useful, to be committed to a cause."

During the next eleven years of his life, from the time he was sixteen to his twenty-seventh year, van Gogh was alternately preoccupied with art and religion. He began working as a salesman in art galleries located in The Netherlands, France, and England. Having become an obsessive reader of the Bible, he abruptly abandoned the art business and became a fanatical sermonizer. He then taught for two months in a boarding school, tutored students in German for a short time in an English day school, and worked as a bookseller. In Amsterdam, he studied for entry into a theology school and developed a habit of attending as many sermons as he could in all denominations. Despite his religious fervor, van Gogh failed to gain entry into theology school, because he could not master Greek and Latin. At twenty-seven he seriously took up drawing and—a short time later—painting.

Van Gogh's commitment to art grew very slowly. For a long time he believed that his drawings were the results of, and subordinate to, his religious mission in life. Sweetman's detailed portrayal of van Gogh's religious quest, his obsessive self-abasement and fanatical proselytizing, as well as the suffering he seemed to relish during his self-appointed missionary work in coalfields, is remarkably intimate and profoundly engrossing. After van Gogh gradually came to accept that art—and not religion—was the central aim to which to apply his singlemindedness and his huge capacity for hard work, he devoted the remaining ten years of his tormented life to developing his artistic genius and "living out his anguish in paint." Van Gogh was, however, "not a natural artist, he made himself into one . . . , day and night turning out innumerable rough, bad, hopeless sketches but gradually mastering control of eye and hand until he was able to subject both to his will." The result of his self-taught artistic mastery, Sweetman asserts, is "one of the greatest achievements of nineteenth-century art": van Gogh's paintings.

The provider of unyielding emotional and financial support in van Gogh's life was his youngest sibling, Theodorus ("Theo") van Gogh. Theo was a successful and increasingly influential art dealer by the time that his older brother abandoned religion and embraced art as the sole purpose of his existence. Although Theo was never successful in selling his brother's paintings, he never failed to provide the financial support that made possible van Gogh's artistic pursuits and development, and without which there is every reason to believe the world might never have known the artist's greatest achievements. As debilitating as it often proved to be to Theo at times, the emotional support and understanding that Theo provided Vincent to a great extent made possible the large number of letters the artist wrote to his brother. These letters, when taken together (though Sweetman quotes them sparingly here), provide the world with the single most detailed and articulate account of an artist's development and the means by which he sought to achieve his artistic aims. Literally supporting van Gogh until the last moment and breath of his life, Theo cradled his brother's head in his arm at half past one in the morning of Tuesday, July 29, 1890, when the artist died of a self-inflicted gunshot wound. Theo himself died on January 25, 1891, less than six months after his brother's death, of a complicated kidney infection.

Sweetman offers his readers a superb re-creation of the cultural ambience of the late nineteenth century—its cities, ateliers, cafés and caberets. This artful re-creation increases one's opportunity for understanding not only van Gogh in the context of his own world, but also the art world during his epoch. From his discussion of how the daguerreotypes and other forerunners of photography changed painting, to his quite knowledgeable analysis of Impressionism and Post-Impressionism, Sweetman is engagingly instructive as an art historian, and his descriptions of specific paintings are always original and beautifully written. Nowhere are his descriptions better than when he discusses van Gogh's paintings; for example, discussing the artist's sunflowers, Sweetman writes:

> They scream yellow. Some are set in a yellow vase on a yellow table, some are violently alive, burning with sunshine, others are dead, limp, exhausted, but not with the tranquil death of a real sunflower when it passes into a dry-brown state before scattering its polished seeds; this [is] death by self-immolation, a yellow suicide.

Ultimately, it is unimportant whether van Gogh was sane or insane, when one considers the great and profoundly original art he left to the world; yet, considering the countless theories and legends about van Gogh that have been postulated in the hundred years since his death, one can easily understand why Sweetman goes to such great lengths to find explanations for the artist's behavior. Underpinning Sweetman's desire to explain van Gogh is his unswerving evaluation of the artist's paintings as "gloriously, happily 'sane.'" In any case, van Gogh became the most popular painter of the late twentieth century. "In the century since his suicide," Sweetman notes, "we have come to accept that his work, more than that of his contemporaries, speaks directly to us." Van Gogh sold only one of his paintings during his lifetime; his contemporaries were as unresponsive to his art as the two women with whom he fell in love were to him. As with his fanatical sermons, van Gogh wanted to create art "that would speak directly to ordinary folk." Thus, he signed his paintings "Vincent," as if he were "approaching the unknowable spectator with a friendly first name."

David A. Carpenter

Sources for Further Study

Booklist. LXXXVI, June 1, 1990, p. 1866.
The Christian Science Monitor. September 6, 1990, p. 14.
Library Journal. CXV, July, 1990, p. 94.
Los Angeles Times Book Review. September 30, 1990, p. 6.
The New Leader. LXXIII, September 17, 1990, p. 21.
New Statesman and Society. III, July 20, 1990, p. 39.
The New York Times Book Review. XCV, August 12, 1990, p. 1.
Publishers Weekly. CCXXXVII, May 18, 1990, p. 72.
The Times Literary Supplement. June 29, 1990, p. 683.
The Washington Post Book World. XX, July 29, 1990, p. 9.

THE VIGOUR OF PROPHECY
A Study of Virgil's *Aeneid*

Author: Elisabeth Henry
Publisher: Southern Illinois University Press (Carbondale). Illustrated. 228 pp. $24.95
Type of work: Literary criticism

An examination of the various temporal perspectives of Vergil's Aeneid, *this book illustrates how recollection of past events and prophetic knowledge of the future create a philosophical vision of fate and divine will which determines heroic action in the epic*

The prophetic vigor of this book springs from Vergil's *Aeneid*, the Latin epic published soon after the poet's death in 19 B.C. and destined to become a literary focus of the Western world. During much of its existence, this epic has been interpreted as an enthusiastic affirmation of Roman piety and dedication to duty. Aeneas, the Trojan hero of the epic, has been admired for his devotion to his father, Anchises, and for his determination to found a new city in Italy—one from which would eventually spring Romulus and Remus, the legendary founders of Rome. In pursuit of these goals, Aeneas suppressed self-interest and personal emotions, such as his affection for Dido, the queen of Carthage, whom he reluctantly left in order to reach Italy. At the same time, the epic has traditionally been read as a form of political propaganda. Commissioned by the emperor Augustus and celebrating the genealogical ties between the emperor and Aeneas, Vergil's poem is an assertion of Rome's greatness, especially under the rule of Augustus, who brought peace and stability to an empire torn apart by political turmoil and civil war for most of the first century B.C.

In the twentieth century, however, an interpretation emphasizing the fury and brutality of Aeneas toward his antagonist, Turnus, at the end of the epic has tarnished the *Aeneid*'s glorious luster and heroic idealism. This is the point of view of the so-called Harvard school, a group of scholars (represented by Adam Parry in "The Two Voices of Virgil's *Aeneid*," *Arion II*.4 1963) for whom Vergil's epic conveys less moral certainty and a more ambiguous portrayal of the hero and of traditional Roman values. In the process, late twentieth century readings have transformed the propagandistic overtones of Vergil's *Aeneid* into a more cynical questioning of Vergil's attitude toward the glories of Augustan Rome.

Henry's study shows a way to assimilate the traditional view of the pious hero with the ruthless hero seen by the Harvard school. It is thus an important step in the process of restoring the Roman national epic to its place of honor in Western literature. By examining episodes in which past events are recalled or in which future ones are anticipated, Henry is able to illustrate in the *Aeneid* a significant sequence of recollection, moral lesson, divine message, and decisive action which explains the actions and motivations of the epic hero as well as his spiritual growth. At first, Aeneas possesses little sense of mission or direction. At the end of the Trojan War, he contemplates only death at the hands of the Greeks in futile defense of his city and his family. Gradually, however, he is confronted with a series of prophetic signs and reminders that develop in him a growing awareness of his mission. As a result of these experiences, Aeneas displays a stronger sense of purpose and more inner resolve in the second half of the epic as he prepares to found his new city in Italy.

Henry shows how Aeneas' new city is the focal point where the different time levels of the epic meet. As both a second Troy and an anticipation of imperial Rome, this city unites both past and future in the epic present. Aeneas' new city thus directs attention simultaneously to the old city of Troy, abandoned by the gods, and to Vergil's Rome, favored by the gods as mistress of the Mediterranean. All three cities affirm the inevitability of fate and of divine will.

The triple identity of this city is a key to the understanding of Aeneas' own actions in Italy and especially his dealings with Turnus. As a Trojan, Aeneas suffered from his native city's loss of divine favor, but as the ancestor of the Roman people, Aeneas is also the chosen agent of the gods. He is destined to found a city, this time with divine sanction. Like the gods who show neither compassion nor mercy to the Trojans, Vergil's pious hero is neither compassionate nor merciful toward his Italian enemies. Thus, Aeneas displays a furious conviction of righteousness, a sense of the cosmic order of the Roman empire which justifies fury as an appropriate response by a pious man to whatever stands in the way of fate.

Henry explains Vergil's hero in terms of the ancient philosophical school of Stoicism. Aeneas is a Stoic disciple growing toward greater maturity and acceptance of divine providence and moving toward fulfillment of this divine will and fate through appropriate actions. In the epic, Aeneas becomes a willing agent who displays both *providentia* (that is, a vision of future purpose) and *prudentia* (a sense of calculated action). While Stoicism in its purest form discouraged spontaneity and encouraged deliberate, rational actions, Henry shows how the fury, anger, and ruthlessness displayed by Aeneas in the last half of the epic suggest a modified form of Stoicism that did not condemn all forms of emotion but, instead, advocated the channeling of irrational feelings toward proper ends.

Reconciliation and acceptance form an important part of Vergil's Stoic worldview. Thus, the Trojan Aeneas' alliance with the Greek king, Evander of Pallanteum, on the future site of Rome represents a reconciliation of the Trojans with their former enemies, the Greeks. A similar process of reconciliation occurs with the gods. Aeneas is reconciled with his divine antagonists, Minerva and Juno; so too does Juno herself eventually accept the cosmic order that decrees the success of Aeneas and his Roman descendants at the expense of her favorites, the Carthaginians.

Henry notes that a special aspect of this reconciliation is its element of joy. Aeneas speaks to his companions about joyful recollection of past sorrow, a joy that increases with the hero's growing awareness of his fated purpose. Though at Carthage, Aeneas finds only pain in the recollection of past events, such as the fall of Troy, later in the epic he begins to recollect in joy. Only then are death and suffering, such as the death of Aeneas' ally Pallas, seen as part of a larger, divine purpose. Fulfillment of fate requires the same joyful acceptance the Romans expected in a religious rite, and Aeneas can rejoice in the certainty of his victory over Turnus at the end of the epic.

Henry pays particular attention to the role of the goddess Minerva, or Pallas, in the *Aeneid*, a role often overlooked or underestimated in studies of the epic, perhaps because there is no hint in Vergil's Minerva of the personal, protective goddess Athena seen in Homer's epics. Vergil's goddess is an impersonal deity who inspires awe in mortals and whose use of force is limited, calculated, and controlled. Frequently she directs chthonic, or earthly, elements against mortals who have earned her wrath. Thus, she sends sea serpents against the Trojan priest Laocoon and his sons and a storm against the Greeks at sea. Vergil's goddess is ruthless and terrible but not random. Her wrath is part of a larger scheme of cosmic order.

Minerva also teaches others about this cosmic order. Her students include the hero Hercules and the Trojan Nautes, who, in turn, teaches Aeneas. These students absorb not only her knowledge but also her sense of righteousness and her ruthlessness. Thus, in Henry's analysis, Aeneas' ferocity toward Turnus at the end of the epic parallels that of Minerva toward her victims. In both situations, these actions are violent expressions of fate. Minerva also strengthens the temporal multiplicity of Vergil's epic. As tutelary goddess of Rome, Minerva teaches her ruthless sense of righteousness to the imperial Romans, whose treatment of recalcitrant subjects was rarely marked by kindness and mercy. At the same time, Vergil's temporal perspective creates a contrast between the natural and the civilized world, between Carthaginian luxury and the rustic simplicity of Evander's village. Like Minerva the teacher, Aeneas is a mediator between these extremes. He will bring civilization to Italy in the same manner that, on another temporal plane, the Romans spread their laws and civilization throughout the empire.

This sense of cosmic inevitability, reinforced through the epic by moments of recollection and prophecy, is thus not only the key to understanding Vergil's pious but ruthless hero but also a philosophical statement about the Romans themselves and about their worldview. Indeed, an important feature of Henry's reading of the *Aeneid* is her emphasis on this special Roman perspective on the role of gods and fate in human affairs. While these beliefs about morality and ethics can easily be misread and misunderstood, Aeneas' fury toward Turnus is philosophically not that different from an American's sense of manifest destiny or the fanaticism of an anti-abortion activist or an Islamic fundamentalist. In each case, the individual has not eradicated passion but redirected it, with religious sanction, toward apparently proper ends.

Henry's own analysis of the *Aeneid* inevitably expands the temporal layers of the epic in other directions. First, she projects the Latin epic back to its Homeric sources and frequently compares the Vergilian epic with the *Iliad* and the *Odyssey*. By noting critical differences between the way gifts, prophecies, and time are used by both poets, Henry shows how Vergil has put a distinctive Roman mark on the narrative. She also adds the temporal perspective of Roman archaeology, with striking reference to various artifacts and buildings of the Roman era, which reinforce the worldview described by the *Aeneid*. Thus, commemorative statues placed around the temple of Mars Ultor after the defeat of Julius Caesar's assassins at Philippi parallel the Roman use of *imagines*, or death masks, of dead ancestors to remember the past and recall for Henry Vergil's use of gifts and spoils to rouse memory in the epic. A sixth century B.C. architectural terra-cotta group of Hercules and Pallas from Foro Boario suggests not only Hercules' role in the *Aeneid* but also typological parallels with Aeneas and the emperor Augustus, who, like Hercules, performed cosmic tasks with the help of the goddess. So, too, statues of Pallas/Minerva excavated since 1977 near the site of ancient Lavinium reflect the chthonic power of the goddess which Henry finds in the *Aeneid*. A final example—the Altar of Augustan Peace erected in 13 B.C.—allows Henry to link the peacemaking role of Aeneas in the *Aeneid* with that of his imperial descendant. All these artifacts, few of which are illustrated in *The Vigour of Prophecy*, provide strong support for Henry's vision of the *Aeneid*.

A further temporal level is the extensive body of scholarly work on the *Aeneid*, cited by Henry in a select bibliography and in the endnotes and occasionally mentioned in the text (sometimes without clear citation). This temporal level is almost unavoidable in any modern discussion of the *Aeneid*, which brings to the reader at the end of the twentieth century more than two thousand years of scholarly discussion and interpretation. This scholarly history is now as much part of the life of the epic as is the history of Augustan Rome.

Indeed, this expanded temporal layer is part of the very fiber of Henry's book, the title of which is taken from a poem entitled "Aeneas at Washington" by the twentieth century American poet Allen Tate. In this poem, quoted in full in an appendix on modern Vergilian poetry, Tate compares the Trojan Aeneas with a Confederate soldier contemplating past and present as he stands on the shore of the Potomac river and contemplates Washington, D.C., the American Rome. The phrase "vigour of prophecy" is used by Henry in reference to her special concern with the relationship between action and recollection, between strength and prophecy, between human action and divine will or fate. Tate's poem affirms for both the *Aeneid* and Henry's study the need to interpret Vergil's epic and its hero in a multilayered context, from both a contemporary Roman point of view and that of the twentieth century. Vergil's pious hero, accepted on his own ruthless terms, then becomes a vigorous voice that recalls the moral values of the imperial Romans and which prophesies the continuing influence of Vergil and of Greco-Roman culture on Western thought.

Thomas J. Sienkewicz

Sources for Further Study

Choice. XXVII, June, 1990, p. 1685.
Greece and Rome. XXXVII, April, 1990, p. 108.

THE VILLAGE OF LONGING and DANCEHALL DAYS

Author: George O'Brien (1934-   )
First published: 1987 (*The Village of Longing*), 1988 (*Dancehall Days*), in Ireland
Publisher: Viking (New York). 325 pp. $18.95
Type of work: Autobiography
Time: The 1950's and 1960's
Locale: Lismore and Dublin, Ireland

George O'Brien's wry, unpretentious portrayal of his life as artist-in-the-making, alternately oppressed and exhilarated by the dilemmas life poses in both provincial Lismore and metropolitan Dublin

Principal personages:

SEOIRSE, the author, an alert, sensitive chronicler of his own internal changes as he leaves Lismore and boyhood behind in order to join his scholarly father in Dublin

MAM, his duty-bound, tough-minded grandmother, who tries to imbue him with her conservative village values

CHRISSY, his aunt, a charming and frank woman who takes a real interest in her nephew and tries to offer him sisterly advice

GEORGIE, his uncle, who tries to initiate him into the manly arenas of sport and manual work with little result

DA, his father, who lives in Dublin with his new bride and has a keen interest in avant-garde film

KAY, Da's comfort-loving, intellectual wife, who tries her best to make Seoirse feel at home in his father's Monkstown, County Dublin, residence

BID, a loud-voiced, irascible peasant woman who serves as an example of an overly opinionated villager

WILLY, Bid's elderly husband, one of the few imposing "gentlemen" of Lismore

Bound in one volume, George O'Brien's two memoirs *The Village of Longing* and *Dancehall Days* give readers a spirited, essentially good-humored, unromantic rendering of what it was like for a sensitive and creative young man to grow up in and apart from family and place, the family being adopted and the place being rural Lismore, near Waterford, Ireland. Like James Joyce, who recorded a similar struggle in *A Portrait of the Artist as a Young Man* (1916), O'Brien had to contend with the strain and tug of emotion so many young Irish people experience when confronted by the emotional and mental constrictions imposed by clan ties, nation, and religion.

Ultimately the young O'Brien—or Seoirse, as he is called here—chose to escape the nets of rural Ireland with its hurling matches, priestly hoverings, and narrow conformity in speech, thought, and dress, a decision neither simple nor painless. He knew that, while much would be gained by leaving Lismore's provincial ways, so too would he jettison valuable things—the connections with relatives and friends, the cozy sense of place, and a familiar pattern of life would be forever lost. Ireland, however, is the mother of exiles; she cannot afford to keep her most ambitious and questioning sons and daughters, who, like O'Brien, must find jobs and recognition in either England or America.

Much pain is mixed with the exile's elation at having eluded the harshness of Irish life, and the tension experienced by all restless, talented émigrés finds a remarkable voice in O'Brien. He initially offers readers the day-to-day details of life in Lismore—all those petty triumphs and disasters that shape childhood—experienced by a boy who, having lost his mother (she died) and his father (he went to find a teaching job in Dublin), is sent to live with his grandmother, Mam, and his Uncle Georgie and Aunt Chrissy. Then, O'Brien records gradual increase in the boy's awareness of the great world outside Lismore, brought on by contacts with his father, items broadcast on the radio, and rare glimpses of celebrities such as American dancer Fred Astaire, a visitor to the village at the behest of the Duke of Devonshire, whose castle dominates Lismore.

Readers unacquainted with provincial Irish lore stand to learn much about the routines of rural Irish life from O'Brien, although one could not call the family he depicts in any way "typical," given the highly individualistic personalities of the people portrayed. Though his writing could be termed poetic prose, it is poetry of the mundane and everyday, depicting dinners, hurling matches, disputes, vistas, landmarks, shops, and streets without sentimentality or overstatement. The Lismorians are mostly manual laborers like Seoirse's Uncle Georgie, opinionated, practical, resourceful, yet naïve and narrow.

Here is nationalistic Ireland at its most fervent pitch, a place where only Catholics are true Irish, Protestants and Jews being "foreign" and therefore to be shunned. The mythos of Lismore, like that of all rural Ireland, has to do with exploits of star hurlers, the bards of ancient times, the heroes whose military prowess eventually led to Irish freedom from hated Britain, and the purity and beauty of Irish women. The result is a uniquely Irish outlook which is well described in O'Brien's memoirs. Nevertheless the young protagonist is far from being seduced by the Ireland-for-the-Irish sloganeering and posturing he encounters so frequently.

Seoirse feels special—different, set apart from his football-loving, narrowly patriotic, philistine compatriots. Mam, on the other hand, and, to a lesser extent, Georgie and Chrissy, are proponents of Church, village, and country, an outlook Seoirse finds repellently narrow and life-denying, yet at the same time, curiously attractive because safe.

Yet Seoirse cannot, for all his efforts, be the ordinary village "Mike" he at times wishes he could be—a man not unlike Georgie, crude, vibrant, conventional, unthinking, deaf to the siren calls of art and learning. The sense of being an outsider is joined to his growing sense of needing more psychic space in which to develop talents he finds he possesses—preeminently the talent to express himself in writing.

For mentors, he finally finds he cannot turn to anyone in Lismore, since they are too provincial in outlook and too complacent to boot. Thus, the reader sees Seoirse's need for a reliable mentor turn into a search for his father and the Dublin of which his father is part.

Dublin and the narrator's father are inextricably tied together in the boy's mind. The Dublin of the 1960's was a city unlike any other in the world: a place relatively accepting of some foreign ideas and big enough in size and complexity to offer shelter to those escaping the provinces of Ireland, yet still bearing the stamp of the distinctive Irish experience and the years of wartime isolation. The father, a teacher-cum-artist, remarries, a decision which both fascinates and irritates Seoirse, who still dreams about his mother and the life they once had.

When the search for adventure in the greater world beyond Lismore becomes an adolescent's reality rather than a young boy's pipe dream, Seoirse makes the break with Mam, Georgie, and Chrissy and heads to Dublin to join his father and his new bride, Kay.

Along with his growing sense of purpose is a sense of inferiority and impotence, a product of his Lismore background. Seoirse wonders if, in fact, he is not simply a *culchee* (that is, a rube or hick), too raw and crude for city life. He agonizes over his new relationship with his father, a man who obviously loves him and wants only the best for him and who will initiate him into the world of artistic filmmakers and writers, poets, and painters.

His father shares with him a rejection of the village mentality and an interest in the avant-garde, yet one could not term either of them avant-garde in personal habits or artistic direction. Both father and son are more Irish in habit and outlook than they would admit, yet Seoirse is the more daring of the two. (In future volumes of his autobiography, one hopes, O'Brien will show how that sense of daring led Seoirse to an artist's exile in London.)

Complicating Seoirse's relationship with his father is the fact that Seoirse must live not only with him but also with Kay, whom Seoirse admires and yet fears. Purposely or inadvertently (it is not made clear which), Kay makes him feel like an intruder, someone interrupting a happy honeymoon. Slowly, yet ever-so-surely, this sense of himself coming between father and stepmother grows, finally leading to an eruption of anger on Seoirse's part which in turn makes his father and Kay furious enough to throw him out of their home. As a result, Seoirse is able to see his Dublin situation in its true light: as something temporary, a way station en route to his real life and vocation.

By the end of this volume, O'Brien has not only discovered foreign writers, pubs, and, to a limited extent, women, but also what he wants to do with his life (write) and where he wants to pursue his ambitions (abroad, in London). Dublin has let him down but has also given him a new sense of purpose and life's possibilities. No longer the *culchee*, Seoirse has become "citified" and therefore aware of things artistic and cultural happening in other parts of the world. London, with its grand vistas and manner and place in the world, would be a far more suitable place for him to refine his intellectual gold. So, at last, Seoirse leaves not only Dublin but also everything that has defined him for a destination which offers only the barest promise of artistic fulfillment.

O'Brien has given readers one of the most detailed accounts since Joyce's of the education and self-exile of an Irish youth, yet one sees more than one man's exile in this tale. Here too is the feel of life in the late 1950's and 1960's when the popular culture of England and America was becoming preeminent—even in the lives of the most remote villagers. The protagonist cannot miss the excitement of life as it is revealed in radio broadcasts of prize fights, distant football matches, and the news. Lismorians play cowboys and Indians and listen to non-Irish music; young boys wait for the tourist buses to show up so they can ogle blonde American girls and admire the wildly checked clothes of their elders.

The chief British influence on Seoirse and other residents of Lismore is the Castle, the grand Irish home of the Duke of Devonshire and his entourage of aging hangers-on, back from Burma or India to live out their days. Though rarely sighted and apparently uninterested in the villagers, the Duke himself inspires awe and anger, often simultaneously. His imperial manner and Protestant religion are in some ways an affront to the humble Catholics of the area and a reminder of the bitter centuries when England ruled Ireland.

Throughout *The Village of Longing* and *Dancehall Days*, there is a nagging sense of Irish inadequacy, of Ireland's failure to provide the requisite backdrop for talented, restless, and intelligent youth to express themselves. Yet O'Brien is good-humoredly honest enough to admit that many of his problems were of his own making and therefore not to be blamed on Ireland. In fact, self-deprecating humor prevails throughout his work; self pity has no place in it. At heart, O'Brien is a comic writer, a wry, careful observer of folkways, always able to turn amusing characters and situations into art. The Lismore and, to a lesser extent, the Dublin he depicts are full of good-natured evasions, clever turns of phrase, and often bizarre mental gyrations where common sense is turned topsy-turvy. There is real love here and little malice.

Indeed, O'Brien leaves one with the impression that, in the last analysis, the most crucial and memorable events in his life were those which took place long ago and far away in tiny, isolated Lismore. In the end, Mam, Georgie, Chrissy, and Da will form his personal pantheon.

The Village of Longing and *Dancehall Days* won the Irish Book Awards Silver Medal for Literature in 1988. O'Brien's voice is original, poetic, compelling, and honest; never harsh, he re-creates a lost world with tenderness and love.

John D. Raymer

Sources for Further Study

Booklist. LXXXVI, January 1, 1990, p. 886.
The Irish Literary Supplement. VII, Spring, 1988, p. 28.
Kirkus Reviews. LVIII, January 1, 1990, p. 33.
Los Angeles Times Book Review. February 4, 1990, p. 4.

New Statesman and Society. II, July 21, 1989, p. 35.
The New York Times Book Review. XCV, April 15, 1990, p. 15.
Publishers Weekly. CCXXXVII, January 26, 1990, p. 408.
The Spectator. CCLIX, November 28, 1987, p. 36.
The Times Literary Supplement. August 25, 1989, p. 929.
The Washington Post Book World. XX, May 6, 1990, p. 11.

VLADIMIR NABOKOV
The Russian Years

Author: Brian Boyd
Publisher: Princeton University Press (Princeton, New Jersey). Illustrated. 607 pp. $25.00
Type of work: Literary biography
Time: 1899-1940
Locale: St. Petersburg, Berlin, Paris

The first volume of a projected two-volume biography, offering analysis of Vladimir Nabo-kov's works as well as the fullest available account of his life

Principal personages:
VLADIMIR VLADIMIROVICH NABOKOV, poet and novelist
VLADIMIR DMITRIEVICH NABOKOV, his father
ELENA IVANOVNA NABOKOV, his mother
VALENTINA "LYUSSYA" SHULGIN, his first love
VÉRA EVSEEVNA SLONIM, his wife
IVAN LUKASH, an émigré writer and friend of Nabokov
ILYA FONDAMINSKY, a publisher of Russian émigré writing
GEORGY ADAMOVICH, a poet and critic active in the Russian émigré community

The lives of nineteenth and twentieth century Russian writers are as fascinating as the poems and novels they wrote and as enigmatic as the nation they inhabited. Fyodor Dostoevski's own soul was torn by the same explosive spiritual dynamics that brought the Karamazov family to murder and salvation. Leo Tolstoy's battle against serfdom and autocracy had the epic scale of *Voyna i mir* (1865-1869; *War and Peace*, 1886). Aleksandr Solzhenitsyn steeled his opposition to the Soviet state during years of government oppression as multilayered as the structure of *V kruge pervom* (1968; *The First Circle*, 1968). Little wonder the lives of these writers attract both Russian and non-Russian biographers.

Vladimir Nabokov is the latest to offer biographers a life as rich as his writing. Nabokov is a rarity indeed: an author who has written classic novels in two languages. Born in 1899, Nabokov matured with the twentieth century. Truly its child, his life intersected with two cataclysmic revolutions, the 1917 Bolshevik coup d'etat in Russia and the 1933 Nazi ascendancy in Germany. Similarly, his art interwove numerous modern concepts, especially the twentieth century's fascination with the idea of consciousness and the shaping of empirical reality by perception.

Brian Boyd's *Vladimir Nabokov: The Russian Years* studies the first forty years of Nabokov's life and works. Though Nabokov left Russia at age twenty in 1919, after the Red Army's defeat of the White forces, Boyd's subtitle is not inaccurate. Nabokov wrote in Russian while he studied in England and later lived in Russian émigré communities in Berlin and Paris. He wrote about the life of Russian émigrés and the continuing impact of prerevolutionary history, which the Marxists and Leninists were convinced they had undone, upon the lives and consciousness of all Russians. Boyd ends the volume with Nabokov's flight to the United States in 1940 to escape the war in Europe; Nabokov understood that if he were to make a living in America as a writer, he would have to write in English. Only then did his years stop being Russian.

Boyd extensively studies Nabokov's family background and youth. Vladimir was born on April 23, 1899, in St. Petersburg, the first child of Vladimir Dmitrievich and Elena Ivanovna. His father was a prominent lawyer and politician, well-known for advocating liberal principles even as Czar Nicholas II's government grew more conservative. His mother was a keen observer of the rich cultural life of St. Petersburg. Vladimir lived a comfortable existence in a stimulating world. The family spent winters in the city and summers at a country estate; his parents employed a succession of tutors who schooled Vladimir in French and English as well as Russian and who introduced him to the arts.

Vladimir's privileged upbringing provided the leisure to cultivate the art of living. By age ten he was an avid butterfly collector. The hobby engaged him passionately all his life, as a topic for scientific and aesthetic inquiry. As an adolescent he learned chess and delighted in creating chess problems; later, as a writer he explored the analogy between the intricacies of the chessboard and the novel. He read voraciously the classic literary works in three languages from his father's library; on his mother's tea table he found the latest poetry of St. Petersburg's flourishing Symbolist poets. They became his heroes. At age fifteen he wrote his first poem, in the style of the Symbolists' lyrical apprehension of emotional life. A year later Vladimir experienced his first love affair with Valentina Shulgin; he recorded his passion in a series of poems to his "Lyussya." Though his love for her ebbed, his passion for poetry did not. He experimented with the metrical patterns of every important poet from Alexander Pushkin, the father of Russian verse, to Andrei Bely, the most innovative Symbolist.

Young Vladimir remained surprisingly aloof from the political upheavals that marked his youth: the 1905 Rebellion, the Great War beginning in 1914, the October Revolution of 1917. His father did not: He served in the Duma, Russia's attempt at legislative government; he was exiled for opposing conservative reforms; and he helped found the Constitutional Democratic party, which tried to replace the autocracy with a Western-style limited monarchy. Vladimir Dmitrievich supported the Provisional Government which succeeded Nicholas II in 1917; when the Bolsheviks overthrew the Provisional Government, he took his family to the Crimea and held a position with the White government there; when the Red Army overwhelmed the Crimea, he led his family into exile. Though young Vladimir observed these upheavals from a distance, he did absorb his father's earnestly defended political principles: respect for the individual, hatred of anti-Semitism, contempt for ideology, and tolerance for diversity.

The Nabokov family settled in London; Elena sold her jewels for Vladimir's tuition at the University of Cambridge. He enrolled at Trinity College, ostensibly to study European history and literature. Already well-read in these areas, he devoted most of his time to writing poetry in Russian. He wrote late into the night, chain-smoking and drinking coffee, to keep the muse awake. Adopting the pen name Sirin, Nabokov submitted his verse to Russian literary journals newly sprung up in several European capitals to serve the thousands of White Russians who had fled Bolshevik Russia. While he wrote verse, his parents worked with émigré organizations planning the restoration of constitutional government in Russia. In early 1922, however, his father was fatally shot by a monarchist at a political rally in Berlin, having bravely sought to protect the featured speaker. That June Nabokov finished his degree and moved to Berlin with his mother.

Nabokov earned his living by tutoring while publishing poetry and translations into Russian for the burgeoning Russian émigré population of Berlin, which numbered nearly a million. He quickly gained a reputation as an important young poet, with publishers such as Ilya Fondaminsky eager to buy his verse and rival poets such as Georgy Adamovich eager to criticize him. Occasionally he worked on filmscripts with Ivan Lukash, another émigré writer surviving by his pen. Nabokov proposed marriage to Svetlana Siewert, whom he had met when he was twenty-two and she sixteen, but her parents broke off the engagement, afraid that Nabokov lacked a reliable source of income. In 1925, he married Véra Slonim, the daughter of a Russian merchant ruined by the Revolution. Like many other women married to Russian writers, she became her husband's muse, amanuensis, and editor.

Now established as a poet, Nabokov began to write short stories and plays. More substantial, written quickly, and capable of producing immediate income, these works depicted scenes from émigré life, an ever-changing kaleidoscope of nostalgia, political intrigue, and day-to-day survival in a strange environment. Nabokov's first novel, *Mashenka* (1926; *Mary*, 1970), centers on a Russian émigré who learns that his childhood sweetheart, now married to his Berlin neighbor, is about to arrive. He plans to meet her at the station and run off with her; at the last minute he changes his mind, sure that she is now sweeter in his memory than she could actually be in reality after many years. *Mary* is the first of many Nabokov fictional works where characters' perceptions shape, or are preferred to, objective reality.

Over the next decade the routine of Nabokov's life changed little, aside from the birth of his son Dmitri in 1934. His existence took on a rhythm not unlike that of his adolescence: winters in the city, summers on the Mediterranean coast, long nights spent writing. The Nabokovs were never financially secure, but his steady publications and occasional lectures kept the family comfortable. Once in a while circumstances required a move to cheaper lodgings, but even during the worst of Germany's runaway inflation, the Nabokovs were never destitute. The more noticeable change was in Nabokov's art. He concentrated increasingly on novel writing and produced three major works: *Korol, dama, valet* (1928; *King, Queen, Knave*, 1968); *Zashchita Luzhina* (1929; *The Defense*, 1964); and *Dar* (1937-1938, 1952; *The Gift*, 1963).

By 1936 the rise of Nazism had driven many Russian émigrés from Berlin. In addition, the high hopes of many émigrés in the 1920's that the Bolshevik government would be overthrown or self-destruct had faded, robbing their community of the energy which had sustained cultural activities. Increasingly Nabokov sought an audience in Paris, traveling frequently there to consult with agents and publishers. Germany's aggressive xenophobia at home boded ill for resident foreigners, while Adolf Hitler's territorial demands worried neighboring countries. Like many Europeans Nabokov became convinced that war was inevitable. In 1937 the Nabokovs moved to France.

He investigated the possibility of a teaching position in Great Britain or the United States but without success. Instead he sought entry to these countries' literary marketplace; he wrote a novel in English, but it was rejected by several publishers. Thanks to Mark Aldanov, émigré editor and writer, Nabokov finally found in the late summer of 1939 a teaching position at Stanford University in California. A week later, World War II began. To leave France, Nabokov was forced to raise money by benefit readings, borrowing, and begging. By May he had earned enough for their passage; as German armies rolled into France, the Nabokovs sailed for the United States on a liner evacuating Jewish refugees.

Boyd's account of Nabokov's life is clearly the result of extensive research into primary documents: Russian government archives; library collections of diaries, newspapers, and rare editions; family papers and notebooks which survived the upheavals of revolution and war. Though his is not an authorized biography, Boyd acknowledges the extensive help of Véra and Dmitri Nabokov. Boyd's portrait of Nabokov is flattering without being fawning, at once sensitive and objective on delicate topics of family life, friendships, finances, and sex. Boyd's primary interest is not a judgment upon character; rather it is in a portrait of the artist as a young man in order to understand better the artist's work.

Nabokov admitted that he was in many ways an autobiographical writer. Most evident in the poems, which often respond to the events of his life, the autobiographical strain is present in the more complicated, more diffused worlds of the novels. Like a detective, Boyd carefully studies the evidence of Nabokov's early life to find the original of the people, the places, and the events which appear in the novels. Yet his search is neither trivial nor reductionist. What intrigues Boyd is not what Nabokov transformed into art, but how he transformed it. The lesson for Boyd is not the self-evident fact that a writer re-creates experience; it is that when one compares the experience and the art, one realizes the richness of the art as both an expression and an understanding of the experience.

Boyd finds in Nabokov's art a celebration of the fact that human beings have consciousness: the reflective ability to see themselves, to see the possibility of alternative selves, and to choose which self to be. To know consciousness is to know all life's rich possibilities, physical and spiritual, happy and miserable, comic and tragic. Nabokov's philosophy of life rooted in consciousness played a fundamental role in the development of his art. Boyd frequently compares Nabokov to other giants of twentieth century literature who were fascinated by the mystery of self-awareness: James Joyce, Marcel Proust, and Jorge Luis Borges. Like them, Nabokov abandoned the traditional premise that the writer is the educator of readers who presents wisdom in pleasant forms. Instead of the man of letters, he sees the artificer of texts. Texts are important in themselves, not as representations of other things. The old-fashioned novel pretended to be something other than what it was, a fiction. It disguised itself as a truthful report, "a slice of life"; it masqueraded as a diary or a manuscript found in a bottle. The new novel is only itself; the writer focuses the reader on the text itself; narrative is a means to that end, not an end in itself. A reader draws from a work not involvement in fictitious lives but involvement in the process of artistic creation.

Boyd often pauses in his account of Nabokov's life to comment upon a story, a play, or a novel. Though such commentary is generally brief, Boyd devotes a whole chapter each to a reading of *The Defense* and *The Gift*. He clearly regards both as masterpieces of modern Russian literature. He reads them as he guesses Nabokov would want them to be read: with the eye of the butterfly collector fascinated by the tiny, brilliantly colored patterns of gossamer wings; and with the cunning of the chess master attempting to guess, control, and counter an opponent's next move. Less objective as critic than as biographer, Boyd freely judges and ranks Nabokov's achievement from work to work. His opinions cannot hide, however, his evident delight even in works he regards as flawed.

Vladimir Nabokov: The Russian Years is an artful blend of fascinating biographical narrative and perceptive criticism. Widely praised by reviewers as an exemplary literary biography, it was selected by *The New York Times Book Review* as one of the Best Books of 1990.

Robert M. Otten

Sources for Further Study

Booklist. LXXXVII, September 15, 1990, p. 1.
Kirkus Reviews. LVIII, August 15, 1990, p. 1136.
Library Journal. CXV, October 1, 1990, p. 88.
Los Angeles Times Book Review. November 11, 1990, p. 1.
The New Criterion. IX, February, 1991, p. 35.
The New Republic. CCIII, October 15, 1990, p. 37.
The New York Times Book Review. XCV, October 14, 1990, p. 3.
Publishers Weekly. CCXXXVII, August 10, 1990, p. 427.
The Wall Street Journal. November 8, 1990, p. A20.
The Washington Post. XX, October 21, 1990, p. 1.
Washington Times. October 8, 1990, p. F3.

VOICES IN THE MIRROR
An Autobiography

Author: Gordon Parks (1912-   )
Publisher: Doubleday (New York). Illustrated. 351 pp. $22.95
Type of work: Autobiography
Time: 1921-1990
Locale: Kansas; New York; Washington, D.C.; and Paris

*Gordon Parks reflects on the events of his tumultuous life and distinguished career in this
autobiography that ranges through five decades and over as many continents*

> *Principal personages:*
> GORDON PARKS, distinguished African-American photographer, filmmaker,
>   and writer
> ROY STRYKER, his mentor at Standard Oil and the head of Standard Oil's
>   photo archives
> GENEVIEVE YOUNG, Parks's third wife and his book editor at Doubleday

Gordon Parks is one of the happy few able to transform disadvantage into advantage, to turn his life around by sheer will, and to know when to seize the chances
luck or happenstance put in his way. As an African American growing up in the nation's heartland, he knew from an early age daily humiliation at the hands of racists.
He rebelled, but where another man or woman would have resorted to the extremes
of violence or docility, Gordon Parks transformed his anger and hatred into a creative energy that accepted no bounds, that refused to be bridled by what was or was
not expected of the black man.

Eventually, through hard work and self-education, Parks won the right to speak
for his people. His accomplishments in several fields distinguish him not as an African American and not by white standards, but as a true Renaissance man of extraordinary achievement. He calls himself photographer, writer, composer, screenwriter
and director, poet and painter. Any man or woman would be proud to attain distinction in any one of these fields; for one man to be acknowledged as an outstanding
practitioner of them all is surely unprecedented.

Voices in the Mirror recounts how Gordon Parks triumphed over the poverty of
his childhood, how he never settled for just enough, and explains why this man of
insatiable curiosity even today believes his work unfinished; other disciplines, ballet
among them, beckon for his lively and sensitive imagination. In the beginning, in
Kansas, he realized what it would take for him to achieve the only kind of success
that would ultimately matter to him, the personal satisfaction that comes with obstacles, if not overcome, then displaced or circumvented. "I was on a search for pride,"
he says, and this sentence could well serve as his motto.

From the time, in his segregated school, when he first heard the implicit warning
from his class advisers "You were meant to be maids and porters," he knew that he
would have to fight racism both overt and subtle. Values to enjoin the battle he
received from his parents, whom he lovingly remembers for their tenderness and

their strength. The world taught him to scramble, to adjust, but never to accept racial barriers. By the age of fourteen he had not yet learned how to fight except blindly: "in a black and white world anything whiter than I became my enemy." With time and patience, he learned that he need not accommodate himself to a system of inequality he so despised:

> The question frequently asked of me is why I have undertaken so many professions—photography, painting, writing, musical composition and film. At first I wasn't sure that I had the talent for any of them, but I did know I had an intense fear of failure, and that fear compelled me to fight off anything that might abet it—bigotry, hatred, discrimination, poverty or hunger. I suffered those evils, but without allowing them to rob me of the freedom to expand.

In Parks's case, opportunities denied only pointed out alternatives.

Born in 1912, Parks has seen and participated in most of the major events of the twentieth century, at least those that define the modern American experience. Much of it he has recorded, if not in his photographs, then in his writings. He has in fact written three other autobiographical works, but especially with this one he gives narrative voice not only to black America's consciousness but to the sometimes buried national conscience as well.

He is unequivocal in his hatred of racists. He describes eloquently their treachery, whether naked and unadorned, or cloaked in the deceitful mufti of social convention:

> Thorn-wielding is their occupation and I can attest to their proficiency. Throughout my childhood they kept their eyes glued to my tenderest parts, striking me, impaling me, leaving me bloodied and confused—without my knowing what had provoked their hostility. I came at last to think of them as beasts with cold hearts; of lost souls impassioned with hatred, slithering about in misery, their feelings severed of all humaneness and spreading over the universe like prickly cloth. Rancor seems to have been their master. . . .

Witness to racism as well as object of its pernicious effects, Parks regards it as an enemy to be encountered over and over, one that requires all his considerable resources and gifts to vanquish.

Perhaps Parks's strength sprang from the Kansas prairieland as much as from what was, after all, a quintessential American family: hard-working, proud, and loving. Forced by the death of his mother, Sarah, when he was fifteen years old, to live with his sister in Minnesota, Parks found himself unable to abide by an intransigent brother-in-law's rules. Not completely prepared to deal with adulthood, he relied on his wits and talents to survive, whether as a piano player in a bordello or as a janitor in a flophouse. All the time he listened to the voices, both his own and others', that guided his future. To the negative ones, the ones that told him to get along, to accept poverty and discrimination, he turned deaf ears; to the others, the ones of hope, he responded as if to a call-to-arms, with his weapons a ready intelligence and a burning ambition.

Without a formal education, Gordon Parks endured the daily torments of service jobs, rootless wanderings, and encounters violent both to the body and mind. Ever candid, he describes his search for maturity in unflinchingly honest prose. Along the way he realized that "degradation was no respecter of color," and later in his photoessays for *Life* magazine, he revealed the fullness of his empathy for those who suffer through no fault of their own.

Although Parks's first contributions to the arts were probably the songs he composed in brothels, he had initial success as a photographer. He became the first black photojournalist to work for *Life*, and some of the most entertaining parts of his autobiography recount his work with the newsmakers of the day. His intimate record of the sensationalized affair between Ingrid Bergman and Roberto Rossellini humanizes what at the time was a feeding frenzy for the press. Parks's accounts of the deracinated but far-from-dispossessed royalty of Europe are succinct and unsparing, but in the stories of their parasitic existence, he usually finds something to pity. As a fashion photographer, he worked with some of the most beautiful women in the world, but his descriptions of his work are brief and curiously flat. He states plainly, however, the difference between documentary work and fashion photography, an insight that perhaps betrays his belief that the former is of more value: "In one lay the responsibility to capture a prevailing mood, while in the other was the obligation to create a mood."

That observation came with experience, and Parks insists still on truth-gathering through living as his subjects do. In Harlem he shared the daily boredom punctuated by scattershot violence of young gang-members; in Brazil he practically moved in with the denizens of Rio's wretched *favelas*. To study Malcolm X and Eldridge Cleaver, he traveled incessantly and had to turn aside the ever-present suspicion that he was the white man's lackey, an insidious sort of "house nigger" on the fringes rather than in the midst of revolution. He also had to overcome his own fear of placing himself in the middle of the bloody confrontations between police and Black Panthers. Through it all he kept questioning, probing, coming to terms with his own life as well as with those he saw through his ubiquitous lens. He chronicled despair and heroism, frivolity and pain. One of his best photographs, that of Ella Watson, a cleaning lady in Washington, D.C., demonstrates his extraordinary eye for irony, for detail, in short, for the "telling moment" that, once captured, continues to speak volumes. It is entirely appropriate that this portrait of a proud woman with her broom and mop, posed in straightforward defiance against a backdrop of the flag, is entitled "American Gothic." It is one of the too-few photographs included in *Voices in the Mirror* from Parks's distinguished portfolio of such images.

In a section that should be required reading for documentary photographers, Parks agonizes over the role the artist assumes while doing his work. Does he remain entirely behind the camera, as objective and unfeeling as the instrument he holds? Once involved, can he remain aloof, unresponsive to the emotion he provokes within his subjects, within himself? Forced to grapple with these issues by his work with the Fontenelle family, a Harlem family and the subject of one of Parks's celebrated photoessays on poverty in the United States, Parks answers that it is impossible for him to control those subjective, basic, altruistic impulses that led him to bring food to hungry children. Once he had "yielded to a need to help them in some way," he fears that he "played God" by pushing them "toward some improbable dream . . . by digging too deep into their lives." In the misery of the Fontenelles' existence, Parks saw mirrored his own struggles and, for him, "It had been impossible to lie contented in the arms of my own personal deliverance."

Gordon Parks not only wears the caps of fashion, documentary, and fine-arts photographer, but the full-brimmed hats of composer, writer, and director as well. He transformed his autobiographical novel *The Learning Tree* (1963) into a celebrated film (1969) and in the process became the first black person to write, direct, and co-produce a Hollywood film. He directed five other films, among them *Shaft* (1971), the blockbuster in which he offered black youth a hero worth emulating, and *Leadbelly* (1976), an acclaimed documentary sabotaged by the studio just as it found its audience. Even as this book was being prepared, the author was busy mounting his ballet, *Martin*, in Washington, D.C.

As varied as his professional life, Parks's personal life does not escape frank, but never bitter, scrutiny. Married three times, with four children, he implicitly warns others that self-absorption and ambition sometimes hurt those left at home. His portraits of his wives are, unfortunately, one-dimensional, especially that of his first, Sally, whose emotions he "interprets" for the reader as he describes his own wanderings and strivings. One of the most moving passages of the book details his personal pain and confusion when his son, Gordon, Jr., the director of *Super Fly* (1972), dies on location in Africa.

The nature of autobiography is, if not self-congratulatory, self-conscious, and this one is no exception. Parks's remembrances of conversations seem at times manufactured to suit a current conclusion. Occasionally, his relationships appear strangely distant as if he is still walking the fine line between subjective and objective reporting, and in spite of his desire to avoid it, he romanticizes, some would even say distorts, the heady days of black militancy. He emphasizes repeatedly that bigotry is universal, but he finds the crucible of racism in Alabama and Mississippi and effectively buys into the myth of the Old South while ignoring the complexity of its social and economic reality: "At last the easy white days of mint juleps and magnolia blossoms were under threat—and by hands that for centuries had picked the cotton." Given the voice, Southern blueblood and redneck alike would argue that stirrup cups and hoop skirts are the props of legend. Even revisionist historians admit that the white tenant farmer, the millhands, and steelworkers, abject in their own poverty and denied their own security, sought to oppress those who had less as readily as did their Northern counterparts. In this instance, Parks loses sight, perhaps, of a theme he makes clear elsewhere, that victims of privilege-based systems are all colors and that imposed ignorance limits them all.

He also does himself a disservice, although an understandable one, when he worries that he has sidestepped the mainstream of black life. His life is indeed a testament to resilience, to his childhood vow to retain his dignity and pride no matter what. The comfortable suburbs of Westchester County may well be a long way from the mean streets of Harlem, but in getting to White Plains, Parks offers an example for all those, black and white, who dream of fulfillment and accomplishment. "There is nothing ignoble about a black man climbing from the darkness on a white man's ladder, providing he doesn't forsake the others who, subsequently, must escape that same darkness," he says, and in this work, destined to be a benchmark in black literature, he adds his voice to those in the mirror to which all the powerless, the dreamers, must listen.

William U. Eiland

Sources for Further Study

The Atlantic. CCLXVI, December, 1990, p. 132.
Booklist. LXXXVII, November 1, 1990, p. 494.
Essence. XXI, November, 1990, p. 50.
Kirkus Reviews. LVIII, September 15, 1990, p. 1310.
Los Angeles Times Book Review. November 4, 1990, p. 2.
Modern Maturity. XXXIII, October, 1990, p. 20.
The New York Times Book Review. XCV, December 9, 1990, p. 19.
Publishers Weekly. CCXXXVII, October 12, 1990, p. 52.
USA Today. December 17, 1990, p. D6.
The Washington Post Book World. XX, November 18, 1990, p. 4.

THE WANT BONE

Author: Robert Pinsky (1940-   )
Publisher: Ecco Press (New York). 70 pp. $17.95
Type of work: Poetry

The poet struggles to understand the sources of language and the intersections of religions and myth, to grasp the possibilities and the limits of these myths and their gods, and to place his own personal memories against the backdrop of history

Robert Pinsky has published three previous books of poems and three books of prose. *History of My Heart*, his last book of poems, received The Poetry Society of America's William Carlos Williams Prize in 1984. *The Want Bone*, contains twenty-five new poems carefully arranged around a prose piece placed in the middle of the volume. In the new work, Pinsky demonstrates an impressive technical skill as well as an interest in a wide range of subject matter.

Though there are no sections in the book, it divides thematically into two halves, with the prose piece at the center. The first half of the volume addresses more overtly religious issues and the second half seems more secular or personal. Elements of myth and religion found in the first half are continued throughout, however, and personal issues crop up in the first half as well.

"From the Childhood of Jesus" is the opening poem, an impressive debut in slant-rhymed couplets that relates a parable about Jesus at five years old. Playing outdoors, Jesus innocently "modeled twelve sparrows out of the river clay// And scooped a clear pond, with a dam of twigs and mud." It is the Sabbath, and "a certain Jew" comes by, scolds the child, and runs to Joseph to complain.

When Joseph rebukes him, Jesus sends the birds away with a clap of his hands. All seems well until another boy ("The son of Annas the scribe") comes by and begins to destroy the dam and pond which Jesus had made. Emphasizing Jesus' human qualities, Pinsky describes him flying into a rage. Jesus shouts at the other boy and delivers a stinging prophecy: "Now you are going to wither// The way a tree does, you shall bear no fruit/ And no leaves, you shall wither down to the root." The prophecy is immediately fulfilled.

"From the Childhood of Jesus" makes an interesting start to *The Want Bone* with its unlikely portrait of an angry child-Jesus figure acting not compassionately but vindictively. The equilibrium that exists at the poem's end is one of horror and sadness. Everyone sleeps except in the household of the withered boy. Even nature appears stunned; the birds fly "aimlessly . . ./ . . . as if never to alight."

"Memoirs," the book's second poem, moves to the modern world and tells of the poet's Jewish heritage passed in word and icon from generation to generation. With a refrain line, "I am this, and not that," the poet also describes a child's growing awareness of his difference from others. Now an adult, asked questions by his son, the poet tells him of the Jews' past. In both of these early poems, Pinsky seeks to define Judaism and its relationship to Christianity. The two seem to be diametrically opposed at times here, and are often antagonistic.

Besides collective history, another theme in *The Want Bone* is language. "Window" and "The Refinery" both ponder the origins of language. In "Window," the book's third poem, the child learns words in a world filled with sensory detail and the delightful dissonance of culture in a large city. In what sounds like an almost universal first memory, the poet recalls being held up to see "snowfall out the window."

Whether it was the poet's mother teaching him to speak or not (and the poet seems to want to obscure this point), Pinsky describes the child's utter delight in the word *snow*—"you opened your small brown fist/ And closed it and opened again to hold the reflection/ Of torches and faces inside the window glass." Language becomes the poet's "window" to the world. Cloudy or opaque sometimes, it is at other times transparent, and shows the world outside as "that bright confusion."

"The Refinery" is grouped with several poems that use industrial images (refineries, hammers, sweatshops). Almost completely the opposite of "Window," "The Refinery" envisions mythic gods, not a personal memory. The gods wake up hungry for words, as though language is food: "a pollen tinted/ Slurry of passion and lapsed/ Intention, whose imagined/ Taste made the savage deities hiss and snort." In this poem, people in cities are the gods' aphids or worker bees, processing language like honey for them. Indiscriminately, they drink up everything: "Lovecries and memorized Chaucer, lines from movies." This world is far from the child's world of wonder at one word. In "The Refinery," words are merely another substance for consumption like oil, air, or water, though they may be more sweet.

The book's title poem describes a world of sand and sea. At first, this world seems free of all human influence or interference. The want bone is the "dried mouthbones of a shark" and it lies, stripped bare, on a bare beach. Pinsky calls the bone, "A scalded toothless harp, uncrushed, unstrung." This want bone is fixed in a position which shapes an "O," which transforms the poem into a commentary on language. Something primitive—a survival instinct—makes the bones finally "sing." They sing of desire and hunger, and the most repeated word is "my." One of the last lines in "The Want Bone" is this primitive, practically nonsensical, chant: "My food my parent my child I want you my own."

Creation myths as well as language myths interest Pinsky. In "Shiva and Parvati Hiding in the Rain," "The Uncreation," and "Lament for the Makers," the poet seems determined to blur the separations between things. Song and desire, creating and destroying, and endowing and devouring are closer, in the poet's mind, than we usually imagine.

In "Shiva and Parvati Hiding in the Rain," Pinsky's image is the wheel of life, the mandala. Shiva and Parvati, the Hindu god of destruction and his consort, are locked in a sexual embrace that symbolizes oneness. As the wheel turns, "their eight sleek/ Limbs and numberless/ Faces all spokes from one trunk." Despite divisiveness, perhaps we are all from one source after all, the poet surmises—or from the universal combination of yin and yang.

In "The Uncreation," the poet ponders another universal—song and its appeal for people. From ballparks to work songs, in cars and at work, song links humans to

God, and sea to cloud. This poem (and others) shows the risks and leaps in subject matter that Pinsky is willing to make. Using triplet stanzas, a favorite form of his, he animates matter to understand it. To his mind, "sometimes even machines may chant or jingle/ Some lyrical accident. . . ."

In "Lament for the Makers," another poem in the triplet form, Pinsky's range is also wide. From Rome and a frieze of Cronus eating his children to Arthur on a barge with his ladies, Pinsky jumps to Brooklyn and then to bars on San Pablo Avenue. Part celebration of the variety of life, part hymn of praise, the poem acknowledges what is primitive and enduring: desire, music, passion, and the routines of life. At the poem's end, a lone basketball player is tossing up hook shots while "[t]he half-ruined city around him throbs and glows/ With pangs of allure that flash like the names of bars."

"Jesus and Isolt," the center of *The Want Bone* both structurally and thematically, is a recombination of religion and myth. Pinsky brings, in this case, Jesus to the side of Isolt during Tristram's absence. Jesus is in the form of a ciclogriff, which is about the size of a tame rabbit, and has "a pair of soft gray leathery wings, and a compact furry body with strong haunches and gloved forepaws like a raccoon's." Odd as this transformation may be, Jesus is both a comfort to Isolt and a teacher.

Isolt, in turn, teaches Jesus about the love between men and women, about her own past life, and about the Irish dragon who nearly killed Tristram. Their closeness has an inevitable end, however, when Tristram returns. Jesus has revealed himself to them as the Son of Man, and he instructs them in the ways of Heaven in hopes of bringing them there. Tristram, however, especially, cannot give up his old ways. Isolt and Tristram hold hands and descend into Hell, while Jesus ascends to his place. "Jesus and Isolt" ends with a sense of deep loss, especially—and surprisingly—for Jesus. Locked in his spirituality, inevitably alone, he is an object of pity for Mary, who looks on him as "the most unfortunate of all his Father's creatures."

As strong as many poems in the first half of The Want Bone are, the poems in the book's second half are better. Pinsky still shows fine technical gifts and a good ear for language, and the poems continue to show a wide range of subject matter—from contemporary urban slums to labor history, for example. What is especially fine, however, is the emotional intensity reached in several poems, namely "Immortal Longings," "Exile," "An Old Man," "Shirt," "Sonnet," and the volume's concluding poem, "At Pleasure Bay."

"Immortal Longings" opens mysteriously. Pinsky chooses an effectively ambiguous beginning that matches the slow drift of a descending airplane. Before the reader figures that out, though, the image of a "silver body" may be a fish or a boat.

The poet imagines the airplane as a modern god, and the passengers are mere cells or atoms of that creature. It hovers and shudders over the glittering city below, each cell starting to rouse, each person driven by his own needs and dreams. The frenzy is matched by the city below, where cars on the freeways are a bright "[z]odiac of intentions."

"Shirt" is one of the finest poems in *The Want Bone*. Although it sounds like a trivial subject, a meditative poem on the history of one's shirt is a unique challenge. Pinsky handles it masterfully. He moves from yoke and collar to the workers who he imagines made the shirt. Fully realized and not stereotyped, the workers drink tea and eat noodles on a break while "talking money or politics." Pinsky manages to include a dramatic moment from the historic fire at the Triangle shirt factory, in 1911. He skillfully brings in poets, too. He mentions the seventeenth century poet George Herbert, and—closer to home—a line from modern American poet Hart Crane. Examining the shirt's pocket carefully, the speaker exclaims how the careful stitching at its corners is "like a strict rhyme/ Or a major chord." The speaker celebrates every aspect of his shirt, leaving nothing out.

"At Pleasure Bay" is written in blank verse and describes several views of a seaside place called Pleasure Bay. Half-mythical, half typically American, the place is resonant with old rumors of a lovers' suicide pact, drawbridges to the sea, and catbirds singing "[n]ever the same phrase twice."

The sea and the birds are constant, despite the coming and goings of humans. After the star-crossed lovers, another story is told. The setting is Berlin, and the lovers are Adolf Hitler and the daughter of an English lord. The woman takes possession of an apartment—from a Jewish couple, no less—and later kills herself. It is rumored that a Jewish lady in Pleasure Bay was the displaced Berlin apartment owner.

Pinsky weaves these disparate tales together, with a tone sometimes meditative, sometimes mournful, but ultimately optimistic. The point of view in "At Pleasure Bay" is from the constant of nature, not the fluctuation of a human being. The poet imagines a state after death, to be more precise, and it sounds like a liberating kind of reincarnation.

> You lie down and embrace one body, the limbs
> Heavy with sleep reach eagerly up around you
> And you make love until your soul brims up
> And burns free out of you and shifts and spills
> Down over into that other body, and you
> Forget the life you had and begin again
> On the same crossing. . . .

"At Pleasure Bay" is Pinsky at his finest—celebrating life and the sensual, sensory world, while not ignoring negative and disturbing aspects. *The Want Bone* is a consistently fine volume of new work in which Robert Pinsky reaches new heights of expression.

Patricia Clark

Sources for Further Study

Chicago Tribune. August 5, 1990, XIV, p. 3.
Library Journal. CXV, June 1, 1990, p. 132.

The New Republic. CCIII, September 24, 1990, p. 46.
The New York Times Book Review. XCV, November 18, 1990, p. 24.
Poetry. CLVII, October, 1990, p. 39.
Publishers Weekly. CCXXXVII, March 30, 1990, p. 44.

WARRENPOINT

Author: Denis Donoghue (1928-   )
Publisher: Alfred A. Knopf (New York). 194 pp. $19.95
Type of work: Memoir
Locale: Warrenpoint, County Down, Northern Ireland

An autobiographical meditation on the author's origins and on the types of relationships he has entered into with them

The author of this complex book has been professor of Modern English and American Literature at University College, Dublin, and in 1981 was appointed to the Henry James Chair of English and American Letters at New York University. An internationally renowned literary critic and teacher, he has produced, either as author or editor, eighteen favorably received academic works, ranging in interest from Jonathan Swift through modern verse drama (*The Inner Voice*, 1959) to a dissection of contemporary literary theory (*Ferocious Alphabets*, 1981). Donoghue is perhaps best known for his critical readings of modern poetry, particularly that of T. S. Eliot and William Butler Yeats. Equipped with a formidable range of learning and an incisive prose style, his name stands with those of Hugh Kenner and Frank Kermode as being synonymous with such distinguishing features of postwar critical activity at the academic level as the internationalization of the range of critical inquiry and the corresponding enlargement of the critic's ambit. In addition, Donoghue is the first Irish literary critic to attain widespread recognition outside his own country, an achievement emblematic of Ireland's increasingly prominent membership in the international cultural community.

In a number of respects, however, *Warrenpoint* is far from being the book the reader might expect. It is not a reconstruction of the author's childhood in the Northern Irish market town that gives the work its name. On the other hand, *Warrenpoint* is not an account of how the author left his native place and rose to eminence in the academic world, a narrative spiced with revealing insights of the international intelligentsia. The work is unconventional in a number of ways. Although firmly anchored in the author's boyhood, and in his relationship with his father, it is not a straightforward narrative. Parallel to the impressionistic recollections of the author's growing up, and carrying more obvious weight than them, are gleanings from the mature adult intellectual's capacious mind. These gleanings typically succeed episodes recollected from the past and have the effect of interrogating these episodes, or rather—in the manner of the professional critic—questioning and challenging the possibility that meaning inheres in them and that identity may be established on the basis of such meaning.

In a sense, therefore, like many great autobiographical texts (citations from both Saint Augustine's and Jean-Jacques Rousseau's confessions, as well as from William Wordsworth's *The Prelude* [1850], are made with due deliberation), *Warrenpoint* is a philosophical disquisition on the nature and object of its confessional activity, and is more philosophical in its overall interests and tendencies than it is affective or

872 Magill's Literary Annual 1991

reconstructive. *Warrenpoint* should not be regarded as a companion piece to its illustrious avatars, however, being deliberately limited in scope and lacking originality of thought. It does read, however, as if one of the author's strong impulses were to subsume his particular experiences in some less fragile framework than the context in which they occurred. Hardly an experience is rendered or a thought entertained without invoking some dictum or exemplum from the canon of Western thought. Poets on whom Donoghue has written persuasively elsewhere (Eliot, Wallace Stevens, and Yeats, for example) have some of their thought and work analyzed—in particular, there are some brilliant pages on Eliot's *Four Quartets* (1943). Philosophers as heterogeneous as G. W. Leibniz, Walter Benjamin, and Emmanuel Levinas are availed of intermittently, and the same is true of certain literary critics, Kenneth Burke and William Empson being the clearest cases in point. In *Warrenpoint*, the intellectual atmosphere is bracing.

The danger that this atmosphere may prove suffocating to the raw material of the author's boyhood is not altogether avoided. This danger is compounded by a desire on Donoghue's part to see his childhood as not particularly exceptional. He is clear that it was distinctive, but he emphasizes its conformism and security with a firmness that borders on the ideological. Such an emphasis is perhaps inevitable, given the circumstances in which Donoghue grew up. Warrenpoint is a typical provincial town in Northern Ireland, by which is meant that its Protestant population, in addition to being in the majority, was culturally and socially in the ascendant, producing conditions of what might be described as moral apartheid for its Catholic fellow-citizens. This state of affairs was particularly true of the years of Donoghue's childhood, when the Northern Irish state—established by the Government of Ireland Act, 1920—had consolidated its effectively unchallenged authority in the name of Protestantism and loyalty to the British crown.

Background information of this kind—much of it provided in *Warrenpoint*, though, typical of the book's stimulating, idiosyncratic organization, toward the end—is essential, since the Donoghue family had a high degree of visibility in the local community. The author's father was sergeant of the local police, a rare appointment for a Catholic, and rarer still for somebody born in the South of Ireland. No childhood could be entirely immune from the cultural and political tensions of such circumstances, yet the main impression given of growing up in such an environment is of being sheltered. Life largely took place under the protective shadow of the father, and a tissue of hints and insinuations throughout the text suggest that it is such stability and authority that the author finds reproduced in books. Thus the arguably unusual decision to use for an autobiography a title without any obvious personal connotations emerges with expressive force. The Warrenpoint in question is not the place that has subsequently (like many Northern Irish towns in recent history) become notorious for Irish Republican Army (IRA) attacks on British forces and civilians alike. It is, rather, not so much a place as a condition consisting of, on the one hand, an encoded system of social constraints and discriminations so elaborate and consistent as to be virtually tribal and, on the other hand, a seemingly corresponding degree of freedom to develop an inner life, largely through study, and perhaps particularly through the activity of questioning that study demands but that social conditions seemed to inhibit. Warrenpoint emerges as a metaphysic of survival.

Donoghue's decision to conclude the book with newspaper accounts from *The Irish Times* of the two incidents of IRA violence that have drawn the world's attention to his native place is an implicit rebuke to all that Northern Ireland has come to denote in the public mind. The news items, in the starkness of their style, form, and content, are clearly at odds with the ethos of his own work. Yet they also draw attention to one of the main themes of *Warrenpoint*, which is how to keep faith with that which has been lost. The various afflictions of Northern Ireland and the peculiar state of arrested institutional development that the military and paramilitary violence there attests are not the author's subject. Although he does try to keep faith with some version of the Irish nationalism inculcated by the Christian Brothers during the years in secondary school, the effort seems halfhearted. It is to be regretted that, given the intellectual tone of the memoir—given that the work is as much an essay in intellectual good faith as it is an act of recollection—Donoghue has not brought the full weight of his formidable mind to bear on such difficult questions as tribal affiliation, dreams of unity, and kindred motifs of the Irish nationalist outlook, particularly when Donoghue himself regrets in passing the debasement of nationalism by many contemporary Irish intellectuals.

It may be that Donoghue feels compromised in confronting the issue of nationalism in contemporary Ireland, North and South, because of his family's unusual social position in Northern Ireland, a position that articulated loyalty to the law of an alien political dispensation. In any case, it is to his Catholic origins that he most clearly desires to remain true, rather than to any identifiable political influence. Certain of Donoghue's pronouncements regarding Catholicism, and his general inclination to uphold Catholic tradition (as opposed to Protestant or Christian), may strike the reader as controversial and uncongenial. A moment is recalled, for example, when Donoghue found himself incapable of uttering the word "chorister," because it was a Protestant term, its Catholic equivalent being "choirboy" (this matter arises as an aside in one of the discussions of the author's musicality). The inclusion of such moments and the unfashionable discussions of religious faith and sectarian observance suggest a potentially dogmatic element in Donoghue's makeup. Their inclusion is also, however, the strongest instances of the unsparing honesty that informs *Warrenpoint* throughout.

Moreover, a far greater presence in his young life was that of his father, and it is in that presence—authoritative, remote, stolid, responsible—that Donoghue wishes to believe. Sergeant Donoghue emerges from these pages as a not particularly knowable or even especially likable figure, and is recalled without a vestige of sentimentality. He is, however, the model of the real by virtue of which young Denis could base his sense of life's adequacy and negotiability. For this sensitive and ungainly child—though the reader rejoices in imagining what a commanding figure he cut as a six-foot-tall fourteen-year-old dancing on rollerskates—the sheltered world of the police barracks, where the family was quartered, was embodied and authenticated in the image of stability and human adequacy presented by his father. Such an image is all the more important since the family history also contains a potent embodiment of stability's alternative. This embodiment is Donoghue's brother John, who died in infancy—an event that constitutes the author's first specific memory. Somewhat unnervingly, *Warrenpoint* is dedicated to this unknown, unknowable infant.

The father's rigidity of manner and scrupulous observance of his role, his evidently all-consuming policemanship, is a sharp reminder of the degree of scrutiny to which he was subject as a Catholic of rank maintaining the law of the British crown for an overwhelmingly Protestant populace. In addition to its cultural nature, however, the sergeant's demeanor offered a psychological profile of fixity of purpose and concentration of energy which enabled his gifted younger son to withstand the limitations of his circumstances, whether the trauma of his baby brother's death, the town's stifling cultural atmosphere, the generalized but all-pervasive sense of being a second-class citizen, the banalities of provincial life, or his own temperamental and even physical difference from his contemporaries (Warrenpoint seems not to have been a place for friendships).

The father exists as the unquestioned and the unchallengeable one, and the life lived in his father's house by his youngest son was similarly unquestioned and unchallenging. It is with this life that the author seeks to maintain continuity, even though the form of the work that recuperates the nature of that life is discontinuous, moving with an air of unforced but surreptitious urgency from matter of fact to matter of speculation, from data to idea, from the securities of childhood to the interrogations endemic to maturity. Rather than dismantling the integrity of his childhood, however, Donoghue's formal approach renders it more secure than ever. The ostensible discontinuity of *Warrenpoint* on the formal level draws attention more effectively than a continuous narrative would to the author's concerns with continuity, tradition, and acceptance, all rendered here in a sustained and profound gesture of filial obeisance. The interrogation of his childhood, apart from yielding the unusual but not remarkable verdict of not guilty, also has the effect of restating its values, from which Donoghue has never deviated and which he publicly reclaims. The acceptance of an identity that was begotten, not made, that was instilled rather than fabricated, and that is best spoken of in terms of fidelity rather than rebellion— a set of attitudes that seems to gain support from Donoghue's apparent hostility to Freudian psychology—articulates his indebtedness to his father's exemplary presence by means of an uncritical desire to remain attached to that presence.

It is tempting to see *Warrenpoint* as an elaborate enactment of the critical process, in which the commentator's role is to maintain the viability and integrity of the necessarily remote and problematic text. Adapting this perspective as a metaphor for Denis Donoghue's relationship with his past, his father attains the status of a beloved, intriguing, formally impermeable text, complete in every respect and offering inexhaustible opportunities for understanding, commitment, and above all homage. The critic's protocols become identical to the son's fealty. Warrenpoint, too, is transformed beyond its local cultural, social, and political limitations to become the place, as unlikely but as real as many others, where such acts of devotion and attention were revealed.

George O'Brien

Sources for Further Study

Booklist. LXXXVII, October 15, 1990, p. 410.
Chicago Tribune. October 21, 1990, XIV, p. 1.
Kirkus Reviews. LVIII, July 15, 1990, p. 977.
Library Journal. CXV, August, 1990, p. 118.
Los Angeles Times. October 4, 1990, p. E13.
The New Republic. CCIII, September 24, 1990, p. 44.
The New York Review of Books. XXXVII, October 25, 1990, p. 48.
The New York Times Book Review. XCV, October 14, 1990, p. 13.
Publishers Weekly. CCXXXVII, July 13, 1990, p. 46.
The Washington Post Book World. XX, October 7, 1990, p. 3.

W. B. YEATS
A New Biography

Author: A. Norman Jeffares (1920-   )
First published: 1989, in Great Britain
Publisher: Farrar, Straus & Giroux (New York). Illustrated. 374 pp. $30.00
Type of work: Literary biography
Time: 1865-1939
Locale: Ireland and England

A *definitive biography of the Irish poet William Butler Yeats*

> *Principal personages:*
> WILLIAM BUTLER YEATS, the Irish poet
> JOHN BUTLER YEATS, his father
> MAUD GONNE, his great love
> LADY AUGUSTA GREGORY, his helpmate in the Abbey Theater

Scholars know more about William Butler Yeats than any other twentieth century poet. He consciously created his own self in his memorable autobiographical works. Nevertheless, A. Norman Jeffares' new biography of William Butler Yeats is very welcome; it is the first full-length biography of the poet since Joseph Hone's *William Butler Yeats* in 1943. Jeffares' 1952 book on Yeats, *William Butler Yeats: Man and Poet*, is more an analysis of the poems than a pure biography. The present biography is able, moreover, to include much information about Yeats that has come to light in the nearly forty years since Jeffares' earlier work, as well as up-to-date scholarship on the thought and background of the poet. Much has come to light about Yeats's life, friendships, love affairs, and membership in various Irish and occult groups and societies such as the Abbey Theatre and the Order of the Golden Dawn, and Jeffares uses this knowledge skillfully to produce a thorough and engaging portrait of a great poet and a fascinating man.

Jeffares traces in great detail the social and economic background of the Yeats family. The family was Anglo-Irish and originally in the linen trade. It was also related by marriage to the powerful Butler clan; one of the Butlers was Duke of Ormonde. William's father, John Butler Yeats, married Susan Pollexfen in 1863; the Pollexfens were involved in shipbuilding and prospered in the western part of Ireland in Sligo—an area the poet was to celebrate as the essential Ireland, a land where old traditions had not died and the fairies were part of everyday existence.

John Butler Yeats had a private income of four hundred pounds and decided not to enter a profession such as law but to be an artist. Jeffares' portrait of the poet's father is beguiling. He was a gifted artist, but he never seemed able to finish a picture: He valued art so highly that he could not accept anything less than a masterpiece. Commissions had to be forfeited because of this inability. As a result, the fortunes of the family gradually declined. John Butler Yeats believed in the gospel of art and passed this commitment on to his son William; he educated him by reading William Shakespeare and the Romantic poets. Thus William's education was rather incomplete, and in 1884 he finally decided to enroll in the Metropolitan School of Art, where he remained until 1886; he was not to be a painter, although his brother Jack was to become a distinguished one.

During this period, Yeats became interested in what were to be lifelong obsessions—Ireland and the occult. Ireland was at this time a hotbed of political ferment. Charles Stewart Parnell had taken control of the Irish Party in the British Parliament and skillfully led the agitation for Home Rule. His fall in the late nineteenth century divided the country into two factions. Yeats was a nationalist, but he was also a poet. He wished to create an "Ireland beautiful in the memory" through his art more than he sought political liberation. His earliest poems were on Irish subjects and used Irish myths. Yet these were not the only influences on the poet; a late Romantic, he was strongly attracted by Pre-Raphaelism and the Decadent movement of the 1890's. The subject may have been Irish, but the style was Romantic. As the first poem in the *Collected Poems* (1933) declared: "Words alone are certain good."

Yeats passionately needed a religion but had not had a conventional religious upbringing; thus he turned to occult systems such as Theosophy. He longed to receive evidence of the spirit world but maintained a healthy skepticism. Many of the groups he joined, especially the Order of the Golden Dawn, were filled with backbiting and rivalries involving such fantastical people as McGregor Mathers and Florence Farr, yet he persisted in the search for religious reality. The spiritualist movements in which he was involved gave him metaphors, subjects, and symbols for his poetry, as his second book, *The Rose* (1893) makes clear. Yeats never abandoned the occult, but he did become more subtle about its use in his poetry.

In 1889, at the age of twenty-three, Yeats met the person who was to be the great love of his life and the subject of many of his greatest poems, Maud Gonne. Maud Gonne was a revolutionary and an ardent believer in Irish nationalism; in contrast to Yeats, she believed in direct and if need be violent action to accomplish political goals. Her involvement in politics was to be one of the many elements that separated the couple and kept them from the marriage he so passionately desired. Yet Jeffares makes clear there were other reasons for Gonne to reject Yeats; she was involved in a lengthy affair with a Frenchman which resulted in the birth of a son who died very young. She also may have been aware of her value to Yeats the poet as a symbol of the unattainable woman; this symbol had much more poetic value than Maud the wife of the poet. Her later marriage to the brutal Major John McBride was, as Jeffares makes clear, very unhappy and short-lived. Yeats proposed to Gonne after McBride's death in 1916, but she refused once more.

By the early twentieth century, Yeats was a recognized poet. He had published *The Wanderings of Oisin* (1889) and two volumes of lyrics, *Crossways* (1889) and *The Rose*. He was also involved in a number of literary societies to promote the culture of Ireland. In 1902, he met Lady Augusta Gregory, who helped him form the Irish Dramatic Society, later to become the Abbey Theatre. Jeffares is very skillful at tracing the quarrels and divisions among those involved in this collaborative enterprise. The management of the Abbey was never satisfactory to Yeats; he supported

Lennox Robinson, but Robinson was a bumbling manager. Jeffares reveals more about the relationship between Yeats, Lady Gregory, and the financial sponsor of the theater, Annie Horniman, than had earlier biographies: The two women were engaged in a rivalry for the poet's attention and affection, while he tried to keep both satisfied. On the other hand, Jeffares is curiously reticent about J. M. Synge and his special place in the Abbey Theatre. Jeffares even slights the famous riots at the Abbey over *The Playboy of the Western World* (1907), and he is no better at dealing with the complicated relationships between Yeats and Sean O'Casey. Nevertheless, Jeffares does help the reader understand the backgrounds and contexts of Yeats's plays, thereby making them more accessible.

In 1913, Yeats met Ezra Pound, the apostle of modernism. Yeats had come to a dead end with his earlier Romanticism and needed to change his style, to make it harder and leaner. Jeffares does not have much to say about Yeats's shifts in style and does not give particularly insightful interpretations of some of Yeats's greatest poems. He does, however, give information about the poems and provides a context by which they might be more clearly and accurately understood. Jeffares performs as a biographer in this book, not a literary critic. Here the poems illuminate the life, and the life illuminates the poems; the poems are not independent entities to be interpreted.

During this period, the controversy about the collection of Lady Gregory's nephew, Hugh Lane, erupted. The Irish refused to build a gallery for Lane's collection of Impressionist paintings until it could be "proved the People wanted Pictures." For all Yeats's nationalism, he had many difficulties with the Irish, especially the Catholic middle classes, who were more interested in material gain or political action than in poetry. Yeats wished to bring into being an Ireland based on heroic and aristocratic virtues—virtues to be found in an earlier Anglo-Irish society but decidedly absent from one based on patriotism and profit. As Jeffares shows, however, Yeats turned everything he encountered, even his anger at his "fool driven land," into poetry. The change from occult and dreamy poetry to social satire was very important in Yeats's development as a poet.

The famous revolt in 1916 which after a long struggle brought independence to twenty-six counties of Ireland was not seen at first as heroic by Yeats. A rebellion by shopkeepers and fanatics was a violation of his aristocratic code. He did have the imagination, however, to seize the opportunity to become Ireland's bard in such poems as "Easter 1916" and "The Rose Tree." In addition, Yeats supported the Free State Party against the Diehards and even saw some aristocratic virtues in such leaders as Kevin O'Higgins. Later, he became a senator in the Irish Free State, but it was never to become the society he imagined.

In 1927, despairing of marrying Maud Gonne, Yeats finally decided to marry Georgia Hyde Lees. She was not a great beauty, but she did give Yeats the comfort and ease he had lacked throughout his life. In addition, she participated in a project of "automatic writing" which led to *A Vision* (1925), the fullest exposition of Yeats's religious and historical beliefs. Jeffares does not say very much about the system of *A Vision*, but he does make its purpose clear: It gave Yeats subjects for his poetry and a way of controlling the cycles of history by understanding them. It was also a way of classifying the different types of human personality and of bringing into an imaginative synthesis the opposites to which Yeats was drawn.

In 1923, Yeats won the Nobel Prize for his contribution to Irish and world literature. He had become by this time an established figure. His later years were spent, in part, at the tower near Lady Gregory's estate at Coole. He did not, however, submit to old age peacefully. He took Steinach injections to revitalize his sexual powers, since he equated a loss of those powers with a loss of poetic creativity. His poems, also, spoke more frankly of sexuality, especially the Crazy Jane sequence. Yeats adopted the persona of a wild and wicked old man, continually striving, rather than a worn-out sage. He wrote some of his greatest poems in this period, including "Among School Children" and "The Second Coming."

Although he remained active and creative, Yeats's health was failing. He was forced to spend time in warmer and less stressful areas such as the French Riviera. He died in France on January 28, 1939. The war that broke out soon afterward prevented the removal of his body to Ireland. In 1948, a warship of the now-independent Republic of Ireland brought the body back to his ancestral home in Sligo. He was buried under the epitaph he had written for himself:

> Cast a cold eye
> On life, on death.
> Horseman, pass by.

Jeffares' biography is likely to become the definitive one. It is unlikely that new facts will emerge to make this book obsolete. There certainly will be new interpretations of the meaning and significance of Yeats's poems and plays, but those will not reduce the importance of Jeffares' work. *W. B. Yeats: A New Biography* is a delightful and informative book with marvelous photographs of Yeats and those who were closest to him. It will help new readers of Yeats to understand and enjoy this great poet and provide new facts and insights for Yeats scholars.

James Sullivan

Sources for Further Study

American Theatre. VI, March, 1990, p. 37.
Booklist. LXXXVI, December 15, 1989, p. 808.
Chicago Tribune. November 19, 1989, XIV, p. 5.
Choice. XXVII, July, 1990, p. 1827.
The Christian Science Monitor. March 15, 1990, p. 13.
The Irish Literary Supplement. VIII, Fall, 1989, p. 6.
Library Journal. CXIV, December, 1989, p. 124.

New Statesman and Society. II, February 3, 1989, p. 44.
The New York Times. January 2, 1990, p. C17.
The Times Literary Supplement. March 10, 1989, p. 252.
The Washington Post Book World. XX, February 25, 1990, p. 6.

WHAT I SAW AT THE REVOLUTION
A Political Life in the Reagan Era

Author: Peggy Noonan (1950-   )
Publisher: Random House (New York). 353 pp. $19.95
Type of work: Political memoirs
Time: The 1980's
Locale: New York City and Washington, D.C.

An "insider's" political memoir that humanizes the Reagan White House while attempting to rehabilitate a faltering presidential image, written by the improbably famous speechwriter of Reagan's second term

> *Principal personages:*
> PEGGY NOONAN, White House speechwriter
> RONALD REAGAN, the fortieth president of the United States, 1981-1989
> NANCY REAGAN, his wife
> GEORGE BUSH, Vice-President during Reagan's term of office
> DONALD REGAN, Secretary of the Treasury and later White House Chief of Staff
> PAT BUCHANAN, White House Communications Director
> RICHARD DARMAN, high ranking presidential aide
> OLIVER NORTH, National Security Council member
> DAN RATHER, a CBS News anchorman

"The Reagan revolution," as many within and without the Reagan campaign and staff referred to it, is clearly one of the more curious political phenomena of the second half of the twentieth century—if only for its grand successes and profound failures. Oddly, the Reagan presidency has as many critics on the right as on the left, and, predictably, the feats regarded as triumphs by one side are regarded as defeats by the other. Such ambivalence has prompted more than one prominent member of the Reagan Administration to offer up that most contemporary genre of political volumes: the insider's memoir intended to "set the record straight."

Thus, there has been a spate of rather self-serving and hard-hearted tomes about Reagan's political fortunes, written from putatively superior vantage points and dwelling typically on the President's supposed flaws. In contrast, there is the sprightly and entertaining book by Peggy Noonan, an insightful and informed set of reflections on the Reagan years by the former and somewhat notorious White House speechwriter. Though it is an "insider's memoir," Noonan's "outsider" spirit of irreverence makes *What I Saw at the Revolution: A Political Life in the Reagan Era* a disarmingly funny and incisive volume. Noonan's work is a breezy show-and-tell tapestry of anecdotes and encounters. The book is a well-tempered if sometimes ego-enhancing report of her extended expedition inside the bowels of America's often-wounded executive branch.

Noonan's memoir begins with a brief but helpful contextualizing look at her apparently unremarkable childhood: "Like most baby boomers, I live this paradox:

Nothing really memorable happened in my childhood, yet I think about it all the time." This observation prepares the reader for Noonan's offbeat characterization of much that occurred in the White House during her sojourn. What emerges as strikingly memorable are not events but persons; in particular, the reader is impressed by the impact of one particular person on her sense of political reality: Ronald Reagan. Noonan's immigrant, working-class Irish background would hardly seem to have prepared her for the celebrity or the political allegiances she currently enjoys. Actually, her ethnic pedigree is only one of the curious historical circumstances and character traits she shares with her beloved president, who is the real central character of this volume.

Early in her narrative, Noonan evinces the same earthy, even religious appreciation that she believes Reagan has for ordinary folk and their abilities to cope with, or even overcome, problems with a minimum of governmental intrusion. This overarching principle helps explain why, in her years at Fairleigh Dickinson University, she embraced a healthy skepticism toward the utopian visions of social improvement generally brokered by the political left. As an English literature major, Noonan sharpened her writing skills and her wit, which served her well in her subsequent landing of a position as a news and editorial writer for CBS radio news. Her successful career there eventually brought her to the attention and appreciation of Dan Rather, the veteran CBS news anchor, whose friendship continued throughout her stint in the Reagan Administration.

From this biographical base, Noonan takes the reader on a fast-paced tour of her eventual interest in and initiation into the White House speechwriting corps. She provides a mostly chronological and day-to-day view of the life and craft of a White House speechwriter. Entailed in this travelogue are Noonan's intriguing histories of certain famous speeches of Reagan and her part in their eventual delivery. These speeches become the unusual but effective pegs upon which the narrative hangs for its coherence and overall organization. What might have been dry or trivial details in the hands of a less adept and winsome writer become riveting insights into Noonan's own work and the interaction of Reagan and his staff.

Upon leaving the "enemy-occupied" territory of CBS, she found herself submerged in a new but not completely different culture, whose prime directive was to shape the public's perceptions of its president. Sprinkled within this narrative are some immortal vignettes of the more infamous and interesting characters associated with the Reagan White House: a catalog of charming rogues and true believers whose allegiance to their president rises and falls with the political tides. For example, Donald Regan, former Treasury Secretary and Chief of Staff, appears as a George Raft sound and lookalike singularly unsuited to the delicacies of Beltway negotiation; Oliver North, the fallen Iran-Contra figure beloved to many conservatives, comes across as a jargon-spewing technocrat whose loyalties are more than ambiguous; and Nancy Reagan emerges as manipulative and overprotective, more comfortable consorting with astrologers than with the religious right who helped elect her husband. Others, such as policy aide Gary Bauer and Education Secretary

William Bennett, are portrayed by Noonan as principled statesmen; and she laments their lack of enduring influence on the Oval Office.

In effect, Noonan intends to portray her own political life in the administration as emblematic of how the Reagan revolution went sour in the second term. She believes that the second term failed because Reagan himself was left foundering in the shadows of bureaucratic politics and twisting in the wind before an obdurate Congress and a media hell-bent for another Watergate exposé. Consequently, Noonan's sympathetic but cockeyed look at what centrist and right-wing Republicans attempted in the 1980's has infuriated as many conservatives as it has liberals, and prompts the wry heading to her book's first chapter: "I Am Often Booed Because of Who My Friends Are." Noonan's "friends" range all over the political spectrum, inside and outside the Beltway, and, more important, inside and outside the media that conservatives have long learned to loathe. The same style and stance that have ingratiated Noonan among liberals have alienated her from those who believe her speechwriting shenanigans and subsequent public prominence were born of an uncivil and untoward ambition.

Therein lies one of the more interesting tales integral to the book's purpose of rehabilitating the Reagan image: how a woman speechwriter rose from obscurity within the domineering male bastion of White House staff politics to become almost as famous and, in certain respects, as influential as some of Reagan's own aides. Noonan was primarily responsible for many of President Reagan's most memorable speeches, including the heartrending text that Reagan delivered following the tragedy of the space shuttle Challenger explosion.

Noonan's blossoming kinship with Reagan, her rising notoriety in the public eye, and her behind-the-scenes impertinence quickly scandalized the more traditional and sedate onlookers within the Republican Party and in the White House. Pressure was placed on her immediate superior, Ben Elliott, to either discipline or dismiss her. The behavioral rules of proper decorum for a speechwriter had to be rewritten for an attractive, vivacious, and articulate woman. In a domain dominated by dutifully ambitious men, political tricksters, and silent yes-men, Noonan, by her account, refused to go along. In the end, she resigned rather than buckle under an administration disintegrating in the throes of the Iran-Contra debacle.

White House speechwriters, indeed speechwriters generally, are rarely "credited." Their identity is intentionally kept a secret, lest the aura of eloquence and institutional authority be undermined by attention to the skill and the ideas of the lowly wordsmith, who labors in anonymous loyalty to the man or woman at the head of the party. Noonan's battle for greater latitude in both speechwriting rhetoric and substance was representative of the larger struggle experienced by conservatives in Reagan's second term.

Against the jealousy and interference of some of her comrades and even the First Lady, there are times, says Noonan, when it is the loyal speechwriter's duty not to set policy but to help clarify it and keep it broadly consistent with implicit goals heralded in party platform and campaign promises. In her estimation, the President was frequently compromised by his second-term advisers: non-ideological and closed-minded pragmatists who unwittingly blunted Reagan's true strengths in their attempts to salvage what they believed was an increasingly weakening presidency. It was her job, Noonan argues, to write so as to allow Reagan to be Reagan, which was a difficult accomplishment in the closing months of the administration.

In the most poignant chapter of the book, Noonan details the evolution of one of her speeches and the censoring sessions precipitated by it, thereby providing a window into the inner workings of policy-making and political maneuvering calculated to provide soundbites.

> Great speeches have always had great soundbites. The problem now is that the young technicians who put together speeches are paying attention only to the soundbite, not to the text as a whole, not realizing that all great soundbites happen by accident, which is to say, all great soundbites are yielded up inevitably, as part of the natural expression of the text. They are part of the tapestry, they aren't a little flower somebody sewed on.

Her own best example of such a tapestry is delineated toward the end of the book. After Noonan recounts her departure from the White House, she depicts an anxious and appreciative George Bush summoning her to help revive his faltering presidential campaign. She provides a fascinating overview of the construction of Bush's dynamic acceptance speech at the close of the 1988 Republican National Convention. This "Thousand Points of Light" speech helped to catapult Bush's public image from that of a second-banana "wimp" to that of a conquering warrior.

In the end, political enemies of Reagan or his brand of conservatism will find little in Noonan's book to fuel their criticism, though they will be able to confirm their suspicions of intrastaff rivalry, opportunism, and deceit. While forthrightly identifying herself with the vision of America that she believes helped elect Reagan over President Jimmy Carter in 1980, Noonan nevertheless questions the degree of commitment maintained by others in his entourage. Clearly, Noonan is no James Boswell and Reagan no Samuel Johnson, but her purposes coincide with those of the venerable biographer: an unabashed apologia for a man with wholesome, decent ideals, whose worthy character should not be overshadowed by the failures of his subordinates. Her admiration for Reagan the man is well-captured in this pithy if somewhat hyperbolic summary:

> He was a modest man with an intellect slightly superior to the average. His whole career, in fact, was proof of the superior power of goodness to gifts. "No great men are good men," said Lord Acton, who was right, until Reagan. Toward mankind he had the American attitude, direct and unillusioned: He figured everybody is doing as much bad as he has to, as much good as he can.

The Reagan who emerges from her book is unfailingly endearing. In the midst of partisan squabbling over policy, he towers above fellow Republicans as a man of charity and grace. He is as concerned about the plight of an Alabama school girl who wants to talk about God in her valedictory address as he is about meeting a head of state. Finally, he is pictured consistently as one not well served by a cabinet and staff content to feed and nurture his distractions and to divert him from what he did best: to raise America's spirits and renew its self-confidence.

Bruce L. Edwards

Sources for Further Study

Commentary. LXXXIX, May, 1990, p. 58.
Human Events. L, May 5, 1990, p. 11.
Library Journal. CXV, March 15, 1990, p. 96.
Los Angeles Times Book Review. February 4, 1990, p. 2.
National Review. XLII, February 19, 1990, p. 49.
The New York Review of Books. XXXVI, December 21, 1989, p. 3.
The New York Times Book Review. XCV, February 4, 1990, p. 1.
Newsweek. CXIV, November 27, 1989, p. 85.
Publishers Weekly. CCXXXVII, January 19, 1990, p. 88.
Time. CXXXV, February 19, 1990, p. 84.
The Washington Post Book World. XX, February 4, 1990, p. 1.

WHAT KIND OF LIFE
The Limits of Medical Progress

Author: Daniel Callahan (1930-   )
Publisher: Simon & Schuster (New York). 318 pp. $19.95
Type of work: Medical ethics

Callahan explores what can be done about the rapidly escalating cost of health care and attempts to formulate the appropriate aims of the health-care delivery system in the United States

The ever-expanding medical system in the United States faces a genuinely serious financial crisis, with costs increasing at a rate about double that of general inflation. The national cost of health care in 1989 was $550 billion.

Energetic efforts have been directed in the past toward eliminating waste from the system, since most Americans believe that good health care would be affordable if the system were more efficient. For example, Medicare has limited unnecessary hospital stays, insurance companies have come to require advance approval for certain operations, health maintenance organizations that can reduce costs have proliferated; yet, these measures have had no significant success in addressing the problem.

In *What Kind of Life: The Limits of Medical Progress*, Daniel Callahan, a well-known expert on medical ethics and cofounder of the Hastings Center, the biomedical ethics think tank, tries to look at the health-care crisis from beginning to end, "to carry the problem through from philosophical premises to general policy recommendations, . . . hoping that the result will add something fresh to the debate."

Callahan argues that cost-containment programs can provide only a temporary solution to the problem. The public's demand for the best care that medical technology can provide and the huge growth in the number of health-care consumers offset any gains achieved by cost-containment efforts. This trend is particularly evident among the elderly, a segment of the population that is increasing in number and requires more complex care. Ironically, the very success and popularity of new medical technology defeat efforts to control costs: Successful technology increases the number of people who come for service, ultimately driving up the costs of care.

The solution to the crisis in the health-care delivery system, according to Callahan, is not simply a matter of eliminating waste or improving efficiency. While acknowledging that waste in the system and the enormous profits that physicians and the manufacturers of medical goods make are real and important problems, Callahan says that the ultimate problem lies in the cherished goals and ideals on which the American health-care system is based. The only way to deal with the crisis in health care, he writes, is to change the way Americans think about and understand illness, life, health, and death. Basic questions—"Where are we going? Where *should* we be going?"—must be raised. Beginning with philosophical premises and ending with general policy recommendations, Callahan attempts "to set forth an alternative way of thinking about health that will lead to the devising of a reasonable and just healthcare system," one that is "rooted in a plausible understanding of the human condition and . . . coherent, feasible, and humane in its practical policy implications."

Callahan calls into question the pursuit of unlimited medical progress, or the assumption that modern medicine must overcome all disease and extend all life. He claims that Americans' obsession with endless medical progress has led both the public and professionals to deny the unpleasant reality that everyone is subject to aging, decline, and death. In Callahan's words, "We have found our mortality wanting, and we have tried to modernize it . . . an extraordinarily expensive economic venture, consuming resources at a rapid and growing rate." The solution is painful: People must learn to curb their aspirations and set limits, he warns, or they will be spending more and more on health care with fewer benefits and less satisfaction. Americans must be willing to settle for "reasonable" health, or health "as a means to achieve some positive good," and accept the reality that illness and death can be postponed but never permanently conquered.

A second cherished ideal Callahan attacks is the American health-care system's preoccupation with the needs of the individual, rather than a concern for the common good. Focusing on the needs of the individual, or "an unlimited pursuit of individual cure," has fostered a steady escalation of "needs" and unrealistic expectations. People have come to believe that they "should get what they want and think they need." Furthermore, the American ideal of equality would extend all benefits to everyone, regardless of the ability to pay, an economic burden the public is unwilling (and unable) to carry. The system has responded by trying to become more efficient, but Callahan contends that the goal of efficiency cannot be met unless the goal of meeting individual need is changed. It is an illusion to think that individuals can all get all they need if only health care is delivered efficiently: "We will never get all we think we need as individuals and will have to settle for something less." He challenges the Universal Declaration of Human Rights assertion that "everyone has a right to a standard of living adequate for the health and well-being of himself and his family, including food, clothing, housing, medical care and necessary family services." According to Callahan, the concept of rights has become so overloaded that it has become meaningless, and Americans' claim of open-ended rights to health care implies that their neighbors (through the government) are obliged to provide for their needs.

It is mistaken to assume that better health and a longer life will result in human happiness, Callahan asserts. In fact, the actual improvement of health over the years has not been accompanied by a subjective sense of better health. He faults the World Health Organization's 1967 open-ended definition of health as "a state of complete physical, mental, and social well-being and not merely the absence of disease or infirmity" for defining all human problems as "illness." This misconception has turned every social problem into a medical problem and led to a maldistribution of the nation's resources, so that other important aspects of society that contribute to happiness, such as education and housing, have been neglected. Health, Callahan affirms, should not be the most important goal in life; it is a relative good, a means to an end, but it should not be a value in its own right.

As an alternative to the present predicament, Callahan proposes a "societal perspective on health," one that puts health in its proper place in the common life. He defines three fundamental human needs that require "some basic level of curative medicine"—the need to exist, to think and to feel, and to act (body needs, psychological needs, and function needs)—but he denies the possibility of ever reaching a consensus on a definition of individual curative "need" or finding an identifiable baseline of health care for all, since the definition of terms such as "adequate care," "minimal needs," and "normal" constantly shifts. If intractable individual need is the criterion, then anyone, however sick or old, is a candidate for care, and there is no way to limit claims. (An example of this dilemma, cited by Callahan, is the trend for older and sicker patients to be on renal dialysis.)

Callahan asserts that the highest priority of the health-care system should be that of promoting the health of society and ensuring that the great majority of citizens are able to contribute to the ends of society and live effectively in their communities. He argues that Americans already have a decent level of health care and must stop trying to push back all frontiers. The social and economic costs of further progress are too high.

Given the impossibility of curing everyone, the health-care system must give primacy to caring—to relieving pain and providing care, counseling, and support. One cannot expect that all individual needs for cure will be met, but everyone can expect a minimally adequate level of caring. Aspirations for meeting the curative needs of individuals must be balanced with society's need to set limits. Within this framework, body needs are met when most people are enabled to live out a full life span, psychological needs are met when they are mentally and emotionally stable, and function needs are met when they can function in society.

Just as limits must be set on the pursuit of cure for the individual, they must also be set on prolonging life beyond "a decent biographical life span," by which Callahan means late seventies or early eighties. Trying to keep people alive as long as possible regardless of the quality of life is not a legitimate goal.

Callahan proposes a more just and economically feasible health-care system, in which government plays a strong role in meeting public health needs, shaping the direction of research, and allocating resources. Care will be rationed, and health promotion that benefits the greatest number of people will take precedence over organ transplants. Care for all who cannot care for themselves, infectious disease control, and general medical and surgical care will be priorities ranked ahead of therapy dependent upon advanced technology. Biomedical research will be directed toward improving the quality of life and producing long-term benefits without increasing the long-term cost of care.

No informed person can argue with Callahan's basic premises that the American health-care system is desperately sick and that the success and popularity of new technologies, together with this society's obsession with the health of the individual, are much to blame. One has only to pick up a newspaper to see almost daily support for his position. The number of women age forty and older who have had mammograms to detect breast cancer had risen from 37 percent in 1987 to 64 percent in 1990; the number of annual coronary artery bypass operations rose from 61,000 to 250,000 between 1975 and 1985; and the number of cataract operations quadrupled between 1978 and 1990. (In the past patients were hospitalized for a week after surgery and required glasses with thick lenses; cataract surgery became popular when costs were reduced, patients could go home the day of surgery, and plastic lenses could be inserted into the eye.)

Callahan admits that he is not the first to suggest that cost-containment efforts will not solve the problem over the long haul. What he does contribute to the debate is a relentless focus on the central issue: that the crisis in health care is a crisis of values. Through repetition and frequent summaries, he rivets the reader's attention on the basic problem—the nature of health and the goals of medicine must be reconceptualized, and, in order to achieve some measure of individual health, people must put the "common good" first.

As a philosophical treatise, the book is wonderful, but the practical implementation of Callahan's alternative will be very difficult. Americans who have been shielded from the pain of rising health-care costs by third-party payments will not readily accept the difficult choices demanded in the health-care system he envisions. The logic of "the greatest good for the greatest number" is appealing, but when the individual who must forgo treatment is a personal friend or relative, logic may not prevail over sentiment. The idea of rationing health care and adhering to a formula that determines who is worth saving and who is not is frightening.

Two observations are in order. First, Callahan does not really address the many other factors that contribute to rising health-care costs. He has mounted a convincing argument to debunk the myth that waste is the basic problem of the health-care system and that cost-containment is the solution. Yet in the new order of things, physicians will continue to seek enormous profits, bureaucrats in the sprawling health-care bureaucracy will protect their privileges, and there will be considerable resistance from all the self-interest groups. While Callahan discusses the responsibility that society must accept for the costs of care to those who neglect their own health, he does not discuss the tremendous burden that social problems such as teenage pregnancy, drug addiction, smoking, and alcoholism place on the system. In a world where health care is rationed, people will surely resent footing the bill for those who refuse to help themselves. If these values are not amenable to change now, will fundamental values such as the belief in medical progress and the individual's right to health care be easier to change in the future?

Second, Callahan has not exhausted all the alternatives to the present system. For example, he does not explore the possibility of using other care providers, such as nurses and paramedics, to perform many of the functions that physicians currently perform. Numerous studies indicate that nurse-practitioners and nurse-midwives can deliver quality care at reduced costs. Will doctors relinquish their power any more easily under the new system?

These are observations, not criticisms. Callahan would probably say that raising these issues is begging the question. He is certainly aware of the complexity of the problem, and in his intent to drive home his message, he has done readers a great service by forcing them to focus on the need to change values. If others will focus with equal fervor on other problems, then perhaps there is hope for a more just and affordable health-care system. Change is inevitable. The war to reform the system, however, must be fought on all fronts.

Edna B. Quinn

Sources for Further Study

America. CLXIII, June 30, 1990, p. 20.
Booklist. LXXXVI, December 1, 1989, p. 706.
Commonweal. CXVII, May 18, 1990, p. 328.
The Guardian Weekly. CXLII, April 1, 1990, p. 20.
Library Journal. CXV, January, 1990, p. 139.
Los Angeles Times. February 6, 1990, p. E7.
The New England Journal of Medicine. CCCXXIII, August 9, 1990, p. 424.
The New York Times Book Review. XCIV, December 24, 1989, p. 1.
The New Yorker. LXVI, March 5, 1990, p. 106.
SciTech Book News. XIV, March, 1990, p. 17.
The Washington Post Book World. XX, January 7, 1990, p. 11.

WILDLIFE

Author: Richard Ford (1944-   )
Publisher: Atlantic Monthly Press (New York). 177 pp. $18.95
Type of work: Novel
Time: 1960-1961
Locale: Great Falls, Montana

In this concise coming-of-age novel, first-person narrator Joe Brinson recalls a time of family disintegration when his father went off to fight a forest fire and his mother had a love affair with another man

Principal characters:
> JOE BRINSON, the sensitive, caring narrator, who looks back from adulthood to his troubled family life when he was sixteen
> JERRY BRINSON, Joe's handsome father, who loses his job as a golf pro and takes a new one fighting a timber fire
> JEANETTE BRINSON, Joe's mother, who becomes a swimming teacher and has an affair with one of her students
> WARREN MILLER, a stout, prosperous businessman in his fifties, who has an affair with Jeanette

Wildlife, Richard Ford's fourth novel, further enhances his stature as one of the premier narrative stylists in contemporary American fiction. Heir to the minimalist tradition forged by Ernest Hemingway in the 1920's and revived by Raymond Carver in the 1970's, Ford shares with these predecessors a gift for deftly paced storytelling and vividly dramatized characters and a lean, understated style. In *Wildlife*, a reworking and expansion of the tale "Great Falls" from his acclaimed short story collection *Rock Springs* (1987), Ford performs an interesting variation on the familiar minimalist theme of isolation. By sustaining a restrained, nonjudgmental tone—largely free of the irony and bitterness that often prevails in minimalist or hardboiled fiction—Ford ultimately delivers an unexpected sweetness.

This sweetness derives from the love that Ford's narrator, Joe Brinson, feels for his parents and from Joe's nostalgia for a time when his parents seemed "good-looking, young, happy"—at the peak of their powers and optimism. Looking back on the year 1960, Joe remembers his father Jerry as "a natural athlete," "a smiling handsome man," who moves his family from Lewiston, Idaho, to Great Falls, Montana. Jerry hopes to benefit from the Gypsy Basin oil boom, using the personal connections he plans to make while teaching golf at a local country club. Joe's mother Jeanette, "a pretty, small woman" who had formerly worked as a bookkeeper and substitute teacher, is somewhat less confident about their prospects in Great Falls. Both parents are college educated, and Joe thinks that his mother "must've believed at the time that this was a normal life she was living, moving, and working when she could, having a husband and a son, and that it was fine."

Through all these details, Ford sketches an archetypal American family: a firm unit (even their first names are unified through alliteration) in quest of the American

Dream, willing to relocate, and hopeful of upward mobility. In the short story "Great Falls," the father, Jack Russell, is a working-class airplane mechanic who supplements his income through his skills at hunting and fishing. In *Wildlife*, Ford changes both the father's attitude toward social class and his chosen sport. Early in the novel, Jerry considers changing his party affiliation from Democratic to Republican, and his dream of assimilating into the upper class through his skill at golf—President Dwight D. Eisenhower's favorite sport—places the family even more firmly in the optimistic Republican mood of the 1950's.

The story is actually set, however, in "the fall of 1960"—a season that suggests a pivotal shift toward a more explosive decade and turns out to be a time of considerable change, of a fall from innocence, for the Brinson family as well. Ford's metaphor for this impending change is the wildfire that burns out of control to the west of Great Falls. Though no one believes that it is close enough to threaten the town, the fire creates an uneasiness, a feeling that, according to Joe, was "like discouragement." Smoke from the fire pollutes the town air and deters people from playing golf, which contributes to Jerry's loss of his job.

From the beginning of *Wildlife*, Ford's simple, monosyllabic diction and crafted, laconic sentences show marked similarities to Hemingway's style. In the scene where Jerry loses his job, Ford's deeper affinities with Hemingway's narrative method begin to emerge. Hemingway once explained his minimalist method by saying, "I always try to write on the principle of the iceberg. There is seven eighths of it under water for every part that shows." To achieve such rich suggestiveness through few words in many of his early, greatest stories, Hemingway uses his protagonist, young Nick Adams, in a manner that is revealingly similar to Ford's use of Joe Brinson. Once Hemingway establishes that Nick is innocent, observant, and sensitive, the author need comment neither on the shocking violence of the events that Nick sees, nor on the derangement of the other characters he encounters; the reader is all the more shocked and disturbed by imagining the impact of these events and characters on Nick. Similarly, Ford achieves remarkable tension and suspense in *Wildlife* by presenting the unpredictable behavior of his adult characters through the eyes of Joe—a young man whose sensitivity, stability, and self-control make the "wildlife"—the impulsive and ill-considered actions of his parents—all the more disquieting to the reader. In the scene where Jerry loses his job, for example, Joe is shocked to hear his father use obscene language, and is even more disturbed when his father takes the money from the pro shop cash register and urges Joe to take any of the expensive clothing and equipment that he wants. Joe attempts to excuse his father's actions ("I thought maybe Clarence Snow [Jerry's boss] had told him to clean out the cash register before he left and all that money was his to keep"), but the reader realizes that on a deeper level Joe is hurt and worried to witness a previously hidden intemperate and immoral side to his father.

Ford constructs the novel with a wildfire burning in the background—a wildfire that he seems to realize is perhaps too obvious as a symbol for the "wildlife," the unruly emotions and potentially destructive behavior that sweep through the Brinson family. Thus, Ford carefully controls the metaphoric implications of the fire, allowing them to surface only occasionally and subtly. The discouragement brought to Great Falls by the fire hits home when Jerry loses his job and goes through several weeks of depression and dissipation. Finally, Jerry takes a job as a fire fighter. From this point, all three family members have occasion to comment on the possible meanings of the fire and of Jerry's move.

Along with the fear that Jerry may be hurt or killed when fighting the fire, the family is also aware that this new job represents a severe social setback. Joe notices, for example, that many of the men on board the bus that will take Jerry to the fire are transients and Indians. Although Jerry tells Joe not to categorize other people, he also acknowledges the low social status of his new job when he urges his son, "Don't let what your parents do disappoint you." Similarly, Jeanette shares an important fear when she tells Joe, "I don't want to be poor"; and she expresses her disappointment in saying that though both she and Jerry were graduated from college, "you wouldn't know it" because of their lack of social success. She conceives the idea that Jerry might take advantage of the fire to leave her permanently, and she begins to cultivate the attentions of Warren Miller, an older but prosperous businessman whose wife has left him and who is attracted to Jeanette as a potential lover.

Although the Brinsons fear the physical danger and social setbacks brought about by the fire, they also—along with Warren Miller—recognize the attraction of the fire and the potential for renewal that it symbolizes. As Jerry is about to depart on the bus, Joe notes that his father is "happy that he was going to a fire now to risk whatever he cared about risking." Later, when Joe first meets Warren Miller, the older man comments on Jerry's departure with a sly remark that also expresses his justification for the adulterous affair that he hopes will develop with Joe's mother: "Sometimes you have to do the wrong thing just to know you're alive." When Jeanette takes Joe on a drive to see the fire, she comes to a similar realization about forest fires: "[T]here was something good about them . . . they replenished where they burned, and that for humans, my mother said, it was sometimes a good thing to be near a thing so uncontrollable. . . . People were drawn to things they shouldn't be." Only Joe, however, seems fully aware of how quickly the beauty and allure of fire can turn to destruction. As he watches a tall spruce tree explode into flame, Joe muses, "It all happened in an instant, and I knew it was dangerous though in a beautiful way. And I understood . . . what I thought dangerous was: it was a thing that did not seem able to hurt you, but quickly and deceivingly would."

Joe turns out to be right about how quickly something dangerous can move: The next day, Jeanette becomes Warren's lover; the day after that Jerry returns and tries to set Warren's house on fire; and within a few days after that, Jeanette moves out of the Brinson home and away from Great Falls. Looking back on the changes in his family life that happened so quickly, Joe realizes that at the time he faced a choice: to try to shield himself from what his parents did and experienced, or to try to understand it. The reader knows, without Joe having to say it, that Joe chooses the second option largely because he loves his parents and wants to do what he can to keep his family together. The reader also comes to appreciate Joe's stated reasons for his quest for understanding. If a young person shields himself or herself, Joe says, "what's lost is the truth of your parents' life and what you should think about it, and beyond that, how you should estimate the world you are about to live in."

Even if Joe was more inclined to try to preserve his ignorance and innocence, his parents persistently drag him into their emotional struggles and misadventures—in ways that sometimes seem perverse and even improbable. For example, when Jeanette goes to Warren's house for dinner and dancing, she takes Joe with her. Similarly, Jerry takes Joe with him when he goes to Warren's house to set it on fire. Furthermore, both parents have the odd habit of speaking to Joe with a calm running commentary on their behavior—even when they seem most out of control.

Ultimately, however, the reader comes to suspend his or her possible disbelief in the parents' odd behavior with Joe. One reason for the reader's credence is that the parents' strange behavior toward Joe seems consistent with their irrational behavior in general. A deeper, more poignant reason is that they, like Joe, are struggling to understand behavior that at times seems as mysterious and uncontrollable to them as it does to him. To Jerry and Jeanette, Joe must seem the most stable and reasonable member of the family; because he is not driven by the parents' conflicting passions, he may seem to each parent to be the family member most capable of providing understanding and support. Furthermore, their persistent inclusion of Joe in situations that other parents would hide from their children is perhaps a poignant sign that they want desperately to hold on to their family attachments and responsibilities.

In addition to exploring the isolation that the Brinsons feel from each other, *Wildlife* also dramatizes the stark isolation of the family itself from the rest of society. Even for such a brief novel as *Wildlife*, it seems strangely underpopulated. Besides the three Brinsons and Warren Miller, Ford characterizes only two other people: Clarence Snow (the country club president) and the unnamed fireman who investigates Jerry's arson. The author portrays the Brinsons as having no friends to speak of and few hobbies, interests, or ties to the general culture. This isolation adds resonance to Joe's realization, looking back, that

> It should have been a time when I cared about more things—a new girlfriend, or books—or when I had an idea of some kind. But I only cared about my mother and my father then, and in the time since then I have realized that we were not a family who ever cared about much more than that.

This isolation and fundamental connectedness of the Brinson family help to explain why Jeanette returns to the family in March, 1961, and why Joe's parents resume their life together. The ending of *Wildlife* is thus a curious one: only partially happy, not productive of any resoundingly conclusive truths, yet neither sad nor inconclusive. Ultimately, *Wildlife* has an authentic ending that rings true to the way life feels as it is being lived. Throughout the novel, Joe Brinson struggles mightily to understand his parents; yet even when he cannot understand them, he never ceases to try, and he never—even in his mind—withdraws his love from them. It is this remarkable staying power of a son's love, his enduring refusal to judge his parents harshly, that gives *Wildlife* its subtle and lasting sweetness.

Terry L. Andrews

Sources for Further Study

Chicago Tribune. May 27, 1990, XIV, p. 3.
The Christian Science Monitor. July 25, 1990, p. 12.
Commonweal. CXVII, August 10, 1990, p. 461.
Library Journal. CXV, June 1, 1990, p. 176.
Los Angeles Times Book Review. June 10, 1990, p. 3.
New Statesman and Society. III, August 10, 1990, p. 35.
The New York Times Book Review. XCV, June 17, 1990, p. 3.
Newsweek. CXV, June 11, 1990, p. 64.
Publishers Weekly. CCXXXVII, April 13, 1990, p. 55.
Time. CXXXV, June 4, 1990, p. 86.
The Times Literary Supplement. August 10, 1990, p. 4558.

WILLA CATHER
Double Lives

Author: Hermione Lee (1948-   )
First published: 1989, in Great Britain
Publisher: Pantheon Books (New York). Illustrated. 410 pp. $29.95
Type of work: Literary criticism and biography

An analysis of Cather's major novels and short stories based on her use of language, imagery, and significant events in her life

> *Principal personage:*
> WILLA CATHER, American novelist, journalist, and poet

Willa Cather: Double Lives is an extraordinarily rich work, weaving together biographical material and close readings of Cather's fiction to illuminate the major themes and literary techniques of this important twentieth century American novelist. Like her subject, Hermione Lee conveys complex ideas with clarity and subtlety; her own prose style is one of the delights of the book. Lee also brings to her study the same kind of broad cultural background that Cather drew upon in her fiction, moving comfortably through discussions of classical literature, Wagnerian operas, and early American history.

Lee's study is grounded on the premise that "Cather's work gets its energies from contraries," from the tensions between Romanticism and realism, Europe and America, the natural and the artificial, the individual and the group. These tensions are revealed in many different ways: in direct plot conflicts, in characters who are themselves split or who serve as doubles for others, in landscape and imagery, in subtle variations of language.

Many of these tensions, Lee suggests, developed out of Cather's early experiences. She devotes much of the first quarter of her study to the author's childhood and adolescence in Nebraska and to the period in her twenties and thirties when Cather worked as a journalist in Pittsburgh and New York. Lee points out that the struggle of the young artist to escape the pressures of provincial life is a recurrent theme in Cather's work. Although Lee takes issue with contemporary critics who read Cather's work as "an encoding of covert, even guilty, sexuality," she finds Cather's attraction to women and her questions about the nature of womanhood another strong source of conflict throughout her career. Lee also suggests that Cather's ambivalent feelings about her mother underlie a number of her female characters, the "lost ladies" who entrance but disillusion their younger admirers. These characters also owe something to Isabelle McClung, Cather's closest friend during her years in Pittsburgh.

Cather's path to artistic success was not an easy one; she was in her early thirties before she published her first volume of short stories and almost forty when she completed *O Pioneers!* (1913), her first major success. Lee's discussion of her life suggests that there were few, if any, periods of unalloyed pleasure in Cather's mature years. Her greatest satisfaction seems to have come from her trips to the Southwest, whose Indian ruins gave her a vision of a society in which art and life were unified. This region forms the backdrop for her most affirmative novel, *Death Comes for the Archbishop* (1927). Cather's trips to France in 1902 and in later years were also significant in a more ambivalent way, arousing her recognition of the marvels of European culture, but also underlining the destructive effects of World War I.

Lee incorporates biographical material, but the heart of her study is in her thoughtful, detailed discussions of Cather's novels and major short works. She treats these works chronologically, providing enough plot summary to make her comments understandable for readers who are not familiar with them, then exploring in detail theme, characterization, language, and imagery.

Cather's earliest published works—the short-story collection entitled *The Troll Garden* (1905) and her 1912 novel, *Alexander's Bridge*—show her preoccupation with the struggle of an artist to survive in a hostile environment, a theme carried out, Lee notes, in "powerful images . . . of a landscape which crushes and resists attempts to shape or transform it." The struggling artist-protagonist of *Alexander's Bridge* is destroyed by the conflict between freedom and conventionality.

The Song of the Lark (1915) provides a more positive treatment of the same theme. Cather used details of her own childhood in describing the youth of her heroine, Thea Kronberg, who, like her creator, felt trapped by her Midwestern environment. Thea transcends the limitations of past and gender to become a great Wagnerian soprano. Lee finds Cather's symbolic use of landscape particularly effective here. In Panther Canyon, Arizona, a distinctively female place filled with caves and fissures, Thea discovers a culture in which there is not division for women between art and life. Thea's voice is her equivalent of the ancient Indian women's beautiful, functional pottery; like them, she "can make shapes in which to catch life."

O Pioneers! and *My Ántonia* (1918), the works written immediately before and after *The Song of the Lark*, are placed by Lee in the tradition of the classical pastoral, the centuries-old literary form that rests on artful simplicity in its search for a golden age in rural life. In each novel, Cather portrays a strong female figure: the almost mythic Alexandra Bergson, who successfully manages her family farm in *O Pioneers!*, and the warm, resilient immigrant girl, Ántonia Shimerda of *My Ántonia*.

While each work is on one level positive and affirmative, Lee finds in both an underlying melancholy. Both are books of coming home and reconciliation, but these homecomings are inextricably linked with death. The marriage of Alexandra to her steady, reliable friend Carl at the end of *O Pioneers!* "seems more like a burial." The narrator of *My Ántonia*, Jim Burden, seems to embody Cather's own search for wholeness in her rural past. His adult life, Lee notes, was "made up of dislocation and absence." He returns to his childhood home and to his memories of Ántonia to find his place in the world. Again Lee sees the ending as somber: "a heavy burden is being placed on the past to make it console us for, even replace, the present."

World War I was for Cather a watershed event. For the last thirty years of her life, she chafed at the materialism and vulgarity of postwar society. Her first attempt to deal with the war and its effects was her 1922 novel, *One of Ours*, which draws on the lives of two young war victims she had known: a Nebraska-born cousin and a talented violinist friend. The novel received considerable criticism for idealizing the war, but Lee suggests that this work should not be evaluated as a commentary on war at all. She reads it as another exploration of a familiar Cather theme: the end of a golden past—in this case, the old West. Cather mourns a second lost paradise in her depiction of prewar France. As in her earlier work, resolution comes not in victory but in acceptance of defeat. Lee describes the main character, Claude, as "a Wagnerian knight questing for redemption . . . in the wasteland." Like Wagner's Parsifal, Claude is a "blameless fool" ennobled by his experience. Yet he is also "a miserable, repressed Nebraskan boy who gets killed in a horrible war." Cather does not, Lee believes, entirely reconcile these two strains, yet the book reflects the tensions of this stage in her career. As Lee perceptively observes, in Cather's earlier works, memory was the force by which one countered death; the novelist's special mission, thus, is to preserve memory. For Claude, however, amnesia is the only way to escape horror, and if that is the case, Lee observes, "the function of the novelist is thus put at risk, and may become more difficult, alienated and obscured."

The bleak worldview of *One of Ours* informs the next group of works, two novellas and a novel that Lee finds Cather's most powerful. *A Lost Lady* (1923), *The Professor's House* (1925), and *My Mortal Enemy* (1926) show new literary subtleties—an emphasis on the creation of mood, the use of objects in symbolic ways, a reliance on suggestion rather than explicit statement. While Cather publicly rejected the experiments of her modernist contemporaries, Lee compares her work with theirs in her emphasis on "the fractures with the past, the need for order, memory and its gaps, heroism, myth."

Two of these works, *A Lost Lady* and *My Mortal Enemy*, grow out of Cather's lifelong fascination with a particular type of woman, one characterized by charm, beauty, selfishness, and power over others. The respective central characters, Marian Forrester and Myra Henshawe, are depicted through the eyes of younger admirers, each of whom is finally disillusioned by the actions of the idealized woman, as Cather may have been by her mother and Isabelle McClung. Yet Lee suggests that the narrator's disillusionment may not be Cather's only judgment on these figures. Marian Forrester, at least, may be seen not only as an "Arcadian ghost" but also as one of Cather's strong women, a survivor like Alexandra or Ántonia.

Lee's discussion of *The Professor's House* is perhaps the high point of her book, a detailed and perceptive analysis of Cather's handling of language and symbols. The professor of the title, Godfrey St. Peter, shares with his author a sense of alienation in a crass, materialistic world symbolized by his pretentious, confining home. From his young friend, Tom Outland, dead before the novel begins, he has received a vision of a more open life, again symbolized by Cather's beloved Southwest. The differences between the lives of these two men, Lee demonstrates, are most visible in the language Cather uses for each. St. Peter's narrative is formal, constrained; Outland's story comes in a fresher, more colloquial voice. The novel, Lee concludes, "is an epitome of all Cather's writing, in which she divides herself between two 'writers': Tom as the instinctual explorer and the Professor as the conscious reviser." Lee finds the work more positive than others, in spite of its elegiac tone, for at the end St. Peter seems to have integrated the instinctual qualities of Tom into himself.

This affirmative note carries over into one of Cather's best, most popular works, *Death Comes for the Archbishop*, a tribute to the missionary priests of the Southwest into which Cather poured her love for New Mexico. Lee compares the narrative structure of this work with that of a medieval saint's legend. Working freely with her historical sources, Cather rejected a realistic, chronological approach in favor of a series of scenes and interlaced stories. Lee writes, "this redistributed narrative makes its centre a conception of time, not as linear accumulation, but as a conjunction of 'timeless moments.'" The language is deliberately stylized to give the effect of an "old translation," and the tone of the whole is triumphant, in tune with the pervasive imagery of light.

For her next novel, *Shadows on the Rock* (1931), Cather again turned to the early history of North America, this time to French Canada at the end of the eighteenth century. As Lee points out, however, this work is more muted than its predecessor. Again, the mood is conveyed in the setting—which is, as the title suggests, gray and misty. Lee attributes the melancholy note to the recent death of Cather's father, her mother's debilitating stroke, and her own health problems. Although the novel is superficially historical, Lee reads it as "a meditation on childhood, family security, and maternal influence."

For her last major novel Cather reached further into her family's past, setting *Sapphira and the Slave Girl* (1940) in antebellum Virginia. Lee finds this study of two families—one black, one white—somewhat disturbing to a modern admirer of Cather: Her treatment of slavery is equivocal and her characterization of blacks at times embarrassingly patronizing. The strength of the novel is again in the portrayal of a strong female figure, the matriarch Sapphira. In this defiant, sometimes cruel old woman, Lee asserts, "Cather is registering her own cold and passionate desire for authorial control, her own experience of the pain and handicap of old age, and her own desire to maintain a stoic dignity in the face of death."

The Willa Cather who emerges from the pages of Lee's book is a complex, introspective, highly conscious artist. She wrote little that was overtly autobiographical and was, in fact, almost obsessive about protecting her privacy. Yet she put much of herself into characters as diverse as Jim Burden and Godfrey St. Peter, Sapphira Colbert and Thea Kronberg. Her struggles to reconcile profound conflicts in her own life became the source for several of the most powerful novels in twentieth century American literature. Lee's fine study illuminates both Cather's life and her work and should be essential reading for any serious student of her fiction.

Elizabeth Johnston Lipscomb

Sources for Further Study

Booklist. LXXXVI, February 15, 1990, p. 1135.
Commentary. XC, September, 1990, p. 60.
Library Journal. CXV, April 1, 1990, p. 116.
Listener. CXXII, October 19, 1989, p. 24.
London Review of Books. XI, December 21, 1989, p. 18.
New Statesman and Society. II, October 6, 1989, p. 43.
The New York Times Book Review. XCV, March 25, 1990, p. 31.
The Observer. October 8, 1990, p. 47.
The Times Literary Supplement. November 17, 1989, p. 1259.
The Washington Post Book World. XX, March 11, 1990, p. 13.

WINDOWS

Author: Robert Creeley (1926-   )
Publisher: New Directions (New York). 160 pp. $19.95; paperback $10.95
Type of work: Poetry

A collection of poems on loneliness, aging, and the limits of language written from Creeley's inimitable angle of vision

Windows, the eleventh book of poetry by Robert Creeley, contains both open-ended, improvisational poems of the type with which he has experimented since *Pieces* (1969) and many elegiac, even lyrical, poems, which, though definitely written in his inimitable style, verge toward more traditional structure and content. Creeley remains the premier American practitioner of minimalism in poetry, working with a short-lined, imagistically spare verse form that struggles to communicate the immediacy of experience without relying on the techniques associated with traditional poetry—for example, simile, metaphor, symbol, extended description, or predictable sound patterns. Within the tight focus of Creeley's poetry, the interaction of the poet's perceiving consciousness and the events that directly impinge upon it become brilliantly highlighted, resulting in a body of poetry that is both personal and profound.

When asked about the circumstances surrounding the composition of *Windows*, Creeley replied that many of the poems resulted from his travels to Austria and Finland. More interesting was his statement that a large number of the poems had to do with painting and painters, representing, in his words, "a frame for/of seeing." It is particularly Creeley's sense of windows as a "frame for/of seeing" that describes his unique sense of poetics. Associated with the Projectivist movement in poetry during the 1950's and 1960's, a movement captained by Charles Olson that promoted open-form, nontraditional composition, Creeley has developed his own idiosyncratic postmodern poetics that abandons all systems which evaluate and interpret experience in favor of direct seeing.

Although Olson also wanted a poetry that presented the perceptual immediacy of direct seeing without the interference of egocentric systems and categories seeking to control and explain experience, he wanted to express as concretely as possible an image of man, a point of view that transcends the purely personal perspective. In *Windows*, Creeley illustrates how rigorously he has relinquished all conceptual schemes: "Trying to get *image of man/* like trying on suit/ too small, too loose,/ too late, too soon—" Like a suit on the rack, the "image of man" will fit neither a specific body nor an individual self. Even more than Olson, Creeley desires a poem unrestrained by any code of significance that would cover experience with meaning, centered purely on the present moment seen from the perspective of the poet. The frame of seeing is immediate and not mediated through any cultural or aesthetic schema.

Besides Charles Olson, Creeley has been heavily influenced by William Carlos Williams, whose object-centered poetics is summed up in the famous line from "A

Sort of a Song" (1944): "No ideas/ but in things." Surpassing his former friend and teacher, Creeley has developed a poetry whose major principle might be stated as no ideas, only words as things. Since *Pieces*, Creeley has used words as physical acts and has constructed poems in the same way that the influential Abstract Expressionist painter Jackson Pollock created paintings from the drip and splatter of paint. The result is a poetry resembling an imprint from experience, rather than a comment on it.

Creeley has described his recent poetic technique as "*scribbling*, of writing for the immediacy of pleasure and without having to pay attention to some final code of significance." A good example of the limitations of this style from *Windows* is the poem "Texas Reverse," which is, simply, "You all/ go." Even if the poem does communicate a feeling of loneliness, the poem is not memorable, based as it is on simple word play.

Although Creeley generates some poetry of this tedious sort whenever he is "scribbling," he can often use this method of juxtaposing words and colloquial phrases to produce poems that reverberate with meaningful potentialities. A successful poem is "Nature Morte": "It's still/ life. It/ just ain't moving." The first line break at "still" emphasizes the horrific lack of movement that characterizes death. The second line beginning with "life," however, changes the grammatical function of "still" from an adjective signifying immobility to an adverb signifying continuation. Also, the hidden phrase "still life" suggests that an art that produces physical stasis, a still life, causes an aesthetic death as terrible as a biological one. In order not to immobilize either life or death, Creeley uses "it" without a discernible referent, illustrating his singular practice of employing ambiguous pronouns so that meaning is not fixed at one source but can enter into the poem from many sources external to the poem. Finally, the colloquial ending does not bring the poem to closure so much as it presents the speaker in a precarious posture of bravado still facing the irresistible force of death manifested in its indefinable it-ness. Much can be accomplished by this poetic method. As Creeley writes elsewhere in *Windows*, "We talk like/ this too/ often someone/ will get wise!"

Because Creeley prefers an abstract, indefinite vocabulary and often relies on nonspecific words such as "edge," "place," "there," and "here" and equivocal pronouns, much of the meaning of his poems must be derived from the subrational impressions engendered by subtle inflections and the timing of the words controlled by line breaks, a technique reminiscent of the musical phrasing in jazz. When confronted, however, with death and aging, Creeley's poetry achieves a remarkable clarity at all levels. Each of the six sections of *Windows* ("The Company," "Window," "Seven," "Dreams," "Eight Plus," and "Helsinki Window") contains poems focused on mortality that transcend his stylistic innovations and join the tradition of the romantic lyric, which, without depreciating the physical world, envisions the possibility of a higher realm of meaning.

The title poem of the first section, "Company," expresses the poet's plaintive desire to be not merely a recording instrument but also to speak to some more common, perhaps communal, purpose: "Recorders ages hence will look for us/ not only in books, one hopes, nor only under rocks/ but in some common places of feeling." This hoped-for participation within a wider arena is offset by the claustrophobic feeling in the last lines: ". . . fearing this/ is the last day, this is the last,/ the last, the last." In these lines echoes the deadening repetitiveness of life where the days succeed one another in an unending, unredeemed sequence.

The poet's struggle to escape the deadly enclosure of mortality is continued in the next section, "Window." Here the title poem of the section describes the poet as writing while leaning "forward at waist,// somewhat stiffly—/ not// old,/ young, young." The insistent reiteration of "young" in these lines betrays Creeley's anxiety about aging and death. Refusing to comprehend death by means of traditional discourse, he bravely ends by asserting "Never just one," acknowledging the multiplicity of possible answers to death's enigmatic questions.

In the middle of a set of improvisations in section "Seven," Creeley intimates some possibilities of escape from mortality. In the short piece "Boat" Creeley opens up to something more than the present moment: "Let me come in,/ come on// board you, sail/ off, *sail off* . . ." In this poem, freedom of movement combines with a lyrical sexuality that breaks restrictions and transforms the confines of a coffin into the hull of a boat. This lyricism finds fuller expression in the poem "The Seasons," an uncharacteristic poem for Creeley since it is structured upon the conventional poetic pattern of seasonal change. Ending with the line "say what it's worth," the poem suggests that Creeley feels a sense of movement and openness; he can look back over the seasons of his life and determine their "worth."

All of Creeley's considerable poetic skills are summoned in the poem "Age," which appears in the fourth section, "Dreams." The poem begins, "Most explicit—/ the sense of trap," presenting the boxed-in, constricted sense of death that Creeley has offered in previous sections of the book. Words themselves can trap the poet's consciousness: "Language of singular/ impedance? A dance? An// involuntary gesture to/ others *not* there? What's wrong here? How/ reach out to the// other side all/ others live on. . . ." A preoccupation with inner, personal problems can prevent the reaching out that effective poetry demands. This excessive inwardness ignores the fact that language in operation naturally produces a speaker and a hearer, an "I" and a "you," and creates a community that salvages loneliness and gives a possible meaning to existence. The struggle to reach out to others can become frustrating. At the end of "Age," the poet is threatened with becoming a "uselessness" that "talks, even if finally to no one,/ talks and talks." As in the art of Samuel Beckett, language may be merely meaningless sounds; there may be nothing to express, coupled with the compulsion to continue the act of expressing. Yet, Creeley does have intimations of a "something" that is the ground of language and, perhaps, existence.

"Eight Plus," the fifth section of *Windows*, includes poems that reinforce the positive sense of movement found in "The Boat." The poem "Consolatio" particularly demonstrates Creeley's ability to question everything, face meaninglessness, and still discover solace. Everything that forms a locus of value in his poetry is scrutinized in this poem: "pulse," the physical rhythms of the body; "mind," the seat of consciousness and source of explanatory systems, "home," the desired place of rest in the middle of confusion; "here," the location of the mind and body in the present moment; and "there," the position of the past and otherness. All of these offer an "echo," not the thing itself. Despite this possible despair, there is a deeper level of meaning, as insistent as the iambic dimeter of the poem's lines, suggesting the stubborn heartbeat of being underlying language. Explicit in the last two lines are movement ("Now to begin") and optimism ("Why fear the end").

This hint of an ineffable ground of meaning underlying existence is amplified in the final section, "Helsinki Window." In this section, the meaning behind existence is presented in images of light and renewal, poetic devices that mirror those associated with romantic lyricism. While visiting the high latitudes of Finland, Creeley notes, "Late sun, late sun,/ this far north you still shine,/ and it's all fine,/ and there's still time enough." Imbued with this sense of light and the sufficiency of time, Creeley can reflect on his life's work. Although his work may not have attained the major illumination of either William Butler Yeats or T. S. Eliot, it can still give a flash of wonder.

Although still besieged by the way that "all/ patterns and plans fixed/ focus death again," Creeley has the suppleness of movement and the freedom of time at the end of this sequence of poems from the far north. The last poem of the book, "Spring Light," is structured around conjecture rather than assurance, asking "Could persons be as this/ fluffed light golden spaces." The anxiety of the questioning has been dampened, however, for "back of dark is summer's/ light that slanting clarity all/ wonders come again the bodies open." As the last line of the poem states, there exists always a "piece of what had not been lost." The illumination from the ground of being and the renewal of spring are both concepts from more traditional poetry that bring a sense of consolation to Creeley's poetry.

Difficult and frustrating as Creeley's poetry may be, his poems in *Windows* disclose a romantic, lyrical intimation of something beyond death and beneath the surface of existence that suffuses all and, in the end, suffices. Whereas other poets have chosen to come to a similar illumination burdened with metaphor and laden with symbols, Creeley has opted for the way of scarcity, lightening his load of stock poetic devices so that, aesthetically unobstructed, he can see the light that permeates the here and now.

Kenneth Gibbs

Sources for Further Study

Publishers Weekly. CCXXXVII, April 13, 1990, p. 59.
San Francisco Chronicle. September 2, 1990, p. REV10.
Small Press. VII, June, 1989, p. 46.
World Literature Today. LXIV, Fall, 1990, p. 640.

WINNING THE CITY

Author: Theodore Weesner (1936-   )
Publisher: Summit Books (New York). 208 pp. $17.95
Type of work: Novel
Time: The 1950's
Locale: Flint, Michigan

A novel chronicling the struggle of a sensitive boy to recover his lost position and security

> *Principal characters:*
> DALE WHEELER, a teenage boy who discovers the unfairness of the world and attempts to alter his situation
> MR. WHEELER, his alcoholic father, who tries to help Dale lead a fuller life
> MR. BOTHNER, a wealthy superintendent at Chevrolet who takes Dale's basketball team and place away from him

Winning the City has for its overt subject a young boy's quest to win the city basketball championship, but it really deals with that boy's search for a place where he can be secure and know who and what he is. He has been displaced from a secure role by the callous action of a wealthy man and needs to recover his place in the world and to find a self that is not dependent on his class or social position. This is Theodore Weesner's fourth novel, and like the others it deals with the outer and inner difficulties a young boy must struggle to overcome; the boy in this novel, like the others, is something of an outcast within a very well defined society with established codes of behavior.

The novel begins with the joyous anticipation of victory in the city basketball championship by the main character, Dale Wheeler, a fifteen-year-old junior high student. He has worked hard all summer on his game; he plays or practices until the lights are shut off at ten P.M.; he sweeps the gymnasium floor so he can have more time to practice on a real court. It is clear that he expects that his hard work will be rewarded and result in changes in his life. Yet he does have a number of recalcitrant problems.

The first problem is his father. Mr. Wheeler is an alcoholic assembly-line worker at the local Chevrolet plant. He is close to his son, but he has problems of his own. In addition to his drinking, he has had his losses. He has lost a family dry-goods store in his native Arkansas; he has lost his wife. Once he showed up drunk at a basketball game in which Dale played and embarrassed his son by dropping a whiskey bottle from his pocket. He does love his son, but he has difficulties in expressing that love; his primary way of conveying affection is to feed Dale, to bring him Coney Island hot dogs or cinnamon doughnuts. He also teaches his son what he can; he initiates him into one ritual of manhood by teaching Dale how to drive. With a realistic perspective, he warns his son not to expect too much from basketball. Dale thinks that he can change his own tenuous social situation and that of his father by his athletic victories. The relationship between father and son is one of the most effective parts of the novel, and the portrayal of a beleaguered father is masterful, especially in the father's rich country language.

When Dale gets to the first practice of the season, Coach Burke introduces Mr. Bothner to the team. New to the area, Bothner has been an All-American basketball player, and his sons have placed first and second in the Soap Box Derby competition. Clearly, this family contrasts with Dale's troubled one. A few days later, Dale learns that Bothner has sponsored a team, the Michigan Truckers, in the city league, eliminated Dale's old team, and left him off the new one. Bothner wants his sons to play together, and the younger one is a point guard, Dale's position. There are also social implications. Bothner is a supervisor at the Chevrolet plant where Dale's father works on the assembly line, and the fathers of the new team have met to establish the team. Dale's father works the 4:00-12:00 P.M. shift and is not considered a socially presentable father.

Enraged at this exercise of power, Dale seeks solace from others. His fellow player Sonny Joe is no help; he wants to play on the new team, and he and the others are impressed by the party Mr. Bothner gives. Dale's junior high coach is also no help: He tells Dale that Bothner created the team so his sons could play on it and there was nothing he could do about it; he merely accepts the injustice. Dale's father also says that there is nothing to be done, although he would visit the principal if Dale thought it might help. Dale does receive daily support from an English teacher, Miss Tarbush, who praises him and challenges his mind. Dale even mentions to her one day that he would like her to become his mother. A young girl, Zona Kaplan, also talks to Dale and makes him feel important, but she has limitations of class and social position, as the book makes clear later.

In desperation, Dale calls a boy from another junior high and asks about their city league team. The team that Dale joins, the Little M's (for Missourians), is very different from the one at his own school. The boys are all sons of immigrants from the South who, like Dale's father, sought work in the automobile factories of Michigan. The team is filled when Dale calls, but the father of one of the boys reacts against the unfairness and puts Dale on the team. It is a very unconventional team; it has no coach, and the boys swear and smoke. Their language and attitudes are very different from that of Dale's school friends. They are rednecks and make no apologies for it; they do not try to ape the manners of their supposed betters. Dale is attracted by their boldness and their storytelling, and he tries to tell a story in their style. Realizing that this language is not natural to him, however, they criticize him. Dale is caught between the group he left and the group he has joined; he belongs to neither. This is also made clear later when his teammates take him on a sexual adventure; they all spend a few minutes with a willing girl in the backseat of a car. Rather than feeling pleased at this sign of acceptance and enjoying the sexual initiation, however, Dale is dismayed that he has soiled his love for Zona. Again, he is caught between two worlds.

There is another dislocation in Dale's life. Mr. Wheeler tells him that they must move to an apartment that is farther away from school. The reason for the move is not clear, but it seems to have something to do with Mr. Wheeler's drinking. At the new apartment, the landlord reminds Dale of his inferior place: When Dale does not bring the landlord's trash cans in, the man calls him a "hillbilly," a lazy and shiftless person who can never change. The change from Dale's early and bright expectations to this humiliation is great.

When the climactic game between the Michigan Truckers and the Little M's takes place at Dale's school, many are surprised that Dale is playing for the rival team. Zona suggests that he is a traitor, and when Dale makes some remarks about the Bothner boys, she rebuffs him by claiming that they are better than he. Dale is made captain of the Little M's, and he immediately protests about the unfair treatment his team is receiving. The Truckers will not supply any practice balls for the Little M's, and Dale argues with the referee. He also argues that the junior high coach should not be on the bench because his name is not on the roster. He does win that battle, and though he is disturbed by cries from the audience that he is a traitor, there is a significant change in him: He no longer broods about the injustices done to him but has begun to act and assert himself.

Dale and the Little M's are surprisingly successful. Dale sinks some long shots, and the team is up by eleven points at the half. There are changes, however, after the halftime break. The Michigan Truckers' defense is more effective. Dale offends the audience by slamming into the younger Bothner boy and is accused of being a dirty player. Then Dale makes a mistake at a critical point near the end of the game: He calls a time-out when his team has no more time-outs, and is given a technical foul. His team never recovers its momentum, and the Michigan Truckers win by five points.

Dale's dream of winning the championship is not realized, but he does learn from the experience. He gives up sports and begins to smoke, since basketball has not changed things for himself and his father; they are still hillbillies and not part of the dominant culture. When he buys cigarettes, another ritual step into manhood, Dale chooses his father's brand, Camels. He now feels at home with his identity, once his place has been defined in his own mind. "It was who he was and what he has been looking for. Being himself." He is no longer touched by the social definitions others would place on him. The place that he had been seeking he now discovers is within himself and cannot be found in the social world of the school or the gymnasium. He resolves "never to play their game. He was this person."

Winning the City is notable for its point of view; everything is seen through the eyes of Dale Wheeler. Weesner captures the intensity and sensitivity of a fifteen-year-old boy very well. In that world, the smallest event, such as his father's playing music, is filled with significance and potential meaning. Also notable is the contrast of styles. There is the folk wisdom of Mr. Wheeler and the rebellious and defiant style of the self-defined rednecks in the Little M's, as well as the middle-class style of most of the people in Dale's junior high, especially Zona, who mentions a number of times that Dale says the oddest things. Dale has difficulty deciding which style of language and attitude is appropriate for him; he does not, in fact, discover his true style until the end of the novel.

The major theme of the novel is the search of the main character to belong, to find a place where he can be his true self. The obstacles to finding that place are primarily social and economic. Curiously, there is no mention of race as a factor; everyone seems to be white, and the important differences are class and origins. Immigrants from the South are seen as lazy and shiftless, lacking the middle-class virtues of the dominant culture. Dale's victory is to see the unfairness beneath that culture and refuse to accept its standards or evaluation of him. His response to unfair labeling by social position is to obliterate class by finding a self that is independent of such categories. He achieves a self-reliance that is not merely negative or defiant, but based on very hard-won experience.

James Sullivan

Sources for Further Study

Booklist. LXXXVI, July, 1990, p. 2074.
Chicago Tribune. July 1, 1990, XIV, p. 3.
Detroit News. August 29, 1990, p. F3.
Kirkus Reviews. LVIII, May 15, 1990, p. 686.
Publishers Weekly. CCXXXVII, June 8, 1990, p. 44.
USA Today. July 26, 1990, p. D2.
The Washington Post Book World. XX, July 29, 1990, p. 4.

A WOMAN OF CONTRADICTIONS
The Life of George Eliot

Author: Ina Taylor (1949-   )
First published: 1989, in Great Britain
Publisher: William Morrow (New York). Illustrated. 255 pp. $19.95
Type of work: Biography
Time: 1819-1880
Locale: Nuneaton and Griff, Warwickshire, England; Coventry; London; and, briefly, Germany, Switzerland, and other parts of the Continent

A brief, incisive biography that offers unconventional insights into the psychology of the great English novelist

        Principal personages:
            GEORGE ELIOT (born MARY ANN EVANS), Victorian novelist, translator,
               and editor
            GEORGE HENRY LEWES, her common-law husband, a journalist
            JOHN WALTER CROSS, her husband for seven months before her death and
               her first biographer

    Ina Taylor's concise, often acidulous study of George Eliot is full of unexpected delights for the reader. But the author fails to prove her central thesis: that Eliot—novelist, translator, editor, and intellectual—was "a woman of contradictions." To be sure, Taylor views her subject in an unfamiliar, decidedly harsher light. Previous biographies—from John Walter Cross's near-idolatrous arrangement of her letters and diaries in *George Eliot's Life as Related in her Letters and Journals* (1881) to Gordon S. Haight's classic *George Eliot: A Biography* (1968)—have emphasized the writer's moral courage, independence, and personal charm. Taylor's biography, in contrast, reveals Eliot as clear-minded and resolute enough to determine her own destiny, no matter what society might expect of her. A woman of strong sexual energy, she enjoyed flirting with (generally older) men; a materialist, she struck a hard bargain to squeeze money from her publishers; an egotist, she used wealth and prestige to shore up her social pretensions and overcome youthful feelings of inadequacy by a show of ostentatious grandeur. For Taylor, George Eliot shrinks in moral dimension to an eccentric Victorian whose lifelong touchstones were needs for security and respectability.

    In the face of conventional judgments far more inclined to pardon Eliot's personal weaknesses and to emphasize instead her plucky rebelliousness against a static, male-dominated social order, Taylor argues that earlier biographers have relied too much upon the exaggerations of Cross, and that suppressed evidence which has recently come to light requires a reevaluation of Eliot's true nature. In an introductory chapter entitled "What's New About George Eliot?" Taylor argues that Cross, who was married to Eliot only seven months before she died, had strong reasons to cover up information hostile to her reputation. In particular, he excluded from his account all references to John Chapman, who was a close—possibly intimate—friend of the writer during her journalistic days as editor of the *Westminster Review.* Cross also neglected to discuss the extent of his wife's earlier friendship with the radical Charles Bray and his circle. By exaggerating the importance of his own role in Eliot's emotional life and by portraying her as a bloodless saint, Cross had attempted, Taylor believes, to atone for his sense of guilt and confusion following her death. Within recent years, scholars have discovered that the couple's honeymoon, which Cross had represented as idyllic, in reality was a disaster. Twenty years his wife's junior, Cross, faced with "the prospect of being tied to an elderly woman for the rest of his life, or hers," had been driven to desperation. He had found "marriage to the greatest novelist of the day so unbearable" that he had tried to commit suicide by drowning in a Venice canal.

Although the couple hushed up any references to the attempt, alluding instead to Cross's "illness," they lived their remaining months together in guarded circumstances. After his wife's sudden death from a cold infection that rapidly worsened, Cross continued to guard Eliot's reputation, and his own, from any suggestion of scandal. In this endeavor he was like most other Victorian biographers, who conventionally concealed from their readers any hints of improprieties. For later scholars of George Eliot, however, Cross's sentimental account of his wife's exemplary moral conduct—taken together with the more solid evidence of letters revealing her kindness, good common sense, tact, and generosity of spirit—influenced commentators to accept a portrait of the master that resembled one of a plaster saint. Taylor breaks the artificial mold and shows instead a living person within.

Taylor's work never proves that George Eliot was a woman of contradictions. Many of the so-called contradictions that Taylor observes are actually paradoxes compounded by Cross and his followers. In other words, the inconsistencies Taylor discovers stem from the contrast between a sentimental image of the writer-saint and the real person. During the course of her industrious life, Eliot rarely pretended to emotions that she did not feel, rarely acted a false role to conform with expectations of society, and rarely spoke or wrote words that she could not authentically defend with the example of her conduct. Among any group of distinguished Victorians, she must stand out as exceptionally honest—judged by either nineteenth or twentieth century standards. An avowed enemy of cant, Eliot fought a lifelong battle to discover truth that she could validate, even at the cost of surrendering her cherished youthful religious dogmas.

Then what "contradictions" can Taylor assert against her subject? Eliot never pretended to remain sexually pure in the Victorian sense; she lived openly—as husband and wife—with George Henry Lewes for nearly a quarter century. Lewes was already married but separated from his wife in an "open" arrangement; the union between the two writers was as committed, mutually respectful, and faithful as any of the more conventional relationships among Victorian notables. Indeed, the Lewes-Eliot relationship was a model of harmony. Taylor cannot fault her subject for moral contradiction, therefore, since her union was without hypocrisy, although clearly in defiance of public views on acceptable wedlock.

A more serious contradiction in Eliot's moral armor, according to Taylor, is the matter of the writer's "mercenary" bent. She was "a woman who claimed her writing as an art form, yet approached it from a mercenary angle"—by which Taylor means that Eliot demanded from her editors and publishers the money that she deserved for her labors. As a matter of fact, Eliot was the first English author to acquire from publishers the right to profit from long-term sales of her books. This bargaining power, for which Lewes' negotiating advice was invaluable, proved in time to be an enormous benefit to other writers, both in Eliot's generation and for succeeding generations as well. How Eliot's shrewd business sense should appear—to Taylor or to her readers—an impulse contradictory to her "art" is a question left unanswered. More relevant is the consistency in her character that made her represent through an inner vision the real world around her, one operating by means of the machinery of money and power. Such a worldview, as seen in *Middlemarch* (1872), springs precisely from the background of the author's life. Her iron-willed father (model for the title character in *Adam Bede* [1859]) and her insufferably superior brother Isaac (who resembles an idealized version of young Tom Tulliver in *The Mill on the Floss* [1860]) were hard-driving businessmen-farmers, ruthless in the exercise of power, especially over the women in their families. As a child, Eliot had learned through bitter experience the hard proscriptions of a social order controlled by wealth. Throughout her life she evidenced a remarkably consistent outlook toward security. Whether as a religious fanatic during adolescence, as a young woman striving for independence from her family, as an aspiring intellectual and journeyman translator and journalist, or as a world-famous writer, Eliot remained constant in her almost single-minded pursuit of financial independence. For her, money and security were bound together; without money, she feared that she would lose her hard-gained independence.

Finally, Taylor faults Eliot as "the woman who was the best advertisement the Woman's Movement had ever had, yet refused to help them." It is true that Eliot's relatively modest contributions to support Girton College, Cambridge—a school that admitted women to higher education—were consistent with the tight-fisted money policy of her family and deeply ingrained in her character. Nevertheless, a fair judgment of Eliot's parsimony cannot extend to hold her guilty of contradictory motives. It is unfair to judge Eliot as an advocate of women's rights by twentieth century standards. During the 1870's, the women's movement in England was in its infancy. What the cause needed least of all was the public support of a notable such as George Eliot, who was stigmatized by respectable society as an unmarried woman living in sin with a married man. Eliot, whose delicate sense of social tact is sharply drawn in her novels, must have realized how vulnerable she must appear as a spokesperson for feminists. Furthermore, she was temperamentally uncomfortable in this type of leadership role. Charming, articulate among select groups of intellectuals and artists, she lacked the magnetism to excite large audiences. In fact, her physical appearance was—according to contemporary accounts and the evidence of the few portraits and photographs she permitted—decidedly unattractive.

Although Taylor's case against Eliot as a woman of contradictions lacks substance, her case is very strong indeed that the writer suffered psychological stress because of her physical appearance. Most readers of Eliot have seen a familiar reproduction of her features: that of a photograph taken in 1858. Even with slight alterations to the original print—the photographic artist had discreetly straightened the subject's nose—the picture shows an animated woman with intelligent eyes, a broad nose, and a pronounced jaw (mostly hidden by her fingers). Judged aesthetically, the picture is not altogether unattractive. But other photographs, especially one taken at Coventry when Eliot was in her mid-twenties, tell a different story. The earliest known photograph shows a woman with a prominent nose (also retouched) and jaw, with a fixity of expression that is poignant. That the photograph of George Eliot—or, as she was known at the time, Mary Ann Evans—represents faithfully the appearance of the writer in her youth is a matter for some reflection.

Generally speaking, a biographer should not devote a disproportionate amount of space to the physical appearance of one's subject; that person's conduct, not his or her physiognomy, usually is the key to his or her psychology. To understand George Eliot, however, a reader must be aware of the physical impact she made upon contemporaries. Taylor is correct in allotting considerable space to reexamine Eliot as a woman who struggled against enormous obstacles—including that of her appearance—to make her way to prominence. A strength of this biography is that Taylor organizes a discussion of Eliot's life according to the identities (or masks) Eliot assumed at crucial stages in her progress.

Born Mary Ann Evans, the plain-featured daughter of a proud, austere landholder, she was taught early in life to accept her place dutifully as an inferior; her solace was in religious devotion so intense that her father and brother finally urged her to relent. In 1849-1850, she fell under the influence of Charles Bray, brightened to the warmth of his curiously irregular household, and changed her name—as she had already changed her nature—to Marian Evans. Her metamorphosis had been a complete break from the past. She was exposed to Charles Christian Hennell's *Inquiry Concerning the Origin of Christianity* (1838), and later to David Friedrich Strauss's *Das Leben Jesu, kritisch bearbeit* (1835-1836; *The Life of Jesus, Critically Examined*, which she translated into English in 1846). As a result, she abandoned her religious fanaticism, left the Church (for which offense she was ostracized by male members of her family), and became a freethinker. In London, living upon a small inheritance after her father's death, she joined a circle of intellectuals, ranging from liberals to radicals, edited *the Westminster Review* for John Chapman, and reviewed diverse books. In 1854, she translated *Das Wesen des Christentums* (1841; *The Essence of Christianity*) by Ludwig Feuerbach into English, and began her career as a journalist.

Using the pseudonym George Eliot, she began writing fiction, encouraged by Lewes, who also acted as her adviser and business manager. Her first sketches were published in 1858 as *Scenes of Clerical Life*. Later books followed with even greater success, including *Adam Bede*, *The Mill on the Floss*, and *Silas Marner* (1861).

These works earned for her not only a worldwide reputation but also a considerable fortune. With each stage of her metamorphosis, Eliot changed her name to mark a change in self-actualization. Taylor never lets the reader forget, however, that the acclaimed English novelist was also an unattractive female. Like the plain-featured Mary Garth in *Middlemarch* (1871-1872), Eliot won hearts because of her common sense, her generosity, and her sweet and forgiving nature.

Taylor neglects to explain the reasons that a woman so blighted psychologically by her masculine-like features was able to win the love of her contemporaries. Not only were Bray and Chapman smitten with her charm, but also the once-cynical Lewes (himself an exceedingly homely man, in spite of his philandering). For Lewes, Eliot proved to be mistress, wife, and loyal companion. Even when Eliot was in her sixties, she won the affection of many people, including that of alleged lesbians such as Elma Stewart and Edith Simcox, whose amorous advances she tactfully spurned. Her young male admirers included Oscar Browning and Alexander Main. J. C. "Johnnie" Cross had also fallen under her spell, and it was to him that she proposed marriage. In addition to her individual admirers, many people flocked to meet Eliot and to bask in her glory. At her "salon," she received notables from England and the Continent, many who would remember her charm, her sound advice, and always her intelligence. The plain woman of Griff had, by the time of her old age, become a raconteur, a sage, and the object of adoring attention.

By insisting upon an unsentimental and unsympathetic revisionist portrait of Eliot, Taylor paradoxically makes her subject appear all the more sympathetic to readers. Far from being a woman of contradictions, Eliot stands out as a person of extraordinary courage. Consistent in her determination to work hard, she overcame limitations—including those imposed by her physical appearance—through solid competence. By the end of the book, even Taylor succumbs to her subject's charm: "Behind the mask was a living breathing woman who made mistakes, distorted the truth, enjoyed sex and was everything a Victorian female was not supposed to be. How much more engaging an individual she was because of that."

Leslie B. Mittleman

Sources for Further Study

Choice. XXVII, June, 1990, p. 1682.
The Christian Century. CVII, February 21, 1990, p. 194.
Listener. CXXII, July 13, 1989, p. 25.
The Observer. July 2, 1989, p. 45.
The Spectator. CCLXIII, August 5, 1989, p. 33.
The Times Literary Supplement. September 20, 1989, p. 1050.
The Washington Post Book World. XX, January 14, 1990, p. 7.

WOMAN OF THE AEROPLANES

Author: Kojo Laing (1946-   )
First published: 1988, in Great Britain
Publisher: William Morrow (New York). 196 pp. $16.95
Type of work: Novel
Time: Unspecified; presumably the late twentieth century
Locale: Tukwan, Ghana, and Levensvale, Scotland

An account of how the citizens of two towns have magically escaped history and the situations that draw them back inevitably to confront time and mortality

Principal characters:
> KWAME ATTA, one of Ghanaian male twins, the "bad" brother; a connoisseur of invention, technology, and capital, and a pragmatist
> KWAKU DE BABO (MR. CORNERSTEP) the other male twin, the "good" brother; a historian, the secretary to the town, a dreamer, and an idealist
> POKUAA, one of the "bosses" of Tukwan, a wheeler-dealer; she is a beautiful woman loved by both Atta and Babo
> DAVID MACKIE, a Scottish businessman, in love with Pokuaa
> ANGUS MACKIE, David's son, in love with Aba
> ABA YAA, a homesick young woman
> CANON BURNS, an Anglican priest
> PASTOR MENSAH, a Ghanaian religious leader

To read *Woman of the Aeroplanes* is to experience wonder and magic, to undertake a glorious journey to a never-never land inhabited by characters whose day-to-day lives exhibit totally human traits and an abundance of positive human values. Citizens of Tukwan in the Asante region of Ghana seem to share a kinship relationship with all objects surrounding them. One man dresses his Mercedes and sleeps under it; the airplanes are landed by ducks more or less attached to the traveling party; a vulture perches on the pipe of one of the Ghanaians and may be the repository of a sacred soul. Ghanaian lawyer Tay says with characteristic solemnity and guile that it may be necessary to redefine living things in a place where ducks talk and goats are artists. In Tukwan, zinnias are ankle-happy and counting the ripples in a lake is a creditable activity for the town scribe.

The delight a reader experiences in participating in a soaring flight of fancy and in sharing the life of the people of Tukwan is anchored by the citizens of Tukwan's twin city Levensvale, a village in Scotland, who also cannot find their geography of time and space. The people of Levensvale are recognizably western in their perceptions; however, the circumstances in which they live (out of time) question basic worldviews of Western culture. These similar circumstances have created in the citizens of both towns an open-mindedness and willingness to accept traditions, perceptions, and practices different from their own. The plot of the novel takes emissaries from Tukwan to Levensvale by means of two airplanes that Pokuaa has purchased from

David Mackie to establish trade and share information and culture for the mutual benefit of the twin cities. It is perhaps 1965 but three other watches register different years. Thus, time is both free and absurdly controlled. The Ghanaians, both those staying and those going, exchange advice and cautions, but only Pastor Mensah voices a dominant concern:

> "What do we want with money or with ideas that we already have enough of . . ." This was Pastor Mensah being pensive through the discomfort he felt at being so high from his crosses. He did not consider that theology should be so tall. And up here he was even more afraid of one thing: The minute Tukwan struck a true balance of life, it would either be invaded or destroyed, he thought.

Soon after the planes take off, Babo accuses Pastor Mensah of being out of date, which serves to corroborate the latter's fears. A consequence of being out of date is immortality. Citizens of Tukwan and Levensvale have at birth a certain expectancy that reincarnation will move them from one form of life to another as their allotted energies are expended. Within that allotment of life, a person is born, is schooled, matures, gives life, ages, and is reincarnated into another being with another allotment. Thus, characters in Tukwan and Levensvale can be and are young and old, wise and foolish, happy and quarrelsome, male and female, sexually productive and nonproductive.

Romance develops among the men and women of the two cities. The twins, Atta and Babo, are both in love with Pokuaa, but she favors them equally. An important plot movement concerns who, if anyone, Pokuaa will choose for a mate. David Mackie, leader of the Levensvale group, is also smitten by Pokuaa, despite his attachment to his wife of thirty years. Angus Mackie, David's son, meets and then persistently pursues Aba, who withholds a positive response until the novel draws to a close. The symbolic joining of Angus and Aba is, at the end, the salvation of the people; for the major thrust of the novel is toward an inevitable return of Tukwan and Levensvale to their own geographies. The enemy Kumasi tribe has spotted aspects of Tukwan and some have even invaded what has been a totally invisible town; yet, the Tukwanians are given another fifty years, a gift from Angus who takes it away from his own life allotment.

Atta and Babo, twin brothers and counterparts, exist in the same relationship to one another as Levensvale and Tukwan. Atta, called the "bad" twin, seems to be so characterized because of his inordinate curiosity and his scientific bent. He is the emerging technocrat whose left brain dominates his actions. Babo, on the other hand, is the "good" twin whose natural bent is toward the literary and artistic. He is both scribe (historian) and poet. Babo is no less inventive than Atta, but his creativity exhibits itself in a different way, and it could be said that Babo, busily writing his way through this novel, is inventing it as he goes along. The eventual joining of Babo and Pokuaa, whose own inventive mind conceives of the merger of Tukwan and Levensvale, signals the author's belief that African and European cultures can be meshed to positive advantage.

It would be a mistake to insist on anything absolute in the dichotomies presented. Rather, positions, interests, traditions, and personalities are multifaceted, each partaking of the other in different ways. The fact that the people of both cultures are so clearly attracted to each other when they allow themselves to interact emphasizes unity rather than separation, and insists on the surreal (and in many minds holy) revelation of the many in the one.

Kojo Laing is the author of a previous novel *Search Sweet Country*, published in 1986. He is also a greatly admired poet, and it is his ability to manipulate language for figurative purposes that leaps to immediate attention. An exuberant and highly original stylist, Laing's images, fast-paced and appearing in multifold manifestations, accomplish on a small scale what the novel as a whole presents. Surrealism is a movement in art and literature that celebrates the imagination, giving to it primary status as a way of knowing. In this manner, Surrealism is antithetical to the dominant view of Western culture that reason points the way to truth. For the Surrealist, the modes of Western culture, such as time, for example, are pure inventions with no relevance to the "real" world. Rather, the imagination released by chance, through dreams, free association, or automatic writing, where there is no conscious control, leads the way to truth.

The surreal juxtaposition is a major technique whereby a comparison is set forth so startling in its implications that it leads to new understandings or helps the reader to realize formerly obscure ideas with greater clarity. The juxtaposition presented in the form of an image meshes the apparently contradictory in a moment of insight that destroys dualities and underscores unity. For the Surrealist, that magic moment is the point where yes and no meet.

Laing's images act in similar ways. Babo's cornerstep, for example, a movement involving hesitation while both turning and not turning a corner is a physical action so characteristic that Babo's nickname is "Mr. Cornerstep." Exterior action is yoked with interior action, for Babo's hesitation is also mental: "Kwaku's cornerstep was dangerous: he was strongest at corners—where several perceptions usually met in his head and strengthened it—and he loved the surprise and space there. Someone somewhere would one day clap at the wonder of his cornerstep."

As the action of the mind is meshed with the action of the body, so also are the human and nonhuman. The bend of Pokuaa's body and her house follow the same curve; her two airplanes stand at the level of her lips—one at her upper lip and the other one at her lower. Pokuaa enters other peoples' dreams and can wed spirits embodied in the blue elephants. In the magic towns of Tukwan and Levensvale and on whatever paths the journeys follow back and forth, the airplanes pull trailers, are guided by ducks, and land piggyback, one on top of the other.

Although images expressed as explicit or implied metaphors dominate the novel, another kind of discourse becomes appropriate during the second visit of emissaries from Tukwan to Levensvale. The culminating event is a conference featuring Canon Burns, representing Western Protestantism, and Pastor Mensah, representing a compilation of Ghanaian religious beliefs. The novel now moves to its climax. The people of Tukwan are aware that the Kumasi will find a way to their town and close their path to eternity. Along with a sense of sorrow, there is also hopefulness, for the Tukwanians know that Babo's pen is able to teach every town that had no twin how to allow the new to create values appropriate to it. The two-story conference of humanity is a joining of head and heart, a time for the people of the twin cities to show Canon Burns how to dance the mystery away, to guide him to an understanding of how to make technology human and to recognize the essential twinning of all things, the sameness of the one rather than the differences of the many. This recognition must include a rejection of racist attitudes which are betrayals of humanity. " 'Every age,' " Pastor Mensah argues, " 'should choose the horrors it can deal with, and the most primitive horror now is the racist.' " Although Canon Burns can understand the anguish and the prayers of Pastor Mensah, he is unable to accept the idea of a free church that merges congregations, a church both men would build together in Levensvale and in Tukwan when the paths to eternity were closed. Canon Burns wants the churches he would build to be Anglican.

The novel, however, does not end in despair. Even if Tukwan is invaded and forced to accept a geography bound by time and space, even if the first things the Tukwanians find when they get home are holes in their forest, airplane crashes all about them, the dirges of elephants, and the dead and disintegrating body of one of their own citizens, they have a kind of remedy. As Babo remarks, the people of the twin cities can themselves live their knowledge simply. For his twin family, his parents and brothers and sisters in Tukwan, Angus Mackie performs an act of incredible generosity. He gives fifty years of his own life's allotment to the Tukwanians, thus allowing them fifty more years to share each other and to regulate their own rate of change as they prepare to reenter a world still trapped in time and tradition.

In the end, life triumphs. Pokuaa chooses Babo to father her children. The ducks guard their house, and Babo realizes that the universe is around the corner, and the corner is free to create the breezes of change.

Woman of the Aeroplanes is not an easy book to read. The language, constructed of dense and startling metaphors as well as an assortment of Ghanaian words and the author's neologisms, underscores the different Ghanaian culture for English-speaking readers outside the region. A reader's patience will be amply rewarded as Laing's fantasy takes hold and the reader is transported to the magical town of Tukwan to share the adventures of its people.

Mary Rohrberger

Sources for Further Study

Booklist. LXXXVI, May 1, 1990, p. 1684.
Kirkus Reviews. LVIII, March 15, 1990, p. 368.
Library Journal. CXV, May 1, 1990, p. 114.

Los Angeles Times Book Review. July 15, 1990, p. 9.
The New York Times Book Review. XCV, July 8, 1990, p. 23.
Publishers Weekly. CCXXXVII, March 9, 1990, p. 53.
The Washington Post Book World. XX, June 17, 1990, p. 1.

THE YEARS OF LYNDON JOHNSON
Volume II: Means of Ascent

Author: Robert A. Caro (1936-   )
Publisher: Alfred A. Knopf (New York). Illustrated. 506 pp. $24.95
Type of work: Biography
Time: 1941-1948
Locale: Texas and Washington, D.C.

A highly critical study of Lyndon Johnson at a turning point in his political career

> *Principal personages:*
> LYNDON BAINES JOHNSON, a Texas congressman and candidate for the Senate in 1948
> LADY BIRD JOHNSON, the wife of Lyndon Johnson
> COKE STEVENSON, a former Governor of Texas and candidate for the Senate in 1948
> GEORGE PARR, the corrupt political boss of Duval County, Texas
> ABE FORTAS, a legal adviser to Lyndon Johnson

In 1982, Robert Caro published the first volume of a projected three-volume biography, *The Years of Lyndon Johnson*. That first volume, subtitled *The Path to Power*, traced Johnson's family history and recounted his early years and growing ambitions. In the second volume, *Means of Ascent* (Caro now says he may need four volumes to tell the whole story), the narrative picks up where the first volume ended, in 1941.

Caro's work-in-progress is a distinguished example of a new class of biography, which in recent years has recaptured the methods and intent of the classical biography of ancient Greece and Rome. The ancient biographers, most notably Plutarch of Chaeronea, were moralists, anxious to edify as well as entertain their audiences. They filled out portraits of their subjects through a subtle blend of narrative and anecdote. In Plutarch's skillful hands, ancient statesmen and generals became exemplars of virtue and vice, models of proper public behavior for students of his and succeeding generations. Ancient biography still makes compelling reading, but the relation of these portraits to the actual characters of their subjects remains problematic.

For Robert Caro, and others like him, such as Roger Morris, author of *Richard Milhous Nixon: The Rise of an American Politician* (1989), biography is once again an instrument with which to inculcate civic virtue. These authors are obsessed with a vision of the decay of American institutions. They regard modern mass politics, with its reliance on messages and imagery communicated by the media, as a degradation of public discourse in America. In their eyes, men such as Lyndon Johnson and Richard Nixon, who created and then dominated modern American political history, are poor successors to the statesmen of earlier generations. But these authors' tale of corruption extends beyond the political realm. For writers such as Caro, the people get the leaders they deserve. Politicians such as Johnson and Nixon rose with the support of the people, their achievements reflecting perversely the deterioration of American citizenship. There could have been no debasement of the political system without a major spiritual crisis affecting the whole of American society.

Thus Caro's *Means of Ascent* is as much jeremiad as biography or history. In his hands Lyndon Johnson, like the subject of an ancient biography, is exhibited as an exemplum, rather than as a man. Caro makes only a half-hearted effort to present a balanced assessment of Lyndon Johnson. He begins the book with a dramatic recounting of the day in March, 1965, when President Johnson threw his administration behind the Voting Rights Act of 1965. Johnson's embrace of the Civil Rights movement would have far-reaching consequences for American society, and must be accounted one of the noblest initiatives ever undertaken by an American president. Johnson's swing toward the cause of civil rights was more than a calculated political maneuver. Johnson had long sympathized with the underprivileged of American society. In his early years as a schoolteacher, he had gone out of his way to help his poverty-stricken and officially neglected Mexican pupils. As a New Deal congressman, he had worked with enthusiasm to better the lot of his constituents. Caro concedes that this was a bright thread running through Johnson's character. But he takes pains to point out that a dark thread ran alongside the bright one. Caro juxtaposes Johnson's speech on voting rights for blacks with his commitment of American ground troops to Vietnam the following month. Soon many of the same people who cheered Johnson's pursuit of equal rights were bitterly protesting the war in Southeast Asia. Johnson's conduct of the war would be characterized by a persistent pattern of lying to the American public. This lying, and the war it obfuscated, squandered America's moral authority and created the famous "credibility gap." Indeed, Caro believes that Johnson's legacy was the undermining of the American people's faith in the presidency, ushering in a period of widespread cynicism regarding American institutions. Caro regards the Vietnam War, and the moral pollution it engendered in America, as a truer expression of Johnson's character and statesmanship than the Great Society.

Thus the real task of Caro's biographical enterprise is to trace the trail of Lyndon Johnson's corruption. This he continues to accomplish with indefatigable thoroughness and obsessive detail. Caro has spent fourteen years thus far on his project, and has combed archives and interviewed dozens of people to accumulate an impressive array of facts and anecdotes. Caro is a skillful writer, and he has masterfully organized his voluminous material into a fast-paced and highly readable narrative. *Means of Ascent* concentrates on a relatively brief period in Lyndon Johnson's life, from 1941 through 1948, when his political career hung in the balance and his life reached a turning point. In Caro's estimation, these were the years when the dark thread in Johnson's life overshadowed the bright one, and he set out on the course which would ultimately lead to the Vietnam War, personal failure, and national trauma.

Caro declares in his introduction that Lyndon Johnson had a "seemingly bottomless capacity for deceit, deception and betrayal." The rest of this lengthy book is simply an extended illustration of this assertion. For Caro, the touchstone of Johnson's character was ambition. Johnson's great failing was to surrender principle and policy to his overweening egotism, making him, ultimately, a moral monster.

Lyndon Johnson's hunger for advancement resulted from a traumatic childhood. For the first decade of his life, Johnson enjoyed the comforts of a middle-class upbringing. His father, Sam Johnson, served six terms in the Texas legislature, winning a reputation for idealism and devotion to the best interests of his constituents. An ill-advised business venture proved Sam Johnson's undoing. The Johnsons were ruined financially, and Sam Johnson swiftly lost the approbation of his neighbors and became an object of ridicule. This sudden loss of status, and the humiliation of his father, whom he had idolized, made a profound impression on the young Lyndon Johnson. Early in life he determined that he would succeed where his father had failed. He developed an obsession with being perceived as tough and shrewd. From the outset of his political career, Johnson displayed ruthlessness and a willingness to cheat, even in situations one might not think worthy of the effort. Thus, Johnson stole elections in college and even the presidency of a social club for congressional assistants.

Means of Ascent takes up Johnson's story in the aftermath of his defeat in the Texas senatorial race of 1941. After a stint of schoolteaching, Johnson had gone into politics, eventually winning a seat in Congress. In Washington, he became a prized protegé of President Franklin D. Roosevelt. He quickly attained a degree of influence unusual in a junior congressman by controlling funds donated by rich oilmen. Always in a hurry to advance his own career, Johnson ran for the Senate in 1941. Enjoying the patronage of the Roosevelt Administration, and liberally distributing largesse, Johnson appeared to have the election sewn up. This led him to commit one of his rare political mistakes. Johnson allowed some of the bosses whose votes he had bought to report their returns early. His opponent took advantage of this by generating enough votes to overtake Johnson and steal the election away from him. Defeat proved a crushing blow to Johnson. Not only had he failed in his bid for higher office, but he, the man who prided himself on hard-edged political sense, had been easily outsmarted. The thought that his overconfident blunder might have forever stalled his career galled and haunted Johnson. He spent the next seven years retrieving that error.

Johnson's quest for power shaped his military service in World War II. In the months leading up to Pearl Harbor, Johnson had repeatedly declared his intention to put on a uniform and place his political career on hold if war came. In the event, Johnson showed no eagerness to go to war, and ultimately entered the Navy because he had trapped himself with his own words. Johnson angled for a high-level political assignment in Washington, and made no effort to get to the combat zone. Military subordination irked him, and for months he frittered away his time on inconsequential inspection tours. At last, when it became politically imperative for Johnson to get near the shooting war, he joined a team sent to investigate the war in the Pacific. As a member of this team, Johnson took part in a hazardous bombing raid which cost the life of one of his colleagues. Johnson behaved well under fire, and upon his return received a Silver Star for gallantry from General Douglas MacArthur. Johnson would later exaggerate his one taste of combat and his politically motivated decoration into a distingished war record.

Johnson left the Navy in obedience to a law which forbade sitting congressmen from active service in the armed forces. Bored with his congressional duties and uncertain about his political future, Johnson next devoted himself to fulfilling another aspect of his capacious ambition. He began to build a fortune. Using his wife, Lady Bird Johnson, as a front, Johnson bought an Austin, Texas, radio station. The previous owners of the station had petitioned the Federal Communications Commission for years in a vain effort to expand its hours and change its frequency to attract more listeners. Johnson used his political influence to facilitate the purchase of the station in his wife's name, and within weeks the Federal Communications Commission granted the station's petition. A few years later, the station was allowed to increase its power greatly, making it one of the most lucrative radio outlets in the region. Eventually Johnson's radio station would form the basis of a broadcasting empire in Texas. By 1948, Johnson was telling intimates that he was worth a million dollars.

In 1948, Johnson decided to sacrifice his safe congressional seat for another chance at entering the Senate. He could no longer endure the slow pace of promotion in the House, which was based entirely on seniority. He saw the Senate as his only opportunity of grasping power before his old age. Johnson's decision was an act of political courage as well as desperation. In the Democratic primary he would face one of the most popular and respected figures in Texas—former Governor Coke Stevenson.

Caro extolls the character of Coke Stevenson, deliberately portraying him as the antithesis of Lyndon Johnson. For Caro, Stevenson was the last of the cowboys, and embodied all the old frontier virtues. Stevenson was born to impoverished parents in the barren hill country of Texas. Through hard work, young Stevenson prospered in business, first running his own freighting business, then working in a bank, and finally becoming a lawyer. With his own hands, Stevenson built himself a ranch which became his chief pride. Stevenson's merit so impressed his neighbors that he was reluctantly drawn into politics. Stevenson rapidly became one of the most respected public figures in the state, serving as Speaker of the state House of Representatives, Lieutenant Governor, and finally Governor. An old-fashioned man, Stevenson believed candidates should be judged on their character and public service. He refused to run an expensive and elaborate campaign for the Senate, contenting himself with driving about the state and meeting voters individually, with only his nephew for a companion.

Against this high-minded style of campaigning, Lyndon Johnson pioneered a new, media-driven approach to politics. Caro sees the Texas Senate race of 1948 as a fateful confrontation between the simpler and more wholesome politics of the past and the modern politics of money and media imagery. Not only did Johnson mobilize vast amounts of money with which to buy radio and newspaper advertisements, but he made use of new technology in other ways as well, including hiring a helicopter to gather attention and ease his travel around the state.

Despite his advantages, Johnson ran well behind Stevenson in the Democratic primary. Facing what seemed like certain defeat in the run-off, Johnson launched a series of attacks on Stevenson, paying little heed to the truth. He also made arrangements with the corrupt political bosses of south Texas, who controlled the votes of the region's Mexican-American citizens. The most notorious of Johnson's allies was George Parr, known as the "Duke of Duval," who virtually owned several counties. Parr made sure that the 1941 mistake was not repeated.

The run-off election proved very close, but it appeared, with most of the returns tabulated, that Stevenson had edged Johnson out by a few hundred votes. Then Parr's men suddenly discovered a ballot box purportedly containing enough ballots to give Johnson an eighty-seven vote lead. Though Stevenson and some of his associates braved Parr's local gunmen and proved to their own satisfaction that the decisive ballots were fraudulent, Stevenson ran afoul of Johnson's political clout. Johnson's friend Abe Fortas devised a cunning legal strategy which enabled him to block Stevenson's attempt to open the disputed ballot box. As a result, Johnson entered the Senate and began his rapid rise to the White House on the strength of this "Eighty-Seven Vote Landslide."

Caro has established without a doubt that Lyndon Johnson stole the election of 1948, something which heretofore has been widely suspected but not decisively proved. This proof of Johnson's culpability must inspire sober reflections on the relation of ends to means in politics, for while Johnson did not honestly earn his first great step to the presidency, certainly the conservative Coke Stevenson in the Senate would never have exerted himself in the struggle for civil rights or against poverty. Confronting such ambiguity in the story of his subject, however, is foreign to Caro's enterprise. He contents himself with a magnificent tale of the skullduggery of a villain. Undoubtedly when Caro's narrative reaches 1968, Johnson's political debacle will be presented as the inevitable product of his sins and the moral of his life will be drawn in vivid colors. Like the works of the ancient biographers, Caro's book is a pleasure to read and an intriguing if rather polemical work of political philosophy. But the whole of Lyndon Johnson is missing in this work. Caro fails to capture the man of humor, the man of vision, the man who inspired loyalty in his followers. The definitive biography of Lyndon Johnson has yet to be written.

Daniel P. Murphy

Sources for Further Study

American Heritage. XLI, July, 1990, p. 10.
The Christian Science Monitor. March 27, 1990, p. 13.
The Houston Post. March 11, 1990, p. C6.
Los Angeles Times Book Review. March 18, 1990, p. 1.

The Nation. CCLI, October 8, 1990, p. 389.
National Review. XLII, April 30, 1990, p. 46.
The New Republic. CCII, June 4, 1990, p. 29.
New York. XXIII, March 5, 1990, p. 100.
The New York Times Book Review. XCV, March 11, 1990, p. 1.
Newsweek. CXV, March 19, 1990, p. 66.
Time. CXXXV, March 5, 1990, p. 67.
The Times Literary Supplement. September 28, 1990, p. 1024.
The Wall Street Journal. March 8, 1990, p. A12.
The Washington Post Book World. XX, March 4, 1990, p. 1.

MAGILL'S
LITERARY ANNUAL
1991

BIOGRAPHICAL WORKS BY SUBJECT
1977-1991

I

BIOGRAPHICAL WORKS BY SUBJECT

III

BIOGRAPHICAL WORKS BY SUBJECT

BIOGRAPHICAL WORKS BY SUBJECT

BIOGRAPHICAL WORKS BY SUBJECT

BIOGRAPHICAL WORKS BY SUBJECT

BIOGRAPHICAL WORKS BY SUBJECT

CUMULATIVE AUTHOR INDEX
1977-1991

Note: Titles from *Magill's History Annual*, 1983, and *Magill's Literary Annual, History and Biography*, 1984 and 1985, have been merged into the Cumulative Author Index, 1977-1991. These titles are indicated parenthetically by an "H" followed by the year of the Annual in which the review appeared.

CUMULATIVE AUTHOR INDEX

CUMULATIVE AUTHOR INDEX

CUMULATIVE AUTHOR INDEX

CUMULATIVE AUTHOR INDEX

CUMULATIVE AUTHOR INDEX

L

CUMULATIVE AUTHOR INDEX

CUMULATIVE AUTHOR INDEX

CUMULATIVE AUTHOR INDEX

CUMULATIVE AUTHOR INDEX